TERRORISM LAW
MATERIALS, CASES, COMMENTS

Fourth Edition

Jeffrey F. Addicott, BA, JD, LLM, SJD

Professor of Law &
Director, Center for Terrorism Law
St. Mary's University School of Law

Lawyers & Judges
Publishing Company, Inc.

This publication is designed to provide accurate and authoritative information in regard to the subject matter covered. It is sold with the understanding that the publisher is not engaged in rendering legal, accounting, or other professional service. If legal advice or other expert assistance is required, the services of a competent professional person should be sought.

—From a *Declaration of Principles* jointly adopted by a Committee of the American Bar Association and a Committee of Publishers and Associations.

The publisher, editors and authors must disclaim any liability, in whole or in part, arising from the information in this volume. The reader is urged to verify the reference material prior to any detrimental reliance thereupon. Since this material deals with legal, medical and engineering information, the reader is urged to consult with an appropriate licensed professional prior to taking any action that might involve any interpretation or application of information within the realm of a licensed professional practice.

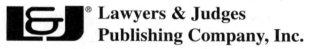

Lawyers & Judges Publishing Company, Inc.

P.O. Box 30040 • Tucson, AZ 85751-0040
(800) 209-7109 • FAX (800) 330-8795
web site: www.lawyersandjudges.com
e-mail: sales@lawyersandjudges.com

Library of Congress Cataloging-in-Publication Data

Addicott, Jeffrey F.
  Terrorism law : materials, cases, comments / Jeffrey F. Addicott. -- 4th ed.
      p. cm.
  Includes bibliographical references and index.
  ISBN-13: 978-1-933264-21-9
  ISBN-10: 1-933264-21-7
  1. War on Terrorism, 2001- 2. Terrorism 3. War (International law) 4. Rule of law. 5. Human rights.
  I. Title. II. Title: Terrorism law.
  KZ6795.T47A33 2007
  345'.02--dc22

                                      2006036100

ISBN 1933264-21-7
ISBN 9-781933264-21-9
Printed in the United States of America
10 9 8 7 6 5 4 3 2 1

Dedication

To R. B. Thieme, Jr.—theologian, soldier, educator, patriot.

Table of Contents

Table of Cases

The principal cases are in bold type. Cases cited or discussed in the text are in roman type. Reference are to pages.

Acknowledgments

The author wishes to acknowledge the invaluable support of Bill Piatt, Dean (1998-2007) and Ryan Professor of Law, St. Mary's University School of Law. Recognizing that "[t]errorism law is an emerging legal discipline critical to understanding the complex balance between global security and civil justice," Dean Piatt helped establish the Center for Terrorism Law in 2003 in order to examine current and potential legal issues related to terrorism in light of the challenge of achieving and maintaining a proper balance between global security and civil justice. This goal is pursued through teaching terrorism law courses, professional exchanges such as symposia and consultations; writing, commenting on and publishing written materials; training; and ensuring access to extensive information resources regarding terrorism (www.stmarytx.edu/ctl).

Among the colleagues, students and friends who expertly dealt with editing and conceptual, bibliographical and organizational problems are Kelly Culpepper and Ema Garcia (bioterrorism), David Irwin (civil liability), R.C. Rondero De Mosier (cyber terrorism), Debby Addicott, Sareta Davis, Kristy Eddings, Robert Guerra, Christian Hack, Stephanie Hoppas, Jason Lemons and Grace Uzomba. The author also wishes to acknowledge with appreciation the University of Kentucky Law Journal, Barry Law Review, University of Richmond Law Review, University of Florida Journal of International Law, Houston Journal of International Law, Military Law Review, Israeli Defense Forces Law Review and The Scholar: St. Mary's Law Review on Minority Issues for permission granted to reprint segments of materials previously published.

Introduction

In any civilized society the most important task is achieving a proper balance between freedom and order. In wartime, reason and history both suggest that this balance shifts to some degree in favor of order—in favor of the government's ability to deal with conditions that threaten the national well-being.

—William H. Rehnquist

Be it the Middle Ages or the Renaissance, the Great War or the Cold War, the trends of human history have always been characterized by epochs or eras. While it is sometimes difficult to find the exact chronological line separating one era from the next, some eras are born in a single dramatic event of such enormity that the very date overshadows the general theme of the times. As December 7, 1941, was to the World War II generation, so too was September 11, 2001, to the new era that many believe has now arrived on the stage of history. Arguably, the post-Cold War period has indeed given way to a new time in history labeled by many commentators as the "War on Terror" or alternatively as the "Global War on Terrorism." Although terrorism is not new, the intensity and frequency of al-Qa'eda and al-Qa'eda-styled terrorism has engulfed the entire civilized world and given rise to new methodologies for combating the rising threat.

Much has changed since the attacks of September 11, 2001—both in law and policy. With the destruction of the al-Qa'eda terror bases in Afghanistan and the removal of the brutal regimes of the Taliban in Afghanistan and Saddam Hussein in Iraq, the United States and the world has faced a plethora of legal and policy challenges. Indeed, the central challenge that the United States is facing, as is the rest of the civilized world, is to realistically fight and win the War on Terror under a democratically based rule of law. Clearly, the protection of human rights and civil liberties is a greater obligation in times of war than in times of peace.

The government has crafted a variety of robust antiterrorism responses designed to disrupt the terrorist network and prevent future terrorist attacks from occurring. Including the passage of the USA PATRIOT Act; the creation of the Cabinet level post of Homeland Security; and the establishment of United States Northern Command, in Colorado; the United States has also engaged in even greater controversial actions such as the preemptive use of military force against the Iraqi regime of Saddam Hussein and the indefinite detention of certain suspected illegal alien terrorists and unlawful enemy combatants. These solutions focus on various pressure points of the problem, but will not prove adequate if America hopes to significantly blunt the scourge of global militant Islamic terrorism. As in all wars, the enemy must be clearly understood and then the battle must be brought to the enemy. Due to the universalist designs of al-Qa'eda and al-Qa'eda-styled militant Islam, the combination of traditional law enforcement with the more muscular use of military force is essential. The one-dimensional use of the criminal justice system, used so ineffectively in the 1990's, cannot confront an ideology of hate able to recruit tens of thousands of followers and field terrorist cells throughout the world. Although many in the world community (and some in America) view the War on Terror as a criminal justice matter, the United States clearly views the struggle as a real "war" against the al-Qa'eda and al-Qa'eda-styled fanatics.

Without question, shifting the tactical focus from punishing those individuals, organizations, or nations who commit terrorist crimes or engage in aggression to new broad methodologies designed to thwart such criminal acts in the first place has caused some to challenge these governmental measures as illegal or at least as inconsistent with American values. As the Global War on Terrorism continues, a deep fissure runs through the legal community. On the one side are those who steadfastly maintain that no or very minor changes need be made to existing laws and processes, while others advocate that significant changes must be implemented to alter the traditional focus of our current legal system from punishing completed crimes to a more aggressive approach capable of preventing crimes, e.g., stopping suicide terrorist attacks before they occur. Understandably, the pivot in every discussion regards where the balance should rest between protecting fundamental freedoms associated with civil liberties and providing adequate safety to the nation from the threat of future al-Qa'eda-styled terrorism.

Considering for instance, that a nuclear truck bomb could obliterate an entire American city and cause a "panicky stampede into truly oppressive police statism, in which measures now unthinkable could suddenly become unstoppable," a 2003 Brookings Institute report aptly argued that "[s]tubborn adherence to the civil liberties status quo would probably damage our most fundamental freedoms far more in the long run than would judicious modifications of rules that are less fundamental." Indeed, should a major weapon of mass destruction event occur, a Pandora's box filled with draconian security measures would truly be opened; we might eventually close it again but we could never get everything back in.

Nevertheless, a fundamental obligation of any State is to protect its citizens from external as well as internal threats to person and property. Nowhere is this obligation more difficult to perform than in the realm of militant Islamic terrorism, particularly when one considers the apocalyptic horrors that might be unleashed through the terrorist use of weapons of mass destruction. In the War on Terror, the United States is concerned not only with those renegade States which might commit or sponsor terror attacks using weapons of mass destruction, but also there is deep consternation about how to best deal with international or domestic terrorist groups, and even individuals.

For those who follow the studies and trends, the lethality of terrorism continues to grow. The number of serious international terror incidents more than tripled in 2004. According to the State Department there were 655 significant terror attacks in 2004, up from 175 in 2003. The increase in 2004 reflected the rise of terrorism in Iraq, but included large scale events in Spain and Russia as well. Of course, such studies are rather inconsequential when one considers the aftermath of a terrorist directed nuclear, biological, chemical, radiological, or cyber attack in an urban area of the United States. The attacks of September 11, 2001, could very well pale in comparison. Furthermore, to the mass casualties and devastating economic disruption, one must add the troubling impact such an event might have on future civil liberties and freedoms that Americans now enjoy. Considering that al-Qa'eda-styled terrorists have targeted the United States more often than any other country in the world, save Israel, the specter of weapons of mass destruction terrorism demands top priority in our thinking and planning.

Karl von Clausewitz once observed that "[e]very age has its own kind of war, its own limiting conditions and its own peculiar preconceptions." One characteristic of the War on Terror is undeniable; the United States stands as the world's bastion of stability and as the foremost sphere of power and influence. Accordingly, it is absolutely critical that our national strategy for winning the War on Terror successfully accomplish three things. First, the United States must fully identify and appreciate the threat of the new breed of al-Qa'eda-styled militant Islamic global terrorism. These Islamo-facists are dedicated murderers who are absolutely convinced that their religion compels them to kill all those that do not accept their worldview. Second, United States strategy must undergo a major metamorphous in order to better bring the battle to the terrorist and to the nations that harbor them. Third, particularly in the context of the new Afghani and Iraqi governments, America must unabashedly promote and sustain a dedicated democracy building campaign in order to drain the totalitarian swamps in which all international terrorism breeds.

This third factor is extremely ambitious and will require decades of commitment. In short, it involves embracing a new paradigm that is intuitively simplistic and yet absolutely vital to winning the War on Terror. Simply put, since democracies do not engage in terrorism the United States must concentrate resources to do more to promote the normative values of democracy, pluralism, and human rights throughout the community of nations. The United States of America must continue to advocate policies which enhance global stability and encourage, at whatever level, a steadfast adherence to established, well-defined norms of international behavior, i.e., maintaining the rule of law rooted in democratic principles. This democracy building initiative must be the basis for a new and dynamic paradigm whose application points to a more effective way to war and terrorism avoidance, especially in regards to State-sponsors of aggression and terrorism. Despite the fact that many elements of militant Islam are migrating from "physical space" to "cyberspace," al-Qa'eda terrorists and their like cannot successfully operate without host nation support from a totalitarian regime.

At the end of the day, terrorism, like crime can never be completely eradicated. Nevertheless, the new specter of al-Qa'eda-styled terrorism can be better contained. The purpose of this introductory text is to survey the dominant characteristics of the War on Terror and to highlight some of the evolving legal and policy implications that confront the United States with special emphasis on the importance of developing capable law-based responses on the one hand and promoting democracy as a long term solution to terrorism avoidance on the other. In this context, even if one is cynical enough to believe that the world politic is ruled primarily by the application or threat of force, it is nevertheless of critical importance from both a national and an international perspective that America rubricate its leadership role by thoughtful concerns for the positive advancement of the rule of law and the protection of cherished civil liberties.

Since the War on Terror is a war between law-abiding nations and lawbreakers, the world's most precious commodities—the promotion of democratic values and human rights—must not become causalities in the War on Terror. Indeed, these are the very tools that will prove of ultimate value in winning the War on Terror. There are moral constants across time and space that are common to all mankind. These powerful forces cannot be defeated.

Finally, as the title of this book indicates, a new body of law called *terrorism law* is now emerging to deal with myriad legal issues associated with terrorism. As set out in the table of contents, this text covers the basic components of terrorism law. It is absolutely vital that lawyers skilled in terrorism law become involved in the national effort to protect the homeland and civil liberties.

Selected Bibliography

Brookings Review, *Rights Liberties and Security*, Vol. 21, Issue1, 2003 WL 11169678, Jan. 1, 2003.

Rehnquist, William H. ALL THE LAWS BUT ONE 222. 1998.

Seelye, Katharine Q., and Elisabeth Bumiller. *After the Attacks: The President; Bush Labels Aerial Terrorist Attacks 'Acts of War,'* N.Y. TIMES, Sept. 13, at A16 (The phrase "war on terror" was first used by President Bush on September 11, 2001, aboard Air Force One. His first major public address the next day also declared the terrorist attacks as "acts of war.")

Uniting and Strengthening America by Providing Appropriate Tools Required to Intercept and Obstruct Terrorism Act (USA PATRIOT Act) of 2001, Pub. L. No. 107-56, 115 Stat. 272. Oct. 26, 2001.

Chapter 1
What Is Terrorism?

The goal of the terrorist is to kill one and frighten 10,000.

—Chinese proverb

Things must be properly defined before they can be intelligently discussed. Although many trace the etymology of the word *terror* to France's "reign of terror" under Robespierre and the Jacobin Committee of Public Safety (*regime de la terreur*), the employment of terror is a phenomenon that has been around for a very long time in human history. Notwithstanding the fact that terrorism is the antithesis of the rule of law, there exists no global consensus on a precise definition of terrorism either in the international community or in the United States. This is due in part to the tensions of the Cold War era when West and East could agree on precious little, but also continues today under the postmodernist cliché, "one man's terrorist is another man's freedom fighter." For instance, a suicide bomber in Israel who intentionally kills innocent Jewish civilians may be considered a "hero" by certain segments of the Palestinian people and a terrorist by others.

1.1 Defining Terrorism

The concept of terrorism is now firmly embedded in the daily lexicon. Yet there is still no specific definition. Recognizing the politics associated with reaching an acceptable global definition for terrorism, the United Nations has very often elected to avoid the term terrorism altogether, use it in a general sense only, or to carefully carve out very specific acts in selected international treaties to characterize as "terrorism." Not only do discussions center on whether a State or just individuals can engage in terrorism, but the issue of using violence in so-called wars of national liberation remains a perennial stumbling block. In fact, definitional agreement is always hindered by whether or not some view terrorists as working for or against one's own national interests. Five examples serve to illustrate this delinquency among the 192 member States of the United Nations.

1

Defining Terror

First, the International Law Commission's 1954 *Draft Code of Offenses Against the Peace and Security of Mankind* contained the following proposed language in Article 25 to define terrorism: "[T]he undertaking or encouragement by the authorities of a State of terrorist activity in another State, or the toleration by the authorities of a State of organized activities calculated to carry out terrorist acts in another State." Even though the proposed sentence failed to define the term, no agreement could be reached. As of this writing, fifty years later, the United Nations General Assembly has still not been able to reach agreement on a final version.

Second, the latest attempt by the United Nations Sub-Commission on Human Rights to come up with a definition of terrorism has met similar troubles. The first draft report of February 2001, listed three essential elements of terrorism. A terrorist act: (1) must be illegal; violating national or international law; (2) must be intended to harm the State for political reasons; and (3) must be capable of generating a state of fear in the general population. However, in order to reach consensus amongst the committee members on its first progress report, the special rapporteur had to delete the entire definition relating to terrorism.

Third, perhaps the greatest missed opportunity for the United Nations to establish a firm international definition of terrorism as it relates to States that sponsor or support terrorists occurred in its failure to employ the word "terrorism" in the context of the key 1957 United Nations General Assembly resolution defining aggression as it relates to when a nation may engage in armed self-defense under Article 51 of the United Nations Charter. The United Nations chose to classify the activities of States that send, organize, or support "armed bands, groups, irregulars, or mercenaries, which carry out acts of armed force against a State," as simply engaging in unlawful aggression in direct violation of the U.N. Charter. It failed to refer to these activities as engaging in terrorism. Terrorism, of course, could have certainly fit into this expression of unlawful aggression, but it was not used.

Currently, there are twelve international conventions related to terrorism and ten criminal acts identified as terrorism in various United Nations conventions and protocols. The acts are: highjacking, aviation sabotage, acts of violence at airports, acts of violence regarding maritime navigation, acts of violence against fixed platforms, crimes against internationally protected persons, unlawful taking and use of nuclear material, hostage taking, terrorist bombings and supporting front organizations serving as financial conduits for terrorists groups. Obviously these ten do not cover terrorism in all its manifestations, but until the international community can form a universal definition, one can certainly reference these documents regarding specific acts of terrorism.

Fourth, in the wake of the September 11, 2001, terror attacks on the United States, the Ad Hoc Committee on Terrorism proposed a definition of terrorism for the General Assembly. This definition was not adopted, however, due to strong opposition from the 56-member Organization of Islamic Conference. In short, the Organization of Islamic Conference wanted the definition to exempt so-called wars of national liberation against foreign occupation (e.g., the Israeli occupation of certain areas in Palestine).

Fifth, on September 28, 2001, the Security Council adopted resolution 1373. The resolution's legal requirements are meant to create a common legal basis for all States to take effective action against terrorists by criminalizing terrorist fundraising and blocking terrorist assets. It is quite impressive on paper. It requires all member States to "[r]efrain from providing any form of support, active or passive, to entities or persons involved in terrorist acts;" "take the necessary steps to prevent the commission of terrorist acts;" "deny safe haven to those who finance, plan, support, or commit terrorist acts;" and "prevent those who finance, plan, facilitate, or commit terrorist acts from using their respective territories for those purposes against other States or their citizens …." To implement these obligations, a Counter-Terrorism Committee (CTC) was created to receive hundreds of State reports on progress in each of the mentioned areas. Amazingly, the CTC has not yet managed to name a single terrorist organization, individual or State sponsor of terrorism.

In the United States, the difficulties in definition are not related to a reluctance to use the term terrorism, but rather they rest in the sheer number of different government instrumentalities that have offered independent interpretations of terrorism which, while similar, are not identical. One of the latest American efforts to define terrorism is found in Section 411 of the PATRIOT Act, signed into law with overwhelming bipartisan support in November of 2001.

Actually, the PATRIOT Act provides similar definitions for "terrorist organization," "domestic terrorism," and "international terrorism." A terrorist organization is defined as one that is:

> (1) designated by the Secretary of State as a terrorist organization under the process established under current law; (2) designated by the Secretary of State as a terrorist organization for immigration purposes; or (3) a group of two or more individuals that commits terrorist activities or plans or prepares to commit (including locating targets for) terrorist activities.

Domestic terrorism is defined in the PATRIOT Act with a slightly different emphasis; domestic terrorism is the "unlawful use, or threatened use, of force or violence by a group or individuals based [in the United States] … committed against persons or property to intimidate or coerce a government, the civilian population … in furtherance of political or social objectives."

International terrorism is set out in the PATRIOT Act as follows:

> International terrorism involves violent acts or acts dangerous to human life that violate the criminal laws of the United States or any state, or that would be a criminal violation if committed within the jurisdiction of the United States or any state. These acts appear intended to intimidate or coerce a civilian population, influence the policy of a government by intimidation or coercion, or affect the conduct of a government by assassination or kidnapping. International terrorist acts occur outside the United States or transcend national boundaries in terms of how terrorists accomplish them, the persons they appear intended to coerce or intimidate, or the place in which the perpetrators operate.

1.2 The Goal of Terrorism

Despite the lack of a fixed universal agreement defining terrorism, the essential goal of terrorism is readily identifiable. As the root word implies, the goal of terrorism is to instill fear in a given civilian population by means of violence. In the oft-repeated Chinese proverb, the objective of the terrorist is to kill one and frighten 10,000. While specific acts of terrorism may appear to be mindless and irrational, terrorism is the exact opposite of confused behavior. Terrorism is a goal-directed, calculated, premeditated use of force. Unfortunately, all too often, terrorist tactics prove effective when those who are targeted respond in a way that reinforces the demands of the terrorists. The March 11, 2004, series of coordinated train bombings in Spain by al-Qa'eda-linked terrorists not only killed just over 200 people, but the attacks caused the newly installed Spanish government to withdraw its military forces from the American led coalition in Iraq, a coalition that is combating some of the very same forces of terror that attacked Spain. On the other hand, sometimes the use of terror tactics can result in unintended consequences for the terrorist network. The al-Qa'eda certainly did not seek the destruction of its primary base of operations in Afghanistan when it attacked the United States on September 11, 2001. At most, al-Qa'eda hoped to spark a massive social and political revolution in the Middle East that would bring to power al-Qa'eda-related governments.

Since the victims of terrorism are invariably innocent civilians, it appears fundamentally logical that a definitional approach should concentrate on the act and not the political, religious, or social causes which motivate the act. Under this regimen, the use of violence on a civilian target with intent to cause fear in a given civilian population for political purposes is easily classified as a terrorist act. In other words, to the common understanding of the general public, terrorism is immediately associated with violence that is directed at the indiscriminate killing of innocent civilians in order to create a climate of fear. Thus, in the 1980s, acts of indiscriminant bombings and burnings of civilians in public places by the "Spear of the Nation," the armed wing of the African National Congress, were acts of terrorism. The ends can never justify the means.

In this light, bombings of public places, the sending of letter bombs or poisons through the mail, hijackings of aircraft, hostage taking, and so on, are all acts of terrorism regardless of the underlying cause said to justify the attack, or whether the attack occurs in peacetime or during war. In a sense, terrorism can simply be described as making "war" on civilians. United States Senator George Mitchell defined terrorism in February 2002 as follows: "Terrorism involves the deliberate killing of randomly selected noncombatants for political ends. It seeks to promote a political outcome by spreading terror and demoralization throughout a population."

In summary, if a universal definition is not practicable, one can at least list four key characteristics of terrorism that better reflect the activity:

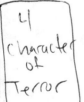

1. The illegal use of violence directed at civilians to produce fear in a target group.
2. The continuing threat of additional future acts of violence.
3. A predominately political or ideological character of the act.
4. The desire to mobilize or immobilize a given target group.

The Secretary General of the United Nations, Kofi Annan, offered this 2005 definition:

> [A]ny action constitutes terrorism if it is intended to cause death or serious bodily harm to civilians or non-combatants, with the purpose of intimidating a population or compelling a Government or an international organization to do or abstain from doing any act.

1.3 Terrorism and Weapons of Mass Destruction

Apart from the normal *modus vivendi* of terrorism, one must now add weapons of mass destruction as a special definitional subset. In Section 1403 of the National Defense Authorization Act for fiscal year 1997, weapons of mass destruction are defined as "any weapon or device that is intended, or has the capability, to cause death or serious bodily injury to a significant number of people through the release of toxic or poisonous chemicals or their precursors, a disease organism, or radiation or radioactivity." Thus, in its broadest sense, weapons of mass destruction include not only nuclear material, but the full range of biological, chemical and radioactive agents.

As is true for any terrorist event, there are three general sources from which a weapon of mass destruction terrorist attack can emanate—States, sub-State groups, or individuals. Tragically, in the so-called information age, all three categories have demonstrated a willingness to use weapons of mass murder in the physical world and there can be no doubt that this thirst for violence will soon spill over into the cyber world as well. States that engage in terrorism and have the potential of using weapons of mass destruction are further divided as either State-sponsors or State-supporters of terrorism.

1.4 State-sponsored and State-supported Terrorism

Perhaps the most easily identifiable category of terrorism is the State-sponsored terrorist attack. In recent times, the international community has been shocked to learn that certain renegade States, such as Saddam Hussein's Iraq, have shown an unabashed willingness to use deadly nerve gas to kill thousands of men, women and children (the Kurds). Indeed, it can be argued that all totalitarian States pose an ever-present threat for the use of weapons of mass destruction at any given time—both against their own people and against other nations. Each year, the U.S. State Department designates certain countries as sponsors of terrorism against other nations. This list always includes: Cuba, Iran, North Korea and Syria. In fact, regarding weapons of mass destruction the number is always larger. For instance, in 1999, John A. Lauder, director of the Central Intelligence Agency's Nonproliferation Center, testified before Congress that a dozen countries "now either possess or are actively pursuing offensive biological weapons capabilities for use against their perceived enemies, whether internal or external." [Taliban]

In the context of a State's use of weapons of mass destruction in a terrorist attack, several commentators seek to distinguish a State-sponsored terrorist act from a State-supported terrorist act. State-sponsored terrorism exists when a State directly but secretly uses its own resources to sponsor acts of terrorism against another country. Since accountability for such acts are denied, the aggressor-State seeks to avoid responsibility. On the other hand, State-supported terrorism [Syria] refers to the practice of a State providing resources or finances to a terrorist group for training and logistics, as occurred in Afghanistan, where the terrorist group headed by Osama bin Laden once took open refuge. In contrast to the State-sponsored scenario, the State-supported terrorist group generally operates in a more independent fashion from the State.

A classic and oft-cited case of a State-sponsored act of terrorism occurred in 1986 when Libyan government agents bombed an American frequented discotheque in then West Berlin, Germany. This secretive act of terror was followed by a second State-sponsored act of terror in [Libya] 1988: the in-flight bombing of Pan Am Flight 103 over Lockerbie, Scotland, which killed 278 people.

In the final analysis, it is difficult to make a practical distinction between State-sponsored and State-supported terrorism. The terms really speak only to the degree of culpability. Nevertheless, if the rule of law has any force, States that allow terrorist groups to operate with impunity on their soil should never be able to escape the attendant lawful consequences. While it is subject to legal debate whether a particular terrorist act committed apart from the support or sponsorship of a State would be considered an "act of war" under international law, a terrorist attack with the support or sponsorship of a State could very well be deemed an "act of war."

The early days of concern regarding terrorism and the use of weapons of mass destruction saw most of the emphasis focused primarily on the actions of the totalitarian State. Because many believed that ready access to weapons of mass destruction material was limited, sub-State terrorist groups and individual terrorists were generally given less attention. For these later categories of terrorism, the international community generally concentrated on making specific overt acts international crimes (e.g., airline hijacking or hostage taking). In regards to renegade States, however, the major issue turned on the proper application of appropriate sanctions against the State that sponsored or supported the terrorist incident.

1.5 The Diplomatic Bag

A particular early concern, which demonstrates the depth of the debate regarding how to deal with a weapon of mass destruction terrorist event *vis-à-vis* international legal sanctions, was the use of the "diplomatic bag" to import and export with impunity assorted prohibited and illegal items into receiving and transit States. The diplomatic bag issue continues to stir disagreement even today. Modern international practice has witnessed the use (or attempted use) of the diplomatic bag to transport illegal foreign currency, illegal drugs, weapons and even people. While all *malum in se* acts committed under the cover of this diplomatic shield are sorely objectionable, the most insidious and disconcerting activities are those in which the diplomatic bag might be used as a vehicle to commit clearly defined acts of terrorism, especially those related to the employment of a weapon of mass destruction.

Currently, the diplomatic privileges and immunities accorded to the diplomatic bag under treaty and customary international law are set out in Article 27 of the Vienna Convention on Diplomatic Relations. In short, the diplomatic bag is deemed by international law to be inviolable and not subject to detention or search. The central thrust of those who periodically call for a change to the Vienna Convention argue that the protected status given to the diplomatic bag must be significantly revised to account for the legitimate security interests of the receiving State. Again, the major concern is that the diplomatic bag could be used by a foreign actor to commit an act of terrorism with a weapon of mass destruction.

Perhaps the most widely publicized abuse of the diplomatic bag to date, and one which clearly illustrates the controversy over the status of the bag, was committed by the Libyan government of Colonel Muammar al-Qaddafi. In April of 1984, two Libyans gunned down eleven demonstrators and one British constable as they stood outside of the Libyan embassy in London. Despite substantial suspicions that the weapons and other evidence connected with this heinous act of terrorism were put inside of Libyan diplomatic bags, the British authorities allowed the Libyans to carry the diplomatic bags out of the country without searching or scanning them. This incident caused a chorus of protest that the rules of diplomatic immunity were obsolete.

Responding to public fears that diplomatic privileges could be used as a vehicle to commit State-sponsored terrorism related to weapons of mass murder, then Secretary of Defense Caspar Weinberger publicly indicated in 1986 that the entire doctrine of diplomatic immunity should be greatly limited. Arguing that State-sponsored terrorists were abusing the doctrine, Weinberger called upon "diplomats, with the assistance of the legal profession" to define new limits that would help solve the problem of diplomatic privileges being extended to those States who were connected with terrorists. Weinberger's call to action was not heeded.

No one can argue that all conventional terrorist acts fade in significance when compared to fears that the diplomatic bag might be used illegally to transport weapons of mass destruction. In the wake of the large-scale destruction that would result from even a single weapon of mass destruction event, the demands for security safeguards would seem to far outweigh any status quo that the international rules might seek to maintain. In short, if ordinary weapons can be neatly and easily sent into the receiving State via the diplomatic bag, why not a weapon of mass destruction? One terrorist from a hostile country, for example, could smuggle in a vile of lethal biological material for insertion in a city water supply in the United States. Although this argument is true enough, the privileged status of the diplomatic bag has never been successfully curtailed. This is true for three reasons.

First, most people understand that if the diplomatic bag privilege is limited then the determined terrorist will find yet another way to smuggle materials for mass murder into the United States. In an open society, such as the United States, the State-sponsored terrorist, or any terrorist, can obtain much, if not most, of the needed materials on the domestic open market and, more importantly, can do so without leaving a signature.

Second, since nations have an inherent right of self-defense to search out and otherwise protect themselves against viable threats to their national security, the State which sponsored such blatant aggressive behavior takes an inordinate risk by using the diplomatic bag in such a manner. Deterrence would keep the renegade State in check.

Third, like all international agreements, the Vienna Convention can never hope to maintain any form of functional integrity unless it is strictly adhered to. Nations who demand inspection of even the most suspicious diplomatic bags must do so only at the risk of having their own bags subjected to the same process by the sending State. And that practice would quickly undermine the entire process of free diplomatic intercourse. The only real guarantee that other nations, friendly or otherwise, will generally follow international rules rests in this reciprocity analysis— the red thread of international law. We follow the rules because the other guy follows the rules.

As discussed in Chapter 2, the way to deal with a State-sponsored terrorist attack, if linkage is established, is to seek redress under the rule of law—financially, judicially, or militarily. Historically, if a State sponsors a terrorist act, the United States has generally demonstrated that it has the capability and willingness to retaliate under the well-recognized venue of self-defense. Unlike other international disputes between nations, terrorist attacks should never be handled by a third-party in the context of dispute resolution. The renegade State must be neutralized in a legitimate manner and forum. Ultimately, the aggrieved State can turn to the classical rules of self-defense, depending on the severity of the terrorist incident. Realistically, if the United States had hard evidence that a State was behind a terrorist attack, it would likely respond under the traditional notions of self-defense and forcible self-help. This, of course, is precisely what occurred in response to the September 11, 2001, attack on the United States. Any nation will certainly do what is necessary to protect itself from illegal acts of violence or the imminent threat of aggression.

1.6 Sub-State Terrorism

Sub-State terrorist groups can either be domestic or international terrorist organizations and are generally categorized by either religious or political ideologies. In 1995, for example, a RAND study found that "25 of 58, or 42 percent of known, active, international terrorist groups had a predominately religious component or motivation." In addition, from a rule of law perspective sub-State terrorist organizations do not operate with the approval or sponsorship of the host nation.

The first use of a weapon of mass destruction by a sub-State group occurred on March 20, 1995, when members of the Aum Shinrikyo cult in Japan released a lethal nerve agent, sarin, in a Tokyo underground subway. This weapon of mass destruction attack killed twelve people and injured 3,000 others, clearly demonstrating that the scenario of terrorists using a weapon of mass destruction was not the stuff of fiction.

While attacks by sub-State groups against United States interests have yet to use weapons of mass destruction (as of this writing), many groups have shown a viciousness and disregard for human life that clearly points to a willingness to use such weapons in the future. For instance, an Islamic radical group with ties to al-Qa'eda and headed by Ramzi Ahmad Yousef conducted the 1993 bombing of New York City's World Trade Center in an attempt to topple one of the twin towers onto the other to kill thousands, an act clearly in the spirit of a weapons of mass destruction event. In fact, it has been reported that those behind the 1993 World Trade Center bombing were also gathering the ingredients for a chemical weapon that could have brought the death toll into the tens of thousands. Some reports indicated that the bomb might have been laced with cyanide, but the poison burned up in the detonation.

In early 2000, United States and Israeli intelligence sources reported that Hamas, the militant Palestinian terrorist group now elected to represent the Palestinians, was experimenting with chemical weapons in their rocket attacks against Israeli targets. Although no radical Islamic group has yet to use chemical or biological agents in their terror attacks on Israel, the potential for such acts certainly exists. With the increasing availability of high-tech weapons and nuclear materials from former communist countries and the ease with which some chemical and biological agents can now be manufactured, there is growing concern that sub-State groups will now actively cross over into the weapons of mass destruction domain. Indeed, the fear also exists that one of the world's dictators might simply give weapons of mass destruction to a sub-State terrorist group. This was certainly a major consideration for the United States led preemptive attack on Saddam Hussein's regime in 2003 and continues to be an issue in the quest to stop the radicalized Iranian regime from developing nuclear weapons.

1.7 Individual Terrorism

Perhaps the most troubling aspect of weapons of mass destruction terrorism is one not often heard in the War on Terror. It is the prospect of an individual not affiliated with any terror organization setting off a weapon of mass destruction in a major urban area. Because they operate on their own, without affiliation to any known group or State, individuals who engage in "lone-wolf" terrorism are far harder to predict, track, or deter.

To demonstrate the seriousness of individual terrorism, on March 3, 1999, William C. Patrick, III, a leading American expert on biological warfare, walked through the security check system at the Rayburn House Office Building in downtown Washington D.C., carrying 7.5 grams of powdered anthrax, enough to kill everyone in the building, in a small plastic bottle. Not only was he rubricating the ease with which a single determined terrorist could breach security systems and target, in this case, a major federal government installation, Patrick's action certainly should have provided the needed wake up call to United States government officials and the public at large. Unfortunately, it did not.

Patrick told a Congressional committee that he was trying to show how a hostile or aggressor State could smuggle powdered anthrax in to the United States in a secure diplomatic pouch. What Patrick was really demonstrating, however, was the ease with which any individual terrorist—domestic or international—could unleash untold bioterrorism horror, almost at will. In his testimony, Patrick related that he had also carried other similar deadly materials and, "like Sherman went through Georgia," had "been through all the major airports, and the security systems of the State Department, the Pentagon, and even the CIA, and nobody [has] stopped me."

The most notorious example of an individual terrorist attack in the United States occurred in April 1995 with the bombing of the Murrah Federal Building in Oklahoma City by Timothy McVeigh. The bomb killed 167 people, including women and children. Although McVeigh did not employ a weapon of mass destruction in his attack, his actions clearly raised the issue of individual domestic terrorism in the context of weapons of mass destruction. While one can ponder the bizarre "anti-government" sentiments that motivated McVeigh, the greater issue really revolves around individual access to material which can cause widespread damage of life and property.

Furthermore, not all individual terrorism can be associated with fanatical political or religious ideologues. Individual terrorism can be committed by persons seeking personal rather than political gain, or by individuals who are mentally ill. Considering the number of "Timothy McVeighs" in any given open society, the prospect of individuals obtaining access to weapons of mass destruction is chilling and will unfortunately continue to grow with time.

1.8 Al-Qa'eda-Styled Terrorism and Militant Islam

The War on Terror is predominantly focused on defeating the al-Qa'eda terrorist network, although the United States is now targeting well over a dozen Islamic terror groups. The Department of Defense's 2005 *National Military Strategic Plan for the War on Terrorism* now recognizes that the number one terrorist threat to the United States is Islamic extremism. The "posterchild" for militant Islam is still the al-Qa'eda organization which is a new type of terrorism that combines all of the forms of terror identified in this chapter. They were, at one time, State-sponsored by the Taliban government of Afghanistan and continue to be State-supported by any number of radical regimes including Iran, the Palestinian territories, Syria and so on. They also qualify as a sub-State terrorist organization because they have secretly infiltrated and established "sleeper" terrorist cells in various nations throughout the world including the United States, Canada, Britain, France, England, Spain, Italy, Australia, Germany, etc.

In addition, al-Qa'eda also influences individual terrorism. Their ideology of hate and intolerance has reached the minds of individuals who, although not directly tied to the organization, choose to commit terrorist acts because they have adopted the general theme and goal of the al-

Qa'eda mindset. This certainly occurred in the shooting murder of several innocent civilians in California at Los Angeles International Airport on July 4, 2002, by Hesham Mohamed Hadayat; although law enforcement officials did all they could to downplay the impact that radical Islamic ideology had in the attack.

Some have described the al-Qa'eda terrorist group as an entirely new type of entity in the world—not just a terrorist group but a "virtual-State" that normal criminal law processes simply cannot curtail. The virtual-State description is fundamentally valid. The al-Qa'eda virtual-State exhibits many of the characteristics of the classic nation-State, but is able to walk in and out of the shadows of international law because it has no fixed national boundaries. For instance, the al-Qa'eda virtual-State certainly has a political arm and media section that directs its policy, a military composed of thousands of devoted killers, a treasury that raises funds across the globe, a large number of supporters and adherents, direct and indirect links to the leaders of other nation-states, etc. Indeed, for this reason, the United States has been obliged to reach beyond the tools of normal law enforcement and to utilize its military power to make war with this virtual-State. This new approach, employing the laws of war, has resulted in numerous legal challenges in both domestic and international law.

Certainly, the War on Terror demands that the United States fully come to grips with the *modis vivendi* of the al-Qa'eda as well as all sister Islamic militant groups that seek to wage war by conducting large scale terrorist attacks on America. Again, America must know the enemy if it is to ever defeat him. In this context, there are three basic reasons why the al-Qa'eda virtual State and al-Qa'eda-styled militant Islam is vastly different from all previous terror groups that civilized nations have had to cope with.

First, threatened by the normative values of democracy, freedom and human rights, the al-Qa'eda and like minded militant Islamic terror groups are dedicated to the destruction of the West and all those who adopt Western ideals, including those moderate Muslim and Arab governments that refute their view of Islam. The fanaticism runs so deep that they are eagerly willing to commit suicide in the furtherance of their cause. Unlike previous terrorist groups, al-Qa'eda suicide bombers have no "exit" strategy to save themselves, making it almost impossible for law enforcement to stop them. (The failed al-Qa'eda-styled plot to detonate liquid explosives on as many as ten U.S. bound airplanes coming from London in August 2006 provided an intelligence bonanza for British and American law enforcement.) The predominantly young male suicide bombers are lured into death (euphemistically called martyrdom) by the religious promise of automatically securing a place in Paradise for themselves where they will receive "fleshly delights [virgins] and the expectation that they will be allowed to choose seventy friends and family members to join them in heaven."

Furthermore, democracies offer a plethora of targets that can easily be attacked, particularly if one is not concerned with surviving the assault. There are, for example, 15,000 chemical plants, refineries and hazardous material sites in the United States. With almost 1,000 of these sites located near large population centers, the death toll from a terror attack could easily total in the tens of thousands. Thus, employing suicide as the method of choice to inflict terror, a dedicated terrorist can target almost any public place, e.g., in New York City there are 468 subway stations, and in

Chicago there are over 2,000 bus stops. Tragically, these new terrorists have successfully used the openness of the democratic society to attack from within, placing great strains on civil liberties.

Second, militant Islam has learned to use the super highway of modern technology to establish ties across the globe and provide logistical support for terror cells in practically every country in the world. In fact, the next generation of fanatics will be far more adept at using the Internet and will no doubt engage in cyber terrorism attacks to disrupt, for instance, power plants, airports, banking institutions and even nuclear power plants. Even now, militant Islamic terrorists use the Internet to assist in recruiting and organizing. Moreover, cyber terrorism is unique because it makes normal physical security measures totally irrelevant. There are no borders to sneak across, no security cameras to avoid and no bombs to manufacture. Terrorists can use a medium of attack that is virtually risk free.

Third, the al-Qa'eda and their like have shown an intense desire to obtain any and all forms of weapons which can inflict mass casualties on civilians, including weapons of mass destruction. Their appetite for killing knows no limits. The greatest fear is that a terrorist will obtain a nuclear weapon and smuggle it into an American port of entry. In fact, such a weapon can be smuggled into the United States with very little risk of failure. Only a tiny fraction of the millions of people (400+ million), cars (130+ million), trucks (12+ million), rail freight cars (2+ million) and maritime containers (8+ million) entering the U.S. at over 3,700 terminals and 301 ports of entry are ever subjected to inspection of any kind.

1.9 Why They Hate

Some terrorists have tried to depict the current Global War on Terrorism as a war against Islam. This is obviously not true. The War on Terror is against those militant Islamic groups that have declared "war" on the United States, such as al-Qa'eda. The ideological motivations of these militant Islamic terror organizations are focused on the advancement of cult-like "religious" objectives rather than the more typical aspirations of traditional old-styled terrorist groups that are primarily concerned with the achievement of political or territorial goals. Driven by extremist pseudo-Islamic radicalism, the new breed of terrorists are bent on destroying through violence those individuals and things which are deemed to be outside of a very narrow *weltanschauung* (world view). Since the establishment of the new Iraqi government in 2004, well over 500 car-bombs driven by al-Qa'eda operatives and other jihadists have murdered about 10,000 innocent civilians, mostly fellow Muslims. Abu Mousab al-Zarqawi, the former leader of al-Qa'eda in Iraq (he was killed by U.S. firepower in June 2006), believed that "slaughtering fellow Arabs who followed different forms of Islam was as important as killing Westerners."

The 9/11 Commission found that the Untied States is facing a loose confederation of people, maybe numbering in the tens of thousands, who believe in a perverted strain of Islam and are busy building the groundwork for decades of struggle. Although militant Islam is not restricted to just the al-Qa'eda-styled belief system—the current Iranian regime has its own radicalized view of Islam—the roots of al-Qa'eda come from a narrow radicalized strain of Islam known as the Wahhabi movement. The movement arose in the eighteenth century under Mohammed Ibn Abd al-Wahab in the desert of Najd in the Arabian Peninsula. Ibn Abd al-Wahab converted a group of illiterate Bedouins under Muhammad Ibn Sa'ud and declared himself the religious leader, or *Sheik*, and Sa'ud the political leader, or *Emir*. Amazingly, one of al-Wahab's first acts was to issue a *fatwa*, a religious decree, casting all non-Wahhabi Muslims as apostates and idol worshippers. In this way, Sa'ud's men were now all cloaked in the role of fighters for *jihad* (holy war) against anyone not in the new Wahhabi movement, including other Muslims whom they killed in large numbers.

Funded by Saudi Arabia, the Wahhabi movement has spread across much of the Islamic world. In fact, the greatest achievement of the sect has been to present Wahhabism to a large segment of the Arab world as an accepted part of Islam, even as the "true" Islam. At its heart, the extreme view of Wahhabism adopts the same ideology of the fascists and communists except that it cloaks itself by manipulating the Islamic religion to gain political power and social domination. Militant Islam is truly an anachronistic mind set, in complete conflict with modern concepts of plurality, human rights and democracy. The rich tradition of religious tolerance in America is the antithesis of militant Islam. Speaking in 2003 before the Senate Subcommittee on Terrorism, Technology and Homeland Security, Alex Alexiev, Senior Fellow at the Center for Security Policy noted:

> A key postulate of Wahhabi's teaching asserts that Muslims who do not believe in his doctrines are ipso facto non-believers and apostates against whom violence and Jihad were not only permissible, but obligatory. This postulate alone transgresses against two fundamental tenets of the Quran—that invoking Jihad against fellow-Muslims is prohibited and that Muslim's profession of faith should be taken at face value until God judges his/hers sincerity at judgment day. This extreme reactionary creed was then used as the religious justification for military conquest and violence against Muslim neighbors of the House of Saud. Already in 1746, just two years after Wahhabism became Saud's religion, the new Saudi-Wahhabi state proclaimed Jihad against all neighboring Muslim tribes that refused to subscribe to it. Indeed, well into the 1920s the history of the House of Saud is replete with violent campaigns to force other Muslims to submit politically and theologically, violating yet another fundamental Quranic principle that prohibits the use of compulsion in religion.

There are numerous terrorist organizations that fit the mold of militant Islam, although not all of the militant groups are at "war" with the United States. The State Department's 2006 list of foreign terrorist organizations (FTO) contains 42 groups; at least 23 of these FTOs cloak themselves in a militant view of Islam. The list includes: Abu Sayyaf Group, Al-Aqsa Martyrs Brigade, Ansar al-Sunna, Armed Islamic Group, Asbat al-Ansar, Gama'a al-Islamiyya, HAMAS, Harakat ul-Mujahedin, Hizballah, Islamic Jihad Group, Jaish-e-Mohammed, Jemaah Islamiya Organization, Al-Jihad, Libyan Islamic Fighting Group, Moroccan Islamic Combatant Group, Mujahedin-e Khalq Organization, Palestinian Islamic Jihad, al-Qa'eda and al-Qa'eda in Iraq. As previously noted, a 1995 RAND-St. Andrews Chronology of International Terrorism study revealed that "25 of 58, or 42 percent of known, active, international terrorists groups had a predominately religious component or motivation." Many of these radical Islamic groups are associated with Islamic fundamentalism spewed from radicalized *madrasas* (religious schools) which operate with impunity in such countries as Saudi Arabia, Pakistan, and Iran. In fact, in the case of many militant Islamic terrorist organizations, direct links have been established to various *Deobandi* religious schools, which are known for openly advocating the most violent forms of terrorism against Western interests. In addition, radical clerics in Western nations also preach this brand of hate to their followers. For instance, many terrorists associated with the July 7 and 21, 2005, bombings in London had direct links to the infamous Findsbury Park Mosque in London (Muslim cleric Abuy Hamza al-Masri was subsequently arrested on suspicion of terrorism links).

The number of adherents of militant Islam is large and growing, perhaps reaching into the hundreds of thousands if one counts the strongly messianic strain of Twelver Shiism in Iran (belief that the twelfth legitimate successor of the prophet Muhammad who is said to have disappeared in the tenth century will return to reign over a world where Islam is universal). Pakistan and other Middle Eastern nations teem with al-Qa'eda sympathizers. But the most chilling hallmark associated with the spread of militant Islam is not the operation of terror training camps for the terror jihadists, but rather the established methodology of inculcating an ideology of hatred into the minds of innocent children from the moment of birth. In the homes, communities, and the *madrasas*, countless numbers of innocent children are brainwashed each and every day of their lives with no opportunity to escape. The radical *madrasas* are like conveyor belts of death where an unlimited number of suicide bombers emerge convinced that their religion demands the murder of Westerners, Jews, or anyone holding a contrary worldview. Up to 20 percent of all *madrasas* may be actively spreading radical ideologies.

Simply stated, the goal of al-Qa'eda-styled militant Islam is to conquer the world. In 2006 alone, Ayman al-Zawahiri and Osama bin Laden made almost 20 videotaped pronouncements on the global war. In August 2006, Zawahiri told his followers: "All the world is a battlefield open in front of us." This idea of global *jihad* is one of the defining threads that bring together suicide murders from Baghdad to Bali. In this light, al-Qa'eda is both a cohesive terror organization and a source of inspiration for all like-minded fanatics. In an April 24, 2006 tape, Osama bin Laden declared: "It is the duty for the Umma [nation] with all its categories of men, women and youths, to give away themselves, their money, experiences and all types of material support ... Jihad today is an imperative for every Muslim. The Umma will commit sin if it did not provide adequate material support for jihad." The never-ending struggle is encompassed in their view of the seventh-century jihad—the spread of Islam by force of arms. Unless they are shut down, the War on Terror cannot be won. Secretary of Defense Donald Rumsfeld made this point in a October 2003 memorandum he sent to General Richard Myers, Chairman of the Joint Chiefs of Staff, entitled: Global War on Terrorism. In the memorandum, Rumsfeld asked, "Are we capturing, killing or deterring and dissuading more terrorists every day than the madrassas [sic] and the radical clerics are recruiting, training, and deploying against us?"

Ultimately, of course, this means that only Muslims can provide the cure to militant Islam. In the aftermath of the July 7, 2005, bombing in London that killed 52 people, this theme was echoed by both the British and leading Muslim leaders in England. The key to winning the conflict is addressing the ideological aspect regarding how terrorists recruit and indoctrinate new followers. Interestingly, the suicide foot-soldiers defy simplistic political, sociological or psychological profiling. They come from extremely diverse educational, economic and social backgrounds. The only common red thread that binds them together is an unrelenting devotion to their radicalized Islamic belief system. *USA v. Koubriti, 199 F. Supp. 2d 656 (E.D.Mich. S.D. 2002) at 1:*

> Wahhabis, Takfiris, and Salafists…These groups regard the Islam that most Muslims practice today as unpure and polluted by idolatry and Western influence …. These radical fundamentalist-Islamic groups see the world divided in two spheres; that is, Dar-al-Islam (House of Islam or Islamic Zone), where peace reigns (Sallam), and the Dar-al-Harb (House of War or War Zone), which prevents a true Islamic state. The latter is viewed by these radical fundamentalist-Islamic groups to include all infidel areas that must ultimately be conquered. Global jihad is the constant effort to achieve this goal.

Perhaps one of the most chilling revelations of the vicious mindset of militant Islam is found in the "bin Laden videotape," released to the public on December 13, 2001. The tape clearly illustrates the twisted religious machinations of the al-Qa'eda terrorists and their like who pervert religion to justify the mass murder of innocent civilians. In the conversation between bin Laden and Sheik Khaled al-Harbi (who surrendered to Saudi officials in 2004) regarding the attacks of September 11, 2001, numerous references are made to "Allah," "Muhammad," the "*fiqu* [holy war] of Muhammad," and so on. At one point, bin Laden boasts that the attacks were beneficial to a "true" understanding of Islam. "The attacks made people think (about true Islam), which benefited them greatly." The video closes with the guest praising bin Laden in the name of Allah, "By Allah my Shaykh [bin Laden]. We congratulate you for the great work. Thank Allah."

Osama bin Laden and his followers are not simply another isolated sub-State religious terror cult like Japan's Aum Shinriko. According to a thought provoking special report from 2001 *Newsweek* entitled, "Why Do They Hate Us," these terrorists "come out of a culture that reinforces their hostility, distrust and hatred of the West—and of America in particular." Incredibly, a Gallup poll taken in late February 2002, indicated that a majority of the Arab world condemned the September 11, 2001, attack on the United States, but believed that Arabs did not carry it out. This opinion was shared throughout the region despite the fact that all nineteen of the hijackers were Arabs.

Similarly, these Islamic zealots are far different from mere criminals. Unlike criminals, they are not in it for monetary gain. They do not wish to circumvent the system, rather they desire to destroy the system. Their fantastic goal is to create an Islamic caliphate that controls the world. Still, al-Qa'eda has cited numerous grievances against the United States to justify their use of terror including American support of "puppet" Arab governments, importation of oil, support for Israel, support for the new Iraq and Afghanistan, Westerners living in Arab lands, morally corrupt Western culture, and so on. These complaints are hollow. Like all enemies of freedom and pluralism, be it the German Nazis or the Stalinist Communists, the radical Islamic terrorists' attack the West for what it is, not for what it has done. In a nutshell, whether the anti-Americanism is motivated by religious enmity, radical idiosyncrasies, or just blind hatred, militant Islamic terrorist groups have no regard or respect for human life let alone the human rights and fundamental freedoms of others. In this light, the problem is not the acts of terror but the mindset of those behind the terror attacks. To be sure, the U.N. Charter's rule of law and expression of human rights are viewed as hateful concepts of Western domination and not self-evident truths pointing the way to the betterment of mankind.

Related to the inherent dangerousness of al-Qa'eda-styled terrorist groups, is the fact that States providing support to these people suffer from the scourge of totalitarianism and open hostility to America and the West. This is an important phenomenon not only because terror groups could probably not flourish into sophisticated networks without the overt support of a State, but also because they can use those States to launch catastrophic terror attacks that will far exceed the horrors of September 11, 2001. Essentially, time is not on the side of civilized nations, as renegade regimes will sooner or later provide weapons of mass destruction to the radical disciples of hate. More terrifying is the realization that, unlike the situations in the Cold War, terrorists in the post 9/11 world do not require a sophisticated delivery system. The suicide terrorist bomber is the delivery system. With the advent of modern technology, the power to wage large scale destruction has now passed from the arena of the nation-state into the realm of the terrorist.

Conversely, a topic covered later in this book argues that democracies do not sponsor or support terrorism, dictatorships do. There exists an abundance of empirical evidence that stable democracies do not engage in international terrorism, instigate war, engage in democide (genocide and mass murder), or abuse the human rights of their people. As Anthony Lake, a Clinton era special assistant to the president for national security affairs, related in an address at John Hopkins University: "Democracies tend not to wage war on each other and they tend not to support terrorism—in fact, they don't. They are more trustworthy in diplomacy and they do a better job of respecting the ... human rights of their people." Certainly, in the preamble to the U.N. Charter and in Article 1 of the Charter, it is evident that the drafters also understood that nations who respect human rights and fundamental freedoms are less likely to engage in terrorism. This truth is axiomatic and democracies should be much more critical of totalitarian regimes.

1.10 Questions for Discussion

1) *One man's terrorist is another man's freedom fighter.* "The causes of terrorism or the political motivation of the individual terrorists are relevant to the problem of definition." Under this proposition, many have argued that acts of violence against "colonialism" or in wars of "national liberation" fall outside of the definition of terrorism. Hence, the dilemma of "[o]ne man's terrorism is another man's heroism." *See* John Norton Moore & Robert F. Turner, NATIONAL SECURITY LAW 2ND EDITION, (2006).

2) *International definitions.* U.N. Sec. Coun. Res. 1368 (Sept. 12, 2001). The Security Council resolution uses the word terror or terrorism six times in the short one page document. Like all other United Nations efforts in this area, SC 1368 uses the term terrorism but offers no definition of terrorism other than to affirm that the September 11, 2001, attacks on the United States was a "horrifying terrorist attack." Is it possible for the international community to reach an agreement on the definition of terrorism? What benefit would a totalitarian regime have for agreeing to an international definition for terrorism?

3. *Congressional definitions of terrorism.* The provision of the United States Code referenced in the PATRIOT Act, defines international terrorism as "terrorism involving citizens or the territory of more than one country." 22 U.S.C. § 2656f (d)(1). Furthermore, "terrorism" is defined as "premeditated, politically motivated violence perpetrated against noncombatant targets by sub-national groups or clandestine agents." 22 U.S.C. § 2656f(d)(2). Section 411 of the PATRIOT Act defines "terrorist activity" at length, as well as what it means to "engage in terrorist activity." 8 U.S.C. § 1182(b)(3)(B). Does the language in the different provisions of the United States Code listed above leave gaps in interpretation? In what way might the provisions be inadequate?

4. *Who is the enemy*? Following the failed August 2006 plot by British Muslims to blow up more than ten jetliners bound for the United States, President Bush said that the foiled plot was a "stark reminder" that "the nation is at war with Islamic fascists." Was this an appropriate characterization of the enemy in the War on Terror?

5. *Is the War on Terror a battle of religions*? The 2006 National Security Strategy of the United States of America states:

> While the War on Terror is a battle of ideas, it is not a battle of religions. The transnational terrorists confronting us today exploit the proud religion of Islam to serve a violent political vision: the establishment, by terrorism and subversion, of a totalitarian empire that denies all political and religious freedom. These terrorists distort the idea of jihad into a call for murder against those they regard as apostates or unbelievers—including Christians, Jews, Hindus, other religious traditions, and all Muslims who disagree with them. Indeed, most of the terrorist attacks since September 11 have occurred in Muslim countries—most of the victims have been Muslims.

Is any one religion more likely to engage in terrorism than another? Although biblical Christianity is distinguished from all other major world religions in that it rejects any system of human good deeds, morality, or ritual as the vehicle to achieve eternal relationship with God, Christians have engaged in terrorism. *See* Jeffrey F. Addicott, *The Misuse of Religion in the War on Terror*, ___ BARRY L. J. ___ (2006).

6. *Hatred in the classroom.* Learning why some come to hate the United States and its allies can be gleaned from what is taught in some Pakistani religious schools. In *Preachers of Hate: Islam and the War on America* (2003), Kenneth R. Timmerman writes:

> In third grade, children learn hate through vocabulary. "The Zionist enemy—attacked—civilians with its aircraft." (*Our Arabic Language for Third Grade*) In sixth grade, hate became a drill. "Who is the thief who has torn our homeland?" (*Our Arabic Language for Sixth Grade*) By seventh grade, students are expected to have internalized anti-Semitism so they can recite it on their own. "Why do the Jews hate Muslim unity and want to cause division among them?" Give an example of the evil attempts of the Jews, from events hap-

pening today." (*Islamic Education for Seventh Grade*) In ninth grade students are told, "One must beware of Jews, for they are treacherous and disloyal." (*Islamic Education for Ninth Grade*).

What is the best way to combat this dissemination of information? Is it right to do so?

Selected Bibliography

1954 Draft Code of Offenses Against the Peace and Security of Mankind, 9 U.N. GAOR Supp. (no. 9) at 11-12, U.N. Doc. A/2693. 1954.

Albright, Madeleine. The Mighty And The Almighty. 2006.

Bergen, Peter L. The Osama bin Laden I Know. 2006.

Carr, Caleb. The Lessons of Terror: A History of Warfare Against Civilians, Why It Has Always Failed and Why It Will Fail Again. 2002.

Chasey, William C. The Lockerbie Coverup. 1995.

Cohen, William S. *Preparing for a Grave New World*, Wash. Post, July 26, 1999, at A19.

Combating Terrorism: Threat and Risk Assessments Can Help Prioritize and Target Program Investments, U.S. GAO Report to Congressional Requesters, Apr. 1998.

Gabriel, Mark A. Islam and Terrorism. 2002.

Gerges, Fawaz A. Journey of the Jihadist. 2006.

Hartigan, Richard Shelly. Lieber's Code and the Law of War. 1983.

Lesser, Ian O., Bruce Hoffman, John Arquilla, David Ronfeldt and Michele Zanini. Countering the New Terrorism. Santa Monica, CA: RAND, 1999, at 17.

Lifton, Robert Jay. Destroying the World to Save It: Aum Shinrikyo, Apocalyptic Violence, and the New Global Terrorism. 2000.

Loeb, Vernon. *Anthrax Vial Smuggled In To Make A Point At A Hill Hearing*, Wash. Post, Mar. 4, 1999, at A1.

Michel, Lou, and Dan Herbeck. American Terrorist: Timothy McVeigh and the Tragedy at Oklahoma City. 2001.

Moore, John Norton, and Robert F. Turner. National Security Law. 2d ed. 2006.

Nelson, William. *Opening Pandora's Box: The Status of the Diplomatic Bag in International Relations*, 12 Fordham Int'l L. J. 494. 1989.

Report of the International Law Commission on the Work of its Thirty-Eighth Session, U.N. Doc. A/41/ 10. 1986.

Sun-tzu, The Art of War, Ralph D. Sawyer trans., 1994.

The Complete Works of Flavius Josephus, William Whiston trans., 1981. The Hebrew Zealots conducted random acts of assassination against the occupying Romans in Judea prior to Jerusalem falling to the Roman legions under Titus in 70 A.D.

Timmerman, Kenneth R. Preachers of Hate: Islam and the War on America. 2003.

USA/PATRIOT Act of 2001, 115 Stat. 272; Pub. Law 107-56 §411. Oct. 26, 2001.

Wedgewood, Ruth. *Responding to Terrorism: The Strikes Against bin Laden*, 24 Yale J. Int'l L. 599. 1999.

Chapter 2
The War on Terror

As we gather tonight, our nation is at war ... and the civilized world faces unprecedented dangers.

—George W. Bush

Synopsis

By definition, the traditional approach to combating terrorism is encompassed in two terms—antiterrorism and counterterrorism. Although most associate the term *counterterrorism* to cover both concepts, strictly speaking, antiterrorism involves all those steps and actions taken by authorities to decrease the probability of a terrorist act from occurring. Antiterrorism, the proactive, preventative stage of stopping terrorism, includes techniques designed to harden potential high profile targets (e.g., government buildings or military installations), as well as actions taken to detect a planned terrorist attack before it occurs. For example, to prevent future terrorist attacks the Pentagon and private industry are both experimenting with video surveillance, modeling techniques and commercial technologies such as those used to identify automatic teller machine customers by scanning their faces.

One of the facets of the War on Terror is the realization that antiterrorism relies heavily on the efforts of ordinary citizens who, when observing suspicious behavior, are willing to notify law enforcement. Sometimes the suspicions prove profitable, as with the September 2002 arrest of six members of the "Lackawanna" sleeper terrorist cell in New York (based on a tip by an Arab American) or the August 2006 arrest of 24 al-Qa'eda-styled radicals in the failed plot to detonate liquid bombs on ten planes bound to the United States from Britain (based also on a tip from the British Muslim community). However, sometimes the suspicions prove incorrect, as in the 2003 case of three men of Middle Eastern descent that were overheard "joking" at a Georgia restaurant about a terrorist plot to be conducted in Miami, Florida (the three were subsequently stopped in Florida and, after a day-long investigation, were released). Therefore, antiterrorism is very much a bottom-up approach. Ordinary citizens are the best first line of defense.

America allows free speech in most circumstances, but never allows illegal violence. Another innovative antiterrorism program is designed to ease tensions between the government and anti-government organizations. Following the 1995 Oklahoma terror bombing, for instance, this approach saw Federal Bureau of Investigation (FBI) agents talking directly to various militia leaders. From Montana to Indiana, federal agents opened dialogues with leaders of several militia organizations to provide a forum for discussion in the hope that these channels of communication would help prevent acts of violence. While this approach will bear little fruit with al-Qa'eda-styled terrorists, it is still wise to explore all avenues of prevention measures—perhaps an informant can be recruited to work against the terror group.

Counterterrorism measures are those tactical actions taken by authorities in response to an actual terrorist incident. In this vein, planning and training will have a great impact on the success or failure of real world counterterrorist measures. While the Department of Justice, through the FBI, is still the lead agency in the event of a terrorist attack with a weapon of mass destruction, the expected mass casualties, physical damage and potential for civil disorder resulting from such an incident will undoubtedly see a shift to the Department of Defense (DOD) as the *de facto* lead federal agency for many counterterrorism issues.

2.1 September 11, 2001

Terrorism is not an enemy, it is simply a method employed by a specific enemy—a method that intentionally targets innocent civilians. Thus, the War on Terror is not a war against a method, but a war against an identifiable enemy—al-Qa'eda-styled terrorists who cloak themselves in militant Islamic rhetoric. To be sure, the War on Terror is not against all militant Islamic groups in the world, but only against those militant Islamic groups that have targeted the United States with open-ended violence. This would be the al-Qa'eda and all other similar militant Islamic groups who adopt their goal of making "war" on the United States.

In 1996, Osama bin Laden, the founder of al-Qaeda, issued his first declaration that he was at war with the United States. After listing a rambling series of so-called grievances against the "Zionist-Crusaders," he stated:

> The walls of oppression and humiliation cannot be demolished except in a rain of bullets. The freeman does not surrender leadership to infidels and sinners. My Muslim Brothers of the World: Your brothers in Palestine and in the land of the two Holy Places are calling upon your help and asking you to take part in fighting against the enemy—your enemy and their enemy—the Americans and the Israelis.

On May 10, 1997, CNN aired a March 22, 1997 interview with Osama bin Laden by Peter Arnett. Bin Laden stated, "We declared jihad against the U.S. government, because the U.S. government is unjust, criminal and tyrannical." On February 22, 1998, Bin Laden and his so-called "World Islamic Front" again declared a religious *fatwa* (a formal statement backed by a religious declaration) urging in the strongest terms that all Muslims should engage in violence against "Jews and Crusaders." Rooting his hatred in his interpretation of the religion of Islam, he proclaimed:

All these crimes and sins committed by the Americans are a clear declaration of war on Allah, his messenger, and Muslims. And *ulema* (clerics) have throughout Islamic history unanimously agreed that the jihad is an individual duty if the enemy destroys Muslim countries. On that basis, and in compliance with Allah's order, we issue the following fatwa to all Muslims: The ruling to kill the Americans and their allies—civilians and military—is an individual duty for every Muslim who can do it in any country in which it is possible to do it, in order to liberate the al-Aqsa Mosque [in Jerusalem] and the holy mosque [in Mecca] from their grip.

The War on Terror began for the United States on September 11, 2001, with coordinated suicide attacks using hijacked domestic airplanes by 19 members of a sophisticated international terrorist network known as al-Qa'eda ("the Base"). The simultaneous attacks occurred in New York, Washington, D.C. and Pennsylvania, killing 3,000 people and destroying billions of dollars in property. Prior to this attack, America responded to al-Qa'eda and al-Qa'eda-styled terrorism with traditional criminal law tools. After 9/11 America realized that it would have to resort to the tools associated with the regulation of armed conflict or international war.

Al-Qa'eda is an umbrella organization founded in 1989 by a Saudi Arabian named Osama (or Usama) bin Laden. Osama bin Laden formed the group out of elements of the Maktab al-Khidamat, an organization founded by Osama bin Laden and Abdallah Azzam (a member of a group called the Palestinian Moslem Brotherhood) in the early 1980s to provide money, equipment and manpower to the Afghan resistance against the Soviet Union's occupation of Afghanistan. With the withdrawal of the Soviets in 1989, bin Laden started al-Qa'eda in order to redirect his efforts to "attack the enemies of Islam all over the world." The religious view embraced by militant Islam is a fixed, comprehensive ideology that targets for death anyone that disagrees with its very narrow set of mandates In 2004, Jordanian Abu Musab al Zarqawi proclaimed his allegiance to Osama bin Laden and headed al-Qa'eda in Iraq. He specifically targeted Muslims and their houses of worship, killing them by the hundreds.

From the early 1990s until the end of 2001, the al-Qa'eda operated openly in the country of Afghanistan with the complete support of the Pashtun-dominated Taliban government. During the tenure of the Taliban regime, the relationship between the Taliban and the al-Qa'eda terrorist organization provided a seminal example of State-supported terrorism. In fact, under the Taliban, Afghanistan became a terror training ground for tens of thousands of Arab and non-Arab al-Qa'eda militants including Saudis, Kashmirs, Chechens, Uzbeks, Uighurs and others (including a number of Americans). These training camps sent cells of well-trained terrorists into numerous countries where they were encouraged to recruit additional members and carry out terrorist attacks on command. While al-Qa'eda has tens of thousands of supporters and low-level operatives worldwide, only carefully selected Muslim males are offered full membership. Interestingly, the al-Qa'eda leadership does not allow volunteers to join the group. Instead, al-Qa'eda seeks out candidates for full membership. These recruits must sign an oath of allegiance called a *bayat*, swearing to carry out the dictates of al-Qa'eda leaders on penalty of death. They are then indoctrinated and trained extensively in assassination, kidnapping, explosives, small arms, hijacking and torture.

Any reasonable doubts as to the involvement of Osama bin Laden's terrorist network in the attacks of September 11, 2001, were dispelled by the December 13, 2001, public release of the so-called "bin Laden videotape." The tape established that bin Laden: (1) knew when the hijackers would strike; (2) knew that the hijackers understood that they were on a "martyrdom operation," but had no details until shortly before the attacks; (3) was pleasantly surprised by the total collapse of the two towers of the World Trade Center in New York; (4) listened with anticipation to radio broadcasts to confirm the terror attacks; and (5) expressed joy and amusement as he detailed the story of the attacks. Perhaps the most damning segment of the thirty-nine-minute tape occurred when bin Laden stated:

> We calculated in advance the number of casualties from the enemy who would be killed based on the position of the tower. We calculated that the floors that would be hit would be three or four floors. I was the most optimistic of them all. Due to my experience in this field, I was thinking that the fire from the gas in the plane would melt the iron structure of the building and collapse the area where the plane hit and all the floors above it only. This is all that we had hoped for.

Almost a year to the day after the attack of September 11, 2001, the al-Qa'eda terrorist organization released another videotape claiming full credit for the attacks. The video specifically mentioned the World Trade Center attack, the Pentagon attack and the attempted attack on the United States Capitol.

2.2 An Act of War

"America is at war." So states President Bush's letter of introduction to the March 2006 *National Security Strategy of the United States of America*. The phrase "war on terror" was first used by President Bush on September 11, 2001, aboard Air Force One. His first major public address the next day also declared the terrorist attacks as "acts of war." The Bush Administration has never departed from the position that the fight against al-Qa'eda and al-Qa'eda-styled terrorism constitutes a global war. For the government of the United States, the War on Terror is not a metaphor similar to the "war on poverty" or the "war on drugs." With the passage of the Military Commissions Act of 2006, there can be no question that both the executive and the legislative branches of the United States clearly view the Global War on Terrorism as real war or, in the vernacular of modern usage, a real international armed conflict. In turn, as federal courts rule on various aspects of the conflict, it is apparent that they too are willing to accept the fact that the powers used by the United States are more associated with international armed conflict than not. In a speech delivered in 1984, Ambassador Jeanne J. Kirkpatrick spoke of a coming "terrorist war [against the United States], [that] is part of a total war which sees the whole society as an enemy, and all members of a society as appropriate objects for violent actions." Her words became reality on September 11, 2001, and the world community came to understand terrorism as "an act of war." Viewing terrorism as an act of war is a new manifestation of the changing nature of armed conflict. As such, it poses a new challenge for the historically fixed international rules relating to international armed conflict.

Apart from the enormity of the al-Qa'eda attack, what made the events of September 11, 2001, so vastly different from all previous incidents of terror was that the United States and the North Atlantic Treaty Organization (NATO) both specifically characterized the attack as an "armed attack" on the United States. The unprecedented armed attack determination was significant because it, in turn, immediately signaled that the United States intended to frame the terror attack as an event equivalent to an "act of war" under international law and not simply a criminal affair to be dealt with by means of traditional law enforcement tools.

The use of the terms "war" or "act of war" traditionally refers to the use of aggressive force against a sovereign State by another State in violation of the United Nations Charter and customary international law. Historically, such illegal acts most often occur without a formal declaration of war. The aggressive act itself triggers the ensuing international armed conflict.

Accordingly, following September 11, 2001, a "use of force" joint resolution was passed by the United States Congress; the President labeled the attack "an act of war;" and, for the first time in its history, NATO invoked its collective self-defense clause should a NATO member suffer an armed attack. Thus, from its inception, the War on Terror was legally couched by the United States in terms of traditional international law of war terminology, even though the actual attack was carried out, strictly speaking, by a non-State actor.

Understanding the need for international approval for prosecuting the War on Terror under the rule of law, the United States turned to the United Nations Security Council on the day after the attack in hope of obtaining a strong use of force resolution to address the attacks. The United States received something very close to that in United Nations Security Council Resolution 1368:

 The Security Council,

Reaffirming the principles and purposes of the Charter of Nations,

Determined to combat by all means threats to international peace and security caused by terrorist acts,

Recognizing the inherent right of the individual or collective self-defense <u>in accordance with the Charter</u> [emphasis added], see p. 440

1. Unequivocally condemns in the strongest terms the horrifying terrorist attacks which took place on 11 September 2001 in New York, Washington, D.C. and Pennsylvania and regards such acts, like any act of international terrorism, as a threat to international peace and security; …

3. Calls on all States to work together urgently to bring to justice the perpetrators, organizers and sponsors of these terrorist attacks and stresses that those responsible for aiding, supporting or harboring the perpetrators, organizers and sponsors of these acts will be held accountable;

4. Calls also on the international community to redouble their efforts to prevent and suppress terrorist acts by increased cooperation and full implementation of the relevant international anti-terrorist conventions and Security Council resolutions, in particular resolution 1269 (1999) of 19 October 1999;

5. Expresses its readiness to take all necessary steps to respond to the terrorist attacks of 11 September 2001, and to combat all forms of terrorism, in accordance with its responsibilities under the Charter of Nations; ….

Because of the structured magnitude of the terrorist attack, Resolution 1368 specifically recognized America's "inherent right of individual and collective self-defense in accordance with the Charter" and specifically called on "all States to work together urgently to bring to justice the perpetrators, organizers and sponsors of these terrorist attacks." Resolution 1368 further addressed the issue of responsibility for those States who supported or sponsored the terrorist attacks by "stressing that those responsible for aiding, supporting or harboring the perpetrators, organizers and sponsors of these acts will be held accountable." Taken as a whole, it can be argued that Resolution 1368 provided the United States and its allies with the international legal authority necessary to respond to the terrorist attacks through the use of military force in self-defense should a State[s] who supported, sponsored, or harbored the terrorists refuse to cooperate in bringing those responsible to justice.

2.3 The Rule of Law—Use of Force

If the mark of a civilized State is measured by how well it follows the rule of law, it is necessary to understand what that term means, particularly in the realm of waging war. The concept "rule of law" was first coined by Western legal scholars in the late sixteenth century. The term was initially used to refer to the common law system of jurisprudence with particular emphasis on equality before the courts. However, the more modern and common meaning is directly associated with all of those rules and legal standards of behavior recognized and practiced between civilized States in the context of the community of nations.

In this setting, one can logically trace the origins of the rule of law back to the 1648 Peace of Westphalia, which concluded the Thirty Years' War in Europe. At that time a number of Christian European States officially recognized themselves as being in a community of sovereign nation-states and guided by certain rules of international and social intercourse. The utility of the nation-state concept soon spread throughout Europe, typified by the colonial powers of Europe holding themselves out as the "self-appointed executive committee of the family of nations." With the Treaty of Paris in 1856, non-Christian nations were also admitted and periodic international conferences were held in such international cities as Vienna and Geneva.

In early days, this community of nations was not deemed to be anything other than a loose association bound together by only a few international agreements and the thinnest of diplomatic threads. Although the primary purpose of this association was to promote world peace and to mitigate, when necessary, "the miseries of war," independent sovereignty reigned supreme because the association lacked any legal character or corporate personality. Thus, the rule of law remained a concept with little viability behind it.

After World War I reflected the total impotence of the association to deter those nations bent on aggression, the victorious European nations created the first international organization with legal parameters, the League of Nations. Formed in large part with the direct assistance of President Woodrow Wilson, the much-heralded League of Nations was the first truly international organization specifically directed toward the curtailment of war. As laudable as that goal might be, the League of Nations' efforts to maintain the peace were totally ineffective. In fact, they were actually counterproductive.

First, accepting the false premise that World War I had somehow been caused by a combination of misunderstandings and entangling collective security alliances, the League of Nations naively adopted a series of procedural requirements focused on third-party dispute settlement processes. The framers assumed that wars, like all disputes, could be settled through negotiation and arbitration. This approach is best reflected in Article 12 of the Covenant of the League of Nations:

> The members of the League agree that if there should arise between them any dispute likely to lead to a rupture, they will submit the matter either to arbitration or to inquiry by the council, and they agree in no case to resort to war until three months after the award by the arbitrators or the report of the Council.

Second, the League of Nations concentrated almost solely on disarmament as the best guarantee of world peace. Somehow the founders of the League of Nations believed that there existed a direct correlation between the number of weapons in existence and the probability of armed conflict. In short, they naively believed that the threat of war could be reduced or eliminated if the League of Nations implemented international agreements which called for the destruction of weapons and the reduction of military forces. In the next two decades, disarmament treaties such as the London Naval Conferences (1930) saw England, France and the United States completely emasculate their military while Germany and her allies, Japan and Italy, embarked on a massive buildup of their armies, navies and air forces.

During this rush to disarm, other international agreements relating to armed conflict were drafted and adopted by the world community, of which the Geneva Conventions of 1929 were the most prominent. Perhaps, the most controversial document that came out of the post-World War I era was the Kellogg-Briand Pact. Signed by almost all of the major world powers, the Pact wishfully prohibited war as the solution to international disputes or as an instrument of national policy.

Although the Kellogg-Briand Pact was viewed by many as an idealistic proscription against war, the abolition of war did not mean that States gave up the inherent right of self-defense; all signatories strongly asserted that the defensive use of military force was absolutely legitimate under the Pact. Paradoxically, the Pact, spawned by a sincere desire to rid mankind of the scourge of war, was actually a dramatic and positive shift in the focus of the rule of law pertaining to war.

The Kellogg-Briand Pact shifted the emphasis from procedural and moral issues related to the legitimacy of war to simply prohibiting all *aggression* under "any circumstances." In effect, a red line of distinction was made between the aggressive use of force, which was always prohibited, and the defensive use of force in response to aggression, which was always lawful. Unfortunately, the Pact did not specifically spell out what it so strongly implied concerning permissive self-defense. The Kellogg-Briand Pact did not devote a single word to the traditional and inherent right of self-defense.

In summation, most of the League of Nations' activities were rooted in the sincere but naive assumption that war was intrinsically irrational and that rational man could solve his differences simply through negotiation and reason. Incredibly, many nations thought this philosophy, coupled with a massive disarming effort, would lead to the abolition of war.

In the first major application of this philosophy of negotiation and so-called reason, Neville Chamberlain, Prime Minister of England, tried to appease the Nazi dictator Adolf Hitler by traveling to Munich, Germany, in October of 1938. The resulting Munich Agreement prompted Chamberlain to foolishly remark, "I believe it is peace for our time … peace with honor." Of course, the fruits of appeasement produced the exact opposite. The clear signal given to the aggressor—peace at any price—prompted the Axis powers to launch the most destructive war in the history of mankind. A similar pattern has developed with how some nations have chosen to deal with the forces of Islamic terrorism. Many countries have simply decided that they will not engage in the Global War on Terrorism. Prior to the events of September 11, 2001, this attitude was also widely held in the United States.

When World War II ended in 1945, the international community once again sought to create a new methodology to reduce or to eliminate armed international conflict, just as they had done following World War I. Work quickly began on a series of international agreements and instruments designed to accomplish this ideal. Many of the efforts, ranging from the creation of the United Nations in 1945 to the 1949 Geneva Conventions, produced widespread and immediate acceptance throughout the world. In this regard, the civilized world recognized the necessity of anchoring its desire for world peace on ideas that would inhibit both the external and, to a lesser degree, the internal dimensions of State sovereignty. The unfettered power of member States to pursue activities and policies that threatened international peace and security had to be squarely addressed. In addition, great concern was voiced about the acts of States in regard to the treatment of their own citizens.

Since the sovereignty of each State would serve as the basis for the new world organization, internationally recognized legal constraints and attendant enforcement mechanisms had to be placed on those nations that threatened the peace. In leading the effort to create such an organization, the United States held out to the world community the vision of a world order based on four essential human freedoms. These four freedoms were first articulated in President Franklin Roosevelt's major speech before Congress on January 6, 1941: freedom of speech, freedom of religion, freedom from want, and freedom from fear. Echoing these ideals, the victorious powers of World War II formed the United Nations.

With the emergence of the United Nations and the principles of international behavior embodied in the Charter of the United Nations, the deficiencies in the Kellogg-Briand Pact were largely corrected. Along with the prohibition of all forms of armed aggression, the U.N. Charter specifically recognized a nation-state's inherent right of self-defense if attacked. Today, in the search for a workable model to address conflict management, the U.N. Charter is considered by many to be synonymous with the international rule of law.

As embodied in Articles 2(3) and 2(4) of the U.N. Charter, the maintenance of "international peace and security" is, in fact, the very purpose of the United Nations. Since all members of the United Nations are recognized as sovereign equals, no nation may resort to "threat or [the] use of force against the territorial integrity or political independence of any State" to settle any form of dispute. This, as well as the clear prohibition in Article 1 against any nation committing "acts of aggression or other breaches of the peace," resulted in a workable, legal framework dedicated to curtailing unlawful aggression. It established a concrete legal framework by which behavior could be gauged.

Recognizing that even the most brilliantly crafted legal framework is useless without an enforcement mechanism, the drafters of the U.N. Charter also established an extensive and flexible international framework for responding to those rogue nations which might choose to violate the provisions of the U.N. Charter and engage in unlawful aggression. Chapter VI of the U.N. Charter authorizes the Security Council to investigate any situation that might endanger the maintenance of international peace and security and to make recommendations for the peaceful resolution of such disputes. Chapter VII of the U.N. Charter authorizes the Security Council to determine the existence of a threat, a breach of peace, or act of aggression, and to take appropriate measures in response. Even though Article 43 provides for the mechanism for member nations to make troops available on the call of the Security Council, no such agreements have ever been concluded. Instead, to enforce the peace, the Security Council relies on the forces of member nations, contributed and organized on an ad hoc basis for each situation.

Finally, recognizing the utopian absurdity of outlawing war, but building upon the framework of the Kellogg-Briand Pact, the U.N. Charter does not restrict all uses of force; it only restricts the unlawful use of force: aggression. Thus, the final element in this legal structure, and the one that is of immeasurable value in the real world, rests upon the U.N. Charter's recognition of the lawful use of force to deter unlawful armed aggression.

Explicitly acknowledging the long-standing customary right of self-defense, Article 51 states that "nothing in the present Charter shall impair the inherent right of individual or collective self-defense if an armed attack occurs against a Member of the United Nations ...." While there still exists lingering controversy over such matters as to what constitutes an armed attack and the utility of the term inherent, the modern rule of law specifically recognizes the fundamental distinction between unlawful aggression and lawful self-defense. In the overall picture, the rule of law has evolved from a vision of an "ideal aspiration towards universal values of law," to the reality of a world that acknowledges the existence and validity of established legal norms. If a nation operates in accordance with this rule of law, it can rightly claim the legal and moral high ground in any conflict.

In summary, there are four primary provisions of the U.N. Charter under which the use of force is analyzed. The starting point, of course, requires a firm understanding that the U.N. Charter does not outlaw the use of force; it only outlaws the use of *aggressive* force.

First, Articles 2(3) and 2(4) set out the general obligations of member States to settle disputes in a peaceful manner and to refrain from "the threat or use of force." U.N. Charter Article 2(3) requires that, "[a]ll Members shall settle their international disputes by peaceful means in such a manner that international peace and security, and justice are not endangered." U.N. Charter Article 2(4) states, "[a]ll Members shall refrain in their international relations from the threat or use of force against the territorial integrity or political independence of any State, or in any other manner inconsistent with the purposes of the United Nations."

Second, if a State engages in the use of aggressive force, Article 24 of the U.N. Charter actually gives the Security Council the "primary responsibility for the maintenance of international peace and security." Then, Article 27 requires that all permanent members of the U.N. Security Council must agree on enforcement provisions, e.g., the use of armed force. These five permanent members are listed in Article 23 of the U.N. Charter. They are China, France, Russia, the United States and Britain. Still, even if the Security Council issues an enforcement ruling, there is no standing U.N. military force to enforce it. Historically, the United States has provided the lion's share of military muscle to back up the Security Council.

The third element of the analytical framework is Article 51 of the U.N. Charter, which sets out the codification of the "inherent right of self-defense." The inherent right of self-defense refers to the right of a country to unilaterally engage in acts of self-defense; regardless of what any other nation or organization, to include the United Nations, may or may not do. This is a well-known and ancient component of international law.

Article 51 of the U.N. Charter states:

> Nothing in the present Charter shall impair the inherent right of individual or collective self-defense if an armed attack occurs against a Member of the United Nations, until the Security Council has taken measures to maintain international peace and security. Measures taken by Members in the exercise of the right of self-defense shall be immediately reported to the Security Council and shall not in any way affect the authority and responsibility of the Security Council under the present Charter to take at any time such action as it deems necessary in order to maintain or restore international peace and security.

Finally, to complete the analysis, one must determine what is meant by the term "armed attack." In order to clearly define when an unlawful use of force in violation of Articles 2(3) and (4) occurs, international law looks primarily at the definition of aggression as adopted by resolution of the U.N. General Assembly. A State engages in aggression in the following ways according to the U.N. Definition of Aggression:

Article 1

Aggression is the use of armed force by a State against the sovereignty, territorial integrity, or political independence of another State, or in any manner inconsistent with the Charter of the United Nations ....

Article 2

The first use of armed force by a State in contravention of the Charter shall constitute prima facie evidence of an act of aggression ....

Article 3

Any of the following acts, regardless of a declaration of war, shall ... qualify as an act of aggression:
(a) The invasion or attack by the armed forces of a State ... of another State or part thereof;
(b) Bombardment by the armed forces of a State against the territory of another State ...
(c) The blockade of the ports or coasts of a State by the armed forces of another State;

(d) An attack by the armed forces of a State on the land, sea, or air forces, or marine and air fleets of another State;

(e) The use of armed forces of one State ... in contravention of the conditions provided for in the agreement or any extension of their presence in such territory beyond the termination of the agreement;

(f) The action of a State in allowing its territory, which it has placed at the disposal of another State, to be used by that other State for perpetrating an act of aggression against a third State;

(g) The sending by or on behalf of a State of armed bands, groups, irregulars, or mercenaries, which carry out acts of armed force against another State of such gravity as to amount to the acts listed above, or its substantial involvement therein.

2.4 NATO

NATO, of which the United States is a full member, also viewed the attacks of September 11, 2001, an "armed attack" under international law. NATO invoked its collective self-defense clause under Article 5 of the NATO Charter where ["an armed attack on one or more of [its members] shall be considered an attack on all,"] and that the members may exercise the right of self-defense which includes the "use of armed force, to restore and maintain the security of the North Atlantic area." The real significance of invoking Article 5, of course, rested more in the European recognition that the terrorist attacks were, in fact, tantamount to an armed attack or act of war against the United States, and not just criminal acts of terrorism.

Armed with the Congressional Joint Resolution, U.N. Resolution 1368 and the NATO Resolution, President George W. Bush exercised his authority as the Commander in Chief, under Article 2, Section 3, of the Constitution, and quickly set about gathering the necessary evidence to find those who committed the attacks and to establish linkage to the State or States that may have provided material support to the terrorists. The President has consistently held that the Untied States is in a state of international armed conflict with al-Qa'eda to which the law of war applies.

2.5 Congressional War-Making Power

Congress was also quick to address the attacks in a manner that clearly established the premise that America was engaged in a real "war." Although Congress elected not to exercise its power to "declare war" under Article 1, Section 8, of the Constitution (it has enacted eleven formal declarations of war relating to only five different conflicts of the 200+ wars that the United States has fought), it did issue a strongly worded joint resolution which authorized the President to use military force, if necessary, to respond to the attacks with "all necessary and appropriate force against those nations, organizations, or persons he determines" were associated with the terror attacks of September 11, 2001. In addition, the resolution also authorized the executive to take action to "prevent any future acts of international terrorism against the United States." The joint resolution is cited as the "Authorization for Use of Military Force." In an unprecedented show of unity of support, this resolution was passed by every member of the Senate and every member of the House of Representatives, save one member from California.

AUTHORIZATION FOR THE USE OF MILITARY FORCE
Public Law 107-40, 107th Congress
Joint Resolution

To authorize the use of United States Armed Forces against those responsible for the recent attacks launched against the United States. NOTE: Sept. 18, 2001—[S.J. Res. 23]

Whereas, on September 11, 2001, acts of treacherous violence were committed against the United States and its citizens; and

Whereas, such acts render it both necessary and appropriate that the United States exercise its rights to self-defense and to protect United States citizens both at home and abroad; and

Whereas, in light of the threat to the national security and foreign policy of the United States posed by these grave acts of violence; and

Whereas, such acts continue to pose an unusual and extraordinary threat to the national security and foreign policy of the United States; and

Whereas, the President has authority under the Constitution to take action to deter and prevent acts of international terrorism against the United States: Now, therefore, be it

Resolved by the Senate and House of Representatives of the United States of America in Congress assembled, NOTE: Authorization for Use of Military Force.

SECTION 1. SHORT TITLE.
This joint resolution may be cited as the "Authorization for Use of Military Force."

SEC. 2. AUTHORIZATION FOR USE OF UNITED STATES ARMED FORCES.
(a) In General.—That the President is authorized to use all necessary and appropriate force against those nations, organizations, or persons <u>he determines</u> planned, authorized, committed, or aided  the terrorist attacks that occurred on September 11, 2001, or harbored such organizations or persons, in order to prevent any future acts of international terrorism against the United States by such nations, organizations or persons.

(b) War Powers Resolution Requirements—

    (1) Specific statutory authorization—Consistent with section 8(a)(1) of the War Powers Resolution, the Congress declares that this section is intended to constitute specific statutory authorization within the meaning of section 5(b) of the War Powers Resolution.

    (2) Applicability of other requirements—Nothing in this resolution supercedes any requirement of the War Powers Resolution.

Approved September 18, 2001.

Even without a Congressional resolution, the President's authority to order the military to action is unquestioned under the terms of the United States Constitution. In fact, there is a long history of American presidents utilizing military forces abroad in situations of armed conflict or potential conflict to protect United States citizens or promote United States interests. The number of instances where the president has used military forces abroad without, for example, a Congressional declaration of War, well exceeds 250 in number. Selected instances include: 1798–1800, undeclared naval war with France; 1801–1805, the First Barbary War (Tripoli declared war but not the United States); 1806, Mexico Incursion; 1806–1810, Gulf of Mexico Incursion; 1810, West Florida Incursion; 1812, Amelia Island in Florida; 1813, West Florida; 1813–1814, Marquesas Islands; 1814–1825, Caribbean (engagements between pirates and American war ships in response to over 3,000 pirate attacks on merchantmen between 1815–1823); 1815, Second Barbary War; 1950–1953, Korean War; 1958, Lebanon; 1962, Cuba; 1962, Thailand; 1964, Congo; 1964–1973, Vietnam War; 1965, Dominican Republic; 1980, Iran; 1981, El Salvador; 1982, Lebanon; 1983, Honduras; 1983, Chad; 1983, Grenada; 1986, Libya; 1989, Panama; 1989, Andean Region; 1991, Persian Gulf War; 1993, Bosnia; 1993–1995, Somalia; 1993–1995, Haiti; 1997, Serbia; 2001, Afghanistan; and 2003, Iraq. In fact, the last time Congress "declared" war was in December 1941.

Nevertheless, the president's authority to use the armed forces and the authority of Congress to declare war or to otherwise share in the process of war making has been the source of much debate over the life of the Republic. Clearly the framers gave each branch of government war making powers in furtherance of their vision of a government of "checks and balances." This check also ensured a built-in source of friction between the two branches.

The most well known source of contention between Congress and the executive branch led to the War Powers Resolution, enacted over President Richard Nixon's veto in 1973. The War Powers Resolution seeks to curtail or limit the power of the executive in the employment of American forces abroad. It requires the President to consult with Congress if American forces are introduced into hostilities or into situations where hostilities are imminent and, after a time set at a maximum of ninety days, either obtain Congressional approval of any continued military action or withdraw. Needless to say, the War Powers Resolution raises serious separation of powers issues which, to date, the United States Supreme Court has not squarely addressed. In any event, no American president from either political party has directly complied with the War Powers Resolution. At most, when presidents have employed United States armed forces in hostile situations or in places where conflict was imminent, Congress has simply been notified in writing "consistent with the War Powers Resolution."

While Congress continues to pass legislation consistent with the idea that the War on Terror is a real armed conflict, e.g., the September 2006 law establishing military commissions for the trial of enemy combatants, one power that Congress clearly has in war making is over "the purse." Ultimately, Congress has the power to cut off funding to any protracted use of military forces. As a practical matter, the ongoing combat in Iraq could not continue without Congressional approval.

2.6 Article III Courts

The War on Terror has created much tension in American society. Recognizing that the struggle between civil liberties and increased security faces every democracy in time of conflict, courts have traditionally avoided involvement in national security matters, leaving the matter to the legislature and executive, which are accountable to the people. Courts realize that bad decisions will become entrenched in the case law of the nation and can serve as a magnet for the development of even more problematic decisions. Nevertheless, because the enemy in the War on Terror falls outside of the traditional definitions associated with armed conflict, the federal courts have issued a variety of rulings in the years since 2001, the most important ones, of course, coming in 2004 and 2006 from the United States Supreme Court. In 2004, both critics and supporters of the United States government waited with great anticipation to see whether or not the Supreme Court would insert itself in the conflict. On June 28, 2004, a badly fractured Supreme Court issued three decisions—*Hamdi v. Rumsfeld*, *Rumsfeld v. Padilla* and *Rasul v. Bush*. A fair reading of the cases indicate that the Court is not asserting a co-equal role in the Global War on Terrorism, but is rather reminding the other two branches that some due process concerns need to be better addressed.

Hamdi

In *Hamdi*, a plurality opinion (8–1) by Justice O'Connor, the Court affirmed the notion that a state of "war" existed. The Court noted that "there is no bar to this Nation's holding one of its own citizens as an enemy combatant." However, the Court remanded the case to give United States citizen Hamdi a "fair opportunity to rebut the Government's factual assertions [that he was an enemy combatant] before a neutral and detached decision maker." In October 2004, without charging him with any crimes, the United States released Hamdi from military detention and sent him back to Saudi Arabia (he denounced his U.S. citizenship). In *Padilla* (5–4), the Court sidestepped the legal issues and dismissed Padilla's habeas petition without prejudice since, they concluded, he had filed in the wrong federal district court. In *Rasul*, the Court held (6–3) that suspected al-Qa'eda and Taliban personnel have a right to file petitions for writs of habeas corpus to contest their detention. The Court held that "aliens held at the base [Guantanamo, Cuba], no less than American citizens, are entitled to invoke the federal court's authority," and "what is presently at stake is only whether the federal courts have jurisdiction to determine the legality of the Executive's potentially indefinite detention of individuals who claim to be innocent of wrongdoing."

If anything, the Court exhibited the fact that it too was struggling to find the line where traditional criminal law jurisprudence ends and law of war jurisprudence begins. In *Hamdi*, Justice O'Connor said the Court "made it clear that a state of war is not a blank check for the president when it comes to the rights of the nation's citizens." Still, the decision certainly upheld the right of the government to do what it had traditionally done in previous wars—detain indefinitely without criminal charge enemy combatants outside the regular parameters of the judicial system.

In the much anticipated 2006 decision of *Hamdan v. Rumsfeld*, a deeply divided Court again provided much needed guidance when it ruled that military commissions to try illegal enemy combatants had to be created by Congress, not the President. In so doing, the Court held that Common Article 3 of the Geneva Conventions applied to the detainees.

2.7 The Employment of Lawful Violence

In the days immediately following the September 11, 2001 attacks, a conclusive body of evidence pointed directly to the al-Qa'eda terrorist organization as the perpetrators of the attacks, and to Afghanistan's Taliban as the State-supporter of the terrorist al-Qa'eda organization. Determined to respond if necessary under the inherent right of self-defense, the Bush administration offered the Taliban government a time certain ultimatum to turn over the al-Qa'eda leaders and to shut down all terrorist camps in Afghanistan. President Bush issued the ultimatum in a solemn speech given to a joint session of Congress on September 20, 2001. The pertinent part reads:

> And tonight, the United States of America makes the following demands on the Taliban: Deliver to the United States authorities all the leaders of al-Qa'eda who hide in your land ... [c]lose immediately and permanently every terrorist training camp in Afghanistan, and hand over every terrorist, and every person in their support structure, to appropriate authorities. Give the United States full access to terrorist training camps, so we can make sure they are no longer operating. These demands are not open to negotiation or discussion. The Taliban must act, and act immediately. They will hand over the terrorist, or they will suffer their fate.

When the Taliban leadership refused to comply with any aspect of the demand, the United States exercised, in conjunction with NATO and its other allies, the lawful use of military force to accomplish those aims. Numerous nations contributed assistance to the American led effort including Pakistan, Saudi Arabia, Britain, Russia, Germany, Australia, France, Canada, Japan and so on. In addition, much of the actual ground combat was borne by indigenous Afghan tribal fighters, primarily the so-called Northern Alliance under the guidance and support of United States Army Special Forces and other United States Special Operations Forces conducting direct action and unconventional warfare missions. The military campaign to dislodge the Taliban and al-Qa'eda took approximately three months, from October 7 to December 23, 2001. Approximately 6,500 air combat missions were flown which attacked over 120 fixed targets. Four hundred vehicles were destroyed and an undetermined number of combatants were killed (some have put the figure as high as 10,000).

In tandem with the removal of the Taliban regime from power, the United States and its allies were able to destroy the al-Qa'eda camps and dismantle much of the infrastructure of the terrorist group in Afghanistan by the end of December 2001. By any account, the Bush strategy of using American air power, American Special Operations Forces and the ground forces of various Afghan resistance groups worked brilliantly in terms of mitigating the loss of life to American forces and reducing civilian suffering. Early critics of the Bush approach incorrectly predicted that the United States could not achieve victory without the use of massive American ground forces and an attendant heavy loss of life. This same pessimism was seen in exaggerated predictions of American lives that would be lost in the 1991 Gulf War should the United States attempt to expel Iraq from Kuwait in accordance with U.N. Resolution 678.

Since the fall of the Taliban government, the al-Qa'eda no longer operates with the open support of a State, but has been forced to revert to clandestine operations primarily as a sub-State terror group. As of early 2007, States throughout the world have arrested or detained well over 4,000 members of the al-Qa'eda network on a variety of terror related charges. The number of terrorists that have been killed is unknown. Of the top 37 al-Qa'eda leaders identified after 9/11 over half have been captured or killed to include Mohammad Atef (killed in Afghanistan), Khalid Shaikh Mohammed (in custody), Abu Zubaydah (in custody), and Ramzi bin al-Shibh (in custody). Bin Laden and his number two confederate Ayman al-Zawahiri still remain at large.

As of early 2007 there were approximately 32,000 coalition troops on the ground in Afghanistan, about 12,000 members coming from the United States. The coalition troops are under the command of NATO's ISAF (International Security Assistance Force) and are drawn from 37 nations. In addition, there are another 10,000 American troops, including Special Forces, that operate under U.S. command. The coalition soldiers are assisting in improving security, tracking down al-Qa'eda and Taliban holdouts, and most importantly, assisting in building a new Afghan army and civilian government. They are supported in the rebuilding effort by tens of thousands of civilian contractors. If the efforts in Afghanistan are successful, it will be a rare example of foreign powers accomplishing nation building.

2.8 Questions for Discussion

1. *War or simply a metaphor*? Is the War on Terror a real war or just political rhetoric? Can "war" be made against a group? In *Montoya v. United States* 180 U.S. 261 (1901), the Court considered whether or not a band of Indians that had broken away from the Mescalero Apache Indian reservation in Arizona to commit a series of hostile and murderous acts would activate the Indians Depredation Act, holding the tribe and the United States government liable for civil damages. The Court held that the tribe could not be held liable for the terrorist acts of the group that "was carrying on a war against the Government as an independent organization." Why is determining whether the War on Terror is a real war the central premise from which all legal issues should be viewed?

2. *Does al-Qa'eda qualify as a virtual-State*? The so-called *Al Qaeda Training Manual,* captured by British authorities in a 2000 raid on the home of Nahihal Wadih Rashie, (available at www.fas.org/irp/world/para/aqmanual.pdf) is considered by some to be irrefutable evidence of al-Qa'eda's ability to wage global war.

3. *Realistic expectations*. Is it realistic to expect nations to adhere to international law when pursuing a "war" on terrorists? Article 2(4) of the United Nations Charter states: "All Members shall refrain in their international relations from the threat or use of force against the territorial integrity or political independence of any state, or in any other manner inconsistent with the purposes of the United Nations." What roadblocks exist to international conformity on a use of force doctrine aimed specifically against terrorism?

4. *Congressional resolutions*. Following the attacks of September 11, 2001, Congress authorized the President "to use all necessary and appropriate force against those nations, organizations, or persons he determines planned, authorized, committed, or aided the terrorist attacks that occurred on September 11, 2001, or harbored such organizations or persons." *See* Authorization For Use of Military Force, P.L. 107-40 (Sept. 18, 2001). How does such a resolution conflict with the United Nations Charter if at all? Does such a resolution violate international law?

Selected Bibliography

Cordesman, Anthony H. TRANSNATIONAL THREATS FROM THE MIDDLE EAST: CRYING WOLF OR CRYING HAVOC? 1999.

Countering Terrorism on U.S. Army Installations, TC 19-16, Apr.1983, at 1-2.

Fenwick, Charles G. INTERNATIONAL LAW. 1965.

Grotius, Hugo. PROLEGOMENA TO THE LAW OF WAR AND PEACE. 1957.

Kellogg-Briand Pact of Aug. 27, 1928, 2 U.S.B.S. 732 (1930).

Kirkpatrick, Jeanne J. Speech at the Jonathan Institute's Conference on International Terrorism. Washington, D.C. June 25, 1984.

League of Nations Covenant, Treaty of Versailles, 2 U.S.B.S. 43.

Lord Lloyd of Hampstead and M. D. A. Freeman. LLOYD'S INTRODUCTION TO JURISPRUDENCE. 1985.

McNeill, William H. THE PURSUIT OF POWER. 1982.

Petrochilos, George. *The Relevance of the Concepts of War and Armed Conflict to the Law of Neutrality*, 31 VAND. J. TRANSNAT'L L. 575. 1998.

President George W. Bush, State of the Union Address. Jan. 23, 2002.

Chapter 3
Expanding the War on Terror

The United States of America will not permit the world's most dangerous regimes to threaten us with the world's most destructive weapons.

—George W. Bush

The Iraqi War, named Operation Iraqi Freedom, began on March 19, 2003, with a coordinated air attack by coalition forces against Iraqi military targets in Baghdad. Forming a "coalition of the willing" made up of like minded democracies, President Bush acted under his Article II authority as the Commander in Chief and a Congressional use of force resolution passed by a healthy majority of both houses of Congress. Although the war occurred without specific approval for the "use of force" from the United Nations Security Council, the Security Council did pass Resolution 1441 just prior to the Iraqi War. Resolution 1441 warned Saddam Hussein's regime of "serious consequences" if Iraq failed to comply with full inspections by United Nations personnel regarding the regime's suspected possession of illegal biological and chemical weapons in violation of U.N. Security Council Resolution 687. Exactly what those "serious consequences" would be was left open.

With the establishment of a democratically elected government under the leadership of Hamid Karzai in Afghanistan and the current Iraqi Government headed by prime minister Nuri al-Maliki, the United States-led coalition continues its mission of tracking down the remnants of the al-Qa'eda and Taliban, as well as helping to quell the continuing Iraqi insurgency. From a foreign policy stance, the United States has attempted to parlay the resounding success it achieved in removing two renegade regimes from power into a deterrence signal to other States who either support or sponsor terrorism. But was the expansion of the Global War on Terrorism to Iraq necessary and/or legal?

The expansion of the War on Terror from Afghanistan to other targeted regimes was first announced by President Bush in his State of the Union Address on January 29, 2002, when the President cautioned the American people that even though Afghanistan was no longer a supporter of terrorist organizations, the War on Terror was not over. Apart from the fact that the United

States would surely use its armed forces against any State that openly harbored al-Qa'eda, the President clearly alerted the nation that he intended to embark on a policy that was certain to expand the War on Terror.

3.1 The Bush Doctrine

In a bold shift of direction, President Bush signaled that renegade regimes that either possessed or were seeking to acquire weapons of mass destruction posed "a grave and growing danger" to world peace that could no longer be ignored. President Bush specifically labeled those rogue regimes— Saddam Hussein's Iraq, Iran and North Korea—as an "axis of evil" because of their continuing support and sponsorship of terrorist groups and their desire to acquire weapons of mass destruction. The President's key point in the message to the nation was to demonstrate his resolve that the "United States of America will not permit the world's most dangerous regimes to threaten us with the world's most destructive weapons."

In short order, President Bush's remarks led to the formulation of the so-called Bush Doctrine for the preemptive use of armed force against certain rogue nations. In September 2002, the White House issued its *National Security Strategy of the United States* where it spelled out both the emerging threat posed by al-Qa'eda-styled terrorism and the criteria for the preemptive use of force. The 49 page March 2006 *National Security Strategy of the United States* continued the preemptive theme under a section entitled, Summary of National Security Strategy of 2002:

> The security environment confronting the United States today is radically different from what we have faced before. Yet the first duty of the United States Government remains what it always has been: to protect the American people and American interests. It is an enduring American principle that this duty obligates the government to anticipate and counter threats, using all elements of national power, before the threats can do grave damage. The greater the threat, the greater is the risk of inaction—and the more compelling the case for taking anticipatory action to defend ourselves, even if uncertainty remains as to the time and place of the enemy's attack. There are few greater threats than a terrorist attack with WMD.

> To forestall or prevent such hostile acts by our adversaries, the United States will, if necessary, act preemptively in exercising our <u>inherent right of self-defense</u>. The United States will not resort to force in all cases to preempt emerging threats. Our preference is that nonmilitary actions succeed. And no country should ever use preemption as a pretext for aggression.

Art. 51 UN charter

Within a year of the 2002 *National Security Strategy*, the application of the Bush Doctrine would see the United States and its allies topple the totalitarian regime of Saddam Hussein and cause the once terrorist State of Libya to abandon its weapons of mass destruction program and embark upon limited democratic reforms.

The Bush Doctrine has raised much debate—both as a policy matter and as a legal matter. Considering that the use of armed force can only be justified under international law when used in "self-defense," is it lawful for the United States to go beyond the rhetoric and actually carry the Global War on Terrorism to those rogue nations identified as supporters and sponsors of terrorist activities, but who have not physically engaged in a specific act of aggression against the United States? Furthermore, even if the United States has legal justification to employ its military force against, for example, Iran, there are practical matters which must be carefully weighed. At a minimum, the United States must certainly demonstrate from the particular circumstances that the use of armed force will not create an even greater danger to international peace and security. Accordingly, in the months leading up to the 2003 war in Iraq, Vice President Cheney repeatedly argued that "[d]eliverable weapons of mass destruction in the hands of a terror network or a murderous dictator, or the two working together, constitutes as grave a threat as can be imagined. The risks of inaction are far greater than the risk of action." Clearly, the two justifications for the Iraqi war were the issues of weapons of mass destruction and support for terrorist networks as reflected in the Congressional authorization for the use of force against Iraq, set out herein.

107th CONGRESS

2d Session

H. J. RES. 114

To authorize the use of United States Armed Forces against Iraq.

IN THE HOUSE OF REPRESENTATIVES

October 2, 2002

JOINT RESOLUTION

To authorize the use of United States Armed Forces against Iraq.

Whereas in 1990 in response to Iraq's war of aggression against and illegal occupation of Kuwait, the United States forged a coalition of nations to liberate Kuwait and its people in order to defend the national security of the United States and enforce United Nations Security Council resolutions relating to Iraq;

Whereas after the liberation of Kuwait in 1991, Iraq entered into a United Nations sponsored cease-fire agreement pursuant to which Iraq unequivocally agreed, among other things, to eliminate its nuclear, biological, and chemical weapons programs and the means to deliver and develop them, and to end its support for international terrorism;

Whereas the efforts of international weapons inspectors, United States intelligence agencies, and Iraqi defectors led to the discovery that Iraq had large stockpiles of chemical weapons and a large scale biological weapons program, and that Iraq had an advanced nuclear weapons development program that was much closer to producing a nuclear weapon than intelligence reporting had previously indicated;

Whereas Iraq, in direct and flagrant violation of the cease-fire, attempted to thwart the efforts of weapons inspectors to identify and destroy Iraq's weapons of mass destruction stockpiles and development capabilities, which finally resulted in the withdrawal of inspectors from Iraq on October 31, 1998;

Whereas in Public Law 105-235 (August 14, 1998), Congress concluded that Iraq's continuing weapons of mass destruction programs threatened vital United States interests and international peace and security, declared Iraq to be in 'material and unacceptable breach of its international obligations' and urged the President 'to take appropriate action, in accordance with the Constitution and relevant laws of the United States, to bring Iraq into compliance with its international obligations';

Whereas Iraq both poses a continuing threat to the national security of the United States and international peace and security in the Persian Gulf region and remains in material and unacceptable breach of its international obligations by, among other things, continuing to possess and develop a significant chemical and biological weapons capability, actively seeking a nuclear weapons capability, and supporting and harboring terrorist organizations;

Whereas Iraq persists in violating resolution of the United Nations Security Council by continuing to engage in brutal repression of its civilian population thereby threatening international peace and security in the region, by refusing to release, repatriate, or account for non-Iraqi citizens wrongfully detained by Iraq, including an American serviceman, and by failing to return property wrongfully seized by Iraq from Kuwait;

Whereas the current Iraqi regime has demonstrated its capability and willingness to use weapons of mass destruction against other nations and its own people;

Whereas the current Iraqi regime has demonstrated its continuing hostility toward, and willingness to attack, the United States, including by attempting in 1993 to assassinate former President Bush and by firing on many thousands of occasions on United States and Coalition Armed Forces engaged in enforcing the resolutions of the United Nations Security Council;

Whereas members of al Qaida, an organization bearing responsibility for attacks on the United States, its citizens, and interests, including the attacks that occurred on September 11, 2001, are known to be in Iraq;

Whereas Iraq continues to aid and harbor other international terrorist organizations, including organizations that threaten the lives and safety of United States citizens;

Whereas the attacks on the United States of September 11, 2001, underscored the gravity of the threat posed by the acquisition of weapons of mass destruction by international terrorist organizations;

Whereas Iraq's demonstrated capability and willingness to use weapons of mass destruction, the risk that the current Iraqi regime will either employ those weapons to launch a surprise attack against the United States or its Armed Forces or provide them to international terrorists who would do so, and the extreme magnitude of harm that would result to the United States and its citizens from such an attack, combine to justify action by the United States to defend itself;

Whereas United Nations Security Council Resolution 678 (1990) authorizes the use of all necessary means to enforce United Nations Security Council Resolution 660 (1990) and subsequent relevant resolutions and to compel Iraq to cease certain activities that threaten international peace and security, including the development of weapons of mass destruction and refusal or obstruction of United Nations weapons inspections in violation of United Nations Security Council Resolution 687 (1991), repression of its civilian population in violation of United Nations Security Council Resolution 688 (1991), and threatening its neighbors or United Nations operations in Iraq in violation of United Nations Security Council Resolution 949 (1994);

Whereas in the Authorization for Use of Military Force Against Iraq Resolution (Public Law 102-1), Congress has authorized the President 'to use United States Armed Forces pursuant to United Nations Security Council Resolution 678 (1990) in order to achieve implementation of Security Council Resolution 660, 661, 662, 664, 665, 666, 667, 669, 670, 674, and 677;

Whereas in December 1991, Congress expressed its sense that it 'supports the use of all necessary means to achieve the goals of United Nations Security Council Resolution 687 as being consistent with the Authorization of Use of Military Force Against Iraq Resolution (Public Law 102-1)', that Iraq's repression of its civilian population violates United Nations Security Council Resolution 688 and 'constitutes a continuing threat to the peace, security, and stability of the Persian Gulf region,' and that Congress, 'supports the use of all necessary means to achieve the goals of United Nations Security Council Resolution 688';

Whereas the Iraq Liberation Act of 1998 (Public Law 105-338) expressed the sense of Congress that it should be the policy of the United States to support efforts to remove from power the current Iraqi regime and promote the emergence of a democratic government to replace that regime;

Whereas on September 12, 2002, President Bush committed the United States to 'work with the United Nations Security Council to meet our common challenge' posed by Iraq and to 'work for the necessary resolutions,' while also making clear that 'the Security Council resolutions will be enforced, and the just demands of peace and security will be met, or action will be unavoidable';

Whereas the United States is determined to prosecute the war on terrorism and Iraq's ongoing support for international terrorist groups combined with its development of weapons of mass destruction in direct violation of its obligations under the 1991 cease-fire and other United Nations Security Council resolutions make clear that it is in the national security interests of the United States and in furtherance of the war on terrorism that all relevant United Nations Security Council resolutions be enforced, including through the use of force if necessary;

Whereas Congress has taken steps to pursue vigorously the war on terrorism through the provision of authorities and funding requested by the President to take the necessary actions against international terrorists and terrorist organizations, including those nations, organizations, or persons who planned, authorized, committed, or aided the terrorist attacks that occurred on September 11, 2001, or harbored such persons or organizations;

Whereas the President and Congress are determined to continue to take all appropriate actions against international terrorists and terrorist organizations, including those nations, organizations, or persons who planned, authorized, committed, or aided the terrorist attacks that occurred on September 11, 2001, or harbored such persons or organizations;

Whereas the President has authority under the Constitution to take action in order to deter and prevent acts of international terrorism against the United States, as Congress recognized in the joint resolution on Authorization for Use of Military Force (Public Law 107-40); and

Whereas it is in the national security interests of the United States to restore international peace and security to the Persian Gulf region: Now, therefore, be it

Resolved by the Senate and House of Representatives of the United States of America in Congress assembled,

SECTION 1. SHORT TITLE.

This joint resolution may be cited as the 'Authorization for Use of Military Force Against Iraq Resolution of 2002.

SEC. 2. SUPPORT FOR UNITED STATES DIPLOMATIC EFFORTS.

The Congress of the United States supports the efforts by the President to—

(1) strictly enforce through the United Nations Security Council all relevant Security Council resolutions regarding Iraq and encourages him in those efforts; and

(2) obtain prompt and decisive action by the Security Council to ensure that Iraq abandons its strategy of delay, evasion and noncompliance and promptly and strictly complies with all relevant Security Council resolutions regarding Iraq.

SEC. 3. AUTHORIZATION FOR USE OF UNITED STATES ARMED FORCES.

(a) AUTHORIZATION—The President is authorized to use the Armed Forces of the United States as he determines to be necessary and appropriate in order to—

(1) defend the national security of the United States against the continuing threat posed by Iraq; and

(2) enforce all relevant United Nations Security Council resolutions regarding Iraq.

(b) PRESIDENTIAL DETERMINATION—In connection with the exercise of the authority granted in subsection (a) to use force the President shall, prior to such exercise or as soon thereafter as may be feasible, but no later than 48 hours after exercising such authority, make available to the Speaker of the House of Representatives and the President pro tempore of the Senate his determination that—

(1) reliance by the United States on further diplomatic or other peaceful means alone either (A) will not adequately protect the national security of the United States against the continuing threat posed by Iraq or (B) is not likely to lead to enforcement of all relevant United Nations Security Council resolutions regarding Iraq; and

(2) acting pursuant to this joint resolution is consistent with the United States and other countries continuing to take the necessary actions against international terrorist and terrorist organizations, including those nations, organizations, or persons who planned, authorized, committed or aided the terrorist attacks that occurred on September 11, 2001.

(c) WAR POWERS RESOLUTION REQUIRMENTS

(1) SPECIFIC STATUTORY AUTHORIZATION—Consistent with section 8(a)(1) of the War Powers Resolution, the Congress declares that this section is intended to constitute specific statutory authorization within the meaning of section 5(b) of the War Powers Resolution.

(2) APPLICABILITY OF OTHER REQUIREMENTS—Nothing in this joint resolution supersedes any requirement of the War Powers Resolution.

SEC. 4. REPORTS TO CONGRESS.

(a) REPORTS—The President shall, at least once every 60 days, submit to the Congress a report on matters relevant to this joint resolution, including actions taken pursuant to the exercise of authority granted in section 3 and the status of planning for efforts that are expected to be required after such actions are completed, including those actions described in section 7 of the Iraq Liberation Act of 1998 (Public Law 105-338).

(b) SINGLE CONSOLIDATED REPORT—To the extent that the submission of any report described in subsection (a) coincides with the submission of any other report on matters relevant to this joint resolution otherwise required to be submitted to Congress pursuant to the reporting requirements of the War Powers Resolution (Public Law 93-148), all such reports may be submitted as a single consolidated report to the Congress.

(c) RULE OF CONSTRUCTION—To the extent that the information required by section 3 of the Authorization for Use of Military Force Against Iraq Resolution (Public Law 102-1) is included in the report required by this section, such report shall be considered as meeting the requirements of section 3 of such resolution.

Accompanying the 2003 military defeat of Saddam Hussein's dictatorship in Iraq was a failure to discover significant stocks of weapons of mass destruction and only some evidence of a collaborative relationship with al-Qa'eda (the 2004 Congressional 9/11 Commission's report found "extensive" and "troubling" contacts between Hussein and al-Qa'eda, but no "collaborative operational relationship"). These two revelations caused much consternation by some about whether the War on Terror should have been expanded to Iraq. Nevertheless, it seems clear that the United States—both the Executive and the Congress—acted appropriately given the basis of the information it had at the time. Indeed, considering the track record of the Hussein regime, the argument that he would acquire (if he did not still have them) and then pass on weapons of mass destruction to terrorists in the post-9/11 world still remains convincing. When President Bush provided a final ultimatum to Saddam Hussein to relinquish power and avoid war, his actions were certainly colored by the realities of the post-9/11 environment in light of the following factual information:

- Saddam Hussein aggressively attacked two other nations—Iran and Kuwait—in direct violation of the principles of the Charter of the United Nations.
- Saddam Hussein launched ballistic missiles at Israel and Saudi Arabia—acts of aggressive war.
- Saddam Hussein used poison gas (a weapon of mass destruction) against Kurdish civilians in Iraq and against Iranian soldiers. In addition, Saddam Hussein's regime murdered untold tens of thousands for political purposes.
- Saddam Hussein's final declaration to the Security Council in response to Security Council Resolution 1441 was patently false.
- Saddam Hussein failed to comply with 17 United Nations Security Council resolutions regarding inspection of weapons of mass destruction. December 16, 1998, in response to Iraq's ejection of all U.N. inspectors, the United States and Britain conducted four days of air strikes with aircraft and cruise missiles against Iraqi targets (Operation Desert Fox).
- In 1998, Congress passed a resolution that President William Clinton signed entitled the "Iraq Liberation Act," indicating that it should be the policy of the United States to support efforts to remove from power the regime of Saddam Hussein and to promote the emergence of a democratic government in Iraq.

- Saddam Hussein continued aggressive military attacks against the United States and Britain after the formal cessation of hostilities in 1991 by firing thousands of times on coalition aircraft patrolling the United Nations imposed "no fly zones" created in accordance with the cease fire of 1991. These attacks on American and British aircraft continued even after U.N. Resolution 1441 was passed and constituted an ongoing state of war under international law.

In any event, 25 million Iraqi people were liberated from the brutal regime of Saddam Hussein and the new government of Iraq has processed him in their criminal justice system for his crimes. Perhaps more importantly, the war in Iraq has sent a clear message to other totalitarian regimes that the United States may very well take action to remove those governments supporting and harboring al-Qa'eda-styled terrorists. Governments which have traditionally been sympathetic to radical terror groups in the past are now taking notice of the United States' position and are certainly adjusting their policies to adapt to this new global paradigm. As stated, the most immediate example is found in the once terrorist State of Libya which has taken significant steps to destroy its weapons of mass destruction and embark upon limited democratic reforms.

The Bush Doctrine has departed from the policies of all previous administrations, from Reagan to Clinton, which, when it came to dealing with terrorist attacks on the United States, were content to "swat the mosquito." For example, the terror attacks on the United States embassies in Kenya and Tanzania in August 1998, which resulted in over 250 deaths, prompted only ineffectual cruise missile attacks against suspected al-Qa'eda targets in Afghanistan and Sudan. Limited responses were also taken in regards to the 1996 Khobar Towers barracks attack in Saudi Arabia, which killed nineteen American airmen, and the attack on the *U.S.S. Cole* in 2000, which killed seventeen American naval personnel.

In contrast, the Bush Doctrine is certainly focused on an ambitious campaign to "drain the swamps"—to eliminate those regimes that actively sponsor large scale terrorism. Because of the murderous nature of some branches of militant Islam, the Bush Doctrine declares that it is not enough to look for the needle in the haystack; the haystack must be destroyed. The premise upon which the Bush Doctrine rests involves two disturbing trends which in and of themselves pose a direct challenge to the peace and stability of the world and stand at odds with the central goals of the U.N. Charter to "maintain international peace and security" (Article 1(1)) and to "promot[e] and encourag[e] respect for human rights and for fundamental freedoms for all without distinction as to race, sex, language, or religion" (Article 1(3)). The first aspect relates to the radical ideological beliefs of the suicide terrorists and the totalitarian States which either harbor them or, as the Bush Doctrine relates, provides "arms to terrorists, giving them the means to match their hatred." The second aspect relates to the willingness of these al-Qa'eda-styled terrorists to use weapons of mass destruction in their quest to carry out grandiose schemes to kill multitudes of civilians. Taken together, this mix is lethal and a clear and present danger to the international peace and security of the United States and the global community.

The Bush Doctrine also embraces the concept of promoting the spread of democracy as the best long-term solution to defeating the terrorists. The 2006 *National Security Strategy* reaffirms that "[i]n the long run, winning the war on terror means winning the battle of ideas, for it is ideas that can turn the disenchanted into murderers willing to kill innocent victims."

3.2 Weapons of Mass Murder

The world must wake from its millenary sleep and recognize the real possibility that weapons of mass destruction will be used against large civilian population centers. Clearly, the terror attacks of September 11, 2001, have demonstrated that international terrorism has now "broke us across the threshold" of creating mass casualties. The al-Qa'eda-styled terrorist is not content to kill in the tens or twenties, he aggressively seeks access to weapons of mass destruction in order to murder in the thousands and tens of thousands. Al-Qa'eda has openly boasted that it seeks nuclear weapons. While nuclear weapons may be beyond the reach of international terrorists at this time, biological weapons, chemical weapons and "dirty bombs" are not. Biological and chemical agents are inexpensive, easy to obtain, hard to trace, and capable of killing thousands upon thousands. Dirty bombs are devices which use conventional explosives in conjunction with nuclear, chemical, or biological byproducts. In addition, terrorists may strike "live" nuclear facilities as the arrest of the "Toronto 19" terror cell in August 2003 amplified (the alleged plot was to crash a plane into the Seabrook Nuclear Reactor).

Finally, as terrorists become more sophisticated in the cyber world, they will soon engage in significant cyber-terrorism attacks to disrupt entire networks that control vital infrastructure systems. Even now, al-Qa'eda terror cells routinely depend on the Internet for training and tactical support to for example, provide instructions on how to make a bomb from commercial materials. According to terror expert Gabriel Weimann, the number of terror-related Web sites has risen from 12, just nine years ago, to more than 4,500 as of 2005. Militant Islam's goal of global war fits perfectly with the Internet's anonymity and ability to reach millions. The terror groups need not even use fixed Internet sites that can be monitored, since discussion boards and encrypted messages are nearly impossible to break.

Add into the equation the fact that al-Qa'eda terrorists have demonstrated a clear desire to use weapons of mass murder if possible and President Bush's call for expanding the War on Terror to any State (e.g., the Taliban's Afghanistan) that exhibits a willingness to support terror makes fundamental sense. Even without a renegade State to supply them with weapons of mass murder, terrorists can acquire them in the following ways. According to a *Public Agenda Special Report: Terrorism*, there are four general scenarios regarding the terrorist use of nuclear devices: (1) the terrorist makes a crude nuclear bomb using smuggled uranium or fissile material; (2) an unstable nation falls into the hands of terrorists (e.g., Pakistan is said to have dozens of nuclear weapons); (3) a conventional bomb is employed to explode radioactive materials (so-called dirty bomb); or (4) a nuclear power plant is attacked. Accordingly, a doomsday scenario becomes a central consideration of whether or not the War on Terror should be expanded. Researchers at Stanford University have compiled a "database of lost, stolen and misplaced nuclear material depicting a world awash in weapons grade uranium and plutonium that is not publicly accounted for." Again, even one or two dedicated suicide bombers armed with a chemical, biological, or nuclear weapon could inflict catastrophic death and destruction in an urban environment. The August 2003 arrest of 19 Muslim males in Toronto, Canada, on suspicion that they were planning to drive an aircraft into the Seabrook Nuclear Reactor, located near Boston, Massachusetts, attests to the desire of Islamic radicals to kill in large numbers.

The problem, of course, is how does one deal with an ideology steeped in pseudo-religious fanaticism which compels its foot soldiers of terror to gladly commit suicide in order to kill innocent civilians? The phenomenon of martyrdom in the name of God is known as "*Istishad*" and it represents a chilling development in four aspects.

- Suicide bombings can result in massive casualties and infrastructure damage.
- Suicide bombings attract wide media attention and vividly portray the determination of the suicide bomber to the "cause."
- Because there is no exit strategy for the suicide bomber to save himself, the suicide attack can be executed at the optimum time and place to ensure success.
- Since the suicide bomber is killed in the attack, there is no possibility to interrogate the attacker for information.

If it seems obvious that third party dispute mechanisms will bear no fruit with terrorists who are filled with such hate, one is left with the unpleasant truism voiced by the ancient Romans—*oderint dum metuatant* ("let them hate us as long as they respect us"). In the short term the United States was not able to reason with either the Taliban regime or Saddam Hussein. Neither of them wished to comply with the principles of peace embodied in the U.N. Charter. Fortunately, America was able to employ the proper application of force under the rule of law to, as President Bush pledged in his first major speech following the September 11, 2001 attack, "bring them to justice or bring justice to them."

In addition, America was extremely fortunate that the War on Terror began prior to the al-Qa'eda gaining access to a stockpile of weapons of mass murder. September 11, 2001, could have happened at any time, but at least now the United States has embarked on a worldwide War on Terror without having suffered the devastation of a true "weapons of mass destruction" event. Clearly, the use of the military arm of the United States must not cease until the States that support al-Qa'eda-styled terrorism have been neutralized and the al-Qa'eda network is destroyed.

On the other hand, particularly in Europe where the Muslim population is large (the Muslim population in France is 10 percent, Britain's is almost 3 percent and America's is about 1 percent (seven million Muslims and 2,000 Mosques), the task for law enforcement is to weed out the radical clerics and terrorists without creating a climate of fear and intimidation in the Muslim community. In addition, the London and Madrid bombings clearly demonstrate that one cannot simply blame "outsiders" for the attacks. The Muslim terrorists that packed acetone peroxide (the bomb of choice which is known as the Mother of Satan) into four rucksacks and then murdered 52 innocent people on July 7, 2005, were all members of British society. Likewise, the 24 arrests made in the August 2006 London raids that disrupted the bombing of up to ten transatlantic airliners were British Muslims, as were the dozen Canadian Muslim terrorists arrested in Canada in 2006 who had about three tons of ammonium nitrate in their possession and planned to behead the prime minister.

3.3 The Bush Doctrine and the Rule of Law

The challenging question for the United States and the entire civilized world is how to legally frame a rule of law that speaks to preventing future attacks by sophisticated State-supported or State-sponsored terrorist groups, particularly in light of their use of weapons of mass destruction and the existence of renegade States. If the employment of a weapon of mass murder is on the near horizon, do the current international rules relating to the use of force (i.e., only used in self-defense) actually work in the post-9/11 world? In other words, must a State wait for a catastrophic State-sponsored or State-supported terrorist attack before it can respond, or does a threatened State have the right to engage in anticipatory self-defense, or perhaps even in a controversial legal theory known as "counter proliferation self-help," against a regime it believes capable of such acts?

The concept of anticipatory self-defense is also termed alternatively as "preemption self-defense" or "preventative self-defense," and has been used by the Israelis, as illustrated by Israel's preemptive air strike on Arab airfields in the 1967 War and against individual Palestinian terrorists, as demonstrated by the ongoing Palestinian conflict.

The United States has long recognized the right of <u>anticipatory self-defense</u> to counter threats to *Anticipatory* its national security. In the United States, scholars regularly cite the famous Caroline Doctrine, which domestically defines the circumstances permitting forcible self-help or self-defense. The Caroline Doctrine grew out of an 1837 raid by Canadian troops to burn a ship harbored in New York. Responding to the Canadian military attack on the ship (which was being used by Canadian rebels) under the concept of self defense or, more precisely, anticipatory self defense, United States Secretary of State, Daniel Webster penned the Caroline Doctrine. Under the Caroline Doctrine a nation may resort to necessary and proportional acts of self-defense if such acts arise out of an instant and overwhelming necessity, leaving no choice of means and no moment of deliberation.

The problem, of course, is that a State may claim the right of anticipatory self-defense as a pretext for aggression. To weigh the validity of the concept of anticipatory self-defense, international law views the employment of this doctrine in the context of an <u>"imminent" armed attack</u> and most often as a part of the inherent right of self-defense found in Article 51 of the U.N. Charter. Traditionally, the analysis was fairly clear cut; imminent was viewed in terms of the actual mobilization by the aggressor State of its conventional military forces in preparation for an armed attack. In the War on Terror, however, the enemy is not a nation-state and does not rely on conventional forces. Al-Qa'eda-styled suicide terrorists may rely on the use of weapons of mass murder targeted at civilians which, in their hands, may very well satisfy the rule of law requirement of "imminent." Regardless, the use of force in preemption must be reasonably proportionate to the specific danger that is to be averted.

Former United States Deputy Secretary of Defense Paul Wolfolwitz was an early and vocal proponent of anticipatory self-defense, speaking with approval for the Israeli military's use of preemptive force in regards to the killing of known Palestinian terrorists and embracing the idea as a necessary instrument of United States policy in the War on Terror. According to Wolfolwitz, "Our approach has been to aim at prevention and not merely punishment. We are at war. Self-defense requires prevention and sometimes preemption." The White House's 2002 *National Security Strategy of the United States* clearly spelled out America's intention to employ the concept of preemption. As noted, this strategy is also known as the Bush Doctrine.

> The United States has long maintained the option of preemptive actions to counter a sufficient threat to our national security. The greater the threat, the greater the risk of inaction— and the more compelling the case for taking anticipatory action to defend ourselves, even if uncertainty remains as to the time and place of the enemy's attack. To forestall or prevent such hostile acts by our adversaries, the United States will, if necessary, act preemptively.

The 2002 *National Security Strategy* (retained in the 2006 *National Security Strategy*) document spells out a three-part approach to weigh the use of preemption.

> We will always proceed deliberately, weighing the consequences of our actions. To support preemptive options, we will:
> - build better, more integrated intelligence capabilities to provide timely, accurate information on threats, wherever they may emerge;
> - coordinate closely with allies to form a common assessment of the most dangerous threats; and
> - continue to transform our military forces to ensure our ability to conduct rapid and precise operations to achieve decisive results.

The concept of counter-proliferation self-help takes the matter of anticipatory self-defense to the next level, although in the 2002 *National Security Strategy* the distinction has essentially been swallowed under preemption. Counter-proliferation self-help is focused specifically on rogue totalitarian States that seek to acquire weapons of mass destruction. The concept argues that when the threat of a totalitarian State or terrorist group using a weapon of mass destruction directly threatens the national survival of another State, a new international legal regimen should allow for the threatened State to engage in "preventive or preemptive use of force to either deter acquisition plans, eliminate acquisition programs, or destroy illicit weapons of mass destruction sites at any stage in the proliferators acquisition efforts."

The 1981 Israeli air attack on Iraq's Osiraq nuclear reactor is the best illustration of this emerging and much-needed doctrine. Although the international community condemned the Israelis for violating the rule of law regarding the use of force in self-defense, both history and common sense prove their actions were entirely justified.

Tragically, the totalitarian Iranian regime under Mahmoud Ahmadinejad (the real power is held by the supreme religious leader Ayatollah Ali Khamenei) is now approaching the same level of development for its own nuclear program. Some Israelis believe that Iran will have nuclear capability by 2008, although most estimates think that a nuclear weapon capability will occur sometime around 2012. Not only does Iran support and sponsor terrorist organizations like Hizballah, but the findings of the 9/11 Commission amplify the danger of a nuclear Iran, recognizing that Iran provided al-Qa'eda operatives pass-through rights without border stamps. In fact, eight to ten of the hijackers passed through Iran between October 2000 and February 2001.

Although Iran is acting in direct defiance of the United Nations Security Council by refusing to cooperate with the International Atomic Energy Agency (IAEA) and is violating its own treaty obligations, it remains to be seen if free nations will simply do nothing or engage in preemptive force to shut down the Iranian program before Iran either uses the nuclear weapons it is developing or passes them on to terrorists for use against the United States or other free nations. The United Nations Security Council has taken some limited action, but few anticipate that the use of force will ever be authorized. In many respects, Iran represents a greater danger than Saddam Hussein. With Iran's 18 to 30 nuclear-related facilities dispersed around the country, the West may have to focus its efforts on Cold War deterrence strategies rather than preemption.

The argument that the War on Terror must be enlarged because of the overwhelming danger to the global community is the only reasonable position to advance in an era of Islamic militant terrorism and weapons of mass destruction. Again, the reason that Iraq was targeted for a preemptive military strike was not because Saddam Hussein could not be deterred. It was because Saddam was likely to provide weapons of mass murder to an al-Qa'eda-styled terrorist organization which could not be deterred. Again, the delivery system for a weapon of mass destruction is a terrorist seeking martyrdom. In the post-9/11 world, any rogue nation that exhibits the potential to pass on weapons and support to al-Qa'eda-styled terrorists threatens the world and is a candidate for swift military action.

Finally, a less-discussed legal basis for military intervention against a rogue nation falls under the evolving legal theory known as humanitarian intervention. For example, although conducted with the specific approval of the United Nations, the December 1992 United States military intervention in Somalia was motivated purely on humanitarian grounds to alleviate human suffering and, even without United Nations sanction, would appear on its face to be a proper exercise of the developing customary legal theory of humanitarian intervention.

The theory of humanitarian intervention, recognized by many modern international scholars, holds that when the government and infrastructure of a country have disintegrated to the point that its people are being subjected to a widespread pattern of gross human rights violations over a prolonged period of time, another nation may intervene to stop the loss of life and to assist in the restoration of law and order. The caveat to the theory, of course, is that once the loss of life has stopped and law and order has been restored, the intervening force must immediately depart.

3.4 Power versus Words—The Rule of Law

The argument is sometimes made, rather cynically, that what really matters in achieving a particular goal is the possession of the necessary power to influence the desired outcome. Accordingly, since the overriding goal of the War on Terror is the protection of American interests and the maintenance of global stability through prevention of terrorism and unlawful aggression, the United States should depend upon dispositions of effective power without concern for the rearrangement of authoritative words to color that power. In weighing the use of force in the War on Terror, some argue that concentration should simply rest on the use of power, downplaying the necessity or impact of words. This approach might be termed a power versus word argument, a phenomenon which rests particularly well with totalitarian regimes, but is also periodically raised by members of democratic societies facing peril.

Thus, when Iraq invaded and conquered the sovereign nation of Kuwait in 1990, no amount of words, treaty obligations or diplomacy halted their exercise of total and brutal aggression against the territory, people and environment of Kuwait. Exercising what was termed the law of the jungle, Iraq simply took what it wanted. The fact that Iraq was a member of the United Nations and bound by the principles relating to dispute settlement through means other than the use of force had no effect whatsoever on its activities. In this regard, the words and ideas contained in the U.N Charter deterred neither Iraq's open and brutal aggression of Kuwait, nor Saddam Hussein's lust for power and territory.

In fact, throughout the entire Gulf crisis, Iraq made no real attempt to conceal, let alone justify, its violations of the U.N. Charter, the Geneva Conventions or other applicable treaties. In the end, it was only the application of power through the superior military might of the allied coalition headed in chief by the United States which succeeded in halting Iraq's aggression.

Other examples of the apparent disconnect of power *vis-à-vis* words can be found in the arena of human rights. The willingness of many States to eagerly endorse numerous human rights covenants that are never put into practice shows that this cynical model finds some basis in fact. If power is all that ultimately counts, then what use do words have in the real world of dealing with international conflict?

Casting the use of power as the dominant factor in the use of force captures only a portion of the issue at hand. Words without corresponding force have little effect in the deterrence of unlawful activities; such a model incorrectly dismisses the role of words in the process. Of course, aggression can never be halted by words alone, no matter how much those words reflect accepted norms. However, the deficiency of this reasoning rests on misunderstanding the critical role which universally defined norms play in the process of deterrence. Clearly defined norms actually provide stimulus and sinew for subsequent action. Such norms are the very building blocks necessary to generate the support to defeat unlawful activities.

If words are the basis for viable action, words must impart unambiguous understanding. A basic tenet of providing instruction is simplicity, appropriately known in the vernacular of the military as KISS (keep it simple stupid). To be efficacious to a wide audience, concepts should be kept as simple as possible. Additionally, since each discipline of study has its own unique system of terminology, effective communication mandates that the more complex the body of material to be learned, the greater one must rely on shorter concepts which take the place of longer chains of thought.

Along with simplicity, concepts must be thoroughly inculcated to be retained. Repetition is also key to all learning; it alone can ensure comprehension and, hence, meaningful communication. Thus, the more complex the body of learning, the greater the need for repetition.

In the War on Terror the Bush Administration has, to be sure, made mistakes, but it has demonstrated a high level of sophistication concerning the need to couch actions in simple, yet meaningful terminology. And, more importantly, that terminology is largely cemented in the rule of law as it pertains to the use of force.

One of the lessons of contemporary science about human behavior is that it helps in creating the conditions necessary for the achievement of a goal to have the goal more sharply delineated. The clarification in detail of distinctions between lawful and unlawful coercion will not, of course, by itself establish all the necessary conditions for restraint of unlawful coercion. But it may perform the very necessary task of outlining the major contours of the effects sought in terms of which alternative choices in the rearrangement of effective power and in the adoption of new modalities in practice must be appraised.

As previously outlined, when President George W. Bush formed the allied coalition against the Taliban, he firmly rooted the campaign in the norms of the U.N. Charter and under the domestic law of the United States. The subsequent force applied by the United States and its allies had the full backing of a universally recognized set of lawful standards contained in Article 51 of the

U.N. Charter. Similarly, the primary Security Council resolution dealing with the attack on America was based upon the lawful authority of the U.N. Charter. Conversely, the Taliban regime had no legal basis in which to frame its aggression and, apart from a few non-democratic States, almost no supporters within the community of nations.

As the decade worth of U.N. Security Council resolutions over weapons inspections in Iraq also demonstrated, words issued without the necessary power to enforce them are almost as counterproductive as power applied without the framework of words. Unfortunately, the same pattern of behavior is unfolding in the context of Iran's nuclear ambitions. Still, to emphasize power in the power-versus-words analysis fails completely in the long run because words are the very basis for establishing acceptable norms of agreed behavior which, in turn, distinguish lawful actions from those that are unlawful.

Furthermore, most of the world can quickly grasp the idea of following the democratically based rule of law in halting an aggressor who has broken the law, or who threatens the employment of weapons of mass murder. In this light, America is only defending itself against rogue nations; *they* have been at war with the United States for a long time.

The rule of law has its problems, but those problems are more in the context of application rather than definition; the meaning is simply framed, the application is not. In its strict meaning, the rule of law has immediate association. The meaning of the rule of law will always refer to that body of accepted and well-recognized principles of international law accepted by democratic nations, the most critical being in the context of the use of force. It is safe to say, in terms of international behavior, that the phrase rule of law will always bring to mind the illegality of the use of aggressive force. The struggle is not so much in meaning—the primary strength of the rule of law—it is whether the rule of law will prevail as the means of justification in a given situation.

If respect for the rule of law is to survive as the measure of civilized behavior, it does not contribute to the discussion to advocate the use of force apart from legal parameters. The United States must abide by the international principles as they now exist. While it is certainly prudent to sternly warn States that support or sponsor terrorism that they will be held absolutely accountable for any acts of aggression, anticipatory self-defense can only be used if the United States reasonably makes the case to the nation that a significant attack by terrorists using weapons of mass murder is imminent.

Thus, even if the attacks of September 11, 2001, are considered an act of war by the al-Qa'eda and the Taliban, the United States cannot unilaterally expand the Global War on Terrorism to nations not directly linked to the September 11, 2001, assault unless it articulates a credible self-defense argument. As noted previously, in considering whether the war should have been expanded to Saddam's Iraq, for example, there was at least evidence that Iraq had plans to develop weapons of mass destruction in violation of U.N. Security Council resolutions as well as a disposition to support terrorism. Both Congress and the Bush Administration presented their case to the American people and the rest of the civilized world. Under domestic American law, the war was legal; both Congress and the Executive approved. While one can argue that the intelligence part was terribly flawed, the war was certainly not "illegal" in light of the applicable U.N. resolutions and the history of the Iraqi regime for duplicity. On the contrary, the U.N. Security Council has never condemned the United States for the war in Iraq (as a practical matter the United States would simply veto any such resolution), but it has passed resolutions supporting the reconstruction of the country under the U.S. led coalition.

Interestingly, despite the fact that the U.N. did not pass a use of force resolution, the United Nations Security Council voted unanimously (14–0) in May of 2003 to grant the United States and the United Kingdom effective legal control over all aspects of the Iraqi economy and political process pending the creation of an internationally recognized interim government. This action was tantamount to recognizing that the use of force against Saddam Hussein was acceptable to the international community. Similarly, in June 2004, the Security Council again voted unanimously (14–0) to fully recognize the legitimacy of the interim Iraqi government which took power on June 28, 2004.

Historically, the United Nations has only authorized armed force on two occasions; both instances related to stopping clearly defined acts of aggression. In a stunning show of world solidarity immediately following the Cold War era, President George H. Bush was able to obtain a clear "use of force" resolution from the U.N. Security Council prior to using lawful violence to expel the 1990 illegal Iraqi invasion and occupation of Kuwait. Resolution 678 reads in relevant part:

> The Security Council …
> Authorizes member States cooperating with the government of Kuwait, unless Iraq on or before January 15, 1991 fully implements … the foregoing Resolutions, to use all necessary means to uphold and implement the Security Council Resolution 660 and all subsequent relevant Resolutions and to restore international peace and security in the area ….

The only parallel to the Security Council's authorization for the use of force in the 1991 Gulf War was in the Korean War. On July 7, 1950, responding to North Korea's armed aggression into South Korea, the Security Council authorized the creation of a unified command under the authority of the United States. The resolution was passed, however, only due to the temporary absence of the Soviet Union.

While the end to major combat operations in Iraq was declared by President Bush in mid-2003, a new and deadly chapter in the Iraqi War quickly took hold—coalition forces and Iraqi civilians were now targeted for murder by various groups of guerrilla fighters, common criminals and terrorists. Even the capture of Saddam Hussein on December 13, 2003, has not significantly stemmed the growing volume of unconventional warfare.

The continued sectarian fighting between Shia and Sunni Muslims, as well as the al-Qa'eda terrorist attacks in Iraq, required the United States to alter its occupation strategy. Instead of reducing the number of troops on the ground in Iraq as hoped for in the occupation phase of the campaign, the United States was obliged to keep about 150,000 military and between 50,000 to 100,000 civilian personnel in Iraq (the exact number of civilian contractors is unknown due to the large number of security contractors). In turn, because of the associated strain on its active duty military forces, the United States found that it had to utilize a great number of its reserve personnel to maintain the troop strength. As the death toll encompasses 3,000 American soldiers (slightly less than 1/5 of the casualties are from non-combat related accidents), the United States is attempting to train a dependable Iraqi military and police force to better quell the violence that has claimed thousands of lives (e.g., 6,599 civilian deaths were recorded in July and August

2006). In addition, the major coalition partners in Iraq—Britain, Italy, Poland, Ukraine, Spain, Netherlands, Australia, Romania, South Korea and Denmark—have about 27,000 troops on the ground, with the United Kingdom supplying about 10,000.

Considering the new threats which the War on Terror presents in terms of rogue terrorist States and large militant al-Qa'eda-styled terrorist organizations, American policy makers can and must develop an active global-based strategy designed to deter and defeat future terror attacks both in areas where American forces are located and on the homeland. At a minimum—added to the new 2006 *National Security Strategy*—this means new thinking in four areas.

First, the United Nations must be energized to immediately address the issue of reaching a consensus on a universal definition for terrorism. This effort should also include language regarding when a particular act of terrorism may be considered as an act of war.

Second, the United States must insist that the concept of counter-proliferation self-help be placed on the table as a viable addition to the international rule of law regarding the use of force against a radical State seeking access to weapons of mass destruction. Most certainly, the United States will do well to obtain the direct assistance and input of the major powers, particularly the Russians.

Third, juxtaposed to pressing the international community for concrete definitions and new legal approaches on how to fight terrorism in the post-9/11 world, the United States should continue to earnestly endorse the spread of democratic values as the absolute best avenue to promote terrorism avoidance over the long term. Democracy is not an American value; democracy and human rights are normative world values. The world community has wisely made assistance to the new Afghan government to build roads, schools, factories, homes, and so forth, contingent on its movement towards the adoption of democratic values; more must be done in this region of the world. At the end of the day, the totalitarian ponds that foster terrorism must be drained. The goal is extremely ambitious, but the cost of inaction is too great. As long as there is a reasonable chance for some level of measured success, the United States cannot unilaterally pull out of Iraq. The country would surely descend into an orgy of bloodshed which would have serious negative economic and geo-political consequences for the region and the world. The cause of radical Islamic terror would increase ten-fold.

Finally, whatever the future may hold, the United States must continue to reinforce the basic truism that a democracy never answers terror with terror in the context of the employment of military force in self-defense. The United States is absolutely obligated under international law to follow the laws of war as well as all applicable international and customary laws. By all level headed assessments, the American military has done an outstanding job in the combat activities in Afghanistan and Iraq in abiding by the law of armed conflict while caring for basic humanitarian needs of civilians caught up in the conflict. As the world's leading democracy, it is imperative that the United States continues to exercise the lawful use of military force in accordance with the letter and spirit of the rule of law or face the possibility that it will be battling the children of hate and terrorism in the next generation.

The twenty-first century is still young, but it does not appear that the road to promoting democracy in Iraq or other parts of the Islamic world will be an easy task. Although the bitter sectarian violence in Iraq may prove to be beyond America's capability to control, the principle of promoting the rule of law must never be abandoned.

3.5 Questions for Discussion

1. *Roots of militant Islamic aggression.* The 9/11 Commission, convened by Congress tried to explain the root of militant Islamic thought:

> They (Bin Laden and al Qaeda) say that America had attacked Islam; America is responsible for all conflicts involving Muslims. Thus Americans are blamed when Israelis fight with Palestinians, when Russians fight with Chechens, when Indians fight with Kashmiri Muslims, and when the Philippine government fights ethnic Muslims in its southern islands. America is also held responsible for the governments of Muslim countries, derided by al Qaeda as "your agents." Bin Laden has stated flatly, "Our fight against these governments is not separate from our fight against you." These charges found a ready audience among millions of Arabs and Muslims angry at the United States because of issues ranging from Iraq to Pales-tine to America's support for their countries' repressive rulers.

How does the Bush Doctrine help or hinder the War on Terror? If the hatred is as pervasive as the 9/11 Commission found, then are there any viable alternatives to the Bush Doctrine?

2. *Preemptive self-defense.* Preemptive use of military force is a central tenet of the Bush Doctrine. Preemptive use of force is designed to prevent enemy attacks by attacking the enemy before they have a chance to strike. Do preemptive measures inherently violate international law?

3. *Will cold-war deterrence work against al-Qa'eda? See* David Rising, *Iraq Terror Boss Seeks Nuke Experts*, SAN ANTONIO EXPRESS NEWS, Sept. 29, 2006, at A1 (Al-Qa'eda's new chief in Iraq, Abu Ayyub al-Masri, calling for nuclear scientists to join his group's holy war against the West).

Selected Bibliography

Addicott, Jeffrey F. *U.S. Must Follow the Law of War or Battle Enemy's Children*, BIRMINGHAM NEWS, Oct. 28, 2001, at C5.

Lake, Anthony. Special Assistant to the President for National Security Affairs, Address to Johns Hopkins University, School of Advanced International Studies. Oct. 21, 1993.

Lesser, Ian O., et al. COUNTERING THE NEW TERRORISM. 1999.

Lillich, Richard. HUMANITARIAN INTERVENTION AND THE UNITED NATIONS. 1973.

Living with Faith and Hope After September 11, U.S. Conference of Catholic Bishops, Dec. 2001. Pub. No. 5-491 USCCB Pub. Wash. D.C.

McDougal, Myers S., and Florentino P. Feliciano. LAW AND MINIMUM WORLD PUBLIC ORDER. 1961.

McHugh, William. *Forcible Self-help in International Law*, NAVAL WAR COLLEGE REVIEW, No. 25, 1972.

President George W. Bush, State of the Union Address. January 29, 2002.

Quinn, Andrew. *Loss of Nuclear Material Tabulated*, SAN JOSE MERCURY NEWS, Mar. 7, 2002, at A1.

Roberts, Guy B. *The Counterproliferation Self-Help Paradigm: A Legal Regime for Enforcing the Norm Prohibiting the Proliferation of Weapons of Mass Destruction*, DENVER JOURNAL OF INTERNATIONAL LAW & POLICY, Summer 1999, at 485.

Rummel, R. J. DEATH BY GOVERNMENT: GENOCIDE AND MASS MURDER IN THE TWENTIETH CENTURY. 1994.

Stone, Andrea. *In Poll, Islamic World Says Arabs Not Involved in 9/11*, USA TODAY, Feb. 27, 2002 at A1.

The 9/11 Commission Report: The National Commission on Terrorist Attacks Upon the United States, 107th Cong. 51. 2004.

Von Glahn, Gerhard. LAW AMONG NATIONS. 6th ed. 1992.

Zakaria, Fareed. *Why Do They Hate Us?* NEWSWEEK, Oct. 22, 2001, at 24.

Chapter 4
Civil Liberties and the War on Terror

The boisterous sea of liberty is never without a wave.

—Thomas Jefferson

The probability that terrorist organizations like al-Qa'eda may employ chemical, nuclear, or biological weapons of mass destruction in suicide attacks poses not only a direct threat to the well-being of tens of thousands of innocent people, but also raises new controversies regarding the possible curtailment of long recognized civil liberties. In creating greater domestic security from future terrorist attacks, the United States government must not trample on American liberties in the name of preserving them. This concern speaks to the matter of "due process." The term due process is most commonly used to describe the rights that Americans enjoy as spelled out in the Fourteenth Amendment of the United States Constitution:

> All persons born or naturalized in the United States, and subject to the jurisdiction thereof, are citizens of the United States and of the State wherein they reside. No State shall make or enforce any law which shall abridge the privileges or immunities of citizens of the United States; nor shall any State deprive any person of life, liberty, or property, without due process of law; nor deny to any person within its jurisdiction the equal protection of the laws.

The term also has come to be associated with American values of fairness and reasonableness in the treatment of others.

Currently, there are <u>seven main areas</u> of concern that have been voiced in the public square as the government struggles to develop durable legal and policy underpinnings to what promises to be a long conflict with al-Qa'eda-styled terrorism. They involve: (1) the use of military tribunals; (2) the power of the United States to investigate, detain and question terrorist suspects; (3) the expansion of the use of the United States military to enforce domestic law; (4) immigration; (5) the use of new information-gathering technologies; (6) the presidential executive order on assassination; and (7) the protection of Constitutional rights.

4.1 Past Efforts to Address Terrorism

As the world watched helplessly while hijacked planes smashed into the World Trade Center and the Pentagon, the attack exposed gaping vulnerabilities in both United States military and law enforcement strategies to guard the nation against a full-fledged terrorist assault by suicidal murderers. Although the threat of a significant terrorist attack on American soil was not an unknown topic of discussion prior to the events of September 11, 2001, very little was done by the federal government in the area of antiterrorism. In 2004, the 567 page report produced by the *National Commission on Terrorist Attacks Upon the United States*, better known as the 9/11 Commission, not only traced the movements of the nineteen hijackers as they circumvented various law enforcement and administrative barriers without detection, but also pointed out in detail how the entire intelligence community failed to stop the attacks.

Prior to 9/11, the actions to address the threat of organized terrorism, particularly militant Islamic groups that targeted American interests, were piecemeal and misguided. Methods were long on rhetoric but short on action. After the dual bombings of two American embassies in Africa in the summer of 1998 left more than 300 people dead, President Clinton vowed that "[n]o matter how long it takes, or where it takes us, we will pursue terrorists until the cases are solved and justice is done." Militarily, President Clinton launched seventy-five cruise missiles at some al-Qa'eda terrorist training camps in Afghanistan and a suspected VX nerve gas production facility at the Shifa Pharmaceuticals plant in Khartoum, Sudan. Nancy Soderberg, a former National Security Council senior aide in the Clinton administration later admitted: "In hindsight, it wasn't enough, and anyone involved in policy would have to admit that." In the kindest light to all administrations (including Ronald Reagan) before September 11, 2001, action by the government was ineffectual because the United States had no frame of reference in which to gauge the magnitude of the threat. The government was mired in old thinking and, as the 9/11 Commission related, a lack of imagination by our intelligence community.

In the international sphere, a brief survey of the American approach to global terrorism prior to September 11, 2001, reveals that America was content to enter into a handful of specific international conventions aimed at encouraging multilateral cooperation in punishing certain narrowly defined acts of terrorism such as hostage taking and hijacking of aircrafts. Some examples of specific antiterrorist conventions include: The Convention on Offenses and Certain Other Acts Committed on Board Aircraft (Tokyo Convention, 1963); Convention for the Suppression of Unlawful Seizure of Aircraft (Hague Convention, 1971); Convention for the Suppression of Unlawful Acts Against the Safety of Civil Aviation (Montreal Convention, 1973); Convention on the Prevention and Punishment of Crimes Against Internationally Protected Persons, Including Diplomatic Agents (New York Convention, 1976-1977); and the International Convention Against the Taking of Hostages (Hostages Convention, 1979). As impressive as the titles sound for these ad hoc conventions, the general position of the United States was simply a mirror of the world community's ineffective approach to the problem of global terrorism. Washington seemed content to react to terrorism incidents, using the criminal justice system when it could.

In the domestic arena, apart from various criminal reforms making terrorist acts abroad a crime under United States domestic law, most of the attention of the executive and legislative branches of government were focused on passing various domestic counterterrorism legislation, such as the 1996 Defense Against Weapons of Mass Destruction Act, commonly referred to as the NLD Act after its sponsors' names, Senators Nunn, Lugar and Domenici. This legislation was limited in scope and designed primarily to assist in planning and training efforts for the use of emergency personnel responding to a major terrorist incident involving a weapon of mass destruction. Early on, these initiatives received much deserved criticism as a band-aid approach to the real world problem of a major terrorist attack.

In most areas of management, meaningful reorganizations of large bureaucracies only occur in response to crisis. Counterterrorism initiatives are no exception. Since the 1980s, there have been numerous legislative initiatives that address terrorist activities, most enacted on the heels of some type of terrorist attack. The central focus of any umbrella security program must involve the coordinated efforts of key federal and state agencies designed to protect United States personnel and property.

4.2 Addressing Terrorism Since 9/11

As is often the case in addressing new threats, the exact scope of the danger posed by al-Qa'eda-styled terrorism is often very difficult to assess. Speculation concerning asymmetric tactics can run from biological terrorism to nuclear terrorism to cyber terrorism, but only probabilities serve to gauge the scenarios. In turn, any new security measure is going to threaten, to some degree, the lifestyle and perhaps some basic rights that American's have long enjoyed. Proclaiming that any changes in the name of national security will entail a "slippery slope" that will see the nation slide into a draconian police state, some so-called civil libertarians prefer to remain frozen at the top, vehemently opposed to all changes. The proper approach, of course, is for one to identify specific notches in the slope—bright and clearly defined lines where the new rule of law will be established for a particular security measure.

The government has taken two major steps to fulfill its obligation to protect the American people from future attacks by al-Qa'eda-styled terrorists. The first is the creation of a new cabinet-level department entitled the Office of Homeland Security and the second is the passage of an exhaustive piece of anti-terror legislation known by short title as the PATRIOT Act and amended in 2006 by the USA PATRIOT Improvement and Reauthorization Act (PATRIOT ACT II).

The Homeland Security Act of 2002 consolidated the federal government's emergency response capabilities under the Department of Homeland Security (DHS). The Act directs the Secretary of DHS to oversee the personnel and assets of the Federal Emergency Management Agency (FEMA) and other related agencies. The DHS has the authority to coordinate the federal government's response to both natural and man-made disasters, including terrorist attacks, on American soil. DHS houses 170,000 employees from 22 agencies. DHS is divided into four separate entities: (1) Information and Infrastructure Protection; (2) Border and Transportation Security; (3) Science and Technology; and (4) Emergency Response. The most notable agencies under the DHS umbrella include the U.S. Coast Guard, Customs Service, Immigration and Naturalization Service (now abolished and divided into three agencies), Border Patrol, Secret Service, Transportation Security Administration and Federal Management Agency.

The HSA provides for a number of new legal standards regarding security issues. For instance, fearing that terrorists may target any number of the nation's critical infrastructures such as power plants, financial networks, airlines, etc., the HSA included rather broad exceptions to the Freedom of Information Act (FOIA) protecting private entities that voluntarily submit "critical infrastructure information" (CII) to the government. The law also provides that any government employee that willfully discloses CII information to the public shall be held criminally liable.

Another HSA provision that provides a legal liability shield to anti-terrorism technologies is the Support Anti-Terrorism by Fostering Effective Technologies Act (SAFETY Act). The Act provides that the DHS Secretary may exempt "sellers" of anit-terrorism technology from tort liability for injuries sustained by third parties resulting from a terrorist attack. Thus, sellers of "any product, equipment, service, device, or technology designed, developed, modified, or procured for the specific purpose of preventing, detecting, identifying, or deterring acts of terrorism" can apply for government certification from DHS. Once the Secretary has certified that the proposed "goods" conform to the seller's specifications, a rebuttable presumption is established that can "only be overcome by evidence showing that the seller acted fraudulently or with willful misconduct in submitting information to the Secretary during the course of the Secretary's consideration of such technology." The SAFETY Act approach departs from the government contractors defense set out in *Boyle v. United Technologies Corp*, where the private party contractor obtained immunity only if he conformed to the government's specifications.

The PATRIOT Act passed in the Senate by a vote of 98–1. The House of Representatives passed their version by a vote of 377-56. Although a number of provisions of the PATRIOT Act were scheduled to expire on December 31, 2005, Congress passed new legislation in early 2006 that, for all practical purposes, extended the majority of the provisions on a permanent basis.

In tandem with domestic strategies to address terrorism, the 9/11 Commission's 2004 report correctly recommended that the United States had to more sharply define a strategy that would ensure that terror groups would not find sanctuary in what it called "the least governed, most lawless places in the world." The Commission listed western Pakistan, Afghanistan, Saudi Arabia, Yemen, West Africa and Southeast Asia as among the most troubled. Other trouble spots which bear note include places like Morocco, a known sanctuary for al-Qa'eda adherents and the home of most of the seventeen suspects jailed in the March 11, 2004, bombings which killed over 200 people in Spain.

4.3 Detainee Status

After the 2002 military campaign in Afghanistan, the vast majority of the Taliban fighters were processed and released in Afghanistan. Approximately 1,000 al-Qa'eda and Taliban fighters were turned over to American forces for disposition. Those turned over to the United States military were deemed to be either too dangerous to parole or were suspected of committing war crimes. By 2007, over 400 were still being held at Guantanamo Bay, Cuba, to include fourteen high-level al-Qa'eda operatives who had been previously kept in undisclosed locations. All of these individuals are currently being detained until either hostilities cease or, in the cases of many, specific charges are levied against them for associated crimes.

Early on, two questions arose regarding due process concerns for these individuals. First, were they entitled to treatment as prisoners of war under the Geneva Conventions? Second, if the United States opted to try these individuals criminally, should they be tried in a United States federal district court or by means of a United States military commission?

An analysis of the first question regarding the status of al-Qa'eda and Taliban fighters under international law begins with the fact that the United States has long incorporated in its laws the international law of war (the term "laws of war" is also used), both customary and codified. (*Paquete Habana*, 175 U.S. 667) After some internal debate, the Bush Administration affirmed that the Geneva Conventions of 1949 did apply to the conflict in Afghanistan and, hence, the Taliban government. However, President Bush also unilaterally determined that the captured al-Qa'eda and Taliban fighters were not eligible for prisoner of war status nor were they entitled to protections contained in Common Article 3 of the 1949 Geneva Conventions, which sets out the minimum standards of treatment for detainees in armed conflict.

The Bush Administration reasoned that since the al-Qa'eda fighters belong to a terrorist organization and are not recognized members of an armed force, they are unlawful belligerents under the laws of war. *Army Field Manual* (FM) 27-10 codifies the law of land warfare. Paragraph 60(b) of FM 27-10 indicates that "[p]ersons who are not members of the armed forces as defined in [the Geneva Conventions], who bear arms or engage in other conduct hostile to the enemy thereby deprive themselves of many of the privileges attaching to the members of the civilian population." As set out in more detail in Chapter 6, this means that they are responsible for breaches of the laws of war, but are not entitled to the status of prisoners of war. In the view of the Bush Administration, al-Qa'eda engaged in acts of war both in the September 11, 2001, attacks and in fighting alongside the Taliban forces in the internationally recognized armed conflict in Afghanistan. Actually, it can be argued that al-Qa'eda has been engaged in acts of war against the United States government since 1996, due to their direct connections with the 1996 bombing of the United States military barracks at Khobar Towers, Saudi Arabia, followed by the 1998 United States Embassy bombings in Kenya and Tanzania and the 2000 suicide boat attack on the *U.S.S. Cole* in Yemen.

As to the captured Taliban fighters, the United States determined that they were likewise not entitled to prisoner of war status under the Geneva Conventions because of their failure to comply with the Conventions' criterion which requires lawful combatants to wear distinctive military insignia, i.e., uniforms which would make them distinguishable from the civilian population at a distance. In finding that the Taliban "have not effectively distinguished themselves from the civilian population," the United States also added that the Taliban fighters had further forfeited any special status because they had "adopted and provided support to the unlawful terrorist objectives of the al-Qa'eda." While the latter finding would not necessarily indicate that the Taliban fighters would not be entitled to prisoner of war status, the former finding would. Still, the Bush Administration repeatedly indicated that all detainees were to be treated in accordance with the humanitarian concerns set out in the Geneva Conventions even though they were not entitled to the additional protections of the Geneva Conventions, i.e., Common Article 3.

The Bush Administration's technical view of the detainees was rejected by the June 2006 Supreme Court decision in *Hamdan v. Rumsfeld*. The Court found that Common Article 3 of the Geneva Conventions did in fact protect the detainees from being subjected to violence, outrages on personal dignity, torture, and cruel, humiliating, or degrading treatment. Although existing Department of Defense directives, orders, policies and doctrine conformed already with the standards of Common Article 3, the DOD quickly issued new treatment guidelines for detainees that incorporated the basic standards set out in Common Article 3.

The 2003 Iraqi War also mandated that the large number of detainees apprehended had to be categorized and housed. Accordingly, the United States grouped the Iraqi detainees into one of three categories: (1) Iraqi soldiers who qualified as prisoners of war under the Geneva Conventions; (2) those suspected of having links to terrorists groups (to include sectarian militias and Saddam loyalists), called "security detainees;" and (3) common criminals.

Those in the first category were mostly captured during the major combat phase of the Iraqi War and were quickly processed and released back into Iraqi society within a few months. While most of the prisoners were treated in accordance with the protections of the Geneva Conventions, the U.S. military self-reported several separate incidents of physical abuse by American guards, most often physical assaults during the first few hours of the detention. As prisoners of war, this particular class of detainees was not required to give any further information upon additional questioning by American forces. To ensure that all parties to the conflict understood this rule of law, Article 17 of the Third Geneva Conventions provides the following:

> No physical or mental torture, *nor any other form of coercion*, may be inflicted on prisoners of war to secure from them information of any kind whatever. Prisoners of war who refuse to answer may not be *threatened, insulted, or exposed to any unpleasant or disadvantageous treatment of any kind* [emphasis added].

Those in the second category were held for indefinite periods of time pending interrogation and eventual transfer to the new Iraqi judicial system. The reason that these security detainees were not given the protections of the Third Geneva Convention is because they failed to qualify as lawful enemy combatants. In short, prisoner of war status is conferred solely on those persons who are "[m]embers of armed forces of a Party to the conflict" or members of militias and members of other volunteer corps, including those of organized resistance movements, belonging to a Party … provided that such … fulfill[s]" four specific conditions:

a) That of being commanded by a person responsible for his subordinates;
b) That of having a fixed distinctive sign recognizable at a distance;
c) That of carrying arms openly; and
d) That of conducting their operations in accordance with the laws and customs of war.

Accordingly, unless a detainee in the post major combat phase of the Iraqi War meets these requirements he is not entitled to the status of prisoner of war but is rather a security detainee. Those in the last category consisted of common felons who were held until such time as the nascent Iraqi judicial system could accommodate them. Given that the determinations were often hard to make between a security detainee and a common criminal, the Bush Administration repeatedly made it clear that all detainees were to be treated in accordance with the humanitarian concerns set out in the Geneva Conventions. As is the case of the detainees at Guantanamo Bay, the detainees receive regular visits by the International Committee of the Red Cross.

Finally, President Bush exercised his authority as the Commander in Chief to designate certain other individuals as "enemy combatants," e.g., United States citizens Jose Padilla and Yaser Esam Hamdi, and to detain said individuals in military custody without criminal charge. On May 8, 2002, Padilla was apprehended at the Chicago airport by federal agents executing a material witness warrant issued by the United States District Court for the Southern District of New York in connection with its grand jury investigation of the 9/11 terrorist attacks. On June 9, 2002, President Bush issued an order to Secretary of Defense Donald H. Rumsfeld designating Padilla as an "enemy combatant." Padilla was transferred to military custody at the Consolidated Naval Brig in Charleston, South Carolina. In late 2005, Padilla was transferred back to federal jurisdiction and charged with a variety of federal crimes. Hamdi was apprehended in Afghanistan during the conflict and was released subsequent to the 2004 Supreme Court ruling under the terms of an agreement between the government and Hamdi.

On June 28, 2004, the same day that the United States transferred power to the interim government in Iraq, the United States Supreme Court handed down a series of opinions (*Rasul v. Bush*, *Al Odah v. United States* and *Hamdi v. Rumsfeld*) regarding the Bush Administration's authority to designate suspected terrorists as "enemy combatants" and to hold such individuals and others without trial, without access to the courts, without charges and incommunicado. Despite sensationalized news media headlines that the Bush Administration had been chastised by the Court, the Court actually upheld the major thrust of the executive's warmaking power to designate an individual (even a United States citizen) as an enemy combatant and to hold that person indefinitely without charges. In the 8-1 *Hamdi* decision, the Court was divided in its rationale, but agreed that even in "a state of war" the president's decision to designate Hamdi as an enemy combatant would still allow him to "notice of the factual basis for his classification" and a "fair opportunity to rebut the government's factual assertions before a neutral decisionmaker." In other words, in the current "state of war," the president does have the authority to designate a suspected terrorist as an "enemy combatant," which means that the person can be held without charges, but the individual so designated has the right to contest that designation before a neutral decisionmaker.

In a clear effort to get Congress to pass legislation authorizing the establishment of a judicial panel to make those determinations for all detainees held in Guantanamo Bay and for United States citizen Hamdi, the Court did not define what it meant by a neutral decisionmaker. Amazingly, leaving it up to the lower courts, the Congress or the Bush Administration to work out the exact standards, the Court did signal that the hearings might not be very extensive in nature, the burden could be shifted to the detainee and that a reviewing judge could relax the standards for admissibility of evidence. Speaking for four members of the majority, Justice O'Connor (her husband is a former Army officer in the Army's Judge Advocate General Corps) even went so far as to observe that "[t]here remains the possibility that the standards we have articulated could be met by ... [a] military tribunal."

One immediate by-product of the Supreme Court decisions was the creation of a Combatant Status Review Tribunal (CSRT) in July of 2004. The CSRT was established by the Secretary of Defense to make independent determinations about whether the detainees held at Guantanamo Bay "are properly classified as enemy combatants and to permit each detainee the opportunity to contest such designation." The panel, made up of three senior military officers, has reviewed the cases of all individual detainees who wished to appear (Hamdi was released from custody without appearing before the CSRT). To date, over 500 individuals have had their cases heard. Still, it is currently unclear whether the determinations of this military tribunal will play a significant role in, for instance, a federal court's determination as to whether the Bush Administration has properly designated detainees as enemy combatants in compliance with the 2004 Supreme Court decision. Scores of cases have been filed by lawyers on behalf of the detainees in the District Court for the District of Colombia and the issue will certainly be reviewed at some point in time by the Supreme Court.

HAMDI v. RUMSFELD
Supreme Court of the United States
542 U.S. 507; 124 S. Ct. 2633 (2004)

Justice O'CONNOR announced the judgment of the Court and delivered an opinion, in which the Chief Justice, Justice KENNEDY, and Justice BREYER join.

At this difficult time in our Nation's history, we are called upon to consider the legality of the Government's detention of a United States citizen on United States soil as an "enemy combatant" and to address the process that is constitutionally owed to one who seeks to challenge his classification as such. The United States Court of Appeals for the Fourth Circuit held that petitioner's detention was legally authorized and that he was entitled to no further opportunity to challenge his enemy-combatant label. We now vacate and remand. We hold that although Congress authorized the detention of combatants in the narrow circumstances alleged here, due process demands that a citizen held in the United States as an enemy combatant be given a meaningful opportunity to contest the factual basis for that detention before a neutral decisionmaker.

I

On September 11, 2001, the al Qaeda terrorist network used hijacked commercial airliners to attack prominent targets in the United States. Approximately 3,000 people were killed in those attacks. One week later, in response to these "acts of treacherous violence," Congress passed a resolution authorizing the President to "use all necessary and appropriate force against those nations, organizations, or persons he determines planned, authorized, committed, or aided the terrorist attacks" or "harbored such organizations or persons, in order to prevent any future acts of international terrorism against the United States by such nations, organizations or persons." Authorization for Use of Military Force ("the AUMF"), 115 Stat 224. Soon thereafter, the President ordered United States Armed Forces to Afghanistan, with a mission to subdue al Qaeda and quell the Taliban regime that was known to support it.

This case arises out of the detention of a man whom the Government alleges took up arms with the Taliban during this conflict. His name is Yaser Esam Hamdi. Born an American citizen in Louisiana in 1980, Hamdi moved with his family to Saudi Arabia as a child. By 2001, the parties agree, he resided in Afghanistan. At some point that year, he was seized by members of the Northern Alliance, a coalition of military groups opposed to the Taliban government, and eventually was turned over to the United States military. The Government asserts that it initially detained and interrogated Hamdi in Afghanistan before transferring him to the United States Naval Base in Guantanamo Bay in January 2002. In April 2002, upon learning that Hamdi is an American citizen, authorities transferred him to a naval brig in Norfolk, Virginia, where he remained until a recent transfer to a brig in Charleston, South Carolina. The Government contends that Hamdi is an "enemy combatant," and that this status justifies holding him in the United States indefinitely—without formal charges or proceedings—unless and until it makes the determination that access to counsel or further process is warranted.

...

II

The threshold question before us is whether the Executive has the authority to detain citizens who ~~Issue~~ qualify as "enemy combatants." There is some debate as to the proper scope of this term, and the Government has never provided any court with the full criteria that it uses in classifying individuals as such. It has made clear, however, that, for purposes of this case, the "enemy combatant" that it is seeking to detain is an individual who, it alleges, was "part of or supporting forces hostile to the United States or coalition partners" in Afghanistan and who "engaged in an armed conflict against the United States" there. We therefore answer only the narrow question before us: whether the detention of citizens falling within that definition is authorized.

The Government maintains that no explicit congressional authorization is required, because the Executive possesses plenary authority to detain pursuant to Article II of the Constitution. We do not reach the question whether Article II provides such authority, however, because we agree with the Government's alternative position, that Congress has in fact authorized Hamdi's detention, through the AUMF.

Our analysis on that point, set forth below, substantially overlaps with our analysis of Hamdi's principal argument for the illegality of his detention. He posits that his detention is forbidden by *18 U.S.C. §4001(a)* [*18 USCS §4001(a)*]. *Section 4001(a)* states that "[n]o citizen shall be imprisoned or otherwise detained by the United States except pursuant to an Act of Congress." Congress passed *§4001(a)* in 1971 as part of a bill to repeal the Emergency Detention Act of 1950, *50 U.S.C. §811 et seq* [*50 USCS §811 et seq.*], which provided procedures for executive detention, during times of emergency, of individuals deemed likely to engage in espionage or sabotage. Congress was particularly concerned about the possibility that the Act could be used to reprise the Japanese internment camps of World War II. H. R. Rep. No. 92-116 (1971); ("The concentration camp implications of the legislation render it abhorrent").

The Government again presses two alternative positions. First, it argues that *§4001(a)*, in light of its legislative history and its location in Title 18, applies only to "the control of civilian prisons and related detentions," not to military detentions. Second, it maintains that *§4001(a)* is satisfied, because Hamdi is being detained "pursuant to an Act of Congress"—the AUMF. Again, because we conclude that the Government's second assertion is correct, we do not address the first. In other words, for the reasons that follow, we conclude that the AUMF is explicit congressional authorization for the detention of individuals in the narrow category we describe (assuming, without deciding, that such authorization is required), and that the AUMF satisfied *§4001(a)*'s requirement that a detention be "pursuant to an Act of Congress" (assuming, without deciding, that *§4001(a)* applies to military detentions).

The AUMF authorizes the President to use "all necessary and appropriate force" against "nations, organizations, or persons" associated with the September 11, 2001, terrorist attacks. There can be no doubt that individuals who fought against the United States in Afghanistan as part of the Taliban, an organization known to have supported the al Qaeda terrorist network responsible for those attacks, are individuals Congress sought to target in passing the AUMF. We conclude that detention of individuals falling into the limited category we are considering, for the duration of the particular conflict in which they were captured, is so fundamental and accepted an incident to war as to be an exercise of the "necessary and appropriate force" Congress has authorized the President to use.

The capture and detention of lawful combatants and the capture, detention, and trial of unlawful combatants, by "universal agreement and practice," are "important incident[s] of war." *Ex parte Quirin, 317 U.S., at 28, 87 L. Ed. 3, 63 S. Ct. 2.* The purpose of detention is to prevent captured individuals from returning to the field of battle and taking up arms once again. Naqvi, Doubtful Prisoner-of-War Status, 84 Int'l Rev. Red Cross 571, 572 (2002) ("[C]aptivity in war is 'neither revenge, nor punishment, but solely protective custody, the only purpose of which is to prevent the prisoners of war from further participation in the war'" (quoting decision of Nuremberg Military Tribunal, reprinted in *41 Am. J. Int'l L. 172, 229 (1947)*); W. Winthrop, Military Law and Precedents 788 (rev. 2d ed. 1920) ("The time has long passed when 'no quarter' was the rule on the battlefield .... It is now recognized that 'Captivity is neither a punishment nor an act of vengeance,' but 'merely a temporary detention which is devoid of all penal character.' ... 'A prisoner of war is no convict; his imprisonment is a simple war measure.'")

...

There is no bar to this Nation's holding one of its own citizens as an enemy combatant. In *Quirin*, one of the detainees, Haupt, alleged that he was a naturalized United States citizen. *317 U.S., at 20, 87 L. Ed. 3, 63 S. Ct. 2.* We held that "[c]itizens who associate themselves with the military arm of the enemy government, and with its aid, guidance and direction enter this country bent on hostile acts, are enemy belligerents within the meaning of ... the law of war." While Haupt was tried for violations of the law of war, nothing in *Quirin* suggests that his citizenship would have precluded his mere detention for the duration of the relevant hostilities. Nor can we see any reason for drawing such a line here. A citizen, no less than an alien, can be "part of or supporting forces hostile to the United States or coalition partners" and "engaged in an armed conflict against the United States," such a citizen, if released, would pose the same threat of returning to the front during the ongoing conflict.

In light of these principles, it is of no moment that the AUMF does not use specific language of detention. Because detention to prevent a combatant's return to the battlefield is a fundamental incident of waging war, in permitting the use of "necessary and appropriate force," Congress has clearly and unmistakably authorized detention in the narrow circumstances considered here.

Hamdi objects, nevertheless, that Congress has not authorized the *indefinite* detention to which he is now subject. The Government responds that "the detention of enemy combatants during World War II was just as 'indefinite' while that war was being fought." We take Hamdi's objection to be not to the lack of certainty regarding the date on which the conflict will end, but to the substantial prospect of perpetual detention. We recognize that the national security underpinnings of the "war on terror," although crucially important, are broad and malleable. As the Government concedes, "given its unconventional nature, the current conflict is unlikely to end with a formal cease-fire agreement." The prospect Hamdi raises is therefore not far-fetched. If the Government does not consider this unconventional war won for two generations, and if it maintains during that time that Hamdi might, if released, rejoin forces fighting against the United States, then the position it has taken throughout the litigation of this case suggests that Hamdi's detention could last for the rest of his life.

It is a clearly established principle of the law of war that detention may last no longer than active hostilities. See Article 118 of the Geneva Convention (III) Relative to the Treatment of Prisoners of War, Aug. 12, 1949, [1955] *6 U. S. T. 3316, 3406*, T. I. A. S. No. 3364 ("Prisoners of war shall be released and repatriated without delay after the cessation of active hostilities"). See also Article 20 of the Hague Convention (II) on Laws and Customs of War on Land, July 29, 1899, 32 Stat 1817 (as soon as possible after "conclusion of peace"); Hague Convention (IV), *supra*, Oct. 18, 1907, 36 Stat 2301 ("conclusion of peace" (Art. 20)); Geneva Convention, *supra*, July 27, 1929, 47 Stat 2055 (repatriation should be accomplished with the least possible delay after conclusion of peace (Art. 75)); Praust, Judicial Power to Determine the Status and Rights of Persons Detained without Trial, *44 Harv. Int'l L. J. 503, 510–511 (2003)* (prisoners of war "can be detained during an armed conflict, but the detaining country must release and repatriate them 'without delay after the cessation of active hostilities,' unless they are being lawfully prosecuted or have been lawfully convicted of crimes and are serving sentences" (citing Arts. 118, 85, 99, 119, 129, Geneva Convention (III), 6 T. I. A. S., at 3384, 3392, 3406, 3418)).

Hamdi contends that the AUMF does not authorize indefinite or perpetual detention. Certainly, we agree that indefinite detention for the purpose of interrogation is not authorized. Further, we understand Congress' grant of authority for the use of "necessary and appropriate force" to include the authority to detain for the duration of the relevant conflict, and our understanding is based on longstanding law-of-war principles. If the practical circumstances of a given conflict are entirely unlike those of the conflicts that informed the development of the law of war, that understanding may unravel. But that is not the situation we face as of this date. Active combat operations against Taliban fighters apparently are ongoing in Afghanistan. See, e.g., Constable, U. S. Launches New Operation in Afghanistan, Washington Post, Mar. 14, 2004, p A22 (reporting that 13,500 United States troops remain in Afghanistan, including several thousand new arrivals); J. Abizaid, Dept. of Defense, Gen. Abizaid Central Command Operations Update Briefing, Apr. 30, 2004, http://www.defenselink.mil/transcripts/2004/tr20040430-1402.html (as visited June 8, 2004, and available in the Clerk of Court's case file) (media briefing describing ongoing operations in Afghanistan involving 20,000 United States troops). The United States may detain, for the duration of these hostilities, individuals legitimately determined to be Taliban combatants who "engaged in an armed conflict against the United States." If the record establishes that United States troops are still involved in active combat in Afghanistan, those detentions are part of the exercise of "necessary and appropriate force," and therefore are authorized by the AUMF.

Ex parte Milligan, 71 U.S. 2, 4 Wall. 2, 125, 18 L. Ed. 281 (1866), does not undermine our holding about the Government's authority to seize enemy combatants, as we define that term today. In that case, the Court made repeated reference to the fact that its inquiry into whether the military tribunal had jurisdiction to try and punish Milligan turned in large part on the fact that Milligan was not a prisoner of war, but a resident of Indiana arrested while at home there. *Id., at 118, 131, 7 U.S. 2, 18*

L. Ed. 281. That fact was central to its conclusion. Had Milligan been captured while he was assisting Confederate soldiers by carrying a rifle against Union troops on a Confederate battlefield, the holding of the Court might well have been different. The Court's repeated explanations that Milligan was not a prisoner of war suggest that had these different circumstances been present he could have been detained under military authority for the duration of the conflict, whether or not he was a citizen.

…

Quirin was a unanimous opinion. It both postdates and clarifies *Milligan*, providing us with the most apposite precedent that we have on the question of whether citizens may be detained in such circumstances. Brushing aside such precedent—particularly when doing so gives rise to a host of new questions never dealt with by this Court—is unjustified and unwise.

III

…

Even in cases in which the detention of enemy combatants is legally authorized, there remains the question of what process is constitutionally due to a citizen who disputes his enemy-combatant status. Hamdi argues that he is owed a meaningful and timely hearing and that "extra-judicial detention [that] begins and ends with the submission of an affidavit based on third-hand hearsay" does not comport with the *Fifth* and *Fourteenth Amendments*. The Government counters that any more process than was provided below would be both unworkable and "constitutionally intolerable." Our resolution of this dispute requires a careful examination both of the writ of habeas corpus, which Hamdi now seeks to employ as a mechanism of judicial review, and of the *Due Process Clause*, which informs the procedural contours of that mechanism in this instance.

…

B

First, the Government urges the adoption of the Fourth Circuit's holding below—that because it is "undisputed" that Hamdi's seizure took place in a combat zone, the habeas determination can be made purely as a matter of law, with no further hearing or factfinding necessary. This argument is easily rejected. As the dissenters from the denial of rehearing en banc noted, the circumstances surrounding Hamdi's seizure cannot in any way be characterized as "undisputed," as "those circumstances are neither conceded in fact, nor susceptible to concession in law, because Hamdi has not been permitted to speak for himself or even through counsel as to those circumstances." *337 F.3d 335, 357 (CA4 2003)* (Luttig, J., dissenting from denial of rehearing en banc); see also *id.*, *at 371–372* (Motz, J., dissenting from denial of rehearing en banc). Further, the "facts" that constitute the alleged concession are insufficient to support Hamdi's detention. Under the definition of enemy combatant that we accept today as falling within the scope of Congress' authorization, Hamdi would need to be "part of or supporting forces hostile to the United States or coalition partners" and "engaged in an armed conflict against the United States" to justify his detention in the United States for the duration of the relevant conflict. The habeas petition states only that "[w]hen seized by the United States Government, Mr. Hamdi resided in Afghanistan." An assertion that one resided in a country in which combat operations are taking place is not a concession that one was "captured in a zone of active combat operations in a foreign theater of war," *316 F.3d at 459* (emphasis added), and certainly is not a concession that one was "part of or supporting forces hostile to the United States or coalition partners" and "engaged in an armed conflict against the

United States." Accordingly, we reject any argument that Hamdi has made concessions that eliminate any right to further process.

C

The Government's second argument requires closer consideration. This is the argument that further factual exploration is unwarranted and inappropriate in light of the extraordinary constitutional interests at stake. Under the Government's most extreme rendition of this argument, "[r]espect for separation of powers and the limited institutional capabilities of courts in matters of military decision-making in connection with an ongoing conflict" ought to eliminate entirely any individual process, restricting the courts to investigating only whether legal authorization exists for the broader detention scheme. At most, the Government argues, courts should review its determination that a citizen is an enemy combatant under a very deferential "some evidence" standard. ("Under the some evidence standard, the focus is exclusively on the factual basis supplied by the Executive to support its own determination" (citing *Superintendent, Mass. Correctional Institution at Walpole v. Hill, 472 U.S. 445, 455-457, 86 L. Ed. 2d 356, 105 S. Ct. 2768 (1985)* (explaining that the some evidence standard "does not require" a "weighing of the evidence," but rather calls for assessing "whether there is any evidence in the record that could support the conclusion")). Under this review, a court would assume the accuracy of the Government's articulated basis for Hamdi's detention, as set forth in the Mobbs Declaration, and assess only whether that articulated basis was a legitimate one. Brief for Respondents 36; see also *316 F.3d at 473–474* (declining to address whether the "some evidence" standard should govern the adjudication of such claims, but noting that "[t]he factual averments in the [Mobbs] affidavit, if accurate, are sufficient to confirm" the legality of Hamdi's detention).

In response, Hamdi emphasizes that this Court consistently has recognized that an individual challenging his detention may not be held at the will of the Executive without recourse to some proceeding before a neutral tribunal to determine whether the Executive's asserted justifications for that detention have basis in fact and warrant in law. He argues that the Fourth Circuit inappropriately "ceded power to the Executive during wartime to define the conduct for which a citizen may be detained, judge whether that citizen has engaged in the proscribed conduct, and imprison that citizen indefinitely," and that due process demands that he receive a hearing in which he may challenge the Mobbs Declaration and adduce his own counter evidence. The District Court, agreeing with Hamdi, apparently believed that the appropriate process would approach the process that accompanies a criminal trial. It therefore disapproved of the hearsay nature of the Mobbs Declaration and anticipated quite extensive discovery of various military affairs. Anything less, it concluded, would not be "meaningful judicial review."

Both of these positions highlight legitimate concerns. And both emphasize the tension that often exists between the autonomy that the Government asserts is necessary in order to pursue effectively a particular goal and the process that a citizen contends he is due before he is deprived of a constitutional right. The ordinary mechanism that we use for balancing such serious competing interests, and for determining the procedures that are necessary to ensure that a citizen is not "deprived of life, liberty, or property, without due process of law," *U.S. Const., Amdt. 5*, is the test that we articulated in *Mathews v. Eldridge, 424 U.S. 319, 47 L. Ed. 2d 18, 96 S. Ct. 893 (1976)*. *Mathews* dictates that the process due in any given instance is determined by weighing "the private interest that will be affected by the official action" against the Government's asserted interest, "including the function involved" and the burdens the Government would face in providing greater process. *424 U.S., at 335, 47 L. Ed. 2d 18, 96 S. Ct. 893*. The *Mathews* calculus then contemplates a judicious balancing of these concerns, through an analysis of "the risk of an erroneous deprivation" of the private interest if the process were reduced and the "probable value, if any, of additional or substitute safeguards." We take each of these steps in turn.

1

It is beyond question that substantial interests lie on both sides of the scale in this case. Hamdi's "private interest ... affected by the official action," is the most elemental of liberty interests—the interest in being free from physical detention by one's own government. *Foucha v. Louisiana, 504 U.S. 71, 80, 118 L. Ed. 2d 437, 112 S. Ct. 1780 (1992)* ("Freedom from bodily restraint has always been at the core of the liberty protected by the *Due Process Clause* from arbitrary governmental action"); see also *Parham v. J. R., 442 U.S. 584, 600, 61 L. Ed. 2d 101, 99 S. Ct. 2493 (1979)* (noting the "substantial liberty interest in not being confined unnecessarily"). "In our society liberty is the norm," and detention without trial "is the carefully limited exception." *Salerno, supra, at 755, 95 L. Ed. 2d 697, 107 S. Ct. 2095*. "We have always been careful not to 'minimize the importance and fundamental nature' of the individual's right to liberty," *Foucha, supra,* at *80, 118 L. Ed. 2d 437, 112 S. Ct. 1780* (quoting *Salerno, supra, at 750, 95 L. Ed. 2d 697, 107 S. Ct. 2095*), and we will not do so today.

Nor is the weight on this side of the *Mathews* scale offset by the circumstances of war or the accusation of treasonous behavior, for "[i]t is clear that commitment for any purpose constitutes a significant deprivation of liberty that requires due process protection," *Jones v. United States, 463 U.S. 354, 361, 77 L. Ed. 2d 694, 103 S. Ct. 3043 (1983)* (emphasis added; internal quotation marks omitted), and at this stage in the *Mathews* calculus, we consider the interest of the *erroneously* detained individual. *Carey v. Piphus, 435 U.S. 247, 259, 55 L. Ed. 2d 252, 98 S. Ct. 1042 (1978)* ("Procedural due process rules are meant to protect persons not from the deprivation, but from the mistaken or unjustified deprivation of life, liberty, or property"); see also *id.,* at *266, 55 L. Ed. 2d 252, 98 S. Ct. 1042* (noting "the importance to organized society that procedural due process be observed," and emphasizing that "the right to procedural due process is 'absolute' in the sense that it does not depend upon the merits of a claimant's substantive assertions"). Indeed, as *amicus* briefs from media and relief organizations emphasize, the risk of erroneous deprivation of a citizen's liberty in the absence of sufficient process here is very real .... Moreover, as critical as the Government's interest may be in detaining those who actually pose an immediate threat to the national security of the United States during ongoing international conflict, history and common sense teach us that an unchecked system of detention carries the potential to become a means for oppression and abuse of others who do not present that sort of threat. See *Ex parte Milligan, 4 Wall.,* at *125, 71 U.S. 2, 18 L. Ed. 281* ("[The Founders] knew—the history of the world told them—the nation they were founding, be its existence short or long, would be involved in war; how often or how long continued, human foresight could not tell; and that unlimited power, wherever lodged at such a time, was especially hazardous to freemen"). Because we live in a society in which "[m]ere public intolerance or animosity cannot constitutionally justify the deprivation of a person's physical liberty," *O'Connor v. Donaldson, 422 U.S. 563, 575, 45 L. Ed. 2d 396, 95 S. Ct. 2486 (1975)*, our starting point for the *Mathews v. Eldridge* analysis is unaltered by the allegations surrounding the particular detainee or the organizations with which he is alleged to have associated. We reaffirm today the fundamental nature of a citizen's right to be free from involuntary confinement by his own government without due process of law, and we weigh the opposing governmental interests against the curtailment of liberty that such confinement entails.

2

On the other side of the scale are the weighty and sensitive governmental interests in ensuring that those who have in fact fought with the enemy during a war do not return to battle against the United States. As discussed above, *supra*, at ____, *159 L. Ed. 2d, at 592*, the law of war and the realities of combat may render such detentions both necessary and appropriate, and our due process analysis need not blink at those realities. Without doubt, our Constitution recognizes that core strategic matters of warmaking belong in the hands of those who are best positioned and most politically accountable for making them. *Dep't of the Navy v. Egan, 484 U.S. 518, 530, 98 L. Ed. 2d 918, 108 S. Ct. 818 (1988)* (noting the reluctance of the courts "to intrude upon the authority of the Executive in military and national security affairs"); *Youngstown Sheet & Tube Co. v. Sawyer, 343 U.S. 579, 587, 96 L. Ed. 1153, 72 S. Ct. 863, 62 Ohio Law Abs. 417 (1952)* (acknowledging "broad powers in military commanders engaged in day-to-day fighting in a theater of war").

The Government also argues at some length that its interests in reducing the process available to alleged enemy combatants are heightened by the practical difficulties that would accompany a system of trial-like process. In its view, military officers who are engaged in the serious work of waging battle would be unnecessarily and dangerously distracted by litigation half a world away, and discovery into military operations would both intrude on the sensitive secrets of national defense and result in a futile search for evidence buried under the rubble of war. To the extent that these burdens are triggered by heightened procedures, they are properly taken into account in our due process analysis.

3

Striking the proper constitutional balance here is of great importance to the Nation during this period of ongoing combat. But it is equally vital that our calculus not give short shrift to the values ~~War~~ that this country holds dear or to the privilege that is American citizenship. It is during our most challenging and uncertain moments that our Nation's commitment to due process is most severely tested; and it is in those times that we must preserve our commitment at home to the principles for which we fight abroad. See *Kennedy v. Mendoza-Martinez, 372 U.S. 144, 164-165, 9 L. Ed. 2d 644, 83 S. Ct. 554 (1963)* ("The imperative necessity for safeguarding these rights to procedural due process under the gravest of emergencies has existed throughout our constitutional history, for it is then, under the pressing exigencies of crisis, that there is the greatest temptation to dispense with guarantees which, it is feared, will inhibit government action"); see also *United States v. Robel, 389 U.S. 258, 264, 19 L. Ed. 2d 508, 88 S. Ct. 419 (1967)* ("It would indeed be ironic if, in the name of national defense, we would sanction the subversion of one of those liberties ... which makes the defense of the Nation worthwhile").

With due recognition of these competing concerns, we believe that neither the process proposed by the Government nor the process apparently envisioned by the District Court below strikes the proper constitutional balance when a United States citizen is detained in the United States as an enemy combatant. That is, "the risk of erroneous deprivation" of a detainee's liberty interest is unacceptably high under the Government's proposed rule, while some of the "additional or substitute procedural safeguards" suggested by the District Court are unwarranted in light of their limited "probable value" and the burdens they may impose on the military in such cases.

We therefore hold that a citizen-detainee seeking to challenge his classification as an enemy combatant must receive notice of the factual basis for his classification, and a fair opportunity to rebut the Government's factual assertions before a neutral decisionmaker .... These essential constitutional promises may not be eroded. At the same time, the exigencies of the circumstances may demand that, aside from these core elements, enemy combatant proceedings may be tailored to alleviate their uncommon potential to burden the Executive at a time of ongoing military conflict. Hearsay, for example, may need to be accepted as the most reliable available evidence from the Government in such a proceeding. Likewise, the Constitution would not be offended by a presumption in favor of the Government's evidence, so long as that presumption remained a rebuttable one and fair opportunity for rebuttal were provided. Thus, once the Government puts forth credible evidence that the habeas petitioner meets the enemy-combatant criteria, the onus could shift to the petitioner to rebut that evidence with more persuasive evidence that he falls outside the criteria. A burden-shifting scheme of this sort would meet the goal of ensuring that the errant tourist, embedded journalist, or local aid worker has a chance to prove military error while giving due regard to the Executive once it has put forth meaningful support for its conclusion that the detainee is in fact an enemy combatant.

…

We think it unlikely that this basic process will have the dire impact on the central functions of warmaking that the Government forecasts. The parties agree that initial captures on the battlefield need not receive the process we have discussed here; that process is due only when the determination is made to *continue* to hold those who have been seized. The Government has made clear in its briefing that documentation regarding battlefield detainees already is kept in the ordinary course of military affairs. Any factfinding imposition created by requiring a knowledgeable affiant to summarize these records to an independent tribunal is a minimal one. Likewise, arguments that military officers ought not have to wage war under the threat of litigation lose much of their steam when factual disputes at enemy-combatant hearings are limited to the alleged combatant's acts. This focus meddles little, if at all, in the strategy or conduct of war, inquiring only into the appropriateness of continuing to detain an individual claimed to have taken up arms against the United States. While we accord the greatest respect and consideration to the judgments of military authorities in matters relating to the actual prosecution of a war, and recognize that the scope of that discretion necessarily is wide, it does not infringe on the core role of the military for the courts to exercise their own time-honored and constitutionally mandated roles of reviewing and resolving claims like those presented here. Cf. *Korematsu v. United States*, *323 U.S. 214, 233-234, 89 L. Ed. 194, 65 S. Ct. 193 (1944)* (Murphy, J., dissenting) ("[L]ike other claims conflicting with the asserted constitutional rights of the individual, the military claim must subject itself to the judicial process of having its reasonableness determined and its conflicts with other interests reconciled"); *Sterling v. Constantin*, *287 U.S. 378, 401, 77 L. Ed. 375, 53 S. Ct. 190 (1932)* ("What are the allowable limits of military discretion, and whether or not they have been overstepped in a particular case, are judicial questions").

In sum, while the full protections that accompany challenges to detentions in other settings may prove unworkable and inappropriate in the enemy-combatant setting, the threats to military operations posed by a basic system of independent review are not so weighty as to trump a citizen's core rights to challenge meaningfully the Government's case and to be heard by an impartial adjudicator.

…

There remains the possibility that the standards we have articulated could be met by an appropriately authorized and properly constituted military tribunal. Indeed, it is notable that military regulations already provide for such process in related instances, dictating that tribunals be made available to determine the status of enemy detainees who assert prisoner-of-war status under the Geneva Convention. See Enemy Prisoners of War, Retained Personnel, Civilian Internees and Other Detainees, Army Regulation 190-8, § 1-6 (1997). In the absence of such process, however, a court that receives a petition for a writ of habeas corpus from an alleged enemy combatant must itself ensure that the minimum requirements of due process are achieved. Both courts below recognized as much, focusing their energies on the question of whether Hamdi was due an opportunity to rebut the Government's case against him. The Government, too, proceeded on this assumption, presenting its affidavit and then seeking that it be evaluated under a deferential standard of review based on burdens that it alleged would accompany any greater process. As we have discussed, a habeas court in a case such as this may accept affidavit evidence like that contained in the Mobbs Declaration, so long as it also permits the alleged combatant to present his own factual case to rebut the Government's return. We anticipate that a District Court would proceed with the caution that we have indicated is necessary in this setting, engaging in a factfinding process that is both prudent and incremental. We have no reason to doubt that courts faced with these sensitive matters will pay proper heed both to the matters of national security that might arise in an individual case and to the constitutional limitations safeguarding essential liberties that remain vibrant even in times of security concerns.

IV

Hamdi asks us to hold that the Fourth Circuit also erred by denying him immediate access to counsel upon his detention and by disposing of the case without permitting him to meet with an attorney. Since our grant of certiorari in this case, Hamdi has been appointed counsel, with whom he has met for consultation purposes on several occasions, and with whom he is now being granted unmonitored meetings. He unquestionably has the right to access to counsel in connection with the proceedings on remand. No further consideration of this issue is necessary at this stage of the case.

…

The judgment of the United States Court of Appeals for the Fourth Circuit is vacated, and the case is remanded for further proceedings. It is so ordered.

* * *

JUSTICE SOUTER, with whom JUSTICE GINSBURG joins, concurring in part, dissenting in part, and concurring in the judgment.

…

V

Because I find Hamdi's detention forbidden by *§4001(a)* and unauthorized by the Force Resolution, I would not reach any questions of what process he may be due in litigating disputed issues in a proceeding under the habeas statute or prior to the habeas enquiry itself. For me, it suffices that the Government has failed to justify holding him in the absence of a further Act of Congress, criminal charges, a showing that the detention conforms to the laws of war, or a demonstration that *§4001(a)* is unconstitutional. I would therefore vacate the judgment of the Court of Appeals and remand for proceedings consistent with this view.

Since this disposition does not command a majority of the Court, however, the need to give practical effect to the conclusions of eight members of the Court rejecting the Government's position calls for me to join with the plurality in ordering remand on terms closest to those I would impose. See *Screws v. United States, 325 U.S. 91, 134, 89 L. Ed. 1495, 65 S. Ct. 1031 (1945)* (Rutledge, J., concurring in result). Although I think litigation of Hamdi's status as an enemy combatant is unnecessary, the terms of the plurality's remand will allow Hamdi to offer evidence that he is not an enemy combatant, and he should at the least have the benefit of that opportunity.

It should go without saying that in joining with the plurality to produce a judgment, I do not adopt the plurality's resolution of constitutional issues that I would not reach. It is not that I could disagree with the plurality's determinations (given the plurality's view of the Force Resolution) that someone in Hamdi's position is entitled at a minimum to notice of the Government's claimed factual basis for holding him, and to a fair chance to rebut it before a neutral decision maker, see *ante*, at ____, *159 L. Ed. 2d, at 601*; nor, of course, could I disagree with the plurality's affirmation of Hamdi's right to counsel, see *ante*, at ____—____, *159 L. Ed. 2d, at 605*. On the other hand, I do not mean to imply agreement that the Government could claim an evidentiary presumption casting the burden of rebuttal on Hamdi, see *ante*, at ____, *159 L. Ed. 2d, at 602*, or that an opportunity to litigate before a military tribunal might obviate or truncate enquiry by a court on habeas, see *ante*, at ____—____, *159 L. Ed. 2d, at 604–605*.

Subject to these qualifications, I join with the plurality in a judgment of the Court vacating the Fourth Circuit's judgment and remanding the case.

JUSTICE SCALIA, with whom JUSTICE STEVENS joins, dissenting.

Petitioner, a presumed American citizen, has been imprisoned without charge or hearing in the Norfolk and Charleston Naval Brigs for more than two years, on the allegation that he is an enemy combatant who bore arms against his country for the Taliban. His father claims to the contrary, that he is an inexperienced aid worker caught in the wrong place at the wrong time. This case brings into conflict the competing demands of national security and our citizens' constitutional right to personal liberty. Although I share the Court's evident unease as it seeks to reconcile the two, I do not agree with its resolution.

Where the Government accuses a citizen of waging war against it, our constitutional tradition has been to prosecute him in federal court for treason or some other crime. Where the exigencies of war prevent that, the Constitution's Suspension Clause, Art. I, § 9, cl. 2, allows Congress to relax the usual protections temporarily. Absent suspension, however, the Executive's assertion of military exigency has not been thought sufficient to permit detention without charge. No one contends that the congressional Authorization for Use of Military Force, on which the Government relies to justify its actions here, is an implementation of the Suspension Clause. Accordingly, I would reverse the decision below.

…

JUSTICE THOMAS, dissenting.

I agree with the plurality that the Federal Government has power to detain those that the Executive Branch determines to be enemy combatants. See *ante*, at ____, *159 L. Ed. 2d, at 591–592*. But I do not think that the plurality has adequately explained the breadth of the President's authority to detain enemy combatants, an authority that includes making virtually conclusive factual findings. In my view, the structural considerations discussed above, as recognized in our precedent, demonstrate that we lack the capacity and responsibility to second-guess this determination.

This makes complete sense once the process that is due Hamdi is made clear. As an initial matter, it is possible that the Due Process Clause requires only "that our Government must proceed according to the 'law of the land'—that is, according to written constitutional and statutory provisions." In *re Winship*, *397 U.S. 358, 382, 25 L. Ed. 2d 368, 90 S. Ct. 1068* (*1970*) (Black, J., dissenting). I need not go this far today because the Court has already explained the nature of due process in this context.

…

In this context, due process requires nothing more than a good-faith executive determination. To be clear: The Court has held that an executive, acting pursuant to statutory and constitutional authority may, consistent with the *Due Process Clause*, unilaterally decide to detain an individual if the executive deems this necessary for the public safety even if he is mistaken.

For these reasons, I would affirm the judgment of the Court of Appeals.

RASUL v. BUSH

Supreme Court of the United States

542 U.S. 466; 124 S. Ct. 2686 (2004)

OPINION BY: STEVENS, J.

These two cases present the narrow but important question whether United States courts lack jurisdiction to consider challenges to the legality of the detention of foreign nationals captured abroad in connection with hostilities and incarcerated at the Guantanamo Bay Naval Base, Cuba.

I

…

Petitioners in these cases are 2 Australian citizens and 12 Kuwaiti citizens who were captured abroad during hostilities between the United States and the Taliban. Since early 2002, the U.S. military has held them—along with, according to the Government's estimate, approximately 640 other non-Americans captured abroad—at the Naval Base at Guantanamo Bay. The United States occupies the Base, which comprises 45 square miles of land and water along the southeast coast of Cuba, pursuant to a 1903 Lease Agreement executed with the newly independent Republic of Cuba in the aftermath of the Spanish-American War. Under the Agreement, "the United States recognizes the continuance of the ultimate sovereignty of the Republic of Cuba over the [leased areas]," while "the Republic of Cuba consents that during the period of the occupation by the United States … the United States shall exercise complete jurisdiction and control over and within said areas." In 1934, the parties entered into a treaty providing that, absent an agreement to modify or abrogate the lease, the lease would remain in effect "[s]o long as the United States of America shall not abandon the … naval station of Guantanamo."

In 2002, petitioners, through relatives acting as their next friends, filed various actions in the U. S. District Court for the District of Columbia challenging the legality of their detention at the Base. All alleged that none of the petitioners has ever been a combatant against the United States or has ever engaged in any terrorist acts. They also alleged that none has been charged with any wrongdoing, permitted to consult with counsel, or provided access to the courts or any other tribunal.

The two Australians, Mamdouh Habib and David Hicks, each filed a petition for writ of habeas corpus, seeking release from custody, access to counsel, freedom from interrogations, and other relief. Fawzi Khalid Abdullah Fahad Al Odah and the 11 other Kuwaiti detainees filed a complaint seeking to be informed of the charges against them, to be allowed to meet with their families and with counsel, and to have access to the courts or some other impartial tribunal. They claimed that denial of these rights violates the Constitution, international law, and treaties of the United States. Invoking the court's jurisdiction under *28 U.S.C. §§1331* and *1350 [28 USCS §§1331* and *1350]*, among other statutory bases, they asserted causes of action under the Administrative Procedure Act, *5 U.S.C. §§555, 702, 706 [5 USCS §§555, 702, 706]*; the Alien Tort Statute, *28 U.S.C. §1350 [28 USCS §1350]*; and the general federal habeas corpus statute, *§§2241-2243*.

Construing all three actions as petitions for writs of habeas corpus, the District Court dismissed them for want of jurisdiction. The court held, in reliance on our opinion in *Johnson v. Eisentrager, 339 U.S. 763, 94 L. Ed. 1255, 70 S. Ct. 936 (1950)*, that "aliens detained outside the sovereign territory of the United States [may not] invok[e] a petition for a writ of habeas corpus." *215 F. Supp. 2d 55, 68 (DC 2002)*. The Court of Appeals affirmed. Reading *Eisentrager* to hold that "'the privilege of litigation' does not extend to aliens in military custody who have no presence in 'any territory over which the United States is sovereign,'" *321 F.3d 1134, 1144 (CADC 2003)* (quoting *Eisentrager, 339 U.S., at 777-778, 94 L. Ed. 1255, 70 S. Ct. 936*), it held that the District Court lacked jurisdiction over petitioners' habeas actions, as well as their remaining federal statutory claims that do not sound in habeas. We granted certiorari, *540 U.S. 1003, 157 L. Ed. 2d 407, 124 S. Ct. 534 (2003)*, and now reverse.

II

…

Issue The question now before us is whether the habeas statute confers a right to judicial review of the legality of Executive detention of aliens in a territory over which the United States exercises plenary and exclusive jurisdiction, but not "ultimate sovereignty." *A: Yes*

III

Respondents' primary submission is that the answer to the jurisdictional question is controlled by our decision in *Eisentrager*. In that case, we held that a Federal District Court lacked authority to issue a writ of habeas corpus to 21 German citizens who had been captured by U. S. forces in China, tried and convicted of war crimes by an American military commission headquartered in Nanking, and incarcerated in the Landsberg Prison in occupied Germany. The Court of Appeals in *Eisentrager* had found jurisdiction, reasoning that "any person who is deprived of his liberty by officials of the United States, acting under purported authority of that Government, and who can show that his confinement is in violation of a prohibition of the Constitution, has a right to the writ." *Eisentrager v. Forrestal, 84 U.S. App. D.C. 396, 174 F.2d 961, 963 (CADC 1949)*. In reversing that determination, this Court summarized the six critical facts in the case:

> We are here confronted with a decision whose basic premise is that these prisoners are entitled, as a constitutional right, to sue in some court of the United States for a writ of *habeas corpus*. To support that assumption we must hold that a prisoner of our military authorities is constitutionally entitled to the writ, even though he (a) is an enemy alien; (b) has never been or resided in the

United States; (c) was captured outside of our territory and there held in military custody as a prisoner of war; (d) was tried and convicted by a Military Commission sitting outside the United States; (e) for offenses against laws of war committed outside the United States; (f) and is at all times imprisoned outside the United States. *339 U.S., at 777, 94 L. Ed. 1255, 70 S. Ct. 936.*

On this set of facts, the Court concluded, "no right to the writ of *habeas corpus* appears."

Petitioners in these cases differ from the *Eisentrager* detainees in important respects: They are not nationals of countries at war with the United States, and they deny that they have engaged in or plotted acts of aggression against the United States; they have never been afforded access to any tribunal, much less charged with and convicted of wrongdoing; and for more than two years they have been imprisoned in territory over which the United States exercises exclusive jurisdiction and control.

Not only are petitioners differently situated from the *Eisentrager* detainees, but the Court in *Eisentrager* made quite clear that all six of the facts critical to its disposition were relevant only to the question of the prisoners' *constitutional* entitlement to habeas corpus. The Court had far less to say on the question of the petitioners' *statutory* entitlement to habeas review. Its only statement on the subject was a passing reference to the absence of statutory authorization: "Nothing in the text of the Constitution extends such a right, nor does anything in our statutes."

…

Because subsequent decisions of this Court have filled the statutory gap that had occasioned *Eisentrager's* resort to "fundamentals," persons detained outside the territorial jurisdiction of any federal district court no longer need rely on the Constitution as the source of their right to federal habeas review. In *Braden v. 30th Judicial Circuit Court of Ky., 410 U.S. 484, 495, 35 L. Ed. 2d 443, 93 S. Ct. 1123 (1973)*, this Court held, contrary to Ahrens, that the prisoner's presence within the territorial jurisdiction of the district court is not "an invariable prerequisite" to the exercise of district court jurisdiction under the federal habeas statute. Rather, because "the writ of habeas corpus does not act upon the prisoner who seeks relief, but upon the person who holds him in what is alleged to be unlawful custody," a district court acts "within [its] respective jurisdiction" within the meaning of *§2241* as long as "the custodian can be reached by service of process." *410 U.S., at 494-495, 35 L. Ed. 2d 443, 93 S. Ct. 1123 Braden* reasoned that its departure from the rule of Ahrens was warranted in light of developments that "had a profound impact on the continuing vitality of that decision." *410 U.S., at 497, 35 L. Ed. 2d, 93 S. Ct. 1123*. These developments included, notably, decisions of this Court in cases involving habeas petitioners "confined overseas (and thus outside the territory of any district court)," in which the Court "held, if only implicitly, that the petitioners' absence from the district does not present a jurisdictional obstacle to the consideration of the claim."

…

IV

Putting *Eisentrager* and *Ahrens* to one side, respondents contend that we can discern a limit on *§2241* through application of the "longstanding principle of American law" that congressional legislation is presumed not to have extraterritorial application unless such intent is clearly manifested. Whatever traction the presumption against extraterritoriality might have in other contexts, it certainly has no application to the operation of the habeas statute with respect to persons detained within "the territorial jurisdiction" of the United States. By the express terms of its agreements with Cuba, the United States exercises "complete jurisdiction and control" over the Guantanamo Bay Naval Base, and may continue to exercise such control permanently if it so chooses. 1903 Lease Agreement, Art. III; 1934 Treaty, Art. III. Respondents themselves concede that the habeas statute would create federal-court jurisdiction over the claims of an American citizen held at the base. Considering that the statute draws no distinction between Americans and aliens held in federal custody, there is little reason to think that Congress intended the geographical coverage of the statute to vary depending on the detainee's citizenship. Aliens held at the base, no less than American citizens, are entitled to invoke the federal courts' authority under §2241.

Application of the habeas statute to persons detained at the base is consistent with the historical reach of the writ of habeas corpus. At common law, courts exercised habeas jurisdiction over the claims of aliens detained within sovereign territory of the realm, as well as the claims of persons detained in the so-called "exempt jurisdictions," where ordinary writs did not run, and all other dominions under the sovereign's control.

…

Section 2241, by its terms, requires nothing more. We therefore hold that *§2241* confers on the District Court jurisdiction to hear petitioners' habeas corpus challenges to the legality of their detention at the Guantanamo Bay Naval Base.

…

V

Whether and what further proceedings may become necessary after respondents make their response to the merits of petitioners' claims are matters that we need not address now. What is presently at stake is only whether the federal courts have jurisdiction to determine the legality of the Executive's potentially indefinite detention of individuals who claim to be wholly innocent of wrongdoing. Answering that question in the affirmative, we reverse the judgment of the Court of Appeals and remand for the District Court to consider in the first instance the merits of petitioners' claims.

It is so ordered.

CONCUR: Justice Kennedy, concurring in the judgment.

…

DISSENT: Justice Scalia, with whom the Chief Justice and Justice Thomas join, dissenting.

…

Departure from our rule of *stare decisis* in statutory cases is always extraordinary; it ought to be unthinkable when the departure has a potentially harmful effect upon the Nation's conduct of a war. The Commander in Chief and his subordinates had every reason to expect that the internment of combatants at Guantanamo Bay would not have the consequence of bringing the cumbersome machinery of our domestic courts into military affairs. Congress is in session. If it wished to change federal judges' habeas jurisdiction from what this Court had previously held that to be, it could have done so. And it could have done so by intelligent revision of the statute, instead of by today's clumsy, countertextual reinterpretation that confers upon wartime prisoners greater habeas rights than domestic detainees. The latter must challenge their present physical confinement in the district of their confinement, see *Rumsfeld v. Padilla, ante*, whereas under today's strange holding

Guantanamo Bay detainees can petition in any of the 94 federal judicial districts. The fact that extraterritorially located detainees lack the district of detention that the statute requires has been converted from a factor that precludes their ability to bring a petition at all into a factor that frees them to petition wherever they wish—and, as a result, to forum shop. For this Court to create such a monstrous scheme in time of war, and in frustration of our military commanders' reliance upon clearly stated prior law, is judicial adventurism of the worst sort. I dissent.

The Supreme Court remanded the *Padilla* case because it was filed in the wrong federal district court. After filing in the proper district court in South Carolina and receiving a favorable ruling, the United States Court of Appeals for the 4th Circuit, on September 9, 2005, overturned the district court and upheld the President's authority to detain Padilla as an "enemy combatant," observing that Padilla had actually been a member of enemy forces during the combat activities in Afghanistan. Then, following the positive 4th Circuit ruling, Padilla was released from military custody, after being held for over three years, and transferred in November 2005 to federal custody to stand trial in federal court for a variety of federal crimes associated with his terror plots. In April 2006 the Supreme Court voted 6-3 to let the lower court opinion stand.

PADILLA v. HANFT
United States Court of Appeals for the Fourth Circuit
No. 05-6396 (Sept. 9, 2005)

LUTTIG, Circuit Judge:

Appellee Jose Padilla, a United States citizen, associated with forces hostile to the United States in Afghanistan and took up arms against United States forces in that country in our war against al Qaeda. Upon his escape to Pakistan from the battlefield in Afghanistan, Padilla was recruited, trained, funded, and equipped by al Qaeda leaders to continue prosecution of the war in the United States by blowing up apartment buildings in this country. Padilla flew to the United States on May 8, 2002, to begin carrying out his assignment, but was arrested by civilian law enforcement authorities upon his arrival at O'Hare International Airport in Chicago.

Thereafter, in a letter to the Secretary of Defense, the President of the United States personally designated Padilla an "enemy combatant" against this country, stating that the United States is "at war" with al Qaeda, that "Mr. Padilla engaged in conduct that constituted hostile and warlike acts, including conduct in preparation for acts of international terrorism that had the aim to cause injury to or adverse effects on the United States," and that "Mr. Padilla represents a continuing, present and grave danger to the national security of the United States." Having determined that "detention of Mr. Padilla is necessary to prevent him from aiding al Qaeda in its efforts to attack the United States or its armed forces, other governmental personnel, or citizens," the President directed the Secretary of Defense to take Padilla into military custody, in which custody Padilla has remained ever since. The full text of the President's memorandum to the Secretary of Defense reads as follows:

THE WHITE HOUSE
WASHINGTON
FOR OFFICIAL USE ONLY

TO THE SECRETARY OF DEFENSE:

Based on the information available to me from all sources,

REDACTED

In accordance with the Constitution and consistent with the laws of the United States, including the Authorization for Use of Military Force Joint Resolution (Public Law 107-40);

I, GEORGE W. BUSH, as President of the United States and Commander in Chief of the U.S. armed forces, hereby DETERMINE for the United States of America that:

(1) Jose Padilla, who is under the control of the Department of Justice and who is a U.S. citizen, is, and at the time he entered the United States in May 2002 was, an enemy combatant;

(2) Mr. Padilla is closely associated with al Qaeda, an international terrorist organization with which the United States is at war;

(3) Mr. Padilla engaged in conduct that constituted hostile and war-like acts, including conduct in preparation for acts of international terrorism that had the aim to cause injury to or adverse effects on the United States;

(4) Mr. Padilla possesses intelligence, including intelligence about personnel and activities of al Qaeda, that, if communicated to the U.S., would aid U.S. efforts to prevent attacks by al Qaeda on the United States or its armed forces, other governmental personnel, or citizens;

(5) Mr. Padilla represents a continuing, present and grave danger to the national security of the United States, and detention of Mr. Padilla is necessary to prevent him from aiding al Qaeda in its efforts to attack the United States or its armed forces, other governmental personnel, or citizens;

(6) it is in the interest of the United States that the Secretary of Defense detain Mr. Padilla as an enemy combatant; and

(7) it is REDACTED consistent with U.S. law and the laws of war for the Secretary of Defense to detain Mr. Padilla as an enemy combatant.

Accordingly, you are directed to receive Mr. Padilla from the Department of Justice and to detain him as an enemy combatant.

DATE: June 9, 2002 Signature /George Bush/

The exceedingly important question before us is whether the President of the United States possesses the authority to detain militarily a citizen of this country who is closely associated with al Qaeda, an entity with which the United States is at war; who took up arms on behalf of that enemy and against our country in a foreign combat zone of that war; and who thereafter traveled to the United States for the avowed purpose of further prosecuting that war on American soil, against American citizens and targets.

We conclude that the President does possess such authority pursuant to the Authorization for Use of Military Force Joint Resolution enacted by Congress in the wake of the attacks on the United States of September 11, 2001. Accordingly, the judgment of the district court is reversed.

I

Al Qaeda operatives recruited Jose Padilla, a United States citizen, to train for jihad in Afghanistan in February 2000, while Padilla was on a religious pilgrimage to Saudi Arabia. Subsequently, Padilla met with al Qaeda operatives in Afghanistan, received explosives training in an al Qaeda-affiliated camp, and served as an armed guard at what he understood to be a Taliban outpost. When United States military operations began in Afghanistan, Padilla and other al Qaeda operatives moved from safehouse to safehouse to evade bombing or capture. Padilla was, on the facts with which we are presented, "armed and present in a combat zone during armed conflict between al Qaeda/Taliban forces and the armed forces of the United States."

Padilla eventually escaped to Pakistan, armed with an assault rifle. Once in Pakistan, Padilla met with Khalid Sheikh Mohammad, a senior al Qaeda operations planner, who directed Padilla to travel to the United States for the purpose of blowing up apartment buildings, in continued prosecution of al Qaeda's war of terror against the United States. After receiving further training, as well as cash, travel documents, and communication devices, Padilla flew to the United States in order to carry out his accepted assignment.

Upon arrival at Chicago's O'Hare International Airport on May 8, 2002, Padilla was detained by FBI agents, who interviewed and eventually arrested him pursuant to a material witness warrant issued by the district court for the Southern District of New York in conjunction with a grand jury investigation of the September 11 attacks. Padilla was transported to New York, where he was held at a civilian correctional facility until, on June 9, 2002, the President designated him an "enemy combatant" against the United States and directed the Secretary of Defense to take him into military custody. Since his delivery into the custody of military authorities, Padilla has been detained at a naval brig in South Carolina.

On June 11, 2002, Padilla filed a petition for a writ of habeas corpus in the Southern District of New York, claiming that his detention violated the Constitution. The Supreme Court of the United States ultimately ordered Padilla's petition dismissed without prejudice, holding that his petition was improperly filed in the Southern District of New York. *Rumsfeld v. Padilla*, 124 S. Ct. 2711, 2727 (2004). And on July 2, 2004, Padilla filed the present petition for a writ of habeas corpus in the District of South Carolina.

The district court subsequently held that the President lacks the authority to detain Padilla, *id.* at 180-81, that Padilla's detention is in violation of the Constitution and laws of the United States, *id.*, and that Padilla therefore must either be criminally charged or released, *id.* at 183. This appeal followed. We expedited consideration of this appeal at the request of the parties, hearing argument in the case on July 19, 2005.

II

A

The Authorization for Use of Military Force Joint Resolution (AUMF), upon which the President explicitly relied in his order that Padilla be detained by the military and upon which the government chiefly relies in support of the President's authority to detain Padilla, was enacted by Congress in the immediate aftermath of the September 11, 2001, terrorist attacks on the United States. It provides as follows:

> [T]he President is authorized to use all necessary and appropriate force against those nations, organizations, or persons he determines planned, authorized, committed, or aided the terrorist attacks

that occurred on September 11, 2001, or harbored such organizations or persons, in order to prevent any future acts of international terrorism against the United States by such nations, organizations or persons.

Pub. L. No. 107-40, § 2(a), 115 Stat. 224 (September 18, 2001). The Supreme Court has already once interpreted this Joint Resolution in the context of a military detention by the President. In *Hamdi v. Rumsfeld*, 124 S. Ct. 2633 (2004), the Supreme Court held, on the facts alleged by the government, that the AUMF authorized the military detention of Yaser Esam Hamdi, an American citizen who fought alongside Taliban forces in Afghanistan, was captured by United States allies on a battlefield there, and was detained in the United States by the military. The "narrow question," addressed by the Court in *Hamdi* was "whether the Executive has the authority to detain citizens who qualify as 'enemy combatants,'" defined for purposes of that case as "individual[s] who ... [were] '"part of or supporting forces hostile to the United States or coalition partners"' in Afghanistan and who '"engaged in an armed conflict against the United States"' there," The controlling plurality of the Court answered that narrow question in the affirmative, concluding, based upon "longstanding law-of-war principles," that Hamdi's detention was "necessary and appropriate" within the meaning of the AUMF because "[t]he capture and detention of lawful combatants and the capture, detention, and trial of unlawful combatants, by 'universal agreement and practice,' are 'important incident[s] of war.'" The rationale for this law-of-war principle, Justice O'Connor explained for the plurality, is that "detention to prevent a combatant's return to the battlefield is a fundamental incident of waging war."

As the AUMF authorized Hamdi's detention by the President, so also does it authorize Padilla's detention. Under the facts as presented here, Padilla unquestionably qualifies as an "enemy combatant" as that term was defined for purposes of the controlling opinion in *Hamdi*. Indeed, under the definition of "enemy combatant" employed in *Hamdi*, we can discern no difference in principle between Hamdi and Padilla. Like Hamdi, Padilla associated with forces hostile to the United States in Afghanistan. *Compare* J.A. 19-23 (detailing Padilla's association with al Qaeda in Afghanistan and Pakistan), *with Hamdi*, 124 S. Ct. at 2637 (describing Hamdi's affiliation with the Taliban in Afghanistan). And, like Hamdi, Padilla took up arms against United States forces in that country in the same way and to the same extent as did Hamdi. Compare (averring that Padilla was "armed and present in a combat zone during armed conflict between al Qaeda/ Taliban forces and the armed forces of the United States"), (alleging that Padilla was "armed with an assault rifle" as he escaped to Pakistan), *with Hamdi*, 124 S. Ct. at 2642 n.1 (noting that the asserted basis for detaining Hamdi was that he "carr[ied] a weapon against American troops on a foreign battlefield"), at 2637 (quoting Mobbs Affidavit that Hamdi had "'surrender[ed] his Kalishnikov assault rifle'" to Northern Alliance forces (alteration in original)). Because, like Hamdi, Padilla is an enemy combatant, and because his detention is no less necessary than was Hamdi's in order to prevent his return to the battlefield, the President is authorized by the AUMF to detain Padilla as a fundamental incident to the conduct of war.

Our conclusion that the AUMF as interpreted by the Supreme Court in *Hamdi* authorizes the President's detention of Padilla as an enemy combatant is reinforced by the Supreme Court's decision in *Ex parte Quirin*, 317 U.S. 1 (1942), on which the plurality in *Hamdi* itself heavily relied. In *Quirin*, the Court held that Congress had authorized the military trial of Haupt, a United States citizen who entered the country with orders from the Nazis to blow up domestic war facilities but was captured before he could execute those orders. The Court reasoned that Haupt's citizenship was no bar to his military trial as an unlawful enemy belligerent, concluding that "[c]itizens who associate themselves with the military arm of the enemy government, and with its aid, guidance and direction enter this country bent on hostile acts, are enemy belligerents within the meaning of … the law of war."

Like Haupt, Padilla associated with the military arm of the enemy, and with its aid, guidance, and direction entered this country bent on committing hostile acts on American soil. Padilla thus falls within *Quirin's* definition of enemy belligerent, as well as within the definition of the equivalent term accepted by the plurality in *Hamdi*. *Compare Quirin*, 317 U.S. at 37-38 (holding that "[c]itizens who associate themselves with the military arm of the enemy government, and with its aid, guidance and direction enter this country bent on hostile acts, are enemy belligerents within the meaning of … the law of war"), *with Hamdi*, 124 S. Ct. at 2639 (accepting for purposes of the case the government's definition of "enemy combatants" as those who were "'part of or supporting forces hostile to the United States or coalition partners'" in Afghanistan and who "'engaged in an armed conflict against the United States'" there").

We understand the plurality's reasoning in *Hamdi* to be that the AUMF authorizes the President to detain all those who qualify as "enemy combatants" within the meaning of the laws of war, such power being universally accepted under the laws of war as necessary in order to prevent the return of combatants to the battlefield during conflict. Given that Padilla qualifies as an enemy combatant under both the definition adopted by the Court in Quirin and the definition accepted by the controlling opinion in Hamdi, his military detention as an enemy combatant by the President is unquestionably authorized by the AUMF as a fundamental incident to the President's prosecution of the war against al Qaeda in Afghanistan.

B

Padilla marshals essentially four arguments for the conclusion that his detention is unlawful. None of them ultimately is persuasive.

1

Recognizing the hurdle to his position represented by the Supreme Court's decision in Hamdi, Padilla principally argues that his case does not fall within the "narrow circumstances" considered by the Court in that case because, although he too stood alongside Taliban forces in Afghanistan, he was seized on American soil, whereas Hamdi was captured on a foreign battlefield. In other words, Padilla maintains that capture on a foreign battlefield was one of the "narrow circumstances" to which the plurality in Hamdi confined its opinion. We disagree. When the plurality articulated the "narrow question" before it, it referred simply to the permissibility of detaining "an individual who … was "'part of or supporting forces hostile to the United States or coalition partners'" in Afghanistan and who "'engaged in an armed conflict against the United States'" there." Nowhere in its framing of the "narrow question" presented did the plurality even mention the locus of capture.

The actual reasoning that the plurality thereafter employed is consistent with the question having been framed so as to render locus of capture irrelevant. That reasoning was that Hamdi's detention was an exercise of "necessary and appropriate force" within the meaning of the AUMF because "detention to prevent a combatant's return to the battlefield is a fundamental incident of waging war." This reasoning simply does not admit of a distinction between an enemy combatant captured abroad and detained in the United States, such as Hamdi, and an enemy combatant who escaped capture abroad but was ultimately captured domestically and detained in the United States, such as Padilla. As we previously explained, Padilla poses the same threat of returning to the battlefield as Hamdi posed at the time of the Supreme Court's adjudication of Hamdi's petition. Padilla's detention is thus "necessary and appropriate" to the same extent as was Hamdi's.

Padilla directs us to a passage from the plurality's opinion in Hamdi in which, when responding to the dissent, the plurality charged that the dissent "ignore[d] the context of th[e] case: a United States citizen captured in a foreign combat zone." Padilla argues that this passage proves that capture on a foreign battlefield was one of the factual circumstances by which the Court's opinion was limited. If this language stood alone, Padilla's argument as to the limitation of Hamdi at least would have more force, though to acknowledge that foreign battlefield capture was part of the context of the case still is not to say (at least not necessarily) that the locus of capture was essential to the Court's reasoning. However, this language simply cannot bear the weight that Padilla would have it bear when it is considered against the backdrop of both the quite different limitations that were expressly imposed by the Court through its framing of the question presented, and the actual reasoning that was employed by the Court in reaching its conclusion, which reasoning was consistent with the question having been framed so as to render an enemy combatant's point of capture irrelevant to the President's power to detain. In short, the plurality carefully limited its opinion, but not in a way that leaves room for argument that the President's power to detain one who has associated with the enemy and taken up arms against the United States in a foreign combat zone varies depending upon the geographic location where that enemy combatant happens to be captured.

Our conclusion that the reasoning in *Hamdi* does not support a distinction based on the locus of capture is buttressed by the plurality's analysis of *Quirin*. Although at issue in *Quirin* was the authority of the President to subject a United States citizen who was also an enemy combatant to military trial, the plurality in *Hamdi* went to lengths to observe that Haupt, who had been captured domestically, could instead have been permissibly detained for the duration of hostilities. That analysis strongly suggests, if it does not confirm, that the plurality did not regard the locus of capture (within or without the United States) as relevant to the President's authority to detain an enemy combatant who is also a citizen, and that it believed that the detention of such a combatant is not more or less a necessary incident of the President's power to wage war depending upon the locus of eventual capture.

Given the lack of any reference to locus of capture in the plurality's articulation of the "narrow question" before it, the absence of any basis in Hamdi's reasoning for a distinction between foreign and domestic capture of one who has both associated with the enemy and taken up arms against the United States on behalf of that enemy in a foreign combat zone, and the plurality's understanding of and reliance upon *Quirin* as a precedent that would permit the detention of an enemy combatant who had been captured domestically, we simply cannot ascribe to the rejoinder to Justice Scalia the significance, much less the dispositive significance, that Padilla urges.

2

Padilla also argues, and the district court held, that Padilla's military detention is "neither necessary nor appropriate" because he is amenable to criminal prosecution. Related to this argument, Padilla attempts to distinguish *Quirin* from his case on the grounds that he has simply been detained, unlike Haupt who was charged and tried in *Quirin*. Neither the argument nor the attempted distinction is convincing.

As to the fact that Padilla can be prosecuted, the availability of criminal process does not distinguish him from Hamdi. If the mere availability of criminal prosecution rendered detention unnecessary within the meaning of the AUMF, then Hamdi's detention would have been unnecessary and therefore unauthorized, since he too was detained in the United States and amenable to criminal prosecution. We are convinced, in any event, that the availability of criminal process cannot be determinative of the power to detain, if for no other reason than that criminal prosecution may well not achieve the very purpose for which detention is authorized in the first place—the prevention of return to the field of battle. Equally important, in many instances criminal prosecution would impede the Executive in its efforts to gather intelligence from the detainee and to restrict the detainee's communication with confederates so as to ensure that the detainee does not pose a continuing threat to national security even as he is confined—impediments that would render military detention not only an appropriate, but also the necessary, course of action to be taken in the interest of national security.

The district court acknowledged the need to defer to the President's determination that Padilla's detention is necessary and appropriate in the interest of national security. However, we believe that the district court ultimately accorded insufficient deference to that determination, effectively imposing upon the President the equivalent of a least-restrictive-means test. To subject to such exacting scrutiny the President's determination that criminal prosecution would not adequately protect the Nation's security at a very minimum fails to accord the President the deference that is his when he acts pursuant to a broad delegation of authority from Congress, such as the AUMF.

As for Padilla's attempted distinction of *Quirin* on the grounds that, unlike Haupt, he has never been charged and tried by the military, the plurality in Hamdi rejected as immaterial the distinction between detention and trial (apparently regarding the former as a lesser imposition than the latter), noting that "nothing in *Quirin* suggests that [Haupt's United States] citizenship would have precluded his mere detention for the duration of the relevant hostilities." *Hamdi*, 124 S. Ct. at 2640 (emphasis added).

3

Padilla, citing *Ex parte Endo*, 323 U.S. 283 (1944), and relying upon *Quirin*, next argues that only a clear statement from Congress can authorize his detention, and that the AUMF is not itself, and does not contain, such a clear statement.

In *Endo*, the Court did state that, when asked to find implied powers in a wartime statute, it must assume that "the law makers intended to place no greater restraint on the citizen than was clearly and unmistakably indicated by the language [the law makers] used." The Court almost immediately thereafter observed, however, that the "fact that the Act" at issue was "silent on detention [did] not of course mean that any power to detain [was] lacking," an observation that proves that the Court did not adopt or even apply in that case a "clear statement" rule of the kind for which Padilla argues.

Padilla contends that *Quirin* also supports the existence of a clear statement rule. However, in no place in *Quirin* did the Court even purport to establish a clear statement rule. In its opinion, the Court did note that Congress had "explicitly" authorized Haupt's military trial. See 317 U.S. at 28. But to conclude from this passing note that the Court required a clear statement as a matter of law would be unwarranted. In fact, to the extent that *Quirin* can be understood to have addressed the need for a clear statement of authority from Congress at all, the rule would appear the opposite:

> [T]he detention and trial of petitioners—ordered by the President in the declared exercise of his powers as Commander in Chief of the Army in time of war and of grave public danger—are not to

be set aside by the courts without the clear conviction that they are in conflict with the Constitution or laws of Congress constitutionally enacted.

Of course, even were a clear statement by Congress required, the AUMF constitutes such a clear statement according to the Supreme Court. In *Hamdi*, stating that "it [was] of no moment that the AUMF does not use specific language of detention," 124 S. Ct. at 2641, the plurality held that the AUMF "clearly and unmistakably authorized" Hamdi's detention. Nothing in the AUMF permits us to conclude that the Joint Resolution clearly and unmistakably authorized Hamdi's detention but not Padilla's. To the contrary, read in light of its purpose clause ("in order to prevent any future acts of international terrorism against the United States") and its preamble (stating that the acts of 9/11 "render it both necessary and appropriate ... to protect United States citizens both at home and abroad"), the AUMF applies even more clearly and unmistakably to Padilla than to Hamdi. Padilla, after all, in addition to supporting hostile forces in Afghanistan and taking up arms against our troops on a battlefield in that country like Hamdi, *also* came to the United States in order to commit future acts of terrorism against American citizens and targets.

These facts unquestionably establish that Padilla poses the requisite threat of return to battle in the ongoing armed conflict between the United States and al Qaeda in Afghanistan, and that his detention is authorized as a "fundamental incident of waging war," in order "to prevent a combatant's return to the battlefield," *id.* Congress "clearly and unmistakably," authorized such detention when, in the AUMF, it "permitt[ed] the use of 'necessary and appropriate force,'" to prevent other attacks like those of September 11, 2001.

4

Finally, Padilla argues that, even if his detention is authorized by the AUMF, it is unlawful under *Ex parte Milligan*, 71 U.S. (4 Wall.) 2 (1866). In *Milligan*, the Supreme Court held that a United States citizen associated with an anti-Union secret society but unaffiliated with the Confederate army could not be tried by a military tribunal while access to civilian courts was open and unobstructed. *Milligan* purported to restrict the power of Congress as well as the power of the President. ("[N]o usage of war could sanction a military trial ... for any offence whatever of a citizen in civil life, in nowise connected with the military service. Congress could grant no such power ..."). *Quirin*, however, confirmed that *Milligan* does not extend to enemy combatants. As the Court in *Quirin* explained, the *Milligan* Court's reasoning had "particular reference to the facts before it," namely, that Milligan was not "a part of or associated with the armed forces of the enemy." The *Hamdi* plurality in turn reaffirmed this limitation on the reach of *Milligan*, emphasizing that *Quirin*, a unanimous opinion, "both postdates and clarifies *Milligan*." 124 S. Ct. at 2643. Thus confined, *Milligan* is inapposite here because Padilla, unlike Milligan, associated with, and has taken up arms against the forces of the United States on behalf of, an enemy of the United States.

III

The Congress of the United States, in the Authorization for Use of Military Force Joint Resolution, provided the President all powers necessary and appropriate to protect American citizens from terrorist acts by those who attacked the United States on September 11, 2001. As would be expected, and as the Supreme Court has held, those powers include the power to detain identified and committed enemies such as Padilla, who associated with al Qaeda and the Taliban regime, who took up arms against this Nation in its war against these enemies, and who entered the United States for the avowed purpose of further prosecuting that war by attacking American citizens and targets on our own soil—a power without which, Congress understood, the President could well be unable to protect American citizens from the very kind of savage attack that occurred four years ago almost to the day.

The detention of petitioner being fully authorized by Act of Congress, the judgment of the district court that the detention of petitioner by the President of the United States is without support in law is hereby reversed.

4.4 Military Commissions

Ostensibly, if the detainees are correctly designated as enemy combatants, the United States has five options which it may pursue against the detainees: (1) release the detainee to his country of origin; (2) turn the accused over to an appropriate foreign criminal jurisdiction (e.g., the new government in Afghanistan); (3) turn the accused over to an International Tribunal; (4) try the accused in a United States federal district court; or (5) try the accused in a United States military commission. If one is only concerned with expediency, the first option is probably the most attractive and needs little discussion (Some of the host nations have actually refused to take their own nationals back and there are some States that the U.S. cannot send the national to for fear of torture.) Likewise, the use of an International Tribunal is attractive but probably not workable due to concerns over such issues as the absence of a death penalty and possible security compromises of "sources and techniques" for gathering intelligence.

The final forum available to prosecute those individuals taken from Afghanistan (or any other location, e.g., Iraq) who are suspected of committing war crimes is the military commission. On November 13, 2001, President Bush signed an executive (military) order which authorized the creation of military commissions to try certain "non-citizens" for engaging in terrorist acts against the United States or aiding or abetting in terrorist acts against the United States. As noted, the Supreme Court in *Hamdan v. Rumsfeld* found that the military commissions were not consistent with the standards of Common Article 3 which required that the "passing of sentences" had to be "pronounced by a regularly constituted court affording all the judicial guarantees which are recognized as indispensable by civilized peoples." Further, the Court rejected the idea that the 2001 Congressional Authorization to Use Military Force (AUMF) had allowed the President to authorize a military commission. In fact, the majority decided that the President's military commission was not lawful because it was "not regularly constituted" as required by Common Article 3. In short, the Court seemed willing to accept a military commission to try enemy combatants, but only if it was authorized by Congress.

Because military commissions have not been used since the end of World War II, the efficacy of using this forum to prosecute the al-Qa'eda and Taliban fighters for war crimes mandates analysis from both legal and historical perspectives. A score of detainees at Guantanamo Bay are now standing or pending trial by military commission.

Military commissions are non-Article III courts. They derive their basic grant of authority from Articles I and II of the United States Constitution. Respectively, Congress has the power to "define and punish ... offenses against the Law of Nations," and the President is the "Commander in Chief of the Army and Navy."

Historically, military commissions (and military tribunals) have been used in a variety of situations associated with urgent government needs related to war. In *Madsen v. Kinsella*, the Supreme Court spoke at some length on the history of military commissions and tribunals, stating: "Since our nation's earliest days, such commissions have been constitutionally recognized agencies for meeting many urgent governmental responsibilities relating to war." In addition, the Courts have recognized the fact that military commissions have been used without Congress specifically "declaring war." (*Talbot v. Seeman*, 5 U.S. 1) For example, military tribunals were used in the War with Mexico, even though Congress never formally declared war. The War with Mexico lasted from 1846–1848, and broke out when Texas, an American settled province of Mexico that had broken away in 1836, was annexed as a state by the United States in 1845. Congress passed the Act of Congress of May 13, 1846, which did not declare war, but recognized "a state of war as existing by the act of the Republic of Mexico." (*Prize Cases*, 67 U.S. 365)

A military commission consists of a panel of military officers who are authorized to render a verdict and sentence. The historical concern in this instance is not whether military commissions can be used to prosecute United States citizens who may or may not be belligerents, but whether commissions are constitutionally able to prosecute non-citizen belligerents for offenses in violation of the law of war. Regarding the use of military tribunals to try United States citizens who are not belligerents, the Supreme Court rendered its opinion in 1866 in *Ex Parte Milligan*, where it held that as long as the civilian courts were operating, the use of military tribunals to try United States citizens who were not actual belligerents was unconstitutional. In December of 1866, the United States Supreme Court granted a writ of habeas corpus to a civilian noncombatant named Lambdin P. Milligan, a pro-Confederate Indiana resident who was convicted in October 1864 by a military tribunal convened in Indianapolis, Indiana. Milligan was convicted of treason and sentenced to be hanged. The lower federal court denied his petition for habeas corpus. In granting the writ for review, the Supreme Court held that although the American Civil War was still in progress at the time of the trial, the circumstances in Indiana, a Union state not in control by Confederate forces, did not justify the use of a military tribunal to prosecute a United States citizen because the civil courts were open and free to function. As to the use of military commissions to prosecute noncitizen and citizen belligerents for offenses in violation of the law of war, the standard is set out in the World War II case of *Ex Parte Quirin*.

In *Ex Parte Quirin*, the United States Supreme Court upheld the convictions of eight German saboteurs who had been captured in the United States and tried by a military commission ordered by President Franklin Roosevelt. The Germans had been sent to attack public and government facilities. At least one of the Germans claimed American citizenship. The Court upheld the jurisdiction of the military commission against all of the Germans, stating: "By the Articles of War, and especially Article 15, Congress has explicitly provided, so far as it may constitutionally do so, that military tribunals shall have jurisdiction to try offenders or offenses against the law of war in appropriate cases." The Court easily distinguished the case from *Ex Parte Milligan*, holding that offenses against the law of war by actual belligerents were constitutionally authorized to be tried by military commission. Besides the trials of the German saboteurs during World War II, subsequent military commissions were used to prosecute approximately 2,600 members of the Axis for violations of the law of war, including the murder of captured American soldiers at the Battle of the Bulge. The surviving high-ranking war criminals in the German military and government were tried by a special international tribunal in Nuremberg, Germany, at the Nuremberg Trials. The senior Japanese leaders were tried at the International Military Tribunal for the Far East.

Although the Supreme Court has long held that the Constitution's Fifth and Sixth Amendment protections apply to non-United States citizens (*Wong Wing v. United States*, 163 U.S. 228), such protections do not extend to belligerents subject to trial in military commissions for war crimes. Seemingly, the use of military commissions has deeply seeded historical and legal precedent as long as the accused are actual combatants charged with violations of the law of war. In *Application of Yamashita*, the Court traced the history of military commissions and concluded: "By thus recognizing military commissions in order to preserve their traditional jurisdiction over enemy combatants ... Congress gave sanction, as we held in *Ex Parte Quirin* to any use of military commissions contemplated by the common law of war." In its January 2002 report on the lawfulness of using military commissions, the American Bar Association Task Force on Terrorism and Law found that the terror attacks of September 11, 2001, were arguably violations of the law of war that would justify the use of military commissions to prosecute accused terrorists.

Among the detainees facing trial by military commission is Salim Ahmed Hamdan, of Yemen. Hamdan, who acknowledges that he is a former driver for Osama bin Laden, was charged with a variety of offenses including conspiracy to attack civilians. Although the military commission process was halted by a district court ruling in 2004, the D.C. Circuit in July 2005 reversed, upholding the legality of the military commission set up by Executive Order. Then, on June 29, 2006, a bitterly divided Court in *Hamdan v. Rumsfeld* reversed the Court of Appeals.

HAMDAN v. RUMSFELD

Supreme Court of the United States

126 S. Ct. 2749 (2006)

Justice STEVENS announced the judgment of the Court and delivered the opinion of the Court with respect to Parts I through IV, Parts VI through VI-D-iii, Part VI-D-v, and Part VII, and an opinion with respect to Parts V and VI-D-iv, in which Justice SOUTER, Justice GINSBURG, and Justice BREYER join.

Petitioner Salim Ahmed Hamdan, a Yemeni national, is in custody at an American prison in Guantánamo Bay, Cuba. In November 2001, during hostilities between the United States and the Taliban (which then governed Afghanistan), Hamdan was captured by militia forces and turned over to the U.S. military. In June 2002, he was transported to Guantánamo Bay. Over a year later, the President deemed him eligible for trial by military commission for then-unspecified crimes. After another year had passed, Hamdan was charged with one count of conspiracy "to commit ... offenses triable by military commission."

Hamdan filed petitions for writs of habeas corpus and mandamus to challenge the Executive Branch's intended means of prosecuting this charge. He concedes that a court-martial constituted in accordance with the Uniform Code of Military Justice (UCMJ) would have authority to try him. His objection is that the military commission the President has convened lacks such authority, for two principal reasons: First, neither congressional Act nor the common law of war supports trial by this commission for the crime of conspiracy—an offense that, Hamdan says, is not a violation of the law of war. Second, Hamdan contends, the procedures that the President has adopted to try him violate the most basic tenets of military and international law, including the principle that a defendant must be permitted to see and hear the evidence against him.

The District Court granted Hamdan's request for a writ of habeas corpus. The Court of Appeals for the District of Columbia Circuit reversed. Recognizing, as we did over a half-century ago, that trial by military commission is an extraordinary measure raising important questions about the balance of powers in our constitutional structure, *Ex parte Quirin,* 317 U.S. 1, 19 (1942), we granted certiorari.

For the reasons that follow, we conclude that the military commission convened to try Hamdan lacks power to proceed because its structure and procedures violate both the UCMJ and the Geneva Conventions. Four of us also conclude, *See* Part V, *infra,* that the offense with which Hamdan has been charged is not an "offens[e] that by ... the law of war may be tried by military commissions." 10 U.S.C. § 821.

I

On September 11, 2001, agents of the al Qaeda terrorist organization hijacked commercial airplanes and attacked the World Trade Center in New York City and the national headquarters of the Department of Defense in Arlington, Virginia. Americans will never forget the devastation wrought by these acts. Nearly 3,000 civilians were killed.

Congress responded by adopting a Joint Resolution authorizing the President to "use all necessary and appropriate force against those nations, organizations, or persons he determines planned, authorized, committed, or aided the terrorist attacks ... in order to prevent any future acts of international terrorism against the United States by such nations, organizations or persons." Authorization for Use of Military Force (AUMF). Acting pursuant to the AUMF, and having determined that the Taliban regime had supported al Qaeda, the President ordered the Armed Forces of the United States to invade Afghanistan. In the ensuing hostilities, hundreds of individuals, Hamdan among them, were captured and eventually detained at Guantánamo Bay.

On November 13, 2001, while the United States was still engaged in active combat with the Taliban, the President issued a comprehensive military order intended to govern the "Detention, Treatment, and Trial of Certain Non-Citizens in the War Against Terrorism" (hereinafter November 13 Order or Order). Those subject to the November 13 Order include any noncitizen for whom the President determines "there is reason to believe" that he or she (1) "is or was" a member of al Qaeda or (2) has engaged or participated in terrorist activities aimed at or harmful to the United States. Any such individual "shall, when tried, be tried by military commission for any and all offenses triable by military commission that such individual is alleged to have committed, and may be punished in accordance with the penalties provided under applicable law, including imprisonment or death." The November 13 Order vested in the Secretary of Defense the power to appoint military commissions to try individuals subject to the Order, but that power has since been delegated to John D. Altenberg, Jr., a retired Army major general and longtime military lawyer who has been designated "Appointing Authority for Military Commissions."

On July 3, 2003, the President announced his determination that Hamdan and five other detainees at Guantánamo Bay were subject to the November 13 Order and thus triable by military commission. In December 2003, military counsel was appointed to represent Hamdan. Two months later, counsel filed demands for charges and for a speedy trial pursuant to Article 10 of the UCMJ. On February 23, 2004, the legal adviser to the Appointing Authority denied the applications, ruling that Hamdan was not entitled to any of the protections of the UCMJ. Not until July 13, 2004, after Hamdan had commenced this action in the United States District Court for the Western District of Washington, did the Government finally charge him with the offense for which, a year earlier, he had been deemed eligible for trial by military commission.

The charging document, which is unsigned, contains 13 numbered paragraphs ....

Only the final two paragraphs, entitled "Charge: Conspiracy," contain allegations against Hamdan. Paragraph 12 charges that "from on or about February 1996 to on or about November 24, 2001," Hamdan "willfully and knowingly joined an enterprise of persons who shared a common criminal purpose and conspired and agreed with [named members of al Qaeda] to commit the following offenses triable by military commission: attacking civilians; attacking civilian objects; murder by an unprivileged belligerent; and terrorism." There is no allegation that Hamdan had any command responsibilities, played a leadership role, or participated in the planning of any activity.

Paragraph 13 lists four "overt acts" that Hamdan is alleged to have committed sometime between 1996 and November 2001 in furtherance of the "enterprise and conspiracy:" (1) he acted as Osama bin Laden's "bodyguard and personal driver," "believ[ing]" all the while that bin Laden "and his associates were involved in" terrorist acts prior to and including the attacks of September 11, 2001; (2) he arranged for transportation of, and actually transported, weapons used by al Qaeda members and by bin Laden's bodyguards (Hamdan among them); (3) he "drove or accompanied [O]sama bin Laden to various al Qaida-sponsored training camps, press conferences, or lectures," at which bin Laden encouraged attacks against Americans; and (4) he received weapons training at al Qaeda-sponsored camps.

After this formal charge was filed, the United States District Court for the Western District of Washington transferred Hamdan's habeas and mandamus petitions to the United States District Court for the District of Columbia. Meanwhile, a Combatant Status Review Tribunal (CSRT) convened pursuant to a military order issued on July 7, 2004, decided that Hamdan's continued detention at Guantánamo Bay was warranted because he was an "enemy combatant." Separately, proceedings before the military commission commenced.

On November 8, 2004, however, the District Court granted Hamdan's petition for habeas corpus and stayed the commission's proceedings ....

The Court of Appeals for the District of Columbia Circuit reversed ....

On November 7, 2005, we granted certiorari to decide whether the military commission convened to try Hamdan has authority to do so, and whether Hamdan may rely on the Geneva Conventions in these proceedings.

II

[The Government argued that the Detainee Treatment Act of 2005 (DTA) had the effect of divesting the federal courts of all pending challenges, including Hamdan's. Furthermore, the Government argued per *Schelsinger v. Councilman*, 420 U.S. 738 (1975), that civilian courts should await the outcome of "on-going military proceedings before entertaining an attack on those proceedings." The Court rejected both arguments and proceeded to the merits.]

...

IV

The military commission, a tribunal neither mentioned in the Constitution nor created by statute, was born of military necessity. *See* W. Winthrop, Military Law and Precedents 831 (rev.2d ed.1920) (hereinafter Winthrop). Though foreshadowed in some respects by earlier tribunals like the Board of General Officers that General Washington convened to try British Major John Andre for spying during the Revolutionary War, the commission "as such" was inaugurated in 1847. *Id.* at 832; G. Davis, A Treatise on the Military Law of the United States 308 (2d ed.1909) (hereinafter Davis). As commander of occupied Mexican territory, and having available to him no other tribunal, General Winfield Scott that year ordered the establishment of both "*"military commissions"*" to try ordinary crimes committed in the occupied territory and a *"council of war"* to try offenses against the law of war.

When the exigencies of war next gave rise to a need for use of military commissions, during the Civil War, the dual system favored by General Scott was not adopted. Instead, a single tribunal often took jurisdiction over ordinary crimes, war crimes, and breaches of military orders alike. As further discussed below, each aspect of that seemingly broad jurisdiction was in fact supported by a separate military exigency. Generally, though, the need for military commissions during this period—as during the Mexican War—was driven largely by the then very limited jurisdiction of courts-martial: "The *occasion* for the military commission arises principally from the fact that the jurisdiction of the court-martial proper, in our law, is restricted by statute almost exclusively to members of the military force and to certain specific offences defined in a written code."

Exigency alone, of course, will not justify the establishment and use of penal tribunals not contemplated by Article I, § 8 and Article III, § 1 of the Constitution unless some other part of that document authorizes a response to the felt need. And that authority, if it exists, can derive only from the powers granted jointly to the President and Congress in time of war. *See In re Yamashita,* 327 U.S. 1, 11 (1946).

The Constitution makes the President the "Commander in Chief" of the Armed Forces, Art. II, § 2, cl. 1, but vests in Congress the powers to "declare War ... and make Rules concerning Captures on Land and Water," Art. I, § 8, cl. 11, to "raise and support Armies," *id.,* cl. 12, to "define and punish . . . Offences against the Law of Nations," *id.,* cl. 10, and "To make Rules for the Government and Regulation of the land and naval Forces," *id.,* cl. 14. The interplay between these powers was described by Chief Justice

Chase in the seminal case of *Ex parte Milligan,* 4 Wall. 2, 139-40 (1866):

> The power to make the necessary laws is in Congress; the power to execute in the President. Both powers imply many subordinate and auxiliary powers. Each includes all authorities essential to its due exercise. But neither can the President, in war more than in peace, intrude upon the proper authority of Congress, nor Congress upon the proper authority of the President . . . . Congress cannot direct the conduct of campaigns, nor can the President, or any commander under him, without the sanction of Congress, institute tribunals for the trial and punishment of offences, either of soldiers or civilians, unless in cases of a controlling necessity, which justifies what it compels, or at least insures acts of indemnity from the justice of the legislature.

Whether Chief Justice Chase was correct in suggesting that the President may constitutionally convene military commissions "without the sanction of Congress" in cases of "controlling necessity" is a question this Court has not answered definitively, and need not answer today. For we held in *Quirin* that Congress had, through Article of War 15, sanctioned the use of military commissions in such circumstances. Article 21 of the UCMJ, the language of which is substantially identical to the old Article 15 and was preserved by Congress after World War II, reads as follows:

> Jurisdiction of courts-martial not exclusive. The provisions of this code conferring jurisdiction upon courts-martial shall not be construed as depriving military commissions, provost courts, or other military tribunals of concurrent jurisdiction in respect of offenders or offenses that by statute or by the law of war may be tried by such military commissions, provost courts, or other military tribunals.

We have no occasion to revisit *Quirin*'s controversial characterization of Article of War 15 as congressional authorization for military commissions. Contrary to the Government's assertion, however, even *Quirin* did not view the authorization as a sweeping mandate for the President to "invoke military commissions when he deems them necessary." Rather, the *Quirin* Court recognized that Congress had simply preserved what power, under the Constitution and the common law of war, the President had had before 1916 to convene military commissions—with the express condition that the President and those under his command comply with the law of war. That much is evidenced by the Court's inquiry, *following* its conclusion that Congress had authorized military commissions, into whether the law of war had indeed been complied with in that case.[23]

The Government would have us dispense with the inquiry that the *Quirin* Court undertook and find in either the AUMF or the DTA specific, overriding authorization for the very commission that has been convened to try Hamdan. Neither of these congressional Acts, however, expands the President's authority to convene military commissions. First, while we assume that the AUMF activated the President's war powers, *See Hamdi v. Rumsfeld,* 542 U.S. 507 (2004) (plurality opinion), and that those powers include the authority to convene military commissions in appropriate circumstances, *see id.* at 518; *Quirin,* 317 U.S. at 28-29; *See* also *Yamashita,* 327 U.S. at 11, there is nothing in the text or legislative history of the AUMF even hinting that Congress intended to expand or alter the authorization set forth in Article 21 of the UCMJ.

Likewise, the DTA cannot be read to authorize this commission. Although the DTA, unlike either Article 21 or the AUMF, was enacted after the President had convened Hamdan's commission, it contains no language authorizing that tribunal or any other at Guantánamo Bay. The DTA obviously "recognize[s]" the existence of the Guantánamo Bay commissions in the weakest sense, because it references some of the military orders governing them and creates limited judicial review of their "final decision[s]." But the statute also pointedly reserves judgment on whether "the Constitution and laws of the United States are applicable" in reviewing such decisions and whether, if they are, the "standards and procedures" used to try Hamdan and other detainees actually violate the "Constitution and laws."

Together, the UCMJ, the AUMF, and the DTA at most acknowledge a general Presidential authority to convene military commissions in circumstances where justified under the "Constitution and laws," including the law of war. Absent a more specific congressional authorization, the task of this Court is, as it was in *Quirin,* to decide whether Hamdan's military commission is so justified. It is to that inquiry we now turn.

V

[Part V is a plurality opinion, where four justices conclude that the charges against Hamdan regarding conspiracy to commit crimes that occurred before the attacks of September 11, 2001, are not triable by a military commission.]

VI

Whether or not the Government has charged Hamdan with an offense against the law of war cognizable by military commission, the commission lacks power to proceed. The UCMJ conditions the President's use of military commissions on compliance not only with the American common law of war, but also with the rest of the UCMJ itself, insofar as applicable, and with the "rules and precepts of the law of nations," *Quirin,* 317 U.S. at 28—including, *inter alia,* the four Geneva Conventions signed in 1949. *See Yamashita,* 327 U.S. at 20-21, 23-24. The procedures that the Government has decreed will govern Hamdan's trial by commission violate these laws.

A

The commission's procedures are set forth in Commission Order No. 1, which was amended most recently on August 31, 2005—after Hamdan's trial had already begun. Every commission established pursuant to Commission Order No. 1 must have a presiding officer and at least three other members, all of whom must be commissioned officers. The presiding officer's job is to rule on questions of law and other evidentiary and interlocutory issues; the other members make findings and, if applicable, sentencing decisions. The accused is entitled to appointed military counsel and may hire civilian counsel at his own expense so long as such counsel is a U.S. citizen with security clearance "at the level SECRET or higher."

The accused also is entitled to a copy of the charge(s) against him, both in English and his own language (if different), to a presumption of innocence, and to certain other rights typically afforded criminal defendants in civilian courts and courts-martial. These rights are subject, however, to one glaring condition: The accused and his civilian counsel may be excluded from, and precluded from ever learning what evidence was presented during, any part of the proceeding that either the Appointing Authority or the presiding officer decides to "close." Grounds for such closure "include the protection of information classified or classifiable …; information protected by law or rule from unauthorized disclosure; the physical safety of participants in Commission proceedings, including prospective witnesses; intelligence and law enforcement sources, methods, or activities; and other national security interests." Appointed military defense counsel must be privy to these closed sessions, but may, at the presiding officer's discretion, be forbidden to reveal to his or her client what took place therein.

Another striking feature of the rules governing Hamdan's commission is that they permit the admission of *any* evidence that, in the opinion of the presiding officer, "would have probative value to a reasonable person." Under this test, not only is testimonial hearsay and evidence obtained through coercion fully admissible, but neither live testimony nor witnesses' written statements need be sworn. Moreover, the accused and his civilian counsel may be denied access to evidence in the form of "protected information" (which includes classified information as well as "information protected by law or rule from unauthorized disclosure" and "information concerning other national security interests,"), so long as the presiding officer concludes that the evidence is "probative" … and that its admission without the accused's knowledge would not "result in the denial of a full and fair trial." Finally, a presiding officer's determination that evidence "would not have probative value to a reasonable person" may be overridden by a majority of the other commission members.

Once all the evidence is in, the commission members (not including the presiding officer) must vote on the accused's guilt. A two-thirds vote will suffice for both a verdict of guilty and for imposition of any sentence not including death (the imposition of which requires a unanimous vote). Any appeal is taken to a three-member review panel composed of military officers and designated by the Secretary of Defense, only one member of which need have experience as a judge. The review panel is directed to "disregard any variance from procedures specified in this Order or elsewhere that would not materially have affected the outcome of the trial before the Commission." Once the panel makes its recommendation to the Secretary of Defense, the Secretary can either remand for further proceedings or forward the record to the President with his recommendation as to final disposition. The President then, unless he has delegated the task to the Secretary, makes the "final decision." He may change the commission's findings or sentence only in a manner favorable to the accused.

B

Hamdan raises both general and particular objections to the procedures set forth in Commission Order No. 1. His general objection is that the procedures' admitted deviation from those governing courts-martial itself renders the commission illegal. Chief among his particular objections are that he may, under the Commission Order, be convicted based on evidence he has not seen or heard, and that any evidence admitted against him need not comply with the admissibility or relevance rules typically applicable in criminal trials and court-martial proceedings.

The Government objects to our consideration of any procedural challenge at this stage on the grounds that (1) the abstention doctrine espoused in *Councilman,* 420 U.S. 738, precludes pre-enforcement review of procedural rules, (2) Hamdan will be able to raise any such challenge following a "final decision" under the DTA, and (3) "there is … no basis to presume, before the trial has even commenced, that the trial will not be conducted in good faith and according to law." The first of these contentions was disposed of in Part III, *supra,* and neither of the latter two is sound.

First, because Hamdan apparently is not subject to the death penalty (at least as matters now stand) and may receive a sentence shorter than 10 years' imprisonment, he has no automatic right to review of the commission's "final decision" before a federal court under the DTA. Second, contrary to the Government's assertion, there *is* a "basis to presume" that the procedures employed during Hamdan's trial will violate the law: The procedures are described with particularity in Commission Order No. 1, and implementation of some of them has already occurred. One of Hamdan's complaints is that he will be, and *indeed already has been,* excluded from his own trial. Under these circumstances, review of the procedures in advance of a "final decision"—the timing of which is left entirely to the discretion of the President under the DTA—is appropriate. We turn, then, to consider the merits of Hamdan's procedural challenge.

C

In part because the difference between military commissions and courts-martial originally was a difference of jurisdiction alone, and in part to protect against abuse and ensure evenhandedness under the pressures of war, the procedures governing trials by military commission historically have been the same as those governing courts-martial. Accounts of commentators from Winthrop through General Crowder—who drafted Article of War 15 and whose views have been deemed "authoritative" by this Court, *Madsen v. Kinsella,* 343 U.S. 341, 353 (1952)—confirm as much. As recently as the Korean and Vietnam wars, during which use of military commissions was contemplated but never made, the principle of procedural parity was espoused as a background assumption.

There is a glaring historical exception to this general rule. The procedures and evidentiary rules used to try General Yamashita near the end of World War II deviated in significant respects from those then governing courts-martial. *See* 327 U.S. 1. The force of that precedent, however, has been seriously undermined by post-World War II developments.

Yamashita, from late 1944 until September 1945, was Commanding General of the Fourteenth Army Group of the Imperial Japanese Army, which had exercised control over the Philippine Islands. On September 3, 1945, after American forces regained control of the Philippines, Yamashita surrendered. Three weeks later, he was charged with violations of the law of war. A few weeks after that, he was arraigned before a military commission convened in the Philippines. He pleaded not guilty, and his trial lasted for two months. On December 7, 1945, Yamashita was convicted and sentenced to hang. *See id.* at 5; *id.* at 31-34 (Murphy, J., dissenting). This Court upheld the denial of his petition for a writ of habeas corpus.

The procedures and rules of evidence employed during Yamashita's trial departed so far from those used in courts-martial that they generated an unusually long and vociferous critique from two Members of this Court. *See id.* at 41-81 (Rutledge, J., joined by Murphy, J., dissenting). Among the dissenters' primary concerns was that the commission had free rein to consider all evidence "which in the commission's opinion 'would be of assistance in proving or disproving the charge,' without any of the usual modes of authentication." *Id.* at 49 (Rutledge, J.).

The majority, however, did not pass on the merits of Yamashita's procedural challenges because it concluded that his status disentitled him to any protection under the Articles of War (specifically, those set forth in Article 38, which would become Article 36 of the UCMJ) or the Geneva Convention of 1929, 47 Stat.2021 (1929 Geneva Convention). The Court explained that Yamashita was neither a "person made subject to the Articles of War by Article 2" thereof, 327 U.S. at 20, nor a protected prisoner of war being tried for crimes committed during his detention, *id.* at 21.

At least partially in response to subsequent criticism of General Yamashita's trial, the UCMJ's codification of the Articles of War after World War II expanded the category of persons subject thereto to include defendants in Yamashita's (and Hamdan's) position, and the Third Geneva Convention of 1949 extended prisoner-of-war protections to individuals tried for crimes committed before their capture. The most notorious exception to the principle of uniformity, then, has been stripped of its precedential value.

The uniformity principle is not an inflexible one; it does not preclude all departures from the procedures dictated for use by courts-martial. But any departure must be tailored to the exigency that necessitates it. That understanding is reflected in Article 36 of the UCMJ, which provides:

> (a) The procedure, including modes of proof, in cases before courts-martial, courts of inquiry, military commissions, and other military tribunals may be prescribed by the President by regulations which shall, so far as he considers practicable, apply the principles of law and the rules of evidence generally recognized in the trial of criminal cases in the United States district courts, but which may not be contrary to or inconsistent with this chapter.

> (b) All rules and regulations made under this article shall be uniform insofar as practicable and shall be reported to Congress.

Article 36 places two restrictions on the President's power to promulgate rules of procedure for courts-martial and military commissions alike. First, no procedural rule he adopts may be "contrary to or inconsistent with" the UCMJ—however practical it may seem. Second, the rules adopted must be "uniform insofar as practicable." That is, the rules applied to military commissions must be the same as those applied to courts-martial unless such uniformity proves impracticable.

Hamdan argues that Commission Order No. 1 violates both of these restrictions; he maintains that the procedures described in the Commission Order are inconsistent with the UCMJ and that the Government has offered no explanation for their deviation from the procedures governing courts-martial, which are set forth in the Manual for Courts-Martial, United States (2005 ed.) (Manual for Courts-Martial). Among the inconsistencies Hamdan identifies is that between § 6 of the Commission Order, which permits exclusion of the accused from proceedings and denial of his access to evidence in certain circumstances, and the UCMJ's requirement that "[a]ll ... proceedings" other than votes and deliberations by courts-martial "shall be made a part of the record and shall be in the presence of the accused." Hamdan also observes that the Commission Order dispenses with virtually all evidentiary rules applicable in courts-martial.

The Government has three responses. First, it argues, only 9 of the UCMJ's 158 Articles—the ones that expressly mention "military commissions"—actually apply to commissions, and Commission Order No. 1 sets forth no procedure that is "contrary to or inconsistent with" those 9 provisions. Second, the Government contends, military commissions would be of no use if the President were hamstrung by those provisions of the UCMJ that govern courts-martial. Finally, the President's determination that "the danger to the safety of the United States and the nature of international terrorism" renders it impracticable "to apply in military commissions ... the principles of law and rules of evidence generally recognized in the trial of criminal cases in the United States district courts," November 13 Order § 1(f), is, in the Government's view, explanation enough for any deviation from court-martial procedures.

Hamdan has the better of this argument. Without reaching the question whether any provision of Commission Order No. 1 is strictly "contrary to or inconsistent with" other provisions of the UCMJ, we conclude that the "practicability" determination the President has made is insufficient to justify variances from the procedures governing courts-martial. Subsection (b) of Article 36 was added after World War II, and requires a different showing of impracticability from the one required by subsection (a). Subsection (a) requires that the rules the President promulgates for courts-martial, provost courts, and military commissions alike conform to those that govern procedures in *Article III courts*, "so far as *he considers* practicable." Subsection (b), by contrast, demands that the rules applied in courts-martial, provost courts, and military commissions—whether or not they conform with the Federal Rules of Evidence—be "uniform *insofar as practicable*." Under the latter provision, then, the rules set forth in the Manual for Courts-Martial must apply to military commissions unless impracticable.

The President here has determined, pursuant to subsection (a), that it is impracticable to apply the rules and principles of law that govern "the trial of criminal cases in the United States district courts," to Hamdan's commission. We assume that complete deference is owed that determination. The President has not, however, made a similar official determination that it is impracticable to apply the rules for courts-martial. And even if subsection (b)'s requirements may be satisfied without such an official determination, the requirements of that subsection are not satisfied here.

Nothing in the record before us demonstrates that it would be impracticable to apply court-martial rules in this case. There is no suggestion, for example, of any logistical difficulty in securing properly sworn and authenticated evidence or in applying the usual principles of relevance and admissibility. Assuming *arguendo* that the reasons articulated in the President's Article 36(a) determination ought to be considered in evaluating the impracticability of applying court-martial rules, the only reason offered in support of that determination is the danger posed by international terrorism. Without for one moment underestimating that danger, it is not evident to us why it should require, in the case of Hamdan's trial, any variance from the rules that govern courts-martial.

The absence of any showing of impracticability is particularly disturbing when considered in light of the clear and admitted failure to apply one of the most fundamental protections afforded not just by the Manual for Courts-Martial but also by the UCMJ itself: the right to be present. Whether or not that departure technically is "contrary to or inconsistent with" the terms of the UCMJ, the jettisoning of so basic a right cannot lightly be excused as "practicable."

Under the circumstances, then, the rules applicable in courts-martial must apply. Since it is undisputed that Commission Order No. 1 deviates in many significant respects from those rules, it necessarily violates Article 36(b).

The Government's objection that requiring compliance with the court-martial rules imposes an undue burden both ignores the plain meaning of Article 36(b) and misunderstands the purpose and the history of military commissions. The military commission was not born of a desire to dispense a more summary form of justice than is afforded by courts-martial; it developed, rather, as a tribunal of necessity to be employed when courts-martial lacked jurisdiction over either the accused or the subject matter. Exigency lent the commission its legitimacy, but did not further justify the wholesale jettisoning of procedural protections. That history explains why the military commission's procedures typically have been the ones used by courts-martial. That the jurisdiction of the two tribunals today may sometimes overlap does not detract from the force of this history; Article 21 did not transform the military commission from a tribunal of true exigency into a more convenient adjudicatory tool. Article 36, confirming as much, strikes a careful balance between uniform procedure and the need to accommodate exigencies that may sometimes arise in a theater of war. That Article not having been complied with here, the rules specified for Hamdan's trial are illegal.

D

The procedures adopted to try Hamdan also violate the Geneva Conventions. The Court of Appeals dismissed Hamdan's Geneva Convention challenge on three independent grounds: (1) the Geneva Conventions are not judicially enforceable; (2) Hamdan in any event is not entitled to their protections; and (3) even if he is entitled to their protections, *Councilman* abstention is appropriate. Judge Williams, concurring, rejected the second ground but agreed with the majority respecting the first and the last. As we explained in Part III, *supra,* the abstention rule applied in *Councilman,* 420 U.S. 738, is not applicable here. And for the reasons that follow, we hold that neither of the other grounds the Court of Appeals gave for its decision is persuasive.

…

i

The Court of Appeals relied on *Johnson v. Eisentrager,* 339 U.S. 763 (1950), to hold that Hamdan could not invoke the Geneva Conventions to challenge the Government's plan to prosecute him in accordance with Commission Order No. 1. *Eisentrager* involved a challenge by 21 German nationals to their 1945 convictions for war crimes by a military tribunal convened in Nanking, China, and to their subsequent imprisonment in occupied Germany. The petitioners argued, *inter alia,* that the 1929 Geneva Convention rendered illegal some of the procedures employed during their trials, which they said deviated impermissibly from the procedures used by courts-martial to try American soldiers. *See id.* at 789. We rejected that claim on the merits because the petitioners (unlike Hamdan here) had failed to identify any prejudicial disparity "between the Commission that tried [them] and those that would try an offending soldier of the American forces of like rank," and in any event could claim no protection, under the 1929 Convention, during trials for crimes that occurred before their confinement as prisoners of war.

Buried in a footnote of the opinion, however, is this curious statement suggesting that the Court lacked power even to consider the merits of the Geneva Convention argument:

> We are not holding that these prisoners have no right which the military authorities are bound to respect. The United States, by the Geneva Convention of July 27, 1929, 47 Stat.2021, concluded with forty-six other countries, including the German Reich, an agreement upon the treatment to be accorded captives. These prisoners claim to be and are entitled to its protection. It is, however, the obvious scheme of the Agreement that responsibility for observance and enforcement of these rights is upon political and military authorities. Rights of alien enemies are vindicated under it only through protests and intervention of protecting powers as the rights of our citizens against foreign governments are vindicated only by Presidential intervention.

The Court of Appeals, on the strength of this footnote, held that "the 1949 Geneva Convention does not confer upon Hamdan a right to enforce its provisions in court."

Whatever else might be said about the *Eisentrager* footnote, it does not control this case. We may assume that "the obvious scheme" of the 1949 Conventions is identical in all relevant respects to that of the 1929 Convention, and even that that scheme would, absent some other provision of law, preclude Hamdan's invocation of the Convention's provisions as an independent source of law binding the Government's actions and furnishing petitioner with any enforceable right. For, regardless of the nature of the rights conferred on Hamdan, they are, as the Government does not dispute, part of the law of war. *See Hamdi,* 542 U.S. at 520-521 (plurality opinion). And compliance with the law of war is the condition upon which the authority set forth in Article 21 is granted.

ii

For the Court of Appeals, acknowledgment of that condition was no bar to Hamdan's trial by commission. As an alternative to its holding that Hamdan could not invoke the Geneva Conventions at all, the Court of Appeals concluded that the Conventions did not in any event apply to the armed conflict during which Hamdan was captured. The court accepted the Executive's assertions that Hamdan was captured in connection with the United States' war with al Qaeda and that that war is distinct from the war with the Taliban in Afghanistan. It further reasoned that the war with al Qaeda evades the reach of the Geneva Conventions. We, like Judge Williams, disagree with the latter conclusion.

The conflict with al Qaeda is not, according to the Government, a conflict to which the full protections afforded detainees under the 1949 Geneva Conventions apply because Article 2 of those Conventions (which appears in all four Conventions) renders the full protections applicable only to "all cases of declared war or of any other armed conflict which may arise between two or more of the High Contracting Parties." Since Hamdan was captured and detained incident to the conflict with al Qaeda and not the conflict with the Taliban, and since al Qaeda, unlike Afghanistan, is not a "High Contracting Party"—*i.e.,* a signatory of the Conventions, the protections of those Conventions are not, it is argued, applicable to Hamdan.

We need not decide the merits of this argument because there is at least one provision of the Geneva Conventions that applies here even if the relevant conflict is not one between signatories. Article 3, often referred to as Common Article 3 because, like Article 2, it appears in all four Geneva Conventions, provides that in a "conflict not of an international character occurring in the territory of one of the High Contracting Parties, each Party to the conflict shall be bound to apply, as a minimum," certain provisions protecting "[p]ersons taking no active part in the hostilities, including members of armed forces who have laid down their arms and those placed *hors de combat* by … detention." One such provision prohibits "the passing of sentences and the carrying out of executions without previous judgment pronounced by a regularly constituted court affording all the judicial guarantees which are recognized as indispensable by civilized peoples."

The Court of Appeals thought, and the Government asserts, that Common Article 3 does not apply to Hamdan because the conflict with al Qaeda, being "'international in scope,'" does not qualify as a "'conflict not of an international character.'" That reasoning is erroneous. The term "conflict not of an international character" is used here in contradistinction to a conflict between nations. So much is demonstrated by the "fundamental logic [of] the Convention's provisions on its application." Common Article 2 provides that "the present Convention shall apply to all cases of declared war or of any other armed conflict which may arise between two or more of the High Contracting Parties." High Contracting Parties (signatories) also must abide by all terms of the Conventions vis-à-vis one another even if one party to the conflict is a nonsignatory "Power," and must so abide vis-à-vis the nonsignatory if "the latter accepts and applies" those terms. Common Article 3, by contrast, affords some minimal protection, falling short of full protection under the Conventions, to individuals associated with neither a signatory nor even a nonsignatory "Power" who are involved in a conflict "in the territory of" a signatory. The latter kind of conflict is distinguishable from the conflict described in Common Article 2 chiefly because it does not involve a clash between nations (whether signatories or not). In context, then, the phrase "not of an international character" bears its literal meaning.

Although the official commentaries accompanying Common Article 3 indicate that an important purpose of the provision was to furnish minimal protection to rebels involved in one kind of "conflict not of an international character," *i.e.,* a civil war, the commentaries also make clear "that the scope of the Article must be as wide as possible." In fact, limiting language that would have rendered Common Article 3 applicable "especially [to] cases of civil war, colonial conflicts, or wars of religion," was omitted from the final version of the Article, which coupled broader scope of application with a narrower range of rights than did earlier proposed iterations.

iii

Common Article 3, then, is applicable here and, as indicated above, requires that Hamdan be tried by a "regularly constituted court affording all the judicial guarantees which are recognized as indispensable by civilized peoples." While the term "regularly constituted court" is not specifically defined in either Common Article 3 or its accompanying commentary, other sources disclose its core meaning. The commentary accompanying a provision of the Fourth Geneva Convention, for example, defines "'regularly constituted'" tribunals to include "ordinary military courts" and "definitely exclud[e] all special tribunals." And one of the Red Cross' own treatises defines "regularly constituted court" as used in Common Article 3 to mean "established and organized in accordance with the laws and procedures already in force in a country."

The Government offers only a cursory defense of Hamdan's military commission in light of Common Article 3. As JUSTICE KENNEDY explains, that defense fails because "[t]he regular military courts in our system are the courts-martial established by congressional statutes." *Post* (opinion concurring in part). At a minimum, a military commission "can be 'regularly constituted' by the standards of our military justice system only if some practical need explains deviations from court-martial practice." As we have explained, *see* Part VI-C, *supra,* no such need has been demonstrated here.

iv

Inextricably intertwined with the question of regular constitution is the evaluation of the procedures governing the tribunal and whether they afford "all the judicial guarantees which are recognized as indispensable by civilized peoples." Like the phrase "regularly constituted court," this phrase is not defined in the text of the Geneva Conventions. But it must be understood to incorporate at least the barest of those trial protections that have been recognized by customary international law. Many of these are described in Article 75 of Protocol I to the Geneva Conventions of 1949, adopted in 1977 (Protocol I). Although the United States declined to ratify Protocol I, its objections were not to Article 75 thereof. Indeed, it appears that the Government "regard[s] the provisions of Article 75 as an articulation of safeguards to which all persons in the hands of an enemy are entitled." Among the rights set forth in Article 75 is the "right to be tried in [one's] presence." Protocol I, Art. 75(4)(e).

We agree with JUSTICE KENNEDY that the procedures adopted to try Hamdan deviate from those governing courts-martial in ways not justified by any "evident practical need," *post,* and for that reason, at least, fail to afford the requisite guarantees. We add only that, as noted in Part VI-A, *supra,* various provisions of Commission Order No. 1 dispense with the principles, articulated in Article 75 and indisputably part of the customary international law, that an accused must, absent disruptive conduct or consent, be present for his trial and must be privy to the evidence against him. That the Government has a compelling interest in denying Hamdan access to certain sensitive information is not doubted. But, at least absent express statutory provision to the contrary, information used to convict a person of a crime must be disclosed to him.

v

Common Article 3 obviously tolerates a great degree of flexibility in trying individuals captured during armed conflict; its requirements are general ones, crafted to accommodate a wide variety of legal systems. But *requirements* they are nonetheless. The commission that the President has convened to try Hamdan does not meet those requirements.

VII

We have assumed, as we must, that the allegations made in the Government's charge against Hamdan are true. We have assumed, moreover, the truth of the message implicit in that charge—viz., that Hamdan is a dangerous individual whose beliefs, if acted upon, would cause great harm and even death to innocent civilians, and who would act upon those beliefs if given the opportunity. It bears emphasizing that Hamdan does not challenge, and we do not today address, the Government's power to detain him for the duration of active hostilities in order to prevent such harm. But in undertaking to try Hamdan and subject him to criminal punishment, the Executive is bound to comply with the Rule of Law that prevails in this jurisdiction.

The judgment of the Court of Appeals is reversed, and the case is remanded for further proceedings.

It is so ordered.

THE CHIEF JUSTICE took no part in the consideration or decision of this case.

Justice BREYER, with whom Justice KENNEDY, Justice SOUTER, and Justice GINSBURG join, concurring.

The dissenters say that today's decision would "sorely hamper the President's ability to confront and defeat a new and deadly enemy." *Post,* (opinion of THOMAS, J.). They suggest that it undermines our Nation's ability to "preven[t] future attacks" of the grievous sort that we have already suffered. That claim leads me to state briefly what I believe the majority sets forth both explicitly and implicitly at greater length. The Court's conclusion ultimately rests upon a single ground: Congress has not issued the Executive a "blank check." Cf. *Hamdi v. Rumsfeld,* 542 U.S. 507, 536 (2004) (plurality opinion). Indeed, Congress has denied the President the legislative authority to create military commissions of the kind at issue here. Nothing prevents the President from returning to Congress to seek the authority he believes necessary.

Where, as here, no emergency prevents consultation with Congress, judicial insistence upon that consultation does not weaken our Nation's ability to deal with danger. To the contrary, that insistence strengthens the Nation's ability to determine—through democratic means—how best to do so. The Constitution places its faith in those democratic means. Our Court today simply does the same.

Justice KENNEDY, with whom Justice SOUTER, Justice GINSBURG, and Justice BREYER join as to Parts I and II, concurring in part.

Military Commission Order No. 1, which governs the military commission established to try petitioner Salim Hamdan for war crimes, exceeds limits that certain statutes, duly enacted by Congress, have placed on the President's authority to convene military courts. This is not a case, then, where the Executive can assert some unilateral authority to fill a void left by congressional inaction. It is a case where Congress, in the proper exercise of its powers as an independent branch of government, and as part of a long tradition of legislative involvement in matters of military justice, has considered the subject of military tribunals and set limits on the President's authority. Where a statute provides the conditions for the exercise of governmental power, its requirements are the result of a deliberative and reflective process engaging both of the political branches. Respect for laws derived from the customary operation of the Executive and Legislative Branches gives some assurance of stability in time of crisis. The Constitution is best preserved by reliance on standards tested over time and insulated from the pressures of the moment.

These principles seem vindicated here, for a case that may be of extraordinary importance is resolved by ordinary rules. The rules of most relevance here are those pertaining to the authority of Congress and the interpretation of its enactments.

It seems appropriate to recite these rather fundamental points because the Court refers, as it should in its exposition of the case, to the requirement of the Geneva Conventions of 1949 that military tribunals be "regularly constituted"—a requirement that controls here, if for no other reason, because Congress requires that military commissions like the ones at issue conform to the "law of war." Whatever the substance and content of the term "regularly constituted" as interpreted in this and any later cases, there seems little doubt that it relies upon the importance of standards deliberated upon and chosen in advance of crisis, under a system where the single power of the Executive is checked by other constitutional mechanisms. All of which returns us to the point of beginning—that domestic statutes control this case. If Congress, after due consideration, deems it appropriate to change the controlling statutes, in conformance with the Constitution and other laws, it has the power and prerogative to do so.

I join the Court's opinion, save Parts V and VI-D-iv. To state my reasons for this reservation, and to show my agreement with the remainder of the Court's analysis by identifying particular deficiencies in the military commissions at issue, this separate opinion seems appropriate.

...

II

In assessing the validity of Hamdan's military commission the precise circumstances of this case bear emphasis. The allegations against Hamdan are undoubtedly serious. Captured in Afghanistan during our Nation's armed conflict with the Taliban and al Qaeda—a conflict that continues as we speak—Hamdan stands accused of overt acts in furtherance of a conspiracy to commit terrorism: delivering weapons and ammunition to al Qaeda, acquiring trucks for use by Osama bin Laden's bodyguards, providing security services to bin Laden, and receiving weapons training at a terrorist camp. Nevertheless, the circumstances of Hamdan's trial present no exigency requiring special speed or precluding careful consideration of evidence. For roughly four years, Hamdan has been detained at a permanent United States military base in Guantánamo Bay, Cuba. And regardless of the outcome of the criminal proceedings at issue, the Government claims authority to continue to detain him based on his status as an enemy combatant.

Against this background, the Court is correct to conclude that the military commission the President has convened to try Hamdan is unauthorized. The following analysis, which expands on the Court's discussion, explains my reasons for reaching this conclusion.

To begin with, the structure and composition of the military commission deviate from conventional court-martial standards. Although these deviations raise questions about the fairness of the trial, no evident practical need explains them.

Under the UCMJ, courts-martial are organized by a "convening authority"—either a commanding officer, the Secretary of Defense, the Secretary concerned, or the President. The convening authority refers charges for trial, and selects the court-martial members who vote on the guilt or innocence of the accused and determine the sentence. Paralleling this structure, under Military Commission Order No. 1 an "'Appointing Authority'"—either the Secretary of Defense or the Secretary's "designee"—establishes commissions subject to the order, approves and refers charges to be tried by those commissions, and appoints commission members who vote on the conviction and sentence. In addition the Appointing Authority determines the number of commission members (at least three), oversees the chief prosecutor, provides "investigative or other resources" to the defense insofar as he or she "deems necessary for a full and fair trial," approves or rejects plea agreements, approves or disapproves communications with news media by prosecution or defense counsel (a function shared by the General Counsel of the Department of Defense), and issues supplementary commission regulations (subject to approval by the General Counsel of the Department of Defense, unless the Appointing Authority is the Secretary of Defense).

Against the background of these significant powers for the Appointing Authority, which in certain respects at least conform to ordinary court-martial standards, the regulations governing the commissions at issue make several noteworthy departures. At a general court-martial—the only type authorized to impose penalties of more than one year's incarceration or to adjudicate offenses against the law of war—the presiding officer who rules on legal issues must be a military judge. A military judge is an officer who is a member of a state or federal bar and has been specially certified for judicial duties by the Judge Advocate General for the officer's Armed Service. To protect their independence, military judges at general courts-martial are "assigned and directly responsible to the Judge Advocate General or the Judge Advocate General's designee." They must be detailed to the court, in accordance with applicable regulations, "by a person assigned as a military judge and directly responsible to the Judge Advocate General or the Judge Advocate General's designee." Here, by contrast, the Appointing Authority selects the presiding officer; and that officer need only be a judge advocate, that is, a military lawyer.

The Appointing Authority, moreover, exercises supervisory powers that continue during trial. Any interlocutory question "the disposition of which would effect a termination of proceedings with respect to a charge" is subject to decision not by the presiding officer, but by the Appointing Authority. Other interlocutory questions may be certified to the Appointing Authority as the presiding officer "deems appropriate." While in some circumstances the Government may appeal certain rulings at a court-martial—including "an order or ruling that terminates the proceedings with respect to a charge or specification"—the appeals go to a body called the Court of Criminal Appeals, not to the convening authority. The Court of Criminal Appeals functions as the military's intermediate appeals court; it is established by the Judge Advocate General for each Armed Service and composed of appellate military judges. This is another means in which, by structure and tradition, the court-martial process is insulated from those who have an interest in the outcome of the proceedings.

Finally, in addition to these powers with respect to the presiding officer, the Appointing Authority has greater flexibility in appointing commission members. While a general court-martial requires, absent a contrary election by the accused, at least five members, the Appointing Authority here is free, as noted earlier, to select as few as three. This difference may affect the deliberative process and the prosecution's burden of persuasion.

As compared to the role of the convening authority in a court-martial, the greater powers of the Appointing Authority here—including even the resolution of dispositive issues in the middle of the trial—raise concerns that the commission's decisionmaking may not be neutral. If the differences are supported by some practical need beyond the goal of constant and ongoing supervision, that need is neither apparent from the record nor established by the Government's submissions.

It is no answer that, at the end of the day, the Detainee Treatment Act of 2005 (DTA) affords military-commission defendants the opportunity for judicial review in federal court. As the Court is correct to observe, the scope of that review is limited, and the review is not automatic if the defendant's sentence is under 10 years. Also, provisions for review of legal issues after trial cannot correct for structural defects, such as the role of the Appointing Authority, that can cast doubt on the factfinding process and the presiding judge's exercise of discretion during trial. Before military-commission defendants may obtain judicial review, furthermore, they must navigate a military review process that again raises fairness concerns. At the outset, the Appointing Authority (unless the Appointing Authority is the Secretary of Defense) performs an "administrative review" of undefined scope, ordering any "supplementary proceedings" deemed necessary. After that the case is referred to a three-member Review Panel composed of officers selected by the Secretary of

Defense. Though the Review Panel may return the case for further proceedings only if a majority "form[s] a definite and firm conviction that a material error of law occurred," only one member must have "experience as a judge;" nothing in the regulations requires that other panel members have legal training. By comparison to the review of court-martial judgments performed by such independent bodies as the Judge Advocate General, the Court of Criminal Appeals, and the Court of Appeals for the Armed Forces, the review process here lacks structural protections designed to help ensure impartiality.

These structural differences between the military commissions and courts-martial—the concentration of functions, including legal decisionmaking, in a single executive official; the less rigorous standards for composition of the tribunal; and the creation of special review procedures in place of institutions created and regulated by Congress—remove safeguards that are important to the fairness of the proceedings and the independence of the court. Congress has prescribed these guarantees for courts-martial; and no evident practical need explains the departures here. For these reasons the commission cannot be considered regularly constituted under United States law and thus does not satisfy Congress' requirement that military commissions conform to the law of war.

Apart from these structural issues, moreover, the basic procedures for the commissions deviate from procedures for courts-martial, in violation of § 836(b). As the Court explains, the Military Commission Order abandons the detailed Military Rules of Evidence, which are modeled on the Federal Rules of Evidence in conformity with § 836(a)'s requirement of presumptive compliance with district-court rules.

Instead, the order imposes just one evidentiary rule: "Evidence shall be admitted if ... the evidence would have probative value to a reasonable person." Although it is true some military commissions applied an amorphous evidence standard in the past, the evidentiary rules for those commissions were adopted before Congress enacted the uniformity requirement of 10 U.S.C. § 836(b) as part of the UCMJ. And while some flexibility may be necessary to permit trial of battlefield captives like Hamdan, military statutes and rules already provide for introduction of deposition testimony for absent witnesses and use of classified information. Indeed, the deposition-testimony provision specifically mentions military commissions and thus is one of the provisions the Government concedes must be followed by the commission at issue. That provision authorizes admission of deposition testimony only if the witness is absent for specified reasons—a requirement that makes no sense if military commissions may consider all probative evidence. Whether or not this conflict renders the rules at issue "contrary to or inconsistent with" the UCMJ under § 836(a), it creates a uniformity problem under § 836(b).

The rule here could permit admission of multiple hearsay and other forms of evidence generally prohibited on grounds of unreliability. Indeed, the commission regulations specifically contemplate admission of unsworn written statements; and they make no provision for exclusion of coerced declarations save those "established to have been made as a result of torture." Besides, even if evidence is deemed nonprobative by the presiding officer at Hamdan's trial, the military-commission members still may view it. In another departure from court-martial practice the military commission members may object to the presiding officer's evidence rulings and determine themselves, by majority vote, whether to admit the evidence.

As the Court explains, the Government has made no demonstration of practical need for these special rules and procedures, either in this particular case or as to the military commissions in general, nor is any such need self-evident. For all the Government's regulations and submissions reveal, it would be feasible for most, if not all, of the conventional military evidence rules and procedures to be followed.

In sum, as presently structured, Hamdan's military commission exceeds the bounds Congress has placed on the President's authority in §§ 836 and 821 of the UCMJ. Because Congress has prescribed these limits, Congress can change them, requiring a new analysis consistent with the Constitution and other governing laws. At this time, however, we must apply the standards Congress has provided. By those standards the military commission is deficient.

III

In light of the conclusion that the military commission here is unauthorized under the UCMJ, I see no need to consider several further issues addressed in the plurality opinion by JUSTICE STEVENS and the dissent by JUSTICE THOMAS.

First, I would not decide whether Common Article 3's standard—a "regularly constituted court affording all the judicial guarantees which are recognized as indispensable by civilized peoples"—necessarily requires that the accused have the right to be present at all stages of a criminal trial. As JUSTICE STEVENS explains, Military Commission Order No. 1 authorizes exclusion of the accused from the proceedings if the presiding officer determines that, among other things, protection of classified information so requires. JUSTICE STEVENS observes that these regulations create the possibility of a conviction and sentence based on evidence Hamdan has not seen or heard—a possibility the plurality is correct to consider troubling.

As the dissent by Justice THOMAS points out, however, the regulations bar the presiding officer from admitting secret evidence if doing so would deprive the accused of a "full and fair trial." This fairness determination, moreover, is unambiguously subject to judicial review under the DTA. The evidentiary proceedings at Hamdan's trial have yet to commence, and it remains to be seen whether he will suffer any prejudicial exclusion.

There should be reluctance, furthermore, to reach unnecessarily the question whether, as the plurality seems to conclude, Article 75 of Protocol I to the Geneva Conventions is binding law notwithstanding the earlier decision by our Government not to accede to the Protocol. For all these reasons, and without detracting from the importance of the right of presence, I would rely on other deficiencies noted here and in the opinion by the Court—deficiencies that relate to the structure and procedure of the commission and that inevitably will affect the proceedings—as the basis for finding the military commissions lack authorization under 10 U.S.C. § 836 and fail to be regularly constituted under Common Article 3 and § 821.

I likewise see no need to address the validity of the conspiracy charge against Hamdan—an issue addressed at length in Part V of JUSTICE STEVENS' opinion and in Part II-C of JUSTICE THOMAS' dissent. In light of the conclusion that the military commissions at issue are unauthorized Congress may choose to provide further guidance in this area. Congress, not the Court, is the branch in the better position to undertake the "sensitive task of establishing a principle not inconsistent with the national interest or international justice."

Finally, for the same reason, I express no view on the merits of other limitations on military commissions described as elements of the common law of war in Part V of JUSTICE STEVENS' opinion.

With these observations I join the Court's opinion with the exception of Parts V and VI-D-iv.

Justice SCALIA, with whom Justice THOMAS and Justice ALITO join, dissenting.

On December 30, 2005, Congress enacted the Detainee Treatment Act (DTA). It unambiguously provides that, as of that date, "no court, justice, or judge" shall have jurisdiction to consider the habeas application of a Guantánamo Bay detainee. Notwithstanding this plain directive, the Court today concludes that, on what it calls the statute's *most natural* reading, *every* "court, justice, or judge" before whom such a habeas application was pending on December 30 has jurisdiction to hear, consider, and render judgment on it. This conclusion is patently erroneous. And even if it were not, the jurisdiction supposedly retained should, in an exercise of sound equitable discretion, not be exercised.

…

For the foregoing reasons, I dissent.

Justice THOMAS, with whom Justice SCALIA joins, and with whom Justice ALITO joins in all but Parts I, II-C-1, and III-B-2, dissenting.   *Dissent*

For the reasons set forth in JUSTICE SCALIA's dissent, it is clear that this Court lacks jurisdiction to entertain petitioner's claims. The Court having concluded otherwise, it is appropriate to respond to the Court's resolution of the merits of petitioner's claims because its opinion openly flouts our well-established duty to respect the Executive's judgment in matters of military operations and foreign affairs. The Court's evident belief that *it* is qualified to pass on the "[m]ilitary necessity," of the Commander in Chief's decision to employ a particular form of force against our enemies is so antithetical to our constitutional structure that it simply cannot go unanswered. I respectfully dissent.

…

Prompted by the Supreme Court's holding in *Hamdan v. Rumsfeld*, an energized Congress understood that they could no longer remain on the sidelines in the War on Terror. In late 2006, Congress established the creation of military commissions, affirming quite satisfactorily that the Military Commission Act of 2006 (MCA) was consistent with the requirements of Common Article 3 of   *MCA*
the Geneva Conventions—the military commissions so established constitute a "regularly constituted court," affording all the necessary "judicial guarantees which are recognized as indispensable by civilized peoples." Indeed, with the passage of the MCA, Congress has firmly committed itself to the view that the nation is at war and that the legislative branch of government has a significant role to play in a variety of legal issues associated with the "enemy combatants"—both legal and illegal—that seek to do great physical harm to the United States and its allies. While the Detainee Treatment Act of 2005 provided an advanced signal that Congress was at last willing to get involved in a limited manner in some of the thorny legal aspects of the War on Terror, the MCA represents a major Congressional shift in scope. In short, the MCA is a resounding statutory broadside that impacts forcefully and with great effect across the entire legal landscape.

Above all, the MCA has certainly washed away all doubt regarding Congress' willingness to characterize the War on Terror as a real global war against real enemies who desire to murder and terrorize. Accordingly, Congress has demonstrated that it is more than willing to employ the full weight of the rule of law pertaining to armed conflict against our enemies.

Not only does the MCA provide crystal clear guidance in the context of the establishment and operation of military commissions to try "any alien unlawful enemy combatant" (al-Qa'eda and al-Qa'eda-styled Islamic terrorists) it provides concrete statutory definitions concerning a wide variety of terms that have been previously hotly debated. The MCA also clearly places a large legal "seal of approval" on many of the initiatives taken by the Bush Administration in the War on Terror. For instance, the MCA defines "unlawful enemy combatants" in precise language while recognizing in the same breath the lawful functioning of the Combatant Status Review Tribunal for enemy combatant determination set up by the Department of Defense in response to the 2004 *Hamdi v. Rumsfeld* ruling. The MCA reads:

> (i) a person who has engaged in hostilities or who has purposefully and materially supported hostilities against the United States or its co-belligerents who is not a lawful enemy combatant (including a person who is part of the Taliban, al Qaeda, or associated forces); or
>
> (ii) a person who, before, on, or after the date of the enactment of the Military Commissions Act of 2006, has been determined to be an unlawful enemy combatant by a Combatant Status Review Tribunal or another competent tribunal established under the authority of the President or the Secretary of Defense.

The MCA also lists in detail the criminal offenses that fall within the jurisdiction of the military commission. Apart from the traditional list of war crimes the MCA appropriately includes "conspiracy" and "providing material support for terrorism," drawing definitional language from the Material Support provisions at Section 2339A for the latter offense. In addition, reaffirming the fact that the United States is in a state of hostilities, the MCA addresses the matter of streamlining the process for dealing with the large number of petitions filed by lawyers on behalf enemy combatants in the federal court system. Again, if one recognizes the government's premise that the nation is at war and the laws of war apply, then the MCA properly deals with restricting habeas corpus and providing for other limitations on the jurisdiction of civilian courts.

In the sphere of authorizing trial by military commission, the Congress wisely allows for the military commission to operate in the traditional manner of all previous military commissions (hundreds were tried by military commissions in World War II, some were even U.S. citizens) and consider, for example, hearsay evidence and information gathered without a search warrant. The MCA holds that "[e]vidence shall be admissible if the military judge determines that the evidence would have probative value to a reasonable person" and "[e]vidence shall not be excluded from trial by military commission on the grounds that the evidence was not seized pursuant to a search warrant or other authorization." While the MCA correctly excludes all statements obtained by use of torture, the MCA also tackles the hard question of statements taken from an illegal enemy combatant where a "degree of coercion is disputed." Such statements may be admissible under strict guidelines depending on when they were obtained. Statements obtained before the enactment of the Detainee Treatment Act "in which the degree of coercion is disputed may be admitted only if the military judge finds that (1) the totality of the circumstances renders the statement reliable and possessing sufficient probative value; and (2) the interests of justice would best be served by admission of the statement into evidence." Statements obtained after enactment of Detainee Treatment Act in which the degree of coercion is disputed may be admitted only if the military judge finds that in addition to (1) and (2) above, "(3) the interrogation methods used to obtain the statement do not amount to cruel, inhuman, or degrading treatment."

Ironically, some view the common sense evidentiary provisions in the MCA as a violation of Common Article 3's requirement that the accused be afforded all the necessary "guarantees … recognized as indispensable by civilized peoples." Such ethnocentric views are quickly dispelled when one considers the day-to-day activity of most modern European criminal courts where hearsay is regularly considered and far different legal avenues regarding the introduction of evidence are regularly employed. Even the International Criminal Court allows hearsay. In fact, earlier calls by some (including uniformed judge advocates who should have known better) that a military commission should include the same due process standards that American soldiers enjoy at a military courts martial under the Uniformed Code of Military Justice were wisely disregarded by Congress. Obviously, these "relaxed" provisions in the MCA are necessary due to the exigencies of war—witnesses and victims may be dead, investigators are not able to get to the crime scene, etc. The MCA does provide the following rights for the accused who is charged:

- a copy of the charges in English and a language he understands;
- a presumption of innocence for the accused;
- guilt must be proven by the government beyond a reasonable doubt;
- access to evidence that the prosecution plans to present at trial;
- access to evidence known to the prosecution tending to exculpate the accused;
- right to remain silent;
- right to testify subject to cross-examination;
- right to obtain witnesses and documents for defense;
- right to present evidence and cross-examine witnesses;
- the appointment of interpreters to assist defense;
- right to be present at every stage of trial (except when proceedings are closed for national security) unless disruptive;
- access to sentencing evidence;
- cannot be tried again by military commission once verdict is final;
- right to submit a plea agreement;
- two-thirds of the military officers on the panel must agree on findings of guilt;
- unanimous decision for death sentence;
- right to a free military attorney or to hire a civilian attorney;
- trial would be open to public (exceptions recognized for physical safety of participants).

As various legal challenges to portions of the MCA make their way through the lower courts, e.g., the MCA revokes all U.S. court's jurisdiction to hear habeas corpus petitions by alien enemy combatants in U.S. custody, it is highly doubtful that the Supreme Court will strike down very much of the MCA as unconstitutional. Indeed, in time of war the Court has traditionally been most reluctant to intervene in matters of national security, particularly when the executive and legislative branches have joined together in such a seamless fashion.

Prior to the MCA, Congress had seemed content to sit on the sidelines in the War on Terror. While rational people understand that the unique threat of al-Qa'eda-styled terrorism can only be addressed by employing the laws established for armed conflict, it is equally true that said laws of war need to be updated to encompass the new paradigm. For over five years, Congress has simply watched as the executive branch, with occasional mandates from the judicial branch, crafted and implemented an emerging rule of law. It was extremely supportive of the rule of law and vital to the issue of legitimacy that the legislative branch of the government finally joined the process.

4.5 Federal Courts

It is well settled that federal district courts of the United States have the legal authority under both domestic and international law to prosecute nonresident aliens for terrorist crimes committed on foreign soil as well as for war crimes. This power has been exercised many times against militant Islamic terrorists, both prior to and after 9/11. In this context, the courts have often been called on to balance the need between the government's desire to protect national security and the defendant's right to a fair and open trial.

A widely cited precedent which amplifies just how far the jurisdictional reach extends in this regard is the case of *U.S. v. Yunis*. The *Yunis* case involved the federal criminal trial of Fawaz Yunis, an Arab terrorist who participated in the hijacking of a Royal Jordanian Airlines airplane at Beirut International Airport in June 1985. The only connection the act had with the United States was the fact that a handful of American citizens were on board the hijacked plane. After reviewing the pertinent international agreements relating to hostage taking and hijacking, the federal district court denied a defense motion to dismiss for lack of jurisdiction and Yunis was convicted of conspiracy, hostage taking and air piracy.

On appeal of his conviction, the Court of Appeals for the D.C. Circuit said the following about the concept of customary international law as it applied to certain criminal acts: "Nor is jurisdiction precluded by norms of customary international law. The district court [correctly] concluded that two jurisdictional theories of international law, the 'universal principle' and the 'passive personal principle,' (*United States v. Benitez*, 741 F.2d. 1312) supported assertion of United States jurisdiction to prosecute Yunis on hijacking and hostage-taking charges." According to the appellate court, the "universal principle" of jurisdiction allows states to prosecute those "offenses recognized by the community of nations as of universal concern, such as piracy, slave trade, attacks on or hijacking of aircraft, genocide, war crimes, and perhaps certain acts of terrorism." Under the passive personal principle, a State may prosecute non-nationals for crimes committed against its nationals outside of its territory.

A constant dilemma for the government in prosecuting Islamic militants is the need to protect national security concerns associated with intelligence gathering while providing the defendant with the full range of rights accorded by the Constitution. By law and custom federal prosecutors are authorized the discretion to decline cases brought to them by investigative agencies. According to unclassified sources, from September 2001 until August 2006, investigative agencies have characterized nearly 6,500 individuals arrested as "international terrorists." Of that number, 1,329, or 27 percent, were convicted in federal district courts. Only 14 received a sentence of 20 years or more in confinement, with 67 receiving sentences of five or more years and 327 receiving sentences less than one year. 704 received no confinement. Although the 1,329 were designated as "international terrorists" by the Justice Department, the actual crimes they were charged with often had no direct connection to terrorist activity. The primary lead charges for these international terrorist cases were 18 U.S.C. § 1001 (fraud/false statements), 14.5 percent; 18 U.S.C. § 2332 (terrorism, criminal penalties), 14.4 percent; 18 U.S.C. § 2339 (providing material support to terrorists), 11.6 percent; 18 U.S.C. § 2371 (conspiracy to commit an offense or to defraud the U.S. government), 4.7 percent; and "not stated," 17.7 percent. In turn, the top lead charge from those convicted of some crime was 18 U.S.C. § 1001 (fraud/false statements), 56.8 percent.

Interestingly, only one American, Adam Gadahn (aka Azzam al-Amriki) has been charged with treason, making him the first U.S. citizen charged with treason since WW II (seditious conspiracy charges were used against the terrorists who conducted the 1993 bombing on the World Trade Center). Gadahn converted to Islam in 1995 and later moved to Pakistan where he has since appeared in a series of videos, calling for terrorist attacks on Americans. Treason, the only crime spelled out in the Constitution, is codified at 18 U.S.C. § 2381. The indictment alleges that Gadahn, owing allegiance to the United States, knowingly adhered to al-Qa'eda and provided it aid-and-comfort, with intent to "betray the United States." The indictment then provides extensive quotations from five separate al-Qa'eda videos in which he appeared and urged others to attack the United States. He is also charged with providing material support in violation of 18 U.S.C. § 2339B.

The violation of immigration laws served as the primary authority for the FBI and immigration officials to detain approximately 1,000 individuals across the United States in the wake of the 9/11 terrorist attacks. Within four months, about two-thirds of those detained accepted voluntary departure orders or were deported. It is unclear how many of these deported illegal aliens actually were terrorists or had firm links to militant Islamic groups. However, in the past six years, the FBI has broken up numerous al-Qa'eda and al-Qa'eda-styled sleeper cells in the United States. One major radical Islamic terrorist cell operating in the Detroit area was broken up in late August 2002 and four extremists were charged. In September 2002, another terrorist cell in New York was broken up by the FBI, leading to the arrests of six Arab-Americans who had trained in al-Qa'eda terror camps in Afghanistan in the summer of 2001. All were subsequently convicted under the material support provisions. In October 2002, six more suspected terrorists were arrested in Oregon (the so-called "Portland Seven") and Michigan. Four members were indicted in federal court in Oregon on charges of trying to join or help the Taliban and al-Qa'eda in Afghanistan wage war on the United States. In 2005, federal authorities broke up an al-Qa'eda cell in Lodi, California, when they arrested a father and his son as part of a larger investigation. In September 2005, the FBI arrested an Egyptian man suspected of plotting the bombing of an airport or plane, but only charged him with wire fraud and the fraudulent use of a social security card. In 2006, an al-Qa'eda-styled group that was plotting to bomb buildings was arrested in Miami, Florida.

In addition, the Justice Department has targeted institutions that provide financial and logistical support to terror groups. In July 2004, for example, a Muslim charity called the Holy Land Foundation for Relief and Development was closed by the government and charged, along with seven of its officers, with supporting terrorist groups by illegally funneling millions of dollars to the terrorist organization Hamas.

Charging considerations also raise unique issues, as do defenses of freedom of religion and privacy, as illustrated in the case of Sheik Omar Abdel Rahm, one of the most notorious Islamic militants prosecuted to date. The so-called blind Sheik was associated with the 1993 terror bombing of the World Trade Center.

UNITED STATES v. RAHMAN

United States Court of Appeals for the Second Circuit

189 F.3d 88 (1999)

NEWMAN, LEVAL, and PARKER, Circuit Judges.
PER CURIAM:

INTRODUCTION

These are appeals by ten defendants convicted of seditious conspiracy and other offenses arising out of a wide-ranging plot to conduct a campaign of urban terrorism. Among the activities of some or all of the defendants were rendering assistance to those who bombed the World Trade Center, planning to bomb bridges and tunnels in New York City, murdering Rabbi Meir Kahane, and planning to murder the President of Egypt. We affirm the convictions of all the defendants. We also affirm all of the sentences, with the exception of the sentence of Ibrahim El-Gabrowny, which we remand for further consideration.

BACKGROUND

Defendants-Appellants Sheik Omar Abdel Rahman, El Sayyid Nosair, Ibrahim El-Gabrowny, Clement Hampton-El, Amir Abdelgani ("Amir"), Fares Khallafalla, Tarig Elhassan, Fadil Abdelgani ("Fadil"), Mohammed Saleh, and Victor Alvarez (collectively "defendants") appeal from judgments of conviction entered on January 17, 1996, following a nine-month jury trial in the United States District Court for the Southern District of New York (Michael B. Mukasey, District Judge).

The defendants were convicted of the following: seditious conspiracy (all defendants); soliciting the murder of Egyptian President Hosni Mubarak and soliciting an attack on American military installations (Rahman); conspiracy to murder Mubarak (Rahman); bombing conspiracy (all defendants found guilty except Nosair and El-Gabrowny); attempted bombing (Hampton-El, Amir, Fadil, Khallafalla, Elhassan, Saleh, and Alvarez); two counts of attempted murder and one count of murder in furtherance of a racketeering enterprise (Nosair); attempted murder of a federal officer (Nosair); three counts of use of a firearm in relation to a crime of violence (Nosair); possession of a firearm with an obliterated serial number (Nosair); facilitating the bombing conspiracy by shipping a firearm in interstate commerce and using and carrying a firearm in relation to a crime of violence (Alvarez); two counts of assault on a federal officer (El-Gabrowny); assault impeding the execution of a search warrant (El-Gabrowny); five counts of possession of a fraudulent foreign passport, and one count of possession with intent to transfer false identification documents (El-Gabrowny).

I. The Government's Case

At trial, the Government sought to prove that the defendants and others joined in a seditious conspiracy to wage a war of urban terrorism against the United States and forcibly to oppose its authority. The Government also sought to prove various other counts against the defendants, all of which broadly relate to the seditious conspiracy. The Government alleged that members of the conspiracy (acting alone or in concert) took the following actions, among others, in furtherance of the group's objectives: the attempted murder of Hosni Mubarak, the provision of assistance to the bombing of the World Trade Center in New York City on February 26, 1993, and the Spring 1993 campaign of attempted bombings of buildings and tunnels in New York City. In addition, some members of the group were allegedly involved in the murder of Rabbi Meir Kahane by defendant Nosair.

The Government adduced evidence at trial showing the following: Rahman, a blind Islamic scholar and cleric, was the leader of the seditious conspiracy, the purpose of which was "jihad," in the sense of a struggle against the enemies of Islam. Indicative of this purpose, in a speech to his followers Rahman instructed that they were to "do jihad with the sword, with the cannon, with the grenades, with the missile ... against God's enemies." Rahman's role in the conspiracy was generally limited to overall supervision and direction of the membership, as he made efforts to remain a level above the details of individual operations. However, as a cleric and the group's leader, Rahman was entitled to dispense "fatwas," religious opinions on the holiness of an act, to members of the group sanctioning proposed courses of conduct and advising them whether the acts would be in furtherance of jihad.

According to his speeches and writings, Rahman perceives the United States as the primary oppressor of Muslims worldwide, active in assisting Israel to gain power in the Middle East, and largely under the control of the Jewish lobby. Rahman also considers the secular Egyptian government of Mubarak to be an oppressor because it has abided Jewish migration to Israel while seeking to decrease Muslim births. Holding these views, Rahman believes that jihad against Egypt and the United States is mandated by the Qur'an. Formation of a jihad army made up of small "divisions" and "battalions" to carry out this jihad was therefore necessary, according to Rahman, in order to beat back these oppressors of Islam including the United States.

Although Rahman did not arrive in the United States until 1990, a group of his followers began to organize the jihad army in New York beginning in 1989. At that time, law enforcement had several of the members of the group under surveillance. In July 1989, on three successive weekends, FBI agents observed and photographed members of the jihad organization, including (at different times), Nosair, Hampton-El, Mahmoud Abouhalima, Mohammad Salameh, and Nidal Ayyad (the latter three of whom were later convicted of the World Trade Center bombing, see *Salameh*, *152 F.3d at 161*), shooting weapons, including AK-47's, at a public rifle range on Long Island. Although Rahman was in Egypt at the time, Nosair and Abouhalima called him there to discuss various issues including the progress of their military training, tape-recording these conversations for distribution among Rahman's followers. Nosair told Rahman "we have organized an encampment, we are concentrating here."

On November 5, 1990, Rabbi Meir Kahane, a former member of the Israeli parliament and a founder of the Jewish Defense League, gave a speech at the Marriot East Side Hotel in New York.

Kahane was a militant Zionist, who advocated expelling Arabs from Israel. The content of this speech was a plea to American Jews to emigrate and settle in Israel. Nosair and possibly Salameh and Bilal Alkaisi, another member of the group, attended the speech. After the speech, as Kahane stood talking with the crowd, two shots were fired and Kahane was hit in the neck and chest.

Nosair, whom witnesses observed with a gun in hand immediately after the shooting, then ran toward the rear door of the room, trailed by one of the onlookers. At the door, seventy-year-old Irving Franklin sought to impede Nosair's flight. Nosair shot Franklin in the leg, and fled the room. Outside the hotel Nosair encountered uniformed postal police officer Carlos Acosta. Acosta tried to draw his weapon and identify himself, but before he these shots hit Acosta in the chest but was deflected into his shoulder by a bullet-proof vest he was wearing, [sic] and the second just missed Acosta's head. Despite being shot, Acosta returned fire, hitting Nosair in the neck. Nosair fell to the ground, dropping his weapon, a .357 caliber magnum revolver, at his side. Acosta recovered the weapon and detained Nosair. Ballistics testing showed that the weapon recovered from Nosair was the weapon that fired projectiles found in the room in which Kahane and Franklin had been shot, as well as in the area Acosta had been shot.

Subsequent to these events, law enforcement personnel executed search warrants for Nosair's home, car, and work lockers. Among the items seized in these searches was a handwritten notebook, in which Nosair stated that to establish a Muslim state in the Muslim holy lands it would be necessary:

> to break and destroy the morale of the enemies of Allah. (And this is by means of destroying) (exploding) the structure of their civilized pillars. Such as the tourist infrastructure which they are proud of and their high world buildings which they are proud of and their statues which they endear and the buildings in which they gather their heads (leaders).

While Nosair was at the prison ward of Bellevue Hospital following the shooting, Nosair stated in response to a question from a treating physician that he had no choice but to kill Kahane, and that it was his "duty." After Nosair was moved from Bellevue to Rikers Island, he began to receive a steady stream of visitors, most regularly his cousin El-Gabrowny, and also Abouhalima, Salameh, and Ayyad. During these visits, as well as subsequent visits once Nosair was at Attica, Nosair suggested numerous terrorist operations including the murders of the judge who sentenced him and of Dov Hikind, a New York City Assemblyman, and chided his visitors for doing nothing to further the jihad against the oppressors. Nosair also tape recorded messages while in custody, including one stating:

> God the Almighty … will facilitate for the believers to penetrate the lines no matter how strong they are, and the greatest proof of that [is] what happened in New York. God the Almighty enabled His extremely brave people, with His great power, to destroy one of the top infidels. They were preparing him to dominate, to be the Prime Minister some day. They were preparing him despite their assertion that they reject his agenda … and that he is a racist.

During Nosair's state trial in 1991, an FBI informant, Emad Salem, began to befriend various of Rahman's followers in an attempt to infiltrate the jihad organization. At that trial, Salem met El-Gabrowny, Nosair's cousin, who was raising money to aid in Nosair's defense. Salem also met other regular attendees such as Siddig Ibrahim Siddig Ali, Abouhalima, Ali Shinawy, Hamdi Moussa, and Ahmed Abdel Sattar. Salem, accompanied by El-Gabrowny, also met with Nosair. El-Gabrowny introduced Salem as "a new member in the family."

As a result of these contacts, Salem traveled to Detroit with Rahman and others to attend a conference on the Islamic economy. During this trip, Salem, seeking to ingratiate himself to Rahman, informed Rahman of his prior service in the Egyptian military during the 1973 conflict with Israel. Rahman told Salem that this was not jihad because he had been paid to fight by an infidel government. Rahman also told Salem that he could make up for this, however, by assassinating Mubarak, a "loyal dog to the Americans."

Before the Nosair trial ended, Salem was invited for dinner at El-Gabrowny's house. During dinner, El-Gabrowny indicated he was concerned about being bugged by the FBI, turned up the television, and then discussed construction of high-powered explosives with Salem. Salem testified that after this dinner at El-Gabrowny's house, bombing became a frequent topic of conversation between them. By early 1992, Rahman had also welcomed Salem into the group. Rahman specifically praised Salem for attempting to restart paramilitary training with the group, noting that there would come a day when the training would be needed.

Mohammad Saad, the cousin of Sattar and a participant in the jihad group, developed a plan to get Nosair out of jail and confided the plan to Salem. Salem repeated the plan to El-Gabrowny, who cautioned them to slow down and await the outcome of Nosair's appeal. After being badgered by Nosair to take action, El-Gabrowny met with Salem and told him that he was in touch with "underground people" who could help them construct bombs. El-Gabrowny instructed Salem on the superiority of remote detonators rather than timers, describing to Salem how a remote detonator could assist in bombing Dov Hikind.

In June 1992 El-Gabrowny visited Nosair again in prison. Upon his return, he instructed Salem and Shinawy that Nosair wanted to see them. Salem testified that, when they made the visit, Nosair berated them for not proceeding with bombing plans and directed Shinawy to seek a fatwa from Rahman approving the bombings. On the way home from the visit, Shinaway told Salem that the planned operation would involve twelve bombs. Shinawy also explained that they would need guns in case they encountered police during the deployment, indicating that his source for firearms was Hampton-El.

Two days later Salem went to El-Gabrowny's house and found Shinawy already there. The three agreed that they would try to secure a "safehouse" for constructing bombs, and El-Gabrowny committed to attempt to obtain detonators from Afghanistan. A few days later, Shinawy summoned Salem to the Abu Bakr Mosque where he introduced Salem to Hampton-El. Salem and Shinaway explained to Hampton-El that they were making bombs but that they were having trouble getting detonators. Hampton-El said that he had access to "ready-made bombs" for $900 to $1,000 apiece. He also offered to obtain a handgun for Salem. A few days later Shinaway gave Salem a handgun presumably from Hampton-El.

In early July 1992, a rift developed between Salem and the FBI, and it was agreed that Salem's undercover investigation would be terminated. To explain his disappearance, Salem told El-Gabrowny that he needed to go to Spain for a while to take care of a problem in his jewelry business.

In late 1992, the paramilitary training resumed, led by Siddig Ali and Hampton-El on weekends between October 1992 and February 1993. Defendants Amir and Fadil Abdelgani and Elhassan all participated in the training camp, as did Abdo Haggag, an Egyptian spy who testified for the Government during the trial. The purpose of the training was to teach the participants jihad tactics. There was talk that jihad was needed in Bosnia, and that some of the trainees might go there. As Siddig Ali later explained to Salem, the training was meant to prepare the trainees for jihad wherever it was needed. During training, Siddig Ali reported to Rahman, and Rahman offered his insights into the training.

In the midst of this training, Hampton-El sought detonators and "clean" guns from Garrett Wilson, a cooperating witness for the U.S. Naval Investigative Service, who testified for the Government at trial. Hampton-El explained that he wanted to train a group of people in "commando tactics" and discussed training techniques and bomb identification.

During this time, Ramzi Yousef (another compatriot who was later convicted of the World Trade Center bombing, see *Salameh, 152 F.3d at 161*) arrived in the United States. Rahman was making numerous calls to overseas numbers, including a Pakistan number which Yousef had inscribed in a bomb making pamphlet. Rahman, Salameh, and Yousef also made several calls to the same number in Pakistan in November. Nosair, speaking with his wife from prison, said, "And what will happen in New York, God willing, it will be … because of my prayers."

In January 1993, Rahman appeared at a conference in Brooklyn, and voiced his beliefs in violent jihad. Rahman further stated that being called terrorists was fine, so long as they were terrorizing the enemies of Islam, the foremost of which was the United States and its allies. While building the World Trade Center bomb, the builders kept in close phone contact with El-Gabrowny and Rahman. Salameh and Yousef repeatedly called El-Gabrowny at home and at the Abu Bakr Mosque and Rahman at home. In December 1992 and January 1993, El-Gabrowny visited Nosair at Attica and later arranged for the World Trade Center bombers to visit Nosair in the weeks preceding the bombing (Abouhalima visited Nosair on January 2 and February 7, and Salameh visited him on February 13).

On February 24, 1993, Salameh rented a van to be used in the World Trade Center bombing. As identification, he used a New York license bearing his own name and El-Gabrowny's address. As Ayyad was making arrangements to purchase the hydrogen gas to be used in the World Trade Center bomb, he called El-Gabrowny. On February 26, 1993, the World Trade Center complex was bombed, causing six deaths and massive destruction.

On March 4, 1993, federal agents executed a search warrant for El-Gabrowny's home. Salameh's use of El-Gabrowny's address when renting the van used in the bombing provided the basis for the warrant. The warrant allowed a search for explosives and related devices. The search of El-Gabrowny's home revealed, among other things, stun guns and taped messages from Nosair urging fighting and jihad in response to the Jewish immigration to Israel. Just prior to executing the search warrant, the agents encountered El-Gabrowny as he left the building and then, seeing them, started back toward it. The agents stopped and frisked him. El-Gabrowny became belligerent and assaulted two agents. On his person, the agents found five fraudulent Nicaraguan passports and birth certificates with pictures of Nosair and his wife and children.

After the bombing of the World Trade Center, Salem again began working for the FBI as an informant. In March of 1993, President Mubarak was scheduled to visit New York. Certain members of Rahman's group saw this visit as an opportunity to assassinate him, in the words of Siddig Ali, "to execute the desire of the Sheik." In seeking financing for this plan, Siddig Ali called a man in the United Arab Emirates for funding, stating that Rahman would vouch for him. Siddig Ali also contacted a source in the Sudanese government to get a copy of Mubarak's itinerary while in New York. Siddig Ali described the plan to Abdo Mohammed Haggag, an Abdel Rahman confidant who later cooperated with the Egyptian and United States authorities, and noted that it would be carried out by participants in the paramilitary training including Elhassan and Amir Abdelgani. Siddig Ali said that those men would assist and did not need to be told anything until the last moment. Haggag confronted Amir about the plan. Amir said that Siddig Ali had not informed him but that he was ready for any operation when called. Nothing came of this plan because Haggag secretly gave the Egyptian government information about the plot, and the New York part of Mubarak's trip to the United States was canceled.

Siddig Ali then proposed a new round of bombings. In late April 1993, he became friendly with Salem, who was, by that point, tape recording his conversations for the FBI. Salem agreed to assist Siddig Ali in putting together the bombs but stated that he would have no part in deploying them. After contemplating bombing a U.S. armory, Siddig Ali proposed bombing the United Nations complex. When initially discussing this plan with Salem, he stated that Rahman had approved the attack on the United Nations, and had called it not merely permissible, but a "must" and a "duty." Siddig Ali invited Salem to discuss these matters directly with Rahman, but reminded him that because of the surveillance, to use caution in so doing. Caution, as defined by Siddig Ali, included phrasing statements in a broad and general manner, and assuring that Rahman was insulated from active involvement in the plot.

Salem met with Siddig Ali again on May 12, pretending that he had surveyed locations for use as a bomb-making safehouse and that he had settled on a garage in Queens that was renting for $1,000 a month. This safehouse was actually rented by the FBI, and the FBI installed videocameras and surveillance equipment in the safehouse before members of the group began using it.

Taking Siddig Ali up on his earlier invitation, Salem had a private conversation with Rahman on the night of May 23, 1993. At the bidding of Siddig Ali, Salem began the conversation by pledging allegiance to Rahman. Salem then told Rahman that he and Siddig Ali were planning to "do a job." Salem explicitly asked Rahman about the United Nations. Rahman replied that bombing the United Nations was "not illicit, however will be bad for Muslims." Rahman instead told Salem to "Find a plan, find a plan ... to inflict damage on the American army itself." Salem then asked about a strike on the FBI headquarters in New York. Rahman told him to "wait for a while," and to "plan carefully."

Salem recounted this conversation to Siddig Ali, who stated that when he had discussed the United Nations issue with Rahman, Rahman had been in favor of the plan. Subsequently, in discussing the plan to bomb the United Nations with Hampton-El, Siddig Ali told him that he had received an "official fatwa" from Rahman regarding the plan. Siddig Ali also told Khallafalla and Amir Abdelgani the same thing, stating that Rahman's approval was necessary whenever one did something "basically unlawful," which would be wrong unless the "mission [was] under the flag of God and his messenger."

As a result of the failure of the plan to execute Mubarak, there was some speculation by members of the group that Siddig Ali was an informer. Siddig Ali and Salem conversed one day with Rahman about the issue. Rahman voiced his suspicions that Siddig Ali was the informer. Ironically, Salem secretly tape recorded this conversation for the Government. During the conversation, Rahman revealed that Abouhalima, one of the World Trade Center bombers, was supposed to have fled to Sudan, not to Egypt, where he was subsequently arrested after the bombing. After the discussion, Siddig Ali told Salem that Rahman had ordered that they be circumspect when discussing their plans with him so that he would not be incriminated.

On May 27, 1993, Siddig Ali introduced Salem to Amir Abdelgani and Fares Khallafalla near the Medina Mosque. The four then traveled to the safehouse where they discussed the bombing plans. At that time Siddig Ali indicated he wanted to bomb the United Nations and the Lincoln and Holland Tunnels. Siddig Ali outlined the proposed plan for three explosions five minutes apart, sometimes sketching on a piece of cardboard. The cardboard was later recovered at the safehouse.

Over the next few days, Siddig Ali and Amir Abdelgani (once accompanied by Salem) drove together to the Lincoln and Holland tunnels, the United Nations, and the Federal Building in Manhattan to scout the targets and examine traffic conditions. During one of these scouting trips, Amir suggested that they consider bombing the diamond district in Manhattan because that would be like "hitting Israel itself." At the United Nations, Siddig Ali noted that a bomb detonated at the entrance would topple the building. The men later gathered at the safehouse to discuss the operation.

On May 30, 1993, Hampton-El met with Siddig Ali and Salem at Hampton-El's safehouse, which he used for conducting business. Siddig Ali and Salem explained that they needed detonators, and Hampton-El said he would try to locate some for them. The three discussed the plan to blow up the United Nations and the tunnels. On June 4, 1993, Siddig Ali arranged to go with Salem to meet Mohammed Saleh. Siddig Ali explained to Salem that Saleh was an important supporter of jihad activities who might assist in the bombing campaign. Saleh was the owner of two gasoline stations in Yonkers, New York. During dinner at Saleh's house, Siddig Ali explained the bombing plan to Saleh, noting the different targets on a piece of paper. Salem was asked by Siddig Ali to eat the piece of paper once Siddig Ali felt that Saleh understood the plan. During dinner, Saleh agreed to help purchase military equipment.

Over the next few weeks, Siddig Ali brought Alvarez and Elhassan into the group. Various members of the group began to collect the items they believed were needed to prepare the bombs. The group also met frequently to refine the bombing plan. On June 13, 1993, Salem and Khallafalla purchased two timers for the bombs in Chinatown. On June 15 and 18, Hampton-El left messages for Siddig Ali indicating that he was still searching for detonators. On June 19, Amir Abdelgani, Khallafalla, Salem, Alvarez, and Siddig Ali met at Siddig Ali's house to discuss the details of the plan, including the number of people and bombs needed to carry it out. Siddig Ali indicated that they needed fertilizer, fuel, and stolen cars.

Amir, Alvarez, and Salem attempted on the evening of June 19 to buy stolen cars to deliver the bombs and to use as getaway cars during the bombing. Although they located a source for stolen cars, they did not have sufficient funds to purchase the cars. That same day, Elhassan met with a friend who was an engineer to discuss the feasibility of blowing up the tunnels and to determine where the weakest points of the tunnels were located.

On June 21, 1993, the group met at the Mosque and drove to the safehouse. Amir, Siddig Ali, and Elhassan discussed a method of communicating at the tunnels so that both of them would blow up at the same time, and planned their escapes after the bombing. Amir and Siddig Ali advised everyone that, if they were caught, not to talk until their lawyers were present. That evening Alvarez tried again, unsuccessfully, to obtain cars for the operation.

On June 22, 1993, after buying five 55-gallon steel barrels from a Newark drum business, Siddig Ali and Amir went to Saleh's gas station to get fuel for the bombs. Saleh agreed over the phone to provide the fuel. Belhabri, Saleh's employee, filled two of the drums with $140 worth of diesel fuel. Saleh agreed to keep two of the empty barrels in his garage. Siddig Ali and Amir did not pay for the fuel, but Belhabri made out a receipt on which he recorded the license plate of the van. Siddig Ali wrote a phony signature on the receipt.

The next day, June 23, Amir returned to Saleh's gas station with Fadil to fill the remaining three 55-gallon drums with diesel fuel. They met Saleh who called his employee at the other station to tell him to wait for the two so that they could get fuel before the station closed. Amir called Siddig Ali and asked if he could tell Fadil the bombing plan since Amir thought that Fadil would eventually catch on. Siddig Ali gave him permission to tell Fadil. Amir and Fadil obtained fuel. When Belhabri wrote out a receipt, Amir objected and called Saleh who then told Belhabri not to put the license number on the receipt but just to write "Sudanese." Belhabri provided $151 worth of fuel. At the same time, SiddigAli and Salem were purchasing more fertilizer for the bombs.

Later in the day, Alvarez gave Siddig Ali a 9mm semi-automatic rifle with an empty 25-round magazine. Siddig Ali and Salem took the gun from Alvarez's apartment in New Jersey to the safehouse. A little after 8 P.M. that evening, Amir and Fadil arrived at the safehouse with the fuel. Amir then washed down the van so that there would be no traces left of the fuel. For the next hour, Amir, Fadil, Siddig Ali, and Salem discussed the bombing plan. At one point, Fadil was asked whether he would participate, and he responded that he had to perform an Istikhara prayer (a prayer seeking divine intervention to guide one's decision in a course of action). After going to the Mosque to pray, Fadil met Elhassan and Alvarez, and they drove back to the safehouse.

Back at the safehouse, Amir began mixing the fuel and the fertilizer, and watched a videotape showing the tunnels that had been shot earlier in the day by Siddig Ali and Salem. Elhassan, Alvarez, and Fadil then returned, joined Amir, and began stirring the fuel and fertilizer together. They discussed the timers and the placement of bombs. At about 2 A.M. on the morning of June 24, FBI agents raided the safehouse and arrested the defendants, seizing the fuel and fertilizer mixture and the cardboard diagram Siddig Ali had periodically used to sketch the bombing plan.

A few hours before arrests were made at the safehouse, FBI agents arrested Saleh at his apartment in Yonkers. At FBI headquarters, Saleh denied having sold fuel to the men but said that Salem had come to his station demanding fuel on two occasions. About a week later on July 5, 1993, Saleh called one of his employees from prison and instructed him to tell Belhabri to destroy the two receipts documenting the fuel given to the Abdelganis and Siddig Ali. Saleh said that it would be "dangerous" for Belhabri if he failed to follow these instructions.

II. The Defense Case

The defendants presented their case for two months, calling 71 witnesses. Hampton-El, Elhassan, Alvarez, and Fadil Abdelgani each testified on his own behalf. The specific defenses put forth by the individual defendants will be set out below as they become relevant to particular claims on appeal. Siddig Ali, among others, was charged in the same indictment as the defendants but was not part of the trial because he pleaded guilty to all counts with which he was charged and cooperated, to a degree, with the Government.

III. Verdicts and Sentences

The jury trial in the case ran from January 9, 1995, to October 1, 1995. The jury returned verdicts finding defendants guilty on all submitted charges, except that Nosair and El-Gabrowny obtained not guilty verdicts on the Count Five bombing conspiracy charges. The defendants were sentenced as follows: Rahman and Nosair, life imprisonment; El-Gabrowny, 57 years; Alvarez, Hampton-El, Elhassan, and Saleh, 35 years; Amir Abdelgani and Khallafalla, 30 years; Fadil Abdelgani, 25 years. The sentences are more fully explained in Part IV(A), infra.

DISCUSSION

I. Constitutional Challenges

A. Seditious Conspiracy Statute and the Treason Clause

Defendant Nosair (joined by other defendants) contends that his conviction for seditious conspiracy, in violation of *18 U.S.C. §2384*, was illegal because it failed to satisfy the requirements of the Treason Clause of the U.S. Constitution, Art. III, 3.

Article III, Section 3 provides, in relevant part:

> Treason against the United States, shall consist only in levying War against them, or in adhering to their Enemies, giving them Aid and Comfort. No Person shall be convicted of Treason unless on the Testimony of two Witnesses to the same overt Act, or on Confession in open Court.

The seditious conspiracy statute provides:

> If two or more persons in any State or Territory, or in any place subject to the jurisdiction of the United States, conspire to overthrow, put down or to destroy by force the Government of the United States, or to levy war against them, or to oppose by force the authority thereof, or by force to prevent, hinder or delay the execution of any law of the United States, or by force to seize, take, or possess any property of the United States contrary to the authority thereof, they shall each be fined under this title or imprisoned not more than twenty years, or both.

18 U.S.C. §2384.

Nosair contends that because the seditious conspiracy statute punishes conspiracy to "levy war" against the United States without a conforming two-witness requirement, the statute is unconstitutional. He further claims that because his conviction for conspiracy to levy war against the United States was not based on the testimony of two witnesses to the same overt act, the conviction violates constitutional standards.

It is undisputed that Nosair's conviction was not supported by two witnesses to the same overt act. Accordingly the conviction must be overturned if the requirement of the Treason Clause applies to this prosecution for seditious conspiracy.

The plain answer is that the Treason Clause does not apply to the prosecution. The provisions of Article III, Section 3 apply to prosecutions for "treason." Nosair and his co-appellants were not charged with treason. Their offense of conviction, seditious conspiracy under Section 2384, differs from treason not only in name and associated stigma, but also in its essential elements and punishment.

In the late colonial period, as today, the charge of treason carried a "peculiar intimidation and stigma" with considerable "potentialities ... as a political epithet."

At the time of the drafting of the Constitution, furthermore, treason was punishable not only by death, but by an exceptionally cruel method of execution designed to enhance the suffering of the traitor. See 4 William Blackstone, Commentaries 92 (observing that the punishment for treason is "terrible" in that the traitor is "hanged by the neck, then cut down alive," that "his entrails [are then] taken out, and burned, while he is yet alive," "that his head [is] cut off," and that his "body [is then] divided into four parts"). In contrast, lesser subversive offenses were penalized by noncapital punishments or less brutal modes of execution. The Framers may have intended to limit the applicability of the most severe penalties—or simply the applicability of capital punishment for alleged subversion—to instances of levying war against, or adhering to enemies of, the United States. Today treason continues to be punishable by death, while seditious conspiracy commands a maximum penalty of twenty years imprisonment.

In recognition of the potential for political manipulation of the treason charge, the Framers may have formulated the Treason Clause as a protection against promiscuous resort to this particularly stigmatizing label, which carries such harsh consequences. It is thus possible to interpret the Treason Clause as applying only to charges denominated as "treason."

...

Seditious conspiracy by levying war includes no requirement that the defendant owe allegiance to the United States, an element necessary to conviction of treason. See *18 U.S.C. §2381* (defining "allegiance to United States" as an element of treason). Nosair nevertheless maintains that "the only distinction between the elements of seditious conspiracy under the levy war prong and treason by levying war is that the former requires proof of a conspiracy while the latter requires proof of the substantive crime." Noting that the requirement of allegiance appears explicitly in the treason statute, but not in the Treason Clause, Nosair suggests that allegiance to the United States is not an element of treason within the contemplation of the Constitution. He concludes that, for constitutional purposes, the elements constituting seditious conspiracy by levying war and treason by levying war are identical, and consequently that prosecutions for seditious conspiracy by levying war must conform to the requirements of the Treason Clause.

The argument rests on a false premise. The Treason Clause does not, as Nosair supposes, purport to specify the elements of the crime of treason. Instead, in addition to providing evidentiary safeguards, the Clause restricts the conduct that may be deemed treason to "levying war" against the United States and "adhering to their Enemies, giving them Aid and Comfort." It does not undertake to define the constituent elements of the substantive crime.

...

B. Seditious Conspiracy Statute and the First Amendment

Rahman, joined by the other appellants, contends that the seditious conspiracy statute, *18 U.S.C. §2384*, is an unconstitutional burden on free speech and the free exercise of religion in violation of the First Amendment. First, Rahman argues that the statute is facially invalid because it criminalizes protected expression and that it is overbroad and unconstitutionally vague. Second, Rahman contends that his conviction violated the First Amendment because it rested solely on his political views and religious practices.

1. Facial Challenge

a. *Restraint on Speech. Section 2384 provides:* If two or more persons in any State or Territory, or in any place subject to the jurisdiction of the United States, conspire to overthrow, put down, or destroy by force the Government of the United States, or to levy war against them, or to oppose by force the authority thereof, or by force to prevent, hinder, or delay the execution of any law of the United States, or by force to seize, take, or possess any property of the United States contrary to the authority thereof, they shall be fined under this title or imprisoned not more than twenty years, or both.

18 U.S.C. §2384.

As Section 2384 proscribes "speech" only when it constitutes an agreement to use force against the United States, Rahman's generalized First Amendment challenge to the statute is without merit. Our court has previously considered and rejected a First Amendment challenge to Section 2384.

...

2. Application of Section 2384 to Rahman's Case

Rahman also argues that he was convicted not for entering into any conspiratorial agreement that Congress may properly forbid, but "solely for his religious words and deeds" which, he contends, are protected by the First Amendment. In support of this claim, Rahman cites the Government's use in evidence of his speeches and writings.

There are two answers to Rahman's contention. The first is that freedoms of speech and of religion do not extend so far as to bar prosecution of one who uses a public speech or a religious ministry to commit crimes. Numerous crimes under the federal criminal code are, or can be, committed by speech alone. As examples: Section 2 makes it an offense to "counsel," "command," "induce" or "procure" the commission of an offense against the United States. *18 U.S.C. §2(a)*. Section 371 makes it a crime to "conspire ... to commit any offense against the United States." *18 U.S.C. §371*. Section 373, with which Rahman was charged, makes it a crime to "solicit, command, induce, or otherwise endeavor to persuade" another person to commit a crime of violence. *18 U.S.C. §373(a)*. Various other statutes, like Section 2384, criminalize conspiracies of specified objectives, see, e.g., *18 U.S.C. §1751(d)* (conspiracy to kidnap); *18 U.S.C. §1951* (conspiracy to interfere with commerce through robbery, extortion, or violence); *21 U.S.C. §846* conspiracy to violate drug laws). All of these offenses are characteristically committed through speech. Notwithstanding that political speech and religious exercise are among the activities most jealously guarded by the First Amendment, one is not immunized from prosecution for such speech-based offenses merely because one commits them through the medium of political speech or religious preaching. Of course, courts must be vigilant to insure [sic] that prosecutions are not improperly based on the mere expression of unpopular ideas. But if the evidence shows that the speeches crossed the line into criminal solicitation, procurement of criminal activity, or conspiracy to violate the laws, the prosecution is permissible.

The evidence justifying Rahman's conviction for conspiracy and solicitation showed beyond a reasonable doubt that he crossed this line. His speeches were not simply the expression of ideas; in some instances they constituted the crime of conspiracy to wage war on the United States under Section 2384 and solicitation of attack on the United States military installations, as well as of the murder of Egyptian President Hosni Mubarak under Section 373.

For example:

Rahman told Salem he "should make up with God ... by turning his rifle's barrel to President Mubarak's chest, and killing him."

On another occasion, speaking to Abdo Mohammed Haggag about murdering President Mubarak during his visit to the United States, Rahman told Haggag, "Depend on God. Carry out this operation. It does not require a fatwa ... You are ready in training, but do it. Go ahead."

The evidence further showed that Siddig Ali consulted with Rahman about the bombing of the United Nations Headquarters, and Rahman told him, "Yes, it's a must, it's a duty."

On another occasion, when Rahman was asked by Salem about bombing the United Nations, he counseled against it on the ground that it would be "bad for Muslims," but added that Salem should "find a plan to destroy or to bomb or to ... inflict damage to the American Army."

Words of this nature—ones that instruct, solicit, or persuade others to commit crimes of violence—violate the law and may be properly prosecuted regardless of whether they are uttered in private, or in a public speech, or in administering the duties of a religious ministry. The fact that his speech or conduct was "religious" does not immunize him from prosecution under generally-applicable criminal statutes.

Rahman also protests the Government's use in evidence of his speeches, writings, and preachings that did not in themselves constitute the crimes of solicitation or conspiracy. He is correct that the Government placed in evidence many instances of Rahman's writings and speeches in which Rahman expressed his opinions within the protection of the First Amendment. However, while the First Amendment fully protects Rahman's right to express hostility against the United States, and he may not be prosecuted for so speaking, it does not prevent the use of such speeches or writings in evidence when relevant to prove a pertinent fact in a criminal prosecution. The Government was free to demonstrate Rahman's resentment and hostility toward the United States in order to show his motive for soliciting and procuring illegal attacks against the United States and against President Mubarak of Egypt. See *Mitchell, 508 U.S. at 487* ("The First Amendment … does not prohibit the evidentiary use of speech to establish the elements of a crime or to prove motive or intent."); *United States v. Hoffman, 806 F.2d 703, 708-09 (7th Cir. 1986)* (evidence of religious affiliation relevant to show defendant's motive to threaten President, because defendant leader of religious group was imprisoned by Government at time of threats).

Furthermore, Judge Mukasey properly protected against the danger that Rahman might be convicted because of his unpopular religious beliefs that were hostile to the United States. He explained to the jury the limited use it was entitled to make of the material received as evidence of motive. He instructed that a defendant could not be convicted on the basis of his beliefs or the expression of them—even if those beliefs favored violence. He properly instructed the jury that it could find a defendant guilty only if the evidence proved he committed a crime charged in the indictment.

We reject Rahman's claim that his conviction violated his rights under the First Amendment.

…

3. Rahman

Rahman argues that the evidence presented by the Government was insufficient to support a conviction for any of the counts with which he was charged. Rahman asserts that he had limited contact with most of the other defendants, that he was physically incapable, due to his blindness, of participating in the "operational" aspects of the conspiracies, and that there was little direct evidence of his knowledge of many of the events in question. We find Rahman's claims unavailing.

a. Seditious Conspiracy and Bombing Conspiracy. To support a conviction for seditious conspiracy under *18 U.S.C. §2384*, the Government must demonstrate that: (1) in a State, or Territory, or place subject to the jurisdiction of the United States, (2) two or more persons conspired to "levy war against" or "oppose by force the authority of" the United States government, and (3) that the defendant was a member of the conspiracy. *18 U.S.C. §2384*.

First, we find ample evidence in the record to support the jury's finding that there was indeed a conspiracy to "levy war" against the United States. Over the course of the trial, the jury was presented with considerable evidence of a conspiracy. The evidence included the fact that many of the defendants in this case, as well as many the World Trade Center defendants, participated in military training exercises the purpose of which was to train members to carry out jihad "operations." Appellant Nosair murdered Kahane in 1990, assisted by Salameh (who had been present at the training sessions). Among Nosair's possessions, the Government found notebooks describing "war" on the enemies of Islam and the manner of prosecuting such, including "exploding … their high world buildings," as well as manuals on guerilla warfare tactics and explosives.

Salameh, Yousef, and Abouhalima, the bombers of the World Trade Center, had considerable phone contact and/or direct contact with El-Gabrowny, Nosair, and Rahman in the weeks leading up to the bombing. Siddig Ali assisted Abouhalima's flight from the United States following the bombing. Rahman also encouraged Salem to murder Mubarak and issued a fatwa calling for the murder. In accordance with this call to duty, Siddig Ali plotted to assassinate Mubarak in March of 1993. The Abdelganis, Saleh, Elhassan, Hampton-El, and Alvarez engaged in a plot to bomb the Lincoln and Holland Tunnels and the United Nations. They purchased fuel, fertilizers, and timers and actively sought detonators. They had begun construction of the explosives when they were arrested. Each of these acts was connected by myriad contacts between the defendants. These illustrative acts, coupled with other evidence presented at trial, convince us that there is ample evidence to support the jury's conclusion that there was a conspiracy to "levy war" on the United States, and that the conspiracy contemplated the use of force.

As to Rahman's individual claim, there is also sufficient evidence to support the conclusion that he was in fact a member of the conspiracy. While there is no evidence that Rahman personally participated in the performance of the conspiracy, when conspiracy is charged, the Government is not required to show that the defendant personally performed acts in its furtherance: it is sufficient for the defendant to join in the illegal agreement. The evidence showed that Rahman was in constant contact with other members of the conspiracy, that he was looked to as a leader, and that he accepted that role and encouraged his co-conspirators to engage in violent acts against the United States.

Rahman discussed the results of the paramilitary training with Abouhalima and Nosair, and encouraged his followers to conduct jihad, including acts of violence, against the United States. During a visit to Nosair at Attica, Nosair instructed Shinawy to seek a fatwa from Rahman regarding a plan to bomb various targets. Siddig Ali reported to Rahman concerning the resumed paramilitary training. Rahman encouraged Salem to conduct jihad by killing Mubarak and issued a fatwa for Mubarek's death. Rahman made numerous calls overseas, including calls to a number in Pakistan that was inscribed in a bombing manual carried by convicted World Trade Center bomber Yousef. Rahman also had frequent contact with other members of the conspiracy including El-Gabrowny, Abouhalima, and Salameh in the weeks leading up to the World Trade Center bombing.

Siddig Ali told Salem that Rahman had referred to the Spring 1993 bombing campaign as a "must" and a "duty." Siddig Ali also told Salem that he was free to discuss the plot with Rahman, but to do so in general terms so as to keep Rahman insulated. Although Rahman did advise against making the United Nations a bombing target because that would be bad for Muslims, he advised Salem to seek a different target (U.S. military installations) for the bombings, and to plan for them carefully. In that same conversation, he also warned Salem to be careful around Siddig Ali, who he suspected was a traitor. Rahman then sought out the traitor in his group, having a long discussion with Salem and Siddig Ali over who was the traitor. This evidence shows that a reasonable trier of fact could have found that Rahman was a member of the conspiracy and that he was in fact its leader.

As to the bombing conspiracy count, the Government must prove: (1) that Rahman was a member of a conspiracy to "destroy, by means of fire or explosives, any building, vehicle or other real or personal property" in interstate commerce, *18 U.S.C. §§371*, 844(i); and (2) that one or more of the conspirators did "any act to effect the object of the conspiracy." *18 U.S.C. §371*. Even if we assume that this count is limited to the Spring 1993 plot, there is clear evidence to support a reasonable conclusion that there was a conspiracy of which Rahman was a member, and that the conspirators had taken overt acts "to effect the object" thereof. The conspirators had, among other things: (1) scouted the Lincoln and Holland Tunnels; (2) contributed rent for a place to make the bombs; (3) purchased fuel oil, fertilizer, and timers from which to make the bombs; and (4) begun mixing the fuel and fertilizer.

Particularly relevant to the finding of Rahman's membership are the statements of Siddig Ali to Salem that Rahman had issued a fatwa for the Spring 1993 bombing plot, and had called it a "must" and a "duty." Although Rahman wavered on the target of the bombing during his conversation with Salem, he nonetheless approved bombing as the method and suggested alternative targets. Rahman and Siddig Ali met together several times during the bombing preparations. On June 17, 1993, less than two weeks before the anticipated bombing, Rahman held a press conference (using Siddig Ali as his translator) during which he warned that the United States would pay a terrible price for supporting Mubarak.

This evidence, taken together, was sufficient to support a reasonable conclusion that Rahman was guilty of the bombing conspiracy.

...

Rahman submitted lengthy offers of proof on the subjects to be covered by the proposed testimony. These offers, from which we quote extensively below, were submitted in a letter from one of Rahman's lawyers. Counsel argued that this testimony would help the jury to understand Rahman's ministerial relationship with his co-defendants, and would show that his conversations with them amounted only to "legitimate and well-recognized religious practice" rather than a criminal conspiracy. The points to be covered by the proposed expert testimony fell into several different categories. Most of the material provided general information about Islam and suggested that Rahman's actions and statements were governed by Islamic law. These included the following statements:

"Islam" means submission to the will of God.

[A] strict monotheism is at the heart of Islamic theology.

Polytheism (shirk) is the concept of worshiping more than one god and is anathema to the strict monotheism of Moslems.

Muslim clerics' sermons are frequently combined with Quranic references ....

The Arabic word "sharia" refers to the corpus of Islamic law which is derived from two main sources, the Quran and the sayings of the Prophet as well as analogical reasoning and the consensus of scholars ....

Islam ... started in the 7th Century A.D. and now claims one billion adherents in the world.

The five pillars or basic precepts of Islam [are] Faith, Prayer, Alms, Pilgrimage, and Fasting.

Muslim clerics and scholars have preached about ... a Muslim's necessity to engage in jihad ....

Jihad [had its] origins in Islam after Prophet Mohammed began preaching in the 7th Century ....

Jihad is cast in the mold of a legal doctrine ….

Jihad has come to mean … the combatting of oppression ….

The Muslim community as a whole has a collective duty or obligation to engage in armed struggle in the path of God [, which] must be organized and announced by a Caliph or Sultan. It is only when the enemy attacks Muslim territory that jihad becomes an individual duty ….

It is an individual obligation for able-bodied Muslims from all over to come to the aid of their brethren [and] jihad is governed by a very clear set of rules such as an invitation to embrace Islam, treatment of prisoners and division of spoils.

[A] person who provides a fatwa is called a Mufti.

According to Islamic law a leadership cannot be conferred on a blind person.

An Imam … leads communal prayer and … a sheik is … an elder who is accorded respect and deference.

[A] sheik may also be a scholar in which case he has … certain duties [including] to lead the Muslims in prayer and deliver a Friday sermon, … provide lessons and religious instruction, … to provide advice, counsel and mediation in situations of dispute, and … where he is questioned on a matter involving the interpretation of Islamic law, to provide … a nonbinding advisory opinion ….

When a scholar is being asked to render an opinion about a subject matter for which he knows the answer he may not simply dismiss the questioner and … to do so would erode his authority ….

Letter from Abdeen Jabara, counsel for Rahman, to Andrew C. McCarthy, Asst. U.S. Atty. (July 7, 1995) (hereinafter "Jabara Letter").

We find no abuse of discretion in Judge Mukasey's rejection of this testimony. The vast majority of what was proffered was not relevant to the issues before the jury. If the evidence showed that Rahman conspired to levy war against the United States or solicited others to commit crimes of violence—including mass killing and destruction through the blowing up of buildings and tunnels—it would not constitute a defense that he was justified in doing so within a framework of Islamic law.

One of the issues stressed by defense counsel in the argument on the admissibility of the testimony was the fact that an Islamic scholar, when asked to render an opinion, "may not simply dismiss the questioner … [without] eroding his authority, stature and position as a scholar." We agree with the District Judge that such details of Islamic tradition were irrelevant to the issues before the jury. As a matter of United States law, the fact that a Mufti or scholar must render an opinion when asked would neither explain nor excuse solicitation to commit acts of terrorism and violence when rendering that opinion.

…

CONCLUSION

The ten defendants were accorded a full and fair jury trial lasting nine months. They were vigorously defended by able counsel. The prosecutors conducted themselves in the best traditions of the high standards of the Office of the United States Attorney for the Southern District of New York. The trial judge, the Honorable Michael B. Mukasey, presided with extraordinary skill and patience, assuring fairness to the prosecution and to each defendant and helpfulness to the jury. His was an outstanding achievement in the face of challenges far beyond those normally endured by a trial judge.

We have considered all of the other claims raised on appeal by all of the defendants, beyond those discussed in this opinion, and conclude that they are without merit. The convictions of all ten defendants are affirmed. With the exception of the sentence of defendant El-Gabrowny, which is remanded for further proceedings as set forth in this opinion, the sentences of all the other defendants are affirmed.

Another member of al-Qa'eda that the government chose to prosecute in federal court, rather than a military commission, was Richard Reid, the so-called shoe bomber who, in December 2001, attempted to blow up an airliner while in flight. Reid raised a variety of issues to include a violation of First Amendment rights.

UNITED STATES v. REID
United States Court of Appeals for the First Circuit
369 F.3d 619 (1st Cir. 2004)

LYNCH, Circuit Judge:

On December 22, 2001, Richard Reid tried unsuccessfully to destroy American Airlines Flight 63 over the Atlantic Ocean by detonating explosives hidden in his shoes. The plane was diverted to Boston, where Reid was arrested. On October 4, 2002, Reid pleaded guilty to eight terrorism-related offenses, n1 and on January 30, 2003, he was sentenced to serve the remainder of his life in prison. At the sentencing hearing, Reid declared his continuing allegiance to the terrorist Osama bin Laden, adding: "I think I ought not apologize for my actions. I am at war with your country ...." A few days later, Reid was transferred from Massachusetts to a maximum security federal prison in Florence, Colorado (ADX Florence), where he remains today.

This interlocutory appeal concerns the conditions of Reid's pre-sentence confinement. Reid contends that the government violated his *First Amendment* rights by restricting his access to news media while he was detained in Massachusetts. As a federal prisoner housed at the Massachusetts Correctional Institute at Cedar Junction, Reid was permitted to use funds from his prison account to purchase a subscription to *Time* magazine. Under a set of "special administrative measures" imposed on Reid by the U.S. Marshals Service (USMS) at the direction of the Attorney General, an FBI special agent removed the "letters to the editor" section from each issue of *Time* (the *Time* letters) before giving the magazine to Reid. The special agent also clipped two articles about terrorism from the magazine and withheld them from Reid. Reid petitioned the district court for access to the withheld material on *First Amendment* grounds. After a hearing on January 21, 2003, the district court denied Reid's request.

We conclude this appeal has been overtaken by changes in the factual and legal circumstances of Reid's confinement. Although there remains a substantial dispute between the parties concerning Reid's access to Time, we nonetheless dismiss the appeal under the branch of the mootness doctrine barring courts from deciding a case when no practical consequences would flow from the decision.

I

A. Special Administrative Measures

(SAM)

Reid challenges the "special administrative measures" (SAMs) that governed his confinement while in Massachusetts. The Attorney General's power to promulgate SAMs for individual prisoners derives from *28 C.F.R. §501.3* ("Prevention of acts of violence and terrorism"). See *Yousef v. Reno, 254 F.3d 1214, 1219 (10th Cir. 2001)*. That regulation permits the Attorney General, who has plenary power over the management of federal prisons, see *18 U.S.C. §4001(b)*, to impose on any individual prisoner "special administrative measures that are reasonably necessary to protect persons against the risk of death or serious bodily injury." *§501.3(a)*. To impose such SAMs, the Attorney General or the head of any federal law enforcement or intelligence agency must certify that, with respect to the prisoner in question, there is a substantial risk that [the] prisoner's communications or contacts with persons could result in death or serious bodily injury to persons, or substantial damage to property that would entail the risk of death or serious bodily injury to persons.

Once authorized, SAMs may impose restrictions on the inmate's housing or privileges, including correspondence, visiting, interviews with representatives of the news media, and use of the telephone, as is reasonably necessary to protect persons against the risk of acts of violence or terrorism. The affected prisoner must be notified of the SAMs and the basis for their imposition. *§501.3(b)*.

SAMs are not indefinite in duration. Before the September 11, 2001 terrorist attacks, the risk assessment underlying a set of SAMs was deemed valid for 120 days; when that period expired, a new risk assessment had to be conducted before the SAMs could be reimposed. *Yousef, 254 F.3d at 1219*; *United States v. Johnson, 223 F.3d 665, 672 (7th Cir. 2000)*. After the September 11 attacks, the Bureau of Prisons amended *§501.3* to permit SAMs to remain in force for up to a full year with the approval of the Attorney General. *§501.3(c)*; see *66 Fed. Reg. 55062, 55062 (Oct. 31, 2001)*. The agency justified the extension by stating that the September 11 attacks had demonstrated "beyond question" that some terrorist conspiracies "are carried out over a long period—far in excess of 120 days." *66 Fed. Reg. at 55063*. Though a prisoner might have limited ability to assist such efforts, the agency found, that fact "does not diminish the urgent need for law enforcement authorities to curb the inmate's ability to participate in planning or facilitating those acts through communications with others within or outside the detention facility."

B. SAMs Imposed on Reid

In February 2002, approximately two months after Flight 63 landed in Boston, the Attorney General authorized the USMS to issue SAMs regulating Reid's pre-trial confinement. Cf. *28 C.F.R. §501.3(f)* allowing branches of the Justice Department other than the Bureau of Prisons to issue SAMs for persons in their custody. After the district court objected to the initial version of Reid's SAMs, see *United States v. Reid, 214 F. Supp. 2d 84, 92 (D. Mass. 2002)*, a new version was issued on June 19, 2002. It was under the June 2002 SAMs that the USMS restricted Reid's access to *Time* magazine.

The June 2002 SAMs purported to control all of Reid's written and recorded communications, including his receipt of written materials. Under the caption "Inmate Communications Prohibitions," the document provided:

> The inmate is prohibited from passing or receiving any written or recorded communications to or from any other inmate, visitor, or anyone else except as outlined and allowed by this document.

The SAMs then set forth detailed rules governing Reid's access to visitors, telephone calls, and legal, consular, and non-legal mail. Reid's *Time* subscription qualified as incoming non-legal mail:

> (Non-legal/Non-consular) Mail—Any mail not clearly and properly addressed to/from the inmate's attorney and marked privileged, or consular mail (incoming or outgoing):
>
> i. Copied—Shall be copied (including the surface of the envelope) by the warden, or his/her designee, of the facility in which the inmate is housed.
>
> ii. Forwarded—Shall be forwarded, in copy form, to the location designated by the FBI ....
>
> iv. Mail Seizure—If outgoing/incoming mail is determined by USMS or FBI to contain overt or covert discussions of or requests for illegal activities, the soliciting or encouraging of acts of violence or terrorism, or actual or attempted circumvention of SAM, the mail shall not be delivered/forwarded. The inmate shall be notified in writing of the seizure of any mail.

These were the only provisions in the June 2002 SAMs pertaining to Reid's *Time* subscription.

C. Reid's Motions for Access to Time

Reid initially challenged these restrictions in June 2002, when he indicated his intent to subscribe to *Time* and filed a motion to prevent the government from interfering with the magazine's delivery. Because Reid had not yet subscribed to Time, however, the district court denied the motion as not ripe.

Reid actually began subscribing to *Time* in September 2002. Initially, it appears, the magazine was delivered to him complete and without undue delay. Then, on October 30, the government informed defense counsel that it had removed an article about terrorism from Reid's October 21, 2002 issue of *Time* under the "Mail Seizure" provision of the SAMs. Reid tried to challenge that decision through administrative channels, cf. *28 C.F.R. §501.3(e)* providing that inmates subjected to SAMs may seek review through an administrative process, but the government successfully took the position that administrative remedies were unavailable to Reid, apparently because he had not yet been sentenced.

Reid responded by filing a renewed motion in the district court to enjoin the government from interfering with his *Time* subscription. He argued that government's censorship of his subscription violated his *First Amendment* rights. Reid also sought permission to purchase a radio, which was prohibited by the SAMs.

The government defended the SAMs and their application to Reid's *Time* subscription and radio request as reasonably necessary for valid penological and national security purposes. The government justified this argument in part by reference to materials filed under seal. Certain outbound correspondence from Reid had been seized during his confinement in Massachusetts. The substance of that correspondence is not at issue in this case; the government submitted it simply to substantiate its claim (articulated in public) that Reid had indeed attempted to communicate with others while in custody. The government also emphasized that Reid is an admitted member of al Qaeda, a terrorist organization that, according to the government, trains its members to exploit "innocent-looking" communications to relay coded messages to and from prison in the event of capture.

On January 2, 2003, the district court held a hearing on Reid's motion. As to the radio, the motion was denied, and Reid has not appealed that decision. As to *Time* magazine, the court denied Reid's motion as moot after the government offered to give Reid the only two *Time* articles it had yet seized under the SAMs. The court agreed to be available on short notice if the government further interfered with Reid's access to the magazine.

Approximately one week later, Reid filed another motion concerning his *Time* subscription. He explained that the government had informed him after the January 2 hearing that (1) all further issues of *Time* magazine would be held by the USMS for thirty days before delivery, with the possibility that some terrorism-related materials would be withheld longer or even permanently, and that (2) all letters to the editor would be removed and withheld permanently. He again sought to enjoin the government from interfering with the complete and prompt delivery of the magazine.

A new hearing was scheduled for January 21. The government told the district court that withholding the *Time* letters was necessary to ensure that *Time* did not unwittingly become a vehicle for al Qaeda agents to convey coded messages to Reid in prison. The defense attacked that argument, pointing out that *Time* publishes only 2 to 3 percent of the letters it receives and that those letters are subject to fact-checking and other editorial control. The government responded that deleting the letters was a reasonable exercise of penological discretion under the SAMs because coded messages in the letters—the possibility of which, the government said, could not be ruled out completely—might provoke "outbursts" by Reid and might enable him to continue his criminal activities through outgoing correspondence.

The district court expressed some skepticism about the government's argument, observing:

> Mr. Reid is a very tall individual. But he's not ten feet tall. And this constant reiteration of we've got to keep data away from him, we've got to keep his data out of the hands of the public lest disaster befall, respectfully, is wearing a bit thin.

Nevertheless, the court denied Reid's motion on the ground that the SAMs permitted the restriction:

> I don't see any right that [Reid] has articulated to receive Time Magazine that would overcome the appropriate general concerns set forth in the SAMs. I've respected the SAMs throughout …. And while I see nothing wrong with letting him have Time Magazine … I see no right for him to have Time Magazine.

The court added that it was persuaded to rule for the government in part because of Reid's "ongoing intent" to harm the United States: "I make no bones about that. This man shows an ongoing intent of hostility to the United States and I, I have that very much in mind."

Reid filed this interlocutory appeal on January 27, 2003. Three days later, on January 30, Reid was sentenced to life in prison, and on the following day he was committed to the custody of the Bureau of Prisons (BOP). On February 4, 2003, the BOP transferred Reid from Massachusetts to ADX Florence, the maximum security facility in Colorado where he will serve his sentence.

II

On appeal, Reid asks this court to decide three questions: (i) whether the June 2002 SAMs were procedurally invalid; (ii) whether those SAMs were unconstitutionally overbroad under the *First Amendment*; and (iii) whether the USMS's withholding of the *Time* letters under the June 2002 SAMs violated Reid's *First Amendment* rights. The government defends the SAMs but also urges dismissal on a variety of grounds, including (1) that this court lacks appellate jurisdiction over

Reid's interlocutory appeal, and (2) that this appeal has been mooted by events after the district court denied Reid's motion, including the expiration of the June 2002 SAMs and Reid's February 2003 transfer to ADX Florence.

For the reasons explained below, we conclude that Reid's appeal to this court is moot. Accordingly, we do not reach the government's challenge to our appellate jurisdiction.

…

In lay terms, we recognize, it might be somewhat odd to describe Reid's claims in this case as "moot." Without a doubt, there is a substantial and continuing dispute between Reid and the government concerning his access to *Time* magazine. The government still has not turned over the *Time* letters that it seized; Reid still demands access to those letters. In that pragmatic sense, the controversy remains "live" and the parties adverse.

The problem is that even if this court decided the questions raised in Reid's appeal, the pragmatic dispute between the parties would be unaffected. That is because the factual and legal circumstances surrounding Reid's case have changed so dramatically that Reid no longer asserts an injury that is "likely to be redressed by a favorable judicial decision" in this proceeding. *Spencer v. Kemna, 523 U.S. 1, 7, 140 L. Ed. 2d 43, 118 S. Ct. 978 (1998)* (quoting *Lewis, 494 U.S. at 477*). Any opinion on the merits of Reid's appeal to this court would be merely advisory. Accordingly, we have no choice but to dismiss the case as moot.

We reach this conclusion for several reasons. First, the June 2002 SAMs—the regulations that Reid challenges on constitutional and procedural grounds—are no longer in effect. By regulation, those SAMs expired on June 19, 2003, one year after their adoption. See *28 C.F.R. §501.3(c)*. No interest of Reid's would be served by invalidating them now: the June 2002 SAMs no longer determine his conditions of confinement, and there is no claim for damages (actual or nominal) for Reid's alleged deprivations while those SAMs were still in effect. Cf. *Mr. & Mrs. R., 321 F.3d at 17* (changed circumstances do not moot claims for money damages). As we observed in the Daley case, which similarly involved an attack on a regulation that expired while the litigation was pending, "this court has no means of redressing either procedural failures or substantive deficiencies associated with a regulation that is now defunct." 292 F.3d at 88.

Moreover, the BOP has imposed on Reid a new set of SAMs, effective August 14, 2003, at the ADX Florence facility in Colorado (the Colorado SAMs). Unlike the June 2002 SAMs, the Colorado SAMs contain provisions specifically regulating Reid's access to the mass media. The *Time* letters initially seized by the USMS in Massachusetts have been forwarded to ADX Florence, where the FBI has seized them anew under the mass media provisions of the Colorado SAMs. As a result, even an order from this court finding that the June 2002 SAMs were unconstitutional would not result in Reid's recovery of the seized *Time* letters. The Colorado SAMs—the only basis for the government's continued withholding of the *Time* letters—are not before us.

In relevant part, the SAMs governing Reid's confinement at ADX Florence provide:

Access to Mass Communications: To prevent the inmate from receiving and acting upon critically-timed information or information coded in a potentially undetectable manner, the inmate's access to materials of mass communication is restricted as follows:

a.   Periodicals/Newspapers

…

ii. Sections of the periodical/newspaper which offer a forum for information to be passed by unknown and/or unverified individuals, including but not limited to classified advertisements

and letters to the editor, should be removed from the periodicals/newspapers prior to distribution to the inmate.

...

Nor has Reid articulated any persuasive reason why this court should decide his appeal notwithstanding the expiration of the June 2002 SAMs and his transfer to ADX Florence. This is not
a case involving a defendant's property interest in something taken by the government—defense
counsel made clear at oral argument that Reid is not interested in an order declaring that the *Time*
letters are his property and must be returned to his family or to his lawyer. Cf. *Fed. R. Crim. P.
41(g)* (authorizing motions for the return of seized property).

Rather, Reid contends that this appeal is not moot because a judgment from this court would
assist him in future litigation against BOP officials in Colorado. We disagree. This is not an appeal
in a civil case; it is an interlocutory appeal from the denial of a motion in a criminal prosecution. If
Reid were to prevail, his remedy would be simply the reversal of the district court's January 21,
2003 order. Plainly, the Colorado SAMs would not be affected by our reversal of that order, which
was predicated on the now-expired June 2002 SAMs and which the district court itself did not
believe would apply beyond the date of sentencing.

...

The appeal is dismissed and the district court order below is vacated. So ordered.

A cornerstone law enforcement tool for prosecuting those accused of engaging in domestic
terrorism is the so-called Material Support Act contained in the Antiterrorism and Effective Death
Penalty Act of 1996. The Material Support Act is an independent substantive offense used as a
basis for early intervention where the alleged terrorist activity is "nipped in the bud." Embodied
in two sections, the law makes it a criminal offense for anyone to provide *material support or
resources* to a terrorist group so designated by the Secretary of State (18 U.S.C. §1189 (2000)).
This means that it is a federal crime to provide almost anything of value, including training,
money, or personnel to such terror groups. If no deaths are involved, the maximum penalty is up
to fifteen years in jail. On the other hand, if the death of any person results from the support activities, the offender can be incarcerated for any term or for life. The impact of the Material Support
Act on law enforcement is significant; it "may be the most significant doctrinal development in
the federal criminal law since the enactment of RICO and the other organizational crime statutes,
the money laundering statutes, and the criminal forfeiture laws [because] [t]hey show how each
new federal criminal 'war'—from Prohibition through the wars on organized crime, on illegal
drugs, and now on terror—has spawned new laws or legal doctrines designed to expand the
[grasp] of the federal government's criminal enforcement arm."

Despite concerns regarding the expansiveness of the Material Support Act and its effect on
civil liberties, it must be acknowledged that the Act has become a vital weapon on the homefront
in addressing the breakup of "sleeper" cells in the Global War on Terrorism. Indeed, because
many of the dozens of cases have been resolved by guilty pleas, relatively few have produced
lower court opinions interpreting the provisions.

Providing material support to terrorists
18 U.S.C.A. §2339A (West 2000 & Supp. 2004)

(a) Offense—Whoever provides material support or resources or conceals or disguises the nature, location, source, or ownership of material support or resources, knowing or intending that they are to be used in preparation for, or in carrying out, a violation of section 32, 37, 81, 175, 229, 351, 831, 842(m) or (n), 844(f) or (i), 930(c), 956, 1114, 1116, 1203, 1361, 1362, 1363, 1366, 1751, 1992, 1993, 2155, 2156, 2280, 2281, 2332, 2332a, 2332b, 2332f, or 2340A of this title, section 236 of the Atomic Energy Act of 1954 (42 U.S.C. 2284), or section 46502 or 60123(b) of title 49, or in preparation for, or in carrying out, the concealment of an escape from the commission of any such violation, or attempts or conspires to do such an act, shall be fined under this title, imprisoned not more than 15 years, or both, and, if the death of any person results, shall be imprisoned for any term of years or for life ….

(b) Definition—In this section, the term "material support or resources" means currency or monetary instruments or financial securities, financial services, lodging, training, expert advice or assistance, safehouses, false documentation or identification, communications equipment, facilities, weapons, lethal substances, explosives, personnel, transportation, and other physical assets, except medicine or religious materials.

Providing material support or resources to designated foreign terrorist organizations
18 U.S.C.A. § 2339B (West 2000 & Supp. 2004)

(a) Prohibited activities.

   (1) Unlawful conduct. Whoever, within the United States or subject to the jurisdiction of the United States, knowingly provides material support or resources to a foreign terrorist organization, or attempts or conspires to do so, shall be fined under this title or imprisoned not more than 15 years, or both, and, if the death of any person results, shall be imprisoned for any term of years or for life ….

(g) Definitions. As used in this section …

   (4) the term "material support or resources" has the same meaning as in section 2339A; …

   (6) the term "terrorist organization" means an organization designated as a terrorist organization under section 219 of the Immigration and Nationality Act.

The Material Support Act provides the government with the ability to obtain convictions without having to prove a specific intent to engage in or to further acts of terrorism. While the law does not penalize membership in a terror group, it does outlaw material support. Thus, the government need only show that the individual knowingly provided the proscribed group with some material support, which in many of the cases so far adjudicated has involved attendance at a terror training camp in Afghanistan. To date, federal judges have largely upheld the legality of the statute and numerous members of terror sleeper cells have been convicted, including New York's Lackawanna Six.

Many have expressed concern that the Material Support Act, as it is currently enforced, grants the Secretary of State too much latitude in designating which organizations qualify as terrorist organizations. Some have even argued that terrorist organizations savvy enough to compartmentalize themselves into different sub-organizations would still be able to receive contributions to assist their non-military activities. Moreover, the designation of a terrorist organization by the State Department under the statute remains subject to a rigorous administrative procedure which requires all conclusions to be supported with exhaustive fact finding, the opportunity for congressional members to object to the designation prior to its publication in the Federal Register and the organization itself allowed to appeal its designation to the D.C. Circuit of the U.S. Court of Appeals. These facts alone demonstrate that the United States is determined to vigorously fight terror before it strikes without succumbing to a "Star Chamber" mentality that threatens the civil liberties of all in the name of security.

UNITED STATES OF AMERICA v. HAMMOUD
United States Court of Appeals for the Fourth Circuit
381 F.3d 316 (4th Cir. 2004)

WILKINS, Chief Judge:

Mohammed Hammoud appeals the sentence imposed following his convictions of numerous offenses, all of which are connected to his support of Hezbollah, a designated foreign terrorist organization (FTO) .... We now set forth the reasoning for our judgment.

I. Facts

The facts underlying Hammoud's convictions and sentence are largely undisputed. We therefore recount them briefly.

A. Hezbollah

Hezbollah is an organization founded by Lebanese Shi'a Muslims in response to the 1982 invasion of Lebanon by Israel. Hezbollah provides various forms of humanitarian aid to Shi'a Muslims in Lebanon. However, it is also a strong opponent of Western presence in the Middle East, and it advocates the use of terrorism in support of its agenda. Hezbollah is particularly opposed to the existence of Israel and to the activities of the American government in the Middle East. Hezbollah's general secretary is Hassan Nasserallah, and its spiritual leader is Sheikh Fadlallah.

B. Hammoud

In 1992, Hammoud, a citizen of Lebanon, attempted to enter the United States on fraudulent documents. After being detained by the INS, Hammoud sought asylum. While the asylum application was pending, Hammoud moved to Charlotte, North Carolina, where his brothers and cousins were living. Hammoud ultimately obtained permanent resident status by marrying a United States citizen.

At some point in the mid-1990s, Hammoud, his wife, one of his brothers, and his cousins all became involved in a cigarette smuggling operation. The conspirators purchased large quantities of cigarettes in North Carolina, smuggled them to Michigan, and sold them without paying Michigan taxes. This scheme took advantage of the fact that Michigan imposes a tax of $7.50 per carton of cigarettes, while the North Carolina tax is only 50 [cents]. It is estimated that the conspiracy involved a quantity of cigarettes valued at roughly $7.5 million and that the state of Michigan was deprived of $3 million in tax revenues.

In 1996, Hammoud began leading weekly prayer services for Shi'a Muslims in Charlotte. These services were often conducted at Hammoud's home. At these meetings, Hammoud—who is acquainted with both Nasserallah and Fadlallah, as well as Sheikh Abbas Harake, a senior military commander for Hezbollah—urged the attendees to donate money to Hezbollah. Hammoud would then forward the money to Harake. The Government's evidence demonstrated that on one occasion, Hammoud donated $3,500 of his own money to Hezbollah.

Based on these and other activities, Hammoud was charged with various immigration violations, sale of contraband cigarettes, money laundering, mail fraud, credit card fraud, and racketeering. Additionally, Hammoud was charged with conspiracy to provide material support to a designated FTO and with providing material support to a designated FTO, both in violation of *18 U.S.C.A. §2339B (West 2000 & Supp. 2004)*. The latter *§2339B* charge related specifically to Hammoud's personal donation of $3,500 to Hezbollah.

At trial, one of the witnesses against Hammoud was Said Harb, who grew up in the same Lebanese neighborhood as Hammoud. Harb testified regarding his own involvement in the cigarette smuggling operation and also provided information regarding the provision of "dual use" equipment (such as global positioning systems, which can be used for both civilian and military activities) to Hezbollah. The Government alleged that this conduct was part of the conspiracy to provide material support to Hezbollah. Harb testified that Hammoud had declined to become involved in providing equipment because he was helping Hezbollah in his own way. Harb also testified that when he traveled to Lebanon in September 1999, Hammoud gave him $3,500 for Hezbollah.

…

II. Constitutionality of *18 U.S.C.A. §2339B*

Section 2339B, which was enacted as part of the Antiterrorism and Effective Death Penalty Act of 1996 (AEDPA), Pub. L. No. 104-132, 110 Stat. 1214, provides for a maximum penalty of 15 years imprisonment for any person who "knowingly provides material support or resources to a foreign terrorist organization, or attempts or conspires to do so." *18 U.S.C.A. §2339B(a)(1)*. The term "material support" is defined as "currency or other financial securities, financial services, lodging, training, safehouses, false documentation or identification, communications equipment, facilities, weapons, lethal substances, explosives, personnel, transportation, and other physical assets, except medicine or religious materials." *18 U.S.C.A. §2339A(b) (West 2000)*.

Hammoud maintains that *§2339B* is unconstitutional in a number of respects. Because Hammoud failed to bring these challenges before the district court, our review is for plain error. To establish plain error, Hammoud must show that an error occurred, that the error was plain, and that the error affected his substantial rights. Even if Hammoud makes this three-part showing, correction of the error remains within our discretion, which we "should not exercise … unless the error seriously affects the fairness, integrity or public reputation of judicial proceedings."

A. Freedom of Association

Hammoud first contends that *§2339B* impermissibly restricts the *First Amendment* right of association. See *U.S. Const. amend. I* ("Congress shall make no law … abridging … the right of the people peaceably to assemble …."). Hammoud concedes (at least for purposes of this argument) that Hezbollah engages in terrorist activity. But, he also notes the undisputed fact that Hezbollah provides humanitarian aid to citizens of Lebanon. Hammoud argues that because Hezbollah engages in both legal and illegal activities, he can be found criminally liable for providing material support to Hezbollah only if he had a specific intent to further the organization's illegal aims. Because *§2339B* lacks such a specific intent requirement, Hammoud argues that it unconstitutionally restricts the freedom of association.

…

Hammoud's argument fails because *§2339B* does not prohibit mere association; it prohibits the conduct of providing material support to a designated FTO. Therefore, cases regarding mere association with an organization do not control. Rather, the governing standard is found in *United States v. O'Brien, 391 U.S. 367, 20 L. Ed. 2d 672, 88 S. Ct. 1673 (1968)*, which applies when a facially neutral statute restricts some expressive conduct.

…

§2339B is clearly within the constitutional power of the government, in view of the government's authority to regulate interactions between citizens and foreign entities. Second, there can be no question that the government has a substantial interest in curbing the spread of international terrorism. Third, the Government's interest in curbing terrorism is unrelated to the suppression of free expression. Hammoud is free to advocate in favor of Hezbollah or its political objectives—*§2339B* does not target such advocacy.

Fourth and finally, the incidental effect on expression caused by *§2339B* is no greater than necessary. In enacting *§2339B* and its sister statute, *18 U.S.C.A. §2339A*, Congress explicitly found that "foreign organizations that engage in terrorist activity are so tainted by their criminal conduct that any contribution to such an organization facilitates that conduct." AEDPA §301(a)(7). As the Ninth Circuit reasoned,

> it follows that all material support given to [foreign terrorist] organizations aids their unlawful goals. Indeed … terrorist organizations do not maintain open books. Therefore, when someone makes a donation to them, there is no way to tell how the donation is used. Further … even contributions earmarked for peaceful purposes can be used to give aid to the families of those killed while carrying out terrorist acts, thus making the decision to engage in terrorism more attractive. More fundamentally, money is fungible; giving support intended to aid an organization's peaceful activities frees up resources that can be used for terrorist acts.

Humanitarian Law Project, 205 F.3d at 1136. In light of this reasoning, the prohibition on material support is adequately tailored to the interest served and does not suppress more speech than is necessary to further the Government's legitimate goal. We therefore conclude that *§2339B* does not infringe on the constitutionally protected right of free association.

B. Overbreadth

Hammoud next argues that *§2339B* is overbroad. A statute is overbroad only if it "punishes a substantial amount of protected free speech, judged in relation to the statute's plainly legitimate sweep." The overbreadth must be substantial "not only in an absolute sense, but also relative to the scope of the law's plainly legitimate applications." It is also worth noting that when, as here, a statute is addressed to conduct rather than speech, an overbreadth challenge is less likely to succeed.

Hammoud argues that *§2339B* is overbroad because (1) it prohibits mere association with an FTO, and (2) it prohibits such plainly legitimate activities as teaching members of an FTO how to apply for grants to further the organization's humanitarian aims. As discussed above, *§2339B* does not prohibit mere association with an FTO and therefore is not overbroad on that basis. Regarding Hammoud's second overbreadth argument, it may be true that the material support prohibition of *§2339B* encompasses some forms of expression that are entitled to *First Amendment* protection. Cf. *Humanitarian Law Project, 205 F.3d at 1138* (holding that "training" prong of material support definition is vague because it covers such forms of protected expression as "instructing members of a designated group on how to petition the United Nations to give aid to their group"). Hammoud has utterly failed to demonstrate, however, that any overbreadth is substantial in relation to the legitimate reach of *§2339B*.

C. Vagueness

Hammoud next argues that the term "material support" is unconstitutionally vague. "The void-for-vagueness doctrine requires that penal statutes define crimes so that ordinary people can understand the conduct prohibited and so that arbitrary and discriminatory enforcement is not encouraged." In evaluating whether a statute is vague, a court must consider both whether it provides notice to the public and whether it adequately curtails arbitrary enforcement.

Section 2339B easily satisfies this standard. As noted above, the term "material support" is specifically defined as a number of enumerated actions. Hammoud relies on Humanitarian Law Project, in which the Ninth Circuit ruled that two components of the material support definition—"personnel" and "training"—were vague. The possible vagueness of these prongs of the material support definition does not affect Hammoud's conviction, however, because he was specifically charged with providing material support in the form of currency. See *United States v. Rahman, 189 F.3d 88, 116 (2d Cir. 1999)* (per curiam) (rejecting vagueness challenge because allegedly vague term was not relevant to Appellant's conviction). There is nothing at all vague about the term "currency."

D. Designation of an FTO

Hammoud's final challenge to the constitutionality of *§2339B* concerns his inability to challenge the designation of Hezbollah as an FTO. Section *2339B(g)(6)* defines "terrorist organization" as "an organization designated [by the Secretary of State] as a terrorist organization under [8 U.S.C.A. §1189 (West 1999 & Supp. 2004)]." *Section 1189(a)(8)* explicitly prohibits a defendant in a criminal action from challenging a designation. Hammoud argues that his inability to challenge the designation of Hezbollah as an FTO is a violation of the Constitution.

Hammoud primarily argues that *§1189(a)(8)* deprives him of his constitutional right to a jury determination of guilt on every element of the charged offense. This right has not been violated, however. "In determining what facts must be proved beyond a reasonable doubt the …

legislature's definition of the elements of the offense is usually dispositive ....." *McMillan v. Pennsylvania, 477 U.S. 79, 85, 91 L. Ed. 2d 67, 106 S. Ct. 2411 (1986)*. Here, Congress has provided that the fact of an organization's designation as an FTO is an element of *§2339B*, but the validity of the designation is not. Therefore, Hammoud's inability to challenge the designation is not a violation of his constitutional rights. the classification was not an element of the offense).

...

For the reasons set forth above, we reject each of Hammoud's challenges to his convictions and sentence. We therefore affirm the judgment of the district court in its entirety.

In summary, then, United States federal district courts have jurisdiction to try individuals for terrorist related offenses under a variety of statutes. However, instead of charging suspected al-Qa'eda war criminals with violations of the laws of war, the federal courts apply parallel statutes related to the *malum in se* crime or apply the appropriate terrorist statute. Some of the al-Qa'eda members are sent to federal court, such as Richard Reid, Zacarias Moussaoui and Jose Padilla, while other members face trail by military commission. Obviously, this disjointed policy allows a great amount of flexibility for the government where, in many cases, federal investigators are not able to gather sufficient evidence to convict suspects for the more serious offenses and have to settle instead for convictions on less serious charges such as immigration violations and lying to federal investigators. On the other hand, the policy of sending some al-Qa'eda terrorists to federal court while others are faced with military commission proves confusing to the assertion that the War on Terror demands the full use of the laws of war.

4.6 Investigating Terrorist Suspects

One of the first issues of concern to draw the attention of the public following the terrorist attacks of September 11, 2001, was the possibility that other al-Qa'eda terrorist cells were at large on American soil. Federal, state and local law enforcement personnel were put on the highest alert and an immediate search for suspected terrorists associated with the attacks on America began under the direction of the Department of Justice.

To better assist law enforcement to prevent future acts of terrorism against the United States, Congress passed the PATRIOT Act which contains a variety of criminal procedure provisions. Many of the revisions are related to the Foreign Intelligence and Surveillance Act (FISA) and the anonymous judges of the FISA court. These judges are federal judges assigned from elsewhere on the federal bench. They have the authority to authorize FBI agents conducting foreign intelligence investigations to wiretap and conduct physical searches.

In early 2006, Congress extended most all of the provisions in the original PATRIOT Act. Because almost all of the provisions in the PATRIOT Act amend or add language to existing federal statutes, it will be some time before the meaning and impact of many of the provisions can be fully evaluated in terms of constitutionality. For example, Section 203 of the Act amends the *Federal Rules of Criminal Procedure* (FRCP) to allow the sharing of grand jury information with other interested federal agencies if it relates to foreign intelligence. Section 203 also allows law enforcement and intelligence officers to break down the so-called "wall" that once prohibited the two agencies from sharing information in cases associated with national security. Amazingly, the ability to exchange terrorist related information did not exist prior to the PATRIOT Act. Currently, federal law enforcement and federal intelligence officers share a wide variety of information associated with criminal investigations and foreign intelligence.

Similarly, Section 218 allows FISA court orders in cases where "a significant purpose" of the investigation is obtaining foreign intelligence. This provision also breaks down the wall between law enforcement and intelligence officers. In fact, Section 218 authority was instrumental in the disruption of the 2002 terror sleeper cell known as the "Portland Seven" out of Portland, Oregon. Six of these militant Islamic terrorists were convicted and sentenced to terms in prison ranging from three to 18 years; the remaining terror suspect was killed in a gun battle with Pakistani authorities in 2003.

Section 219 amends the FRCP to authorize nationwide search warrants for terrorism cases. Section 209 permits stored voicemail to be obtained by a search warrant and not a wiretap court order. Section 214 provides for FISA courts to issue pen-register and trap-and-trace orders in terrorist cases similar to the process used in the context of criminal investigations. Previously, the order could not be issued unless the subject was contacting a foreign power.

Section 215 amends the old "business records" authority of the FISA. At one time, Section 215 was perhaps the most controversial provision of the PATRIOT Act, which authorizes investigators to seek a court order compelling the production of *any tangible item no matter who held it*, relevant to certain counterintelligence and counterterrorism investigations. Despite the fact that the Justice Department indicated that as of March 2005 the Section 215 authority had been used on only 35 occasions, some continue to raise a variety of civil rights concerns, e.g., it could be used to look at library cards (the Justice Department indicated in 2005 that Section 215 had never been used to secure library, bookstore, gun sale or medical records).

Section 213 adds a subsection to 18 U.S.C. § 3103a in order to authorize a delayed notice of execution of a search warrant (under specific conditions). The search warrant grants federal agencies the ability to conduct secret searches when armed with the appropriate probable cause judicial warrant. Section 213 of the PATRIOT Act simply codifies a law enforcement tool that has been in use for decades by federal judges. The statute eliminates the requirement that law enforcement provide a person subject to a search warrant with contemporaneous notice of the search. Known as "sneak and peek," these searches allow law enforcement officers the authority to search and seize any tangible object or record with delayed notification to the owner or possessor when the court finds necessity for action.

Sneak and peek authority has stirred debates over the provision's value to the defense of the nation and its attendant harm to civil liberties. Representative C.L. "Butch" Ottor (R-Idaho) offered his view at a floor debate: "Sneak-and-peek searches give the government the power to repeatedly search a private residence without informing the residents that he or she is the target of an investigation. Not only does this provision allow the seizure of personal property and business records without notification, but it also opens the door to nationwide search warrants and allows the CIA and the NSA to operate domestically."

Despite the rhetoric of those who oppose the provision, sneak and peek searches cannot be carried out without a probable cause search warrant issued by a neutral and detached magistrate.

In addition, in order to perform this type of search, the court must find "reasonable cause to believe that providing immediate notification of the execution of the warrant may have an adverse effect" on the investigation. Furthermore, the law does not allow for searches to be conducted without any notification; instead, it simply allows for a delay in notification when there is reasonable belief that prior notification could damage the investigation. Obviously, the sneak and peek provision is an extremely valuable tool because it allows the authorities to gather evidence without "tipping their hand." Often, many terrorists, or groups of terrorists in "sleeper cells," maintain only temporary domiciles and are known to move locations very quickly. This provision aids officials in gathering valuable information from a suspect's house without alerting the suspect of the investigation. In this context, the property that could possibly be seized (or copied) could include laptop computers and other computer records.

Section 206 allows the FISA court to authorize the use of roving wiretap surveillance, permitting the interception of any communications made to or by a suspect without identifying a specific telephone line or computer system to be monitored. In other words, the wiretap authorization is attached to the particular terrorist suspect as opposed to a particular communication technology. Because terrorists are likely to quickly change communication devices to avoid detection, Section 206 provides a vital tool to law enforcement in monitoring their activities. As of March 2005, this provision had been used 49 times against international terrorists and spies. Similarly, Section 207 of the PATRIOT Act extends the initial FISA court order time duration from 90 days to 120 days, and such court orders can now be extended for up to one year as opposed to the former requirement of renewable 90 day periods.

Section 212 expands the original law which required that third parties, such as common carriers, be specified in a court order to provide any assistance necessary to conduct a surveillance. The new law extends that obligation to any unnamed and unspecified third party. Those parties would include, for instance, any libraries that provide internet access to the public, university computer labs and internet cafes. This allows federal agencies the ability to monitor these facilities if they have probable cause to believe that a terrorist or intelligence target is using the facility to transmit communications. Furthermore, the FBI may issue so-called national security letters demanding a limited amount of information from financial or communication entities.

4.7 Use of the Military in Domestic Law Enforcement

There have been a number of new developments associated with the Global War on Terrorism that impact on the use of the United States military. Recognizing the need to increase military preparedness to fight the War on Terror, Congress has increased defense spending by large percentages over the past five years. Since 2001, the DOD budget has increased about 40 percent, from 306 billion to 440 billion in 2007. More importantly, the Pentagon issued its long-awaited *Quadrennial Defense Review* (QDR) on October 1, 2001. The Congressionally mandated QDR is the official strategic policy of how the United States armed forces should be utilized. The 2001 QDR eliminated the long-standing vision of structuring the United States military to fight two simultaneous wars and now envisions a military that is based on a "capabilities-based model" flexible enough to fight asymmetrically and to deal with, among other things, international terrorism. In short, the 2001 QDR placed homeland security as the primary mission of the DOD. In addition, the creation of a new four-star general combatant command responsible for coordinating military support for defending the territory of the United States has been created. The command is called United States Northern Command and is based in Colorado Springs, Colorado. Northern Command has no forces other than the approximately 500 personnel at the headquarters. When needed, Northern Command will draw its forces from other commands, depending on the mission.

But even with these changes, the United States has yet to cross the mental bridge from waging conventional warfare on foreign soil to developing action-oriented tactics and strategies to combat international terrorism in the homeland. The 2006 QDR, for the first time, took into account the nation's war against terrorism and the acknowledgement that the War on Terror could be a "long war." This long war is a combination of prolonged irregular combat against al-Qa'eda-styled terror activity that includes Afghanistan, Iraq and even such places as Somalia or the Philippines. The 2006 QDR recognizes that the forces have to do a better job in addressing non-traditional asymmetric challenges.

One of the areas that is being looked at in the context of new missions for the American military is the question of whether a long standing law prohibiting the use of the active military to support domestic law enforcement within the borders of the United States should be revoked or modified. This law is the 1878 Posse Comitatus Act (PCA), 10 U.S.C. § 375; 18 U.S.C. § 1385, which prohibits the use of the military to execute the civil laws of the United States. In full text, the PCA states:

> Whoever, except in cases and under circumstances expressly authorized by the Constitution or Act of Congress, willfully uses any part of the Army or the Air Force as a posse comitatus or otherwise to execute the laws shall be fined under this title or imprisoned not more than two years, or both.

Posse comitatus is Latin for "the force of the country" and refers to the English common law doctrine which empowered the local sheriff to summon able-bodied men to help enforce the law in an emergency situation. With the end of Reconstruction, federal troops employed as a standing army of occupation were finally withdrawn from the South in 1877. In 1878, Congress passed the PCA which stopped the practice of local or federal civilian law enforcement being able to conscript military troops into their posse's. The Act came about due to the use of federal troops in the Southern States to assist civilian law enforcement of the Reconstruction Act of 1867 following the American Civil War. It originally only applied to the United States Army, but was extended in 1947 to the Air Force. Nevertheless, the DOD views the Act as applying to all services. However, the PCA does not apply to a member of the Reserve component when not on active federal duty, nor to a member of the State National Guard when not in federal service. Finally, the Act does not apply to the Coast Guard.

Several laws grant specific exceptions to the application of the PCA. United States Code, Title 18, Section 831, provides that if nuclear material is involved in an emergency, the Secretary of Defense may provide assistance to the Department of Justice, notwithstanding the PCA. The Act does not prevent the President from using the military in cases of civil disorders or emergencies. In fact, the military has been used hundreds of times in such domestic operations. The Act also does not apply to the use of United States armed forces personnel who either arrest or assist in the arrest of international criminals outside the territory of the United States. In addition, a variety of United States courts have held that military support to domestic law enforcement, short of actual search, seizure, arrest or similar confrontation with civilians, does not violate the Act. Specific examples of permitted support to domestic law enforcement include traffic direction and the provision of information, equipment and facilities.

With the creation of Northern Command the issue of the PCA is sure to be raised again. Arguments that the Act is a Congressional statute and can be repealed in toto does not rest well with the long national tradition of excluding the military from domestic law enforcement. Americans clearly have an aversion to the use of soldiers as a policing force. In a letter sent to Defense Secretary Rumsfeld in October of 2001, Senator John Warner (R-VA) asked if the PCA should "now be changed to enable our active-duty military to more fully join other domestic assets in this war against terrorism?" For now, the answer appears to be no. But the question remains on the table.

One alternative to the use of active duty military force to conduct law enforcement or to respond to a major terrorist attack would be the use of National Guard and Army Reserve to create a rapid deployment force for each state with the attendant funding to develop and train the necessary personnel. Following the 1991 war with Iraq, this idea was quickly put into full force in Israel, where a Home Defense Command was set up. Composed of 97 percent reservists, Israel has established sixty-seven stations throughout the nation in order to better deal with the aftermath of a weapons of mass destruction event. This same idea has not taken hold of policymakers in the United States.

The primary hindrance to a weapon of mass destruction rapid response force in each state rests in the massive amount of funding and training. One way to help reduce costs for developing such a force comes from the State Defense Forces model. United States Code, Title 32, Section 109, provides: "In addition to its National Guard, if any, a state or territory may, as provided by its laws, organize and maintain defense forces." State legislatures in twenty-four states and Puerto Rico have created State defense forces to perform a wide variety of functions from light infantry duties (the Virginia Defense Force) to military police functions (Ohio Military Reserve).

Of particular interest in the mechanics of creating rapid-response forces (RRF) to deal with weapons of mass destruction is the example set by the Texas State Guard. During 1998, for example, units of the Texas State Guard rapid reaction force "participated in 122 events, which involved 1,865 members who contributed 24,663 man-hours and saved the state's cities $490,860." Activities included crowd control, traffic control, and search-and-rescue operations—just the type of activities sorely needed in the aftermath of a weapon of mass destruction terrorist attack. During the emergency created by Hurricane Katrina in 2005, the Texas State Guard again did active service in a variety of areas.

4.8 Immigration

As of 2007, estimates place the number of illegal aliens living in the continental United States at between 11 and 12 million people. On the other side of the equation, there are about 2,000 Homeland Security personnel to police them. Following 9/11 many blamed the Immigration and Naturalization Service (INS) for the attacks. In 2002 Congress abolished the INS and replaced it with three separate agencies under the DHS: the Bureau of Citizenship and Immigration Services (BCIS), the Bureau of Immigration and Customs Enforcement (BICE) and the Bureau of Customs and Border Protection (BCBP).

Although an in-depth analysis of the new changes authorized by the PATRIOT Act is beyond the scope of this book, the provision giving the attorney general broad powers to take into custody and detain illegal aliens suspected of terrorism will most likely prove to be the most controversial and bears analysis here. The power to indefinitely detain illegal aliens raises at the very least a constitutional due process issue under the Fifth Amendment, a matter which will most certainly require resolution by the federal judiciary.

Specifically, Section 412(a) of the PATRIOT Act adds Section 236A to the Immigration and Nationality Act, allowing the Attorney General to take into custody any alien certified to be inadmissible or deportable on one of six grounds: (1) espionage, (2) sabotage, (3) export restrictions, (4) attempt to overthrow the United States Government, (5) terrorist activities, and (6) any other "activity that endangers the national security of the United States." Section 412(a)(5) then requires the government to either begin criminal or deportation proceedings within seven days of the detention. Ostensibly, however, Section 412(a)(6) empowers the government to indefinitely detain certain certified illegal alien terrorists who are not likely to be deported in the foreseeable future due to the continuing nature of the investigation. The question of concern regards the matter of how long a certified individual terrorist may be detained and under what conditions.

The United States Supreme Court has yet to rule on the constitutionality of Section 412(a)(6). Nevertheless, because of a 2001 decision entitled *Zadvydas v. Davis*, it seems likely that the Court will probably find that Section 412(a)(6) is constitutional. In *Zadvydas*, the Court was concerned with the constitutionality of whether the government could detain a removable illegal alien beyond the removable period (i.e., indefinitely, or "only for a period reasonably necessary to secure the alien's removal from the country"). The Court construed the applicable section of the Immigration and Nationality Act narrowly, firmly disapproving the indefinite detention of aliens who were not likely to be deported. Still, the Court in *Zadvydas* did recognize in the opinion that suspected terrorists could be held for indefinite periods in preventive detention. The Supreme Court understood that illegal aliens detained for "terrorism or other special circumstances where special arguments might be made for forms of preventive detention," should not be affected by the general rule disapproving the indefinite detention of resident aliens not likely to be deported. *Zadvydas* seemingly exempted suspected alien terrorists as a "small segment of particularly dangerous individuals" that the government could subject to indefinite detention.

The PATRIOT Act's provision on indefinite detention for certified detainees is likely to pass constitutional muster because it actually exceeds the *Zadvydas* standard regarding suspected terrorists held on an indefinite basis. First, Section 412(b) specifically provides that judicial review of detentions of suspected alien terrorists is available via habeas corpus. Second, the new law proscribes fixed time limits for review of the attorney general's certification. Section 412(a)(6) provides that an alien whose "removal is unlikely in the reasonably foreseeable future, may be detained for additional periods of up to six months if release threatens national security or the safety of an individual or the community." Furthermore, Section 412(a)(7) requires the attorney general to review said certification every six months and allows the suspected illegal alien terrorist to request a reconsideration of the certification every six months. If these provisions are satisfied, the said terrorist suspect may be held indefinitely.

Concerns for security measures have caused the United States to revisit the issue of immigration laws regarding who is allowed into the country and under what conditions they are allowed to remain. According to the latest statistics, over 30 million visas were granted to foreign nationals in 1998 to enter the United States. The reason for entry into the United States generally includes reasons related to study, teach, travel, or to conduct business. Of paramount concern in weighing this figure is the fact that about 40 percent of the nation's undocumented immigrants have overstayed their visas. Still, the government has done little to correct the problem.

In the final analysis, whatever new changes Congress may make to existing immigration law, it is painfully obvious that a far better job has to be done. This critique extends from screening and background checks of individuals seeking visas to enter the borders of the United States to tracking the millions of illegal aliens who have overstayed their visas. Despite these troubling facts, concerns must be voiced in the public square that an inordinate tightening of immigration laws may promote "racial profiling" (racial profiling is the practice of targeting individuals on the basis of their race or ethnicity in the belief that a particular group is more likely to engage in certain unlawful behavior) or encourage an untoward atmosphere of bigotry and fear in the general population. Changes in the law should not negatively affect the vast majority of law-abiding aliens; no American wishes to see a return to the poisoned atmosphere that occurred when, for instance, President Franklin Roosevelt ordered the internment of American citizens of Japanese descent during World War II.

4.9 New Information-Gathering Technologies

The absolutely revolutionary advancements in the field of technology have made the world a smaller place. Even without the threat of terror, the impact on privacy issues has been phenomenal. Nevertheless, if the ability to engage in preventive measures to defeat terrorism are to be realized, the government will most certainly seek to employ new information-gathering technologies which will include at the very least the increased use of video surveillance in public places, image-recognition modeling to scan faces, computer data mining and eavesdropping on electronic message traffic. Within days after September 11, 2001, the Attorney General proposed a laundry list of new wiretap and electronic eavesdropping powers to enable law enforcement officials to "act more quickly in fast-moving cases [of terrorism]." Many of these requests, such as a revision of wiretapping laws pertaining to cell phones and so on, have already been enacted into law; many more issues are sure to be debated as the balance between privacy and security is stretched to the limit. While there exists no specific constitutional right to privacy in public places, some privacy advocates early on feared that the next wave of government requests might "short-circuit constitutional safeguards under the guise of counterterrorism." A survey of some of the new proposals for combating terrorism clearly adds to the discussion of where the line should be drawn between privacy and security.

For instance, while x-ray technology has long been used to screen things and people who enter certain government facilities and airports, a new technology called backscatter is now being used to screen airline travelers in a number of American airports. Backscatter technology uses beams of low power energy that does not penetrate the subject (as does x-ray technology) to produce a detailed picture image. It is superior to metal detectors in that it can detect with great precision things such as non-metallic weapons, drugs, or bombs. On the other hand, it also reveals the traveler's breasts, buttocks and genitalia with a detail that can count the number of hairs on a person's back. Does such an intrusion constitute a violation of the Fourth Amendment? Recalling that the Fourth Amendment does not create an absolute right to privacy, but a qualified one to protect individuals from "unreasonable searches," the courts will ultimately decide where the line is to be drawn.

A new idea currently in the mill involves the use of electronic profiling. Since the beginning of the Global War on Terrorism, the Pentagon has stepped up its testing of various image-recognition technology hardware through the Defense Advance Research Projects Agency (DARPA). DARPA is developing sophisticated technology that is superior to new automatic teller machines which can scan a customer's face for positive identification. This technology has already been tested in England where over 200 outdoor cameras are used in the London Borough of Newham to keep watch on "pedestrians and passerby, employing a facial-recognition system that can automatically pick out known criminals and alert local authorities to their presence." These cameras can compare hundreds of thousands of faces on file against a particular subject face within seconds.

Despite the complaints regarding invasion of privacy, "pod" cameras are rapidly becoming a part of the modern landscape. In fact, the 6,000 cameras set in London's subway system were pivotal in solving the July 7 and July 21, 2005, bombings by al-Qa'eda operatives. Cities across the United States are following suit. In Chicago, for example, over 2,000 camera pods are now in place in high-crime areas and on transit and public buildings. In 2005, the Department of Homeland Security gave over $800 million to 50 cities for surveillance cameras.

Baggage screening has also received renewed attention, particularly in wake of the failed August 2006 London based plot to blow up jet airliners bound to the United States. Acting primarily through the rule-making power delegated to administrative agencies such as the DHS, the United States is steadily increasing the security of various public transportation facilities, with a particular emphasis on airports. Congress continues to pass a number of new pieces of legislation including the 2002 Aviation Transportation and Security Act, which requires increased airport screening through the use of advanced detection devices, physical searches and positive passenger bag match. This new law has proven a burden to both passengers and to the industry in general. For instance, a proposed 12 billion dollar expansion to LAX International Airport in Los Angeles, California, was delayed until a new baggage-inspection facility and screening machines required by the FAA were built. Indeed, attacks could come from outside the plane in the form of surface to air missiles, or through the thousands of privately owned planes that can be easily rented. In addition, the 1995 attack on the Tokyo subway by the Aum Shinrikyo religious cult highlights the security challenge posed by terrorists using chemical or biological agents.

The DHS has also implemented a new Homeland Security Advisory System (HSAS) created by Presidential Directive 3. Utilizing a color-coded warning system, HSAS is an advisory system for federal, state, and local authorities to improve coordination and communication among all levels of government and the public.

More sophisticated biometric and cryptographic technologies, such as fingerprints on identification cards or iris scans at airports, may soon become common fare. Privacy issues of concern relate to how this data is stored, who should have access and for what purposes?

In New York City, doormen at apartment complexes, dock workers and other workers are being trained by the City to look for things out of the ordinary. In all, over 28,000 workers have been trained by the police department at a cost of over one million dollars. Other federal programs to train, for example, interstate truck drivers to report possible terrorist situations are also active.

It appears that increased security at public facilities and other public places is rapidly becoming a part the "new normal." It is perhaps the most obvious signpost that Americans are living in a new time. Paradoxically, it is not only our elected representatives who will decide how much security Americans will receive. Those decisions will be made in part, and implemented in the main, by administrative agencies—the so-called headless "fourth branch" of government.

For example, in late 2005, the DHS Research Projects Agency issued a solicitation to the private sector to provide 26 research and development prototypes in the areas of explosives detection, chemical and biological countermeasures protection, law enforcement, threat assessment and vulnerability testing, critical infrastructure protection, borders and transportation security, emergency preparedness and response, and cyber security in the following areas:

1. Maritime Safety and Security Team (MSST) Explosive Trace Detection—a prototype system demonstrating improved capabilities for explosive trace detection in the maritime environment.

2. Non-invasive Portable Object Examination System—a multi-sensor, person-portable system to assist trained users in expedient, non-invasive examination of unattended bags, mail packages, and other objects.

3. Advanced Capability X-ray System for Bomb Squad—an advanced capability X-ray system that provides improved penetration and resolution to conduct radiographic examination and diagnostics of suspected packages and confirm the presence of Improvised Explosive Devices.

4. Portable Entry Point Screening Portal—a robust, portable, fully automated, walk-through portal that can detect explosive material on clothing or skin using a non-intrusive, non-contact technique that meets the TSA T&E detection criteria and methods.

5. Escape Hood—a small concealable escape mask that will allow personnel to safely leave potentially contaminated areas.

6. Rapid Suspected Bio-agent Screening—a tool and method for rapidly screening suspicious "white powders" to eliminate the probability that the substance is a biological threat agent.

7. Aircraft "Spot" Decontamination—a kit and method for use to provide "spot" decontamination of common aircraft cabin materials.

8. Biosurveillance Detection Algorithms—an algorithmic procedure/model to provide earliest detection of bioterrorist attacks on humans, plants, animals, food, water, or the environ-

ment based on correlations between a broad range of low confidence biosurveillance data streams.

9. Rapid Field Identification of High Priority Plant Pathogens (RFIP)—person-portable system that will provide minimally trained user's assistance in field identification of plant pathogens.

10. One-Person Portable Chemical Detector—a lightweight, chemical detection device for use in ports of entry (both land and seaport environments) to simultaneously detect and identify high priority chemical threat agents and Toxic Industrial Chemicals (TICs).

11. NIOSH CBRN 60 Tactical Escape Mask—a lightweight, one-time use, NIOSH-approved tactical escape mask with 60-minute endurance in CBRN environments.

12. Transportation Route Risk Analysis and Resource Allocation Tool—a prototype to facilitate transportation route risk analysis. The primary output of the tool will be a list of transportation routes ranked according to relative risk.

13. Significant Encounters Visual Environment (SIEVE)—a real-time port and border encounter monitoring system. This system must incorporate GIS layered data-mapping technologies with established reporting and watch procedures.

14. Modeling the Complex Urban Environment (MCUE)—a near real-time system that maps group and tactic-specific threats to specific vulnerabilities and to emergency preparedness and response within a complex urban environment.

15. Improved Heartbeat Detector System Prototype—a heartbeat detector system for finding concealed passengers or detecting motion in conveyances and cargo containers, using vibration sensors and analysis software with a user interface.

16. Extreme Wide Field-of-View IR/NV Capability—a marine and land-based system that provides vessel and vehicle operators a wide-peripheral awareness, stereoscopic, low moment arm, night-vision system.

17. Tactical Information Sharing System (TISS) Image Analysis Capability—software that performs facial image comparisons for the purpose of identifying possible criminals and terrorists from low resolution images. The system will generate full frontal facial images from partial images and perform digital image comparisons.

18. Advanced 3-D Locator System—a system to accurately locate and track incident responders inside threatened buildings, collapsed buildings, subterranean facilities, or underground.

19. Geospatial Modeling of Homeland Security Capabilities—a capability model in a geospatial system to allow planners to visualize preparedness information and perform quantitative analysis (such as coverage area, deployment time, and mutual aid dependencies).

20. Resource Awareness Data Portal—a shared, virtual data repository of emergency management/emergency response resource data constructed and maintained in a "just in time" manner.

21. Advanced Urban Search and Rescue (US&R) Breaching Approach—an advanced breaching (cutting, coring, burning) and breaking system for faster and safer extrication of victims from disaster sites.

22. BOTNET—a cyber security tool for identifying bots (software agents that interact with network services intended for people as if it were a real person. The term is derived from "robot") and botnets (a collection of such software robots, or bots, which run autonomously, from unwitting host computers, usually for nefarious purposes).

23. Control System Cyber Assessment Tool—a web-based, self-assessment tool for process control systems to assist owners and operators in performing self-assessments of the cyber security of their control system architecture.

24. Exercise Scenario Modeling Tool—a collaborative web-based tool to assist exercise planners in developing cyber security exercise scenarios for use in cyber training incident response teams.

25. Blue Force Tracking Tool and Evaluation of Multi-Agency Maritime Blue Force Tracking (BFT) System—This effort develops a prototype Blue Force Tracking (BFT) Command Center tool to enable the watchstander to simultaneously manage up to 100 Blue Force vessels. Automatic Identification System BFT hardware specified by the Coast Guard will be fabricated and installed in Coast Guard and port partner vessels in the Port of New York. A six month evaluation will be conducted to assess the performance and Command and Control benefits of this new capability.

26. USCG Sector Command Center (SCC) Simulator Testbed—a USCG Sector Command Center Testbed to systematically evaluate the integration of new technologies and improved command and control concepts into SCC operations. The testbed will be simulator based in that vessel movement and sensor output will be synthetic, although based upon realistic performance and behavior.

4.10 Assassination

Osama bin Laden is quoted as saying that "[t]he confrontation that Islam calls for with these godless and apostate regimes does not know Socratic debates, Platonic ideals, nor Aristotelian diplomacy. But it knows the dialogue of bullets, the ideals of assassination, bombing and destruction, and the diplomacy of the cannon and the machine gun." In contrast, the United States is deeply concerned with fighting the War on Terror under the rule of law—domestically and internationally. From a domestic perspective, the continuing dilemma for democratic policymakers is how to protect the nation without curtailing long-recognized civil liberties. From an international perspective, American policymakers are likewise concerned with following all those international laws associated with both the lawfulness of the use of force and the appropriate application of that force. Without question, the most pressing issue in the international realm centers on the Bush Administration's promotion of a legal rationale for the preemptive use of military force against al-Qa'eda-styled terrorists or rogue States who pose a direct or gathering threat to the United States by means of weapons of mass destruction.

Juxtaposed to the issue of crafting a legal basis for the use of preemptive military force is the recurring issue of whether certain individuals—such as high level al-Qa'eda officials or leaders of totalitarian States which support or sponsor terrorism—can be legally targeted for "assassination." In other words, if preemptive military force is an acceptable addition to the rule of law, can the United States simply kill selected high-level leaders without having to employ large-scale military forces against the offending rogue nation or terrorist organization?

Currently, there are two principle documents associated with these two legal concerns. Respectively, they are the groundbreaking 2002 *National Security Strategy of the United States of America* released by the White House on September 17, 2002 and the Presidential Executive Order 12333 banning assassination.

The purpose of this section is to provide a policy and legal analysis of the United States' position regarding assassination as viewed in the context of the lawful use of preemptive military force. In doing so, this section examines the deficiencies of the current Executive Order 12333 and suggests that it should be replaced by a new executive order which clearly defines the circumstances under which individuals may be lawfully targeted for death by military forces—either in peacetime or war. Alternatively, if a new and more precise executive order is not issued to replace Executive Order 12333, there are two interlocking principles that argue against overturning Executive Order 12333. The first of these reasons regards properly understanding the most common definition of assassination and the second relates to the proper use of armed force under the rule of law. Taken together, those who advocate that the ban on assassination should be lifted without modification in order to allow the United States to engage in assassination are essentially advocating that the United States should be able to engage in unlawful killing, or murder.

In the days following the September 11, 2001, attacks on the United States the question of retaliation and self-preservation weighed heavily on the minds of policymakers. Instinctively, many in Washington called for an immediate response to the perpetrators behind the attacks, even if it meant engaging in assassination which some clearly viewed to be in violation of longstanding Executive Order 12333 prohibiting assassination by agents of the United States government. Then, prior to the March 2003 war in Iraq, many expressed the idea of toppling the dictator Saddam Hussein by simply killing him. These views represent a misunderstanding of Executive Order 12333 and the legal basis for responding to aggression.

The genesis of Executive Order 12333 can be traced back to 1977, when President Gerald Ford issued the first executive order prohibiting political assassination. President Ford was prompted to action by a 1975 Congressional Report (commonly known as the Church Commission) headed by Senator Frank Church which held hearings on the question of whether or not the United States had engaged in assassination or assassination plots against certain foreign leaders. The most damning portion of the report found that between 1960 and 1965, "the United States was implicated in several assassination plots to kill Fidel Castro," the ruler of communist Cuba.

The Church Commission found that the Central Intelligence Agency's (CIA) Operation Mongoose sought to eliminate Castro with a number of unlikely weapons, such as poison tipped pens and cigars, and an exploding seashell that was to be placed near Castro's favorite scuba spots. Issuing a document consisting of hundreds of pages, the Church Commission was unable to make a finding that "assassination plots were authorized by the Presidents or other people above the governmental agency or agencies involved," but the commission did find that the "system of executive command and control was so ambiguous that it [was] difficult to be certain at what levels assassination activity was known and authorized." The Church Commission strongly concluded that assassination was both legally and morally repugnant to a democratic people and should never be associated with the United States of America: "[A]ssassination is incompatible with

American principles, international order, and morality. It should be rejected as a tool of foreign policy."

Curiously, despite the exhaustive research done by the Church Commission on assassination and the call for "intervention by Congress to proscribe it as a matter of law," Congress never enacted legislation to legally ban the use of assassination as an instrument of foreign policy, leaving the matter to the Executive Branch via an executive order. Although presidential executive orders are policy and not law, this distinction is functionally irrelevant, particularly in regard to the politically charged issue of assassination.

President Ford's executive order on assassination read: "Prohibition of Assassination. No employee of the United States Government shall engage in, or conspire to engage in, political assassination." Shortly thereafter, President Jimmy Carter followed suit with his own slightly modified version which deleted the term "political," and in 1981, President Ronald Reagan issued Executive Order 12333 on assassination. It reads in full text: "No person employed by or acting on behalf of the United States government shall engage in, or conspire to engage in, assassination." Subsequent presidents have not changed the Reagan order banning assassination by agents of the United States. Executive Order 12333 remains in effect.

A common and reoccurring theme of frustration runs across the arguments of those who seek the repeal of Executive Order 12333. This frustration actually reflects a lack of understanding of what assassination actually means or entails, not what Executive Order 12333 actually prohibits. In short, the central problem is that people use the same word—assassination—and assume that everyone is talking about the same meaning. Of course, this situation is aggravated both by the brevity of the executive order, which provides no definition whatsoever for the term assassination, and the fact that it makes no attempt to distinguish between instances of lawful killing verses instances of assassination, or unlawful killing.

Former conservative United States Senator Jesse Helms from North Carolina amplified this confusion when he remarked on September 11, 2001, that he was in favor of taking whatever action was necessary, to include assassination, to punish those responsible for the attacks on the United States: "I hope I will live to see the day when it will once again be the policy of the United States of America to go after the kind of sneaky enemies who created this morning's mayhem." Then, just over a week after the terrorist attacks, liberal minded National Public Radio senior news correspondent Daniel Schorr forcefully urged policymakers to do away with the ban on assassination. Schorr wrote: "A 25 year old executive order reflecting the reaction to mindless cold war plotting against President Castro and other third world leaders seems completely anachronistic after Sept. 11th. It is time to rescind an assassination ban that has no more reason for existing." In fact, in the days immediately after the attacks on America, Congressman Bob Barr of Georgia proposed a bill in the House of Representatives which would have nullified Executive Order 12333.

Fortunately, cooler heads prevailed and Congress passed no legislation regarding Executive Order 12333. Shortly thereafter, then White House spokesman Ari Fleischer correctly related to reporters that the assassination ban "does not limit America's ability to act in self-defense." The elimination of terrorists could require, Fleischer remarked, "acts which involve the lives of others."

Although Fleischer rightly understood in September 2001 that the ban on assassination did not prohibit the United States from taking actions in self-defense against specific threats, he later seemed to have lapsed into misunderstanding. At an October 1, 2002, press conference, Fleischer voiced support for non-American actors assassinating Saddam Hussein. When asked about the cost of a possible war with Iraq, spokesman Fleischer remarked, "I can only say that the cost of a one-way ticket is substantially less than that [the estimated cost of nine billion dollars a month]. The *cost of one bullet*, if the *Iraqi people* take it on themselves, is substantially less than that [emphasis added]." While the assassination of Saddam Hussein by his own people would not violate Executive Order 12333, reporters immediately asked Fleischer if the Bush Administration was encouraging assassination. Fleischer shrewdly stopped short of using the term assassination in reference to Saddam Hussein, perhaps remembering that such a call to the Iraqi people would violate the customary law on assassination.

Without question, the traditional concept of assassination absolutely prohibits one nation from encouraging others, in this case the Iraqi people, to murder the leader of an unfriendly government. Nevertheless, as the United States geared up for possible war with Iraq, national news media sources continued to speculate about the assassination of the Iraqi dictator. Numerous newspapers cited "senior intelligence reports" that Saddam Hussein would probably be assassinated by "members of his inner circle in the final days or hours before U.S. forces launch a major ground attack."

Those who call the loudest for abandoning Executive Order 12333 mistakenly feel that it might impede the expeditious prosecution of the War on Terror—either against al-Qa'eda leaders or the senior leaders of those handful of totalitarian regimes that back terrorism. To date, however, neither the Congress nor the President have taken steps that would blunt the ban on assassination. The reason for this inactivity rests in a mixed bag of historical, legal and policy considerations. Still, there are several strong arguments for abandoning the current executive order on assassination, not because it impedes the War on Terror but because it is more confusing than helpful in defining the application of the lawful use of military force against legitimate targets—whether in peacetime or war—to include the senior leadership of hostile governments or terrorist groups.

Before a thing can be properly discussed it must be properly defined. Nowhere is this more applicable than in addressing the issue of assassination *vis a vis* Executive Order 12333. Assassination is defined in leading dictionaries as follows:

- *Webster's Dictionary*: "The act of killing or murdering by surprise or secret assault."
- *American Heritage College Dictionary*: "1. To murder (a prominent person) by surprise attack, as for political reasons. 2. To destroy or injure treacherously."
- *Black's Law Dictionary*: "The act of deliberately killing someone, especially a public figure, usually for hire or political reasons."
- *Random House Dictionary*: "1. To kill suddenly or secretively. Murder premeditatedly and treacherously. 2. To destroy or denigrate treacherously and viciously."

A comparison of most definitions reveals that the common meaning associated with the term assassination is that it is "murder by surprise" usually carried out for "political purposes." In a law review article on the topic, Tyler Harder believes that the best way to capture the meaning of assassination is to view it as a combination of three essential elements: "(1) a murder, (2) of a specifically targeted figure, (3) for a political purpose." Thus, an assassination must contain all three elements or the killing will not meet the requirements of an assassination. Harder's approach is a good starting point because it focuses on the elements of murder—always an illegal concept—and politics—a concept generally reserved for activities not in the sphere of warfare.

Since assassination is universally regarded as murder, it is important to distinguish the concept of murdering another human being, which is always illegal *per se*, from the concept of killing another human being, which may or may not be illegal. Unfortunately, the distinction between murder and killing is often blurred in modern society contributing to a lack of clarity on the subject of assassination. Many postmodernists erroneously believe, for example, that it is somehow immoral for the State to take the life of another human being under any circumstances. For them, the concept of *nullen crimen sine poena* (no crime without punishment) does not extend to taking the life of another human. Hence, in their minds, all killing is both immoral and illegal.

Interestingly, definitional problems regarding the lawfulness of killing another human being can be traced back to the Biblical prohibition on this matter found in the Decalogue at Exodus 20:13 and Deuteronomy 5:17, which many widely regarded English translations, such as the King James version of the Bible, incorrectly render as: "Thou shalt not kill." In fact, the correct translation of the Hebrew into the English is: "Thou shalt not *murder* [emphasis added]." The Hebrew word for kill is not used in the prohibitions of Exodus 20:13 and Deuteronomy 5:17. The Hebrew word that is used is *lo tirtzach* and "refers only to the criminal act of homicide, not [for instance] taking the life of enemy soldiers in legitimate warfare." In fact, the Mosaic law is filled with detailed laws that specifically mandate that the State should lawfully kill certain humans convicted under the rule of law for such crimes as murder, kidnapping, etc. The Old Testament principle is properly seen as centering on the duty of the State to protect its citizens on interior lines from domestic criminal behavior.

In turn, the Mosaic law also sets out a detailed law of war codex which provides for the protection of citizens on exterior lines by specifically authorizing the killing of enemy combatants. From the Judeo tradition, killing enemy combatants in battle is not murder.

Assassination, then, is clearly identified and properly classified as a type of killing that is unlawful, i.e., a form of murder, and murder is always defined as "the *killing* of a human being with malice aforethought [emphasis added]." Although Executive Order 12333 does not define assassination, this silence certainly provides no legitimacy to advocating a "new" definition of assassination which would somehow characterize the concept as anything other than what it is— murder. Furthermore, since murder is an intrinsically illegal act, the definitional problem automatically defeats any reasoned advancement of the proposition that murder, e.g., assassination, can somehow be made lawful.

In other words, if murder is a violation of both domestic United States law and international law, Executive Order 12333 really does not make illegal something that was not already illegal. Therefore, doing away with Executive Order 12333 would not allow the United States to engage in assassination, either in peace or war. Indeed, revoking Executive Order 12333 would only send a negative signal, suggesting to the world that the United States did away with the ban so that it could commit an illegal act of murder.

The word "assassination" is derived from the Arabic word *hashishiyyin*, which refers to the practice of an eleventh century Muslim "brotherhood" that was specifically devoted to killing their religious and political enemies in any manner available. To be sure, the concept of assassination is far more ancient and can apply with equal validity to various infamous incidents in history to include the murder by surprise for political purposes of Gaius Julius Caesar by Brutus and his fellow plotters in 44 B.C., as well as to Hebrew Zealots who conducted random acts of assassination against the occupying Romans and those who supported the Romans in Judea prior to the fall of Jerusalem by the legions of Rome under Titus in 70 A.D. Because American history has witnessed the assassination of several presidents by assassins, to include President Abraham Lincoln, most Americans view assassination as something that is carried out against political figures.

There are even historical instances where the concept of assassination was incorporated as an integral part of certain religious beliefs. For example, when the British entered India in the nineteenth century, they encountered a Hindu cult devoted to the goddess Kali that required its members to commit murder by surprise upon random victims as a form of worship. In contrast to other assassinations, these murders by surprise were not for political purposes, but for religious purposes.

Early Western scholars discussed the matter of assassination both in the context of war and peace. They all viewed assassination as an act directed against the leader of a country. Interestingly, some of the earliest commentators, such as theologian and philosopher Thomas Aquinas, felt that killing an evil sovereign for the common good might be legally justified. However, Aquinas' view held little sway with subsequent scholars, particularly following the 1648 Peace of Westphalia and the rise of the nation-state.

In fact, extremely sensitive to the concept of reciprocity as the key element in international intercourse between nation-states, most seventeenth century scholars rejected the idea of assassinating a leader in peacetime under any circumstances and equally frowned on the use of assassination as a legitimate use of armed force during war. Regardless of the method of attack employed during warfare, the attack should never involve treachery, a term commonly associated with assassination but seldom defined. Influenced by Europe's Code of Chivalry, many international jurists in the area felt that assassination should not be employed in order that the "honor of arms be [sic] preserved and public order and safety of sovereigns and generals not be unduly threatened."

Hugo Grotius, the so-called father of international law and author of the first real codification of rules relating to the conduct of warfare, spent a great deal of time exploring the matter of assassination in the context of war. Grotius used treachery or treacherous murder as an analytical starting point in his commentaries. Understanding the issue of reciprocity, he discussed assassination as something that violates an express or tacit obligation between countries. For Grotius, a violation of natural law or the law of nations certainly occurred if a leader was killed by those that had an obligation to him; such an act of assassination would be treacherous. Conversely, if an enemy leader is ambushed or tricked into a trap by opposing soldiers and killed, then natural law was not violated. Grotius wrote, "It is in fact permissible to kill an enemy in any place whatsoever. According to the law of nations, not only those who do such deeds, but also others who instigate others who do them, are considered free from blame." In any event, Grotius strongly disapproved of putting a monetary price on the head of an enemy leader, reasoning that this would encourage the leader's subjects to kill him treacherously, i.e., by assassination.

Alberico Gentile, another prominent scholar of his day, voiced a similar line of argument regarding assassination. A bit more pragmatic in his approach, Gentile cautioned that killing an enemy leader treacherously—by assassination—might actually incite more anger in the enemy population, causing the enemy population to actually fight harder in order to avenge the murder. In addition, Gentile felt that the very act of assassination itself lacked the valor that one might gain in victory on the field of battle. As did Grotius, Gentile distinguished killing an enemy leader by treacherous means from killing an enemy leader in combat. Death on the battlefield was a lawful "battle circumstance."

Writing in the eighteenth century, scholar Emmerich de Vattel of Switzerland also defined assassination as "murder committed by a means of treachery." In his book entitled *Le Droit des Gens, ou Principes de la Loi Naturelle, appliqués a la Conduite dt aux Affaires des Naions et des Souverains*, De Vattel believed that assassination could apply in both peacetime and war, and applied with equal effect whether the deed was done by the people of the leader or subjects of an opposing country. De Vattel wrote:

> Hence I mean by assassination a murder committed by means of treachery, whether the deed be done by persons who are subjects of him who is assassinated, or his sovereign, and who are therefore traitors, or whether it be done by any other agent who makes his way in as a suppliant or refugee, or as a turncoat, or even as an alien; and I assert that the deed is a shameful and revolting one, both on the part of him who executes and of him who commands it.

Furthermore, De Vattel felt that punishing those individuals who assassinated the sovereign was the responsibility of the world community. De Vattel encouraged all civilized nations "[i]n the interest of the common safety of mankind to join forces and unite to punish" those who engaged in assassination.

Thus, the weight of authority from early Western scholars might be encapsulated as follows: First, most defined assassination as an illegal act most commonly associated with targeting and killing enemy leaders in peacetime or war. Second, all early commentators recognized the lawfulness of targeting and killing the enemy leader in war, although some authorities considered killing the enemy leader in a treacherous manner off the battlefield as an act of assassination.

The early American position on the matter held assassination as an illegal tool in both peacetime and wartime. The first significant mention of assassination occurred during the American Civil War with the adoption by Union forces of a codification of the law of war known as the Lieber Code. On April 24, 1863, the Lieber Code was promulgated as Army General Orders Number 100 by the Secretary of War, E.D. Townsend. In a merger of peacetime and wartime scenarios, Section IX, paragraph 148 states:

The law of war does not allow proclaiming either an individual belonging to the hostile army, or a citizen, or a subject of the hostile government an outlaw, who may be slain without trial by any captor, any more than the modern law of peace allows such international outlawry; on the contrary, it abhors such an outrage. The sternest retaliation should follow the murder committed in consequence of such proclamation, made by whatever authority. Civilized nations look with horror upon offers of rewards for the *assassination of enemies* as relapses into barbarism [emphasis added].

Since the somewhat confusing definition of the Lieber Code, subsequent American legal views on assassination have improved only slightly. Surprisingly, the next significant mention of the concept of assassination is not found until 1956, in *Field Manuel 27-10, Department of the Army Field Manual of the Law of Land Warfare* (FM 27-10). Paragraph 31 of FM 27-10, entitled "Assassination and Outlawry," quotes Article 23, paragraph b of the *Annex to the Hague Convention Number IV, dated 18 October 1907*: "It is especially forbidden to kill or wound treacherously individuals belonging to the hostile nation or army." FM 27-10 then goes on to describe this sentence in the context of American military law:

This article is construed as prohibiting assassination, proscription, or outlawry of an enemy, or putting a price upon an enemy's head, as well as offering a reward for an enemy "dead or alive." It does not, however, preclude attacks on individual soldiers or officers of the enemy whether in the zone of hostilities, occupied territory, or elsewhere.

To date, one of the very best efforts to handle the legal aspects of assassination *vis a vis* Executive Order 12333 is contained in a 1989 legal memorandum written by H. Hays Parks, the Chief of the International Law Branch, International Affairs Division, Office of the Judge Advocate General. In his memorandum entitled "Executive Order 12333 and Assassination," Parks does an excellent job explaining the term assassination "in the context of military operations across the conflict spectrum." In essence, Parks correctly concludes that the targeting and killing of hostile or enemy leaders in an act of self-defense is not an act of assassination, even if by surprise.

It is well settled in modern international law that no nation may engage in aggression against any other nation. The definition of aggression is spelled out at in the 1957 General Assembly's United Nations Definition of Aggression and certainly includes the act of assassination. According to Article 2(4) of the Charter of the United Nations (U.N. Charter), all member states: "[s]hall refrain in their international relations from the threat or use of force against the territorial integrity or the political independence of any state, or in any manner inconsistent with the Purposes of the United Nations." With this premise so stated, it is equally well recognized that the legitimate use of force is rooted in the inherent right of every nation to act in self-defense if it is the object of aggression.

It is also important to realize that aggressive acts are often carried out by one nation against another without the intent to provoke full scale hostilities or war. Likewise, the nation that is attacked with aggressive force will respond in self-defense with proportional military action with no intention of going to war.

Article 51 of the U.N. Charter codifies the right of a nation attacked with aggressive violence to engage in self-defense. The doctrine of self-defense, of course, is a customary right of ancient origin not created by the United Nations Charter. In pertinent part, Article 51 reads: "Nothing in the present Charter shall impair the inherent right of individual or collective self-defense if an armed attack occurs against a Member of the United Nations." Thus, the State that engages in acts of aggression, or the unlawful use of force, may never claim that it is acting under the self-defense provisions of Article 51 of the U.N. Charter. Furthermore, apart from the fundamental requirement of proportionality in the employment of violence in self-defense, the use of self-defense can occur in peace as well as war.

On numerous occasions, the United States has lawfully exercised the inherent right of self-defense against individuals or States in both peacetime and wartime environments. President William Clinton, for example, sent cruise missiles against several al-Qa'eda terrorist training camps in Afghanistan following the 1998 al-Qa'eda attack on the United States embassies in Africa. This military action occurred during peacetime and was permitted under the rule of law regarding self-defense. Even if the leader Osama bin Laden was targeted in the attacks, President Clinton's actions would not be classified as attempted assassination.

Similarly, in the 1991 Gulf War (and the 2003 campaign), Saddam Hussein himself was a legitimate military target and his death by coalition forces would not have been an assassination. As the commander in chief of the Iraqi military, Saddam Hussein could have been legally targeted and killed. In war, enemy combatants are legitimate targets for attack so long as the hostile forces are not killed with treachery, e.g., while legitimately visiting a protected place such as a hospital. The fact that Hussein was not specifically targeted was clearly a political decision, although President George H. Bush is said to have remarked: "We're not in the position of targeting Saddam Hussein, but no one will weep for him when he is gone." Despite the lawfulness of killing the enemy leader in wartime, there often exists an unwillingness to specifically target that individual.

Parks correctly recognizes that a State may use military force in peacetime if it is acting in self-defense. Such acts are not assassination:

> Historically, the United States has resorted to the use of military force in peacetime where another nation has failed to discharge its international responsibilities in protecting U.S. citizens from acts of violence originating in or launched from its sovereign territory, or has been culpable in aiding and abetting international criminal activities.

After listing several historical examples of the United States' use of military force in self-defense, including the 1986 bombing of "terrorist related targets in Libya," Parks concludes: "Hence there is historical precedent for the use of military force to capture or kill individuals whose peacetime actions constitute a direct threat to U.S. citizens or U.S. national security."

Indeed, immediately following the terrorist attacks of September 11, 2001, the Congress of the United States clearly recognized the inherent right of self-defense in peacetime. While the Congress never "declared war" under the provisions of Article 1 of the Constitution, they quickly passed a joint resolution which left no doubt as to their desire to authorize the President of the

United States to use military force in self-defense. Among other things, the Congressional Resolution recognized the inherent right of self-defense,

> under the Constitution to take action to deter and prevent acts of international terrorism against the United States … [and] authorized [the President] to use all necessary and appropriate force against those nations, organizations, or persons he determines planned, authorized, committed, or aided the terrorist attacks that occurred on September 11, 2001, or harbored such organizations or persons, in order to prevent any future acts of international terrorism against the United States by such nations, organizations or persons.

The Congress clearly understood that targeting individual terrorists associated with the attacks on the United States was not assassination, but the appropriate response in self-defense to unlawful aggression.

From a legal perspective, the most challenging issue associated with the continuing War on Terror is the fact that both the nature of the enemy and the nature of the threat has changed dramatically, and so the response under the rule of law has to change. In his State of the Union message of January 29, 2002, President George W. Bush signaled his resolve that the United States of America would "not permit the world's most dangerous regimes to threaten us with the world's most destructive weapons."

In the context of killing individuals, can the United States go beyond the rhetoric and target for death a known terrorist or individual leader of a nation that sponsors or supports terrorism? If the use of a weapon of mass destruction by a fanatical terrorist is on the near horizon, do the traditional international rules related to the use of force, i.e., only used in self-defense, actually work in the real world of the al-Qa'eda virtual State? In other words, must the United States idly wait for a catastrophic terrorist attack before it can respond, or does a threatened nation have the right to engage in preemptive self-defense against those individuals that are planning the attack?

As previously covered, the most striking instance in modern history occurred in the 1967 Six Day War when Israel, anticipating a full-scale armed attack from Egypt, Syria, Jordan, and others, attacked Arab airfields first. The doctrine of preemptive self-defense holds that when a State is faced with an imminent armed attack it may resort to proportional acts of preemptive self-defense. Other scholars view the concept of anticipatory self-defense as inconclusive. For example, one textbook on national security law writes: "Past practice is inconclusive, but it suggests that a state facing an imminent and potentially devastating armed attack may escape condemnation for a preemptive response."

Parks lists three forms of self-defense that the United States recognizes as appropriate for unilateral action under the inherent right of self-defense: "(a) Against an actual use of force, or hostile act. (b) Preemptive self defense against an imminent use of force. (c) Self defense against a continuing threat." Parks agrees that the preemptive use of military force against terrorists would be permissible and would not be assassination. Parks specifically asserts:

> This right of self defense would be appropriate to the attack of terrorist leaders where their actions pose a continuing threat to U.S. citizens or the national security of the United States. As with an attack on a guerrilla infrastructure, the level to which attacks could be

carried out against individuals within a terrorist infrastructure would be a policy rather than a legal decision.

Nevertheless, the fact that a nation is acting under the rubric of self-defense does not allow that nation to employ military force in any manner it so desires. The State acting in self-defense is still required to adhere to a set of binding international rules associated with how that force is employed. In time of war, these rules are known as the law of war or the law of armed conflict. However, in the modern era, where the line between war and peacetime is inexorably blurred, many of the most basic rules regarding military necessity, unnecessary suffering and proportionality apply equally to the peacetime use of military force.

The law of armed conflict describes lawful targets which can be destroyed in the proper context of military operations. The general principal is that the military acting in self-defense—whether in a peacetime or wartime environment—may kill the enemy, whether lawful combatants or unprivileged belligerents, and may include in either category civilians who take part in the hostilities. An enemy combatant, whether part of an organized military or a civilian who undertakes military activities, is a legitimate target at all times and may be lawfully killed, even if by surprise. This includes the leader of the hostile forces.

Thus, unannounced attacks do not preclude the use of violence involving the element of surprise. All "combatants are subject to attack if they are participating in hostilities through fire, maneuver and assault; providing logistic, communications, administrative, or other support." In addition, there is "no distinction made between an attack accomplished by aircraft, missile, naval gunfire, artillery, mortar, infantry assault, ambush, land mine or booby-trap, a single shot by a sniper, a commando attack, or other, similar means." It is not an act of assassination to kill individuals in this context.

In turn, the law of armed conflict absolutely prohibits the killing of noncombatants, except as a matter of collateral damage where civilians may be killed ancillary to the lawful attack of a military objective. Civilians that maintain close proximity to a military objective assume the risk of being killed by enemy fire. Since they are neither specifically targeted individuals nor are they killed by the use of treachery, the killing of such civilians is not assassination. On the other hand, specifically targeting innocent civilians as a military objective is always illegal and criminal.

As the United States tests the new doctrine of preemptive self-defense against renegade States, it is efficacious to consider how the Israelis have employed the concept to target and kill known senior terrorist leaders in the on-going Palestinian conflict. In fact, the United States has generally supported the Israeli military's use of preemptive force in regards to the killing of certain Palestinian terrorists. United States Deputy Secretary of Defense, Paul Wolfolwitz has often cited the Israeli use of preemption with approval, drawing an early parallel to what Americans must do to win the War on Terror. Wolfolwitz noted, "Our approach has been to aim at prevention and not merely punishment. We are at war. Self-defense requires prevention and sometimes preemption."

In this light, the killing of known Islamic militant terrorists is not assassination, but an act of preemptive self-defense. Israel, of course, does not call these acts assassination, although the term is often used by various individuals to describe the killings of those responsible for the waves of suicide bombings against innocent Israeli citizens. Instead, the Israelis refer to the acts of killing as "targeted thwarting, liquidation, or elimination." A June 2001 poll taken at Tel Aviv University found that 77 percent of Israeli Jews approved of the policy. Dr. Ely Karmon of the Israel based Institute for Counter Terrorism believes that the Israeli use of preemptive self-defense is in fact the best means of responding to the terrorists as the practice is largely carried out with concern for collateral civilian causalities. "They [the Israeli military] are not bombing indiscriminately or using heavy weapons as necessary to hit Hezbolla outposts in Lebanon. Here we have much greater control, greater intelligence, and the ability to act."

One of the most high-level public killings was of the Secretary General of the Popular Front for the Liberation of Palestine, Mustapha Zibri, on August 27, 2001. An Israeli helicopter fired two rockets and obliterated his office in Ramallah. Zibri's office was three doors down from Yassir Arafat's. The mechanics for how the killings are carried out generally start with Israeli intelligence that process reports and information from a variety of sources to include Palestinian collaborators. Using this information the government compiles a list of people that they have concluded are definitely involved in terrorist activity. The next step is to give the Palestinian Authority the list of suspects for arrest, which proves futile due to the fact that the Palestinian Authority refuses to act on the information. Thus, when an opportunity to kill the terrorist presents itself, the approval to kill is given and Israeli helicopters or snipers kill the terrorist by surprise attack at a location calculated to reduce collateral damages to civilians.

In summary, assassination is an unlawful killing in violation of the rule of law. Whether conducted in peacetime or wartime, assassination is absolutely forbidden under international law even in the absence of an executive order supposedly banning the practice. Anyone who carries out an act of assassination would be guilty of either murder or a war crime, depending on the circumstances. Furthermore, anyone who ordered the assassination would be guilty of either murder or a war crime under the concept of command responsibility.

On the other hand, the use of force in legitimate acts of self-defense does not qualify as assassination. Those who think that the United States is somehow restricted by Executive Order 12333 from targeting terrorists or rogue nations that threaten to conduct terrorist acts are mistaken. If it is the case that Executive Order 12333 causes more confusion than not in understanding the applicable rule of law, should it be repealed? One commentator has argued that the "failure of the executive order to outline exactly what it prohibits has set planners and operators adrift." But a stronger case can be made by pointing out that it is the public, politicians and commentators that are most confused by the executive order, not the military planners and operators. The military generally understands that the proper application of force in self-defense does not violate Executive Order 12333. Politicians and commentators seem most susceptible to succumbing to the temptation to associate an overbroad interpretation to the ban on assassination.

As a practical matter, it is fundamentally obvious that no American president will ever repeal Executive Order 12333 unless he immediately replaces it with a better product. The resulting negative repercussions in the sphere of public relations alone would render such a move remarkably insensate. The better product, of course, would require a document consisting of some pages that clearly defines assassination and then distinguishes those circumstances where the lawful use of force could be applied. As America continues its War on Terror, it is vitally important to operate under clearly framed principles under the rule of law and not shrouded ambiguities and innuendos. Our enemies as well as our friends and allies need to understand that the Untied States of America operates under the rule of law. As Professor John Norton Moore of Virginia so aptly put it:

> Law, however, is vitally important. Even in the short run, law serves as a standard of appraisal for national actions and as a means of communicating intentions to both friend and foe, and perceptions about lawfulness can profoundly influence both national and international support for particular actions.

4.11 The Constitution and the War on Terror

To some, the War on Terror portends a society in which the rights of the individual will more and more have to give way in favor of ever increasing security measures designed to vindicate the expanding desire of protecting the safety of the public from global terrorism. It may be a correct assessment that the continuing War on Terror makes our civil rights *vulnerable* to erosion, but the so-called "slippery slope" argument which resists all changes in the law must be viewed against the clear and present threat of al-Qa'eda-styled terrorist organizations and their possible use of weapons of mass destruction. The all too real specter of mass casualties, billions of dollars in physical damage and civil disorder absolutely demands that the federal government fulfill its primary mission of ensuring the safety of its citizens and the viability of its citizens. As Supreme Court Justice Robert Jackson remarked in *Terminello v. Chicago*, "[t]he constitutional Bill of Rights … [is not] a suicide pact." Jackson went on to say: "The choice is not between order and liberty. It is between liberty with order and anarchy without either."

On the other hand, there are many who object to law enforcement tools such as the PATRIOT Act as an unconstitutional violation of civil liberties. According to Gregory Nojeim, the Associate Director of the ACLU's Washington Office: "These new and unchecked powers could be used against American citizens who are not under criminal investigation, immigrants who are here within our borders legally and also those whose First Amendment activities are deemed to be threats to national security by the Attorney General." Interestingly, a handful of states and many local governments around the nation have expressed opposition to the PATRIOT Act in the form of resolutions or even local statutes. In February 2004, the city of New York approved a resolution condemning the PATRIOT Act. In doing so, New York City joined 246 other municipalities and counties, along with three states, that have enacted legislation in opposition to the PATRIOT Act. One New York City council member spoke out about the new measure stating: "The Patriot Act [sic] is really unpatriotic, it undermines our civil rights and civil liberties."

Despite efforts to demonize the PATRIOT Act, the provisions are actually a judicious effort to stop future terror attacks and in 2006 a majority of the members of Congress voted to extend the vast majority of the provisions. Commenting on the number of local governments that had passed resolutions or laws against the PATRIOT Act, a Justice Department spokesman noted that many of the ordinances were based on "erroneous" information and that the PATRIOT Act "has been one of the most important tools Congress has given the government to fight terrorism and prevent terrorist attacks." In order to thwart future attacks, law enforcement must have the legal ability to gather information on suspected terrorists in order to stop them before they attack.

Another issue of debate that occurred in 2006 was the Bush Administration's "data mining" program that targeted the international calls between terrorist suspects abroad and individuals in the United States. This warrantless program was conducted without a FISA court order by the National Security Agency (NSA) with the help of the nation's largest telecommunications firms. While the program did not include listening to telephone calls, legal and security experts debated the government's argument that President Bush was acting under his wartime authority as the Commander in Chief under Article 2 of the Constitution and the Congressional Authorization for Use of Military Force after 9/11. Indeed, echoing Chief Justice John Marshall announcement in *Marbury v. Madison* that "a legislative act contrary to the Constitution is not law," the FISA Court of Review in 2002 affirmed that FISA did not prohibit the president from exercising his independent constitutional power.

In times of crisis, the government has always taken steps to curtail civil liberties. In the past some of the measures have been clearly unconstitutional, e.g., President Lincoln's suspension of the writ of habeas corpus for jailed "Northern" American citizens, or President Roosevelt's internment of thousands of U.S. citizens of Japanese descent. Compared with these abuses, the government's efforts in the War on Terror may not seem extreme at all. In fact, the American people have overwhelmingly approved of the overall performance of the government in finding a working balance between defending their freedoms and protecting their freedoms. Nevertheless, as the federal government makes policy and moves the nation in the Global War on Terrorism, it is prudent to well recall the caution of George Washington: "the price of freedom is eternal vigilance." Accordingly, all measures employed to combat terrorism must be within the bounds of democratic principles and the rule of law. More importantly, so-called extraordinary laws should be proportionate to the terrorist threat and frequently reviewed, revised and rescinded if no longer needed. For instance, the London bombings of July 2005 caused the British to develop new security laws that seriously challenge the foundation of freedom of speech by making it illegal to glorify or indirectly incite terrorism. Obviously, the line between free speech and security is greatly stressed in the War on Terror because this is not a war in the classic sense. This war will not end with a formal surrender. Thus, changes in law that appear necessary in the name of security for the moment may become an unwanted fabric of our society for future generations. If one is to avoid the slippery slope, then marked and clear legal notches must be set out beyond which we as Americans will not pass.

4.12 Questions for Discussion

1. *Legitimate targets.* A major debate exists surrounding the relationship terrorist agents must have to a terrorist organization in order to be considered legitimate military targets in the War on Terror. Considering the different classifications for terrorism discussed in Chapter 1, who is a legitimate target in the War on Terror, individuals or countries? Should individual terrorists be targeted militarily or judicially? Why might the favored response for a nation to a terrorist attack be to use military force as opposed to other methods? If the events of September 11, 2001, had not occurred would your answer be the same?

2. *Financing terrorism.* The United States Code provides: "Whoever knowingly provides material support or resources to a foreign terrorist organization, or attempts or conspires to do so, shall be fined under this title or imprisoned not more than 15 years, or both, and, if the death of any person results, shall be imprisoned for any term of years or for life." 18 U.S.C.A. § 2339B(a)(1). In *United States v. Hammoud*, 381 F.3d at 316. (4th Cir. 2004) defendant, Mohammed Hammoud challenged his conviction in district court after he was found to have given aid to the foreign terrorist organization, Hizballah. Can this law aimed at criminalizing financial contributions to terrorist organizations do more to deter terrorism than laws which punish terrorist acts?

3. *Why did the United States refuse to sign Protocol I to the Geneva Conventions*? The United States is not a signatory to Protocol Additional to the Geneva Conventions of August 12, 1946, and Relating to the Protection of Victims of International Armed Conflicts, June 8, 1977, 1125 U.N.T.S. 3. Protocol I seeks to extend coverage to non-international conflicts in which "peoples are fighting against colonial domination and alien occupation and against racist regimes in the exercise of their right to self-determination." See generally Abraham Sofaer, *The U.S. Decision Not to Ratify Protocol I to the Geneva Conventions on the Protection of War Victims*, 82 Am. J. Int'l. L. 784 (1988).

4. *Lawful detention*? In September 1868, the U.S. District Court for the Southern District of Florida denied a writ of habeas corpus for Dr. Samuel Mudd, a civilian citizen of Maryland, who had been convicted by a military tribunal for his part in the Lincoln assassination of April 14, 1865. *Ex Parte Mudd*, 17 F. Cas. 954 (S.D. Fla. 1868) (No. 9,899). On June 30, 1865, the military tribunal convicted Dr. Mudd and sentenced him to life in prison. Dr. Mudd was transferred to a prison in Florida where he filed a writ of habeas corpus relying on *Ex Parte Milligan*. In denying the petition, Judge Thomas J. Boynton distinguished the murder of Lincoln as a military crime, even though the war had arguably ended prior to the assassination of Lincoln. The appeal of this decision reached the United States Supreme Court in February 1869, but was dismissed by Chief Justice Chase as moot due to the fact that President Andrew Johnson had pardoned Dr. Mudd and two other civilians. Was Mudd's detention lawful?

5. *Defining enemy combatants.* DOD Directive 2310.01E, entitled *The Department of Defense Detainee Program,* dated September 5, 2006, describes an enemy combatant as "a person engaged in hostilities against the United States or its coalition partners during *armed conflict* [emphasis added]. Is the DOD term "armed conflict" consistent with the Military Commission Act definition of enemy combatants?

6. *Military commission or federal court*? Richard Reid, a.k.a. Abdel Rahim, is a British citizen with direct ties to the al-Qa'eda network. He attempted to explode bombs hidden in his shoes while aboard a flight over the Atlantic Ocean. Each shoe contained about 4 oz. of an explosive named pentaerythritoltetranitrate. The crew and passengers subdued him. On January 16, 2002, Mr. Reid was indicted by a federal grand jury on nine counts, including the use of a

weapon of mass destruction and attempted murder. Admitting his ties to al-Qa'eda and hatred for America, Reid pled guilty in October 2002 to eight charges including attempted use of a weapon of mass destruction, attempted homicide and placing an explosive device on an aircraft. Should Reid have been transferred to military custody and tried by military commission? Is it appropriate or legal for the Bush Administration to process some al-Qa'eda members through federal district court while others are processed through a military commission per the 2006 Military Commission Act? Should U.S. citizenship really make a difference?

7. *Free speech vs. material support.* In October 2006, Adam Yahiuye Gadahn, an American citizen from California was indicted by a federal grand jury and charged with treason and providing material support to al-Qa'eda per 18 USC § 2339B. Gadahn has appeared in numerous al-Qa'eda videos where he praises the terror group and calls on others to participate in murder and violence against the United States. The form of support is identified as "personnel" and "services." Presumably the theory is that Gadahn provided himself as personnel to al-Qa'eda. Can 2339B lawfully function as the equivalent of a membership prohibition? Due to the expansive reach of the Material Support Act, Professor Norman Abrams urges legal observers to "ask whether and to what extent the residual and preventative uses of these sections are beginning to trespass upon fundamental values of liberty." (Norman Abrams, *The Material Support Terrorism Offenses: Perspectives Derived from the (Early) Model Penal Code*, 1 J. NAT'L SEC. L. POL. 5, 6-7 (2005). Do you agree?

8. *Privacy concerns*. Bomb-sniffing dogs that are trained to smell bomb components that screening devices might miss are being employed at some airports. Is this approach more or less objectionable than the proposed use of TSA airport screeners trained to spot "suspicious behavior" among passengers? What privacy issues are raised?

9. *Advancing the proper rule of law.* In February 2006, the U.N. Commission on Human Rights issued a joint report on the situation of the detainees at Guantanamo Bay. Based on interviews of "former Guantanamo Bay detainee's currently residing or detained in France, Spain and the United Kingdom," lawyers for detainees and "information available in the public domain" (the Rapporteur's refused to visit the detention facility at Guantanamo Bay for a first hand inspection) they concluded that the United States was engaging in "torture" in violation of international law. The Rapporteur's also found that the detention itself was illegal and that the "United States Government should either expeditiously bring all Guantanamo Bay detainees to trial [via domestic criminal or an international tribunal] or release them without further delay." What premise did the Rapporteur's reject in making the second finding? Why is the first finding flawed?

Selected Bibliography

Aquinas, St. Thomas. ON POLITICS AND ETHICS. (Paul E. Sigmund trans. 1988).

Bank, Aaron. OSS To Green Berets. 1986.

De Vattel, E. The Law Of Nations Or The Principles Of International Law Applied To The Conduct And To The Affairs Of Nations And Of Sovereigns. (Charles G. Fenwick trans. 1916).

Dep't of Army, Field Manual 27-10. *The Law of Land Warfare*. July 1956.

Dunoff, Jeffrey L., Steven R. Ratner, and David Wippman. International Law Norms, Actors Process. 2002.

Elliott, H.W. The Trial And Punishment Of War Criminals In The "New World Order." (unpublished doctoral of juridical science thesis 1996) (available at the Rare Book Room, U. of Virginia School of Law).

Ford, Franklin L. Political Murder: From Tyrannicide To Terrorism. 1985.

Franck, Thomas M., and Michael J. Glennon. Foreign Relations And National Security Law. 1993.

Geneva Convention of August 12, 1949, Relative to the Treatment of Prisoners of War, 6 U.S.T. 3316, T.I.A.S. No. 3364, 75 U.N.T.S. 135.

Gentile, Alberico. De Iure Belli Libri Tres. (John C. Rolfe trans. 1933).

Grotius, Hugo. The Law Of War And Peace (1625), *reprinted in* The Law Of War: A Documentary History. L. Freidman. (ed.) 1972.

Hague Convention No. IV, October 118, 1907. Regulations Respecting the Laws and Customs of War on Land.

Hartigan, Richard Shelly. Lieber's Code And The Law Of War. 1983.

Heddings, Raymond E. U.S. Roles in Providing Humanitarian Assistance following NBC Accidents/ Incidents: The Legal Considerations. 1999.

Kerwin, Cornelius M. Rulemaking: How Government Agencies Write Law And Make Policy. 1999.

McHugh, William. *Forcible Self-help in International Law*. 25 Naval War C. Rev. 61. 1972.

Moore, John Norton. Law And The Grenada Mission. 1984.

Parks, W. Hays. *Memorandum of Law: Executive Order 12333 and Assassination*. The Army Lawyer, Dec.1989, at 4.

Pumphrey, Carolyn W. (ed.) Transnational Threats: Blending Law Enforcement And Military Strategies. available at http://carlisle-www.army.mil/usassi/welcome.htm. 2000.

Scales, Robert H., Jr. Future Warfare. 1999.

Schindler, Dietrich, and Jiai Toman. The Laws Of Armed Conflict 3. 1988.

Schmitt, Michael N. *State Sponsored Assassination in International and Domestic Law*. 17 Yale J. Int'l L. 679. 1992.

Sloan, Steven. Beating International Terrorism. 1986.

Thieme, R.B., Jr. Freedom Through Military Victory. 1977.

Chapter 5

Necessity and Rationale for the Law of War—Lessons from My Lai

Nothing is new under the sun.

—Ecclesiastes 1: 9-10

It is often remarked that we learn from history that we learn nothing from history. This truism has been attributed to the German philosopher Georg Hegel but the principle is certainly one of ancient origins, reflecting the fact that the human race has generally exhibited a total inability to learn even the most elementary historical lessons. Of course, the tragedy is that this need not be so, mankind can learn from history. Indeed, if history teaches mankind anything about avoiding the mistakes and disasters of the past, it is that he must first understand the historical lessons—lessons often realized only after the expenditure of incredible amounts of human blood and treasure—and then inculcate those lessons in each succeeding generation.

In the War on Terror, the most critical lesson is that the application of lawful violence is a necessary ingredient in defeating those who employ, or seek to employ, violence in an unlawful manner. The concept of lawful violence, of course, refers to the requirement that the international law of war must be fully followed. Those who violate the law of war commit war crimes.

To a large degree, from Valley Forge (1778) to Afghanistan (2001) and Iraq (2003), the United States military can take full credit for a commendable record in its adherence to the law of war. This is because of its commitment to institutionalizing certain truisms which might be encapsulated in the old saw that "[a] right thing must be done in a right way or it is wrong."

Thus, defeating the enemy—a right thing—must be done under the law of war—in a right way—or the entire activity is wrong. This assessment is not only true in a democratic society, it is fundamentally necessary for the continuation of that democracy. On the other hand, there is no such thing as a "clean" war. In its War on Terror, America has suffered a significant number of tactical errors in the use of its military ranging from friendly fire incidents that have killed American soldiers and the soldiers of its coalition partners, to the unintended deaths of non-combatants by coalition military fire power. While these tragedies have been leveraged by some in order to criticize the legitimacy of the American led effort to employ force against its enemies on the battlefield, all such attempts to denigrate the United States pale in the wake of the prisoner abuse scandal at Abu Ghraib. The 2003 release of photographs of American soldiers abusing Iraqi detainees at the Abu Ghraib prison in Iraq created a firestorm of concern that threatened to derail several of the most fundamental policy and legal pillars on which America conducts the War on Terror. While it is now well established that the abuses were not systemic, they provided a propaganda bonanza to the terrorists. The War on Terror is not won or lost on the battlefield, it is won or lost in the sphere of public opinion. Indeed, if the allegations of a command "cover-up" regarding the alleged murder of 24 Iraqi civilians at Al-Haditha by Marines proves true, the political damage could prove devastating to the war effort.

Accordingly, it is necessary to explore the law of war and the rationale and necessity for abiding by those rules. Because these lessons are timeless, the very best lesson plan for the United States flows not from Abu Ghraib, but from a notorious war crime committed by American forces in the Vietnam War—the My Lai massacre.

The War on Terror has involved the use of traditional combat techniques last seen in the 2003 war against Saddam Hussein, where two armed groups of soldiers engage in open combat. It also involves the more troubling type of combat which Americans are now facing in Iraq and encountered in larger measure in the Indo-China conflict, where the Viet Cong and their communist allies regularly violated the law of war by refusing to wear distinctive uniforms, hiding amongst the civilian population, torturing and murdering American prisoners of war, and murdering noncombatants by the thousands. Tragically, in the Vietnam War, this led to several instances of abuse of the law of war by American soldiers, the most notorious being the massacre at My Lai. While American forces in Afghanistan and Iraq have generally exhibited broad compliance with the law of armed conflict and an understanding that ethical conduct and military prowess go hand in hand, it is absolutely imperative that the significance of the lessons learned at My Lai are revisited and impressed on every American soldier as the nation once again faces an illegal combatant who engages in the same tactics as the Viet Cong and views our adherence to the rule of law as a weakness.

For many Americans, the knowledge of enemy violations of the law of war elicits a negative reaction to the United States being required to follow the law of war. If the terrorists and allies of the terrorists do not abide by the rules, e.g., militants in Iraq have decapitated several American soldiers and engaged in the wholesale slaughter of innocent civilians, why should America? For this reason it is imperative that individuals who are unfamiliar with the law of war understand both the basic rationale and necessity for the law of war. This applies to the American people in general and, more importantly, to the soldiers who actually fight the enemy in the War on Terror.

Again, while it may seem out of place to discuss the law of war in the Global War on Terrorism against the lessons learned at My Lai, there is no better model to serve as the perfect vehicle for learning or relearning the necessity and rationale for the rules of armed conflict. Furthermore, it is equally necessary that American forces impress on their allies the need to comply with the law of war. In fact, reports filtered out of Afghanistan in 2002 that some of our Afghan allies had engaged in violations of the law of war. One incident is said to have occurred in the case of the deaths of 200 Taliban prisoners of war that died while being transported in shipping containers from the battlefield to internment camps. Similarly, abuses by Iraqi security forces are becoming regular fare. Not only is America relentlessly scrutinized and judged on how it complies with the law of war, but the conduct of our allies is also factored into the assessment. Criminal behavior casts a cloud over both the forces and the new governments of Afghanistan and Iraq.

As a nation that is governed by the rule of law, it is vital that America validate—for itself and for the civilized world—the legitimacy of its War on Terror by the manner in which it conducts that war. Clearly, the United States cannot claim that its forces are the "good guys" unless the rules of armed conflict are meticulously observed. Enforcement of the rules of war is a demonstration to the world and the American people that America is waging a *jus in bello*. No doubt, the attention of the world has shifted from the murderous machinations of the al-Qa'eda, the Iraqi illegal combatants and their like, to an extreme focus on how well the United States and its allies adhere to all aspects of the rule of law in battling these people. For better or worse, this phenomenon is a reality. No one shows interest regarding the fact that the "bad guys" behave in gross violation of the law of war as their very *modus vivendi*. After all, that is precisely why they are the bad guys. On the other hand, the world has an intense interest in how the "good guys" perform. If a military claims that their cause is just, they must act accordingly.

5.1 The Law of War

Warfare is not a novel phenomenon: it is as old as human history itself. Even a cursory review of the practice reveals that all cultures and societies have participated in warfare, either in defense or in aggression. Prior to the adoption of the U.N. Charter, which mandates that the analysis for determining the legitimate use of force turn under the self-defense provisions of Article 51, the concept of waging a just war was known as *jus ad bellum*. *Jus ad bellum* encompassed several elements to include: (1) the nation had a just cause; (2) the nation was acting under the legitimate governing authority; (3) the nation had just intentions; (4) the nation issued a public declaration of the causes for the use of force and the intentions associated with the use of that force; (5) the nation considered the proportionality in the results; (6) the nation demonstrated that the use of force was only used as a last resort; and (7) there existed a reasonable hope of success.

As stated, international law no longer recognizes *jus ad bellum* as a viable legal tool in determining when military force is lawful. Nevertheless, as a practical matter, *jus ad bellum* still has great moral weight in the context of demonstrating the validity of the use of force and ensuring the continuation of public support in a pluralistic society for the Global War on Terrorism.

In tandem with the concept of *jus ad bellum*, the term *jus in bello* refers to just conduct in war or abiding by the law of war. This means that a nation that goes to war engages enemy targets under the concepts of military necessity, proportionality and unnecessary suffering. In contrast to *jus ad bellum*, *jus in bello* is still a recognized concept in international law. As a matter of fact, as long as mankind has practiced war there have been rules to lessen and regulate the attendant sufferings associated with warfare.

To the uninitiated in the study of war, it seems somewhat incongruent that one of man's most violent activities should be governed by rules of conduct. Some writers, such as Leo Tolstoy, have even argued that the very establishment of rules which seek to regulate warfare are per se immoral because such rules wrongfully cloak war with a form of legitimacy and are therefore counterproductive to the goal of eliminating the scourge of war. Tolstoy advanced the notion that the waging of war should not be regulated at all, "when it becomes too horrible, rational men will outlaw war altogether."

Fortunately, most serious thinkers reject this utopian attitude, acknowledging the necessity of rules of conduct to mitigate the various categories of sufferings that are the natural consequence of war. The law of war was never intended to be an idealistic proscription against war.

The current corpus of the law of war consists of all of those laws, by treaty and customary principles, that are applicable to warfare. Most nations have bond themselves by international agreements to follow the law of war. Those nations that have not signed these international agreements are nevertheless bound by them if the rules have reached the status of customary international law. Customary international law comes from observing past uniformities among nations of a norm or standard that has reached widespread acceptance in the international community. Evidence of customary international law may be found in judicial decisions, the writing of noted jurists, diplomatic correspondence, and other evidence concerning the practices of States.

The cornerstone of the law of war is the Geneva Conventions of 1949. In the modern era, every nation on the planet is absolutely obligated to abide by the Geneva Conventions of 1949, whether they have signed the Conventions or not. The 1949 Geneva Conventions cover four categories:

- Geneva Convention of August 12, 1949, for the Amelioration of the Condition of the Wounded and Sick in Armed Forces in the Field;
- Geneva Convention of August 12, 1949, for the Amelioration of the Condition of the Wounded, Sick, and Shipwrecked Members of Armed Forces at Sea;
- Geneva Convention of August 12, 1949, Relative to the Treatment of Prisoners of War; and
- Geneva Convention of August 12, 1949, Relative to the Protections of Civilian Persons in Time of War.

In general, the rules of warfare are focused both on the proper targeting of military objectives and the treatment of enemy detainees, prisoners of war and other noncombatants. Examples of the law of war include such common sense rules as the requirement to treat prisoners and detainees humanely; they may not be abused under any circumstances. Also, the probation on targeting for military attack civilians or protected places, such as hospitals and religious sites, and the duty to treat all noncombatants with dignity and respect are integral components of the law of war.

In the War on Terror, Congress has not declared war under the authority granted in Article I of the Constitution. This fact makes absolutely no difference in regards to America's obligation to follow the law of war. In fact, the law of war immediately applies whenever there is an international armed conflict involving two or more States, regardless of how the parties to that conflict care to label the conflict.

Mirroring the Geneva Conventions, the United States military has codified the law of war in FM 27-10. FM 27-10 affirms that the basic goal of the law of war is to limit the impact of the inevitable evils of war by:

- protecting both combatants and noncombatants from unnecessary suffering;
- safeguarding certain fundamental human rights of persons who fall into the hands of the enemy, particularly prisoners of war, the wounded and sick, and civilians; and
- facilitating the restoration of peace.

Violations of the law of war are called war crimes. In FM 27-10: "The term war crime is the technical expression for a violation of the law of war by any person or persons, military of civilian. Every violation of the law of war is a war crime." The definition in FM 27-10 would include both customary and treaty law within the parameters of the law of war. War crimes are categorized as either grave breaches or simple breaches. The term grave breaches is technically only related to those violations set out as such in the Geneva Conventions. Grave breaches would include the following acts committed against persons or property specifically protected by the Geneva Conventions: willful killing; torture or inhuman treatment, including biological experiments; or willfully causing great suffering or serious injury to body or health.

Under the Geneva Conventions, each nation is under a strict obligation to search for all persons alleged to have committed war crimes. They must investigate the allegations of war crimes and if a grave breach of the law of war is discovered, the nation must either prosecute or extradite those so accused. As previously related, it is the policy of the United States that all American military personnel so accused are prosecuted by military courts marital under the substantive provisions of the UCMJ.

5.2 Voices from the Past—My Lai

Every army has its own mythology, its symbols of heroism as well as its symbols of shame. The army of the United States is no exception. In the sphere of heroism the American military has an incredible reservoir of noble and fantastic figures to draw from—men whose military proficiency and ethical conduct in combat have maintained an impeccable American reputation for both battlefield excellence and strict adherence to the laws regulating warfare. More than any other army in modern history, the American army is able to proudly claim as its own some of the greatest soldiers in the history of warfare. Robert E. Lee and Douglas MacArthur certainly are two of the very best this country has ever produced and therefore the subject of much study in American military schools.

Unfortunately, the United States military also has its figures of shame; soldiers who have engaged in blatant violations of the most fundamental and civilized rules regulating behavior in combat. While American misconduct is certainly an aberration and not the norm, this fact does not lessen the severity of the shame. Without question, each and every grave breach of the law of war represents a horrible scar on the credibility of the American armed forces, as well as on the civilized democracy which they protect.

The greatest emblem of American military shame in the twentieth century occurred during the Vietnam War, a war few Americans have yet to properly understand. While there were several cases of unlawful killings of unarmed civilians committed by American troops during the Indo-China War, by far the most violent, and hence the most infamous, has come to be called the My Lai massacre.

Of course, any discussion of American violations of the law of war during Vietnam, in general, and at My Lai, in particular, must be viewed against the background of the enemy's activities. In this context, American violations absolutely pale in comparison to the thousands upon thousands of command directed slaughters that were committed by the communist regime of then, North Vietnam and their Viet Cong allies. With respect to the American presence in Vietnam, My Lai can certainly be characterized as an aberration. Professor Rummel noted:

> The American record in Vietnam with regard to observance of the law of war is not a succession of war crimes and does not support charges of a systematic and willful violation of existing agreements for standards of human decency in time of war, as many critics of the American involvement have alleged. Such charges were based on a distorted picture of the actual battlefield situation, on ignorance of existing rules of engagement, and on a tendency to construe every mistake of judgment as a wanton breach of the law of war.

As was the case for the Taliban and al-Qa'eda in Afghanistan and the terrorists in Iraq, blatant violations of numerous provisions of the law of war, to include murder, torture and intimidation, were the *modus operandi* for the communists. In the estimate of Rummel, North Vietnam sponsored the slaughter of over one and a quarter million of its own people from 1945 to 1987. Included in this figure, since the fall of South Vietnam in 1975, are over 250,000 boat people and 250,000 other civilians who were either ruthlessly murdered outright or who perished in communist death camps set up to "re-educate" non-communists. Sadly, these massive crimes have never been punished, much less acknowledged by numerous human rights groups. "In sum, re-education was a label for revenge, punishment, and social prophylaxes. But unlike the Khmer Rouge who were too public about their mass killing, the Vietnamese regime at first cleverly hid it from the outside world."

Nonetheless, the enemy's barbaric conduct offers little solace to the American conscience in the wake of My Lai. Misconduct by the enemy, be it the Communists of North Vietnam, the al-Qa'eda-styled terrorists, or the minions of Saddam Hussein in no way justifies American violations of the law of war. For the Viet Cong and North Vietnamese, the strategy for a communist victory was intentionally predicated on terror and propaganda; for the United States, the massacre at My Lai was a horrible contradiction.

5.3 Facts of My Lai

The hard facts relating to the My Lai massacre are now fairly certain, thanks to a thorough criminal investigation aimed at the perpetrators of the crime and a collateral administrative investigation ordered by the Secretary of the Army and headed by Lieutenant General W. R. Peers. Despite an initial cover-up by some of those associated with the crime, the enormity of the atrocity made it unlikely that it could long be kept secret, although for well over a year the general public knew nothing of the incident.

On March 16, 1968, an American combat task force of the 23rd Infantry Division (the Americal Division) launched an airmobile assault into the village complex of Son My in the province of Quang Ngai, South Vietnam. As was the case for all such operations, the attack was executed only after the commander of the task force, Lieutenant Colonel Frank Barker (the task force was called Task Force Barker), had assembled the key junior commanders for a final review of the details of the combat operation. This briefing, which took place on March 15, 1968, involved discussions on the positioning of helicopters, artillery preparation and the specific assignments of the three companies that comprised the task force. While the other two companies provided blocking and support functions, Charlie Company, commanded by Captain Ernest Medina, would take the primary responsibility for battling any enemy resistance encountered in the village.

At the briefing the commanders were reminded that intelligence reports had indicated that the village complex was a staging area for the 48th Viet Cong local force battalion and that the Americans could expect an enemy force of up to two hundred and fifty soldiers. In short, the United States soldiers anticipated that they would be outnumbered by the enemy. Still, having yet to engage any enemy forces in direct combat, the Barker Task Force saw the operation as an opportunity to finally fight the ever-elusive Viet Cong in the open.

The intelligence regarding a large enemy force proved to be incorrect. When the American combat forces landed they soon found that the village was occupied almost totally by noncombatants. Although the civilians offered no resistance whatsoever, some of the members of Charlie Company went on a command directed killing spree. Under the direct supervision of several company grade officers, First Lieutenant William L. Calley, Jr., being the most notorious, American troops murdered well over 200 unarmed South Vietnamese civilians.

The largest killing of civilians occurred in the hamlet of My Lai, known to the Americans by the nickname of "Pinkville," a part of the Son My complex. Thus, the entire massacre came to be known as the My Lai massacre. The murdered consisted primarily of women, children and old men; some shot in groups, others as they fled. At My Lai proper most of the civilians had been methodically herded into large groups and then gunned down, primarily under the direct supervision of Lieutenant William Calley.

In addition to the unlawful killing of civilians, the soldiers engaged in the destruction of most of the homes and in the killing of the domestic animals in the village. Several cases of rape were also reported to have taken place during the massacre. When it was over, the statistics told the story: one American soldier in Charlie Company had been wounded by friendly fire and hundreds of South Vietnamese women, children and old men were dead.

The only positive aspect of the incident was the fact that some of the American solders had either refused to participate or had openly attempted to halt the killings. Chief Warrant Officer Two (CW2) Hugh C. Thompson, Jr., was one of those who took specific actions to halt the killings. Tasked with piloting one of the helicopters during the operation, CW2 Thompson testified that he noticed large numbers of "wounded and dead civilians everywhere." Assuming that the

Americans on the ground would assist those who were wounded—as was the standard procedure—CW2 Thompson began to mark the location of the wounded Vietnamese civilians with smoke canisters as he flew overhead. To his horror, he witnessed the exact opposite. Drawn to the smoke, American soldiers were shooting the wounded that CW2 Thompson had so accurately marked. Still only partially realizing the full impact of what was happening on the ground, CW2 Thompson immediately landed his helicopter in My Lai, near a large drainage ditch filled with dead and dying civilians. As he began to assist those Vietnamese who were still alive to leave the area, Lieutenant Calley and a handful of troops approached.

When CW2 Thompson asked for assistance in caring for the civilians, Lieutenant Calley made it clear that he intended to kill the remaining noncombatants. CW2 Thompson recalled that Lieutenant Calley said: "The only way you'll get them [the civilians] out is with a hand grenade." However, instead of backing down from the clear designs of his superior officer, CW2 Thompson quickly ordered his M60 machine gunner, Private First Class Lawrence Colburn, to open fire on the American soldiers if they came any closer to the remaining civilians. CW2 Thompson then placed all the civilians he could on his helicopter and ferried them to safety.

5.4 My Lai Comes to Light

The initial attempts to cover up the crime could not quell the nightmares of those who had witnessed the murders. Rumors of the massacre persisted, coming to a boiling point when an ex-serviceman named Ron Ridenhour sent a second hand account of the massacre to President Richard Nixon, "twenty three members of Congress, the Secretaries of State and Defense, the Secretary of the Army, and the chairman of the Joint Chiefs of Staff." Ridenhour had written a four-page letter that chronicled detailed information from several of the soldiers who had either taken part in the bloody killings or had witnessed it first hand.

Ron Ridenhour's letter received prompt attention both in the media and in the legislative and executive branches of government. Needless to say, the initial military reaction was one of disbelief; no one believed that a massacre of that magnitude could have been committed by American soldiers or that the massacre "could have remained hidden for so long."

As the horrible truth of the crime became known, the army quickly launched the comprehensive Peers Commission investigation, popularly known as the Peers Report. At the same time the general public tasted the horror of the My Lai massacre through a series of gruesome photographs of the dead which had been taken by a former army photographer named Ronald Haeberle. The color photographs appeared in the December 1969 issue of *Life* magazine.

5.5 Impact of My Lai

In the subsequent judicial actions associated with the murders at My Lai, charges were preferred against four officers and nine enlisted men. Twelve other officers were charged with military type offenses associated with the cover-up. Of these, only Lieutenant William Calley was convicted. The other officers and enlisted men either had the charges against them dismissed or were found not guilty at their courts martial.

Tried before a military panel composed of six officers, Lieutenant Calley was found guilty of the premeditated murder of twenty-two noncombatants and of assault with intent to murder a two-year-old child. Although Calley was sentenced to a dismissal and confinement at hard labor for life, the convening authority reduced this to a dismissal and twenty years at hard labor, and the Secretary of the Army further reduced the sentence to a dismissal and ten years at hard labor.

Aside from the issue of individual culpability for those involved in the massacre, My Lai had a devastating impact on the outcome of the Vietnam War. Given the total lack of any semblance of a grand strategy on the part of the United States to win the war, it can be argued that this atrocity did as much to harm the survival of an independent South Vietnam as any other single event in the Indo-China War. The public revelation of this massacre not only solidified the anti-war movement in the United States, but it cast a pall of confusion and shame over the nation at large that significantly contributed to the eventual abandonment of South Vietnam to the Communist forces in the North. Beginning in 1969, a vocal and radical minority of war protestors incorporated opposition to the American ground soldier to their general opposition to the War. For these people, the enemy was now the American soldier, not the Communists. The revelation of what happened at My Lai dealt a blow to the *esprit de corps* and professionalism of the United States Army that can still be felt today.

5.6 Why Did My Lai Happen?

Taken out of the context of the social and political climates that were brewing in the United States in the late 1960s and early 1970s and viewed from a purely objective perspective, the immediate focus in the aftermath of the crime was summed up in a single word: "Why?" Why did it happen? How could so many American boys have become involved in such a heinous war crime? And, more importantly, how could the officers in command of the operation have ordered such atrocities or participated in the attempt to cover them up? To realize that some civilians were killed as a collateral matter through military action against legitimate military targets was one thing, to have ground forces intentionally shoot innocent noncombatants in cold blood was incomprehensible.

The Peers Report did not cite any one factor as the cause for the massacre at My Lai. While the panel observed that "what may have influenced one man to commit atrocities had had no effect on another," General Peers was determined that the final report should reflect some explanation as to why the massacre had occurred. Recognizing the inherent difficulty in finger pointing, the panel nonetheless identified several factors that seemed to be conducive to an environment which might have led to the violations of the law of war. In fact, the Peers factors are a witches' brew that would similarly apply to any war, particularly a conflict like Iraq and Afghanistan in which the enemy has no regard for the rule of law.

The lack of proper training in the law of war was a common theme in the interviews of the witnesses and subjects involved in My Lai. Perhaps the most graphic illustration of this factor was reflected at the trial of Lieutenant Calley when he testified that the classes on the Geneva Conventions conducted during Officer Candidate School were inadequate. In any event, the Peers Report entered specific findings that the soldiers that made up Task Force Barker had not received sufficient training in the "Law of War (Hague and Geneva Conventions), the safeguarding of noncombatants, or the Rules of Engagement." Although the requirements set out in United States Army Republic of Vietnam (USARV) Regulation 350-1, dated November 10, 1967, made it clear that, at a minimum, all soldiers were required to have annual refresher training on the Geneva Conventions, in many cases, there was no command emphasis on this requirement. Hence, to that degree, the individual soldier did not know what was required of him.

Pocket sized guidance cards, which were a mandatory issue item to all soldiers to assist in learning and abiding by the law of war, were usually never read and seldom lasted past the first monsoon rains. In addition, Military Assistance Command Vietnam (MACV) Directive 20-4, which required the immediate reporting of all violations of the law of war, was seldom stressed by the command structure.

Regardless of the deficiencies in providing training in the law of war, the Peers Report did not find this to be a significant reason for the grave breaches of multiple murders which occurred at My Lai. Such deficiencies in training might excuse minor or technical breaches of the law of war, but not the grave *malum in se* breaches. The members of the Commission correctly noted that "there were some things a soldier did not have to be told were wrong—such as rounding up women and children and then mowing them down, shooting babies out of mother's arms, and raping." It was patently obvious to the Commission that some of the members of the company were simply cold-blooded criminals dressed in military uniforms, both enlisted and officers. Clearly these individuals found themselves in an environment where there was little, if any, deterrence to the overt expression of their criminal propensities.

A tendency by some of the members of Charlie Company to view the Vietnamese people as almost subhuman was thought to be another factor which may have contributed to the massacre. Of course, the use of derogatory terms to describe the Vietnamese as nothing but "gooks," "dinks," or "slopes" was not uncommon during the Vietnam War. In fact, soldiers in all wars have developed derogatory phrases to describe their enemies; it is easier to dispatch an enemy who can be characterized as different. In the My Lai case, however, the Peers Report concluded that some of the members of Charlie Company had carried this tendency to dehumanize the enemy to an unreasonable extreme, viewing the "Vietnamese [people] with contempt, considering them subhuman, on the level of dogs."

To discover the reason for this degree of hatred, the Peers Report had a detailed background analysis done on each individual in Company C. The results showed nothing unusual. The company was an average unit with 70 percent of the troops having high school diplomas and nineteen having some college credits. The reason for the hatred was a result of a combination of several factors, the greatest of these merely a reflection of the locked-in arrogance inherent in the criminal mind, and the least, but more common, related to the frustration of having to fight an enemy who refused to abide by the law of war.

One of the most telling factors listed in the Peers Report dealt with examining the nature of the enemy that infested South Vietnam, with the implicit criticism that the United States military was never allowed to take the war to the real enemy—North Vietnam. In the South, the United States military was asked to carry out primarily defensive operations against a well-trained and well-equipped guerilla force that could not be distinguished from the local population and that refused to abide by the established principles of the law of war.

> They would set up their bunkers in villages and attack from the midst of helpless civilians. Thus, surrounding themselves with and using innocent civilians to protect themselves is in

itself a war crime and makes them criminally responsible for the resulting civilian dead ....
[T]hey would also directly attack villages and hamlets, kill the inhabitants, including children, in order to panic the civilians in the area and cause social chaos that the communist
then could exploit.

Like the al-Qa'eda and the sectarian murderers in Iraq, the Viet Cong and regular North Vietnamese Army soldiers knew their environment; they knew every path, trail, and hut in their areas
of operation. In addition, whether by brute force, which included public torture and execution, or
by psychological intimidation, the Viet Cong could count on the local support of the civilian
population for shelter, food, and intelligence. As such, it was not uncommon for women and children to actively participate in military operations against American forces. With women and children participating in combat activities, by laying booby traps, serving as scouts or actually bearing arms, the American soldier had to disregard the traditional indicators such as sex and age as
criteria for categorizing the noncombatant and concentrate instead on the extremely difficult issue of hostile intent. The Peers Report recognized this dilemma:

> The communist forces in South Vietnam had long recognized our general reluctance to do
> battle with them among the civilian populace and had used that knowledge to our tactical
> and strategic disadvantage throughout the history of the war in Vietnam. Exploitation of
> that reluctance by ... [the enemy] forces caused a distortion of the classic distinction be-
> tween combatants and noncombatants.

The difficulty of determining friend from foe was also woefully apparent in regards to the
military-aged male Vietnamese. Having developed an incredible system of underground tunnels
and caves, members of the Viet Cong and North Vietnamese Army were able to appear and disap-
pear at will. Also, when under pressure, it took only seconds to remove all military insignia or
equipment and to blend in with the local population.

Without question, the use of guerilla tactics, characterized by a heavy reliance on booby traps
and hit-and-run missions, had a tremendous adverse psychological impact on the American commanders and their troops. In numerous interviews, the Peers Report noted that the general attitude
of the soldier was one of extreme tension at engaging this unseen enemy; an enemy who hid behind women and children and would not come out in the open to do battle.

Consequently, every civilian was viewed as a potential threat, every inch of ground as hiding
a potential booby trap or mine. Descriptive terms such as "keyed up" were frequently used to
describe the apprehension and frustration associated with going out on patrol or, in many cases,
just being in friendly villages. It was not uncommon for a friendly village to be visited by the
Communists on any given night, setting landmines that would kill Americans the next day. Consequently, some of those who testified before the Peers Commission naturally assumed that the
"effects of mines and booby traps were the main reason for the atrocities committed by the task
force." This view is incorrect. While such factors undoubtedly contributed to the extraordinary
level of tension in the Barker task force, it would be far too simplistic to rely on the illegal
warfighting tactics of the enemy as the primary reason for the atrocity. If this factor was the main
cause for My Lai, one would have expected many massacres similar to My Lai to have taken
place throughout Vietnam.

Taking strong note of the overall organizational problems throughout the Army structure in Vietnam, the Peers Report actually believed that certain specific organizational problems in Task Force Barker "played the most prominent part in the My Lai incident." In focusing on Task Force Barker, it was apparent that the lack of staff personnel was a serious impediment to effective command and control. The task force "could hardly function properly, particularly in such matters as development of intelligence, planning and supervision of operations, and even routine administration."

One of the dominant characteristics of the Vietnam War was the lack of effective organization in the United States Army's force structure. From brigades to platoons, shortages of personnel and frequent rotations resulted in ad hoc arrangements regarding the composition of military units. Adding to the organizational deficiencies was the influx of poorly trained or ill-disciplined troops who were on "short" tours of a year. The short tour ensured problems in command and control; by the time the soldier had gained the necessary experience to be an effective member of the unit, he was eligible for transfer back to the "States." In the realm of directing combat operations, the lack of effective command and control can be disastrous. Indeed, the majority of abuses of detainees in the Global War on Terrorism have occurred at the hands of ill-trained and ill-disciplined National Guard and Reserve units.

Along with the general organizational problems in the task force, there was the lack of clear plans and orders concerning the operation into Son My. Because the entire operation was based on intelligence that anticipated a large enemy force in the area, the American soldiers initially expected that they were going to be outnumbered by at least two to one. In addition, the task force leaders regularly employed the term "search and destroy" without providing an adequate definition to the troops. The phrase search and destroy was never meant to provide license to kill whatever was encountered on an operation, despite the connotation of the term. In this regard, the Peers Report found that no instructions were ever given as to how to handle the civilians that might be encountered during the Son My operation.

In the final analysis, the organizational problems outlined above contributed to an overall atmosphere that made the events at My Lai possible. But the real pin in the grenade was the most fundamental aspect of the command and control problem—lack of leadership at the ground level of the operation.

5.7 Leadership

The constant mental and emotional strain associated with combat conditions is certainly exacerbated by having to face enemies like the al-Qa'eda and Iraqi insurgents who engage in violations of the law of war, but the factor that weighed the heaviest in explaining the massacre at My Lai was none of the four discussed above. Rather, it was the lack of responsible leadership at the very level where it was most critical—at the junior officer level. Although the Peers Report faulted all levels of command—"[i]t appears … that at all levels, from division down to platoon, leadership or the lack of it was perhaps the principal causative factor in the tragic events before, during, and after the My Lai operation"—the direct underlying deficiency most certainly rested at the company and platoon level. One of the participants of the massacre, Private Paul Meadlo recalled the orders of his officer:

You know what to do with them, [Lieutenant] Calley said, and walked off. Ten minutes later he returned and asked, "Haven't you got rid of them yet? I want them dead. Waste them." ... We stood about ten to fifteen feet away from them [a group of 80 men, women and children herded together] and then he [Lieutenant Calley] started shooting them. I used more than a whole clip—used four or five clips.

By virtue of the chain of command structure of the military, the primary responsibility for ensuring adherence to the law of war rests on the officer corps, with particular professionalism demanded of those junior officers at the platoon and company level, where soldiers are most apt to encounter the vast majority of issues associated with the law of war. Simply put, soldiers are expected to obey the law of war and their officers are expected to see that they do.

In their 300-page report on the Abu Ghraib abuse cases, the Department of the Army Inspector General mirrored the Peers Commission finding that "in some cases, abuse was accompanied by leadership failure at the tactical level." Another 2003 report, entitled the Taguba Report, issued by Major General Antonio Taguba, found that leadership failure was a critical problem within the chain of command at the Abu Ghraib prison. Interestingly, although several of the soldiers who were charged with abuse contented that they were ordered to commit the abuses, both reports concluded that the abuses at Abu Ghraib were not the result of soldiers following orders from superiors.

Of course, the difficult issue is not how to deal with those soldiers or officers who in their individual capacities violate the law of war—they are punished by military courts martial. Rather, the real difficulty is presented by the officer who orders his soldiers to commit war crimes, or who knowingly fails to control those under his command who violate the law of war. Clearly, the difficulty at My Lai was a result of command-directed breaches of the law of war in the context of lawful versus unlawful orders. Beginning with the premise that all soldiers are expected to obey lawful orders and are subject to courts martial if they do not, how should one expect the soldier to react to an unlawful order, assuming, of course, that the soldier can even recognize the order as unlawful?

In considering the question of whether a superior order constitutes a valid defense, military courts must take into consideration the fact that obedience to lawful military orders is the duty of every member of the armed forces; that the latter cannot be expected, in conditions of war discipline, to weigh scrupulously the legal merits of the orders received; that certain rules of warfare may be controversial; or that an act otherwise amounting to a war crime may be done in obedience to orders conceived as a measure of reprisal. At the same time, it must be borne in mind that members of the armed forces are bound to obey only lawful orders.

Furthermore, soldiers may not normally rely on the defense of superior orders should they obey an unlawful order; they are responsible for their own acts or omissions. When the defense of superior orders is raised, however, a two-tier test is applied. The first tier is a subjective one concentrating on whether or not the accused knew that the order was illegal. If the accused did not know that the order was illegal then the inquiry shifts to what the accused could reasonably have been expected to know regarding the legality of the order. "The fact that the law of war has been violated pursuant to an order of a superior authority ... does not constitute a defense ... unless [the accused] did not know and could not reasonably have been expected to know that the act ordered was unlawful." Although the objective tier of the two-part test draws upon the reasonable man standard, it is really a reasonable man under the stresses present in that particular combat environment.

Moreover, the job of distinguishing the legitimacy of the orders of a superior must be viewed against the backdrop of the entire concept of enforced discipline, extending from boot camp until discharge. The requirement for enforced discipline is absolutely essential to ensure that in the unnatural conditions of the combat environment soldiers will be able to function properly. No army could ever survive without a system promoting genuine and enforced discipline, which is firmly rooted in the requirement to obey the directions of superiors. It follows then, that if soldiers are expected to obey all lawful orders, they cannot be expected to scrupulously weigh the legal merits of orders received under the stresses of combat.

Accordingly, this means that the officer corps of any army must be filled with only the finest available men and women. Nowhere is this requirement more essential than in the selection and placement of the men who serve as officers in combat units. Only men of the highest moral caliber and military skill should be assigned the responsibility of command. In commenting on leadership skills for officers, General George S. Patton, Jr., correctly stated, "If you do not enforce and maintain discipline, you [officers] are potential murderers."

Under the concept of command responsibility or indirect responsibility, commanders can be charged with violations of the law of war committed by their subordinates if they ordered the crimes committed or knew that a crime was about to be committed, had the power to prevent it, and failed to exercise that power. In the United States, this standard has come to be called the Medina standard, so named for Captain Ernest Medina.

A second standard for indirect responsibility for commanders that has been the object of much debate and is recognized only in the United States is the Yamashita standard. The Yamashita standard is named for the World War II Japanese general, Tomoyuki Yamashita, who was tried before a military commission for war crimes committed by soldiers under his command. The primary charge against Yamashita revolved around the 20,000 Japanese sailors who went on a murder and rape rampage in Manila near the end of the war. Although the prosecution was unable to prove that Yamashita ordered the crimes or even knew about them, he was convicted under a "should-have-known" standard. This should-have-known theory held that if, through normal events, the military commander should have known of the war crimes and did nothing to stop them, he is guilty of the actions of his soldiers. This should have known standard applies only when the war crimes are associated with a widespread pattern of abuse over a prolonged period of time. In such a scenario, the commander is presumed to have knowledge of the crime or to have abandoned his command.

Herein is the underlying tragedy at My Lai and the essential lesson for battling terrorists, be it in Iraq or Afghanistan: several of the junior officers on the scene were totally inadequate, not only in moral character and integrity, but also in basic military skills. As exhibited by their gross behavior, these officers were completely unworthy of the responsibility of command.

When one details the background of William Calley, the centerpiece of the command directed killings, it is not surprising to discover that he was not the type of individual who should have been charged with leadership responsibilities of any nature. Having flunked out of a junior college in Miami, Florida, Calley moved west before enlisting in the army in 1966. Once in the army, Calley was somehow selected to attend Officers Candidate School, where he graduated despite poor academic marks. Assigned to the field as a platoon leader in a combat unit, the soldiers under his command quickly discovered that Lieutenant Calley did not even understand basic military combat skills. As one rifleman in the platoon put it, "I wonder how he ever got through Officer Candidate School. He [Calley] couldn't read no darn [sic] map and a compass would confuse his ass."

In summation, the factor that most directly resulted in the crimes at My Lai clearly rests on the shoulders of a few junior officers on the ground, Lieutenant William Calley being one of the worst. All the evidence suggests that it was Lieutenant Calley who initiated much of the murdering, acting both in his individual capacity and, far more shamefully, in his capacity as an officer in charge of subordinates. Abusing the authority of his position, Lieutenant Calley directly ordered the soldiers under his command to commit murder; some of the men obeyed while a few did not. While no one can pardon the behavior of those who carried out the illegal orders, the real tragedy of My Lai was the absence of competent and virtuous leadership.

Instead of setting the standard for moral conduct, Calley performed in the exact opposite fashion. He represented the antithesis of what a commander should be. As Sun Tzu laid out almost 500 years before Christ, "[t]he commander stands for the virtues of wisdom, sincerity, benevolence, courage, and strictness."

5.8 Lack of a Grand Strategy on the Part of the United States

A final factor that must be explored in any war and one that few commentators on Vietnam have properly gauged is the full impact that the lack of a grand strategy by the United States had on the outcome of the Indo-China conflict. In this regard, My Lai was possible due to the total and complete absence of a strategy to deal with the communist sponsored aggression against South Vietnam. President George W. Bush has established clear objectives in the War on Terror and appears to be achieving those objectives in measured steps as American forces have held rogue nations like Iraq and Libya to account. Regardless of one's political views, his unequivocal vision for the total defeat of the Taliban government of Afghanistan and the regime of Iraq's Saddam Hussein could not have been clearer. The American military understood that vision and carried it out in a magnificent manner. In the War on Terror, it is imperative that the government continue to clearly define objectives as they appear and, just as important, to carefully ensure that those objectives are achieved. Obviously, missteps have occurred, particularly in regard to the faulty intelligence on weapons of mass destruction supplied to both the Clinton and Bush Administrations, as well as the European allies and the United Nations.

If the concept of a grand strategy is defined as the use of a nation's full national power to achieve a particular objective, it is clear that at no time did the United States have a grand strategy in Vietnam for dealing with the communist aggression. On the other hand, it is just as obvious that the communists had from the very beginning a complete and dedicated grand strategy for conquering all of Indo-China through the use of revolutionary warfare. Similarly, the al-Qa'eda attack on September 11, 2001, was certainly motivated by a grand strategy to incite the whole of the Arab world in a crusade against the West and against "moderate" Arab rulers.

The basic mechanics of a sound grand strategy takes advantage of one's strengths and the enemy's vulnerabilities, while neutralizing the enemy's strengths and one's own vulnerabilities. In practically every category of factors associated with the art of waging war, the Communists in Vietnam were able to fulfill this formula; the United States was not. Thus, while the communists mobilized all of the people under their control in a unity of effort—from the military to the political—the United States consistently sought to disassociate the American people from the war. Fortunately, in the War on Terror, the al-Qa'eda has failed to realize their grand strategy and if a pivot of normalcy can be established in Afghanistan or Iraq, al-Qa'eda will not find a safe-haven for planning and training.

In the sphere of combat operations in Vietnam, the communists were particularly effective in drawing on their strengths. Conversely, the Americans typically refused to rely on their strengths. Aware that they were no match for the far superior power of American combat forces, the communists primarily employed small hit and run tactics against selected targets; like the Saddam loyalists, they quickly discovered that engaging the United States military in conventional warfare was pure folly. Coupled with guerilla tactics deliberately focused on becoming the unseen enemy, the communists illegally took advantage of the American respect for the law of war. By hiding themselves in civilian populations, the communists intentionally sought to blur the distinction between the combatant and the noncombatant, "hoping either for immunity from attack or to provoke … indiscriminate attack."

Establishing well-stocked sanctuaries in neighboring Cambodia and Laos, they were immune from defeat as long as the United States refused to seriously attack these bases. In the War on Terror, the United States faces a similar situation with al-Qa'eda and Taliban forces taking sanctuary in various countries in the Middle East, including Pakistan and Syria. In the war in Vietnam, the United States never effectually used the overwhelming strength of its military to subdue and defeat North Vietnam. Instead, American measures were confined to patrolling efforts in reaction to communist attacks in the territory of South Vietnam. In the War on Terror, the Bush administration acknowledges that it must target the enemy wherever they go. Whether through cooperation with friendly nations or on its own initiative, the United States seems correctly focused on going after the enemy—in the words of President Bush, to "smoke them out."

Finally, in tandem with their guerilla tactics, the Communists relied heavily on all forms of propaganda placing special emphasis on the ambiguity of words to erode the will of the United States to continue the war. For example, they falsely portrayed the conflict as a protracted war waged by agrarian reformers with no end in sight, while simultaneously promising a negotiated settlement at any moment. Al-Qa'eda, on the other hand, has not entirely failed in its use violence and propaganda. Before his death by U.S. forces in June 2006, Abu Musab al-Zarqawi managed to organize so many attacks on Shias and their holy places of worship that a bitter sectarian war broke out with such violence that the nation may very well never recover.

In summation, the ultimate success of the communist strategy in Vietnam rested primarily in the fact that the United States never developed a coherent overall strategy of its own. Necessarily, this mandated that the communist's grand strategy would eventually prevail. What is surprising is that it was not until 1968 that the impact of not having a viable grand strategy became apparent to the American soldier. When it did, however, the painful beginning of the demoralization of the

United States military quickly followed. As the attendant anti-war protests at home increased, many soldiers questioned the efficacy of their sacrifices in Vietnam. More importantly, the soldiers realized that the emphasis of the American leadership was not on achieving peace through a military victory, but on peace through negotiations—negotiations which constantly promised an end to the war at any time. As a consequence, no one wanted to be the last casualty in a war that was not supported at home and which the United States government refused to let the military win.

5.9 Lessons of My Lai

The massacre at My Lai cannot be undone. However, in developing a methodology for preventing future atrocities which could occur in the War on Terror, the images of the horror of My Lai perfectly illustrate the necessity for abiding by the law of war. Certainly, the Peers Report was a valuable tool in attempting to explain some of the factors that seemed to create an environment in which violations of the law of war were more likely to occur. Taken together, these factors can be reduced to three fundamental lessons.

One of the most troubling issues for American soldiers is the realization that in many of the wars the United States has fought, the enemy has openly and repeatedly violated numerous provisions of the law of war. In the Vietnam War, the communist forces regularly engaged in command-directed atrocities on a massive scale. Just in relation to the treatment of prisoners, for example, every single American prisoner of war was subjected to torture and maltreatment in flagrant violation of the Geneva Conventions.

For many American soldiers, knowledge of enemy violations presents an immediate negative response to the law of war. The realization that the enemy may often refuse to abide by the law of war prompts an immediate gut response: Why should I care about the rules if the enemy doesn't? Faced with such questions, it is not enough to simply inform the soldier that he will be punished for violations, it is imperative that the soldier understand the rationale for abiding by the law of war. Thus, it is critical that the soldier's question be answered so that he possesses a basic understanding of the entire concept of the development of rules regulating combat.

5.10 Lesson One—Rationale for the Law of War

Many people have some vague notion that rules regulating warfare came out of the aftermath of World War II or, at the most, World War I. Nothing could be further from the truth. As long as there have been wars there have been rules established to reduce the suffering to both the environment and to other humans. While some of these ancient rules would not be consistent with the modern humanitarian concepts reflected in the current law of war, it is interesting to note that many of the provisions in the modern law of war are derived directly from some of the earliest formulations of rules regulating warfare.

For example, in the book of Deuteronomy, the ancient Hebrews were given specific instructions on the protections that were to be afforded to the persons and property of an enemy city under siege. Generally, if the city surrendered, the inhabitants were not to be harmed. If the city refused to surrender, but was subsequently captured, no women or children were to be molested. In all cases, torture was absolutely prohibited. Similarly, protection for the environment was also codified; fruit trees located outside of a besieged city were protected from unnecessary damage; the fruit could be eaten but it was unlawful to cut down the trees.

To observe that the modern law of war rests firmly upon an ancient foundation of humanitarian concerns that are intrinsically acceptable is only one reason why the rules have enjoyed universal acceptance through time—the fact that such rules are morally valuable axioms only captures part of the truth as to their development and utility. Clearly, the historical development of rules regulating warfare also follows a general pattern of what might be termed pragmatic necessity. While many of the rules limiting suffering were undoubtedly based on humanitarian concerns, it can be argued that the basic rationales for having a law of war are rooted in several collateral principles of self-interest.

First, under the concept of reciprocity, nations would develop and adhere to laws of war because they were confident that the enemy would also do the same under a quid-pro-quo theory. This mutual assurance theory has long been recognized as not only a primary motivator for establishing rules regulating warfare, but as the centerpiece in almost every other function of international intercourse.

The second element in the historical development of the law of war centers on a similar vein of self interest, reflected so aptly by Alexander the Great's admonitions to his incredible army on the eve of practically every battle: "Why should we destroy those things which shall soon be ours?" Under this reasoning, particularly in the context of securing limited amounts of spoil, the destruction of anything beyond military targets to subdue the enemy's military forces would be neither beneficial nor reasonable. Under modern principles, similar violations of the law of war would not contribute to the goal of the collection of legitimate reparations, a measure often employed against the aggressor nation.

A third line of reasoning draws on the related fact that abuses seldom shorten the length of the conflict and are never beneficial in facilitating the restoration of peace. The targeting of nonmilitary property usually produces unwanted effects for those who engage in such activities. The event in American history most often used to illustrate this point comes from the activities of Union General William T. Sherman during the American Civil War. General Sherman's widespread looting and burning of civilian homes and personal property, coupled with the deliberate slaughter of all domesticated animals on his march through Georgia and the Carolinas in the last two years of the War did not significantly contribute to the collapse of the Confederacy. On the contrary, his brutal actions simply strengthened the resolve of Southerners to resist while sowing the seeds of hatred for generations to come.

Clearly, the intelligent warfighter makes every effort to comply with and even exceed the requirements of the law of war, particularly in regards to the treatment of prisoners of war and noncombatants. Not only does humane treatment demonstrate the best evidence that your side is the one that is waging a *jus in bello*, but it often serves as the best avenue to counter enemy propaganda concerning law of war violations. As the pragmatic Prussian soldier and author, Karl von Clausewitz observed, "If we find that civilized nations do not … devastate towns and countries, this is because their intelligence exercises greater influence on their mode of carrying on war, and has taught them a more effectual means of applying force …."

A fourth factor approaches the matter from a purely military perspective. Plainly put, the use of limited military resources for the destruction of civilian targets is a waste of assets and hence, detrimental to the goal of defeating the enemy's military. In short, such conduct is simply counter-productive because "it rarely gains the violator a distinct military advantage."

The final rationale, albeit of greater impact in an era characterized by the widespread dissemination of information, rests in the very nature of the modern civilized nation-state. States that adhere to the principles of democratic institutions and fundamental human rights will not tolerate activities that are conducted in defiance of the rule of law. As brought out so strongly by the My Lai incident, civilized societies will not provide the necessary homefront support for an army that is perceived as acting in violation of the law of war. Although in the radical totalitarian regime this factor is generally ignored, in the United States, as in all democratic societies, this element of homefront support is absolutely essential to any deployment and sustainment of military forces. The basic minimum "standards of morality transcend national boundaries."

The necessity of homefront support is not always easy for the military to sustain. In part the difficulty rests in the associated phenomenon of "imputed responsibility." With reference to any military in a democratic society, the term imputed responsibility recognizes the fact that the acts of a few soldiers who engage in egregious abuses of the law of war are immediately imputed to the entire military establishment. For instance, because Lieutenant Calley and a handful of others murdered babies at My Lai, large segments of the public might tend to view all American soldiers in Vietnam as baby killers. To a large degree the mass media feeds this phenomenon, as reflected by almost every Hollywood movie concerning the Vietnam War. In American cinema, the soldier is routinely depicted as engaging in abuses of the law of war or ingesting large quantities of illegal drugs. The fact that the vast majority of American soldiers did neither is not shown. Accordingly, the best way for the military to combat the concept of imputed responsibility is to make every effort to see that abuses do not occur and, if they do, promptly investigate and punish those proven to be guilty. Complete transparency but be the guide. Under no circumstances can a cover-up be justified—the light must be shed promptly and fully on all allegations of war crimes. The U.S. military learned this lesson from My Lai as demonstrated by the handling of the prisoner abuse cases in Iraq. Again, the military self-reported the individual acts of criminal behavior to the media and also launched its own investigation (the Taguba Report) prior to the photographs appearing in the media.

In the modern era, then, the law of war is based on a combination of rationales reflecting a mixture of pragmatism and moral concerns. The competent warfighter should understand that the factors include:

- humanitarian concerns based on moral precepts;
- the concept of reciprocity in behavior;
- the desire for reparations;
- the desire to limit the scope and duration of the conflict and to facilitate the restoration of peace;
- the effective use of military resources; and
- the necessity for securing homefront support.

5.11 Lesson Two—Soldiers Must Be Trained in the Law of War

The second lesson from My Lai needs little introduction—to be effective the law of war must be constantly taught to soldiers. To a large degree the United States military has long held an outstanding reputation for adherence to the law of war because of its commitment to training. Unfortunately, there have been periods where training has not been properly emphasized, providing fertile ground for violations of the law of war. If nothing else, the massacre at My Lai served as the "catalyst for a complete review of Army training in the law of war."

The United States Army has proponency for the law of war for all branches of the military. This means that the army is responsible for developing and publishing the written doctrine. The current methodology for teaching the law of war attempts to tailor the training to the particular unit.

Since Special Operations Forces are a primary tool used on the ground in the War on Terror, it is efficacious to review the current level of training that these forces receive in the law of war. In short, Special Operations Forces not only receive constant classroom instruction on the law of war but also have difficult law of war questions dealing with special operations built into their training missions which are constantly practiced. The much-reported event in the Gulf War in which an Army Special Forces team had to choose between killing an Iraqi girl or being discovered by enemy forces was actually a well-rehearsed scenario resulting in a correct application of a very difficult law of war issue. The girl was spared.

A red thread that runs throughout the issue of training in the law of war is the role of the military lawyer or judge advocate. Since Vietnam, the Army has dramatically expanded its use of military attorneys to ensure that its forces comply with all aspects of the law of war. All combat forces have an operational law attorney assigned at the Division level. Likewise, all Army Special Forces groups have a specialized military attorney assigned. The function of this judge advocate is not only to ensure compliance with and adherence to the law of war, but to examine the full range of international and domestic laws that affect specifically "legal issues associated with the planning for and deployment of United States forces overseas in both peacetime and combat environments." This is a major change from the role of the judge advocate in Vietnam—a role primarily delegated to the administration of criminal law, well behind the front lines of combat.

Currently, the function of the judge advocate in the field can be divided into two elements—he has both preventive and active roles. In the preventive role, the judge advocate advises commanders on potential issues dealing with rules of engagement, targeting enemy military objectives, and all other relevant aspects of the law of war. In addition, the judge advocate is deeply involved in providing instruction and training to soldiers within his particular command.

In the active role, the judge advocate is involved in the investigation of allegations of war crimes. The requirement to investigate is either carried out directly by the legal officer or is closely monitored by the judge advocate. Finally, judge advocates will be called upon to either prosecute or defend those charged with violations.

5.12 Lesson Three—Preventing Violations of the Law of War in the War on Terror

As noted, the importance of professional conduct on the battlefield extends to both the strategic, political, and social realms. In turn, the primary responsibility for inculcating professional conduct falls directly on the officer corps. Nowhere is the need for training in the law of war more critical than in the proper development of the military's officer corps. Thus, no officer should be given the responsibility of leadership without two essential factors: (1) technical proficiency in the profession of arms; and (2) the highest ethical and moral courage. Under the ancient Roman adage that no man can control others until he can first control himself, officers must be thoroughly prepared in both of these areas. Combat command should only be offered to officers who have been thoroughly scrutinized and put through extensive field training exercises designed to test their reaction under combat pressures.

There can be no question that the primary cause of My Lai was the lack of disciplined control (i.e., the lack of any real leadership). Such leadership is absolutely essential in preventing war crimes. The associated tensions set out by the Peers Report were not the real problem at My Lai—tensions of combat will always be present in one form or another. The real problem was in the effective control of those tensions. Control of warfighting pressures rest not only with the individual soldier but directly with his commanding officer. Sadly, many of the officers in Charlie Company not only allowed the illegal manifestations of battlefield stress to be exhibited by their troops, but through their orders and example they initiated and actively participated in the atrocities. There can be little doubt that proper officer leadership could have prevented the murders at My Lai. Consequently, the primary responsibility for these crimes is on their heads. The function of leadership is to hold up the professional torch at all times, at all costs.

Great armies are neither created, nor sustained, by accident. To a large degree, great armies are maintained by officers who understand, and then are able to apply, the lessons of military history. In this respect, no officer can truly be called a professional without a firm commitment to the moral and ethical rules regulating combat. Quite naturally, this objective requires constant training, as well as a comprehensive understanding of one's moral roots. Consequently, the military of the United States constantly must reaffirm its commitment to the positive values of military proficiency and ethical integrity.

Currently, U.S. Army training doctrine places a great deal of emphasis on the concept of duty and uses General Robert E. Lee as its illustration to all soldiers. For instruction, inspiration and inculcation, American officers can find no better role model than General Lee. While some may forget, ignore, or purposefully deny the role that Lee has had in shaping our modern military, to those who are objective his impact on American tactics and humanitarian concerns never can be obscured.

Lee's tactics and civility have become ingrained into the character of the United States military establishment. Although these qualities certainly existed before the emergence of Lee the general, his genius and humanity have epitomized and translated them into the very fabric of subsequent American military doctrines. For this reason, any analysis of the United States military, either in terms of tactics or comportment with the law of war, that ignores the tremendous contributions of General Lee can never be more than a fraction of the truth.

For example, although some Southerners criticized Lee for not authorizing lawful reprisals to deter Union violations of the law of war, General Lee firmly believed that reprisals were not the answer. Responding to a letter from the Confederate Secretary of War regarding possible Confederate responses to Union atrocities, Lee reiterated his position in the summer of 1864:

As I have said before, if the guilty parties could be taken, either the officer who commands, or the soldier who executes such atrocities, I should not hesitate to advise the infliction of the extreme punishment they deserve, but I cannot think it right or politic, to make the innocent … suffer for the guilty.

With Americans fighting Americans, Lee knew that the long-term effects of engaging in reprisals would not be profitable for the nation or the South. He was undoubtedly correct; Lee's strict adherence to the rules regulating warfare, coupled with his firm policy prohibiting reprisals, contributed greatly to the healing process after the War. This same thinking colors the activities of American forces who face the cowardly and unlawful tactics of the terrorists.

One of the driving forces that created the legend of Lee, the ultimate gentleman, was his unmatched sense of humanity. "Lee was the soldier-gentleman of tradition, generous, forgiving, silent in the face of failure … a hero of mythology." No matter how great the temptation for legitimate reprisals, a concept well recognized in international law, R. E. Lee would not stoop to the level of his enemies. This is one of the reasons he has been called the "Christian General," as reflected in his address to the troops as they marched into Pennsylvania during the Gettysburg campaign of 1863: "It must be remembered that we make war only on armed men, and that we cannot take vengeance for the wrongs our people have suffered without lowering ourselves in the eyes of … Him to whom vengeance belongeth." Instructing his officers to arrest and punish all soldiers who committed any offense on the person or private property of civilians, he reminded them that "the duties exacted of us by civilization and Christianity are not less obligatory in the country of the enemy than in our own."

Perhaps the most telling tribute to Lee came from his former enemies. When General Lee died in 1870, newspapers throughout the North universally praised his military genius and morality. The *New York Herald* said, "In him the military genius of America was developed to a greater extent than ever before. In him all that was pure and lofty in mind and purpose found lodgment. He came nearer the ideal of a soldier and Christian general than any man we can think of."

Unfortunately, despite America's rich tradition in fairness in combat operations, even the best lessons of history quickly fade unless they are inculcated. Future My Lai's cannot be prevented unless the answers to the "why" of My Lai are repeated over and over until they are ingrained into every warfighter in uniform. Just as Americans must never forget their rallying cries of honor and nobility—"Remember the Alamo"—they must be forced to deal with their nightmares—"My Lai." On the other hand, it is precisely because of its horror and repulsiveness that My Lai is uniquely suited to serve as the primary vehicle to address the entire issue of adherence to the law of war as well as the necessity for effective leadership in the extremely trying War on Terror.

The final caveat in the War on Terror is that the American military cannot afford to take these lessons lightly. Given the fact that knowledge acquired beyond basic trial and error methodologies requires varying degrees of academic effort, it is not surprising that over time, both individually and collectively, many lessons of history will be forgotten and thus, repeated. This fact is particularly devastating when viewed in the context of man's efforts to reduce the continuing pattern of human warfare and terrorism. Accordingly, not only must the lessons of My Lai be remembered—they must be inculcated.

5.13 Questions for Discussion

1. *Responding to war crime allegations.* Considering the lessons of My Lai, what is the best course of action for the military command to take when it receives allegations of war crimes committed by American forces?

2. *Role of propaganda in the War on Terror.* How does the al-Qa'eda terror network employ the media as a tool of warfare? Is it effective?

3. *Grand strategy.* What impact does a grand strategy have in the War on Terror? Is there a clearly focused grand strategy in Iraq?

4. *Why follow the laws of war if the enemy does not?* The Roman practice of offering Roman citizenship to tribes who agreed to serve in the Roman army as auxiliary troops greatly benefited the expansion of the empire. For example, the *Honariani Atecotti Seniores* were formed from captured pirates from the Scottish Atecotti tribe circa 300 A.D. and served in the *Auxilium Palatinum*. On the other hand, the later Roman practice of slaughtering civilians only stiffened resistance amongst the barbarians who eventually conquered Rome. Caleb Carr, THE LESSONS OF TERROR: A HISTORY OF WARFARE AGAINST CIVILIANS, WHY IT HAS ALWAYS FAILED AND WHY IT WILL FAIL AGAIN (2002).

5. *Did the Calley trial follow the rules of war that were set in the aftermath of World War II at the Tokyo and Nuremberg War Crimes Tribunals?* The Tribunals had set the precedent that no soldier could rely on the excuse that he was following orders from a superior in order to excuse his war crimes. Then Secretary of the Army Howard H. Callaway stated to the *New York Times* that Lt. William Calley believed he was following orders, and thus his sentence was reduced. This contradicted the standards set in Tokyo and Nuremberg, where some Japanese and German soldiers were executed for their purported war crimes despite the fact that they raised the defense of superior orders. *See* Burke Marshall and Joseph Goldstein, *Learning From My Lai: A Proposal on War Crimes,* NY TIMES, Apr. 2, 1976 at 26. In light of these facts did the United States set a precedent that it did not have to abide by international law? Could a subordinate in a terrorist organization rely on the same defense Lt. Calley used if he were charged with a war crime?

Selected Bibliography

30 SOUTHERN HISTORICAL SOCIETY PAPERS 94. 1902.

Addicott, Jeffrey F. *Operation Desert Storm: R. E. Lee or W. T. Sherman?* 136 MILITARY LAW REVIEW 115. 1992.

Elliott, H. Wayne. *Theory and Practice: Some Suggestions for the Law of War Trainer*, THE ARMY LAWYER, July 1983, at 1.

Generous, Kevin M. VIETNAM, THE SECRET WAR. 1985.

Goldstien, Joseph, et al. THE MY LAI MASSACRE AND ITS COVER-UP: BEYOND THE REACH OF LAW? 1976.

Graham, David E. *Operational Law (OPLAW)—A Concept Comes of Age*, THE ARMY LAWYER, July 1987, at 9.

Hall, David K., et al. FORCE WITHOUT WAR. 1979.

Henkin, Louis, et al. MIGHT V. RIGHT. 1991.

Jones, J. William. LIFE AND LETTERS OF GENERAL ROBERT EDWARD LEE. 1906.

Moore, John Norton. LAW AND THE INDO-CHINA WAR. 1972.

Nagel, Paul C. THE LEES OF VIRGINIA. 1990. Lee's view on Christian salvation was devoid of any form of human merit or morality although by the measure of any society, his own moral standards were impeccable. Grace oriented to biblical Christianity, he wrote, "I can only say that I am a poor sinner, trusting in Christ alone for salvation."

O'Brien, William V. THE CONDUCT OF JUST AND LIMITED WAR. 1981.

Peers, Lt. Gen. W.R. THE MY LAI INQUIRY. 1979.

Samenow, Stanton E., Jr. INSIDE THE CRIMINAL MIND. 1984.

Schindler, Dietrich, ed., and Jiri Toman. THE LAWS OF ARMED CONFLICTS. 1988.

Taylor, Lawrence. A TRIAL OF GENERALS. 1981.

Tinkle, Lon. 13 DAYS TO GLORY: THE SIEGE OF THE ALAMO. 1958.

Tolstoy, Leo. WAR AND PEACE. 1983.

von Clausewitz, Karl. ON WAR. J. Graham trans. 1918.

Walsh, Gary L. *Role of the Judge Advocate in Special Operations*, THE ARMY LAWYER, Aug. 1989, at 6-8.

Weigley, Russel F. HISTORY OF THE UNITED STATES ARMY. 1984.

Williamson, Porter B. PATTON'S PRINCIPLES: A HANDBOOK FOR MANAGERS WHO MEAN IT. 1979.

Chapter 6
Interrogation Techniques

If interrogators step over the line from coercion to outright torture, they should be held personally responsible. But no interrogator is ever going to be prosecuted for keeping Khalid Sheikh Mohammed awake, cold, alone and uncomfortable. Nor should he be.

—Mark Bowden

In discussing the issue of interrogation practices, most are reminded of the Abu Ghraib prison abuse incident. Was the prison abuse a reflection of a systemic policy—either *de jure* or *de facto*—on the part of the United States to illegally extract information from detainees, or was the abuse simply isolated acts of criminal behavior on the part of a handful of soldiers amplified by a grossly incompetent tactical chain of command at the prison facility? The primary concern is over the alleged American practice known as "stress and duress" interrogation—the use of various forms and levels of physical and physiological force to extract information. Juxtaposed to this matter is the issue of rendition, where it is alleged that the United States purposefully sends detainees to other nations knowing that they are subjected to interrogations that employ torture or other illegal techniques.

Allegations of torture roll off the tongue with ease. In the context of American interrogation practices and treatment of both terrorist detainees and enemy combatant detainees, charges of torture are regularly raised by a wide variety of individuals and interest groups. Recognizing that not every alleged incident of mistreatment necessarily satisfies the legal definition of torture, it is imperative that one views such allegations with a clear understanding of the applicable legal standards set out in law and judicial precedent. In this manner, claims of illegal interrogation practices can be properly measured as falling above or below a particular legal threshold. Only then can one hope to set aside the rhetoric by such groups as Amnesty International, who called the Guantanamo detention facility the "gulag of our time," and objectively establish whether or not the United States stands in violation of the rule of law.

In tandem with investigating American interrogation practices the matter of how authorities should deal with the so-called "ticking time bomb" terrorist merits serious scrutiny in America's war against the unrestrained savagery of fanatical suicide bombers bent on using weapons of mass destruction. The concern is so great that a number of prominent voices both in and outside of the government have advocated that a judicial exception should be carved out to allow torture as an interrogation tool in special instances. Perhaps one of the most prominent and unexpected voices to advocate such a position is Professor Alan Dershowitz.

While some may claim that Dershowitz is reluctantly reflecting a new and ugly pragmatism associated with blunting these terrorists, America cannot allow itself to slip into a Star Chamber mentality where torture is mandated by the State as a necessary evil. Understanding the need to find the appropriate balance between civil liberties and security concerns, the purpose of this chapter is twofold. First, the interrogation practices used by the United States to get information from various categories of detainees will be measured in light of both the domestic and international laws on torture and other forms of mistreatment. Bluntly put, is the United States using illegal interrogation methods in the War on Terror as some have charged? Second, in the special case of the ticking time bomb terrorist, should the United States openly disregard the rule of law and officially sanction the use of torture?

6.1 Defining Torture

Torture as an instrument of the State to either punish or extract information from certain individuals has a long and dark history which need not be fully recounted here. Suffice it to say that in the West, the practice can be traced to the Romans who codified the use of torture as part of the Roman criminal law.

In England, the earliest authoritative records regarding State use of torture appears in the Privy Council registers in the year 1540, which extends, with some gaps in the reports, for a hundred years. (Anyone familiar with the reign of Henry VIII knows that the state practice surely predated these official warrants.) The number of official warrants issued by the Crown during this period was less than 100, an amazingly low figure relative to the number of felony investigations which occurred in any given year. This low statistic demonstrates that the predominant use of torture was interrogational in nature and not for punishment. The 1597 case of Jesuit priest John Gerard typifies the goal of torture. The Crown's warrant directed Gerard's torture in the Tower of London by means of "the manacles" and other "such torture" in order to make Gerard "utter directly and truly his uttermost knowledge" concerning certain traitors to the Crown.

In the modern era, by fixed law and customary practice the prohibition on torture is now universal in nature; a majority of States have ratified the various international agreements associated with banning torture. Nevertheless, even though no State allows torture in its domestic law, the practice continues to flourish. It is estimated that one in four States regularly engages in the torture of various prisoners and detainees. Added to this paradox is the dilemma that some of the acts that should clearly constitute torture do not enjoy a uniformity of definition within the international community. As one legal commentator rightly pointed out, "The prohibition of torture … is not, itself, controversial. The prohibition in application, however, yields endless contention as each perpetrator [State actor] seeks to define its own behavior so as not to violate the ban."

6.2 International Agreements

Before exploring the common international legal definition of torture, it is useful to survey the general understanding of the term. Torture comes from the Latin verb "torquere" (to twist) and is defined in leading dictionaries as follows: "Infliction of severe physical pain as a means of punishment or coercion;" "[t]he act of inflicting excruciating pain, as punishment or revenge, as a means of getting a confession or information, or for sheer cruelty;" "[t]he infliction of intense pain to the body or mind to punish, to extract a confession or information, or to obtain sadistic pleasure."

Certainly the red thread in these definitions is a combination of two essential elements: (1) the infliction of severe physical pain to the body or mind used to (2) punish or obtain information. International law adopts this formula but sharpens it by stipulating that a State actor must carry out the act of torture. Thus, one may describe certain criminals as torturing their victims during the commission of a particularly gruesome murder, but such criminal acts carried out by non-State actors are not violations of the international law on torture. In addition, international law expands the prohibition of torture to include other less abusive acts commonly designated in the world community as "other acts of cruel, inhuman, or degrading treatment or punishment," which is shortened simply to "ill-treatment."

Like the concept of human rights, international law really had little to say about the practice of State torture until the close of World War II. With the establishment of the United Nations in 1945, the prohibition of torture and ill-treatment are core rights found in all of the most important international documents.

Article 5 of the 1948 Universal Declaration of Human Rights serves as the foundation for all subsequent efforts on torture. Article 5 of the Declaration consists of only one brief sentence: "No one shall be subjected to torture or to cruel, inhuman, or degrading treatment or punishment." Later, the widely influential and legally binding International Covenant on Civil and Political Rights followed on the heels of the Universal Declaration of Human Rights. In pertinent part, Article 7 of the Covenant utilizes the exact same language found in the Universal Declaration on Human Rights: "No person shall be subjected to torture or to cruel, inhuman or degrading treatment or punishment." In binding itself to the International Covenant on Civil and Political Rights, the United States Senate sought to clarify the meaning of Article 7 and attached a reservation which defined "cruel, inhuman or degrading treatment or punishment" as meaning "the cruel and unusual treatment or punishment prohibited by the Fifth, Eighth and /or Fourteenth Amendments to the Constitution of the United States."

In 1975 the United Nations adopted the Declaration on the Protection of all Persons from Being Subjected to Torture or Other Cruel, Inhuman or Degrading Treatment or Punishment.18 Although this document was a declaration only, it served as the basis for the 1984 United Nations Convention Against Torture, and Other Cruel, Inhuman or Degrading Treatment or Punishment (Torture Convention), the primary international agreement governing torture and ill-treatment. As suggested by the title, the point which had served as a source of controversy was more fully addressed in the Torture Convention—the distinction between "torture" and "other acts of cruel, inhuman, or degrading treatment or punishment." While both acts were previously prohibited in other documents, for the first time, the Torture Convention spelled out the obligations and consequences attendant to each type of act. Still, the Torture Convention did not exhibit the same care in defining what it meant by "other cruel, inhuman or degrading treatment or punishment" as it did with regard to torture. Without question, the Torture Convention devoted far more attention to crafting the meaning of the term torture, which it defined as:

UN
define
torture

> [A]ny act by which severe pain or suffering, whether physical or mental, is intentionally inflicted on a person for such purposes as obtaining from him or a third person information or a confession, punishing him for an act he or a third person has committed or is suspected of having committed, or intimidating or coercing him or a third person, or for any reason based on discrimination of any kind, when such pain or suffering is inflicted by or at the instigation of … a public official or other person acting in an official capacity. It does not include pain or suffering arising only from, inherent in or incidental to lawful sanctions.

According to the Torture Convention, for torture to exist in the context of an interrogation the following criteria must be present: (1) the behavior must be based on an intentional act; (2) it must be performed by a State agent; (3) the behavior must cause severe pain or suffering to body or mind; and (4) it must be accomplished with the intent to gain information or a confession. In adopting the Torture Convention, the United States Senate provided the following reservations which require specific intent and better define the concept of mental suffering:

> [T]he United States understands that, in order to constitute torture, an act must be specifically intended to inflict severe physical or mental pain or suffering and that mental pain or suffering refers to prolonged mental harm caused by or resulting from: (1) the intentional infliction or threatened infliction of severe physical pain or suffering; (2) the administration or application, or threatened administration or application, of mind altering substances or other procedures calculated to disrupt profoundly the senses or the personality; (3) the threat of imminent death; or (4) the threat that another person will imminently be subjected to death, severe physical pain or suffering, or the administration or application of mind altering substances or other procedures calculated to disrupt profoundly the senses or personality.

Article 2 of the Torture Convention absolutely excludes the notion of exceptional circumstances to serve as an excuse to the prohibition of torture. "No exceptional circumstances whatsoever, whether a state of war or a threat of war, internal political instability or any other public emergency, may be invoked as a justification for torture."

As noted, the phrase "other acts of cruel, inhuman, or degrading treatment or punishment," e.g., "ill-treatment," is not defined in the Torture Convention. It is just stated. The Torture Convention certainly obliges each State party to the document to "undertake to prevent … other acts of cruel, inhuman, or degrading treatment or punishment," but Article 16 of the Torture Convention is the only part of the treaty that addresses ill-treatment.

Since the Torture Convention desires to "make more effective the struggle against torture and other cruel, inhuman or degrading treatment or punishment throughout the world," the distinction rests in the fact that torture and ill-treatment are viewed as two limbs of the same formula with torture, quite understandably, being predominant. Thus, while all acts of torture must necessarily include ill-treatment, not all acts of ill-treatment constitute torture. Clearly, a greater stigma is associated with the insidious evil of torture so that all intuitively realize that international law forbids torture, even if few are cognizant of the fact that ill-treatment is also prohibited. In turn, interrogation practices that do not rise to the level of ill-treatment may be repugnant by degree, but would be perfectly legal under international law. This being the case, it is efficacious to begin the discussion by pointing out the differences between torture and ill-treatment as they have significant ramifications regarding State Party obligations.

Article 3 of the Torture Convention prohibits any State Party to "expel, return ("refouler") or extradite any person to another State where there are substantial grounds to believe that the person will be subjected to torture." The more common term for this practice is "rendition." In making this determination, the State Party is required at Article 3(2) "to take into account all relevant considerations" with particular regard to whether or not there exists "a consistent pattern of gross, flagrant or mass violations of human rights." Eventhough the combined factors of "substantial grounds" with "a consistent pattern of gross, flagrant or mass violations of human rights" provide considerable flexibility for a State Party to justify a particular rendition, at least the prohibition is established and a standard is established, albeit a subjective one. In contrast, Article 16 has no similar requirement regarding ill-treatment. This means that a State Party to the treaty is absolutely free to hand over an individual to a State that it knows engages in ill-treatment.

Article 4 requires each State Party to ensure that torture is a criminal offense under its domestic criminal law and Article 12 dictates that each State Party investigate any allegations of torture under its jurisdiction when reasonable grounds exist to believe that such acts have occurred. Article 7 further requires the State Party to either extradite the alleged torturer or "submit the case to competent [domestic] authorities for the purpose of prosecution." Also, Article 15 excludes all statements elicited through torture from evidence, while Article 14 requires the Party State to make compensation to the victims of torture.

In contrast, Article 16 has no similar requirements mandating that ill-treatment be criminalized in domestic penal codes, requiring the prosecution of individuals charged with ill-treatment, or limitations on rendition. In addition, Article 16 has no requirement that victims of ill-treatment be compensated or that statements obtained as the fruit of ill-treatment must be excluded from evidence at a criminal trial. According to one commentator, "[t]he failure to strengthen article 16 appears to have been based on a belief that the concept of cruel, inhuman or degrading treatment or punishment was too vague a legal standard upon which to base legal culpability and judgments."

BELLOUT v. ASHCROFT

U.S. Court of Appeals for the Ninth Circuit

363 F.3d 975 (9th Cir. 2004)

SILVERMAN, Circuit Judge:

Mouloud Bellout, a native and citizen of Algeria, petitions for review of the BIA's summary affirmance of the IJ's denial of Bellout's application for asylum, withholding of removal, and protection under the Convention Against Torture (CAT). The IJ found Bellout statutorily ineligible for relief from deportation because he engaged in terrorist activity when he joined "Armed Islamic Group (GIA)," a State Department-recognized terrorist organization, in 1995 and lived in GIA camps in Algeria for three years. Bellout has been removed to Algeria.

We hold as follows: First, because the IJ found that there are reasonable grounds to believe that Bellout engaged in or is likely to engage in terrorist activity under *8 U.S.C. §1158(b)(2)(a)(v)*, we lack jurisdiction to review the IJ's determination that Bellout is ineligible for asylum by virtue of *8 U.S.C. §1158(b)(2)(D)*. Second, substantial evidence supports the IJ's conclusion that Bellout is ineligible for withholding of removal. Finally, substantial evidence supports the IJ's denial of deferral of removal under CAT.

I. FACTS

Bellout attempted to enter the United States at Los Angeles International Airport on January 6, 1999, using a fraudulent Belgian passport. After the INS initiated removal proceedings, Bellout applied for asylum, withholding of deportation, and relief under CAT, alleging that he would be tortured by terrorists or police if he returned to Algeria. At his hearing, Bellout testified that he joined GIA in 1995, lived in GIA mountain camps, made friends with other members, read GIA's pamphlets and literature, discussed ideology with other members of the group, and carried weapons and ammunition. When GIA divided into a second group in 1996, Bellout went with the second group—"Algamma El-Salafia Lel-Daawa Wal Ketal." He remained with this group until 1998, when he left Algeria.

The IJ found that Bellout was statutorily barred from asylum, withholding of removal and relief under CAT as an alien "who the Attorney General knows, or has reasonable grounds to believe, is engaged in or is likely to engage after entry in any terrorist activity."

8 U.S.C. §1189(a) authorizes the Secretary of State to designate foreign terrorist organizations by providing notice and findings to congressional leaders and publishing the designation in the Federal Register. Unless Congress disapproves the designation, it becomes effective upon publication in the Federal Register. *Id. §1189(a)(2)(B)*. Although the designation is effective for two years, the Secretary may redesignate a foreign terrorist organization after the two years expire. *Id. §1189(a)(4)*.

The Secretary has designated and redesignated the "Armed Islamic Group (GIA)" as a terrorist organization under *8 U.S.C. § 1189. Designation of Foreign Terrorist Organizations, 62 Fed. Reg. 52650 (Oct. 8, 1997); 64 Fed. Reg. 55112 (Oct. 8, 1999); 66 Fed. Reg. 51088 (Oct. 5, 2001); 68 Fed. Reg. 56860 (Oct. 2, 2003)*. According to the State Department Office of Counterterrorism's 1999 Report of Foreign Terrorist Organizations, GIA is an extremely violent terrorist group that frequently and brutally attacks and kills civilians, journalists, and foreign residents. The Report says that GIA uses assassinations and bombings and favors kidnapping victims and slitting their throats. According to the Report, GIA's activities are not limited only to Algeria; GIA hijacked an Air France flight in December 1994 and is suspected of a series of bombings in France in 1995.

Because Bellout had been a member of a State Department-designated terrorist organization, the IJ found that Bellout engaged in terrorist activity and, in the alternative, posed a danger to security in the United States. He was therefore ineligible for asylum. He likewise was ineligible for withholding of deportation. The IJ also concluded that Bellout was not entitled to deferral of removal under CAT because he had failed to establish that he would more likely than not be tortured if he returned to Algeria. The BIA affirmed the IJ's decision, adopting that decision as the final agency determination pursuant to 8 C.F.R. § 3.1(a)(7) (2002).

Bellout argues that the IJ erred in finding that he was ineligible for asylum and withholding of removal because he engaged in terrorist activity, and in denying him relief under CAT.

II. ASYLUM

An alien is ineligible for asylum if he is inadmissible or removable for engaging in terrorist activity or if "the Attorney General determines" that "there are reasonable grounds for regarding an alien as a danger to the security of the United States." *8 U.S.C. § 1158(b)(2)(A) (iv)–(v)*. "Terrorist activities" include membership in "a foreign terrorist organization, as designated by the Secretary [of State] under [8 U.S.C.] *section 1189*." *Id. § 1182(a)(3)(B)(i)(v)*.

The asylum statute deprives this court of jurisdiction to review the Attorney General's determination under *8 U.S.C. § 1158(b)(2)(A)(v)* that an alien is ineligible for asylum because the alien is inadmissible or removable because of terrorist activity. See *8 U.S.C. § 1158(b)(2)(D)*. The statute provides:

> (D) No judicial review
>
> There shall be no judicial review of a determination of the Attorney General under subparagraph (A) (v) [ineligibility for asylum because the alien is inadmissible for terrorist activity].

Thus, this court lacks jurisdiction to review the IJ's determination that Bellout is ineligible for asylum pursuant to *§ 1158(b)(2)(A)(v)* because Bellout is inadmissible or removable because of terrorist activity. This portion of the petition for review is dismissed.

III. WITHHOLDING OF REMOVAL

We affirm the IJ's denial of relief if there is reasonable, substantial, and probative evidence to support the decision based on the record as a whole, and we may not reverse the IJ's findings unless the evidence compels a contrary conclusion. *INS v. Elias-Zacarias, 502 U.S. 478, 481, 117 L. Ed. 2d 38, 112 S. Ct. 812 (1992)*.

An alien is ineligible for withholding of removal if "the Attorney General decides that ... there are reasonable grounds to believe that the alien is a danger to the security of the United States." ... Reasonable grounds exist to believe that an alien is a danger to security if the alien "has engaged, is engaged, or at any time after admission engages in any terrorist activity (as defined in *section 1182(a)(3)(B)(iv)* ...)." Terrorist activities include membership in "a foreign terrorist organization, as designated by the Secretary [of State] under [8 U.S.C. §] *1189*."

Consistent with the statutory provision for withholding of removal, federal regulation provides for mandatory denial of withholding of removal under CAT if the Attorney General has "reasonable grounds to believe that the alien is a danger to the security of the United States." *8 U.S.C. § 1231(b)(3)(B)(iv)*; *8 C.F.R. § 1208.16(d)(2) (2003)*. Thus, if the alien is barred from withholding of removal under *§ 1231(b)(3)(B)(iv)*, he is also barred from withholding of removal under CAT.

Substantial evidence supports the IJ's conclusion that Bellout engaged in or was likely to engage in terrorist activity because Bellout testified that he was a member of GIA for three years. Because Bellout engaged in terrorist activity, there are reasonable grounds to believe that he is a danger to the security of the United States, and he is ineligible for statutory withholding of removal and withholding of removal under CAT. *See 8 U.S.C. §1231(b)(3)(B)*; *8 C.F.R. §1208.16(d)(2)*.

Interpreting a prior version of the asylum statute, we recently held that an alien who engaged in terrorist activity against a foreign country is not necessarily a danger to the security of the

United States. *Cheema v. INS, 350 F.3d 1035, 1040–41 (9th Cir. 2003). Cheema* does not control this case because the court's reasoning in *Cheema* was premised on prior versions of the asylum and withholding statutes. The prior asylum statute barred aliens who engaged in terrorist activity from eligibility for asylum and withholding of removal *unless* the Attorney General found that there were not reasonable grounds for regarding the alien as a danger to the security of the United States. We held that the Attorney General could not collapse the two-prong statutory test and focus only on terrorist activity.

However, the statute has changed so there is no longer a two-prong test. The Illegal Immigration Reform and Immigrant Responsibility Act of 1996 (IIRIRA) amended the asylum statute to provide that an alien is ineligible for asylum if the Attorney General decides that there are reasonable grounds for regarding the alien as a danger to the security of the United States *or* that the alien is inadmissible or removable for terrorist activity. Either ground will support the IJ's denial of asylum. Pub. L. 104-208, § 604, 110 Stat. 3009-691 (1996) (codified at *8 U.S.C. §1158(b)(2)(A) (I(v))-(v))*. In addition, the Antiterrorism and Effective Death Penalty Act of 1996 (AEDPA) amended the withholding of removal statute to specifically provide that an alien who engages in terrorist activity "shall be considered to be an alien for whom there are reasonable grounds for regarding as a danger to the security of the United States." Pub. L. 104-132, § 413(a), 110 Stat. 1214 (1996) (codified at *8 U.S.C. §1231(b)(3)(B)(iv))*.

IV. RELIEF UNDER CAT

Bellout argues that the IJ should have granted him deferral of removal under the Convention Against Torture because, he claims, the police will torture him if he returns to Algeria. Article 3 of the United Nations Convention Against Torture or Punishment prohibits removal to a state where there are substantial grounds to believe the alien would be tortured. *Al-Saher v. INS, 268 F.3d 1143, 1146 (9th Cir. 2001)*. Although barred from "withholding of removal" under CAT, Bellout remains eligible for "deferral of removal" under CAT. *8 C.F.R. §1208.17(a) (2003)*. We review the denial of relief under CAT for substantial evidence. *Zheng v. Ashcroft, 332 F.3d 1186, 1194 (9th Cir. 2003)*.

To be eligible for deferral of removal under CAT, Bellout must establish that he "is more likely than not to be tortured" if he returns to Algeria. *8 C.F.R. § 1208.17(a) (2003)*; *see also Zheng, 332 F.3d at 1194*. Bellout testified to one incident of abuse by the police in 1994 before he joined GIA. There is no evidence in the record that the Algerian government is aware that Bellout joined GIA or is interested in him. The IJ found that there was no evidence that members of militant groups who leave Algeria will be persecuted or tortured upon return and that Bellout did not meet his burden of establishing it is more likely than not that he will face torture if returned to Algeria. The evidence does not compel a contrary conclusion. *Zheng, 332 F.3d at 1194*.

PETITION FOR REVIEW DISMISSED IN PART AND DENIED IN PART.

The inherent vagueness of ill-treatment and the reluctance of the Torture Convention to fully define the concept or to provide even a minimum level of sanction to the practice have been further aggravated by a controversial and often cited European Court of Human Rights ruling, *Ireland v. United Kingdom*. The *Ireland* court found certain interrogation practices of English authorities to investigate suspected terrorism in Northern Ireland to be "inhuman and degrading," i.e., ill-treatment, under the European Convention on Human Rights, but not severe enough to rise to the level of torture. According to the Court, the finding of ill-treatment rather than torture "derives principally from a difference in the intensity of the suffering inflicted." In *Ireland*, the Court considered the use of five investigative measures known as "the five techniques" which were practiced by British authorities for periods of "four or five" days pending or during interrogation sessions.

- Wall-standing: Forcing the detainees to stand for some period of hours in a stress position described as "spreadeagled against the wall, with their fingers put high above their head against the wall, the legs spread apart and the feet back, causing them to stand on their toes with the weight of the body mainly on the fingers." Wall-standing was practiced for up to 30 hours with occasional periods for rest.
- Hooding: Placing a dark hood over the head of the detainee and keeping it on for prolonged periods of time except during interrogation.
- Subjection to noise: Holding the detainees in a room where there was a continuous loud and hissing noise.
- Deprivation of Sleep: Depriving detainees of sleep for prolonged periods of time.
- Deprivation of Food and Drink: Reducing the food and drink to suspects pending interrogations.

Real world enforcement mechanisms to ensure compliance with the Torture Convention's prohibition of torture and ill-treatment are wholly inadequate. This is because the individual State Party is expected to self-police itself and, if this fails, the only remaining hope for meaningful pressure is international condemnation from the court of world opinion. While the Torture Convention did create an investigatory body called the Committee Against Torture, its responsibilities revolve around a complex maze of reports and recommendations which, as one might anticipate, have generally accomplished very little. In fact, the biggest stick that the Committee Against Torture wields is the threat that it may provide an unfavorable summary of a particular country in its yearly report. As always, the chief enforcement tool in a democracy is the rule of law coupled with the judgment of its citizens; civilized peoples are repulsed by the concept of torture and ill-treatment. Levels of compliance in totalitarian regimes are dismal, and the minimal progress that is achieved occurs only through the economic and political pressure applied by democracies.

IRELAND v. UNITED KINGDOM

European Court of Human Rights

2 EHRR 25 (1978)

- Torture
- Ill-treatment
- Stress & Duress
- Common Article 3 of Geneva

PANEL: Judge Balladore Pallieri (President), Judges, Wiarda, Zekia, Cremona, O'Donoghue, Pedersen, Thsr Vilhjalmsson, Ryssdal, Ganshof Van Der Meersch, Sir Gerald Fitzmaurice, Bindschedler-Robert, Evrigenis, Teitgen, Lagergren, Liesch, Gvlc Kl, Matscher, Mr M-A Eissen, Registrar, And Mr H Petzold, Deputy Registrar

AS TO THE FACTS

I. The Emergency Situation and its Background

The tragic and lasting crisis in Northern Ireland lies at the root of the present case. In order to combat what the respondent Government describe as "the longest and most violent terrorist campaign witnessed in either part of the island of Ireland," the authorities in Northern Ireland exercised from August 1971 until December 1975 a series of extrajudicial powers of arrest, detention and internment. The proceedings in this case concern the scope and the operation in practice of those measures as well as the alleged ill-treatment of persons thereby deprived of their liberty.

…

15. Northern Ireland is not a homogeneous society. It consists of two communities divided by deep and long-standing antagonisms. One community is variously termed Protestant, Unionist or Loyalist, the other is generally labeled as Catholic, Republican or Nationalist. About two-thirds of the population of one and a half million belong to the Protestant community, the remaining third to the Catholic community. The majority group is descended from Protestant settlers who emigrated in large numbers from Britain to Northern Ireland during the seventeenth century. The now traditional antagonism between the two groups is based both on religion and on social, economic and political differences. In particular, the Protestant community has consistently opposed the idea of a united Ireland independent of the United Kingdom, whereas the Catholic community has traditionally supported it.

16. The Irish Republican Army (IRA) is a clandestine organisation with quasi-military dispositions. Formed during the troubles prior to the partition of the island and illegal in the United Kingdom as well as in the Republic of Ireland, the IRA neither accepts the existence of Northern Ireland as part of the United Kingdom nor recognises the democratic order of the Republic. It has periodically mounted campaigns of terrorism in both parts of the island of Ireland and in Great Britain. After 1962, the IRA was not overtly active for some years.

   During the time covered by the complaints of the applicant Government, that is from 1971 to 1975, virtually all those members of the IRA living and operating in Northern Ireland were recruited from among the Catholic community.

…

47. At the beginning of 1972, despite a small drop, the level of violence remained higher than at any time before 9 August 1971. On 30 January 1972, 13 people were killed by army gunfire in the course of disorders taking place in the predominantly Catholic town of Londonderry. This incident led to a new upsurge in support for the IRA amongst the Catholic community.

   In the first three months of 1972, 87 people were killed, including 27 members of the security forces. Two assassinations carried out in March, one of a Protestant and the other of a Catholic, were the only deaths attributed to Loyalist activity. 421 explosions, the vast majority attributed to the IRA, were caused during the same period.

48. From August 1971 until 30 March 1972 there had been in Northern Ireland 1,130 bomb explosions and well over 2,000 shooting incidents. 158 civilians, 58 soldiers and 17 policemen had been killed, and 2,505 civilians, 306 soldiers and 107 RUC members injured.

Throughout these months the numbers held under detention or internment orders proceeded to rise until a total of over 900 persons, all suspected of involvement with the IRA, were held at the end of March 1972. At the same time, the ordinary processes of the criminal law continued to be used, against Protestants as well as Catholics, whenever there was thought to be sufficient evidence to ground a criminal conviction. Thus, between 9 August 1971 and 31 March 1972, over 1,600 people were charged with "terrorist-type" offences.

49. In March 1972, in view of the deteriorating circumstances, the Government in London decided that they should assume direct responsibility for the administration of law and order in Northern Ireland if there was to be any hope of political progress This decision was unacceptable to the Government of the province and accordingly it was announced on 24 March 1972 that direct rule from Westminster not only on law and order but on all matters was to be introduced.

Under the Northern Ireland (Temporary Provisions) Act 1972 (hereinafter referred to as the "Temporary Provisions Act"), which was passed by the United Kingdom Parliament and came into force on 30 March 1972, temporary provision was made for the exercise of the executive and legislative powers of the Northern Ireland Parliament and Government by the United Kingdom authorities. The Belfast Parliament was prorogued and the Queen empowered to legislate in its stead by Order in Council. The executive powers of the Belfast Government were transferred to the Secretary of State for Northern Ireland. This was a new office created for the purpose; its holder was a member of the United Kingdom Government and answerable to the United Kingdom Parliament. The legislation was enacted for a period of one year but was subsequently extended.
…

68. On 8 August 1973, the Northern Ireland (Emergency Provisions) Act 1973 (hereafter abbreviated to the "Emergency Provisions Act") came into force. This Act, which was based mainly on the recommendations of the Diplock Commission (see paras. 58 and 59 above), repealed the 1922 Special Powers Act, Regulations 10 and 11(1) and the 1972 Terrorists Order, while retaining in substance the procedure laid down in the latter Order. Briefly, the extrajudicial powers introduced under the Emergency Provisions Act were:

(i) arrest and detention for 72 hours;

(ii) interim custody for 28 days; and

(iii) detention (see paras. 88 and 89 below for a fuller explanation). These emergency powers remained in force for a period of one year unless renewed. The Act also dealt with the trial and punishment by the ordinary courts of certain scheduled offences, for the most part offences concerned with violence. One provision, s.6, is referred to below at para. 136.

69. Between 1 February 1973 and 31 October 1974, interim custody orders were served on 99 Protestants and 626 Catholics; at all times many more Catholics than Protestants were actually held. Shortly before Christmas 1973, 65 detainees, 63 of whom were Catholics, were released.

70. During the same period, 2,478 persons were charged with "terrorist-type offences", the total being made up as follows: 1,042 Protestants, 1,420 Catholics and 16 soldiers. These figures included 60 Protestants and 66 Catholics charged with murder. In addition, searches were being conducted and arms recovered in relation to both sides.
…

III. Allegations of Ill-Treatment

A. Introduction

92. As recounted above at paras. 39 and 41, on 9 August 1971 and thereafter numerous persons in Northern Ireland were arrested and taken into custody by the security forces acting in pursuance of the emergency powers. The persons arrested were interrogated, usually by members of the RUC, in order to determine whether they should be interned and/or to compile information about the IRA. In all, about 3,276 persons were processed by the police at various holding centres from August 1971 until June 1972. The holding centres were replaced in July 1972 by police offices in Belfast and at Ballykelly Military Barracks.

93. Allegations of ill-treatment have been made by the applicant Government in relation both to the initial arrests and to the subsequent interrogations. The applicant Government submitted written evidence to the Commission in respect of 228 cases concerning incidents between 9 August 1971 and 1974 ....

95. The Commission grouped the cases into five categories, according to the place where the ill-treatment was said to have been inflicted, namely:

(1) the unidentified interrogation centre or centres;

(2) Palace Barracks, Holywood;

(3) Girdwood Park Barracks;

(4) Ballykinler Regional Holding Centre; and

(5) various other miscellaneous places.

B. The unidentified interrogation centre or centres

96. Twelve persons arrested on 9 August 1971 and two persons arrested in October 1971 were singled out and taken to one or more unidentified centres. There, between 11 to 17 August and 11 to 18 October respectively, they were submitted to a form of "interrogation in depth" which involved the combined application of five particular techniques.

These methods, sometimes termed "disorientation" or "sensory deprivation" techniques, were not used in any cases other than the fourteen so indicated above. It emerges from the Commission's establishment of the facts that the techniques consisted of:

(a) wall-standing: forcing the detainees to remain for periods of some hours in a "stress position," described by those who underwent it as being "spreadeagled against the wall, with their fingers put high above the head against the wall, the legs spread apart and the feet back, causing them to stand on their toes with the weight of the body mainly on the fingers;"

(b) hooding: putting a black or navy coloured bag over the detainees' heads and, at least initially, keeping it there all the time except during interrogation;

(c) subjection to noise: pending their interrogations, holding the detainees in a room where there was a continuous loud and hissing noise;

(d) deprivation of sleep: pending their interrogations, depriving the detainees of sleep;

(e) deprivation of food and drink: subjecting the detainees to a reduced diet during their stay at the centre and pending interrogations.

The Commission's findings as to the manner and effects of the application of these techniques on two particular case-witnesses are referred to below at para. 104.

97. From the start, it has been conceded by the respondent Government that the use of the five techniques was authorised at "high level." Although never committed to writing or authorised in any official document, the techniques had been orally taught to members of the RUC by the English Intelligence Centre at a seminar held in April 1971.

98. The two operations of interrogation in depth by means of the five techniques led to the obtaining of a considerable quantity of intelligence information, including the identification of 700 members of both IRA factions and the discovery of individual responsibility for about 85 previously unexplained criminal incidents.

99. Reports alleging physical brutality and ill-treatment by the security forces were made public within a few days of Operation Demetrius (described above at para. 39). A committee of enquiry under the chairmanship of Sir Edmund Compton was appointed by the United Kingdom Government on 31 August 1971 to investigate such allegations. Among the 40 cases this Committee examined were 11 cases of persons subjected to the five techniques in August 1971; its findings were that interrogation in depth by means of the techniques constituted physical ill-treatment but not physical brutality as it understood that term. The Committee's report, adopted on 3 November 1971, was made public, as was a supplemental report of 14 November by Sir Edmund Compton in relation to three further cases occurring in September and October, one of which involved the techniques.

100. The Compton reports came under considerable criticism in the United Kingdom. On 16 November 1971, the British Home Secretary announced that a further Committee had been set up under the chairmanship of Lord Parker of Waddington to consider "whether, and if so in what respects, the procedures currently authorized for interrogation of persons suspected of terrorism and for their custody while subject to interrogation require amendment."

The Parker report, which was adopted on 31 January 1972, contained a majority and a minority opinion. The majority report concluded that the application of the techniques, subject to recommended safeguards against excessive use, need not be ruled out on moral grounds. On the other hand, the minority report by Lord Gardiner disagreed that such interrogation procedures were morally justifiable, even in emergency terrorist conditions. Both the majority and the minority considered the methods to be illegal under domestic law, although the majority confined their view to English law and to "some if not all the techniques."

...

102. At the hearing before the Court on 8 February 1977, the United Kingdom Attorney-General made the following declaration:

> "The Government of the United Kingdom have considered the question of the use of the 'five techniques' with very great care and with particular regard to Article 3 of the Convention. They now give this unqualified undertaking, that the 'five techniques' will not in any circumstances be reintroduced as an aid to interrogation."

103. The Irish Government referred to the Commission 8 cases of persons submitted to the five techniques during interrogation at the unidentified centre or centres between 11 and 17 August

1971. A further case, that of T 22, considered in the Commission's report in the context of Palace Barracks, concerned the use of the five techniques in October 1971. The Commission examined as illustrative the cases of T 6 and T 13, which were among the 11 cases investigated by the Compton Committee.

104. T 6 and T 13 were arrested on 9 August 1971 during Operation Demetrius. Two days later they were transferred from Magilligan Regional Holding Centre to an unidentified interrogation centre where they were medically examined on arrival. Thereafter, with intermittent periods of respite, they were subjected to the five techniques during four or possibly five days; neither the Compton or Parker Committees nor the Commission were able to establish the exact length of the periods of respite.

The Commission was satisfied that T 6 and T 13 were kept at the wall for different periods totaling between twenty to thirty hours, but it did not consider it proved that the enforced stress position had lasted all the time they were at the wall. It stated in addition that the required posture caused physical pain and exhaustion. The Commission noted that, later on during his stay at the interrogation centre, T 13 was allowed to take his hood off when he was alone in the room, provided that he turned his face to the wall. It was not found possible by the Commission to establish for what periods T 6 and T 13 had been without sleep, or to what extent they were deprived of nourishment and whether or not they were offered food but refused to take it.

The Commission found no physical injury to have resulted from the application of the five techniques as such, but loss of weight by the two case-witnesses and acute psychiatric symptoms developed by them during interrogation were recorded in the medical and other evidence. The Commission, on the material before it, was unable to establish the exact degree of any psychiatric after-effects produced on T 6 and T 13, but on the general level it was satisfied that some psychiatric after-effects in certain of the fourteen persons subjected to the techniques could not be excluded.

105. T 13 claimed in addition to have been beaten and otherwise physically ill-treated, but the medical evidence before the Commission, as the delegates explained at the hearing before the Court on 21 April 1977, gave reason to doubt that he had been assaulted to any severe degree, if at all. Accordingly, the Commission treated the allegations in regard to T 13 as concerning the five techniques only.

T 6 similarly alleged that he was also assaulted in various ways at, or during transport to and from, the centre. On 17 August 1971 he was medically examined on leaving the centre and also on his subsequent arrival at Crumlin Road Prison where he was then detained until 3 May 1972. The medical reports of these examinations and photographs taken on the same day revealed on T 6's body bruising and contusions that had not been present on 11 August. While not accepting all T 6's allegations, the Commission was:

> "satisfied beyond a reasonable doubt that certain of these injuries ... [were] the result of assaults committed on him by the security forces at the centre."

> As a general inference from the facts established in T 6's case, the Commission also found it "probable that physical violence was sometimes used in the forcible application of the five techniques."

...

107. T 13 and T 6 instituted civil proceedings in 1971 to recover damages for wrongful imprisonment and assault; their claims were settled in 1973 and 1975 respectively for £15,000 and

£14,000. The twelve other individuals against whom the five techniques were used have all received in settlement of their civil claims compensation ranging from £10,000 to £25,000.

…

PROCEEDINGS BEFORE THE COMMISSION

144. In their original application, lodged with the Commission on 16 December 1971, and later supplemented, the Irish Government made various allegations of violations by the United Kingdom of Articles 1, 2, 3, 5, 6 and 14 of the Convention.

145. On 1 October 1972, the Commission declared the application inadmissible as regards Article 2 but accepted the allegations that:

> —the treatment of persons in custody, in particular the methods of interrogation of such persons, constituted an administrative practice in breach of Article 3;

…

147. In its report, the Commission expressed the opinion:

> (i) unanimously, that the powers of detention and internment without trial as exercised during the relevant periods were not in conformity with Article 5(1) to (4), but were "strictly required by the exigencies of the situation" in Northern Ireland, within the meaning of Article 15(1);
>
> …
>
> (iv) unanimously, that the combined use of the five techniques in the cases before it constituted a practice of inhuman treatment and of torture in breach of Article 3;
>
> (v) unanimously, that violations of Article 3 occurred by inhuman, and in two cases degrading, treatment of
>
> > —T 6, in an unidentified interrogation centre in August 1971,
> >
> > —T 2, T 8, T 12, T 15, T 9, T 14 and T 10 at Palace Barracks, Holywood, in September, October and November 1971,
> >
> > —T 16, T 7 and T 11, at various places in August, October and December 1971;
>
> (vi) unanimously, that there had been at Palace Barracks, Holywood, in the autumn of 1971, a practice in connection with the interrogation of prisoners by members of the RUC which was inhuman treatment in breach of Article 3 of the Convention;

…

The report contains various separate opinions.

DECISION-1:

AS TO THE LAW

148. Paragraph (d) of the application of 10 March 1976 states that the object of bringing the case before the Court (r.31(1)(d)) of the Rules of Court) is:

> "to ensure the observance in Northern Ireland of the engagements undertaken by the respondent Government as a High Contracting Party to the Convention and in particular of the engagements specifically set out by the applicant Government in the pleadings filed and the submissions made

on their behalf and described in the evidence adduced before the Commission in the hearings before them."

"To this end," the Court is invited:
"to consider the report of the Commission and to confirm the opinion of the Commission that breaches of the Convention have occurred and also to consider the claims of the applicant Government with regard to other alleged breaches and to make a finding of breach of the Convention where the Court is satisfied that a breach has occurred."

In their written and oral pleadings before the Court, the Irish Government allege breaches of Articles 1, 3, 5 (taken together with Article 15), 6 (taken together with Article 15) and 14 (taken together with Articles 5 and 6).

They also maintain—though they do not ask the Court to make a specific finding—that the British Government failed on several occasions in their duty to furnish the necessary facilities for the effective conduct of the investigation. The Commission does not go as far as that; however, at various places in its report, the Commission points out, in substance, that the respondent Government did not always afford it the assistance desirable. The Court regrets this attitude on the part of that Government; it must stress the fundamental importance of the principle, enshrined in Article 28, sub-paragraph (a) in fine, that the Contracting States have a duty to cooperate with the Convention institutions.

149. The Court notes first of all that it is not called upon to take cognisance of every single aspect of the tragic situation prevailing in Northern Ireland. For example, it is not required to rule on the terrorist activities in the six counties of individuals or of groups, activities that are in clear disregard of human rights. The Court has only to give a decision on the claims made before it by the Irish Republic against the United Kingdom. However, in so doing, the Court cannot lose sight of the events that form the background to this case.

I. On Article 3

150. Article 3 provides that "no one shall be subjected to torture or to inhuman or degrading treatment or punishment."

A. Preliminary questions

151. In their memorial of 26 October 1976 and at the hearings in February 1977, the United Kingdom Government raised two preliminary questions on the alleged violations of Article 3. The first concerns the violations which they no longer contest, the second certain of the violations whose existence they dispute.

1. Preliminary question on the non-contested violations of Article 3

152. The United Kingdom Government contest neither the breaches of Article 3 as found by the Commission (see para. 147 above), nor—a point moreover that is beyond doubt—the Court's jurisdiction to examine such breaches. However, relying inter alia on the case-law of the International Court of Justice (Northern Cameroons case, judgment of 2 December 1963, and Nuclear Tests cases, judgments of 20 December 1974),they argue that the European Court has power to decline to exercise its jurisdiction where the objective of an application has been accomplished or where adjudication on the merits would be devoid of purpose. Such, they claim, is the situation

here. They maintain that the findings in question not only are not contested but also have been widely publicised and that they do not give rise to problems of interpretation or application of the Convention sufficiently important to require a decision by the Court. Furthermore, for them the subject-matter of those findings now belongs to past history in view of the abandonment of the five techniques (1972), the solemn and unqualified undertaking not to reintroduce these techniques (8 February 1977) and the other measures taken by the United Kingdom to remedy, impose punishment for, and prevent the recurrence of, the various violations found by the Commission.

This argument is disputed by the applicant Government. Neither is it accepted in a general way by the delegates of the Commission; they stated, however, that they would express no conclusion as to whether or not the above-mentioned undertaking had deprived the claim concerning the five techniques of its object.

153. The Court takes formal note of the undertaking given before it, at the hearing on 8 February 1977, by the United Kingdom Attorney-General on behalf of the respondent Government. The terms of this undertaking were as follows:

> "The Government of the United Kingdom have considered the question of the use of the 'five techniques' with very great care and with particular regard to Article 3 of the Convention. They now give this unqualified undertaking, that the 'five techniques' will not in any circumstances be reintroduced as an aid to interrogation."

The Court also notes that the United Kingdom has taken various measures designed to prevent the recurrence of the events complained of and to afford reparation for their consequences. For example, it has issued to the police and the army instructions and directives on the arrest, interrogation and treatment of persons in custody, reinforced the procedures for investigating complaints, appointed commissions of enquiry and paid or offered compensation in many cases (see paras. 99-100, 107, 110-111, 116-118, 121-122, 124, 128-130, 132, 135-139 and 142-143 above).

154. Nevertheless, the Court considers that the responsibilities assigned to it within the framework of the system under the Convention extend to pronouncing on the non-contested allegations of violation of Article 3. The Court's judgments in fact serve not only to decide those cases brought before the Court but, more generally, to elucidate, safeguard and develop the rules instituted by the Convention, thereby contributing to the observance by the States of the engagements undertaken by them as Contracting Parties (art 19).

The conclusion thus arrived at by the Court is, moreover, confirmed by para. 3 of r.47 of the Rules of Court. If the Court may proceed with the consideration of a case and give a ruling thereon even in the event of a "notice of discontinuance, friendly settlement, arrangement" or "other fact of a kind to provide a solution of the matter", it is entitled a fortiori to adopt such a course of action when the conditions for the application of this Rule are not present.

…

C. Questions concerning the merits

162. As was emphasised by the Commission, ill-treatment must attain a minimum level of severity if it is to fall within the scope of Article 3. The assessment of this minimum is, in the nature of things, relative; it depends on all the circumstances of the case, such as the duration of the treatment, its physical or mental effects and, in some cases, the sex, age and state of health of the victim, etc.

163. The Convention prohibits in absolute terms torture and inhuman or degrading treatment or punishment, irrespective of the victim's conduct. Unlike most of the substantive clauses of the Convention and of Protocols Nos. 1 and 4, Article 3 makes no provision for exceptions and, under Article 15(2), there can be no derogation therefrom even in the event of a public emergency threatening the life of the nation.

164. In the instant case, the only relevant concepts are "torture" and "inhuman or degrading treatment", to the exclusion of "inhuman or degrading punishment".

1. The unidentified interrogation centre or centres

(a) The "five techniques"

165. The facts concerning the five techniques are summarised at paras. 96-104 and 106-107 above. In the Commission's estimation, those facts constituted a practice not only of inhuman and degrading treatment but also of torture. The applicant Government ask for confirmation of this opinion which is not contested before the Court by the respondent Government.

166. The police used the five techniques on fourteen persons in 1971, that is on twelve, including T 6 and T 13, in August before the Compton Committee was set up, and on two in October whilst that Committee was carrying out its enquiry. Although never authorised in writing in any official document, the five techniques were taught orally by the English Intelligence Centre to members of the RUC at a seminar held in April 1971. There was accordingly a practice.

167. The five techniques were applied in combination, with premeditation and for hours at a stretch; they caused, if not actual bodily injury, at least intense physical and mental suffering to the persons subjected thereto and also led to acute psychiatric disturbances during interrogation. They accordingly fell into the category of inhuman treatment within the meaning of Article 3. The techniques were also degrading since they were such as to arouse in their victims feelings of fear, anguish and inferiority capable of humiliating and debasing them and possibly breaking their physical or moral resistance.

 On these two points, the Court is of the same view as the Commission.

 In order to determine whether the five techniques should also be qualified as torture, the Court must have regard to the distinction, embodied in Article 3, between this notion and that of inhuman or degrading treatment.

 In the Court's view, this distinction derives principally from a difference in the intensity of the suffering inflicted.

 The Court considers in fact that, whilst there exists on the one hand violence which is to be condemned both on moral grounds and also, in most cases, under the domestic law of the Contracting States, but which does not fall within Article 3 of the Convention, it appears on the other hand that it was the intention that the Convention, with its distinction between "torture" and "inhuman or degrading treatment," should by the first of these terms attach a special stigma to deliberate inhuman treatment causing very serious and cruel suffering.

 Moreover, this seems to be the thinking lying behind Article 1 in fine of Resolution 3452 (XXX) adopted by the General Assembly of the United Nations on 9 December 1975, which declares: "Torture constitutes an aggravated and deliberate form of cruel, inhuman or degrading treatment or punishment."

Although the five techniques, as applied in combination, undoubtedly amounted to inhuman and degrading treatment, although their object was the extraction of confessions, the naming of others and/or information and although they were used systematically, they did not occasion suffering of the particular intensity and cruelty implied by the word torture as so understood.

168. The Court concludes that recourse to the five techniques amounted to a practice of inhuman and degrading treatment, which practice was in breach of Article 3.

(b) Ill-treatment alleged to have accompanied the use of the five techniques

169. The applicant Government claim that the fourteen persons subjected to the five techniques, or some of those persons including T 6 and T 13, also had to undergo other kinds of treatment contrary to Article 3.

The Commission has found such treatment only in the case of T 6, although it regarded it as probable that the use of the five techniques was sometimes accompanied by physical violence (see para. 105 above).

170. As far as T 6 is concerned, the Court shares the Commission's opinion that the security forces subjected T 6 to assaults severe enough to constitute inhuman treatment. This opinion, which is not contested by the respondent Government, is borne out by the evidence before the Court.

171. In the thirteen remaining cases examined in this context, including the contested case of T 13, the Court has no evidence to support a finding of breaches of Article 3 over and above that resulting from the application of the five techniques.

172. Accordingly, no other practice contrary to Article 3 is established for the unidentified interrogation centre or centres; the findings relating to the individual case of T 6 cannot, of themselves, amount to proof of a practice.

…

246. The Court accordingly considers that it is not necessary to apply Article 50 in the present case.

FOR THESE REASONS, THE COURT

I. On Article 3

1. holds unanimously that, although certain violations of Article 3 were not contested, a ruling should nevertheless be given thereon;

2. holds unanimously that it has jurisdiction to take cognisance of the cases of alleged violation of Article 3 to the extent that the applicant Government put them forward as establishing the existence of a practice;

3. holds by sixteen votes to one that the use of the five techniques in August and October 1971 constituted a practice of inhuman and degrading treatment, which practice was in breach of Article 3;

4. holds by thirteen votes to four that the said use of the five techniques did not constitute a practice of torture within the meaning of Article 3;

5. holds by sixteen votes to one that no other practice of ill-treatment is established for the unidentified interrogation centres;

6. holds unanimously that there existed at Palace Barracks in the autumn of 1971 a practice of inhuman treatment, which practice was in breach of Article 3;

7. holds by fourteen votes to three that the last-mentioned practice was not one of torture within the meaning of Article 3;

...

As covered in chapter 4, two important developments have shaped U.S. policy and law in terms of interrogation techniques. In the context of "enemy combatants" under the control of the U.S. government, the Detainee Treatment Act of 2006 (P.L. 109-163) adopted some international human rights terminology in setting out interrogation limits. In short, American interrogators may not engage in "cruel, inhuman and degrading treatment or punishment of persons under detention, custody, or control of the United States Government." Further, pursuant to the so-called McCain Amendment, "cruel, unusual, and inhuman treatment or punishment" covers all those acts prohibited by the Fifth, Eighth and Fourteenth Amendments to the Constitution, as stated in U.S. reservations to the Torture Convention. The other development was the 2006 Military Commission Act which applied the provisions of Common Article 3 of the Geneva Conventions.

6.3 United States Domestic Law

The American experience has not been guiltless in terms of the sanctioned use of torture and ill-treatment to elicit confessions in criminal investigations, particularly in the early part of the last century. By 1931, the appalling practice of torture by local law enforcement had become so common throughout the nation that a special government fact-finding commission was set up to investigate the matter. The Wickersham Commission issued a report on abusive police interrogation practices that not only educated the public, but also energized the United States Supreme Court to hand down a string of cases in which police interrogation abuses that "shocked the conscience" of the Court were equated with torture.

Currently, torture is defined in 18 U.S.C. § 2340 as:

> [A]n act committed by a person acting under the color of the law specifically intended to inflict severe physical or mental pain or suffering (other than pain or suffering incidental to lawful sanctions) upon another person within his custody or physical control.

While domestic acts of torture are punished as common law crimes, 18 U.S.C. § 2340A makes it a federal offense for an American national to either commit or attempt to commit torture outside the United States. In 1992, Congress passed the Torture Victim Protection Act of 1991, which opened United States courts to civil law damage suits by any individual "who, under actual or apparent authority, or color of law, of any foreign nation," violates international law regarding torture.

In the context of what techniques would be lawful for interrogators to use in the United States, a 2003 United States Supreme Court decision entitled *Chavez v. Martinez* provides some current guidance. The central issue in *Chavez* involved the issue of coercive questioning by a police officer.

The facts of the case are as follows. While "investigating suspected narcotics activity" near a vacant lot, police in Oxnard, California, stopped Oliverio Martinez as he was riding his bike down a darkened path. The police conducted a patdown frisk of Martinez and discovered a knife in his waistband. An altercation ensued and police officers claim that Martinez took one of the officer's "gun from its holster and pointed it at them." Officer Pea then drew her service pistol and shot Martinez five times, leaving him blinded and paralyzed. Martinez was placed under arrest and taken by ambulance to the hospital. Sergeant Ben Chavez, the patrol supervisor, "accompanied Martinez to the hospital and then questioned Martinez while he was receiving treatment from medical personnel." The interrogation in the emergency room of the hospital "lasted a total of about 10 minutes, over a 45-minute period, with Chavez leaving the emergency room for periods of time to permit medical personnel to attend to Martinez."

During the interrogation, Chavez never read Martinez his Miranda warnings. There can be no question that Martinez was disoriented and in extreme pain throughout the process of interrogation. At first Martinez was uncooperative. "At one point, Martinez said 'I am not telling you anything until they treat me,' yet Chavez continued the interview." Later, Martinez admitted taking the gun and pointing it at police. This act resulted in Martinez being shot by Pea.

Although Martinez was never charged with any crime and his statements were never used against him in a criminal proceeding, he subsequently filed a claim for damages in the United States District Court for the Central District of California under 42 U.S.C. § 1983, alleging that Sergeant Chavez had violated his Fifth Amendment right against self-incrimination as well as his Fourteenth Amendment substantive due process right. The Court of Appeals for the Ninth Circuit affirmed the District Court's denial of Chavez's defense of qualified immunity and entered summary judgment in favor of Martinez for both claims. With Justice Thomas delivering the opinion for the majority, the Supreme Court granted certiorari and reversed and remanded the case.

In seeking guidance for questioning suspected terrorists within the United States, the case is significant for two reasons. First, by overturning the Ninth Circuit's ruling that "the mere use of compulsive questioning, without more, violates the Constitution," the Court clearly established that the Fifth Amendment is not violated when law enforcement agents who do not intend to use statements in subsequent criminal proceedings interrogate with coercion an unwilling suspect without providing Miranda warnings. The Court related that "mere coercion does not violate the text of the Self-Incrimination Clause absent the use of compelled statements in a criminal case against the witness." Thus, the Court held that "the absence of a 'criminal case' in which Martinez was compelled to be a 'witness' against himself defeats his core Fifth Amendment claim" and voids any §1983 action. Still, the Court was quick to note that they were not condoning the use of torture or ill-treatment by law enforcement:

> [O]ur views of the proper scope of the Fifth Amendment's Self-Incrimination Clause do not mean that police torture or other abuse that results in a confession is constitutionally permissible so long as the statements are not used in trial; it simply means that the Four-

teenth Amendment's Due Process Clause, rather than the Fifth Amendment's Self Incrimination Clause, would govern the inquiry in those cases and provide relief in appropriate circumstances.

Second, the ruling left in place the subjective "shock the conscience" standard, taken from the 1952 case of *Rochin v. California*, for determining when the police cross the threshold for conduct that violates the Fourteenth Amendment. In *Rochin*, police officers witnessed the defendant swallow two capsules which they suspected were illegal substances. Rochin was handcuffed and taken to a hospital where a doctor forced an emetic solution through a tube into Rochin's stomach and against Rochin's will. Rochin vomited two morphine capsules and was subsequently convicted. Overturning the conviction, the Supreme Court held that obtaining evidence by methods that are "so brutal and so offensive to human dignity" stands in violation of the Fourteenth Amendment's due process clause:

> [W]e are compelled to conclude that the proceedings by which this conviction was obtained do more than offend some fastidious squeamishness or private sentimentalism about combating crime too energetically. This is conduct that *shocks the conscience* …. They are methods too close to the rack and screw to permit of constitutional differentiation [emphasis added].

As to whether the facts of *Chavez* would constitute a violation of the Fourteenth Amendment, the Court remanded that issue back to the lower court although at least five of the justices apparently were not "shocked" that Sergeant Chavez engaged in a repetitive interrogation even though Martinez was suffering "excruciating pain." Despite the fact that Sergeant Chavez may have indeed benefited from the situation if Martinez subjectively thought that he had to answer questions as a condition of getting medial treatment, this was not the case and medical personnel were treating Martinez throughout the interrogation period. Justice Thomas wrote that "we cannot agree with Martinez's characterization of Chavez's behavior as egregious or conscience shocking." The fact that Chavez did not interfere with medical treatment and did not cause the pain experienced by Martinez (the bullet wounds to Martinez occurred prior to and totally apart from the questioning process) were certainly important factors which influenced some, but not all, of the Justices.

Expressing an opposite view on the matter, Justice Stevens saw the interrogation conducted by Sergeant Chavez as tantamount to torture and a clear violation of the Fourteenth Amendment:

> As a matter of fact, the interrogation of respondent was the functional equivalent of an attempt to obtain an involuntary confession from a prisoner by torturous methods. As a matter of law, that type of brutal police conduct constitutes an immediate deprivation of the prisoner's constitutionally protected interest in liberty.

Unfortunately, the Court did not provide any new approaches to assist in defining what would constitute behavior that would "shock the conscience." The Court was content to cite previous examples from past cases, traced from the 1936 case of *Brown v. Mississippi*.

In *Brown*, the Court ruled that convictions based on confessions extracted by law enforcement through methods tantamount to torture violated the Fourteenth Amendment. The facts of the case involved the hanging and whipping of a murder suspect by local police until a confession was obtained. Other defendants were also tortured—they "were made to strip and ... were laid over chairs and their backs were cut to pieces with a leather strap with buckles on it ... and in this manner the defendants confessed to the crime." All of the defendants were convicted of murder and sentenced to death. In reversing the convictions, the Supreme Court stated the following:

> [The] state is free to regulate the procedure of its courts in accordance with its own conceptions of policy, unless in so doing it offends some principle of justice so rooted in the traditions and conscience of our people as to be ranked as fundamental. But freedom of the state in establishing its policy is the freedom of constitutional government and is limited by the requirement of due process of law. Because a state may dispense with a jury trial, it does not follow that it may substitute trial by ordeal. The rack and torture chamber may not be substituted for the witness stand.

Not all fact patterns are as easy to associate with torture as *Brown*, which is clearly torture at its worst. Indeed, those familiar with the "shock the conscience" test understand that the Court has often interpreted the test with a great degree of flexibility, particularly when judging the actions of law enforcement officers faced with exigent circumstances related to governmental needs such as public safety issues. For example, in the 1998 case of *County of Sacramento v. Lewis* the Court denied a §1983 claim based on an alleged substantive due process violation. In *Lewis*, a passenger on a motorcycle was killed as the result of a high-speed police chase ending when the fleeing motorcycle tipped over and a police car in close pursuit struck and killed the respondent's sixteen-year-old son.

In discussing the threshold for shocking the conscience, the *Lewis* decision "made it clear that the due process guarantee does not entail a body of constitutional law imposing liability whenever someone cloaked with state authority causes harm." Indeed, "[i]n a due process challenge to executive action, the threshold question is whether the behavior of the governmental officer is so egregious, so outrageous, that it may fairly be said to shock the contemporary conscience."

Interestingly, an equally important aspect of *Lewis* centered on the Court's view that not only does the conduct have to be egregious, but that "conduct intended to injure in some way unjustifiable by any government interest is the sort of an official action most likely to rise to the conscience-shocking level." This means that the Court will provide greater deference if the government can demonstrate a justification for its conduct based on the totality of the circumstances. The stronger the justification, the more flexibility allowed.

This deference factor certainly played out in a 1966 Ninth Circuit case entitled *Blefare v. United States*. In a fact pattern similar to *Rochin*, the appellants were suspected of swallowing narcotics which were lodged in their rectums or stomachs. Appellants were searched by U.S. officials at a border crossing from Mexico into the United States where they consented to a rectal probe by a doctor. When the rectal probe found no drugs, a "saline solution was ... given the appellants to drink to produce vomiting." Blefare, one of the suspects, "was seen by the doctor to have regurgitated an object and reswallowed it." Then, without Blefare's consent the doctor forcefully passed a soft tube into the "nose, down the throat and into the stomach," through which fluid flowed in order to induce vomiting. This resulted in the discovery of packets of heroin and the subsequent conviction of Blefare.

The Ninth Circuit refused to hold that the involuntary intrusion into Blefare's stomach shocked the conscience. The Court attempted to distinguish the case from *Rochin* by noting that Blefare had at first consented to the rectal probe and the drinking of saline, and that, in any event, the actions to induce vomiting were not brutal. Arguably, the ruling hinged on the fact that the State had an important governmental interest in keeping heroin from entering the United States. In the Court's view, it would have been shocking had they overturned the conviction based on the due process clause. On the contrary, the Court felt that it would "shock the conscience" if Blefare's conviction were set aside:

> It would shock the conscience of law abiding citizens if the officers, with the knowledge these officers had, were frustrated in the recovery and use of this evidence. It is shocking to know that these appellants swallowed narcotics to smuggle it into and through the United States for sale for profit …. If we were mechanically to invoke Rochin to reverse this conviction, we would transform a meaningful expression of concern for the rights of the individual into a meaningless mechanism for the obstruction of justice.

To be sure, there are a number of cases that proponents of coercive questioning techniques can cite to buttress the view that in exigent circumstances the police may be obliged to use force to get life saving information. For instance, in *Leon v. Wainwright* the Eleventh Circuit brushed aside the fact that police officers had used "force and threats" on kidnap suspect Jean Leon in order to get the suspect to reveal the location of his victim. When apprehended by a group of police officers in a Florida parking lot, Leon refused to reveal the location of his kidnap victim (the victim, Louis Gachelin, had been taken by gunpoint to an apartment where he was undressed and bound). In order to get the suspect to talk, police officers then physically abused Leon by twisting his arm and chocking him until he revealed where the kidnap victim was being held. Later, Leon was taken to the police station were he made a second confession which the Court ruled as admissible at his trail. In speaking to the use of brutal force to get the information needed to protect the victim, the Court deemed that the action of the officers was reasonable given the immediate concern to find the victim and save his life.

> We do not by our decision sanction the use of force and coercion by police officers. Yet this case does not represent the typical case of unjustified force. We do not have an act of brutal law enforcement agents trying to obtain a confession in total disregard of the law. This was instead a group of concerned officers acting in a reasonable manner to obtain information they needed in order to protect another individual from bodily harm or death.

Returning to *Chavez*, the government brief attempted to draw together the concept of governmental interest by arguing that the Court in *Chavez* should take the opportunity to create a "terrorist exception" which would accord protection to police officers from §1983 suits when questioning suspected terrorists. This matter was not directly addressed by the justices. Nevertheless, if one adds *Chavez* to *Lewis* and its progeny, certain constitutional parameters for interrogating a terrorist suspect can now be staked out. Simply put, even if a suspect asks for a lawyer and demands that all questioning cease, law enforcement may justifiably refuse these requests and engage in interrogation that may consist of coercive techniques so long as the techniques utilized fall below the threshold of shocking the conscience (which equates to actions not in violation of the Torture Convention). In addition, under the concept of governmental interest, the more the suspected terrorist matches the scenario of the ticking time bomb terrorist, the more deference given to police interrogators.

Critics of *Chavez*, such as Brooklyn law professor Susan Herman, rightly understand that allowing the use of coercive interrogation techniques short of the ambiguous "shock the conscience" standard leaves open the door for abuse to those not suspected of terrorism. Others are dismayed that the *Chavez* Court refused to even acknowledge the existence of the Torture Convention and its place in the matter of coercive interrogations.

6.4 Allegations of United States Sanctioned Torture

Keeping in mind that the goal of any antiterrorism effort is to stop or eliminate the terrorists before they commit murderous attacks, there are four general law enforcement means that mesh together in this effort: (1) using informants and undercover agents to infiltrate the terror cell (known as HUMINT sources); (2) using surveillance, searches and wiretaps to learn of locations, organizational structure and plans for future attacks; (3) arresting and detaining terrorists before they commit a terrorist attack; and (4) interrogation of terrorists. Only the last category, interrogating those detained as suspected foot soldiers of terrorism, is discussed herein.

Since the advent of the War on Terror, the United States has detained thousands of individuals which can be grouped into one of four categories: (1) those suspected of having links to the al-Qa'eda (or similar radical Islamic fundamentalist groups) terror movement; (2) those designated as enemy combatants; (3) those detained as prisoners of war in the Iraq military campaign; and (4) those who have been apprehended since the close of major combat operations in Iraq and Afghanistan and designated as "security detainees." Most of those detained in the first category were apprehended by federal law enforcement personnel on the heels of the attacks of September 11, 2001, and, after questioning, the majority were deported as illegal aliens. The vast majority of those in the third group have since been released.

Detainees in the second group are members or supporters of the al-Qa'eda network captured on the battlefields of Afghanistan, although the United States has also included other suspected members of al-Qa'eda apprehended in places other than military combat zones. Along with Yaser Esam Hamdi, at least two enemy combatants, Ali Saleh Kahlah Al-Marri and Jose Padilla, have been arrested in the United States. With the 2006 release of the 14 detainees held by the CIA in "undisclosed" locations, many of the individuals in the second category are currently being housed in Guantanamo Bay, Cuba. Some of the detainees have been held in detention without being charged with a crime for over five years. Those in the fourth group are being held in Iraq with the permission of the Iraqi government.

The second and fourth group of individuals—enemy combatants and security detainees—have generally been subjected to extended interrogation, but few have been released from detention. The purpose of detaining enemy combatants is to ensure that they do not return to join enemy forces and, in this unique situation, to allow American officials the opportunity to gather any necessary intelligence about the terrorist's organizational infrastructure, financial network, communication system, weapon supply lines and plans for future terror attacks. As is the practice in all wars, the purpose of detention is not to punish the enemy combatant, but to protect the host nation from future acts of violence by the enemy. In this light, over 400,000 German and Italian enemy combatants were held in the United States during World War II. They were not charged with crimes, afforded lawyers, or allowed access to U.S. courts.

By far the group that has received the most attention consists of the more than 400 men held at Guantanamo Bay, Cuba, at a specially built facility named Camp Delta. Again, the majority of these men were captured on the battlefields of Afghanistan. Although all of the detainees are said to be participants in the War on Terror, the Bush Administration has not recognized these detainees as eligible for prisoner of war status under the Third Geneva Convention nor did the Bush Administration apply Common Article 3 of the Geneva Conventions. As covered previously, the reason that the Third Geneva Convention does not apply is because both the Taliban fighters and the al-Qa'eda fighters fail to qualify as lawful enemy combatants under the applicable provisions of international law. Specifically, prisoner of war status is only conferred on persons who are "[m]embers of armed forces of a Party to the conflict" or "members of other militias and members of other volunteer corps, including those of organized resistance movements, belonging to a Party … provided that such … fulfill[s]" four specific conditions:

[handwritten margin note: Not POWs b/c violate:]

- That of being commanded by a person responsible for his subordinates;
- That of having a fixed distinctive sign recognizable at a distance;
- That of carrying arms openly; and
- That of conducting their operations in accordance with the laws and customs of war.

Despite the fact that the Third Geneva Convention is not applied to these enemy combatants, the Bush Administration pledged that all detainees were treated in accordance with the humanitarian concerns set out in the Geneva Conventions. With the passage of the Detainee Treatment Act in 2005 uniform standards for interrogation of individuals in custody of the DOD were set out. Further, the Act expressly bans cruel, inhuman, or degrading treatment of detainees in the custody of any U.S. agency. Then, in 2006 the Supreme Court in *Hamdan* ruled that the detainees now officially enjoy the provisions of Common Article 3 of the Geneva Conventions. The 2006 Military Commission Act also provides similar protections:

(c) Additional Prohibition on Cruel, Inhuman, or Degrading Treatment or Punishment—

(1) IN GENERAL—No individual in the custody or under the physical control of the United States Government, regardless of nationality or physical location, shall be subject to cruel, inhuman, or degrading treatment or punishment.

(2) CRUEL, INHUMAN, OR DEGRADING TREATMENT OR PUNISHMENT DEFINED—In this subsection, the term 'cruel, inhuman, or degrading treatment or punishment' means cruel, unusual, and inhumane treatment or punishment prohibited by the Fifth, Eighth, and Fourteenth Amendments to the Constitution of the United States, as defined in the United States Reservations, Declarations and Understandings to the United Nations Convention Against Torture and Other Forms of Cruel, Inhuman or Degrading Treatment or Punishment done at New York, December 10, 1984.

(3) COMPLIANCE—The President shall take action to ensure compliance with this subsection, including through the establishment of administrative rules and procedures.

The detainees continue to receive regular visits by the International Committee of the Red Cross, diplomats from their respective nations, military attorneys and various other fact finding groups. Common Article 3 of the Geneva Conventions requires the following:

ARTICLE 3 COMMON TO THE GENEVA CONVENTIONS OF 1949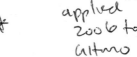

applied 2006 to Gitmo

In the case of armed conflict not of an international character occurring in the territory of one of the High Contracting Parties, each Party to the conflict shall be bound to apply, as a minimum, the following provisions:

(1) Persons taking no active part in the hostilities, including members of armed forces who have laid down their arms and those placed *hors de combat* by sickness, wounds, detention, or any other cause, shall in all circumstances be treated humanely, without any adverse distinction founded on race, colour, religion or faith, sex, birth or wealth, or any other similar criteria.

To this end, the following acts are and shall remain prohibited at any time and in any place whatsoever with respect to the above-mentioned persons:

(a) violence to life and person, in particular murder of all kinds, mutilation, cruel treatment and torture;

(b) taking of hostages;

(c) outrages upon personal dignity, in particular humiliating and degrading treatment;

(d) the passing of sentences and the carrying out of executions without previous judgment pronounced by a regularly constituted court, affording all the judicial guarantees which are recognized as indispensable by civilized peoples.

(2) The wounded and sick shall be collected and cared for.

An impartial humanitarian body, such as the International Committee of the Red Cross, may offer its services to the Parties to the conflict.

The Parties to the conflict should further endeavour to bring into force, by means of special agreements, all or part of the other provisions of the present Convention.

The application of the preceding provisions shall not affect the legal status of the Parties to the conflict.

The precise status of "enemy combatant" is pivotal in determining what interrogation techniques can be used to gather information from the subject detainee. Article 17 of the Third Geneva Convention provides that prisoners of war are only required to give their "surname, first names and rank, date of birth, and army regimental, personal or serial number, or failing this, equivalent information." The prisoner of war is not required to give any further information upon questioning. To leave no doubt on this point, Article 17 goes on to provide the following:

> No physical or mental torture, nor any other form of coercion, may be inflicted on prisoners of war to secure from them information of any kind whatever. Prisoners of war who refuse to answer may not be *threatened, insulted, or exposed to any unpleasant or disadvantageous treatment of any kind* [emphasis added].

Certainly, if the Third Geneva Convention covered the detainees, American authorities would not be entitled to interrogate them or obtain additional information. Conversely, enemy combatants who are not prisoners of war do not fall under the protections of the Third Geneva Convention and may therefore be questioned by American interrogators on additional topics of interest.

One allegation that has not received treatment in any American court is the charge of torture or ill-treatment by American officials of certain detainees. These claims are generally associated with the issue of interrogations, but also extend to criticisms of the living conditions of the detainees. Some have claimed that even if one agrees that the detainees may be held and questioned, the process of deciding what do to with the more than 400 detainees in Guantanamo Bay is far too lengthy. In response, Secretary of Defense Donald Rumsfeld has pointed out that the process of determining what to do with each detainee is slow because each case has to be reviewed by various federal agencies to include the Central Intelligence Agency (CIA) and the Federal Bureau of Instigations (FBI).

As stated, since the detainees are not entitled to prisoner of war status, international law does not forbid interrogation so long as it is conducted free of torture or ill-treatment. The primary protection against torture or ill-treatment in the case of the detainees would be the Torture Convention which, in effect, is unenforceable by the international community or, more likely, charges of violations of the law of war—war crimes—which also prohibits torture.

The American position on the question of torture is that the United States does not engage in torture or other ill-treatment, either in questioning or housing detainees. United States National Security Council spokesman, Sean McCormack, exemplifies the official stand: "The United States is treating enemy combatants in U.S. government control, wherever held, humanely and in a manner consistent with the principles of the Third Geneva Convention of 1949." Of course, this is not to say that the United States does not fully question detainees at a variety of levels. Government officials responsible for gathering information from detainees certainly employ the full range of permissible interrogation tactics to include offering various incentives such as money or engaging in trickery.

Suggestions by various "unnamed" government sources that American interrogators might be forced to engage in physical pressure, e.g., torture or ill-treatment, to get information from suspected terrorists surfaced almost immediately after the terror attacks of September 11, 2001. In October 21, 2001, a *Washington Post* article served as the information source of choice to those who accuse the United States of engaging in torture. The article quoted the perennial "unnamed" FBI agent as stating:

We are known for humanitarian treatment, so basically we are stuck …. Usually there is some incentive, some angle to play, what you can do for them. But it could get to that spot where we could go to pressure … where we don't have a choice, and we are probably getting there.

Then, in March of 2002, the *Washington Post* once again relied on "unnamed sources" to alert its readers that the United States government had turned over dozens of suspected terrorists "to countries, including Egypt and Jordan, whose intelligence services have close ties to the CIA and where they can be subjected to interrogation tactics—including torture and threats to their families—that are illegal in the United States." The process referred to in the article is known as "rendition." As previously noted, rendition is a common practice which is only improper under international law if, for instance, the United States knowingly delivers a suspect to a nation that it has substantial grounds to believe engages in "a consistent pattern of gross, flagrant or mass violations of human rights." While an "unnamed source" in a media article may view a particular country as a nation that satisfies this test, it is ultimately a question for the government of the United States and the international community to answer.

Without more evidence than that provided by unnamed sources, it is impossible to accurately gauge what interrogation methods are being used in a particular State. In addition, from a legal perspective, there is no international prohibition against rendering a suspected terrorist to a nation that engages in interrogation practices that would constitute ill-treatment. For example, assuming for the sake of argument that Jordan does use some amount of physical or physiological pressure in its interrogation practices, one would need to determine whether or not the type of pressure rises to the level of torture, or is ill-treatment only.

It was not until December 26, 2002, that the public was alerted to the concept of "stress and duress" tactics allegedly used by American interrogators. According to the initial story in the *Washington Post*, various unnamed government sources suggested that the United States was using a laundry list of questionable techniques to get uncooperative detainees housed outside the United States to talk. The article stated: "At times they [uncooperative detainees] are held in awkward, painful positions and deprived of sleep with a 24-hour bombardment of lights—subject to what are known as 'stress and duress'." Other examples of stress and duress listed were so-called "false flag" operations in which the detainee is deceived into believing he has been turned over to a "country with a reputation for brutality," or having female interrogators question the detainee, "a psychologically jarring experience for men reared in a conservative Muslim culture where women are never in control."

The article also alleged that when detainees were first apprehended, "MPs [military police] and U.S. Army Special Forces troops … [would] beat them [detainees] up and confine them in tiny rooms." To buttress this view, the article then quoted another unnamed American official as saying: "[O]ur guys may kick them around a little bit in the adrenaline of the immediate aftermath [of the arrest]."

Ultimately, if such stress and duress tactics failed to glean meaningful results, the article reported that the detainees were rendered to third countries where they could be subjected to mistreatment or "mind-altering drugs such as sodium pentothal." However, the *Washington Post* article piece placed a caveat on its claims about rendition practices by noting that the CIA's "Directorate of Operations instructions, drafted in cooperation with the general counsel, tells case officers in the field that they may not engage in, provide advice about or encourage the use of torture by cooperating intelligence services from other countries." As expected, since the publication of the stress and duress story a handful of similar second hand reports have found their way into the media, most of them loudly claiming that the United States tortures suspects.

6.5 What Exactly Do American Interrogators Do?

Without question, numerous elements of the government have direct roles to play in gathering timely intelligence about the terrorist network in the Global War on Terrorism. The primary responsibilities are shared by the CIA, the FBI and the DOD. The CIA has primary responsibility for terrorist matters outside the United States and the FBI has primary responsibility for terrorist matters in the United States. The DOD relies chiefly on The Defense Intelligence Agency (DIA), a DOD support agency with over 7,000 military and civilian employees stationed throughout the world.

Once a terrorist suspect is detained, what do American interrogators do? One outcome of the Abu Ghraib abuse story was the June 2004 release of a "10-centimetre pile of [classified] internal memos and documents" from senior policy makers in the Bush administration detailing the approved interrogation tactics for conducting interrogations of uncooperative detainees. Prior to the June 2004 release of the memorandums, the public was left to wonder whether the techniques were lawful or actually involved torture.

The reluctance to release the exact interrogation techniques centered on the fear that the release of such information would allow enemy forces to develop counter-intelligence techniques to frustrate efforts to get meaningful intelligence. Consequently, U.S. officials remained silent about the techniques, telling the public that its agents were employing the full range of robust interrogation tactics to include offering various incentives such as money or engaging in trickery.

The public documents associated with interrogation rest in Army Field Manual 34-52, Intelligence Interrogation (FM 34-52), which absolutely prohibits the use of torture or physical stress techniques in conducting interrogation. In April 2002, a *Wall Street Journal* article examined some of the interrogation methods currently taught to students at the Army's interrogation school in Fort Huachuca, Arizona. The reporter began the piece by making the following observation:

> *Interrogators*—the Pentagon renamed them "human intelligence collectors" last year—
> are authorized not just to lie, but to prey on a prisoner's ethnic stereotypes, sexual urges and
> religious prejudices, his fear for his family's safety, or his resentment of his fellows.
> They'll [Army interrogators] do just about anything short of torture, which officials say is
> not taught here, to make their prisoners spill information that could save American lives.

The *Wall Street Journal* piece went on to list some of the techniques that are taught at the school to get prisoners to talk. These techniques include the "incentive" approach, the "fear-up" approach, the "fear-down" approach, the "pride and ego down" approach, and the "pride and ego up" approach. The article concluded by noting that stress positions—placing prisoners in uncomfortable positions until they talk—are not taught at the school and that a military lawyer is "on

the detainees at Guantanamo were individuals with close connections to al Qaeda leadership and planning figures.

These individuals include financiers, bodyguards, recruiters and operators. There were detainees assessed to possess significant information of al Qaeda plans. They were also demonstrating training in al Qaeda resistance methods to the approaches set out in FM 34-52.

On Oct. 11, 2002, the commander of Joint Task Force Guantanamo requested the use of additional interrogation techniques for Muhammad, Mani Ahmed and S'hal Lan al Qahtani, individuals believed to have close al Qaeda connections. The Commander requested approval for 20 other interrogation techniques.

On Oct. 25, 2002, the commander of the U.S. Southern Command forwarded the request to the Chairman of the Joint Chiefs of Staff for approval. The request included 20 techniques.

On November 27, 2002, General Counsel, after discussing the request with Deputy Secretary of Defense, Under Secretary of Defense (Policy) and the Chairman of the Joint Chiefs of Staff, recommended that the Secretary of Defense approve 17 of the 20 techniques requested by Southern Command.

On Dec. 2, 2002, the Secretary of Defense approved the 17 techniques recommended by the General Counsel. The techniques approved were arranged on a three-tiered system that required approval from different levels of the chain of command before they could be used. A number of the techniques that were approved were never used. These guidelines were in effect from Dec. 2, 2002 until Jan. 15, 2003.

On Jan.15, 2003, the Secretary of Defense rescinded the Dec. 2 guidance when he learned of concern about the implementation of the techniques. The Secretary of Defense directed the Department of Defense General Counsel to establish a working group to assess the legal, policy, and operational issues relating to the interrogation of detainees held by the U. S. Armed Forces in the war on terrorism.

The working group consisted of representatives of the military departments, service general counsels, the Judge Advocates General of the armed services, defense policy, the joint staff, and the Defense Intelligence Agency. The Department of Justice advised the working group in its deliberations. The working group reported 35 techniques as appropriate for consideration for use and rejected several as either inappropriate or lacking sufficient information to permit review. The final product of the working group included a list of techniques and procedures.

(Note: This working group was the subject of a Department of Defense background briefing on May 20, 2004. The briefing transcript can be located at http://www.defenselink.mil/transcripts/2004/tr20040520-0788.html.)

After this deliberate and determinative legal and policy review, the Secretary of Defense approved the use of 24 techniques for use at Guantanamo on April 16, 2003. Seventeen of the techniques approved for use at Guantanamo come from FM 34-52. Four of the techniques require notification to the Secretary before use.

It is the policy and practice of the Department of Defense to treat detainees in the War on Terrorism humanely and, to the extent appropriate and consistent with military necessity, in a manner consistent with the principles of the Geneva Convention.

No procedures approved for use ordered, authorized, permitted, or tolerated torture. Individuals who have abused the trust and confidence placed in them will be held accountable. There are a number of inquiries that are ongoing to look at specific allegations of abuse, and those investigations will run their course.

...

On September 6, 2006, the DOD issued its new military detainee and terror suspect treatment guidelines. The DOD Directive 2310.01E is entitled: *The Department of Defense Detainee Program*. In announcing the new rules, President Bush also informed the public that 14 "high value" terror suspects had been transferred from undisclosed CIA locations to Guantanamo Bay. This speech was the first official acknowledgement of the existence of the previously secret CIA detainee program. President Bush said that the CIA program had been authorized by a secret presidential directive issued on September 17, 2001. Relating that the program was subject to internal legal review, the Bush Administration continues the legal view that the CIA detainees are wartime detainees held under the laws of war; international human rights law, which applies in peacetime, is not applicable. Believing that the CIA program had "saved lives," the President confirmed that with the transfer of the 14 there are "now no terrorists in the CIA program." Further, the Bush Administration denies that any of the CIA detainees were subjected to interrogation techniques that violated international or domestic law.

Those associated with the art of interrogation know that the initial goal is to get the suspect to start talking and that the best way to get reliable and useful information is to treat the subject humanly; in other words, to not engage in torture or ill-treatment. In fact, when faced with torture, individuals will most likely say anything to stop the pain, making their statements sometimes questionable. According to a former Colonel in Army intelligence, "Anything you can do to disconnect someone is going to help ... [b]ut it's a myth that torture is effective. The best way to win someone over is to treat them kindly." From a practical perspective, this is certainly a fundamental reason that torture should not be employed—it seldom produces truthful statements, particularly in the case of hardened zealots willing to engage in suicide missions. If they are willing to die for their distorted Nazi-like ideology, they are certainly prepared to withstand torture.

The story of "Half-Dead Bob" reported by U.S. News and World Report typifies the al-Qa'eda mindset while illustrating the American policy of humane treatment of detainees in accordance with the principles of the Geneva Conventions. An Arab captured on the battlefield of Afghanistan was nicknamed "Half-Dead Bob" by the Americans when he arrived at Guantanamo Bay. His nickname derived from the fact that he came to the detention center weighing 66 pounds, suffering from tuberculosis, shrapnel wounds, and having only one lung. The article states:

> Army Maj. Gen. [Major General] Michael Dunlavey vividly remembers his first "encounter with 'Bob.' Dunlavey ran interrogations at the base until November of last year. By the time they met, Bob was making a rapid recovery. He had put on 50 pounds and, sitting

across a table from Dunlavey, he thanked him for the food and medical treatment. 'General, you are probably a good Christian,' Dunlavey recalls him saying. 'And you are probably a good man. But, if I ever get free, I will kill you.'"

6.6 What Can American Interrogators Do?

The Abu Ghraib prison abuse scandal once again brought the issue of acceptable interrogation techniques into the public eye. Domestic law is clear on its prohibition of torture. Under international law, the prohibition on torture is equally clear and many of the practices that constitute torture are universally accepted as illegal. Unfortunately, the water becomes increasingly opaque as one ventures into the realm of ill-treatment and then beyond into techniques which, while questionable, may or may not constitute ill-treatment, e.g., stress and duress. In addition, the legal parameters associated with interrogation techniques depend in part on where the interrogation takes place. Interrogations conducted by law enforcement within the United States must not violate constitutional protections. On the other hand, as seen in *Bellout v. Ashcroft*, interrogations conducted outside the United States, including those conducted by foreign agents as a result of rendition, provide little hope to the detainee for judicial review in an American forum.

Another source of guidance to distinguish a reasonable interrogation from an interrogation that crosses the line into ill-treatment or torture is found in the 1999 Israeli High Court decision entitled *Public Committee Against Torture v. State of Israel* (*Public Committee*). In the context of outlawing certain interrogation practices by Israeli officials, the High Court considered how otherwise reasonable interrogation practices could become illegal if taken to an extreme point of intensity. Playing music to disorient a subject prior to questioning is not illegal per se, but if the music is played in a manner that causes undue suffering, it is arguably a form of ill-treatment or torture. Depriving subjects of sleep during a lengthy interrogation process may be legitimate, but depending on the extent of sleep deprivation, could also constitute ill-treatment or torture. The use of handcuffing for the protection of the interrogators is a common and acceptable practice, so long as the handcuffs are not unduly tightened so as to cause excess pain. Similarly, the use of blindfolds is acceptable if done for legitimate security reasons, while the use of sacks over the head without proper ventilation is unacceptable.

The backdrop for *Public Committee* is as follows. The General Security Service of Israel (GSS) is responsible for conducting investigations of suspected terrorists who commit crimes against the State of Israel. As part of this responsibility, the GSS engages in the detention and interrogation of suspected terrorists. Up until the late 1980s, the official position of the government of Israel was that GSS interrogators did not use "coercive" methods during terrorist interrogations. In 1987, the government appointed the Landau Commission to investigate the methods of interrogation used by the GSS. In November 1987, the Landau Commission issued its report, recognizing the terrorist threat to the nation and the attendant necessity for the GSS to engage in what it termed euphemistically as "a moderate measure of physical pressure" during interrogations of suspected terrorists. In a separate secret part of the report, the Landau Commission set out limits in the types of physical pressure that the GSS might employ. In the publicly released section of the report, the commission advised that GSS agents should combine "non-violent psychological pressure of a vigorous and extensive interrogation … with … a moderate amount of physical pressure." In short, the Landau Commission provided the green light for the GSS to use "moderate ... physical pressure" when conducting interrogations.

Adopting the recommendations of the Landau Commission, the Israeli government issued directives authorizing the GSS to use various physical means in certain cases. In taking the unprecedented step of trying to regulate the use of physical pressure during the interrogation of suspected terrorists, the government contended that such methods did not constituted torture. The Supreme Court of Israel disagreed and found that the primary techniques used by the GSS (which had until then remained secret) involved the following:

- Shaking: The practice of shaking was deemed to be the most brutal and harshest of all the interrogation methods. The method is defined as "the forceful shaking of the suspect's upper torso, back and forth, repeatedly, in a manner which causes the neck and head to dangle and vacillate rapidly."

- Shabach Position: The practice of binding the subject in a child's chair "titled forward towards the ground, in a manner that causes him real pain and suffering." Other reports amplify the method and add that the subject's head is "covered in a hood while powerfully deafening music is emitted within inches of the suspect's head."

- Frog Crouch: The practice of making the subject crouch on the tips of their toes for five-minute intervals.

- Excessive Tightening of Handcuffs: The practice of inflicting injury to a suspect by excessive tightening of handcuffs or through the use of small handcuffs.

- Sleep Deprivation: The practice of intentionally keeping the subject awake for prolonged periods of time.

In ruling that there existed an absolute prohibition on the use of torture as a means of interrogation, the Supreme Court held some of the practices of the GSS violated Israel's Basic Law—Human Dignity and Liberty. Specifically, the Court found that shaking, the use of the shabach, the use of the frog crouch, and, in certain instances, the deprivation of sleep, were all illegal and prohibited investigation methods.

PUBLIC COMMITTEE AGAINST TORTURE IN ISRAEL v. ISRAEL
H.C.J. 5100/94 (1999)
Supreme Court of Israel Sitting as High Court of Justice

OPINION by President A. Barak:

The General Security Service (hereinafter, the "GSS") investigates individuals suspected of committing crimes against Israel's security. Is the GSS authorized to conduct these interrogations? The interrogations are conducted on the basis of directives regulating interrogation methods. These directives equally authorize investigators to apply physical means against those undergoing interrogation (for instance, shaking the suspect and the "Shabach" position). The basis for permitting such methods is that they are deemed immediately necessary for saving human lives. Is the sanctioning of these interrogation practices legal? These are the principal issues presented by the applicants before us.

Background

1. The State of Israel has been engaged in an unceasing struggle for both its very existence and security, from the day of its founding. Terrorist organizations have established as their goal Israel's annihilation. Terrorist acts and the general disruption of order are their means of choice. In employing such methods, these groups do not distinguish between civilian and military targets. They carry out terrorist attacks in which scores are murdered in public areas, public transportation, city squares and centers, theaters and coffee shops. They do not distinguish between men, women and children. They act out of cruelty and without mercy (For an in depth description of this phenomenon see the Report of the Commission of Inquiry Regarding the GSS' Interrogation Practices with Respect to Hostile Terrorist Activities headed by (ret.) Justice M. Landau, 1987—hereinafter, "Commission of Inquiry Report") published in the Landau Book 269, 276 (Volume 1, 1995).

The facts presented before this Court reveal that one hundred and twenty one people died in terrorist attacks between 1.1.96 to 14.5.98. Seven hundred and seven people were injured. A large number of those killed and injured were victims of harrowing suicide bombings in the heart of Israel's cities. Many attacks—including suicide bombings, attempts to detonate car bombs, kidnappings of citizens and soldiers, attempts to highjack buses, murders, the placing of explosives, etc.—were prevented due to the measures taken by the authorities responsible for fighting the above described hostile terrorist activities on a daily basis. The main body responsible for fighting terrorism is the GSS.

In order to fulfill this function, the GSS also investigates those suspected of hostile terrorist activities. The purpose of these interrogations is, among others, to gather information regarding terrorists and their organizing methods for the purpose of thwarting and preventing them from carrying out these terrorist attacks. In the context of these interrogations, GSS investigators also make use of physical means. The legality of these practices is being examined before this Court in these applications.

...

The Physical Means

8. The physical means employed by the GSS investigators were presented before this Court by the GSS investigators. The State's attorneys were prepared to present them for us behind closed doors (in camera). The applicants' attorneys were opposed to this proposal. Thus, the information at the Court's disposal was provided by the applicants and was not tested in each individual application. This having been said, the State's position, which failed to deny the use of these interrogation methods, and even offered these and other explanations regarding the rationale justifying the use of an interrogation methods or another, provided the Court with a picture of the GSS' interrogation practices.

The decision to utilize physical means in a particular instance is based on internal regulations, which requires obtaining permission from various ranks of the GSS hierarchy. The regulations themselves were approved by a special Ministerial Committee on GSS interrogations. Among other guidelines, the Committee set forth directives pertaining to the rank authorized to allow these interrogation practices. These directives were not examined by this Court. Different interrogation methods are employed depending on the suspect, both in relation to what is required in that

situation and to the likelihood of obtaining authorization. The GSS does not resort to every interrogation method at its disposal in each case.

Shaking

9. A number of applicants (H.C. 5100/94; H.C. 4054/95; H.C. 6536/95) claimed that the shaking
method was used against them. Among the investigation methods outlined in the GSS' interrogation regulations, shaking is considered the harshest. The method is defined as the forceful shaking
of the suspect's upper torso, back and forth, repeatedly, in a manner which causes the neck and
head to dangle and vacillate rapidly. According to an expert opinion submitted in one of the applications (H.C. (motion) 5584/95 and H.C. 5100/95), the shaking method is likely to cause serious
brain damage, harm the spinal cord, cause the suspect to lose consciousness, vomit and urinate
uncontrollably and suffer serious headaches.

   The State entered several countering expert opinions into evidence. It admits the use of this
method by the GSS. To its contention, there is no danger to the life of the suspect inherent to shaking; the risk to life as a result of shaking is rare; there is no evidence that shaking causes fatal damage; and medical literature has not to date listed a case in which a person died directly as a result of
having been only shaken. In any event, they argue, doctors are present in all interrogation compounds, and instances where the danger of medical damage presents itself are investigated and
researched.

   All agree that in one particular case (H.C. 4054/95) the suspect in question expired after being
shaken. According to the State, that case constituted a rare exception. Death was caused by an
extremely rare complication resulting in the atrophy of the neurogenic lung. In addition, the State
argues in its response that the shaking method is only resorted to in very particular cases, and only
as a last resort. The interrogation directives define the appropriate circumstances for its application and the rank responsible for authorizing its use. The investigators were instructed that in every case where they consider resorting to shaking, they must probe the severity of the danger that
the interrogation is intending to prevent; consider the urgency of uncovering the information presumably possessed by the suspect in question; and seek an alternative means of preventing the
danger. Finally, the directives respecting interrogation state, that in cases where this method is to
be used, the investigator must first provide an evaluation of the suspect's health and ensure that no
harm comes to him. According to the respondent, shaking is indispensable to fighting and winning
the war on terrorism. It is not possible to prohibit its use without seriously harming the GSS' ability to effectively thwart deadly terrorist attacks. Its use in the past has lead to the thwarting of
murderous attacks.

Waiting in the "Shabach" Position

10. This interrogation method arose in numerous applications (H.C. 6536/95, H.C. 5188/96, H.C.
7628/97). As per applicants' submission, a suspect investigated under the "Shabach" position has
his hands tied behind his back. He is seated on a small and low chair, whose seat is tilted forward,
towards the ground. One hand is tied behind the suspect, and placed inside the gap between the
chair's seat and back support. His second hand is tied behind the chair, against its back support.
The suspect's head is covered by an opaque sack, falling down to his shoulders. Powerfully loud
music is played in the room. According to the affidavits submitted, suspects are detained in this
position for a prolonged period of time, awaiting interrogation at consecutive intervals.

The aforementioned affidavits claim that prolonged sitting in this position causes serious muscle pain in the arms, the neck and headaches. The State did not deny the use of this method before this Court. They submit that both crucial security considerations and the investigators' safety require tying up the suspect's hands as he is being interrogated. The head covering is intended to prevent contact between the suspect in question and other suspects. The powerfully loud music is played for the same reason.

The "Frog Crouch"

11. This interrogation method appeared in one of the applications (H.C. 5188/96). According to the application and the attached corresponding affidavit, the suspect being interrogated was found in a "frog crouch" position. This refers to consecutive, periodical crouches on the tips of one's toes, each lasting for five minute intervals. The State did not deny the use of this method, thereby prompting Court to issue an order nisi in the application where this method was alleged. Prior to hearing the application, however, this interrogation practice ceased.

Excessive Tightening of Handcuffs

12. In a number of applications before this Court (H.C. 5188/96; H.C. 7563/97), various applicants have complained of excessive tightening of hand or leg cuffs. To their contention, this practice results in serious injuries to the suspect's hands, arms and feet, due to the length of the interrogations. The applicants invoke the use of particularly small cuffs, ill fitted in relation to the suspect's arm or leg size. The State, for its part, denies any use of unusually small cuffs, arguing that those used were both of standard issue and properly applied. They are, nonetheless, prepared to admit that prolonged hand or foot cuffing is likely to cause injuries to the suspect's hands and feet. To the State's contention, however, injuries of this nature are inherent to any lengthy interrogation.

Sleep Deprivation

13. In a number of applications (H.C. 6536/96; H.C. 7563/97; H.C. 7628/97) applicants have complained of being deprived of sleep as a result of being tied in the "Shabach" position, being subjected to the playing of powerfully loud music, or intense non-stop interrogations without sufficient rest breaks. They claim that the purpose of depriving them of sleep is to cause them to break from exhaustion. While the State agrees that suspects are at times deprived of regular sleep hours, it argues that this does not constitute an interrogation method aimed at causing exhaustion, but rather results from the prolonged amount of time necessary for conducting the interrogation.

Applicants' Arguments

14. Before us lie a number of applications. Different applicants raise different arguments. In principle, all the applications raise two essential arguments: First, they submit that the GSS is never authorized to conduct interrogations. Second, they argue that the physical means employed by GSS investigators not only infringe upon the human dignity of the suspect undergoing interrogation, but in fact constitute criminal offences. These methods, argue the applicants, are in violation International Law as they constitute "Torture," which is expressly prohibited under International Law. Thus, the GSS investigators are not authorized to conduct these interrogations. Furthermore, the "necessity" defence which, according to the State, is available to the investigators, is not rel-

evant to the circumstances in question. In any event, the doctrine of "necessity" at most constitutes an exceptional post factum defence, exclusively confined to criminal proceedings against investigators. It cannot, however, by any means, provide GSS investigators with the preemptory authorization to conduct interrogations ab initio. GSS investigators are not authorized to employ any physical means, absent unequivocal authorization from the Legislator pertaining to the use of such methods and conforming to the requirements of the Basic Law: Human Dignity and Liberty. There is no purpose in engaging in a bureaucratic set up of the regulations and authority, as suggested by the Commission of Inquiry's Report, since doing so would merely regulate the torture of human beings.

We asked the applicants' attorneys whether the "ticking time bomb" rationale was not sufficiently persuasive to justify the use of physical means, for instance, when a bomb is known to have been placed in a public area and will undoubtedly explode causing immeasurable human tragedy if its location is not revealed at once. This question elicited a variety of responses from the various applicants before the Court. There are those convinced that physical means are not to be used under any circumstances; the prohibition on such methods to their mind is absolute, whatever the consequences may be. On the other hand, there are others who argue that even if it is perhaps acceptable to employ physical means in most exceptional "ticking time bomb" circumstances, these methods are in practice used even in absence of the "ticking time bomb" conditions. The very fact that, in most cases, the use of such means is illegal provides sufficient justification for banning their use altogether, even if doing so would inevitably absorb those rare cases in which physical coercion may have been justified. Whatever their particular views, all applicants unanimously highlight the distinction between the ability to potentially escape criminal liability post factum and the granting of permission to use physical means for interrogation purposes ab initio.

…

The Means Employed for Interrogation Purposes

21. As we have seen, the GSS investigators are endowed with the authority to conduct interrogations. What is the scope of these powers and do they encompass the use of physical means in the course of the interrogation in order to advance it? Can use be made of the physical means presently employed by GSS investigators (such as shaking, the "Shabach" position, and sleep deprivation) by virtue of the investigating powers given the GSS investigators? Let us note that the State did not argue before us that all the means employed by GSS investigators are permissible by virtue of the "law of interrogation" per se. Thus, for instance, the State did not make the argument that shaking is permitted simply because it is an "ordinary" investigator's method in Israel. Notwithstanding, it was argued before this Court that some of the physical means employed by the GSS investigators are permitted by the "law of interrogation" itself. For instance, this is the case with respect to some of the physical means applied in the context of waiting in the "Shabach" position: the placing of the head covering (for preventing communication between the suspects); the playing of powerfully loud music (to prevent the passing of information between suspects); the tying of the suspect's hands to a chair (for the investigators' protection) and the deprivation of sleep, as deriving from the needs of the interrogation. Does the "law of interrogation" sanction the use of physical means, the like used in GSS interrogations?

22. An interrogation, by its very nature, places the suspect in a difficult position. "The criminal's interrogation," wrote Justice Vitkon over twenty years ago, "is not a negotiation process between

two open and fair vendors, conducting their business on the basis of maximum mutual trust" (Cr. A 216/74 *Cohen v The State of Israel*) 29(1) P.D. 340 at 352). An interrogation is a "competition of minds," in which the investigator attempts to penetrate the suspect's thoughts and elicit from him the information the investigator seeks to obtain. Quite accurately, it was noted that:

> Any interrogation, be it the fairest and most reasonable of all, inevitably places the suspect in embarrassing situations, burdens him, intrudes his conscience, penetrates the deepest crevices of his soul, while creating serious emotional pressure. (Y. Kedmi, On Evidence, Part A, 1991 at 25).

...

23. It is not necessary for us to engage in an in-depth inquiry into the "law of interrogation" for the purposes of the applications before us. These vary from one matter to the next. For instance, the law of interrogation, as it appears in the context of an investigator's potential criminal liability, as opposed to the purpose of admitting evidence obtained by questionable means. Here, by contrast, we deal with the "law of interrogation" as a power activated by an administrative authority (See Bein supra.). The "law of interrogation" by its very nature, is intrinsically linked to the circumstances of each case. This having been said, a number of general principles are nonetheless worth noting:

> First, a reasonable investigation is necessarily one free of torture, free of cruel, inhuman treatment of the subject and free of any degrading handling whatsoever. There is a prohibition on the use of "brutal or inhuman means" in the course of an investigation (F.H. 3081/91 *Kozli v. The State of Israel*, 35(4) P.D. 441 at 446). Human dignity also includes the dignity of the suspect being interrogated. (Compare H.C. 355/59 *Catlan v. Prison Security Services*, 34(3) P.D. 293 at 298 and C.A.4463/94 *Golan v. Prison Security Services*, 50(4) P.D. 136). This conclusion is in perfect accord with (various) International Law treaties—to which Israel is a signatory—which prohibit the use of torture, "cruel, inhuman treatment" and "degrading treatment" (See M. Evans and R. Morgan, Preventing Torture (1998) at 61; N.S. Rodley, The Treatment of Prisoners under International Law (1987) at 63). These prohibitions are "absolute." There are no exceptions to them and there is no room for balancing. Indeed, violence directed at a suspect's body or spirit does not constitute a reasonable investigation practice. The use of violence during investigations can potentially lead to the investigator being held criminally liable. (See, for example, article 277 of the Penal Law: Pressure on a Public Servant; supra at 130, 134; Cr. A. 64/86 *Ashash v. The State of Israel* (unpublished)).

> Second, a reasonable investigation is likely to cause discomfort. It may result in insufficient sleep. The conditions under which it is conducted risk being unpleasant. Indeed, it is possible to conduct an effective investigation without resorting to violence. Within the confines of the law, it is permitted to resort to various machinations and specific sophisticated activities which serve investigators today (both for Police and GSS). Similar investigations—accepted in the most progressive of societies—can be effective in achieve their goals. In the end result, the legality of an investigation is deduced from the propriety of its purpose and from its methods. Thus, for instance, sleep deprivation for a prolonged period, or sleep deprivation at night when this is not necessary to the investigation time wise may be deemed a use of an investigation method which surpasses the least restrictive means.

From the General to the Particular

24. We shall now turn from the general to the particular. Plainly put, shaking is a prohibited investigation method. It harms the suspect's body. It violates his dignity. It is a violent method which does not form part of a legal investigation. It surpasses that which is necessary. Even the State did not argue that shaking is an "ordinary" investigation method which every investigator (in the GSS or police) is permitted to employ. The submission before us was that the justification for shaking is found in the "necessity" defence. That argument shall be dealt with below. In any event, there is no doubt that shaking is not to be resorted to in cases outside the bounds of "necessity" or as part of an "ordinary" investigation.

25. It was argued before the Court that one of the investigation methods employed consists of the suspect crouching on the tips of his toes for five minute intervals. The State did not deny this practice. This is a prohibited investigation method. It does not serve any purpose inherent to an investigation. It is degrading and infringes upon an individual's human dignity.

26. The "Shabach" method is composed of a number of cumulative components: the cuffing of the suspect, seating him on a low chair, covering his head with an opaque sack (head covering) and playing powerfully loud music in the area. Are any of the above acts encompassed by the general power to investigate? Our point of departure is that there are actions which are inherent to the investigation power. Therefore, we accept that the suspect's cuffing, for the purpose of preserving the investigators' safety, is an action included in the general power to investigate. Provided the suspect is cuffed for this purpose, it is within the investigator's authority to cuff him. The State's position is that the suspects are indeed cuffed with the intention of ensuring the investigators' safety or to prevent fleeing from legal custody. Even the applicants agree that it is permissible to cuff a suspect in similar circumstances and that cuffing constitutes an integral part of an interrogation. Notwithstanding, the cuffing associated with the "Shabach" position is unlike routine cuffing. The suspect is cuffed with his hands tied behind his back. One hand is placed inside the gap between the chair's seat and back support, while the other is tied behind him, against the chair's back support. This is a distorted and unnatural position. The investigators' safety does not require it. Therefore, there is no relevant justification for handcuffing the suspect's hands with particularly small handcuffs, if this is in fact the practice. The use of these methods is prohibited. As was noted, "Cuffing causing pain is prohibited." Moreover, there are other ways of preventing the suspect from fleeing from legal custody which do not involve causing the suspect pain and suffering.

27. This is the law with respect to the method involving seating the suspect in question in the "Shabach" position. We accept that seating a man is inherent to the investigation. This is not the case when the chair upon which he is seated is a very low one, tilted forward facing the ground, and when he is sitting in this position for long hours. This sort of seating is not encompassed by the general power to interrogate. Even if we suppose that the seating of the suspect on a chair lower than that of his investigator can potentially serve a legitimate investigation objective (for instance, to establish the "rules of the game" in the contest of wills between the parties, or to emphasize the investigator's superiority over the suspect), there is no inherent investigative need for seating the suspect on a chair so low and tilted forward towards the ground, in a manner that causes him real pain and suffering. Clearly, the general power to conduct interrogations does not authorize seating a suspect on a forward tilting chair, in a manner that applies pressure and causes pain to his back,

all the more so when his hands are tied behind the chair, in the manner described. All these methods do not fall within the sphere of a "fair" interrogation. They are not reasonable. They impinge upon the suspect's dignity, his bodily integrity and his basic rights in an excessive manner (or beyond what is necessary). They are not to be deemed as included within the general power to conduct interrogations.

28. We accept that there are interrogation related considerations concerned with preventing contact between the suspect under interrogation and other suspects and his investigators, which require means capable of preventing the said contact. The need to prevent contact may, for instance, flow from the need to safeguard the investigators' security, or that of the suspects and witnesses. It can also be part of the "mind game" which pins the information possessed by the suspect, against that found in the hands of his investigators. For this purpose, the power to interrogate—in principle and according to the circumstances of each particular case—includes preventing eye contact with a given person or place. In the case at bar, this was the explanation provided by the State for covering the suspect's head with an opaque sack, while he is seated in the "Shabach" position. From what was stated in the declarations before us, the suspect's head is covered with an opaque sack throughout his "wait" in the "Shabach" position. It was argued that the sack (head covering) is entirely opaque, causing the suspect to suffocate. The edges of the sack are long, reaching the suspect's shoulders. All these methods are not inherent to an interrogation. They do not confirm the State's position, arguing that they are meant to prevent eye contact between the suspect being interrogated and other suspects. Indeed, even if such contact should be prevented, what is the purpose of causing the suspect to suffocate? Employing this method is not connected to the purpose of preventing the said contact and is consequently forbidden. Moreover, the statements clearly reveal that the suspect's head remains covered for several hours, throughout his wait. For these purposes, less harmful means must be employed, such as letting the suspect wait in a detention cell. Doing so will eliminate any need to cover the suspect's eyes. In the alternative, the suspect's eyes may be covered in a manner that does not cause him physical suffering. For it appears that at present, the suspect's head covering—which covers his entire head, rather than eyes alone,—for a prolonged period of time, with no essential link to the goal of preventing contact between the suspects under investigation, is not part of a fair interrogation. It harms the suspect and his (human) image. It degrades him. It causes him to lose sight of time and place. It suffocates him. All these things are not included in the general authority to investigate. In the cases before us, the State declared that it will make an effort to find a "ventilated" sack. This is not sufficient. The covering of the head in the circumstances described, as distinguished from the covering of the eyes, is outside the scope of authority and is prohibited.

29. Cutting off the suspect from his surroundings can also include preventing him from listening to what is going on around him. We are prepared to assume that the authority to investigate an individual equally encompasses precluding him from hearing other suspects under investigation or voices and sounds that, if heard by the suspect, risk impeding the interrogation's success. Whether the means employed fall within the scope of a fair and reasonable interrogation warrant examination at this time. In the case at bar, the detainee is found in the "Shabach" position while listening to the consecutive playing of powerfully loud music. Do these methods fall within the scope or the general authority to conduct interrogations? Here too, the answer is in the negative. Being exposed to powerfully loud music for a long period of time causes the suspect suffering. Furthermore, the suspect is tied (in place) in an uncomfortable position with his head covered (all

the while). The use of the "Shabach" method is prohibited. It does not fall within the scope of the authority to conduct a fair and effective interrogation. Powerfully loud music is a prohibited means for use in the context described before us.

30. To the above, we must add that the "Shabach" position includes all the outlined methods employed simultaneously. Their combination, in and of itself gives rise to particular pain and suffering. This is a harmful method, particularly when it is employed for a prolonged period of time. For these reasons, this method does not form part of the powers of interrogation. It is an unacceptable method. "The duty to safeguard the detainee's dignity includes his right not to be degraded and not to be submitted to sub-human conditions in the course of his detention, of the sort likely to harm his health and potentially his dignity."

A similar—though not identical—combination of interrogation methods were discussed in the case of *Ireland v. United Kingdom* (1978) 2 EHRR 25. In that case, the Court probed five interrogation methods used by England for the purpose of investigating detainees suspected of terrorist activities in Northern Ireland. The methods were as follows: protracted standing against the wall on the tip of one's toes; covering of the suspect's head throughout the detention (except during the actual interrogation); exposing the suspect to powerfully loud noise for a prolonged period and deprivation of sleep, food and drink. The Court held that these methods did not constitute "torture." However, since they treated the suspect in an "inhuman and degrading" manner, they were nonetheless prohibited.

31. The interrogation of a person is likely to be lengthy, due to the suspect's failure to cooperate or due to the information's complexity or in light of the imperative need to obtain information urgently and immediately. Indeed, a person undergoing interrogation cannot sleep as does one who is not being interrogated. The suspect, subject to the investigators' questions for a prolonged period of time, is at times exhausted. This is often the inevitable result of an interrogation, or one of its side effects. This is part of the "discomfort" inherent to an interrogation. This being the case, depriving the suspect of sleep is, in our opinion, included in the general authority of the investigator (Compare: H.C. 3429/94 *Shbana v. GSS* (unpublished)). So noted Justice Shamgar, in a similar instance:

> The interrogation of crimes and in particular, murder or other serious crimes—cannot be accomplished within the confines of an ordinary public servant's work day …. The investigation of crime is essentially mental resistance …. For this reason, the interrogation is often carried out at consecutive intervals. This, as noted, causes the investigation to drag on … and requires diligent insistence on its momentum and consecutiveness." (Cr. A. 485/76 *Ben Loulou v. The State of Israel* (unpublished)).

The above described situation is different from those in which sleep deprivation shifts from being a "side effect" inherent to the interrogation, to an end in itself. If the suspect is intentionally deprived of sleep for a prolonged period of time, for the purpose of tiring him out or "breaking" him—it shall not fall within the scope of a fair and reasonable investigation. Such means harm the rights and dignity of the suspect in a manner surpassing that which is required.

32. All that was stated regarding the exceptions pertinent to an interrogation, flowing from the requirement that an interrogation be fair and reasonable, is the accepted law with respect to a regular police interrogation. The power to interrogate given to the investigator GSS investigator by law

is the same interrogation powers the law bestows upon the ordinary police force investigator. It appears that the restrictions applicable to the police investigations are equally applicable to GSS investigations. There is no statutory instruction endowing a GSS investigator with special interrogating powers that are either different or more serious than those given the police investigator. From this we conclude that a GSS investigator, whose duty is to conduct the interrogation according to the law, is subject to the same restrictions applicable to a police interrogation.

Physical Means and the "Necessity" Defence

33. We have arrived at the conclusion that the GSS personnel who have received permission to conduct interrogations (as per the Criminal Procedure Statute [Testimony]) are authorized to do so. This authority-like that of the police investigator—does not include most of the physical means of interrogation which are the subject of the application before us. Can the authority to employ these interrogation methods be anchored in a legal source beyond the authority to conduct an interrogation? This question was answered by the State's attorneys in the affirmative. As noted, an explicit authorization permitting GSS to employ physical means is not to be found in our law. An authorization of this nature can, in the State's opinion, be obtained in specific cases by virtue of the criminal law defense of "necessity," prescribed in the Penal Law. The language of the statute is as follows: (Article 34 (1)):

> A person will not bear criminal liability for committing any act immediately necessary for the purpose of saving the life, liberty, body or property, of either himself or his fellow person, from substantial danger of serious harm, imminent from the particular state of things [circumstances], at the requisite timing, and absent alternative means for avoiding the harm.

The State's position is that by virtue of this "defence" to criminal liability, GSS investigators are also authorized to apply physical means, such as shaking, in the appropriate circumstances, in order to prevent serious harm to human life or body, in the absence of other alternatives. The State maintains that an act committed under conditions of "necessity" does not constitute a crime. Instead, it is deemed an act worth committing in such circumstances in order to prevent serious harm to a human life or body. We are therefore speaking of a deed that society has an interest in encouraging, as it is deemed proper in the circumstances. It is choosing the lesser evil. Not only is it legitimately permitted to engage in the fighting of terrorism, it is our moral duty to employ the necessary means for this purpose. This duty is particularly incumbent on the state authorities—and for our purposes, on the GSS investigators—who carry the burden of safeguarding the public peace. As this is the case, there is no obstacle preventing the investigators' superiors from instructing and guiding them with regard to when the conditions of the "necessity" defence are fulfilled and the proper boundaries in those circumstances. From this flows the legality of the directives with respect to the use of physical means in GSS interrogations. In the course of their argument, the State's attorneys submitted the "ticking time bomb" argument. A given suspect is arrested by the GSS. He holds information respecting the location of a bomb that was set and will imminently explode. There is no way to diffuse the bomb without this information. If the information is obtained, however, the bomb my be diffused. If the bomb is not diffused, scores will be killed and maimed. Is a GSS investigator authorized to employ physical means in order to elicit information regarding the location of the bomb in such instances? The State's attorneys answers in the affirmative. The use of physical means shall not constitute a criminal offence, and their use is sanctioned, to the State's contention, by virtue of the "necessity" defence.

…

35. Indeed, we are prepared to accept that in the appropriate circumstances, GSS investigators may avail themselves of the "necessity" defence, if criminally indicted. This however, is not the issue before this Court. We are not dealing with the potential criminal liability of a GSS investigator who employed physical interrogation methods in circumstances of "necessity." Moreover, we are not addressing the issue of admissibility or probative value of evidence obtained as a result of a GSS investigator's application of physical means against a suspect. We are dealing with a different question. The question before us is whether it is possible to infer the authority to, in advance, establish permanent directives setting out the physical interrogation means that may be used under conditions of "necessity." Moreover, we are asking whether the "necessity" defence constitutes a basis for the GSS investigator's authority to investigate, in the performance of his duty. According to the State, it is possible to imply from the "necessity" defence, available (post factum) to an investigator indicted of a criminal offence, an advance legal authorization endowing the investigator with the capacity to use physical interrogation methods. Is this position correct?

36. In the Court's opinion, a general authority to establish directives respecting the use of physical means during the course of a GSS interrogation cannot be implied from the "necessity" defence. The "necessity" defence does not constitute a source of authority, allowing GSS investigators to make use physical means during the course of interrogations. The reasoning underlying our position is anchored in the nature of the "necessity" defence. This defence deals with deciding those cases involving an individual reacting to a given set of facts. It is an ad hoc endeavour, in reaction to a event. It is the result of an improvisation given the unpredictable character of the events. Thus, the very nature of the defence does not allow it to serve as the source of a general administrative power ....

37. In other words, general directives governing the use of physical means during interrogations must be rooted in an authorization prescribed by law and not from defences to criminal liability. The principle of "necessity" cannot serve as a basis of authority. If the State wishes to enable GSS investigators to utilize physical means in interrogations, they must seek the enactment of legislation for this purpose. This authorization would also free the investigator applying the physical means from criminal liability. This release would flow not from the "necessity" defence but from the "justification" defense ....

...

A Final Word

39. This decision opens with a description of the difficult reality in which Israel finds herself security wise. We shall conclude this judgment by re-addressing that harsh reality. We are aware that this decision does not ease dealing with that reality. This is the destiny of democracy, as not all means are acceptable to it, and not all practices employed by its enemies are open before it. Although a democracy must often fight with one hand tied behind its back, it nonetheless has the upper hand. Preserving the Rule of Law and recognition of an individual's liberty constitutes an important component in its understanding of security. At the end of the day, they strengthen its spirit and its strength and allow it to overcome its difficulties. This having been said, there are those who argue that Israel's security problems are too numerous, thereby requiring the authorization to use physical means. If it will nonetheless be decided that it is appropriate for Israel, in light of its security difficulties to sanction physical means in interrogations (and the scope of these means which deviate from the ordinary investigation rules), this is an issue that must be decided

by the legislative branch which represents the people. We do not take any stand on this matter at this time. It is there that various considerations must be weighed. The pointed debate must occur there. It is there that the required legislation may be passed, provided, of course, that a law infringing upon a suspect's liberty "befitting the values of the State of Israel," is enacted for a proper purpose, and to an extent no greater than is required. (Article 8 to the Basic Law: Human Dignity and Liberty).

40. Deciding these applications weighed heavy on this Court. True, from the legal perspective, the road before us is smooth. We are, however, part of Israeli society. Its problems are known to us and we live its history. We are not isolated in an ivory tower. We live the life of this country. We are aware of the harsh reality of terrorism in which we are, at times, immersed. Our apprehension is that this decision will hamper the ability to properly deal with terrorists and terrorism, disturbs us. We are, however, judges. Our bretheren require us to act according to the law. This is equally the standard that we set for ourselves. When we sit to judge, we are being judged. Therefore, we must act according to our purest conscience when we decide the law.

Again, apart from the moral argument and speaking strictly from a legal perspective, the United States cannot engage in torture. This is in violation of the Torture Convention and is penalized under domestic law. Conversely, the United States may legitimately engage in interrogation practices that do not rise to the level of ill-treatment or, if dealing with a detainedd, do not violate Common Article 3. As discussed, this is an ambiguous zone, subject to interpretation based on the facts and, in many cases, unknowable without judicial guidance. As foreboding as the term stress and duress may sound, there are many techniques that involve acts which are clearly permissible under any analysis. For example, one would be hard pressed to argue that the reported use of female interrogators, trickery, or a day long interrogation session would constitute a prima facie case of torture or even ill-treatment as some have suggested. Further, one cannot simply conclude that the use of awkward positioning of a particular detainee violates legal norms; without more information, the term "awkward positioning" is simply too subjective to evaluate.

Still, if an agent of the United States engages in torture while interrogating, for example, al-Qa'eda suspects, the government is obligated under both domestic and international law to investigate and prosecute those responsible. But if the United States engages in ill-treatment of al-Qa'eda detainees, it is not obligated under international law to either prosecute the offender or turn that person over to any other nation or entity for prosecution. If the offender is a soldier, the proper forum for punishment is a military courts martial under the appropriate criminal article.

Weighing the credibility of charges that the United States engages in torture or ill-treatment as a standard practice is difficult at best. On the one hand, suggestions of torture generally come from media reports based on unnamed sources and anecdotal evidence. On the other hand, the government's penchant for secrecy regarding interrogation tactics makes it next to impossible to make an independent assessment.

Recognizing the dilemma of separating fact from speculation in this type of information environment, some international law experts have provided alternative interpretations of, for instance, the purported use of "stress and duress" interrogation tactics. Yale law professor Ruth Wedgwood opined that, based on the limited information available to the public on this matter, it was debatable whether the American interrogation techniques as reported in the *Washington Post* constituted torture.85 Wedgewood cautioned that she was "somewhat skeptical" of the reports from unidentified sources, wondering how much was swagger and tough talk as opposed to actual conduct. Furthermore, she correctly pointed out that reports of detainees held in "awkward, painful positions" present an ambiguous concept which does not speak to degree or circumstance. Wedgwood noted, "If it's [stress and duress] hanging someone from their wrists, absolutely not— that's prohibited … [b]ut if it's keeping someone in handcuffs or temporarily hooded during transport, maybe yes—as a legal matter, there could be legitimate reasons for that."

A factor that lends a tremendous amount of credibility to the government's contention that it abides by the international law prohibiting torture is the military's continuing commitment to criminally investigate and prosecute those soldiers accused of torture or ill-treatment. From the beginning of the War on Terror, the United States has responded well to verifiable instances of criminal activity that could be even remotely interpreted as torture or ill-treatment with relentless criminal investigation, prosecution and punishment. For instance, a number of convictions have been handed down in a variety of cases as a result of the Army's criminal investigations. Indeed, if the government is sincere about prohibiting torture and ill-treatment, one would certainly expect that those who engaged in such illegal acts would be investigated and punished to the full extent of the law. The sincerity of the United States to reject the practice of illegal interrogations is further boosted by the fact that the initial stories concerning abuse are generally made by military officials. For instance, the initial story about the prisoner abuse at Abu Ghraib was by the military, not the media. The media simply paid no attention to the March 2004 self reported information that several soldiers were going to be punished under the Uniform Code of Military Justice (UCMJ) until a media source was given the photographs in April of 2004. In sum, the military's prompt and thorough investigation of the Abu Ghraib scandal and the transparency of the trials of the soldiers who were involved in these atrocities should reassure observers that the military command structure will not allow torture or ill-treatment tactics to become institutionalized.

The July 2004 Department of the Army Inspector General Report on prisoner abuse found 94 documented cases of prisoner abuse since the War on Terror began, including some 40 deaths, 20 of them homicides. When viewed in light of the thousands and thousands of detainees captured and processed, this figure does not, as the report concluded, reveal a "systemic problem."

Of course, the most direct source of information on torture would obviously come from those detainees who claim to have been tortured by the Americans. Consequently, as small groups of detainees are released from custody, Western reporters have attempted to glean first hand testimony as to the issue of torture. As one would expect from the mouths of ruthless terrorists devoted to a Nazi-like ideology of hate (if one can murder innocent civilians, one can certainly lie), many of these newly released members of the Taliban and al-Qa'eda alleged that they were horribly tortured by their American captors.

Unexpectedly, others in the same group are sometimes quite open in proclaiming that all the detainees were treated well and not tortured. For instance, in a group of 27 detainees released from Guantanamo Bay in July 2003, 16 Afghans were interviewed by *Associated Press* correspondents as they were transferred to a Red Cross bus in Afghanistan. Those who alleged they were tortured complained in general terms of "cold rooms," "crowded rooms" and "beatings." Only one in the group, Abdul Rahman, specifically alleged that he had been "badly punished 107 times," and had been chained and beaten with "a metal rod on his legs and back." Interestingly, when pressed by reporters to show any scars or evidence left by the torture, Rehman "refused to show scars that may have resulted from any abuse."

In contrast, another detainee, Nate Gul, told reporters that none of the detainees were beaten during interrogation: "They didn't beat us during the interrogation. They wrote down anything we said. They interrogated me about 30 to 40 times." One terrorist expert revealed the following comments from two former Pakistani detainees at Guantanamo:

> Shah Muhammad and Sahibzada Osman Ali told me that except for some roughing up immediately after they were captured they were not badly treated at Camp X-Ray. They both felt bored, lonely, frustrated, angry, and helpless (enough for Shah Muhammad to attempt suicide), but neither believed that he would be harmed by his American captors, and both regarded the extreme precautions (shackles, handcuffs, hoods) that so outraged the rest of the world as comical.

In June of 2003, the matter of the treatment of more than 750 illegal aliens detained on immigration charges in the aftermath of September 11, 2001, was addressed before the House Judiciary Committee. Attorney General John Ashcroft responded to critics who alleged "'significant problems' in how law enforcement officials treated some of the 762 people detained." Among other problems, an internal inspector general's report found evidence of "alleged beatings and other abuse at a high-security facility prison [Metropolitan Detention Center] in Brooklyn, N.Y., where 84 of the people were detained." The Attorney General testified that investigations into the allegations were ongoing, but in no way condoned by law enforcement.

At the end of the day, the reasonable observer must conclude that allegations that the United States condones and uses torture and ill-treatment as interrogation tools are vastly overstated and often simply taken for granted by those who should know better. For instance, in his latest book, *The Case for Israel*, Professor Alan Dershowitz charges that the United States engages in "modified forms of torture that include physical and psychological components." He then backs up his charge by citing newspaper articles that rely on unnamed sources. Certainly, there have been isolated incidents of misconduct by soldiers and law enforcement personnel who acted outside the scope of their duty, but so far the government has shown a good faith effort to take corrective and disciplinary action when these cases are brought to light. Even the Army's own popular newsmagazine, the *Army Times*, reflected this matter by devoting the front cover of a January 2004 edition to four military police soldiers who were punished for abusing Iraqi prisoners. In addition, the military has convicted all of the soldiers implicated in the Abu Ghraib prison abuse. The fact that some soldiers or government agents have engaged in misconduct does not mean that the government endorses or condones the practice.

The purpose of detainee interrogation is to glean as much intelligence as possible from individuals who have information associated with the al-Qa'eda terrorist network and all associated terror networks. The goal is to apprehend as many of the terrorists as possible and to prevent future acts of terror on our people with particular concern for the likelihood that our enemies will surely use weapons of mass destruction against us. To date, interrogations have yielded much valuable information. According to the Jacoby Declaration, as of January 2003, the United States has thwarted over 100 terrorist attacks worldwide based on information provided in part form detainee interrogations.

One matter is fundamentally certain: if the al-Qa'eda are to be kept at bay, the United States must rely on detainee interrogation as an integral antiterrorist tool. The need for the interrogator to get information to protect the lives of innocents is a legitimate and perfectly lawful exercise. By its very nature, even the most reasonable interrogation places the detainee in emotional duress and causes stress to his being—both physical and mental. Still, a reasonable interrogation must necessarily be free of torture or ill-treatment. As new techniques are explored, the United States must develop methods that penetrate quickly the consciousness of the detainee without causing pain and suffering.

Those who regularly claim that the United States oversteps the line regarding torture and ill-treatment tend to invoke the worn slippery slope argument, but that does not mean the potential for abuse does not exist. The old saw attributed to Lord Acton that "power tends to corrupt" has validity.

6.7 The Ticking Time Bomb Scenario

Many legal scholars who understand the threat of al-Qa'eda-styled terrorism often paraphrase with approval former Supreme Court Justice Jackson's observation that "the Constitution is not a suicide pact." One issue that gains a tremendous amount of attention in this debate is how to deal with a suspected terrorist in a ticking time bomb scenario. Even noted civil rights advocates like law professor Laurence Tribe understand that the landscape has changed. After 9/11 he wrote: "The old adage that it is better to free 100 guilty men than to imprison one innocent describes a calculus that our Constitution—which is no suicide pact—does not impose on government when the 100 who are freed belong to terrorist cells that slaughter innocent civilians, and may well have access to chemical, biological, or nuclear weapons."

Different commentators have varying turns on the theme, but it commonly goes something like this. Suppose a terrorist suspect is taken into custody in a major city and is found to be in possession of nuclear bomb-making materials and detailed maps of the downtown area. The terrorist blurts out to police that he is a member of al-Qa'eda and that a nuclear car bomb is on a timer set to detonate in ten hours (the time he had estimated he could safely get away from the blast). The suspect then demands a lawyer and refuses to answer any more questions. Of course, law enforcement may legitimately ignore his demands and conduct a reasonable interrogation as long as they do not engage in torture, ill-treatment or employ techniques that would shock the conscience. But what if reasonable interrogation techniques yield no information—the suspect refuses to talk? This Hobson's choice poses one of the strongest arguments for the use of non-lethal torture.

Given the premise of the ticking time bomb scenario, it is difficult to portray oneself as a centrist—either one uses whatever means necessary to get the information to stop the blast or one simply allows the slaughter of innocent civilians. Should a reasonable law enforcement officer with spouse and children residing in the blast zone simply resign himself to the fact that they were all going to perish since it is unlawful under both international and domestic law to use torture?

Or is it more likely that the law officer faced with this scenario would in fact engage in torture and argue the defense of necessity at a subsequent criminal trial?

Alternatively, one might attempt to overcome the moral dilemma if the government created a justification defense which sanctioned the use of torture in special circumstances. In this manner one could eschew hypocrisy—the government would sanction the use of torture and the law officer would not face prosecution for his acts.

As noted in the *Public Committee* decision, the Supreme Court of Israel was clearly apprehensive about the sweeping scope of its decision, particularly in the context of a ticking time bomb terrorist. In rendering its decision, the Court strongly signaled that the Knesset (legislative branch of Israel) might find it efficacious at some point to "sanction physical means in interrogations .... provided, of course, that a law infringing upon a suspect's liberty ... is enacted for a proper purpose, and to an extent no greater than is required." To date, the Israeli legislature has not enacted any such legislation.

In addition, despite its absolute stance rejecting the legality of moderate physical pressure and the associated administrative directives promulgated to regulate the use of moderate physical pressure vis a vis the interrogation of terrorist suspects, the Supreme Court of Israel went on to recognize the defense of necessity if individual GSS investigators were charged with employing such prohibited interrogation techniques in the case of a ticking time bomb scenario. Citing Israeli penal law regarding necessity112—engaging in illegal conduct in order to promote a greater good—the Court recognized that GSS interrogators would have the right to raise the defense of necessity in a subsequent prosecution. The Court stated that "[o]ur decision does not negate the possibility that the 'necessity' defense be available to GSS investigators [in ticking time bomb scenarios] ... if criminal charges are brought against them, as per the Court's discretion." The Court said that "if a GSS investigator—who applied physical interrogation methods for the purpose of saving human life—is criminally indicted, the 'necessity' [defense] is likely open to him in the appropriate circumstances."

Indeed, the Court seemed to anticipate that any reasonable GSS investigator, charged with protecting innocent lives, would apply "physical interrogation methods for the purpose of saving human life" when confronted with a ticking time bomb terrorist. In other words, GSS investigators would use whatever means necessary to avert the explosion of the bomb. The Court noted, however, that the threat of the explosion must be a "concrete level of imminent danger:"

> [The] "necessity" exception is likely to arise in instances of "ticking time bombs," and that the immediate need ... refers to the imminent nature of the act rather than that of the danger. Hence, the imminence criteria is satisfied even if the bomb is set to explode in a few days, or perhaps even after a few weeks, provided the danger is certain to materialize and there is no alternative means of preventing its materialization. In other words, there exists a concrete level of imminent danger of the explosion's occurrence.

The defense of necessity is a doctrine well-known to the common law. It is defined as "[a] justification defense for a person who acts in an emergency that he or she did not create and who commits a harm that is less severe than the harm that would have occurred but for the person's actions." Professor Wayne Lafave's criminal law text amplifies this definition by explaining that "the harm done is justified by the fact that the action taken either accomplished a greater good or prevented a greater harm."

The general understanding of the necessity defense at common law was that it was in response to circumstances emanating from the forces of nature and not from people. "With the defense of necessity, the traditional view has been that the pressure must come from the physical forces of nature (storms, privations) rather than from human beings." When the pressure is from human beings, the defense, if applicable, is duress, not necessity.

In the modern era, the distinction between the pressure coming from nature or human beings has merged. According to Lafave, defense of necessity extends to both instances.

> [T]he reason is of public policy: the law ought to promote the achievement of high values at the expense of lesser values, and sometimes the greater good for society will be accomplished by violating the literal language of the criminal law …. The matter is often expressed in terms of choice of evils: when the pressure of circumstances presents one with a choice of evil, the law prefers that he avoid the greater evil by bringing about the lesser evil.

Still, the defense of necessity is not available to a defendant in situations where the legislature has previously made a determination of values. This concept is clearly stated in the Model Penal Code: "Neither the Code nor other law defining the offense provides exceptions or defenses dealing with the specific situation involved; and a legislative purpose to exclude the justification claimed does not otherwise plainly appear." For instance, a person may not take a human life in order to save himself.

It is no secret to those familiar with the debate on civil liberties in the War on Terror that Harvard Law School's Alan Dershowitz has publicly advocated a far more aggressive approach to dealing with such things as the ticking time bomb terrorist. Dershowitz opposes the use of a necessity defense because relying on a necessity defense allows for torture to be carried on "below the radar screen," which invites greater abuse by law enforcement agents. Without bantering words, Dershowitz acknowledges the utility of nonlethal torture to get life saving information from a ticking time bomb terrorist. To be sure, Dershowitz's views spawned a firestorm of debate, not because he has advocated something new, but because it was Alan Dershowitz, the well-known civil libertarian, who made the case for State approved torture.

According to Dershowitz, such instruments of non-lethal torture could include the use of "a sterilized needle inserted under the fingernails to produce unbearable pain without any threat to health or life." The authority to engage in non-lethal torture would come from a torture warrant issued by a judge. In this manner, Dershowitz argues that the process of torture is judicially sanctioned and the chances of abuse by individual investigators is thereby reduced. "I believe … that a formal requirement of a judicial warrant as a prerequisite to nonlethal torture would decrease the amount of physical violence directed against suspects."

Those who oppose the use of torture under any circumstance whatsoever, to include the ticking time bomb scenario, invariably attempt to change or avoid the premise. Those who flatly reject Dershowitz's proposal for judicial torture warrants for a ticking time bomb terrorist are prone to engage in avoidance. For example, a recent law review article noted that "[b]y expanding the narrow framework of Dershowitz's inquiry, it is possible to focus our debate on alternative means of maintaining national security that do not violate [the] human dignity [of the terrorist]." Of course, the only way to lessen the likelihood of a ticking time bomb scenario is to neutralize the bomb before the fuse is lit, i.e., increasing police powers to break up the terrorist organizations and to prevent the unthinkable from coming to fruition.

No one can disagree that the rule of law and democracy are cherished values that must be protected. However, Dershowitz counters that in time of war it is sometimes necessary to, as Abraham Lincoln advocated, suspend our liberties to protect our liberties. In fact, Lincoln denied habeas corpus and unilaterally jailed thousands of American citizens (in the North).

Interestingly, Dershowitz's argument would require lawyers to chart a legal course around the Fourth, Fifth and Fourteenth Amendment protections of the United States Constitution, while simultaneously ignoring the binding obligations of the Torture Convention which clearly states in Article 2: "No exceptional circumstances whatsoever, whether a state of war or a threat of war, internal political instability or any other public emergency, may be invoked as a justification for torture."

Dershowitz also fails to consider the matter of war crimes in his argument. To add judicial torture warrants to the corpus of America's rule of law would not only make a mockery of the rule of law, it would subject the United States to allegations of international war crimes. As noted, all of the existing international laws relating to armed conflict—to include the Geneva Conventions, the Hague Conventions, and customary principles—are codified by the military in a book called Field Manual 27-10, Department of the Army Field Manual of the Law of Land Warfare (FM 27-10). Violations of the law of war are labeled as war crimes. FM 27-10, paragraph 499 defines the term war crime as a "technical expression for a violation of the law of war by a person or persons, military or civilian." War crimes are divided into simple breaches and grave breaches. Grave breaches are set out in the Geneva Conventions to include such acts as torture or inhuman treatment, including biological experiments, or willfully causing great suffering or serious injury to body or health. FM 27-10, paragraph 502 defines the following acts as "grave breaches" of the Geneva Convention of 1949 if committed against persons or property protected by the Conventions: willful killing, torture or inhuman treatment, including biological experiments, willfully causing great suffering or serious injury to body or hearth, and extensive destruction and appropriation of property, not justified by military necessity and carried out unlawfully and wantonly.

Each nation is under a strict legal obligation to search for all persons alleged to have committed war crimes and to investigate all allegations of war crimes. If a grave breach of the law of war is discovered, that nation has the obligation to either prosecute or extradite the accused offender. FM 27-10, paragraph 498 indicates that:

> [a]ny person, whether a member of the armed forces or a civilian, who commits an act which constitutes a crime under international law is responsible therefore and liable to punishment. Such offenses in connection with war comprise: a. Crimes against peace, b. Crimes against humanity, and c. War crimes.

The United States policy is that American soldiers accused of violations of the law of war will be prosecuted under the provisions of the UCMJ for the substantive offense. For example, killing unarmed civilians is a war crime and also a substantive crime of murder. A deliberate attack on noncombatant civilians clearly violates the codified and customary laws of war. Indeed, the law of war was designed to protect innocent civilians.

If one accepts the premise that the United States is at war with the al-Qa'eda network, then it certainly follows that the law of war is violated should an American investigator, civilian or military, engage in torture. Acts of torture constitute a grave breach of the law of war and the United States has an obligation to investigate and, if allegations of torture are valid, to either prosecute or extradite the offender to a nation that desires to prosecute. There are no exceptions for a ticking time bomb. The al-Qa'eda are clearly illegal enemy combatants, but that does not provide the United States with a license to torture them.

It is easy to choose between a right and a wrong, but the ticking time bomb scenario forces one to choose between the lesser of two wrongs. Disregarding the legal issues associated with torturing a ticking time bomb terrorist, is it possible to morally justify the use of torture to extract information? Those who believe so point to the so-called utilitarian principal best developed by philosopher Jeremy Bentham. Under the concept of utilitarianism the pain inflicted on the ticking time bomb terrorist by means of otherwise prohibited interrogation techniques is weighed against the potential pain and death that would be inflicted on the community. Accordingly, the utilitarian argument is cited with approval by those who believe that the community's welfare is of greater value than the welfare of the terrorist who seeks to destroy the community.

There are a great number of words in the English language to describe a person who not only does the *right thing* in a given situation, but performs that action in the *right way*. Such a person may be described as exhibiting virtue, integrity, honor, courage, etc. The formula of doing a right thing in a right way is an essential ingredient for the establishment and development of a just and democratic society based on the rule of law. Conversely, deviations from the formula are destructive to the individual and to society. For instance, I regularly inform my students that getting an "A" on a Civil Procedure exam in law school is a right thing, but cheating to accomplish this goal can only be characterized as a wrong way to achieve the "A." Thus, doing a right thing (getting an "A") must be done in a right way (by studying and not cheating) or the result is wrong.

In dealing with the ticking time bomb terrorist scenario, the right thing is simple enough to appreciate—law enforcement must get the information that could save the lives of thousands or, if the bomb is a weapon of mass destruction, tens of thousands. The more difficult part of the formula is the second half—getting the needed information in the right way.

Prior to *Public Committee*, the government of Israel had taken the unusual step of trying to regulate the use of torture if not by means of a judicial torture warrant, then by administrative rules. In short, the government directives had provided a justification defense to an interrogator who engaged in torture. This practice was struck down as unlawful. A similar move to regulate torture in the United States would certainly meet the same end—a democracy cannot sanction torture. Once it does, it has abandoned the moral high ground; it is no longer a democracy. Whether justification flows from the legislative, executive or judicial branch, it is anathema to a freedom loving people.

If an interrogator engages in torture, he must be charged for his crimes. Drawn from the Israeli approach in *Public Committee*, a defense of necessity would require him to satisfy a four pronged test: (1) the investigator had reasonable grounds to believe that the suspect had direct knowledge which could be used to prevent the weapon from detonating, (2) that the weapon posed an imminent danger to human life, (3) that there existed no alternative means of preventing the weapon from exploding, and (4) that the investigator was acting to save human life.

The War on Terror provides Americans an opportunity to reexamine much of what this nation represents to the world. In this light, the sanctioned use of torture must surely strike the vast majority as inconsistent with civilized values. Accordingly, while there could very well exist an emergency ticking time bomb scenario in which torture of a particular terrorist is necessary, the interrogator must face criminal liability. To approach the issue in any other manner would send the wrong signal to friends and foe alike. Those who believe that the United States can defend freedom by subverting our own values are as misguided as those who demand that the government fight the War on Terror without altering civil liberties by jot or tittle. Torture is illegal and must remain on the books as such.

6.8 Abu Ghraib and the Search for the Smoking Gun

This chapter would not be complete without a section on the so-called Abu Ghraib scandal and the associated implications for the War on Terror. While the end to major combat operations was declared by President Bush on May 1, 2003, a new and deadly chapter in the Iraqi War quickly took hold—coalition forces and Iraqi civilians were now targeted for murder by various groups of sectarian guerrilla fighters, common criminals and al-Qa'eda linked terrorists. Even the capture of the dictator Saddam Hussein on December 15, 2003, did not stem the growing volume of terrorist attacks.

The continued fighting and terrorist attacks in Iraq required the United States to alter its occupation/exit strategy. Instead of reducing the number of troops on the ground in Iraq as was hoped for in the occupation phase of the campaign, the United States was obliged to keep about 140,000 military personnel in Iraq. Clearly, the United States had underestimated the presence of foreign and host nation terrorists, Iraqi Republican guard fighters, and on down the list.

The rising intensity of the insurgency in mid 2003 also mandated that the large number of detainees that were being apprehended had to be categorized and housed. As already detailed, the United States grouped the detainees into one of three categories: (1) Iraqi soldiers who qualified as prisoners of war (POW) under the Geneva Conventions; (2) those suspected of having links to a variety of terrorist groups (to include Saddam loyalists and radical Islamic fundamentalists), called "security detainees;" and (3) common criminals.

Those in the first category were quickly processed and released back into Iraqi society within a few months. While most of the prisoners were treated in accordance with the protections of the Geneva Conventions, the U.S. military reported numerous incidents of physical abuse by American guards. The most common type of abuse seemed to occur at or near the point of capture and included physical assaults and petty larceny. In general terms, however, the vast majority of POWs were treated in accordance with international law protections. Most importantly, as prisoners of war, this particular class of detainees was not required to give any further information upon additional questioning by American forces.

Those in the second category were held for indefinite periods of time pending interrogation and eventual transfer to the nascent Iraqi judicial system. The reason that these security detainees were not given the protections of the Third Geneva Convention is because they failed to qualify as lawful enemy combatants. Again, prisoner of war status is conferred only on those persons who are "[m]embers of armed forces of a Party to the conflict" or "members of other militias and members of other volunteer corps, including those of organized resistance movements, belonging to a Party … provided that such … fulfill[s]" four specific conditions: (a) being commanded by a person responsible for his subordinates; (b) having a fixed distinctive sign recognizable at a distance; (c) carrying arms openly; and (d) conducting their operations in accordance with the laws and customs of war.

Accordingly, unless a detainee in the post major combat phase of the Iraqi War met these requirements, he was not entitled to the status of prisoner of war but was rather a security detainee. At most, such an individual would be protected only by the Fourth Geneva Convention covering civilians held during the occupation and the humanitarian protections provided by Common Article 3 of the Geneva Conventions. Common Article 3 protects all unlawful combatants taken captive from "(a) violence to life and person, in particular murder of all kinds, mutilation, cruel treatment and torture; (b) taking hostages; (c) outrages upon personal dignity, in particular humiliating and degrading treatment …." Essentially, the detainee must be treated humanely, but can be questioned to gain information.

Although determinations were often hard to make between a security detainee and a common criminal, the Bush Administration repeatedly made it clear that all detainees were to be treated in accordance with the humanitarian concerns set out in the Geneva Conventions. Accordingly, all detention facilities received regular visits by the International Committee of the Red Cross (Red Cross). In fact, the Red Cross served a valuable function in Iraq by alerting the United States to a number of abuse allegations.

The establishment of detention facilities to house the detainees was aggravated by the sheer number of detainees. This required the coalition to utilize prison structures that had been used in the Saddam era to include the infamous prison at Abu Ghraib, located about 20 miles west of Baghdad. Abu Ghraib was the largest U.S. run detention facility and, at a high point in the tempo of operations, housed up to 7,000 detainees in October 2003. It is a vast complex of six separate compounds on a 280 acre site circled by over 2 miles of fences and 24 guard towers. The Red Cross reported that they made regularly scheduled visits to a total of 14 U.S. run facilities to include the infamous Tier 1 (cellblock 1a), "a darkened, two-story isolation wing used for interrogations" and the site of the prisoner abuse at Abu Ghraib. During the visit to Tier 1 at Abu Ghraib, they reported that they did not notice anything "as bad as the abuses portrayed in the … photos." About 35 people where held in Tier 1 during the Red Cross visit.

The public was first shown the infamous photographs taken inside of the U.S. military run prison at Abu Ghraib in a CBS show called *60 Minutes II* aired on April 28, 2004. The widely circulated photos showed a handful of U.S. military police soldiers engaged in a variety of abusive and sexually sadistic acts against mostly blindfolded Iraqi detainees. Among other things, the photos showed naked prisoners stacked in pyramids, connected by wires, on a dog leash, and threatened by dogs. In addition, a handful of U.S. military police charged in the abuse scandal had forced naked prisoners to simulate sex acts.

The chronology of how the Abu Ghraib abuse story was revealed began on January 13, 2004, when Army Specialist Joseph Darby, a military policeman at Abu Ghraib, gave a computer disc containing the abuse photos to a military investigator. On January 14, 2004, the Army immediately initiated a criminal investigation and the United States Central Command (the four-star combatant command located in Florida) informed the media in a press release on January 16, 2004, that it was investigating detainee abuse at an unspecified U.S. prison in Iraq. On February 23, 2004, the military informed the U.S. press that 17 Army personnel had been suspended of duty pending further criminal investigations about the detainee abuse. Then, on March 20, 2004, the military reported to the media that it had charged six soldiers with detainee abuse to include criminal charges of assault, cruelty, indecent acts and mistreatment. Interestingly, however, the press did not fully respond to the growing story as the mere fact that soldiers were being punished for misconduct did not constitute news that was out of the ordinary—the military regularly punishes soldiers who violate the law. In fact, the media only became energized on April 28, 2004, when *60 Minutes II* aired the photos.

Pursuant to evidence of criminal misconduct contained in a U.S. Army Criminal Investigation Division (CID) Report, seven enlisted reserve soldiers, all from the 372nd Military Police Company, 320th Military Police Battalion, 800th Military Police Brigade, were charged with an assortment of violations of provisions of the UCMJ. The central figure in the scandal was a reservist Private First Class (PFC) named Lynndie England who is known for poses in which "she pointed at the genitals of a naked detainee while a cigarette dangled from her lips" and "holding a [dog] leash around a naked prisoner's neck." The other soldiers were Specialist Charles Graner, Staff Sergeant Ivan Frederick, Sergeant Javal Davis, Specialist Jeremy Sivits, Specialist Sabrina Harman, and Specialist Megan Armbuhl. All of those charged were reservists and all worked the night shift at Tier 1 in Abu Ghraib, where the abuses took place in the last months of 2003.

The particulars relating to the Abu Ghraib abuse story are now well settled thanks to the CID's criminal investigation and a number of collateral administrative investigations. In chronological order they are: (1) the April 2004 Taguba Report, prepared by Major General Antonio Taguba; (2) the July 2004 Army Inspector General Report, prepared under Lieutenant General Paul Mikolashek; (3) the August 2004 Fay Report, prepared by Major General George Fay; and (4) the August 2004 Schlesinger Report, headed by the former Secretary of Defense in the Nixon administration, James Schlesinger. In addition, there are other related examinations to include: (1) Vice Admiral Albert Church, Navy Inspector General, looking into interrogation and detention rules in Iraq, Afghanistan and elsewhere; (2) Secretary of Defense Donald Rumsfeld, looking into all prisoner operations and interrogation procedures; (3) CID investigation, looking into prisoner deaths in Iraq and Afghanistan; and (4) Lieutenant General James Helmly, Chief of the Army Reserve, looking into Army Reserve training procedures with special attention to military police and military intelligence.

The overriding question regarding the prisoner abuse echoes the thoughts of Senator Lindsey Graham (R-S.C.), a member of the Armed Services Committee: "How could we let this prison melt down and become the worst excuse for a military organization I've seen in my life?" None of the Reports found that there was an official policy—either written or oral—to torture or abuse prisoners. According to the Schlesinger Report, the most far reaching investigation to date and the one which the *Wall Street Journal* deemed the "definitive assessment of what went wrong," "no approved procedures called for or allowed the kinds of abuse that in fact occurred." In fact, the Schlesinger Report found "no evidence of a policy of abuse promulgated by senior officials or military authorities." In addition, none of the Reports cite any direct abuse of prisoners by officers or by superiors ordering subordinates to commit the abuses. In short, the Schlesinger Report concurs with all the Reports to date in finding that the individuals that conducted the sadistic abuse are personally responsible for their acts.

Nevertheless, taking a broader examination of what happened at Abu Ghraib, the Schlesinger Report did find fault with the senior levels of command; there were "fundamental failures throughout all levels of command, from the soldiers on the ground to [the United States] Central Command and to the Pentagon" that set the stage for the abuses.

The Schlesinger Report agreed with the calls for disciplinary action in the Fay Report for a number of officers in the immediate tactical chain of command who knew, or should have known, about the abuses at Abu Ghraib. "The commanders of both brigades—800 Military Police Brigade Commander Janis Karpinski and Military Intelligence Brigade Commander Thomas Pappas—either knew, or should have known, abuses were taking place and taken measures to prevent them." Certainly, however, this would include not only Brigadier General Janis Karpinski and Colonel Thomas Pappas, but those subordinate commanders and on down the chain of command to the battalion, company and platoon level. The chaotic environment at the prison existed in large part due to the dereliction of tactical commanders on the ground at Abu Ghraib.

The Schlesinger Report and all other investigations find that the culpability of commanders rests at the tactical level. The Schlesinger Report found "no evidence that organizations above 800th MP Brigade—or the 205 MI Brigade—level were directly involved in the incidents at Abu Ghraib.

While all the Reports talked about a number of factors that contributed to an atmosphere that allowed the abuses at Abu Ghraib to occur, the Schlesinger Report did the best job at providing a clear summation. These factors included:

- A lack of planning for detainee operations—from the Pentagon to the commanders on the ground in Iraq—and an inability to react to the marked spike in the insurgency that occurred in the summer of 2003;
- A confusing chain of command at Abu Ghraib where a military intelligence officer, Colonel Pappas, was placed in command of military police units;
- Lack of equipment and troops at Abu Ghraib; and
- A failure of the immediate chain of command to supervise and train soldiers under their command.

Finally, the Schlesinger Report did an excellent job of placing the problem of detainee abuse in a wider "real world" perspective. Noting that the U.S. military has handled about 50,000 detainees from all theaters of conflict since the start of combat operations in Afghanistan in 2001, the Schlesinger Report then compared that figure with the number of reported allegations of abuse, including some deaths. With around 300 cases of abuse reported, the Schlesinger Report noted that about one-third of the allegations occurred at the "point of capture or [at a] tactical collection point." As of August 2004, about half of the 300 cases had been investigated with 66 substantiated cases.

Throughout the War on Terror, the Red Cross has regularly criticized the United States for alleged violations of international law by conducting interrogations of non-uniformed combatants and terrorists taken into custody. The legal basis that the Red Cross asserts is Additional Protocol I to the Geneva Conventions of August 12, 1949, which would accord prisoner of war status to these people. The problem with this charge is that the United States has never ratified Protocol I. On the contrary, the United States specifically rejected Protocol I for the very reason that it bestowed a legal status on non-uniformed combatants. Thus, the idea that Protocol I is binding on the United States as a principal of "customary international law" is correct only in part. The United States is not bound by Protocol I in this regard and is perfectly within its legal rights to interrogate non-uniformed combatants or terrorists; these individuals are not entitled to the protections given to prisoners of war. The Red Cross is unquestionably a valuable early warning system for any democracy that wants to respect the rule of law, but its credibility is weakened each time it uses the guise of Protocol I to criticize the United States.

In the Iraqi campaign, the administration has consistently held the position that the Geneva Conventions will apply to the detainees. As Daniel J. Bell'Orto, the principal deputy Defense general counsel related, it is "all Geneva, all the time." In Iraq, the then head of U.S. forces, Lieutenant General Ricardo Sanchez, issued a one-page directive in October 2003, titled "Interrogation Rules of Engagement" which would be applicable to non-POWs. This directive allowed for practices, vetted by Army lawyers as lawful under the Fourth Geneva Convention and Common Article 3, that included silence, repetition of questioning, emotional love/hate techniques, and the use of fear (where the interrogator behaves in a heavy overpowering manner by yelling or throwing things).

At the end of the day, it seems improbable that the American military engaged in command directed torture or ill-treatment at Abu Ghraib, particularly when it was the military itself that self-reported to the media the fact that individual soldiers were being investigated and punished in accordance with the rule of law for wartime abuses at the prison. Clearly, the best indicator that the senior leadership is not culpable (with the exception of the direct tactical chain of command for dereliction of duty) is found in its continuing commitment to criminally investigate and prosecute those soldiers accused of committing detainee abuses. Numerous soldiers have already been prosecuted and sentenced for their crimes, and criminal trials will continue for others.

When one considers that the number of detainees in the War on Terror—including Afghanistan, Iraq and other operations—is about 50,000, it is unrealistic to expect that abuses will not occur. Violations of rules occur in every human endeavor, to include war. In an interview with the *Wall Street Journal*, Mr. James Schlesinger correctly noted that the "behavior of our troops is so much better than it was in World War II." The so-called "bad apple" syndrome is in fact the primary causative issue at Abu Ghraib—a handful of closely knit reserve personnel engaged in acts of sadism as they worked the night shift from October to December of 2003.

It is equally true that the Abu Ghraib story has been devastating to the United States. While each and every case of abuse is repulsive to American standards of decency and justice, the terrorists have certainly become "media-savvy" in their quest to parlay these individual cases into marketable propaganda. For example, many nations that are opposed to the United States are quick to exploit the individual cases of abuse at Abu Ghraib by painting the entire conduct of all American soldiers as immoral and illegal. Of course, Americans do not need to be told that the abuses are beyond the pale of conduct expected of its military. A CNN Gallup poll taken in May 2004 showed that three in four Americans agreed that the abuses at Abu Ghraib could not be justified.

The investigative reports have done a great service to the American people and the world by dispelling the shrill cries of those who blame a secret Pentagon "culture of permissiveness" for the abuses at Abu Ghraib. While the Schlesinger Report found institutional and even personal responsibility in the tactical chain of command for allowing conditions for abuse to occur at Abu Ghraib, the Report specifically found that "[n]o approved procedures called for or allowed the kinds of abuse that in fact occurred. There is no evidence of a policy of abuse promulgated by senior officials or military authorities." The Reports exonerate the military from any charges of a systemic use of abuse to gain intelligence, although it is certain that some military intelligence soldiers will face charges for their own acts of abuse at Abu Ghraib.

The abuses at Abu Ghraib should not have happened. The damage to American credibility and the War on Terror is incalculable. In the long run, the fact that the military prosecuted the Abu Ghraib offenders speaks volumes to the world about the true character of the United States and its military. To its great credit, the senior military leadership certainly learned the lessons of My Lai. Understanding that the best approach to dealing with war crimes is to act with alacrity and transparency, the tragedy at Abu Ghraib by a few has been thoroughly investigated and justice has been handed out to the perpetrators and, as the process moves forward, it is hopeful that the sword of justice will turn to those in the tactical chain of command. Two quotes sum up the entire affair: Senator Ben Nighthorse Campbell: "I don't know how the hell these people got into our Army;" and Secretary of Defense Donald Rumsfeld: "I failed to identify the catastrophic damage that the allegations of abuse could do to our operations in the theater, to the safety of our troops in the field, to the cause to which we are committed."

6.9 Questions for Discussion

1. *Is it wise to advocate the use of an advance judicial approval for nonlethal torture*? Alan Dershowitz, WHY TERRORISM WORKS: UNDERSTANDING THE THREAT, RESPONDING TO THE CHALLENGE 141, 148 (2002). Dershowitz writes: "When I respond by describing the sterilized needle being shoved under the fingernails, the reaction is visceral and often visible—a shudder coupled with a facial gesture of disgust."

2. *Do we need rules?* In a FOX NEWS channel interview on *DaySide with Linda Vestor* (Oct. 31, 2003), the author supported the pending criminal charges against an Army Lieutenant Colonel charged with assault in the interrogation of an Iraqi detainee. The Colonel allegedly threatened the Iraqi detainee with a pistol to get information about a future ambush of American soldiers. The live audience was largely opposed to the military's criminal investigation of the officer and displayed displeasure with the author's legal support for the referral of courts martial charges. *See also* Rowan Scarborough, *Colonel in Iraq Refuses to Resign*, WASH. TIMES, Oct. 31, 2003, at A3. Why?

3. *Is this a lawful technique?* The "fear-up" approach in interrogation techniques is described as "heavy-handed, table-banging violence," where "[t]he interrogator behaves in a heavy, overpowering manner with a loud and threatening voice" and may "throw objects across the room

to heighten the prisoner's implanted feelings of fear." *See also* Doug Saunders, *War on Terror: U.S. Walks a Fine Line to Make Prisoners Talk, Interrogation Teams Allowed to 'Fear Up' Terror Suspects, but Beating Them is Not Ok,* GLOBE & MAIL (Toronto, Canada), Sept. 17, 2002, at A9.

4. *Releasing enemy combatants.* What dangers face a nation if it releases enemy combatants prior to the end of a conflict? American news media have confirmed U.S. official findings that some detainees released from Guantanamo Bay have returned to Afghanistan and Pakistan in order to rejoin their comrades in fighting the United States and its allies. *See* John Mintz, *Released Detainees Rejoining the Fight,* WASH. POST, Oct. 22, 2004 at A01. How can released enemy combatants be prevented from returning to the fight? How might prolonged confinement help or hinder United States efforts in the War on Terror?

Selected Bibliography

42 U.S.C. § 1983.

> Every person who, under color of any statute, ordinance, regulation, custom, or usage, of an State or Territory or the District of Columbia, subjects or causes to be subjected, any citizen of the United States or other person within the jurisdiction thereof to the deprivation of any rights, privileges, or immunities secured by the Constitution and laws, shall be liable to the party injured in an action at law, suit in equity, or other proper proceeding for redress, except that in any action brought against a judicial officer for an act or omission taken in such officer's judicial capacity, injunctive relief shall not be granted unless a declaratory decree was violated or declaratory relief was unavailable.

Balz, Dan. *Durbin Defends Guantanamo Comments,* WASH. POST, June 17, 2005, at A11 (discussing the reactions of the White House and other politicians to Illinois Senator Richard J. Durbin's speech on the Senate floor, comparing interrogation procedures and conditions for detainees at Guantanamo Bay to those of Nazi concentration camps and Soviet gulags).

Bowden, Mark. *The Dark Art of Interrogation,* ATLANTIC MONTHLY, Oct. 2003, at 76.

Cohn, Marjorie. *Dropping the Ball on Torture: The U.S. Supreme Court Ruling in Chavez v. Martinez,* June 10, 2003, available at http://jurist.law.pitt.edu/forum/forumnew113.php.

Commission of Inquiry Into the Methods of Investigation of the General Security Service Regarding Hostile Terrorist Activity, reprinted in 23 ISR. L. R. 146. 1989.

Cooperman, Alan. *CIA Interrogation Under Fire; Human Rights Group Say Techniques Could Be Torture,* WASH. POST, Dec. 28, 2002, at A9 (detailing Human Rights Watch's accusations that the United States violated international law by torturing detainees and turning detainees over to states that engaged in torture).

Dershowitz, Alan. THE CASE FOR ISRAEL. 2004.

Dershowitz, Alan. WHY TERRORISM WORKS: UNDERSTANDING THE THREAT, RESPONDING TO THE CHALLENGE. 2002.

Gellman, Barton, and Dana Priest. *U.S. Decries Abuse But Defends Interrogations; 'Stress and Duress' Tactics Used On Terrorism Suspects Held in Secret Overseas Facilities,* WASH. POST, Dec. 26, 2002, at A1.

Langbein, John H. TORTURE AND THE LAW OF PROOF. 1987.

Levinson, Sanford. *"Precommitment" and "Postcommitment:" The Ban On Torture In The Wake Of September 11*, 81 Tex. L. Rev., 2013, 2020. 2003.

Parry, John T. *What Is Torture, Are We Doing It, And What If We Are?* 64 U. Pitt L. Rev. 237, 251. 2003.

Schofield, Phillip. First Principles Preparatory To Constitutional Code: Collected Works Of Jeremy Bentham. 1989.

Schulz, William F. *The Torturer's Apprentice*, The Nation, May 13, 2002, at 25 (reviewing Alan M. Dershowitz's 2002 publication "Shouting Fire: Civil Liberties in a Turbulent Age").

Sofaer, Abraham. *The U.S. Decision Not to Ratify Protocol I to the Geneva Conventions on the Protection of War Victims*, 82 Am. J. Int'l. L. 784. 1988.

Taylor, Stuart, Jr. *Rights, Liberties, and Security*, Brookings Review. Volume 21, Issue 1, Jan. 1, 2003.

Willson, David Jarris. A History Of England. 2d ed. 1972.

Chapter 7
Contractors on the Battlefield

Personnel recovery is no longer limited to high-risk, specialized troops as was the case in the past .... Isolated personnel now include U.S. military, contractors and other government civilians, as well as coalition partners.

—LTG Norton Schwartz

Synopsis
7.1 History and Status of Contractors
7.2 Force Protection
7.3 AT Training
7.4 Parent Contractor Company Liability Issues
7.5 Personnel Recovery
7.6 Conclusion
7.7 Questions for Discussion
Suggested Bibliography

Providing adequate protection, antiterrorism [AT] training and, if necessary, personnel recovery for civilian contractors deployed to support United States military operations presents significant legal and policy challenges that both the military and civilian contractor companies have yet to fully appreciate, let alone properly institutionalize. Although many Americans still visualize the United States military as a monolithic force of uniformed personnel only, the reality is far different. Due to federally imposed personnel limitations for the armed forces and the need for specialized skills in the modern high-tech military, hundreds of activities once performed by the military are now privatized and outsourced to thousands of civilian contractors. These civilian contractors routinely provide a wide array of important and essential activities in support of the full range of military operations to include infrastructure improvements and rebuilding. In other words, civilian contractors now work shoulder-to-shoulder with military personnel during both armed conflict and in Military Operations Other Than War (MOOTW). While armed conflict refers to traditional combat operations associated with internationally recognized warfare, MOOTWs are contingency missions, which include activities such as combating terrorism, counter-narcotic operations, peacekeeping operations, and other high-risk missions around the globe.

One of the consequences of the Global War on Terrorism is that American and coalition contractors—particularly in Iraq and Afghanistan—are increasingly subjected to kidnappings, torture and murder by terrorists, criminal elements and other insurgency forces. Without question, civilian contractors will continue to be integral participants in the ongoing War on Terror. Therefore, it is imperative that issues of force protection, AT training and personnel recovery be fully delineated and the related legal contours more clearly defined. This is particularly important in light of the ever-evolving nature of terrorism and the attendant responses.

Both the DOD and the companies that provide civilian contractors have core moral and legal responsibilities to provide contract personnel with adequate security, AT training and, in certain circumstances, rescue from capture. In tandem with identifying the legal and policy considerations associated with these issues, this chapter will also address the matter of civil liability to the parent contracting company should it fail to provide adequate protection and/or appropriate AT training to their civilian employees serving overseas in hostile environments.

7.1 History and Status of Contractors

The military's use of civilian defense contractors certainly did not begin with the military campaigns and counter-terror operations in Afghanistan and Iraq. Since the inception of the American republic over 200 years ago, civilian contractors have provided a wide array of essential goods and services to military personnel operating both in garrison and in the field. The role of and need for contractor support began to expand greatly during the war in Vietnam and has dramatically increased in the Global War on Terrorism. With the accelerated use of civilian contractors who accompany the military, the issue of status looms as a central matter of concern. Are they combatants, non-combatants, or a hybrid?

Civilians accompanying military forces, also known in the DOD Lexicon as contractors deploying with the force (CDF), fall into three broad categories, each governed by somewhat different legal and regulatory guidance. These three categories are: DOD civilian employees, civilian contractor personnel, and other non-affiliated civilians. As the primary topic of interest for these three categories, civilian contractor personnel includes "any individual, firm, corporation, partnership, association, or other legal nonfederal entity that enters into a contract directly with the [DOD] to furnish services, supplies, or both, including construction." In addition, many of the civilian contractors who accompany the military on contingency operations are designated as "mission-essential" (M-E) personnel (similar to the designation of DOD civilian employees as "emergency-essential" personnel). In essence, an M-E contractor is someone who works in a position in an overseas contingency operation that is required to ensure the success of the operation.

Given the scope and pace of the modern military, military planners no longer consider civilian contractors as a luxury or a "nice to have" addition to the force structure. Indeed, contractors accompanying the military on operations are a necessity without which the modern military could not conduct combat or engage in MOOTW. Because contractors now provide a wide range of technical, logistical, maintenance and security support services to DOD missions, America's unparallel military superiority now requires contractor support to maintain military readiness and operational capabilities. As noted, governmental limits on the number of DOD personnel authorized in a particular area, the increasing sophistication of military technologies and the ever present need to conserve DOD resources for other potential activities make contractor personnel support vital. Working for American contractor companies under DOD contracts, thousands of engineers, technicians, construction workers, food service providers, weapon specialists, etc., make up a "privatized Army." This privatized Army is currently deployed closer than ever before to imminently dangerous areas, including the actual battlefield. To be sure, this fact has resulted in untoward consequences. Tragically, as of January 2007, over 300 civilian contractors working in Iraq (many of them Americans) have been killed, with hundreds more wounded.

Furthermore, relative to the size of the uniformed armed forces during the Cold War, today's active duty military is a significantly smaller force. This increases the importance of contractor support to maintain the overall flexibility of the active and reserve forces. While no one really knows exactly how many civilian contractors are currently supporting DOD contingency operations overseas, low ranging estimates reveal that in Iraq alone there is approximately one civilian contractor for every ten active duty military personnel. This amounts to over 20,000 civilian contractors, a number sure to increase over the next few years as the pace of infrastructure support in Iraq (and Afghanistan) increases (the high end number is over 150,000).

All civilian contractors operate under a specific contract, either directly with the DOD or subcontracted to another contractor who is under contract with the DOD. The duties of all contractors are "established solely by the terms of their contract." Usually, the military contract will fall into one of three general categories. First, Theater Support Contracts are contracts associated with providing support to the regional combatant command, for instance, in Colombia the combatant command is United States Southern Command. These contracts are typically for day-to-day recurring services at the deployed site, to include minor construction projects, repair parts, equipment rental, etc. The second type of contracts are called External Support Contracts and are awarded by commands outside the pertinent combatant command, such as the Defense Logistics Agency. Again, under these civilian contracts, civilian contractors are expected to provide services at the deployed locations. Finally, Systems Contracts, the third category of contracts, provide the required logistics support to maintain and operate weapons systems and various mechanical systems used in the field. Regardless of the type of contract, the realities of military exigencies necessitate that civilian contract personnel "shall be prepared to respond rapidly, efficiently, and effectively to meet mission requirements for all contingencies and emergencies."

Furthermore, some contracts may require contractor personnel to be United States citizens, reflecting a security consideration associated with intelligence concerns or other sensitive issues. In fact, vetting contractors who might have access to particular DOD military sites is a necessary force protection measure. For example, the threat posed by in-country contractors with regular access to coalition military facilities was vividly demonstrated in December 2004, at Forward Operating Base (FOB) Marez in Mosul, Iraq. In this tragic incident, a suicide bomber penetrated base security measures and killed twenty-two people, including several civilian contractors. While the suicide bomber was not a civilian contractor (he was most probably a terrorist who disguised himself in an Iraqi military uniform), the event illustrated the fact that a non-American civilian who falsely gained employment under the pretense of an in-country contractor could accomplish the same act of terrorism.

While the United States clearly adopts the international law prohibiting contractors from engaging in hostilities, the reality is that contractors can be deployed throughout the battlefield, including forward-deployed positions (relative to enemy forces) to support operations during armed conflict or in other hostile environments associated with contingency operations. As evidenced by contractor casualties at the FOB Mosul attack, civilian contractors are regularly exposed to the risks of physical harm similar to that of military personnel. An enemy that blends in with the civilian population is far more able to employ violence. To prepare for the physical dangers inherent in such asymmetrical conflicts, contractors must be properly informed, trained and equipped not only to understand their own rights and obligations, but also to understand those of the United States military and the parent contractor company.

Unlike military personnel, civilian contractors accompanying the armed forces in the field do not fit neatly into well-defined arenas of military law and procedure. While the military has always carefully outlined its own command structure for its uniformed personnel, the picture is far less certain for civilians accompanying the forces. In fact, except in a Congressional declaration of war (which last occurred in 1941 during World War II), civilian contractors are not subject to the provisions of the UCMJ, that is, military law. Not only do military commanders have extremely limited authority to take any type of direct disciplinary action against contractors to make them perform their duties, contractors are generally not required to do anything outside of the terms of their specific contract. Simply stated, commanders must look to the contracting officer for enforcement of the terms of the contract. DOD Instruction 3020.41 in paragraph 6.1.1, entitled, "International Law and Contractor Legal Status," states:

> Under applicable law, contractors may support military operations as civilians accompanying the force, so long as such personnel have been designated as such by the force they accompany and are provided with an appropriate identification card under the provisions of the 1949 Geneva Convention Relative to the Treatment of Prisoners of War…. If captured during armed conflict, contingency contractor personnel accompanying the force are entitled to prisoner of war status.

The reason for this dilemma revolves around the exact nature of the civilian contractor vis a vis the concept of armed conflict. To begin with, traditional international law has focused sharply on the distinction between international and internal armed conflict with most of the concern on the former. Even under the international law of war, the precise status of contractors is still the subject of some debate. The current corpus of the law of war, which consists of all laws created by treaty and customary principles applicable to international warfare, is largely encompassed by the 1949 Geneva Conventions. The Geneva Conventions serve as the primary source of law in the event of an international armed conflict. While the Geneva Conventions require all militaries to distinguish between combatants (armed forces) and non-combatants (civilians), civilian contractors are neither combatants nor non-combatants in the traditional sense of the terms. Contractors are simply civilians that are authorized to accompany regular military forces on assorted military operations to include times of international armed conflict (the United States' policy is to handle all hostile adversaries consistent with the spirit and terms of the Geneva Conventions irrespective of the nature of the conflict).

When taking a broader meaning of the term non-combatant, that is, the general civilian population, the concept actually embraces "certain categories of persons who, although members accompanying the armed forces, enjoy special protected status, such as medical officers, corpsmen, chaplain[s], technical (i.e., contractor) representatives, and civilian war correspondents." In fact, the Geneva Conventions provide that prisoner of war (POW) protected status is given to "[p]ersons who accompany the armed forces without actually being members thereof, such as civilian members of military aircraft crews, war correspondents, supply contractors, [and] members of labor units or of services responsible for the welfare of the armed forces…." Thus, contractors are viewed as separate from the general civilian population and must be treated as POWs if captured by enemy forces during an international armed conflict.

As long as the civilian contractor takes no direct part in hostilities, he must be given POW status. Still, this non-combatant status does not insulate contractors from the exigencies of the battlefield, including the possibility of capture, injury or death. This fact should always be stressed to civilian contractors before they are assigned to work in hostile environments outside of the United States.

Furthermore, with the defeat of the radical Taliban regime and the dictatorship of Saddam Hussein, a state of international armed conflict no longer exists between the United States (and its allies) and Afghanistan or Iraq. In this environment, MOOTW, the protections of the Geneva Conventions, are not applicable. In fact, the ongoing terrorist activities in Iraq and Afghanistan would probably not even qualify as an internal armed conflict. Although one could argue that the basic protections associated with basic humanitarian law and human rights law would protect the captured contractor from abuse or torture, the sad reality of the Global War on Terrorism is that civilian contractors are often specifically targeted by terrorists who recognize no law whatsoever and hold no distinction between civilians and the military. Humanitarian law has no value to terrorists. Thus, self-defense, AT training and a personnel recovery policy are best viewed from the perspective of the adversary. In other words, will the hostile forces abide by the applicable legal norms and standards of civilized behavior?

During MOOTW, either the normative law of the host nation or any applicable Status of Forces Agreements (SOFAs) will determine the rights and privileges bestowed on civilian contractors while they are present in the host nation (special diplomatic arrangements may also exist for particular deployments). Unless a state of international armed conflict exists or some other set of special circumstances, e.g., the United States serving in an occupation role as it did in Iraq and Afghanistan, the use of civilian contractors will be strictly limited by these parameters. Again, as stated in the June 2005 Defense Federal Acquisition Regulation Supplement (DFARS): "Contractor personnel are not combatants and shall not undertake any role that would jeopardize their status."

7.2 Force Protection

Force protection is not simply providing armed military escorts to civilian contractors. Instead, it is a process of events that begins long before the civilian contractor is deployed. In recognition of this fact, force protection is defined as "actions taken to prevent or mitigate hostile actions against DOD personnel, resources, facilities, and critical information." Thus, the process of force protection clearly encompasses AT training, to include such things as ensuring that civilian contractors have "an understanding of [the] threat and the development of a system of indications and warnings that will facilitate a proactive, predictive response to enemy and terrorist action."

Force protection is the shared obligation of the military and the contractor company, tempered by the restriction that while accompanying the forces during an armed international conflict, civilian contractors cannot conduct force protection measures that would be tantamount to engaging in hostilities. Further, if armed contractors are used to provide security during a MOOTW, such activities must be spelled out in the contract and "[r]equests for permission to arm contingency contractor personnel to provide security services shall be reviewed on a case-by-case basis by the appropriate Staff Judge Advocate to the geographic Combatant Commander to ensure there is a legal basis for approval. The request will be approved or denied by the geographic Combatant Commander...."

Although the responsibility for force protection "starts with the combatant commander, extends downward, and includes the contractor," the exact extent of force protection afforded to the contractors as a general class is not entirely clear. Even the recently adopted June 2005 DFARS on contractors deployed on contingency operations offers only general guidance for the Combatant Commander. Of course, as a practical matter, the military's failure to adequately protect the civilian contractor may compromise the contractor's ability to perform the tasks (or terms) of the contract, thereby hampering the ability of the deployed military force to conduct operations. With the continuing cycle of violence in Iraq, some contracting companies have decided that the atmosphere is simply too dangerous and have pulled out. For instance, in December 2004, American contracting company Contrack International abandoned a $325 million contract in which they supervised a consortium that rebuilt transportation infrastructure in Iraq. In making their announcement to withdraw, a Contrack spokesman confided that "work [in Iraq] was too dangerous and costly."

As stated, if the contract allows, the military may position civilian contractors anywhere in the theater of operations. While they can never be used in "direct support" of hostile operations, the dangers of the battlefield and the limitations of the military to provide adequate force protection may subject contractors to bodily harm, necessitating the contractors' possession of firearms for self defense.

DOD policy discourages contractor personnel from possessing firearms for self-defense (although United States law does not preclude the possession of firearms for DOD employees under certain conditions). If weapons are authorized, they must be a military specification sidearm (the 9mm automatic pistol), utilizing military specification ammunition. A new draft DOD Instruction provides that the combatant commander may "authorize issuance of standard military side arms or appropriate weapons to selected contractor personnel for individual self-defense" but only on those "rare occasions when military force protection is deemed unavailable." The June 2005 DFARS states that the "Combatant Commander will determine whether to authorize in-theater contractor personnel to carry weapons and what weapons will be allowed."

While a hostile environment and the limits of force protection may favor the possession of weapons by civilian contract personnel, other factors weigh heavily against it. First, arming contractors may distort their battlefield status as civilians accompanying the force. Second, contractors—especially those with prior military experience—may use the weapon in an unauthorized manner, further blurring the line between combatant and noncombatant. Furthermore, possession of a sidearm may cause the enemy to mistake a contractor for a soldier, thereby having the unintended effect of increasing the risk of physical harm to the contractor. To prevent accidents and misuse, contractors must be properly trained in use of firearms for self-defense only and must comply with all applicable local laws.

Even if the contractor gains approval from the Combatant Commander to carry a sidearm in theater, the terms of the contract or parent company policy may forbid it. In reality, contractors who wish to possess a firearm for self-defense must not only gain approval of the Combatant Commander but must also be authorized (or not expressly forbidden) by the terms of the contract under which they are employed. In the majority of cases, civilian contractors may be provided with protective clothing such as bulletproof vests and helmets, but few are ever allowed to carry firearms. Additionally, in some circumstances, host nation law may also prohibit contractors from possessing firearms. The exception, of course, would be those civilian contractors who are specifically hired to provide armed security protection. Depending on the agreement with the host nation, in times of non-international armed conflict, these individuals may be armed with firearms other than pistols.

Army doctrine clearly provides that civilian contractors accompanying the force must be protected: "[T]he Army's policy has become that when contractors are deployed in support of Army operations/weapons systems, they [contractors] will be provided force protection commensurate with that provided to DAC personnel." Still, force protection measures necessary to safeguard contract personnel will vary depending on the circumstances, taking into account known and perceived risks. This is a directly proportional relationship; a more direct threat requires greater force protection to safeguard contractor personnel. For instance, during military operations in Somalia in 1993, the risks to contract personnel supporting DOD operations in theater were acute—armed gangs hostile to the American presence and the humanitarian mission presented a serious threat to the safety of civilian contract personnel. As a result, some contract personnel required an armed military escort at all times. Conversely, other military operations present lower levels of threat. In the late 1990s, civilian contract personnel traveled "nearly one million miles a month on the open roads of Bosnia, Croatia, and Hungary... for the most part without the benefit of any force protection."

In the Global War on Terrorism, ample evidence demonstrates that contractors, particularly those who have not received training on the rudimentary aspects of battlefield risks or how to manage them, are more likely the targets of kidnapping or other acts of violence. Within the general class of contractors, it is apparent that those without prior military experience or those who operate without the benefit of weapons for self-defense are at the greatest risk. Nevertheless, even if the contractor is former military, "the currency of their conditioning, both mental and physical, must be taken into account."

Army policy regarding contractor force protection must be juxtaposed more generally against Joint DOD doctrine, which relates to all the military services. Interestingly, Joint Publication (JP) 4-0, issued by the Chairman of the Joint Chiefs of Staff in 2000, provides that "[f]orce protection responsibility for DOD contractor employees is a contractor responsibility, unless valid contract terms place that responsibility with another party...." Consistent with JP 4-0, DOD force protection makes it clear that contractors are private American citizens and, accordingly, "[t]he Commanders do not have the same legal responsibility to provide security for [DOD] contractors as that provided for military forces or direct hire employees." Thus, while commanders may feel a moral or practical obligation to provide active and comprehensive force protection, in the sphere of legality, "[c]ontractors working within a U.S. military facility or in close proximity of U.S. Forces shall receive incidentally the benefits of measures undertaken to protect U.S. Forces."

The Draft DOD Instruction entitled Contractor Personnel Authorized to Accompany U.S. Armed Forces provides that contractors "shall receive incidentally the benefits of measures undertaken to protect U.S. forces ...." However, the draft also mandates a higher level of responsibility in certain instances: "[C]ommanders shall provide force protection, commensurate with the level of force protection provided to military forces, when contractor personnel are integral to the military forces and providing essential contractor services (e.g., contractor logistics convoys)."

While the Combatant Commander will make the final decision "to provide force protection to participating contractors," the degree of force protection civilian contractors receive can also be a contractual matter that is determined by the contract itself. Consequently, astute negotiations on the part of civilian contractors seeking to provide services to DOD operations in hostile environments could obligate military personnel to provide increased levels of force protection. Yet, even if a particular contract absolves the military of formal force protection responsibilities, military policy maintains that commanders assume some duty to protect civilians accompanying the force, particularly those who are deemed to be M-E personnel." The June 2005 DFARS simply acknowledges that the military should at least provide training to those contractors that are issued special equipment: "The deployment center, or the Combatant Commander, shall issue OCIE [organizational clothing and individual equipment] and shall provide training, if necessary, to ensure the safety and security of contractor personnel."

Obviously, commanders should ensure that contractor security provisions are incorporated into the operational plans (OPLANs) and operational orders (OPORDs) when determining the size of theater security forces. Given the importance of certain categories of contract personnel to certain missions, it is likely that the commander will willingly assume the responsibility of providing appropriate force protection commensurate with the risks and resources available.

Paradoxically, although the military requires force protection for civilian contract personnel accompanying the forces, it is an impossible task to perform. In turn, a lack of precise (and often contradictory) guidance can certainly hamper the ability of contractor companies to fulfill their obligations vis-a-vis providing viable AT training to their employees. In short, to protect their employees from harm (and themselves from time consuming and costly lawsuits), contracting companies must assume high levels of force protection and AT training may not be provided by the military.

Equally disadvantaged by the absence of a uniform standard, military commanders must "work with requirements that vary according to the services and the individual contracts" between the military and the contractor. Indeed, the confusing nature of the contractor force protection doctrine has led "the Combatant Commanders [to request] DOD-wide guidance on the use of contractors to support deployed forces to establish a baseline [force protection policy] that applies to all the services." Until uniform DOD guidance is fully developed regarding force protection, the only alternative is to ensure that proper and adequate AT training is provided by the parent contracting company to help close the gap.

7.3 AT Training

Major General (Ret) Alfred A. Valenzuela remarked at a June 2005 conference on "Contractor's on the Battlefield," sponsored by the Center for Terrorism Law in San Antonio, Texas, and TATE,

Inc., that "[a]lthough AT training is clearly a central theme of force protection in general, it is an area that requires special attention, particularly since the parent contracting company has a much larger role to play in AT training." The current reality of the Global War on Terrorism has merged traditional force protection concerns with antiterrorism policies and security initiatives. It is now DOD policy that "[DOD] Components and the [DOD] Elements and Personnel shall be protected from terrorist acts through a high priority, comprehensive AT program." Again, military commanders have the primary "responsibility and authority to enforce appropriate security measures to ensure the protection of [DOD] Elements and Personnel subject to their control and shall ensure AT awareness and readiness of all [DOD] Elements and Personnel ... assigned or attached." Unfortunately, this Directive does not define what constitutes "appropriate security measures." Instead, the matter is left to the discretion of the commander on the ground, who is in the best position to understand the most salient threats and the proper methodologies to counter them.

DOD policy provides that training—both in certain basic legal issues and in techniques to manage personal security in hostile environments—should always be a prerequisite to deployment. Preventing the need for the military to engage in personnel recovery of captured civilians, military doctrine is clear on the need to provide appropriate AT training:

> Before entering a theater of operations or an area of responsibility ... identified [DOD] civilian employees, [DOD] contractors (under the terms of the contract), and other designated personnel shall receive or already have completed the training necessary to survive isolation in a hostile environment, including captivity, and to return home safely and with honor.

Consistent with military doctrine, it seems entirely logical that all civilian contractors should be processed and trained through a DOD training site. Unfortunately, while a Draft DOD Instruction illustrates this basic need, it is not currently the case. In reality, AT training is approached in an extremely fragmented and ad hoc manner. Although the military may provide AT training at Individual Deployment Sites (IDS) or Continental United States (CONUS) Replacement Centers (CRC), it does not always happen. In fact, the use of IDS or CRC facilities by contract personnel is determined based upon the terms of the contract between the contractor and DOD. Then again, if contract personnel do require IDS or CRC pre-deployment processing, they may not get meaningful AT training since the IDS/CRC is tasked with actions to "screen contractor personnel records, conduct theater specific briefings and training, issue theater specific clothing and individual equipment, verify that medical requirements ... for deployment have been met, and arrange for transportation to the theater of operations." Moreover, CRC focus is on military unit training versus training of individual survival skill sets.

The fact "that [DOD] contracts have varying and sometimes inconsistent language addressing deployment requirements" creates a sloppy training model for contractors engaged in contingency operations. Sending contractors into harm's way, absent a basic understanding of the threat or of the basic principles associated with terrorism law, places the contractors and the military forces they support at great risk. Thus, while military doctrine provides that "[c]ontractors arriving in theater must receive appropriate processing," specified AT training is not a mandatory component of contractor pre-deployment. Certainly, the rise of terrorism and the challenges of providing support to the armed forces in urban settings necessitate additional AT training for contractors in these high-risk environments. Yet, commanders are only required to offer "AT training to contractors under the terms specified in the contract," leaving many contract personnel ill-prepared and under-equipped to operate in locations plagued by the threat of car bombs, suicide bombers or ambushes.

The 2003 DOD guidance on isolated personnel training for civilian contractors does outline certain AT training requirements for contractors accompanying the force, but the level of training is not uniform—it varies based on the level of threat determined by the Combatant Commander. The guidance designates three levels of training regarding specific principles of resistance: Level A, if the perceived threat by hostile forces is low; Level B, for a medium threat level; and Level C, for a high threat level. The mechanics of the training is often accomplished through the use of videos and is designed to help the contractor survive capture and exploitation by hostile forces. The training is not representative of comprehensive SERE (Survival, Evasion, Resistance, Escape) training given to certain categories of military personnel.

Another glaring deficiency associated with AT training is the lack of a Civilian Code of Conduct for civilian contractors who may be captured by hostile forces, to include terrorists. Civilian contractors sorely need "guidelines to increase their chance of survival in captivity, and to avoid potential criminal sanctions upon repatriation." For example, all Americans owe an unconditional allegiance to the United States and that allegiance is not cut-off simply because of capture by hostile forces.

DOD guidance regarding the provision of basic AT training has not kept up with the volume of contractors pouring into Iraq and other places around the globe. In effect, civilian contractor companies operating under the United States Army's Logistics Civil Augmentation Program (LOGCAP) are left to provide their own AT training. Unfortunately, in far too many cases, the AT training is sorely inadequate or is simply not done. The case of Thomas Hamill of Macon, Mississippi, is typical of how this process plays out in the real world. In late 2003, Hamill was hired by Kellogg Brown and Root (KBR) to serve as a driver of large tanker trucks in Iraq. Hamill's case is noteworthy because he is one of the few civilian contractors to have ever survived a terrorist kidnapping—he escaped from his terrorist captors 24 days after a brutal ambush of his truck convoy. His escape in 2004 is all the more amazing because he received only limited training from KBR in basic force protection related solely to his driving duties. He had no training whatsoever from the military in how to survive, evade, resist, or escape from the terrorists. Military SERE experts who interviewed him after the ordeal were impressed by Hamill's level-headed dealings with his terrorist captors, stating, "We don't know how you did it. You aren't a soldier, and you haven't been trained [in AT techniques]."

Hamill was only slightly better prepared from the KBR training than if he had received no AT training at all. When first hired in 2003, Hamill was flown to KBR headquarters in Houston, Texas, for "a seven-day orientation class." A month after the course, Hamill was flown to Kuwait where he was given a second round of training courses. "They had us attend a defensive-driving course where we discussed things such as convoy formations, how to spot explosive devices, booby traps, and how to recognize and avoid suspicious automobiles." Then, before each convoy was started on the road for its destination, Hamill, now a convoy commander, would receive a safety briefing from KBR as to road conditions and possible danger from terrorist attacks. Beyond this, Hamill never received any other type of AT training.

In light of the Hamill experience, it is imperative that either the military or the parent contracting company provides a higher level of meaningful and realistic AT training that prepares DOD contract personnel for high-risk deployments. For the contractor, adequate AT training provides "the first opportunity to get the contractor's head in the current joint operational and tactical situation" present within the theater. Obviously, the preferred point of contact for this obligation should be the military. As it becomes the primer for theater specific force protection and personnel recovery readiness of contractors' en route from [the continental United States] to high-threat overseas venues," the CRC has the potential to provide near real-time information that will improve contractor safety and survivability. Training also facilitates contractor compliance with and understanding of security-related DOD regulations, such as those regarding temporary duty travel abroad, made applicable to contract personnel through the DOD AT Program Directive.

If the military does not provide the proper AT training, parent contracting companies need to hire specialists to provide in-house training to ensure that their employees are as ready as possible to handle the exigencies associated with contingency operations and possible capture by hostiles. Not only is there a moral duty to see that this is accomplished, but the parent company who fails in this regard may be subjecting itself to possible civil liability. Just as contracting companies must ensure that employees have proper equipment, clothing and supplies to perform the contract, they are also responsible to provide AT awareness training to their employees similar to that provided to military personnel.

In short, contractors who receive AT and security-related training prior to deployment are better positioned to avoid and manage the risks encountered on MOOTW or in armed conflict. This, in turn, takes pressure off the Combatant Commander in terms of force protection concerns and the conservation of military resources.

7.4 Parent Contractor Company Liability Issues

With the increasing number of terrorist related deaths and wounding of civilian contractors accompanying the military in the Global War on Terrorism, the question of civil liability for contracting companies has become an important concern. Considering the rapid rate in which individual employee contractors are prepared, processed and trained to go into dangerous environments, such as Iraq, Afghanistan, and Colombia, it is inevitable that civil litigation against parent contract companies will arise. A 2004 civil lawsuit, filed in Wake County Superior Court, Raleigh, North Carolina, against the contracting company Blackwater Security Consulting and other named defendants, illustrates the concern.

Nordan v. Blackwater Security Consulting was filed by the survivors of four deceased independent civilian contractors and is the first in the nation to be lodged against a private military contracting company for death during a MOOTW mission. The four contractors were hired as security consulting contractors and were viciously murdered on March 31, 2004, while escorting a civilian convoy through Fallujah, Iraq, a known hostile environment at the time. Among a list of allegations of wrongdoing, the families contend that Blackwater sent the contractors into this hostile environment without proper equipment or armed escorts as promised in the contract. The families also thought the amount of AT training given to the deceased contractors was insuffi-cient. The formal allegations lodged by the survivors consist of fraud in the inducement of the contract and wrongful death because the contractors had been promised protection and proper information (associated with AT training) when they signed the contracts.

A new development in the *Nordan* case appeared in the summer of 2005, when a federal judge sent the suit back to State court. Not long after the case was first filed in January 2005, Blackwa-ter filed a motion to have the case heard in federal court. Blackwater's rationale for having the case heard in federal court was twofold. First, it argued that the Defense Base Act, a federal law capping death benefits for contractors working outside of the United States, entirely preempted State law relevant to this matter. Second, Blackwater asserted that the question of remedies avail-able to contractors in war zones was an issue of "unique federal interest." U.S. District Judge Louise W. Flanagan, while conceding that the case dealt with "novel and complex" issues, re-jected Blackwater's arguments and ruled that the case was appropriate for the North Carolina court. This decision was widely interpreted as a victory for the plaintiffs, due to the fact that North Carolina permits pecuniary compensation in wrongful death suits. The decision could also be taken as a victory for legal observers interested in clearing up some of the muddier legal questions surrounding the rights and obligations of overseas civilian contractors and their employers.

Before detailing the *Nordan* lawsuit, it is important to consider some of the possible reasons that many civilian contractors might be motivated to sign on to work for overseas companies, particularly in dangerous environments. Apart from fulfilling a sense of patriotism to the nation at war, in all probability, a significant incentive rests in the increased pay that the civilian contractor can receive. Not only do most companies pay danger premiums for work in hostile environments, but much of the pay earned overseas may be excluded from U.S. Federal taxable income. For example, the United States Army allows contracting officers to negotiate increased amounts of pay when the employee operates in areas considered to be equivalent to a war type environment. For many civilians, the increase in pay is a sufficient element to subject themselves to a hostile, even deadly work environment.

On the other hand, many parent contracting companies seek to insulate themselves from any liability whatsoever by crafting language in the contract that leaves the contractor (or his heirs) with virtually no ability to sue the parent company. Again, the *Nordan* case is quite telling con-cerning the methodology of how the contractor company attempts to absolve itself of liability. A typical Blackwater contract related to employment duties in Iraq or Afghanistan contains a clause regarding contract performance during hostilities:

> Contractor agrees and acknowledges that the Services performed in the Duty Station ... have been identified as being essential to BSC's [Blackwater] complete performance un-der the terms of the contract between BSC and the Customer [the United States] and not-withstanding the existence of hostilities or a state of war, whether declared or undeclared, Contractor agrees to perform his or her assigned duties until released from such duties by the Contractor's supervisor or the supervisor's designated representative.

Next, the sample Blackwater contract has a clause headlined as "Contractor Acknowledgement, Release and Waiver." Spelling out an assumption of the risk, the clause graphically reads:

Contractor agrees and acknowledges that due to the hazardous nature of the Duty Station and the Services to be provided hereunder, Contractor hereby expressly and voluntarily agrees to assume any and all risks of personal injury including, without limitation, death and disability which may result from contractor providing Services pursuant to this Agreement. Contractor understands and acknowledges that the Duty Station [place where the contractor works] is volatile, hostile and extremely dangerous and in some instances, military forces may be conducting continuing military operations in the region.

The assumption of the risk clause then continues with a lengthy list of the dangers and risks that the Contractor acknowledges and "voluntarily, expressly and irrevocably assum[es]."

Contractor understands and acknowledges that by voluntarily agreeing to participate in the Engagement [accompanying the military on a contingency operation or actual armed conflict], he is voluntarily, expressly, and irrevocably assuming any and all known and unknown, anticipated and unanticipated risks which could result in physical or emotional injury, paralysis, death, or damage to himself, to his property, or to third parties, whether or not such injury or death is caused by other independent contractors to BSC, known and unknown domestic and foreign citizens or terrorist or U.S. governmental employees.

In addition to the above exculpatory clauses, Blackwater further attempts to release liability for any acts of negligence on its part by including the following language in a clause entitled "Release:"

Contractor, on behalf of Contractor and Contractor's spouse, heirs, administrators, estate, personal representatives, successors and assigns (collectively referred to as "Contractor's Group"), hereby releases and forever discharges BSC ... (collectively referred to as "Releasees") from any and all claims, judgments, awards, actions and causes of action which may be asserted now or in the future by Contractor's Group for any liability whatsoever for accident, injury (including without limitation, death or disability), losses, loss of consortium, expenses, loss of income and other damages based upon or in any way arising from Contractor's performance of Services pursuant to this Agreement and the transportation of Contractor, including, without limitation, loss of life ... *whether as a result of negligence, gross negligence, omissions or failure to guard or warn against dangerous conditions*, use, structure or activity, or any other cause, arising from Contractor's participation in the Engagement ... even if such injury was caused in whole or in part by the negligence of Releasees [emphasis added].

To further reinforce the position that the company cannot be sued in civil court, the contract specifically spells out the following in a separate paragraph entitled "Covenant Not to Sue:"

Contractor further agrees and covenants not to file, prosecute, bring, maintain or in any way proceed on any claim, suit, civil action, complaint, arbitration or administrative action or proceeding of any kind in any municipal, state, federal agency, court, or tribunal against Releasees with respect [sic] any of the foregoing facts, occurrences, events, transactions, damages, injuries, claims, causes of action and other matters released in Section 11.2 [the "Release" clause set out above].

Then, in a separate clause entitled, "Liquidated Damages," the Blackwater contract expressly sets out:

> The parties hereto expressly agree that in the event of Contractor's death or injury based upon or in any way arising from Contractor's performance of Services pursuant to this Agreement and the transportation of Contractor, even if such injury was caused in whole or in part by the negligence of Releasees, Contractor's Group has no recourse whatsoever against BSC. Contractor understands and agrees that if he is hurt or killed during Contractor's performance of Services pursuant to this Agreement or the transportation of Contractor, Contractor has no recourse whatsoever against Releasees.

Finally, at the end of the lengthy contract, the contractor employee agrees to a final waiver:

> By signing this document, Contractor acknowledges that if Contractor is hurt or his property is damaged while providing Services hereunder, the intent is that Contractor and Contractor's Group is bound by this Release and Indemnification and therefore will be found by a court of law to have waived his right to maintain a lawsuit against BSC on the basis of any claim from which Contractor has released them herein.

Obviously, an employment contract such as the detailed Blackwater example serves as a formidable shield to any legal responsibility on the part of the parent company. Because many contracts are interpreted within the "four-corners" of the contract, these iron clad provisions are generally viewed as binding, leaving contract personnel with little recourse against the company if he/she is harmed or killed. Likewise, there appears to be little incentive for the company to take responsibility for its contractors as the contract language precludes the contractor from suing, even for the company's negligent behavior.

In response to the plaintiffs in *Nordan*, Blackwater can raise the following defenses: the contract specifically spelled out the dangers; the workers signed a release giving up most of their rights to sue Blackwater if something untoward happened to them; their families and their estates can't sue either, even if the deaths were the result of Backwater's negligence or gross negligence; and the contractors signed on willingly, were being paid a large sum of money, and were fully aware of all of the risks since all of them were military veterans. Furthermore, Blackwater will argue that the Defense Base Act is the contractor's remedy, particularly if the dependents of the contractors have already started to receive payments for the deaths of the contractors. However, if the court finds that the decedents were independent contractors and not employees, the applicability of the statute is brought into question. The test to determine whether the decedents were independent contractors will center on a number of factors to include: (1) the extent of control exercised over the work by the employer, (2) the presence of independent skills, knowledge and training of the decedents, (3) the method of payment and taxes, (4) the length of time of employment, and (5) the provision of equipment. Indeed, if the court finds that the relationship between the decedents and Blackwater was not that of employee/employer, then the Act will not bar recovery by the plaintiffs.

Aside from relying on the contract provisions themselves, the parent contracting companies can also rely on a "Government Contract Defense" to further absolve themselves of responsibility. First raised in the context of a contractor's liability for a manufacturing defect, this defense is set out by the United States Supreme Court in *Boyle v. United Technologies*. *Boyle* arose in the context of a tort claim asserting that a defense contractor had negligently designed a helicopter escape hatch resulting in the death of the pilot when the helicopter crashed. The Court applied a three-prong test to determine whether the contractor was immune from suit. The Court concluded that the Government Contract Defense was applicable where: (1) the contractor has taken actions at the direction of agency officials exercising their discretionary authority, (2) the directions involved reasonably precise specifications created by the Government with which the contractor complied, and (3) the contractor did not fail to warn the Government of known dangers associated with the Government's design. Therefore, the contractor was immunized from tort liability for damages arising from the alleged helicopter design defects.

Currently, the immunity arising under *Boyle* is a potentially valuable tool for those contract companies that provide a weapons system in a battlefield environment. Providing such equipment in a combat or contingency operation raises the stakes for all parties involved. This is true because the failure of a weapons system can have direct adverse consequences in terms of property damage and combat casualties. Such adverse consequences could then give rise to potentially enormous financial liability for the contractor.

While this scenario no doubt makes reliance on the *Boyle* defense a potentially important shield for contractors, it is important to note that the *Boyle* case involved a contract for production of a weapons system. Currently, many overseas contractor efforts in support of contingency operations usually involve contracts for services. At least two federal district courts have undertaken detailed analyses of this issue, and both have held that the rationale for the defense outlined in *Boyle* and its progeny dictates that the defense is also available to civilian contractors performing service contracts, not just manufacturing.

Another possible line of defense for a contracting company is the so-called "Government Agency Defense." This defense basically holds that if a contractor engages in a valid legal activity in furtherance of the performance of a government contract, he is immune from suit for that activity to the extent that the government would be immune if sued directly. The treatment of this defense by federal courts in recent decades has been woefully inconsistent and, therefore, it unfortunately provides little real guidance.

Despite the rigid language of Blackwater-styled contracts and the above mentioned defenses, plaintiffs (like those in *Nordan*) may still be able to recover significant monetary damages even if they entered into an "iron-clad" contract. First, the claims will be filed in individual State courts and therefore the applicable State law may provide some relief, for example, under a wrongful death statute that allows for financial compensation or an expansive strict liability theory. Apart from the fact that the parent company may be held liable for intentional or reckless conduct, strict liability may prove to be a viable option.

The Second Restatement of Torts establishes strict liability for defendants who engage in ultrahazardous or abnormally dangerous activities. Clearly, sending contractors into hostile combat zones would be considered an abnormally dangerous activity. Section 519 of the Restatement generally declares that "[o]ne who carries on an abnormally dangerous activity is subject to liability for harm to the person, land or chattels of another resulting from the activity, although he has exercised the utmost care to prevent the harm." Naturally, this section also limits the liability "to the kind of harm, the possibility of which makes the activity abnormally dangerous."

The subjective factors for determining whether or not an activity is abnormally dangerous are set out in Section 520 of the Restatement. These factors include: (1) the "existence of a high degree of risk of some harm to the person, land or chattels of others," (2) the "likelihood that the harm that results from it will be great," (3) the "inability to eliminate the risk by the exercise of reasonable care," (4) the "extent to which the activity is not a matter of common usage," (5) the "inappropriateness of the activity to the place where it is carried on," and (6) the "extent to which its value to the community is outweighed by its dangerous attributes."

In assessing each of the factors listed in Section 520, it should be noted that none of them are dispositive, and it is not necessary to prove each of them in order to find that an activity qualifies as abnormally dangerous. Moreover, none of the factors have to be given equal weight. In short, the framers of the Restatement grant courts wide latitude in using these factors to determine the dangerousness of the activity. Section 522 takes things a step further, imposing strict liability on a defendant engaged in an abnormally dangerous activity "for the resulting harm although it is caused by the unexpectable (1) innocent, negligent, or reckless conduct of a third person, or (2) action of an animal, or (3) operation of a force of nature."

Applying all of these factors to the plaintiffs' claims in *Nordan*, it appears on the surface that a solid case for strict liability can certainly be made against the defendants. It is difficult, if not impossible, to argue that the defendant's business does not qualify as an abnormally dangerous activity. The representations made to the plaintiffs when they signed on with Blackwater to serve as security contractors certainly sent a message that their job would include specific hazards that required special equipment and training (to include AT training). It also appears that most of the six factors listed in Section 520 can be applied to the facts of the *Nordan* case. The first four factors are particularly applicable, as it is obvious that the situation the security contractors faced in Fallujah constituted "a high degree of risk of some harm … [to] others," with the likelihood that the resulting harm "will be great" and could not be eliminated with "the exercise of reasonable care." Moreover, it will be difficult for the defendants to demonstrate that the activity they hired the contractors to engage in was "a matter of common usage."

Nevertheless, the last two factors are more problematic for the plaintiff. It is less likely that a court will find the defendants' activities in Fallujah to be inappropriate for that locale. Fallujah was a well-known hostile zone where terrorists regularly operated. Additionally, the court could subjectively find that the valuable service that the defendants supplied to the Iraqi civilian population and American troops in the Fallujah community outweighed the dangerous attributes of the activity itself.

At the end of the day, of course, the Restatement grants the court the power to exercise a great amount of discretion in assessing the criteria. Accordingly, the formula the court would use to assign weight and persuasiveness to each of the factors makes prognostication nearly impossible. Still, Section 519 of the Restatement reveals that a defendant can exercise the utmost care and still be liable for the harm that another suffers as a result of the defendant's abnormally dangerous activity. As such, the precautions taken and the equipment supplied by Blackwater cannot shield them from strict liability for the harms that befell the plaintiffs in Fallujah on March 31, 2004. A *fortiori*, if the plaintiff can show that Blackwater was actually deficient in providing the proper equipment or AT training, the strict liability case becomes stronger.

On the other hand, it must be admitted that other factors make the imposition of strict liability on the defendants, based on their engagement in an abnormally dangerous activity, much more difficult. Most significantly, Section 523 of the Restatement makes a "plaintiff's assumption of the risk of harm from an abnormally dangerous activity" an absolute bar from recovery. The defendants are likely to argue the plaintiff was aware of all of the dangers associated with the job and still signed an employment contract in which they were specifically informed of the risks and assumed the risks. If the court finds this argument to be credible, it could prove fatal to the plaintiffs' claims of strict liability based on the exercise of an abnormally dangerous activity. Nevertheless, many courts view assumption of the risk language to be calculated risks that do not automatically bind contractor employees, particularly when viewed in the light of any promises made by the parent contracting company.

Faced with the assumption of the risk obstacle, which is included as boilerplate contract language for all of the contracting companies, the plaintiffs could still use some of the strict liability elements to buttress their negligence claims. As counter intuitive as it might appear, in arguing for imposition of strict liability, plaintiffs could cite the amount of increased training they were required to undertake as evidence of the abnormal and hazardous nature of the activity. As more often is the case, in arguing a strict liability or negligence theory of recovery, the plaintiffs would argue that they received no extensive AT training and therefore where more likely to suffer the harms that they did, in fact, suffer. Thus, since they were not properly provided AT training, they could not form the required level of understanding to appreciate the dangers they were waiving. In other words, the injuries the plaintiffs suffered were directly attributable to the lack of information and AT training offered by the parent contracting company. Indeed, inadequate and nonexistent training has been cited frequently by contractors in Iraq as an ongoing and potentially dangerous problem.

In addition, plaintiffs can claim, as in *Nordan*, that they relied on the defendant's promises of proper AT training and force protection in making their decision to sign the subject contract. In *Nordan*, the four plaintiffs could allege that the parent company neglected their duty to provide AT training and force protection, or engaged in intentional fraud (perhaps in the interest of greater profits) to induce the deceased to enter the contract. Stated specifically, fraud in the inducement applies when the defendant knowingly makes a false representation of a material fact, intending that action to be acted upon. Additionally, the plaintiff must have incurred damages in its reasonable reliance and action upon the false representation. In the event that fraud in the inducement of a contract is found, the court orders rescission of the entire contract. In short, the so-called "iron clad" contract is gone.

At the end of the day, the repercussions of any lawsuit to the parent contracting company can extend far beyond compensatory or even punitive damages. The injury to reputation can impact negatively on developing new business contacts and cause difficulty in recruiting new hires.

7.5 Personnel Recovery

According to the DOD, "[p]reserving the lives and well-being of ... contractors placed in danger of being isolated, beleaguered, detained, captured or having to evade while participating in U.S.-

sponsored activities or missions is one of the highest priorities of the Department of Defense."

As stated, contractors who have "fallen into the power of the enemy" during an international armed conflict are considered POWs and are to be afforded all the protections of the Geneva Conventions. As such, during captivity the contractor is now a POW and must receive adequate food, water, shelter, and clothing. Following the cessation of active hostilities between the two warring parties, the contractor must be released. Toward this end, DOD policy requires that:

> Before entering a theater of operation or an area of responsibility, identified [DOD] civilian employees, [DOD] contractors (under the terms of the contract), and other designated personnel shall know their personal legal status under the Geneva Conventions. Knowledge of their personal legal status shall assist those who become captured or isolated to apply properly the rights and privileges afforded to them under international law.

Ironically, DOD issued this broad-reaching Instruction on August 20, 2003, more than three months after the cessation of the international armed conflict in Iraq and almost three years after the cessation of the international armed conflict in Afghanistan. Still, since most of the contractor casualties in the Global War on Terroriam have not occurred during the rather brief periods of international armed conflict against totalitarian regimes, international law of war protections are not applicable.

The vast majority of contractor deaths, kidnappings, and woundings have occurred during MOOTW missions, particularly in the context of the ongoing terror attacks by al-Qa'eda, insurgents and other criminals. In contingency operations, civilians accompanying the force represent easy targets for enemy forces set on hostage-taking. There is no question that the terrorists recognize the propaganda value of exploiting the media and sensationalizing the kidnappings. Because contractors are typically unarmed, have little knowledge of or training in evasion techniques (i.e., no AT training), and may receive only incidental protection from combatant personnel, the risk of capture is often high. Once captured, many are viciously tortured and murdered.

Although the terrorist attacks are not considered to be under the umbrella of any international set of rules, the distinction has little meaning to al-Qa'eda-like terror groups who have no regard for any civilized rules regulating armed conflict. Terrorists, insurgents and criminal gangs who prey upon contractors do not subscribe to the law of war or civilized behavior, thereby making the protections afforded by any rule of law hollow with little practical or perceived value. Considering the prospect of torture and other violence likely to befall the captured civilian contractor, the issue of personnel recovery is a pressing matter.

While a primary purpose of AT training is to provide contractors with the skills necessary to avoid capture, it is also concerned with providing skills to allow them to cope with possible capture and return to U.S. control. Thus, AT training should always be viewed as a venue for SERE training. The very purpose of AT training is to avoid potential threats.

> It is DOD policy that preserving the lives and well-being of U.S. military, [DOD] civilian and contract service employees placed in danger of being isolated, beleaguered, detained, captured or having to evade while participating in a U.S.-sponsored activity or mission is one of the highest priorities of the Department of Defense. The Department of Defense has

a moral obligation to protect its personnel, prevent exploitation of its personnel by adversaries, and reduce the potential for captured personnel being used as leverage against the United States.

Nevertheless, it is no secret that personnel recovery matters are fragmented and a National Security Presidential Directive is sorely needed. Although the military has attempted to recover captured contractors in Iraq, whether or not such a rescue attempt is made may not only be limited by operational constraints (e.g., a lack of intelligence as to the location of the contractor), but also due to a lack of clear, high-level guidance. Each military service plan for individual operations, the training/preparation for such operations and even the terminology is defined differently. Indeed, the term "personnel recovery" is defined differently within the military establishment. One source defines personnel recovery as follows:

> [A]ggregation of military, civil, and political efforts to recover captured detained, evading, isolated or missing personnel from uncertain or hostile environments and denied areas. Personnel recovery may occur through military action, action by non-governmental organizations, other U.S. Government-approved action, and diplomatic initiatives, or through any combination of these options.

In effect, the term personnel recovery is an umbrella term that envisions a combination of military, civil and political efforts united to obtain the immediate release of those detained against their will or isolated from a hostile environment either via coordinated negotiation or forcible recovery.

Given the current high-risk environments of not only Iraq and Afghanistan, but also of places like Colombia and other hostile zones around the globe, one might conclude that all personnel recovery operations are conducted by either the Air Force or Special Operations Forces (SOF). This is not the case. While SOF forces provide flexibility as well as the unique knowledge and equipment required for high-risk, personnel recovery missions, there is no "dedicated" personnel recovery force. Based on each case, the Combatant Commander will rely on a combination of assets to form a rescue mission. The much-publicized April 2003 rescue of Jessica Lynch does not represent the model for recovery operations, although in that personnel recovery operation, SOF soldiers successfully rescued Private Jessica Lynch from an Iraqi hospital during a nighttime raid without suffering a single American casualty.

The use of the military to conduct personnel recovery missions is defined, in part, by the DOD policy on Non-Conventional Assisted Recovery, which covers not only United States military personnel, but also "DOD civilian employees, contractors and other designated personnel isolated during military operations or as a direct result of developing or ongoing crisis prior to U.S. military intervention." The significance of this DOD Instruction cannot be overstated for two reasons. First, the DOD Instruction specifically includes, by its terms, "contractors" as a covered entity without limitations or qualification (that is, under the terms of the contract). Second, the DOD Instruction's applicability is broad—arguably, by using the term "military operations," the policy accounts for personnel recovery operations in both war and MOOTW. As such, Non-Conventional Assisted Recovery (NAR) encompasses:

> All forms of personnel recovery conducted by an entity, group of entities, or organizations that are trained and directed to contact, authenticate, support, move and exfiltrate U.S. military and other designated personnel from enemy-held or hostile areas to friendly control through established infrastructure procedures. NAR includes unconventional assisted recovery.

Though frequently the result of hostilities, personnel recovery options are not limited to hostilities *per se*:

> The scope of persons for whom the United States will undertake Personnel Recovery is not limited to situations involving hostile action or circumstances suggestive of hostile action. Personnel Recovery measures may be initiated for personnel (U.S., allied, or coalition) who become unaccounted for as a result of training exercises, operations other than war wherein hostile action is not involved and operational environments not involving hostile action.

Individuals who become missing as a result of non-hostile action do not automatically gain the benefits of personnel recovery operations initiated on their behalf. DOD policy provides that "the specific persons for whom Personnel Recovery may be initiated will vary based upon the circumstances unique to each situation."

While the implementing regulations are the province of DOD, Congress has provided the statutory framework within which DOD conceptualizes and formulates personnel recovery policy specifically and missing person policy more generally. The Secretary of Defense established the Defense Prisoner of War/Missing Personnel Office pursuant to 10 U.S.C. 1501:

> The Secretary of Defense shall establish within the Office of the Secretary of Defense an office to have the responsibility for Department of Defense Policy relating to missing persons .... Subject to the authority, direction, and control of the Secretary of Defense, the responsibilities of the office shall include ... policy, control, and oversight ... of the entire process for investigation and recovery related to missing persons (including matters related to search, rescue, escape, and evasion) ....

The Defense Prisoner of War/Missing Personnel Office (DPMO) is charged with coordinating the full range of policy issues associated with personnel recovery throughout DOD and the interagency community. Perhaps more significant for the civilian contractor, Congress defines the term "missing person" to mean:

> [A] member of the armed forces on active duty who is in a missing status; or a civilian employee of the Department of Defense or an employee of a contractor of the Department of Defense who serves in direct support of, or accompanies, the armed forces in the field under orders and who is in a missing status.

Contractors are also considered "covered persons" for the purposes of DOD action to investigate the circumstances of their absence and, possibly, to evaluate and implement personnel recovery options. As a result, 10 U.S.C 1502 states:

> After receiving information that the whereabouts and status of a [covered] person ... is uncertain and that the absence of the person may be involuntary, the commander of the unit, facility, or area to or in which the person is assigned shall make a preliminary assessment of the circumstances. If, as a result of that assessment, the commander concludes that the person is missing, the commander shall recommend that the person be placed in missing status and ... transmit a report containing that recommendation to the Secretary concerned ....

The application of the statute to personnel recovery provides some overarching bright-lines and the opportunity for Congressional supervision, but does not limit or preclude the need for more clarification of personnel recovery vis á vis the specific and increasingly important role of the contractor.

7.6 Conclusion

There can be no doubt that the use of civilian contractors by the modern United States military is an absolute necessity for successful mission accomplishment. This is certainly true in the context of the Global War on Terrorism, but it is also true in other contingency operations from South America to the Far East. Unfortunately, "the regulatory scheme governing civilians accompanying the force is in a rapid state of flux" and DOD lacks a "comprehensive policy to ensure that contractors are adequately protected ... or that the risks to them are adequately managed in high-threat, overseas locations." In fact, most of the regulatory guidance dealing with civilians accompanying the military was written prior to the Global War on Terrorism.

Congress has recognized a number of the shortcomings in the areas of civilian contractors and personnel recovery, and has taken steps to address some of these gaps. Another encouraging development in terms of advancing the issues associated with civilian contractors is the June 2005 DFARS. This DFARS addresses questions regarding governmental responsibility to contractors deployed on contingency operations overseas, defining their duties in relation to DOD and setting out specific required language in all such contracts. Likewise, the October 2005 DOD Instruction 3020.41 created a comprehensive source for the DOD procedures dealing with CDF. This dialogue is encouraging, but more needs to be done.

Mitigating the risk of injury or capture of civilian contractors is a shared responsibility of the United States and the parent contracting company. Not only does DOD need to fully develop an institutional approach to contractor force protection, it is imperative that parent contracting companies develop a better system of providing the necessary AT training for their employees who are sent to high-risk overseas locations. Until the government develops a systemic approach, (e.g., providing the full range of force protection training at military pre-deployment sites), the prudent parent contracting company will ensure that their employees have the necessary information to prepare them for the exigencies of their overseas assignments. At a minimum, this means that the parent company should include an appropriate level of AT training so that contractors are better able to avoid or survive capture or injury when operating in high-risk environments.

7.7 Questions for Discussion

1. *Civilian or combatant?* Thomas Hamill & Paul T. Brown, ESCAPE IN IRAQ: THE THOMAS HAMILL STORY 150 (2004). When captured by terrorists in Iraq, Hamill noted that he was considered a solider by the terrorists:

> "What do you do?" asked the well-dressed man [Iraqi terrorist].
>
> "I am a civilian contractor," I replied.
>
> "You are a soldier," pronounced the well-dressed man. "You haul supplies and fuel to the solders for the trucks, tanks, and planes that bomb Fallujah."
>
> "You are a soldier!" said the man in the red wrap [Iraqi terrorist].
>
> "No I am not a soldier," I said. "I am here to support the military. I am a truck driver."
>
> "You were driving military trucks, no?" said the well-dressed man.
>
> "Yes, I was, but I am a civilian," I said.
>
> "You are a soldier," he said.

2. *Protection from lawsuits.* What impact will a plaintiff's verdict in the *Nordan* case have on parent contracting companies?

3. *Code of Conduct.* Should independent civilian contractors have a Code of Conduct?

Suggested Bibliography

Campbell, Gordon L. *Contractors on the Battlefield: The Ethics of Paying Civilians to Enter Harm's Way and Requiring Soldiers to Depend on Them*, JOINT SERVICES CONFERENCE ON PROFESSIONAL ETHICS, January 27–28, 2000.

Defense Federal Acquisition Regulation Supplement (DFARS). CONTRACTOR PERSONNEL SUPPORTING A FORCE DEPLOYED OUTSIDE THE UNITED STATES, 70 Fed. Reg. 23790, May 5, 2005 (eff. June 6, 2005).

Dep't of the Army Field Manual 100-21. CONTRACTORS ON THE BATTLEFIELD, Jan. 2003, at ¶ 6-1.

Dep't of the Army Field Manual 100-21, supra note 29, at ¶ 6-1.

U.S. Dep't of the Army Pamphlet 715-16. CONTRACTOR DEPLOYMENT GUIDE ¶ 3-1(c). Feb. 27, 1998.

U.S. Dep't Of Defense Dir. 2000.12. DOD ANTITERRORISM (AT) PROGRAM, ¶ 4.6. Aug. 18, 2003.

Dep't Of Defense Dir. 2310.2. PERSONNEL RECOVERY, ¶ 3.1. Dec. 22, 2000. (defining personnel recovery as the "aggregation of military, civil, and political efforts to recover captured, detained, evading, isolated or missing personnel from uncertain or hostile environments and denied areas").

U.S. Dep't Of Defense instruction 1300.23. ISOLATED PERSONNEL TRAINING FOR DOD CIVILIAN AND CONTRACTORS ¶ E1.1.1. Aug. 20, 2003. (defining DOD civilian employees as "U.S. citizens or foreign nationals employed by the [DOD] and paid from appropriated or non-appropriated funds under permanent or temporary arrangement").

U.S. Dep't Of Defense instruction 1300.23. ISOLATED PERSONNEL TRAINING FOR DOD CIVILIAN AND CONTRACTORS ¶ 4.1. Aug. 20, 2003.

U.S. Dep't Of Defense instruction 2310.5. ACCOUNTING FOR MISSING PERSONS ¶ E3.1.6. Jan. 31, 2000.

U.S. Dep't Of Defense instruction 2310.6. Non-Conventional Assisted Recovery In The Department Of Defense ¶ 1. Oct. 13, 2000.

General Accounting Office. *Military Operations: Contractors Provide Vital Services to Deployed Forces but Are Not Adequately Addressed in DOD Plans*, GAO-03-695, at 2-9. June 2003.

Hamill, Thomas, and Paul T. Brown. Escape In Iraq: The Thomas Hamill Story 150. 2004.

Interagency National Personnel Recovery Architecture: Final Report, Inst. For Defense Analyses, P-3890, July 2004, at F-1.

Legal Lessons Learned From Afghanistan And Iraq, Vol. 1, Center For Law And Military Operations, The Judge Advocate General's Legal Center & School 172. August 1, 2004.

Liegl-Paul, Charlotte M. *Civilian Prisoners of War: A Proposed Citizen Code of Conduct*, 182 Military L. Rev. 106. 2004.

Taylor, Guy. *Legal Limbo Shadows Civilians in War Zone*, Wash. Times, July 6, 2004, at A1.

Tiron, Roxana. *Pentagon Still Undecided on Polices to Protect Contractors*, Nat'l Def., Nov. 2004, at 39.

Turner, Lisa L., and Lynn G. Norton. *Civilians at the Tip of the Spear*, 51 A. F. L. Rev. 1, 4. 2001.

U.S. Dep't of the Army Regulation 715-9. Contractor Personnel In Germany—Technical Expert, Troop Care, And Analytical Support Personnel ¶ 1-4. Apr. 2, 2003.

U.S. Dep't Of Defense. Joint Publication 1-02. Dictionary Of Military And Associated Terms 40 (2001) (defining antiterrorism as "[d]efensive measures used to reduce the vulnerability of individuals and property to terrorist attacks, to include limited response and containment by local military forces").

Yearsley v. W.A. Ross Const. Co., 309 U.S. 18, 20-21 (1940). ("Where an agent or officer of the Government purporting to act on its behalf has been held to be liable for his conduct causing injury to another, the ground of liability has been found to be either that he exceeded his authority or that it was not validly conferred.")

Chapter 8
Cyberterrorism

[Today's networked criminals] operate like cell-based terrorist organizations.

—Barry Collin

While many trace the beginning of the War on Terror to September 11, 2001, it is now clear to all that the United States has been a primary target for terrorist attacks by radical Islamic terrorist groups for many years. Unfortunately, in hindsight, it is equally apparent that the United States was not adequately prepared to defend the homeland from the innovative al-Qa'eda terror attacks of September 11, 2001. The 9/11 Commission Report described the lack of preparedness of American intelligence and law enforcement agencies as a "failure of imagination." The government simply did not take seriously the possibility of terrorists using commercial airlines as precision weapons to attack buildings. The failure to appreciate the sophistication of the al-Qa'eda terrorist network opened the door for devastating attacks. Consequently, the United States was caught completely by surprise, resulting in the loss of 3,000 lives and billions of dollars in property loss.

Since the attacks of September 11, 2001, the government has crafted a variety of robust antiterrorism responses designed to disrupt terrorist networks and lessen the probability of future al-Qa'eda-styled terrorist attacks. Trying to anticipate emerging threats, these responses include the passage of the *National Strategy to Secure Cyberspace*, the *National Strategy for the Physical Protection of Critical Infrastructure and Key Assets* and the passage of the PATRIOT Act. Without question, shifting the tactical focus from punishing those individuals, organizations, or nations who commit terrorist crimes or engage in aggression to new broad methodologies designed to thwart such criminal acts in the first place has caused "a sea of change" in how the government approaches terrorism prevention.

Nevertheless, a new and deadly terrorist threat called cyberterrorism is now emerging that may, as many commentators predict, catch the United States totally off guard. The same failure of recognition and lack of awareness prior to the terrorist air attacks of September 11, 2001, might be mimicking itself in the cyber world, and the attacks could prove to be more crippling and deadly than anything imaginable. Fortunately, some in the government have recognized that if portions of our physical world could be destroyed as it was in the attacks of 9/11, a *fortiori*, our cyber world, which regulates all aspects of modern society, is an extremely vulnerable sector of our society, ripe for terrorist attack. When one considers that terrorist organizations such as al-Qa'eda and Hamas have been using computers, email and encryption to support and finance their organizations for years, it is only logical to conclude that they are fully aware that cyberterrorism offers a low cost method of inflicting major damage and it is very difficult to trace. Indeed, it is simply naïve to believe that terrorists will not adapt their thinking to attack cyber space. Thus, the purpose of this chapter is to briefly outline the threat of cyberterrorism and to address some of the new tools that the United States is employing to address the threat.

8.1 Defining Cyberterrorism

The modern world we have created is totally dependent on the workings of the Internet, computer databases and software of the cyber world. Without question, the cyber realm is fully incorporated into our everyday lives and touches almost everything we do or think. Apart from serving as a fantastic communication medium, the cyber world regulates all aspects of our infrastructure to include water, electricity, banking, transportation, technology, agriculture, medical, nuclear facilities, waste management, government services, etc. This fact has not only spawned the era of cyber crime, costing billions of dollars a year, but it has also given rise to the specter of cyberterrorism.8.1 The Threat of Cyberterrorism Not only does the PATRIOT Act provide an updated list of America's critical infrastructure, it also makes reference to cyber and physical critical infrastructures and describes the national policy toward protecting these assets. Section 1016(b)(2) of the Critical Infrastructures Protection Act of 2001 specifically identifies, "telecommunications, energy, financial services, water, and transportation sectors," all of which have not only physical components, but cyber components as well. Section 1016(b)(3) speaks to the importance of these critical infrastructures and calls for their protection.

SEC. 1016. CRITICAL INFRASTRUCTURES PROTECTION

(a) SHORT TITLE.—This section may be cited as the "Critical Infrastructures Protection Act of 2001."

(b) FINDINGS.—Congress makes the following findings:

(1) The information revolution has transformed the conduct of business and the operations of government as well as the infrastructure relied upon for the defense and national security of the United States.

(2) Private business, government, and the national security apparatus increasingly depend on an interdependent network of critical physical and information infrastructures, including telecommunications, energy, financial services, water, and transportation sectors.

(3) A continuous national effort is required to ensure the reliable provision of cyber and physical infrastructure services critical to maintaining the national defense, continuity of government, economic prosperity, and quality of life in the United States.

(4) This national effort requires extensive modeling and analytic capabilities for purposes of evaluating appropriate mechanisms to ensure the stability of these complex and interdependent systems, and to underpin policy recommendations, so as to achieve the continuous viability and adequate protection of the critical infrastructure of the Nation.

(c) POLICY OF THE UNITED STATES.—It is the policy of the United States—

(1) that any physical or virtual disruption of the operation of the critical infrastructures of the United States be rare, brief, geographically limited in effect, manageable, and minimally detrimental to the economy, human and government services, and national security of the United States;

(2) that actions necessary to achieve the policy stated in paragraph (1) be carried out in a public-private partnership involving corporate and non-governmental organizations; and

(3) to have in place a comprehensive and effective program to ensure the continuity of essential Federal Government functions under all circumstances.

(d) ESTABLISHMENT OF NATIONAL COMPETENCE FOR CRITICAL INFRASTRUCTURE PROTECTION.

(1) SUPPORT OF CRITICAL INFRASTRUCTURE PROTECTION AND CONTINUITY BY NATIONAL INFRASTRUCTURE SIMULATION AND ANALYSIS CENTER.—There shall be established the National Infrastructure Simulation and Analysis Center (NISAC) to serve as a source of national competence to address critical infrastructure protection and continuity through support for activities related to counterterrorism, threat assessment, and risk mitigation.

(2) PARTICULAR SUPPORT.—The support provided under paragraph (1) shall include the following:

(A) Modeling, simulation, and analysis of the systems comprising critical infrastructures, including cyber infrastructure, telecommunications infrastructure, and physical infrastructure, in order to enhance understanding of the large-scale complexity of such systems and to facilitate modification of such systems to mitigate the threats to such systems and to critical infrastructures generally.

(B) Acquisition from State and local governments and the private sector of data necessary to create and maintain models of such systems and of critical infrastructures generally.

(C) Utilization of modeling, simulation, and analysis under subparagraph (A) to provide education and training to policymakers on matters relating to—

(i) the analysis conducted under that subparagraph;

(ii) the implications of unintended or unintentional disturbances to critical infrastructures; and

(iii) responses to incidents or crises involving critical infrastructures, including the continuity of government and private sector activities through and after such incidents or crises.

(D) Utilization of modeling, simulation, and analysis under subparagraph (A) to provide recommendations to policymakers, and to departments and agencies of the Federal Government and private sector persons and entities upon request, regarding means of enhancing the stability of, and preserving, critical infrastructures.

(3) RECIPIENT OF CERTAIN SUPPORT.—Modeling, simulation, and analysis provided under this subsection shall be provided, in particular, to relevant Federal, State, and local entities responsible for critical infrastructure protection and policy.

(e) CRITICAL INFRASTRUCTURE DEFINED.—In this section, the term "critical infrastructure" means systems and assets, whether physical or virtual, so vital to the United States that the incapacity or destruction of such systems and assets would have a debilitating impact on security, national economic security, national public health or safety, or any combination of those matters.

(f) AUTHORIZATION OF APPROPRIATIONS.—There is hereby authorized for the Department of Defense for fiscal year 2002, $20,000,000 for the Defense Threat Reduction Agency for activities of the National Infrastructure Simulation and Analysis Center under this section in that fiscal year.

Like the term "terrorism," no universal definition for cyberterrorim has emerged. In general, however, cyberterrorism is the employment of various computing resources to intimidate or coerce another (usually the government) in furtherance of specific objectives. Mark Pollit has defined cyberterrorism as "the premeditated, politically motivated attack against information, computer systems, computer programs, and data which results in violence against non combatant targets by sub-national groups or clandestine agents." Accordingly, cyberterrorism involves activities that disrupt, corrupt, deny, or destroy information contained in computers or computer networks. Of course, not all acts of cyber crime would meet the definition of cyberterrorism.

Those unfamiliar with the term cyberterrorism simply view the concept to mean an attack on the Internet. This is far too simplistic a view. A cyber attack could be used to destroy not only the electronic, but also the physical infrastructures that hold the nation together. Such a scenario is possible because some of the nation's most important infrastructures, such as defense systems, chemical and hazardous materials, water supply systems, transportation, energy, finance systems and emergency services are electronically controlled by centralized computer networks called Supervisory Control and Data Acquisition (SCDA) systems. In short, SCDA systems provide the "brain power" to manage critical infrastructures. A successful cyber terror attack on even a single SCDA could cause massive economic and physical damage throughout large portions of the United States. For example, in 2002, the FB uncovered information emanating out of the Middle East that certain hackers were studying the electrical generation, transmission, water storage, distribution and gas facilities of SCDA digital systems used to control the utilities of the San Francisco Bay area in California. Theoretically, hackers could disrupt the SCDA or even take command of the system in order to disable the flood gates or control hundreds of thousands of volts of electric energy. In fact, this type of activity has already occurred.

In 2002, a hacker was arrested in Australia for breaking into the SCDA of an Australian sewage and water treatment plant and directing the pumping of one million liters of sewage into the environment. This was the first reported instance of a hacker successfully breaking into a critical infrastructure and causing massive damage. It is a harbinger of things to come.

To be sure, the activity of all kinds of cyber crime is on the increase. A study released in June 2004 found that cyber attacks on financial institutions have more than doubled from the previous year. Studies regularly demonstrate that the majority of Internet professionals believe a major attack on Wall Street or other banking institutions is imminent. It is well known that al-Qa'eda is especially attracted to financial institutions where they can steal funds, disrupt day-to-day business, or even create a major assault on the system to cause panic. A coordinated cyber attack could mean far more than the inconvenience of shutting down an ATM machine. It could encompass the transfer of millions of dollars from banking accounts.

Apart from a cyber attack, law enforcement must also consider a scenario in which terrorists conduct an actual conventional explosives attack on a SCDA or its equivalent, perhaps in conjunction with a cyber attack. A terrorist suicide attack aimed at a building that contains a major Internet service provider would be devastating.

Other possibilities for attack are equally possible. In a 2004 article in *Computerworld* magazine, security expert Peiter Zatka expressed concerns about a different type of cyber threat. Zatka warned that the real destruction might not occur from cyber attacks, but from insider threats. An insider threat exists when a hacker infiltrates an internal network and then, instead of causing an immediate denial of service or other type of harm, remains invisible inside the network in order to spy. The infiltrators use a technique called "sniffing" in order to acquire account information needed to access the network. This allows the interceptors the ability to obtain all the information that passes along the network line, including usernames and passwords.

Remaining undetected, the insider often alters encryption and communication applications in order to copy input and output data from the control terminals to various hidden sections on the system. Universities and network service providers are tempting targets for the harvesting of accounts and credentials. In testimony before the United States Senate in 2004, the Deputy Director of the FBI's cyberterrorism division stated: "The FBI predicts that terrorist groups will either develop or hire hackers, particularly for the purpose of complementing large scale attacks with cyberattacks." There is no doubt that al-Qa'eda-styled terrorists are studying means to attack the West's infrastructure by means of cyber space. If they are successful, the world could suffer an "electronic Pearl Harbor."

Perhaps a more useful attempt to capture the concept of cyberterrorism can be found in a recent Congressional Research Service Report by John Rollins and Clay Wilson. In the report, the authors break cyberterrorism down into two categories:

- Effects-based: Cyberterrorim exists when computer attacks result in effects that are disruptive enough to generate fear comparable to a traditional act of terrorism, even if done by criminals [as opposed to terrorists].
- Intent-based: Cyberterrorism exists when unlawful or politically motivated computer attacks are done to intimidate or coerce a government or people to further a political objective, or to cause grave harm or severe economic damage.

8.2 PATRIOT Act Provisions

Without question, the most well known piece of legislation associated with the terror attacks of September 11, 2001, is the PATRIOT Act. Designed as a tool to assist law enforcement to disrupt terrorist cells and their base of operations, the PATRIOT Act was passed by an overwhelming majority of the Congress and signed into law by President Bush on October 26, 2001, and renewed with amendments on March 26, 2006.

The PATRIOT Act contains a mixed variety of criminal provisions aimed at both the investigation of suspected terrorists and the disruption of the sources of funding and support for terrorist organizations. However, because almost all of the provisions in the PATRIOT Act amend or add language to existing federal statues, it is often difficult to encapsulate the full impact of many of the provisions at first glance. In terms of cyberterrorism, a number of legislative changes were instituted that expanded the ability of both law enforcement and intelligence agencies regarding surveillance and investigative powers. In short, the PATRIOT Act allows federal authorities far greater freedom in monitoring the Internet and provides for a streamlined system of sharing gathered information with other federal and state agencies.

The PATRIOT Act authorizes electronic communications interception for the collection of evidence related to terrorism, computer fraud, and abuse at § 201 and § 202. The Act also clarifies the definition of "protected computers" and increases fines and prison terms for damage at § 814. Other important tools are found in the ability of law enforcement agents to employ "pen registers," "trap and trace" devices, "sneak and peek" searches, and "roving wiretaps" (which permits surveillance on the person and not, for example, on the phone or phone number). Section 214 of the PATRIOT Act is entitled: "Pen Register and Trap and Trace Authority under FISA." This section expands the scope of the Foreign Intelligence Surveillance Act of 1978 (FISA) and provides greater powers to the FISA courts to grant court orders for surveillance.

Section 217 sets out detailed definitions regarding interception of computer trespasser communications. Among other things it clearly defines "wire communications," electronic communications," "user," and "computer trespasser." A computer trespasser "means any person who accesses a protected computer without authorization and thus has no reasonable expectation of privacy in any communication transmitted to, through, or from the protected computer."

In addition, both the PATRIOT Act at § 214 and the Cyber Security and Enhancement Act (CSEA) have eased the warrant and subpoena requirements under the old Electronic Communications Privacy Act of 1986 (ECPA). Under the CSEA (which amends certain sections of Title 18 of the United States Code), the government official need not obtain a warrant if he has a "good faith" belief regarding the prevention of death or serious bodily harm. In addition, the CSEA amends 18 U.S.C. § 3125(a)(1) to allow a government official to use a pen register or a trap and trace device without a warrant or a court order if there is a "threat to national security and an ongoing attack on a protected computer system."

In traditional terms, a pen register is simply a process that collects the outgoing phone numbers from a specific telephone line, while a trap and trace device captures the incoming numbers placed to a specific phone or computer line. Prior to the enactment of the PATRIOT Act, pen registers and trap devices could only be used to intercept the numbers dialed or transmitted on the telephone line that was specifically attached to the device. In addition, the old statutory language limited the use of such devises to telephone lines. Understanding the fantastic growth in electronic devices used to communicate information, the PATRIOT Act redefined pen register to mean "a device or process which records or decodes dialing, routing, addressing, or signaling information transmitted by an instrument or facility from which a wire or electronic communication is transmitted."

In short, the use of pen registers under the PATRIOT Act now allows for the tapping of all sorts of private activity on the Internet and allows law enforcement to collect some private information communicated even from personal e-mails. A pen register and trap and trace device that is used in association with the Internet allows federal agencies to capture all the email headers going to and from an email account, list all servers that a suspect accesses, track anyone that accesses a certain web page and track all web pages that a particular suspect may access. Thus, armed with the new definitions, pen registers and trap and trace now allow federal agencies to include not only telephone lines, but also the Internet, electronic mail, Web surfing and any other form of electronic communication. Although the law prohibits the collection of "content," this can be an ambiguous term—valuable data can still be collected that is more personal than a home telephone number.

Another example of the PATRIOT Act providing an avenue to link the private industry and the government is § 105, which allows the United States Secret Service to develop a national network of Electronic Crimes Task Forces (ECTF). The goal of this section of the Act is to take a formula designed by the United States Secret Service and spread that concept throughout the continental United States. The model is based on the New York Electronic Crimes Task Force, a task force created to combat various forms of electronic crimes, including potential terrorist attacks against critical infrastructure and financial payments. Since it's inception in 1995, the New York Electronic Crimes Task Force has initiated investigations resulting in more than 800 people being charged with computer crimes that resulted in losses exceeding $500 million. In 2002, the New York Task Force was comprised of over 50 law enforcement agencies, 100 private companies and nine regional universities.

Since the passage of the PATRIOT Act, the United States Secret Service has begun operating these task forces all over the United States, including locations in San Francisco, Las Vegas, Los Angeles, Dallas, Houston, Miami, Chicago, Cleveland, Boston, New York, Washington DC, Charlotte and Columbia. These ECTF's are designed to adapt to the type of industry that is prevalent in that geographical area. Since combating cyberterrorism as a partnership is imperative, the addition of private corporations is a pivotal component to the success of the ECTF and is a partnership that not only enhances the role of law enforcement, but provides mutually beneficial rewards for private corporations. The private sector is able to directly bring issues to the ECTF that affect their particular industry and do so in a secure law enforcement environment. Private corporations are also able to view how criminals violate current computer technology, and therefore, they are better able to protect their own corporate assets. One of the many perks for the government is that it is able to connect with companies that have a particular expertise and resources that many law enforcement agencies are lacking. One such example is AT&T Laboratories. AT&T is able to break encryption codes with greater speed than most law enforcement entities and this can be invaluable in an investigation, particularly when gathering evidence in an expeditious manner.

To even the cursory viewer, the advances in technology have caused a shift in law enforcement techniques that are stretching the protections of the Constitution's Fourth Amendment (unreasonable searches and seizures). For example, one area that is not covered in the PATRIOT Act involves the question of whether law enforcement should be able to unscramble an encrypted communication back into a readable form. It is common knowledge that sophisticated terrorists are now using cloaking devices provided by encryption companies to keep police from reading their communications. Thus, even if law enforcement can intercept the scrambled communications sent by terror suspects, they have no way of translating the information back into readable form. Consequently, legislation is probably necessary to more fully force encryption companies to provide a "back door" to allow law enforcement agencies access.

8.3 Prosecuting Cyberterrorism

Intending to reduce "hacking" of computer systems, Congress passed the Computer Fraud & Abuse Act in 1986. It was amended in 1994, 1996 and in 2001 by the PATRIOT Act. Under § 218, the PATRIOT Act increased the scope and penalties associated with hackers—violators only need to intend to cause damage generally, and a second offense can lead to a 20 year prison sentence. In addition, in response to the threat of cyberterrorism various states have enacted legislation which either recognizes the threat of cyberterrorism or defines cyberterrorism and provides for prosecution. Although the number of federal and state criminal prosecutions are small in number, civil actions derived out of the commercial code to respond to unfair competition are also used (U.C.A. 1953 § 13-5a-102).

UNITED STATES v. MITRA

United States Court of Appeals, Seventh Circuit

405 F.3d 492 (2005)

EASTERBROOK, Circuit Judge. Wisconsin's capital city uses a computer-based radio system for police, fire, ambulance, and other emergency communications. The Smartnet II, made by Motorola, spreads traffic across 20 frequencies. One is designated for control. A radio unit (mobile or base) uses the control channel to initiate a conversation. Computer hardware and software assigns the conversation to an open channel, and it can link multiple roaming units into "talk groups" so that officers in the field can hold joint conversations. This is known as a "trunking system" and makes efficient use of radio spectrum, so that 20 channels can support hundreds of users. If the control channel is interfered with, however, remote units will show the message "no system" and communication will be impossible.

Between January and August 2003 mobile units in Madison encountered occasional puzzling "no signal" conditions. On Halloween of that year the "no system" condition spread citywide; a powerful signal had blanketed all of the City's communications towers and prevented the computer from receiving, on the control channel, data essential to parcel traffic among the other 19 channels. Madison was hosting between 50,000 and 100,000 visitors that day. When disturbances erupted, public safety departments were unable to coordinate their activities because the radio system was down. Although the City repeatedly switched the control channel for the Smartnet system, a step that temporarily restored service, the interfering signal changed channels too and again blocked the system's use. On November 11, 2003, the attacker changed tactics. Instead of blocking the system's use, he sent signals directing the Smartnet base station to keep channels open, and at the end of each communication the attacker appended a sound, such as a woman's sexual moan.

By then the City had used radio direction finders to pin down the source of the intruding signals. Police arrested Rajib Mitra, a student in the University of Wisconsin's graduate business school. They found the radio hardware and computer gear that he had used to monitor communications over the Smartnet system, analyze how it operated, and send the signals that took control of the system. Mitra, who in 2000 had received a B.S. in computer science from the University, possessed two other credentials for this kind of work: criminal convictions (in 1996 and 1998) for hacking into computers in order to perform malicious mischief. A jury convicted Mitra of two counts of intentional interference with computer-related systems used in interstate commerce. See *18 U.S.C. § 1030(a)(5)*. He has been sentenced to 96 months' imprisonment. On appeal he says that his conduct does not violate *§ 1030*—and that, if it does, the statute exceeds Congress's commerce power.

Section 1030(a)(5) provides that whoever

(A)

(i) knowingly causes the transmission of a program, information, code, or command, and as a result of such conduct, intentionally causes damage without authorization, to a protected computer;

(ii) intentionally accesses a protected computer without authorization, and as a result of such conduct, recklessly causes damage; or

(iii) intentionally accesses a protected computer without authorization, and as a result of such conduct, causes damage; and

(B) by conduct described in clause (i), (ii), or (iii) of subparagraph (A), caused (or, in the case of an attempted offense, would, if completed, have caused)—

(i) loss to 1 or more persons during any 1-year period (and, for purposes of an investigation, prosecution, or other proceeding brought by the United States only, loss resulting from a related course of conduct affecting 1 or more other protected computers) aggregating at least $5,000 in value;

(ii) the modification or impairment, or potential modification or impairment, of the medical examination, diagnosis, treatment, or care of 1 or more individuals;

(iii) physical injury to any person;

(iv) a threat to public health or safety; or

(v) damage affecting a computer system used by or for a government entity in furtherance of the administration of justice, national defense, or national security ...

shall be punished as provided in subsection (c) of this section.

Subsection (e)(1) defines "computer" as "an electronic, magnetic, optical, electrochemical, or other high speed data processing device performing logical, arithmetic, or storage functions, and includes any data storage facility or communications facility directly related to or operating in conjunction with such device, but such term does not include an automated typewriter or typesetter, a portable hand held calculator, or other similar device." Subsection (e)(2)(B) defines a "protected computer" to include any computer "used in interstate or foreign commerce or communication." Finally, subsection (e)(8) defines "damage" to mean "any impairment to the integrity or availability of data, a program, a system, or information."

The prosecutor's theory is that Smartnet II is a "computer" because it contains a chip that performs high-speed processing in response to signals received on the control channel, and as a whole is a "communications facility directly related to or operating in conjunction" with that computer chip. It is a "protected computer" because it is used in "interstate … communication"; the frequencies it uses have been allocated by the Federal Communications Commission for police, fire, and other public-health services. Mitra's transmissions on Halloween included "information" that was received by the Smartnet. Data that Mitra sent interfered with the way the computer allocated communications to the other 19 channels and stopped the flow of information among public-safety officers. This led to "damage" by causing a "no system" condition citywide, impairing the "availability of … a system, or information" and creating "a threat to public health or safety" by knocking out police, fire, and emergency communications. *See § 1030(a)(5)(A)(i), (B)(iv).* The extraneous sounds tacked onto conversations on November 11 also are "information" sent to the "protected computer," and produce "damage" because they impair the "integrity" of the official communications. This time subsection *§ 1030(a)(5)(B)(v)* is what makes the meddling a crime, because Mitra hacked into a governmental safety-related communications system.

Mitra concedes that he is guilty if the statute is parsed as we have done. But he submits that Congress could not have intended the statute to work this way. Mitra did not invade a bank's system to steal financial information, or erase data on an ex-employer's system, see *United States v. Lloyd, 269 F.3d 228 (3d Cir.2001)*, or plaster a corporation's web site with obscenities that drove away customers, or unleash a worm that slowed and crashed computers across the world, see *United States v. Morris, 928 F.2d 504 (2d Cir.1991)*, or break into military computers to scramble a flight of interceptors to meet a nonexistent threat, or plant covert programs in computers so that they would send spam without the owners' knowledge. All he did was gum up a radio system. Surely that cannot be a federal crime, Mitra insists, even if the radio system contains a computer. Every cell phone and cell tower is a "computer" under this statute's definition; so is every iPod, every wireless base station in the corner coffee shop, and many another gadget. Reading *§ 1030* to cover all of these, and police radio too, would give the statute wide coverage, which by Mitra's lights means that Congress cannot have contemplated such breadth.

Well of course Congress did not contemplate or intend this particular application of the statute. Congress is a "they" and not an "it"; a committee lacks a brain (or, rather, has so many brains with so many different objectives that it is almost facetious to impute a joint goal or purpose to the collectivity). See Kenneth A. Shepsle, *Congress is a "They," Not an "It": Legislative Intent as Oxymoron, 12 Int'l Rev. L. & Econ. 239 (1992)*. Legislation is an objective text approved in constitutionally prescribed ways; its scope is not limited by the cerebrations of those who voted for or signed it into law.

Electronics and communications change rapidly, while each legislator's imagination is limited. Trunking communications systems came to market after 1984, when the first version of *§ 1030* was enacted, and none of the many amendments to this statute directly addresses them. But although legislators may not know about trunking communications systems, they *do* know that complexity is endemic in the modern world and that each passing year sees new developments. That's why they write general statutes rather than enacting a list of particular forbidden acts. And it is the statutes they enacted—not the thoughts they did or didn't have—that courts must apply. What Congress would have done about trunking systems, had they been present to the mind of any Senator or Representative, is neither here nor there. See *West Virginia University Hospitals, Inc. v. Casey, 499 U.S. 83, 100-01, 111 S.Ct. 1138, 113 L.Ed.2d 68 (1991)*.

Section 1030 is general. Exclusions show just *how* general. Subsection (e)(1) carves out automatic typewriters, typesetters, and handheld calculators; this shows that other devices with embedded processors and software are covered. As more devices come to have built-in intelligence, the effective scope of the statute grows. This might prompt Congress to amend the statute but does not authorize the judiciary to give the existing version less coverage than its language portends. See *National Broiler Marketing Ass'n v. United States, 436 U.S. 816, 98 S.Ct. 2122, 56 L.Ed.2d 728 (1978)*. What protects people who accidentally erase songs on an iPod, trip over (and thus disable) a wireless base station, or rear-end a car and set off a computerized airbag, is not judicial creativity but the requirements of the statute itself: the damage must be intentional, it must be substantial (at least $5,000 or bodily injury or danger to public safety), and the computer must operate in interstate or foreign commerce.

Let us turn, then, to the commerce requirement. The system operated on spectrum licensed by the FCC. It met the statutory definition because the interference affected "communication." Mitra observes that his interference did not affect any radio system on the other side of a state line, yet this is true of many cell-phone calls, all of which are part of interstate commerce because the electromagnetic spectrum is securely within the federal regulatory domain. See, e.g., *Radovich v. National Football League, 352 U.S. 445, 453, 77 S.Ct. 390, 1 L.Ed.2d 456 (1957)*; *Federal Radio Commission v. Nelson Brothers Bond & Mortgage Co., 289 U.S. 266, 279, 53 S.Ct. 627, 77 L.Ed. 1166 (1933)*. Congress may regulate all channels of interstate commerce; the spectrum is one of them. See *United States v. Lopez, 514 U.S. 549, 558, 115 S.Ct. 1624, 131 L.Ed.2d 626 (1995)*; *United States v. Morrison, 529 U.S. 598, 608-09, 120 S.Ct. 1740, 146 L.Ed.2d 658 (2000)*. Mitra's apparatus was more powerful than the Huygens probe that recently returned pictures and other data from Saturn's moon Titan. Anyway, the statute does not ask whether the person who caused the damage acted in interstate commerce; it protects computers (and computerized communication systems) used in such commerce, no matter how the harm is inflicted. Once the *computer* is used in interstate commerce, Congress has the power to protect it from a local hammer blow, or from a local data packet that sends it haywire. (Indeed, Mitra concedes that he could have been prosecuted, consistent with the Constitution, for broadcasting an unauthorized signal. See *47 U.S.C. § 301, § 401(c)*.) Section 1030 is within the national power as applied to computer-based channel-switching communications systems.

Mitra offers a fallback argument that application of *§ 1030* to his activities is so unexpected that it offends the due process clause. But what cases such as *Bouie v. Columbia, 378 U.S. 347, 84 S.Ct. 1697, 12 L.Ed.2d 894 (1964)*, hold is that a court may not apply a clear criminal statute in a way that a reader could not anticipate, or put a vague criminal statute to a new and unexpected use. Mitra's problem is not that *§ 1030* has been turned in a direction that would have surprised reasonable people; it is that a broad statute has been applied *exactly as written*, while he wishes that it had not been. There is no constitutional obstacle to enforcing broad but clear statutes. See *Rogers v. Tennessee, 532 U.S. 451, 458-62, 121 S.Ct. 1693, 149 L.Ed.2d 697 (2001)* (discussing *Bouie's* rationale and limits). The statute itself gives all the notice that the Constitution requires.

During deliberations the jury inquired about the meaning of the word "intentionally." The judge referred them to the instructions, which included a definition. Mitra says that the judge should have drafted a new definition, because the first must have been confusing (though he concedes that it was correct). This sort of problem is one for the district judge to resolve on the spot; there would be little point in Monday morning quarterbacking.

Sentencing requires but little discussion. The district judge added offense levels under *U.S.S.G. § 2B1.1(b)(13)(A)(iii) and (B)* after concluding that Mitra had disrupted a "critical infrastructure." (Our citations are to the 2003 Manual, which the district judge used; the current version is substantively identical but numbered a little differently.) Application Note 12 defines that term; Mitra concedes that an emergency radio system fits the definition. Emergency services are one of the note's examples. Once again his argument takes the form that the authors of this language just couldn't have meant what they said. It is not as if the note were a linguistic garble, or that it is impossible to fathom why any sane person would think that the penalty for crippling an emergency-communication system on which lives may depend should be higher than the penalty for hacking into a web site to leave a rude message. The district judge was right to apply the guideline and note as written.

Mitra was sentenced before *United States v. Booker, ____ U.S. ____ , 125 S.Ct. 738, 160 L.Ed.2d 621 (2005)*, and did not argue in the district court that the sixth amendment limits the judge's role in sentencing. Review now is limited to a search for plain error. The approach developed in *United States v. Paladino, 401 F.3d 471 (7th Cir.2005)*, applies to this sentence, which falls within a properly calculated guideline range. Accordingly, although the judgment of conviction is affirmed, we remand to the district court under the terms of *Paladino* so that the district judge may inform us whether the additional discretion provided by *Booker* 's remedial holding would affect Mitra's sentence.

8.4 Protection from Cyberterrorist Attack

On April 23, 2000, Vitek Boden was apprehended during a routine traffic stop in Queensland, Australia. Boden was found in possession of a stolen computer and radio transmitter which he used to turn his vehicle into a mobile "command center." Boden had breached the SCDA system of an Australian water and sewage treatment plant off Australia's Sunshine Coast. Over the course of two months Boden directed the system, on forty-six separate occasions, to pump massive amounts of raw sewage into the local environment. This was the first reported instance of a hacker successfully breaking into a critical infrastructure, causing massive damage and being apprehended.

The fear of cyberterrorism has caused at least 41 states to pass non-release provisions to their state Freedom of Information laws (patterned after the federal FOIA) and state Sunshine laws (providing for public access to government meetings). The thrust of most of these non-release provisions is to keep information out of the hands of potential terrorists in order to limit the possibility of a disabling attack on the critical infrastructure. For instance, the Ohio Revised Code makes specific exceptions to the Ohio Open Government law regarding non-release of information related to *acts of terrorism*, *critical infrastructures*, and *security records*. Under § 149.433(B): "A record kept by a public office that is a security record or an infrastructure record is not a public record under § 149.433 of the Revised Code and is not subject to mandatory release or disclosure under that section." Under § 149.433(A)(3), the term "security records" is broadly construed to include:

(a) Any record that contains information directly used for protecting or maintaining the security of a public office against attack, interference, or sabotage, and

(b) Any record assembled, prepared, or maintained by a public office or public body to prevent, mitigate, or respond to acts of terrorism, to include any of the following:

(i) Those portions of records containing specific and unique vulnerability assessments or specific and unique response plans either of which is intended to prevent or mitigate acts of terrorism, and communication codes or deployment plans of law enforcement or emergency response personnel;

(ii) Specific intelligence information and specific investigative records shared by federal and international law enforcement agencies with state and local law enforcement and public safety agencies; and

(iii) National security records classified under federal executive order and not subject to public disclosure under federal law that are shared by federal agencies, and other records related to national security briefings to assist state and local government with domestic preparedness for acts of terrorism.

The term "infrastructure record" under the Ohio Revised Code § 149.433(A)(2) means:

Any record that discloses the configuration of a public office's critical systems including, but not limited to, communication, computer, electrical, mechanical, ventilation, water, and plumbing systems, security codes, or the infrastructure or structural configuration of the building in which a public office is located." However, the term infrastructure record "does not mean a simple floor plan that discloses only the spatial relationship of components of a public office or the building in which a public office is located.

The term "act of terrorism" under the Ohio Revised Code § 149.433(A)(1) has the same statutory meaning as is found in Ohio Revised Code § 2909.21:

'Act of terrorism' means an act that is committed within or outside the territorial jurisdiction of this state or the United States, that constitutes a specified offense if committed in this state or constitutes an offense in any jurisdiction within or outside the territorial jurisdiction of the United States containing all of the essential elements of a specified offense, and that is intended to do one or more of the following:

(1) Intimidate or coerce a civilian population;

(2) Influence the policy of any government by intimidation or coercion; or

(3) Affect the conduct of any government by the act that constitutes the offence.

Limitations have also been imposed on the federal FOIA. These restrictions have drawn wide and vocal criticism from a variety of sources and leads to the question: "How much information should be suppressed in the interests of national security?"

LIVING RIVERS, INC. v. UNITED STATES BUREAU OR RECLAMATION
United States District Court, D. Utah, Central Division
272 F.Supp.2d 1313 (2003)

CAMPBELL, District Judge. Plaintiff Living Rivers, Inc. ("Living Rivers"), a non-profit, incorporated environmental group, claims that Defendant the United States Bureau of Reclamation (the "BOR") violated the Freedom of Information Act ("FOIA") by refusing to disclose documents that Living Rivers requested under FOIA. The documents are inundation maps prepared by the BOR for the areas below Hoover Dam and Glen Canyon Dam. The BOR contends that disclosure of the maps could endanger the dams and those who live downstream from the dams, and therefore are exempt from disclosure under FOIA. The matter is before the court on the parties' cross-motions for summary judgment. For the reasons set for below, the court GRANTS BOR's motion and denies Living Rivers' motion.

BACKGROUND

I. Procedural Background

On September 19, 2001, Living Rivers requested pursuant to FOIA that the BOR disclose all inundation maps, including those pertaining to dam failure, for the areas below Hoover Dam and Glen Canyon Dam. On November 9 and November 19, 2001, the BOR denied the requests on the ground that the maps were exempt from disclosure under FOIA's Exemption 2. The BOR explained that the inundation maps related to the BOR's internal practices and that disclosure of the maps would risk circumvention of a statute or regulation. Living Rivers appealed the decisions administratively on December 10, 2001. On April 2, 2002, the United States Department of the Interior—of which the BOR is a part—denied the appeal. On July 3, 2002, Living Rivers filed this lawsuit.

II. Factual Background

In support of their motion, the BOR submitted the Declaration of Larry L. Todd. (Todd Decl., Ex. 3, attached to BOR's Mem. in Support of Def. BOR's Cross Mot. for Summ. J. and in Opp'n to Pl.'s Mot. for Summ. J.) Mr. Todd has been the Director of Security, Safety and Law Enforcement of the BOR since June 30, 2002. This position was created after September 11, 2001. Before September 11, security, safety and law enforcement matters were handled by the Director of Operations. Mr. Todd held that position until his present position was created.

Mr. Todd explained that the BOR created the maps to allow evaluation of the effects of dam failure, to protect the public downstream of the dam from the consequences of dam failure, and to assist federal and local law enforcement and emergency officials by providing timely and concise emergency information in the event of dam failure. In addition, the inundation maps are a key element in allowing the BOR to determine the risks at various dams and to set priorities in addressing issues of dam safety.

Mr. Todd described the information shown in the inundation maps:

> Inundation maps show which downstream areas and communities would be flooded and are at risk in the event of a dam failure. The maps reveal populated areas, communities and recreational areas

that would be at risk due to dam failure. The maps also show critical infrastructure, such as power plant sites, that would be affected by the failure. The maps show estimated travel times for the flood progression at key locations, which are usually communities or populated areas. Most of the maps also show estimated flow volumes and water depths at these key locations.

According to Mr. Todd, "[t]he inundation maps include information that is unique and not otherwise readily ascertainable by the public." Therefore, "[t]he precise nature of flood damage that would result from a failure of the dams, as depicted in the inundation maps, is not known by the general public."

Mr. Todd explained that, in his opinion,

[t]he information shown on the inundation maps would comprise dam security and the security of the surrounding populations if the maps fell into the hands of a terrorist or other person intending to harm one or more of the Colorado River dams (collectively, "terrorist"). The inundation maps would give the terrorist information about the amount of damage that could be caused by destroying a dam. Because the inundation maps are based upon a worst-case scenario, they present a broad view of the extent of damage resulting from breaching the dam, thus making the dam a more attractive target to the terrorist.

In addition to identifying the populations that would be affected by the destruction of a dam, the inundation maps could be used to identify critical infrastructures, buildings, and facilities which would be destroyed by attacking the dam. This information too is valuable to terrorists.

Because the inundation maps show flood travel times and water depths, terrorists could use the inundation maps to help plan and execute sequenced attacks, which could include attacks on bridges and roads to cut off evacuation routes or attacks on communications facilities to disrupt emergency response.

Mr. Todd described the measures that the BOR takes to ensure the security of the inundation maps. These include keeping the maps in locked areas and limiting the distribution of the maps to those who "demonstrate a 'need to know' [including State and Federal law enforcement and emergency officials] in accordance with the criteria set forth in the BOR directives."

ANALYSIS

I. The Legal Standard for Summary Judgment in FOIA Cases

"FOIA generally provides that the public has a right of access, enforceable in court, to federal agency records." *Audubon Soc'y v. United States Forest Serv., 104 F.3d 1201, 1203 (10th Cir.1997).* FOIA requires federal agencies to disclose records to the public upon request, "unless the requested records fall within one or more of nine categories of exempt material." *Assassination Archives and Research Ctr. v. Cent. Intelligence Agency, 177 F.Supp.2d 1, 5 (D.C.Cir.2001); see also Audubon, 104 F.3d at 1203.* If a requested document contains exempt information, the agency must release "[a]ny reasonably segregable portion" after deleting exempt portions. *5 U.S.C. § 552(b); see also Anderson v. Dep't of Health & Human Servs., 907 F.2d 936, 941 (10th Cir.1990)* (stating that the district court "may not simply conclude that an entire file or body of information is protected without consideration of the component parts").

"FOIA is to be broadly construed in favor of disclosure, and its exemptions are to be narrowly construed …. The federal agency resisting disclosure bears the burden of justifying nondisclosure." *Audubon, 104 F.3d at 1203* (internal citation omitted). District courts review de novo agency decisions to withhold information requested under FOIA. *See Anderson, 907 F.2d at 941.*

Here, the BOR claimed initially that its inundation maps fit under Exemption 2, which permits withholding of information "related solely to the internal personnel rules and practices of an agency." *5 U.S.C. § 552(b)(2)*. On this review of the agency action, the BOR claims that it also need not disclose its inundation maps pursuant to Exemptions 7(E) and 7(F), *5 U.S.C. § 552(b)(7)*, which pertain to information compiled for law enforcement purposes, and Exemption 3, *5 U.S.C. § 552(b)(3)*, which incorporates nondisclosure provisions of other federal statutes.

II. Exemption 2

As stated above, Exemption 2 exempts disclosure of documents "related solely to the internal personnel rules and practices of an agency." *5 U.S.C. § 552(b)(2)*. The so called "Low 2" approach to Exemption 2 provides that the exemption only applies to "[p]redominantly internal documents that deal with trivial administrative matters." *See Schiller v. Nat'l Labor Relations Bd., 964 F.2d 1205, 1207 (D.C.Cir.1992)*. But the BOR initially denied Living Rivers's FOIA requests under the expansive, "High 2" interpretation of Exemption 2.

At least four circuits have adopted the "High 2" interpretation of Exemption 2. *See Audubon, 104 F.3d at 1203-04, 1204 n. 1* (citing *Schwaner v. Dep't of Air Force, 898 F.2d 793, 794 (D.C.Cir.1990), Caplan v. Bureau of Alcohol, Tobacco & Firearms, 587 F.2d 544, 547 (2d Cir.1978); Kaganove v. Envtl. Prot. Agency, 856 F.2d 884, 889 (7th Cir.1988),* and *Hardy v. Bureau of Alcohol, Tobacco & Firearms, 631 F.2d 653, 656 (9th Cir.1980))*. The Tenth Circuit has neither adopted nor rejected the High 2 interpretation. *See Audubon, 104 F.3d at 1204; Hale v. United States Dep't of Justice, 973 F.2d 894, 902 (10th Cir.1992)* (stating that Exemption 2 "possibly" encompasses "more substantial matters that might be the subject of legitimate public interest *if* the disclosure of the latter might pose a risk of circumvention of lawful agency regulations"), *overruled in later appeal on other grounds, 2 F.3d 1055 (10th Cir.1993)*.

Under the High 2 approach, government information is exempted if: "(1) the information falls within the language of the exemption-that is, it relates to the 'internal personnel rules and practices' of the agency and is 'predominantly internal'; and (2) its disclosure would risk circumvention of federal statutes or regulations." *Audubon, 104 F.3d at 1203-04* (quoting *Crooker v. Bureau of Alcohol, Tobacco & Firearms, 670 F.2d 1051, 1074 (D.C.Cir.1981))*.

Living Rivers contends that the inundation maps fail both prongs of the High 2 test. As regards the first prong of the test, Living Rivers, relying on Tenth Circuit case law, argues that the inundation maps do not relate to the BOR's "personnel" rules and practices and therefore do not fall within the statutory language of Exemption 2. But the BOR contends that because the maps are "predominantly internal," they are covered by Exemption 2. In *Audubon,* a case on which Living Rivers relies, the Tenth Circuit held that the requested maps, which identified specific owl nest sites in Arizona and New Mexico, were "not sufficiently 'related to internal personnel rules and practices' and would therefore fail the first prong" of the High 2 exemption if the court were to adopt that analysis. *Audubon, 104 F.3d at 1204*. The court addressed the Forest Service's argument that the "maps [were] related to agency practices because they assist[ed] Forest Service personnel in their management duties." *Id.* The court emphasized that the phrase " 'internal personnel' modifies both 'rules' and 'practices.' " *Id.* "Therefore, the proper inquiry [was] not whether the owl maps relate[d] to the 'agency practices,' but whether they relate[d] to the '*personnel* practices' of the Forest Service." *Id.* (emphasis in original). The court concluded that "[i]t stretch[ed] the language of the exemption too far to conclude that owl maps 'relate[d]' to personnel practices of the Forest Service." *Id.*

As in *Audubon,* the BOR here argues that the inundation maps are related to agency practices and personnel because they assist the BOR in its law enforcement duties. The BOR gives as an example the fact that BOR personnel "utilize the maps to develop their own emergency response plans." (Def.'s Supp. Mem. at 20.) As Living Rivers points out, however, the maps neither provide instructions nor contain rules or practices for BOR personnel. The court agrees with Living Rivers and concludes that the first prong of the High 2 exemption test has not been met.

III. Exemption 7

At the administrative level, the BOR did not cite Exemption 7 when it refused to disclose the inundation maps to Living Rivers. Because FOIA directs district courts to review agency actions de novo, an agency may raise a particular exemption for the first time in the district court. *See 5 U.S.C. § 552(a)(4)(B)* (providing for de novo review); *Young v. CIA, 972 F.2d 536, 538 (4th Cir.1992)* (stating that "an agency does not waive FOIA exemptions by not raising them during the administrative process"); *see also Ford v. West, 149 F.3d 1190, available at 1998 WL 317561, at *1 (10th Cir.1998)* (unpublished decision) (addressing exemption raised for the first time in district court). Further, Living Rivers does not argue that the BOR's initial reliance on Exception 2 precludes the BOR from now relying on other exemptions.

Exemption 7 prevents disclosure of "information compiled for law enforcement purposes" when producing such information

> (E) would disclose techniques and procedures for law enforcement investigations or prosecutions, or would disclose guidelines for law enforcement investigations or prosecutions if such disclosure could reasonably be expected to risk circumvention of the law, or (F) could reasonably be expected to endanger the life or physical safety of any individual. *5 U.S.C. § 552(b)(7).*

The threshold issue under Exemption 7 is whether the BOR may be classified as a "law enforcement agency." *See Church of Scientology v. United States Dep't of the Army, 611 F.2d 738, 748 (9th Cir.1979); see also Fine v. United States Dep't of Energy, Office of Inspector General, 823 F.Supp. 888, 907 (D.N.M.1993).* Courts have stated that "[a]n agency which has a clear law enforcement mandate … need only establish a 'rational nexus' between enforcement of a federal law and the document for which an exemption is claimed." *Pratt v. Webster, 673 F.2d 408, 420 (D.C.Cir.1982)* (quoting *Church of Scientology, 611 F.2d at 748*). "An agency with both administrative and law enforcement functions must demonstrate that its purpose in compiling the particular document fell within its sphere of enforcement authority." *Fine, 823 F.Supp. at 907.* In *Pratt,* the D.C. Circuit stated that "a court must scrutinize with some skepticism the particular purpose claimed [by a mixed-function agency] for disputed documents redacted under FOIA Exemption 7." *Pratt, 673 F.2d at 418.*

Living Rivers and the BOR disagree on the scope of Exemption 7's "law enforcement purpose" requirement. The BOR contends that materials compiled for purposes of protecting against and preventing violations of law, as opposed to only "the more traditional law enforcement functions of investigation and prosecution," fall within Exemption 7's scope. (*See* Def.'s Supp. Mem. at 8.) Living Rivers claims that to qualify as law enforcement materials, the materials "must involve the detection or punishment of violations of law." (Pl.'s Reply Mem. at 5) (quoting *Allnutt v. United States Dep't of Justice, 99 F.Supp.2d 673, 680 (D.Md.2000)*).

The BOR relies primarily on *U.S. News & World Report v. Dep't of the Treasury,* an unpublished District of the District of Columbia decision. *See U.S. News & World Report v. Dep't of the Treasury,* No. 84-2303, 1986 U.S. Dist. LEXIS 27634, at *5 (D.D.C. Mar. 26, 1986) (unpublished decision). In *U.S. News & World Report,* the court held that the Secret Service properly withheld pursuant to Exemption 7(E) specifications and other information relating to the purchase of two armored presidential limousines, even though such information did not relate to an investigation of a specific violation of the law. *See id.* at *3-5, *8. In its discussion of Exemption 7's law enforcement purpose requirement, the court explained,

> The Secret Service is unique in that its law enforcement efforts are geared primarily towards prevention rather than apprehension. While its activities in this case, therefore, do not involve investigating someone suspected of violating the law, but center instead on its efforts to protect the President, there can be no doubt that they are directly related to the agency's statutory mandate.

Id. at *5. The court withheld information concerning the cars' specifications and components but allowed disclosure of the final, total price of the presidential cars. *Id.* at *8, *10.

Living Rivers correctly points out that the agency involved in *U.S. News & World Report,* the Secret Service, is a per se law enforcement agency. *See U.S. News & World Report,* 1986 U.S. Dist. LEXIS 27634, at *4. The standard for establishing a law enforcement purpose therefore was lower in *U.S. News & World Report* than it is for the BOR, a mixed-function agency. *See Fine, 823 F.Supp. at 907.*

Nevertheless, Congress has provided the BOR with express "law enforcement authority" to "maintain law and order and protect persons and property within Reclamation projects and on Reclamation lands." *43 U.S.C.A. § 373b(a).* Mr. Todd, the BOR's Director of Security, Safety and Law Enforcement, has stated that the BOR uses the inundation maps pursuant to the BOR's law enforcement authority. (*See* Todd Decl. at ¶¶ 8, 10-12); *see also U.S. News & World Report,* 1986 U.S. Dist. LEXIS 27634, at *5 (emphasizing that the agency activities in question were "directly related to the agency's statutory mandate"). For example, Mr. Todd explained that the maps show which downstream areas would be flooded in the event of a dam failure attack. (Todd Decl. ¶ 12.) The BOR uses the inundation maps to develop its Emergency Action Plans and to protect and alert potentially threatened people in the vicinity of the dams. (*Id.* ¶¶ 8, 11.)

Living Rivers has put forth no contrary evidence, but argues that the mere fact that the BOR *uses* the maps in law enforcement does not bring the maps under Exemption 7's scope. But the context in which an agency has currently compiled a document, rather than the purpose for which the document was originally created, determines whether it is "compiled for law enforcement purposes." *See John Doe Agency v. John Doe Corp., 493 U.S. 146, 153-54, 110 S.Ct. 471, 107 L.Ed.2d 462 (1989)* (stating that the phrase "compiled for law enforcement purposes" "seems readily to cover documents already collected by the Government originally for non-law enforcement purposes"); *KTVY-TV v. United States, 919 F.2d 1465, 1469 (10th Cir.1990), abrogated on other grounds recognized by Rosenfeld v. United States Dep't of Justice, 57 F.3d 803, 814 (9th Cir.1995);* (*see also* Def.'s Reply Mem. at 5-6).

Accordingly, the court concludes that the inundation maps are presently used and were compiled in direct relation to the BOR's statutory law enforcement mandate. The BOR therefore satisfies the first prong of Exemption 7.

A. Exemption 7(E)

The BOR contends that public disclosure of the inundation maps would cause the harms set forth in Exemption 7(E). Exemption 7(E) protects from disclosure information compiled for law enforcement purposes where release of the information "would disclose techniques and procedures for law enforcement investigations or prosecutions, or would disclose guidelines for law enforcement investigations or prosecutions if such disclosure could reasonably be expected to risk circumvention of the law." *5 U.S.C. § 552(b)(7)(E)*. The Tenth Circuit has explained that Exemption 7(E) "is to be applied only to techniques and procedures generally unknown to the public." *Hale v. United States Dep't of Justice, 973 F.2d 894, 902 (10th Cir.1992)* (quoting *Dunaway v. Webster, 519 F.Supp. 1059, 1082 (N.D.Cal.1981)), overruled in later appeal on other grounds, 2 F.3d 1055 (10th Cir.1993)*. "However, techniques and procedures may be exempt even if they are known to the public to some extent if disclosure of the circumstances of their use could lessen their effectiveness." *Id.* at 902-03.

The BOR argues that courts have applied Exemption 7(E) to information that would reveal protective and preventive techniques, procedures, or guidelines. In *Librach v. Federal Bureau of Investigation,* a case cited by the BOR, the Eighth Circuit assumed without discussion that documents that "pertain[ed] to the relocation of a witness under the Department of Justice Witness Security Program" could be withheld under "exemptions *5 U.S.C. § 552(b)(3),* 7(C), and 7(E)." *Librach v. Federal Bureau of Investigation, 587 F.2d 372, 373 (8th Cir.1978); see also U.S. News & World Report,* 1986 U.S. Dist. LEXIS 27634, at *7 (discussing *Librach, 587 F.2d at 373*). The BOR again relies upon *U.S. News & World Report,* where the court applied Exemption 7(E) to withhold the Secret Service's presidential limousine specifications. *See U.S. News & World Report,* 1986 U.S. Dist. LEXIS 27634, at *6-7. The court in *U.S. News & World Report* emphasized "the unique [preventative] nature of [the Secret Service's] function," and rejected a "wooden interpretation" of Exemption 7(E). *Id.* at *6.

The BOR argues that disclosure of the maps "could reasonably be expected to risk circumvention of the law because they would assist terrorists in assessing which potential targets of terrorism would cause the maximum damage in terms of loss of life and property." (Def.'s Supp. Mem. at 10; *see also* Todd Decl. ¶ 20.) Mr. Todd explained in his Declaration that the maps show, among other information, which communities and infrastructure would be flooded by a catastrophic breach in the dams. (*See* Todd Decl. ¶¶ 12, 14.) The BOR adds that the inundation maps' "precise, valuable information" about potential flood damage and fatalities is not well known to the public. (Def.'s Supp. Mem. at 11-12; *see also* Todd Decl. ¶¶ 23-26 (describing efforts made to keep maps from the public)).

Nevertheless, as Living Rivers points out, the BOR does not explain how the information in the maps qualifies as "techniques and procedures ... or would disclose guidelines for law enforcement investigations or prosecutions," as required by the "circumvention of law" exemption of *5 U.S.C. § 552(b)(7)(E)*. (Pl.'s Reply Mem. at 7.) The BOR's maps are not like the documents in a case such as *U.S. News & World Report,* where disclosing the requested limousine specifications would have revealed structural *techniques* that served to prevent harm. *See U.S. News & World Report,* 1986 U.S. Dist. LEXIS 27634, at *6-7. This point is arguably too legalistic. However, given the narrow construction courts must give to FOIA's exemptions, the court concludes that the BOR has failed to establish how the inundation maps "would disclose techniques and procedures … or … would disclose guidelines." *5 U.S.C. § 552(b)(7)(E)*; *see Audubon Soc'y v. United States Forest Serv., 104 F.3d 1201, 1203 (10th Cir.1997)* (stating that "FOIA is to be broadly construed in favor of disclosure, and its exemptions are to be narrowly construed").

B. Exemption 7(F)

The BOR also contends that public disclosure of the inundation maps "could reasonably be expected to endanger the life or physical safety of any individual." *5 U.S.C. § 552(b)(7)(F)*; *(see* Def.'s Supp. Mem. at 12). Exemption 7(F) is neither limited to protect the lives of "law enforcement personnel," nor to known, named individuals only. *See Garcia v. United States Dep't of Justice, 181 F.Supp.2d 356, 378 (S.D.N.Y.2002)* (applying Exemption 7(F) to protect private citizen third parties). District courts in the D.C. Circuit and the Second Circuit have stated that "[i]n evaluating the validity of an agency's invocation of Exemption 7(F), the court should 'within limits, defer to the agency's assessment of danger.'" *Id.* (quoting *Linn v. United States Dep't of Justice, Civ. A. No. 92-1406, 1995 WL 631847, at *9 (D.D.C. Aug.22, 1995)*).

The BOR contends that disclosure of the inundation maps "could reasonably place at risk the life or physical safety of those individuals who occupy the downstream areas that would be flooded by a breach of Hoover Dam or Glen Canyon Dam." (Def.'s Supp. Mem. at 13). In his declaration, Mr. Todd referred to a dam failure as a "weapon of mass destruction," mentioned that "[t]he maps show estimated travel times for the flood progression at key locations, which are usually communities of populated areas," and stated that the maps "are vital … to warn and evacuate people from potential flood zones." (Todd Decl. ¶ ¶ 15, 12, 27.) Mr. Todd also stated that "[t]errorists could use the inundation maps to estimate the extent of flooding that would be occasioned by attacking individual features of the dam. Terrorists could also use the inundation maps to compare the amount of flooding and damage that would result from attacking one dam as compared to attacking another dam." (*Id.* ¶ 20.) Mr. Todd's statements concerning risk assessment by terrorists demonstrate that the release of the maps could increase the risk of an attack on the dams.

Living Rivers suggests that the court order the BOR to submit the maps in camera, *see 5 U.S.C. § 552(a)(4)(B)*, and order the release of the portions of the maps that warrant exemption from FOIA. Living Rivers does not oppose exempting information such as "flood travel times and water depths," which could be used in aid of an attack, but contends that "the maps generally, which show the areas that would be flooded, simply do not increase the likelihood or ease of an attack." (Pl.'s Reply Mem. at 9.)

Living Rivers acknowledges that the "material that would actually aid in carrying out a terrorist attack" should be redacted from the maps and exempted. But the court is satisfied, after careful examination of Mr. Todd's declaration, that the BOR has carefully considered what material should be disclosed and what material should be withheld. Therefore, the court concludes that the BOR has satisfied its burden of justifying non-disclosure of the inundation maps.

ORDER

For the foregoing reasons, the BOR's motion for summary judgment is GRANTED and Living Rivers's motion for summary judgment is DENIED.

8.5 Government and Private Sector Partnership

One thing is certain, as the sophistication of all forms of cyber crime increases, so does the threat to the cyber world. Considering that the super highway of the cyber world is composed of hundreds of thousand of interconnected computers, servers, switches and fiber optics that allows our critical infrastructures to function, no institution is truly safe. Furthermore, since 85 to 90 percent of America's critical infrastructure is privately owned, it is imperative that the government and private industry join together in a unified manner to establish both reactive and proactive strategies. In any plan, the need for timely and accurate information is absolutely essential.

Despite the fact that cyber criminals cause businesses and consumers as much as $20 billion a year through viruses and identify fraud, technology companies have largely resisted government calls to produce better software and stronger networks. Similarly, the owners of the critical public infrastructure are equally reluctant to share necessary information about their operations with other companies or the government. In part, they are worried that their competitors will gain access to exclusive company data that is shared with the government through the FOIA or other sources. Other concerns relate to the negative response that stockholders or consumers may have should breaches become public.

Finding an effective way to encourage private industry to respond to the challenge of cyberterrorism has been problematic. The Clinton Administration took the initial steps to address the vulnerabilities of the nation's infrastructure to cyber crime. In a Presidential directive, several of the most critical infrastructures of the nation—both public and private—were identified to include telecommunications, energy, finance and emergency services. Although the Clinton directive called for a voluntary partnership between government and private industry, few private companies exhibited interest in joining the effort, citing loss of valuable information in a competitive market based economy. Two concerns were advanced. First, if a company revealed that a cyber terror event had breached their system, the revelation could cause loss of confidence in the soundness of the business. Second, if a company revealed how its security system operated, competitors might use that information to gain a competitive advantage.

On the other hand, without disclosure of information about hackers and the possible weak points of security systems, it is difficult for institutions to know what vulnerabilities exist within their security systems. One issue is certain, the sooner institutions share information about security vulnerabilities, the quicker all organizations can implement counter measures to protect themselves from cyberterrorism. In April 2000, Congress passed the Internet Integrity and Critical Infrastructure Protection Act which outlined protections regarding sharing of information.

Building on the Clinton approach, the Bush Administration has taken a number of similar steps designed to develop public-private alliances to combat cyberterrorism. Like Clinton, the Bush Administration saw the private sector as best equipped to tackle the potential threat of cyberterrorism. This premise is based on the fact that private sector technologies created cyber space and continues to evolve new avenues in the field. Accordingly, a number of new laws and policy directives have been passed to better secure the nation from a cyberterrorism attack.

The *National Strategy to Secure Cyberspace* and the *National Strategy for the Physical Protection of Critical Infrastructures and Key Assets* were released in early 2003. These two strategies are designed to help America secure the cyber world by establishing three main objectives:

(1) prevent cyber attacks against America's critical infrastructure, (2) reduce national vulnerability to cyber attacks, and (3) reduce damage and recovery time from cyber attacks when they do occur.

The main priority of the *National Strategy to Secure Cyberspace* is the establishment of a national cyberspace security response system. It calls upon the entire society—the federal government, state and local governments, the private sector and the American people—to engage in coordinated and focused efforts to secure cyberspace. While the Department of Homeland Security (DHS) is responsible for identifying and protecting against "vulnerabilities" in the information infrastructure, the Department of Justice (DOJ) is to focus on responding to "threats" presented by intentional, unlawful acts that threaten the confidentiality, integrity and availability of information networks.

In fact, the DHS is in the process of perfecting a response system that joins the government and the private sector together in order to provide for specific analysis, warning information and a crisis management response if a major cyber attack occurs. The plan also creates a national cyberspace security threat and vulnerability reduction program. This program would make an effort to identify and punish possible attackers, locate and remediate the existing vulnerabilities, and develop new systems and technology that would reduce future vulnerabilities.

As stated, the Computer Fraud and Abuse Act prohibits a variety of activities to include accessing classified information unlawfully and damaging protected computers that results in physical injury, a threat to public health or safety, or damage to a computer used for national defense or national security. The lengthiest sentence to date was in December 2004 where the accused was sentenced to nine years confinement.

The Cyber Security Research and Development Act authorizes a multi-year effort to create more secure cyber technologies, to expand cyber security research and development, and to improve the workforce. For certain, if and when the West suffers its first "Pearl Harbor cyber attack," the government will implement programs to force private industry to share information and to develop better security systems. It is perhaps naive to place the burden for securing the nation's infrastructure on the shoulders of private industry—viable software to protect against cyber terrorism is not being fully pursued. For now, apart from suffering economic loss, there are no driving incentives for private industry to work together to combat cyber terrorism. Still, given the expansion of the cyber world, there is no other option.

Indeed, there are several partnerships that are bearing fruit. One example is the Center for Infrastructure Assurance and Security (CIAS), located in San Antonio at the University of Texas at San Antonio. Among its many efforts to better help to secure cyberspace, in 2003, CIAS conducted the first large-scale cyber attack exercise since the terror attacks of September 11, 2001. Called, Dark Screen, the cyber exercise tested the ability of various government and business agencies to respond to attacks that affected the infrastructure, communication and information systems. Working closely with the CIAS, the Center for Terrorism Law at St. Mary's University School of Law has also embarked on several joint projects to include researching the legal aspects of new a technology designed to counter a common form of cyber attack—distributed denial of service (DDoS) attacks which aim to flood the target computer with data packets, thereby making it unavailable to the user or, in the case of a website, unavailable to the website's visitors.

8.6 Conclusion

America's technological advances in cyber technology are unmatched. As often is the case, however, a country's greatest strength can also prove to be a critical weakness. America's dependency on the cyber world opens new vulnerabilities to a different type of terrorist attack. A cyber attack can target an actual computer networking system that can cripple a critical infrastructure. It can also manifest itself in a conventional explosive attack on physical structures. Former FBI Director Louis Freech claimed that "the FBI believes cyber-terrorism, the use of cyber-tools to shut down, degrade, or deny critical national infrastructures, such as energy, transportation, communications, or government services, for the purpose of coercing or intimidating a government or civilian population, is clearly an emerging threat." It is a threat that must be met with the same recognition and gravity as a physical terrorist attack. In order to secure the nation against cyberterrorism, security officials must not be lured into believing that terrorist organizations, such as al-Qa'eda, lack the necessary equipment and knowledge needed to implement such an attack. Top al-Qa'eda officials have already expressed their intent to attack the American economy and infrastructures by using the Internet. Al-Qa'eda suicide bombers routinely depend on the Internet for training and tactical support for terror operations; the migration from the physical world to the cyber world has already begun. It is only a matter of time before a young computer savvy jihadist will deal a devastating blow to the United States.

The United States must heed these warnings. A valuable tool in this effort is the PATRIOT Act coupled with the general framework set out by the *National Strategy to Secure Cyberspace*. In order to thwart future attacks, law enforcement must have the legal ability to gather information on suspected terrorists. Still, cyber security has not benefited from the increase in dollars seen elsewhere in homeland security. Partnering the private industry with the government is in its infancy but it is imperative that long-term research and development be encouraged. Eventually, the government may be forced to implement programs to ensure that private industry shares information and develops security systems. Unfortunately, the complacent habit of dealing only with realized threats has not imparted a sense of urgency that will ultimately be necessary to protect the cyber world. The government must work so that in the upcoming years the cyber world is as safe a place as the physical world.

8.7 Questions for Discussion

1. *Applying the "terrorism" label to a cyberattack.* In *R v Boden*, The Supreme Court of Queensland in Australia upheld 20 of the 26 convictions that Vitek Boden was sentenced to for his cyber attacks on the SCDA system of an Australian water and sewage treatment plant in the year 2000. *2002 WL 969399 (QCA), [2002] QCA 16.* In his appeal, Boden contended that he was not a terrorist, but a disgruntled ex-employee, and the severe sentencing he received hurt his future marketability in the workplace. Boden was not found to have had any known connections to a terrorist organization. Does the fact Boden was a disgruntled ex-employee mean he should have been granted leniency? Was Boden a terrorist?

2. *Developing new tools to fight cyberattacks.* Locating the source of a DDoS attack is important for purposes of criminal prosecution, deploying effective countermeasures and development of new defense tools. Southwest Research Institute (SwRI) and CIAS are partnered on a project to develop an automated IP traceback solution to combat DDoS attacks. Although the IP Traceback concept faces additional challenges such as the need for cooperation among Internet Service Providers (ISPs) and the future potential for government regulation, there are legal concerns as well. What specific legal issues should the project's managers be concerned with? Why?

3. *Open Government laws.* What impact could each state's Open Government laws have on restricting or prohibiting private industry from taking measures to protect themselves from a cyberterrorism attack?

Selected Bibliography

CYBERCRIME LAW REPORT. *On the Hill Hacking for Terror.* March 8, 2004.

Krim, Jonathan. *U.S. Goals Solicited on Software Security; Task Force Suggests Limited Regulation.* WASH. POST, 7. Apr. 2, 2003, at E2.

Malcolm, John. *Virtual Threat, Real Terror: Cyberterrorism in the 21st Century.* Testimony of the Deputy Assistant Attorney General John G. Malcolm on Cyberterrorism, Senate Judiciary Committee, Subcommittee on Terrorism, Technology and Homeland Security. February 24, 2004.

McLemore, David. *On the Cyberterror Front Lines San Antonio Carving a Niche by Helping Protect Vital Systems,* DALLAS MORNING NEWS, Sept. 21, 2003, at A31.

Pollit, Mark. *Cyberterrorism: Fact or Fancy?* PROCEEDINGS OF THE 20TH NATIONAL INFORMATION SYSTEMS SECURITY CONFERENCE. October 1997, at 285–289.

Rollins, John, and Clay Wilson. *Terrorist Capabilities for Cyberattack: Overview and Policy Issues.* CRS Report RL33123. Oct. 20, 2005.

Stohs, Brett. *Protecting the Homeland Exemption: Why the Critical Infrastructure Information Act of 2002 will Degrade the Freedom of Information Act,* BERKELEY TECHNOLOGY LAW JOURNAL. Summer 2003.

Verton, Dan. BLACK ICE: THE INVISIBLE THREAT OF TERRORISM. 2003.

Zatko, Peiter. *Inside the Insider Threat,* COMPUTER WORLD, June 10, 2004.

Chapter 9
A New Paradigm for War and Terrorism Avoidance

Before we bring all the U.S. troops and all the coalition troops out of here [Afghanistan] … we must set conditions that prevent a reintroducing of the sorts of people that caused us to be standing where you and I are standing right now.

—General Tommy Franks

Synopsis

9.1 The Causes of Aggression and Terrorism
9.2 The New Paradigm for War and Terrorism Avoidance
9.3 Defining Democratic Values and Democracy
9.4 Origins of Human Rights
9.5 The Corpus of Human Rights Law
9.6 United Nations Efforts to Promote Human Rights
9.7 Non-Governmental Organizations Devoted to Human Rights
9.8 Regional Organizations to Promote Human Rights
9.9 Traditional Efforts of the United States in Promoting Human Rights
9.10 New Non-Traditional Roles—Human Rights as a Force Multiplier
9.11 The Role of Special Forces
9.12 New Challenges and New Thinking
9.13 Questions for Discussion
Selected Bibliography

Apart from the fact that the United States emerged from the Soviet Cold War as the sole remaining superpower, a promising by-product of the disintegration of the communist dictatorship was the addition of dozens of nascent democracies into the community of nations. At the time, little thought was given to the long-term effect of this phenomenon. Nevertheless, some recognized very quickly that the world was more secure, not only because an evil system of government had been swept into the dust bin of history, but because it was replaced by governments that earnestly wanted to embark on the road to democracy. Strongly advocating the need for the world community to foster the development of these new and struggling democracies, the director of the Center for International Studies at New York University School of Law noted, "The world will certainly miss the boat if it does not use the end of the cold war to create a global system for the new millennium, one which preserves peace, fosters economic growth, and prevents the deterioration of the human physical and environmental condition." In essence, a handful of scholars recognized the efficacy of a very simple truth in both war and terrorism avoidance. As previously noted, this truth was best summed up in the words of Anthony Lake: "[D]emocracies tend not to wage war on each other and they tend not to support terrorism—in fact, they don't. They are more trustworthy in diplomacy and they do a better job of respecting the environment and human rights of their people."

Now, with the arrival of a new century, a new window of opportunity is opening for a similar shift towards democracy. This time the winds of freedom are poised to fan across the Arab world. Separated from all the horror, misery, and tragedy of war associated with the United States led campaign against terrorist aggression in Iraq and Afghanistan, there is comfort in the fact that America and the international community of civilized nations may be able to further advance an often ignored paradigm for reducing the likelihood of terrorism and war, at least at the international level. This hopeful theme has been at the heart and soul of the Bush Administration's war aims. Found throughout the *2002 National Security Strategy*, President Bush best summed up this theme in his second Inaugural Address in 2005: "The best hope for peace in our world is the expansion of freedom in all the world."

Although it is true that the Islamic and Arab community of nations are plagued with nondemocratic governments (with the exception of Turkey), it is erroneous to label that corner of the globe as a monolithic conglomerate of countries that embrace the radical Nazi-like totalitarianism of Iran, Syria and the virtual-state of the al-Qa'eda. In addition, it is equally erroneous to assume that the vast majority of people who live under the tyranny of these dictatorships do so with any welcomed degree of loyalty or enthusiasm. In the words of Secretary of State, Condoleezza Rice, "We reject the condescending view that freedom will not grow in the soil of the Middle East—or that Muslims somehow do not share in the desire to be free." Basic denials of human rights are not a matter of "cultural heritage." Given the choice between freedom and dictatorial rule, rational humans—those who have not been brainwashed in "Hitler youth camps"—will always choose freedom. This basic truth was demonstrated with the fall of the Taliban regime. Even without a viable frame of reference for what democracy really entails, the common people of Afghanistan enthusiastically welcomed the promise of freedom. Over 1.8 million Afghans have returned since the fall of the Taliban, the largest movement in thirty years. The window of opportunity, then, centers on the hope that as dictatorships fall in the War on Terror, they will be replaced with some form of liberal democracy. This certainly is the ultimate goal in Afghanistan and Iraq. This is the hope in the rest of the region.

The international community, especially the well-established democracies led by the United States, has a critical role to perform in the promotion of democratic values and human rights. The task of promoting genuine democratic standards of behavior in whatever new governments take hold will not be a simple undertaking. In far too many instances, forces of intolerance—ethnic, nationalistic, racial, and religious—will certainly permeate both the new governments and the societies from which they are formed. For instance, the new government in Iraq may desire the concepts associated with democracy but a general pattern of ethnic and sectarian fragmentation has introduced an escalating and often uncontrollable level of disorder and violence. Thus, if America and the international community do not find a realistic way to promote and foster at least the most fundamental categories of democratic values and human rights, the flames of terrorism and aggressive war will burn bright once again. Totalitarianism always stands hungrily at the door of freedom.

9.1 The Causes of Aggression and Terrorism

The most troubling aspect of all in addressing terrorism and war avoidance begins with the question of what causes people, or more precisely, governments, to commit gross violations of human rights and unlawful violence. Clearly, this is a critical issue as it is directly related to the attendant matter of how to best halt terrorism and aggression. Thus, the question becomes whether there is a way to rid the planet of these scourges apart from the use of armed force.

In reviewing the human experience of the last six thousand years, one could list a host of factors related to the use of aggression by a country against both its own people and its neighbors to include such things as religious conflict, ethnic strife, territorial disputes, population pressures, and competition for limited resources. While all of these external factors may be catalysts for aggression, any discussion that fails to examine the basic nature of man can never capture more than a part of the real truth. Theologians such as R. B. Thieme, Jr., often stress that the root of the matter centers on the makeup of man: "In our beings are all the seeds of great conflicts." Holocaust victim Anne Frank also amplified this point in her diary:

> I don't believe that the big men, the politicians and the capitalists alone, are guilty of war. Oh no, the little man is just as guilty, otherwise the peoples of the world would have risen in revolt long ago. There's in people simply an urge to destroy, an urge to kill, to murder and rage, and until all mankind, without exception, undergoes a great change, wars will be waged, everything that has been built up, cultivated, and grown will be destroyed and disfigured, after which mankind will have to begin all over again.

Moreover, nations are made up of people. The troubles of the world are not beamed onto earth from some hostile alien force. Since violations of the rule of law in terms of aggression and terrorism are generally associated with corresponding human lusts for power and approbation, one must put the responsibility for violations not only on the external factors created by man, but on the darker angles of mankind itself. Although numerous excuses are always voiced by the perpetrator, violations are ultimately a reflection of the problems that rest inside each individual, who, according to the basic tenets of every major religion, is morally flawed. Thus, the question of what causes a person to commit a *malum in se* crime can be asked collectively of a government that engages in a consistent pattern of aggression and human rights violations.

On the individual level, observations about the sinister side of some societies strongly reinforces the Judeo-Christian doctrine of the total depravity of man. However, the view that there will always be aggressive warfare and terrorism in the world, like crime in society, is only partially correct. Crime on the national level and aggressive violence on the international level can be controlled. The concept of the total depravity of man voiced by Anne Frank applies primarily to theological questions e.g., the mechanics of salvation. The concept does not mean that mankind is in a state of total helplessness and wickedness *vis-à-vis* other people. On the contrary, operating under the principles of freedom and self-determination, civilized peoples have come together to form national entities so that they might produce the by-products of privacy, justice and economic prosperity.

Under such a model, nation-states have prospered and flourished, but only to the extent that they have recognized the collateral need to protect those rights on interior and exterior lines. On interior lines, States must recognize the legitimate functions of a police and judicial system to punish criminal behavior; on exterior lines, nation-states must recognize the need for a strong military establishment to protect the nation from the aggressive behavior of dictatorships and the supporters of terrorism.

Objectively, much of what we know about the nature of governments created by man comes from the record of their histories; records written in streams of blood. For example, to observe that various governments have engaged in horrendous acts of aggression against their own people and others simply describe their behavior, but only partially explains it. In fact, no one has ever satisfactorily explained why certain societies-ancient Assyria, Soviet Russia, Nazi Germany, North Vietnam, Communist China, or Saddam's Iraq-turned into aggressive war machines that committed murderous human rights violations against their own people and neighboring country.

What has been established are the characteristics of those nations that have a high propensity for engaging in aggressive war, terrorism, and human rights abuses. National Security law expert and ABA Director of the Center for National Security Law, Professor John Norton Moore, argues that totalitarian regimes like the Taliban and Saddam's Iraq are considerably more likely to resort to aggressive violence than democracies. Professor Moore terms this phenomenon the "radical regime" syndrome.

Radical Regime Syndrome

> A radical totalitarian regime … seems to blend together a mixture of a failing centrally planned economy, severe limitations on economic freedom, a one-party political system, an absence of an independent judiciary, a police state with minimal human rights and political freedoms at home, a denial of the right to emigrate, heavy involvement of the military in political leadership, a large percentage of the GNP devoted to the military sector, a high percentage of the population in the military, leaders strongly motivated by an ideology of true beliefs including willingness to use force, aggressively anti-Western and anti-democratic in behavior, and selective support for wars of national liberation, terrorism, and disinformation against Western or democratic interests.

Tyrants seek the destruction of freedom loving people. Some, like the Taliban and current Iranian regime, cloak themselves in radicalized versions of Islam; others, like Saddam's Iraq and the current regime in Syria, have no driving religious affiliation. All of these regimes are linked, however, by a common bond of hate, power lust and aggression to gain, maintain and extend power. Human rights, the rule of law and civilian control are alien concepts to totalitarian governments because the freedom inherent in these concepts cannot coexist with tyranny.

9.2 The New Paradigm for War and Terrorism Avoidance

Recognizing a nexus between the nation that mistreats its own citizens and the nation that fosters aggression against its neighbors, "[b]oth the preamble and Article 1 of the United Nations Charter make crystal clear that the drafters were under the impression that the unleashing of aggressive war occurred at the hands of those States in which the denial of the value … of the individual human being … was most evident." Furthermore, with the outstanding research of eminent scholars such as Professor R. J. Rummel, it is now possible to demonstrate numerically the validity of the proposition that totalitarian regimes are the chief abusers of human rights:

> War is not the most deadly form of violence. Indeed, I have found that while about 37,000,000 people have been killed in battle by all foreign and domestic wars in our century, government democide [genocide and mass murder] have killed over 148,074,000

more. Plus, I am still counting. Over 85 percent of these people were killed by totalitarian governments.

So, the new paradigm for war and terrorism avoidance is a very simplistic model: If democracies make better neighbors, *a fortiori*, it is certainly in the best interests of the United States to do all it can to foster democratic values and human rights in the emerging nations and to thereby enlarge respect for the rule of law in international relations. In the words of Professor B. Russett, "[D]emocracies have almost never fought each other ... By this reasoning, the more democracies there are in the world, the fewer potential adversaries we and other democracies will have and the wider the zone of peace."

All can understand the simplicity of Russett's argument. In fact, Professor Moore firmly believes this simple fact represents a "new and more accurate paradigm about war, peace, and democide." It replaces the old thinking of peace through appeasement and rubricates the only hope for reducing the threat of weapons of mass murder, terrorism and human rights abuse. Appeasement leads to more aggression. This view is further amplified by a recent RAND study:

> The failure of regimes to provide for peaceful political change and the phenomenon of economies unable to keep pace with population growth and demands for more evenly distributed benefits can provide fertile ground for extremism and political violence affecting U.S. interests. For this reason, the United States has a stake in promoting political and economic reform as a means of reducing the potential for terrorism, some of which, as in Latin America, the Middle East, and the Gulf, may be directed at us.

Unfortunately, the paradigm seems to be extremely difficult to propagate. In part, this is because democratic ideals are not spread through the use of force—of fire and sword—so that windows of opportunity for change generally only appear in the aftermath of the defeat of a totalitarian regime. This occurred in the Axis powers of Germany, Italy, and Japan following World War II and then again with the end of the Cold War in the former territories of the Soviet Union. In addition, the paradigm is difficult to advance because people in democracies are often lulled into complacency and apathy about the conditions of fellow humans on the planet. They forget the truth that democracies are far better systems of government than any other. To borrow a phrase from the British novelist Rebecca West, "The trouble with man is twofold; he cannot learn those truths that are too complicated and he forgets those truths that are too simple." The realization that democracies do not engage in terrorism or aggressive war is clearly a "simple truth" that must be reinforced at every turn.

In the War on Terror, the United States needs to accelerate efforts to encourage the full development of any fledgling democracy under the truism that democracies do not wage war or allow terrorism to flourish. If the RAND study is correct, this strategy will go far in reducing the root causes of terrorism.

The primary criterion for winning the War on Terror, then, must concentrate on a realistic examination and application of this simple, yet powerful, formula, a formula related directly to the enhancement of United States' interests as it addresses the long-term goal of curtailing the aggressive use of force. In fact, the truism about the behavior of democracies is predicated upon

United States' interests; in no way does it pit American domestic interests against issues of international concern. In the context of either peace or deterrence, they are one and the same.

If one accepts the paradigm as valid, three issues immediately arise. First, what precisely are these values associated with democracy? Second, are these values merely a Western ethnocentric assertion of power over other non-democratic nations or are they self-evident truths? Third, what is the best way to promote these values?

9.3 Defining Democratic Values and Democracy

In 1788, Massachusetts adopted a State Bill of Rights which proclaimed, "A frequent recurrence to fundamental principles is absolutely necessary to preserve the blessings of liberty and to maintain a free government." These fundamental principles generally refer to all of those basic rights associated with democratic forms of government and are best encapsulated in the Constitution's Bill of Rights approved by Congress in 1789 and ratified in 1791.

Before America stood up as a democracy, early Western scholars such as John Locke, David Hume, Baron de Montesquieu and Jean-Jacques Rousseau wrote extensively on the subject of "civic humanism" or "natural rights" and the proper function of government in relation to the citizen. These scholars agreed with the premise that individuals came together to form national entities so that the individual could, within the framework of a government, better protect and advance his inherent rights to life, liberty and property.

Contrary to the practice of the majority of the countries of their day, these men pointed out that the government was formed to be the guardian of basic human freedoms, not the usurper. For instance, in his *Second Treatise of Government*, John Locke wrote, "The legislative or supreme authority cannot assume to itself a power to rule by extemporary, arbitrary decrees, but is bound to dispense justice, and to decide the rights of the subject by promulgated, standing laws, and known authorized judges."

The writings of these early scholars had a tremendous impact on the American rebels of 1776. Faced with the task of articulating a moral justification for their armed secession against the colonial rule of Great Britain, Thomas Jefferson and others were obliged to carefully translate Locke's natural rights into legal and enforceable rights. Apart from properly dealing with the continued evil of human servitude, the American drafters were largely successful. In their Declaration of Independence to the British Crown, they declared that the individual, simply by virtue of his God-given being, possessed the "right to life, liberty, and the pursuit of happiness." The Declaration of Independence's powerful opening showed that the framers were not inventing out of whole cloth the ideas and ideals they embraced. The men who penned the Constitution and the Declaration of Independence were drawing on the wisdom of the ages to bring together a proper balance between freedom and authority. Recognizing that freedom without authority is anarchy, and authority without freedom is tyranny, the Declaration of Independence proclaimed:

> We hold these truths to be self-evident, that all men are created equal, that they are endowed by their Creator with certain inalienable rights that among these are Life, Liberty, and the pursuit of Happiness. That to secure these rights, Governments are instituted among Men, deriving their just powers from the consent of the governed.

In two sentences, the framers laid out a fantastic manifesto that recognized the dignity of man exercising his God-given rights through a democratic government formed to protect the fundamental rights of its citizens. For the Americans, these rights were rooted in Divine providence which made them inalienable and morally justified ab initio. As Benjamin Franklin remarked at the Constitutional Convention in 1787, "I have lived, Sir, a long time, and the longer I live, the more convincing proofs I see of this truth: that God governs the affairs of men."

With their freedom purchased through six long years of bloodshed on the battlefield, the colonial Americans produced one of the most phenomenal documents in the history of mankind—the Constitution of the United States of America. The Constitution established a democratic government operating under principles which forever united the terms freedom and democracy. In the minds of many, the terms are synonymous. Nevertheless, when one speaks of the desirability of promoting democratic values, this does not necessarily imply the adoption of a direct democracy as the ideal form of government.

The United States of America was created as a representative democracy (i.e., a republic); it is not a true direct democracy in the fashion of the ancient Greek city-states. The founding fathers were extremely careful in their choice of government. They rejected the concept of a pure democracy where all citizens have an equal and direct voice in government and chose instead a representative democracy. The framers restricted the franchise of participants and established three separate independent branches of government, with checks and balances to ensure that the authority of the central government was truly limited. *Webster's Third New International Dictionary* defines a representative democracy as "a form of government in which the supreme power is vested in the people and exercised by them indirectly through a system of representation and delegated authority in which the people choose their officials and representatives at periodically held free elections …."

In weighing the usefulness of a direct democracy against a representative democracy, it is interesting to note the words of historian Alexander Fraser Tytler (1748 to 1813), who wrote about the decline and fall of the Athenian Republic. He concluded:

> A [direct] democracy cannot exist as a permanent form of government. It can only exist until the voters discover that they can vote themselves money from the public treasury. From that moment on, the majority always votes for the candidates promising the most benefits from the public treasury with a result that a democracy always collapses over loose fiscal policy always followed by dictatorship.

Mr. Tytler went on to develop a fascinating general trend in the rise and fall of nations. He wrote:

> The average age of the world's greatest civilizations has been 200 years. These nations have progressed through the following sequence:
>
> From bondage to spiritual faith;
> From spiritual faith to courage;
> From courage to liberty;
> From liberty to abundance;

From abundance to selfishness;
From selfishness to complacency;
From complacency to apathy;
From apathy to dependency;
From dependency back to bondage.

If democratic principles do not necessarily mesh with direct democracy as the best form of government, they certainly do equate to what Daniel Webster envisioned as "a state of society characterized by tolerance toward minorities, freedom of expression, and respect for the essential dignity and worth of the human individual with equal opportunity for each to develop freely to his fullest capacity in a cooperative community." It is certainly possible that a government that is honest, accountable, predictable and efficient can conform to democratic principles and protect human rights. However, the modern era has demonstrated repeatedly that a representative democracy is best suited to produce democratic principles and is, therefore, the government of choice in reference to the paradigm for war and terrorism avoidance.

Still, governmental authority in a State may be vested in one person, a small group, a large group, or the entire body. Measured in the light of human rights and democratic principles, none of these systems are necessarily per se worse than any other; it is just that representative democracies have institutional safeguards (such as checks and balances on power) that can guarantee fundamental freedoms over the long term.

For instance, the framers instituted three basic types of activities for the government. First, a system of checks and balances was established to ensure that the government fulfilled its obligation to protect the life, freedom, privacy and property of law-abiding citizens. Second, laws were instituted to better regulate commercial and social disputes between individuals. And third, the government was asked to set up certain physical infrastructures to provide essential services that were beyond individual capabilities, such as providing for basic primary education, law enforcement, and a military establishment.

The factor that divides good government from bad government is in the degree to which the government allows the functioning of democratic principles under the framework of the law. Dictatorships have a pseudo "rule of law," but it is not based on principles of freedom. Accordingly, any so-called elections held in a totalitarian system can never be more than a cruel perversion of the concept. Clearly, a ruling system that provides its citizens with freedom of expression, peaceful assembly, a free market economy and some degree of participation in government rests on democratic principles and a true rule of law. Thus, a monarchy, an aristocracy, or a representative democracy that rules for the common good of the citizen under democratic principles can each be positive manifestations of government. Other forms of government such as a tyranny or an oligarchy wield authority based solely on the self-interest of the ruling elite and refuse to embrace freedom.

In addressing the issue of writing democratic constitutions for the emerging democracies of Europe following the collapse of the Soviet Empire, Professor A. E. Dick Howard of the University of Virginia School of Law commented on this friction concerning what government is all about:

> The Bill of Rights of the United States Constitution declares what government may not do; it is what Justice Hugo Black once called a list of "thou shalt nots." The document reflects

the view that the function of a bill of rights is to limit government's powers. Central and East European drafters have enlarged this meaning of "rights." A legacy of the twentieth-century notion of positive government, an age of entitlements, is bills of rights that declare affirmative rights. Such bills include, of course, the traditional negative rights, but they also spell out claims upon government, such as the right to an education, the right to a job, or the benefits of care in one's old age.

Forced equality through social engineering is the policy and propaganda of the totalitarian system. As Professor Howard has discovered, many of the emerging democracies out of the former U.S.S.R. have still not shaken this old thinking. The true function of good government emphasizes freedom and self-determination which will always lead to varying degrees of social inequality. Faced with Lord Acton's often quoted truism that "power tends to corrupt, and absolute power corrupts absolutely," the government that adheres to principles of freedom is much preferred.

But what if people want to choose a political system that denies fundamental freedoms? Coming out of the Nazi era, the post World War II German government was quick to address this question by enacting in their Basic Law a provision which holds that no citizen may use his freedom to destroy freedom. In other words, no political party that endorses non-democratic principles will be allowed to stand for office. Indeed, once a totalitarian party takes office, it will abolish all systems of freedom because it is the antithesis of freedom. A recent historical example of this strange paradox—where an extremist party manages to win at the ballot box—can be found in the Algerian experience. When the first round of balloting in December 1991 went to the radical Taliban-styled Islamic Salvation Front (better know by its French acronym FIS), the Algerian military intervened to stop the extremists from taking power. Understanding that the FIS would not endorse principles of freedom if they took power, the Algerian army banned the FIS and supported the secular State apparatus. Showing their true colors, the FIS then accelerated a murder and terror campaign (their tactic of choice was to slit the throat of anyone who did not agree with the movement) against the civilian population, resulting in the murder of nearly 200,000 people. Fortunately, the FIS's armed wing, the so-called Islamic Salvation Army, disbanded in January of 2000 and Algerians elected President Abdelaziz Bouteflika shortly thereafter. Although much remains to be done, President Boutelflika's Charter for Peace and National Reconciliation has put the nation on the road to democratic reforms.

In the modern era, the terms democratic principles and fundamental freedoms have been joined by the concept of human rights. The report of the June 1993 World Conference on Human Rights, held in Vienna and attended by 171 States, defined the relationship between democracy, fundamental freedoms and human rights as follows:

> Democracy, development, and respect for human rights and fundamental freedoms are interdependent and mutually reinforcing. Democracy is based on the freely expressed will of the people to determine their own political, economic, social and cultural systems and their full participation in all aspects of their lives …. The international community should support the strengthening and promoting of democracy, development and respect for human rights and fundamental freedoms in the entire world.

Indeed, since some wrongly criticize the concept of democracy as a Western value, it may be more appropriate to speak to the world politic in terms of the normative concept of human rights. Human rights evoke a more inclusive standard, which can apply to all the peoples and nations of the world. As a practical matter, of course, there is no difference between democratic values and human rights.

9.4 Origins of Human Rights

When the framers of the Constitution wrote about the Law of Nations, they were addressing those principles of international law that governed State-to-State contacts. At most, the individual was viewed only as an object in the process. As recently as fifty years ago, the leading treatise on international law reflected the absence of a legal recognition of the issue of international human rights. Lassa Oppenheim wrote, "[A]part from obligations undertaken by treaty, a State is entitled to treat both its own nationals and stateless persons at discretion and that the manner in which it treats them is not a matter with which International Law, as a rule, concerns itself."

While general humanitarian concerns for individuals have always been around in the marketplace of world ideas, it has only been since the close of the Second World War that legal norms in the context of human rights have emerged. Before this period, humanitarian concerns such as eradicating the evil of slavery were handled to a large degree by each individual state. Nevertheless, as each of the Western powers eradicated the institution, the abolition of slavery gradually became a principle of customary international law. Thus, fueled by the formation of the United Nations in 1945, an entire system of human rights legal principles, some by treaty and some by custom, slowly emerged.

In the last half of the twentieth century, no concept has done more to advance positive change in the social and political spheres of human experience than human rights. In the quest for bettering the quality of human life, human rights have had a major impact in shaping world opinion and events. In this context, human rights have increasingly served as the basis for reaching consensus on defining the fundamental pillars upon which all "just" governments should be anchored. As the preamble to the Universal Declaration of Human Rights asserts, human rights serve "as a common standard of achievement for all peoples and all nations."

In the modern era, human rights have emerged as a significant moral and legal force in modern domestic and international relations. In its most comprehensive meaning, human rights encompass all those principles and concerns associated with ensuring respect for the inherent dignity of the individual human being. In this sense alone can individuals ever be called equal, since each human being, regardless of his abilities or handicaps, possesses the same right of respect for his person and property. The problem, of course, is in the extent to which individual governments are willing to define, recognize, and then enforce the inherent human rights each citizen possesses.

Because mankind is organized into national entities or States, human rights have their primary meaning as they relate to the relationship of the individual and the national entity. In contrast to the situation of only a few generations ago, when the sovereignty of the State was the fundamental principle upon which international law was based, the rapid development of international human rights norms and standards now requires the sovereignty of the State to be weighed and measured against what might be called the sovereignty of the individual.

Despite the phenomenal inroads that human rights have made in the world arena, the goal of universal acceptance and adherence has not been achieved; the path continues to be strewn with adversity. Although the term human rights rolls off the tongue with great ease, one of the most frustrating issues associated with the study of human rights is the fact that there is no standard definition of the term human rights. The legal definition of rights usually refers to claims recognized and enforced by law, but human rights can encompass a far broader category of issues, many not deemed to be legally binding in the context of either domestic or international law. Thus, without a clear definition, the range of issues human rights should encompass continues to be debated.

Juxtaposed to the strict definitional problem, another obstacle in reaching a universal consensus on defining human rights rests in the polarization of the term. Without question, the term human rights has numerous connotations, making it extremely popular over the entire political and social spectrum to describe, with equal vigor, almost any and every aspect of the human condition. Furthermore, because the term is freely used by groups with diametrically opposed agendas and ideologies—often without honest assessment or examination—human rights are often treated as a disposable tool to achieve a political end. The result is that the unwary or casual observer is left with a term that is saddled with wide-ranging ambiguities as to its meaning and goals.

For example, during the Cold War both the Soviet Union and the United States routinely accused one another of human rights abuses. The United States would accuse the Soviets of violating human rights, pointing to the systematic denial of all categories of human freedom related to person and property as a function of the totalitarian regime. In turn, the Soviets would vehemently charge the United States and other capitalist countries with "headline grabbing" human rights abuses (in order to divert attention from their own abuses and to further ongoing machinations to advance communist ideology throughout the globe).

Of course, in the debate of which system of government commits the worst violations of human rights, one point is generally clear, totalitarian governments are hypocritical in their professed support for human rights, democracies are not. Although individual acts of human rights abuse can occur under any form of government, there is a vast difference between totalitarian regimes and democratic governments. Totalitarian regimes are guilty of institutional denials of human rights, routinely carried out as the *modus vivendi* of government.

In contrast, human rights violations in democracies are generally caused by individuals operating under their own authority and outside of normal institutional procedures. Accordingly, democracies are far more likely to care about human rights and to investigate and punish those public officials guilty of human rights violations.

Another mark of the phenomenal degree of support for human rights in democracies is that human rights are accepted as vitally important considerations across the entire political spectrum. For instance, in the United States, all major political platforms, be they conservative or liberal, recognize and endorse the need for the promotion of the most fundamental categories of human rights, both in America and throughout the globe. Liberals and conservatives may disagree on the degree or method of promotion, but both advocate the pursuit of human rights as the primary vehicle for the advancement of peace and stability.

As a consequence of the support given to human rights by the democracies, the world community, by treaty and custom formed essentially since the close of World War II, has arrived at a general consensus on certain basic human rights which all mankind should enjoy. Because this basic category of international human rights is universally recognized, it is commonly referred to as "international human rights." In the realm of international law, international human rights can be generally defined as that body of universally recognized inalienable rights that every individual is entitled to and that every government must guarantee.

At least in the sphere of this consensus, international law no longer recognizes the unrestricted right of the State to deal with its citizens or aliens in any manner it so desires. International human rights law transcends international borders. The often-heard quip of England's King George when asked for help during France's reign of terror no longer applies—"If a country chooses to go mad within its own borders, it may do so."

Without question, the lynchpin of international human rights law advocates one of the most fundamental functions of the national entity—to protect the human rights of the individual. In this sense, respect for international human rights is the *sine qua non* of civilized society and failure of the State to afford such protection can lead to a wide range of sanctions—political, economic and even judicial.

Apart from the desire to halt external aggression, the U.N. Charter was also designed to address fundamental issues related to international human rights. If the desire for curtailing aggressive war was the justification for restricting some aspects of the external exercise of a State's sovereignty, the drafters intended human rights to be the justification for examining a State's internal ability to generally treat its citizens in any manner it wished.

Although the references to human rights in the U.N. Charter are set out in extremely general terms, they nonetheless clearly set the tone for all future treaties and covenants related to human rights. For example, the preamble to the U.N. Charter states that the peoples of the United Nations have determined to "reaffirm faith in fundamental human rights, in the dignity and worth of the human person [and] in the equal rights of men and women ...." This is followed by language in Article 1 (3) which, under the purpose of the U.N., calls for member nations to promote and encourage "respect for human rights and for fundamental freedoms for all without distinction as to race, sex, language, or religion ...."

With the creation of the United Nations, work quickly began on a series of international agreements and instruments designed to accomplish the two major themes in the Charter—restricting war and promoting human rights. Many of the efforts resulted in widespread and immediate acceptance of various international agreements throughout the nations of the world, including the 1949 Geneva Conventions. While the Geneva Conventions do not deal with restricting warfare, *jus ad bellum*, they are deeply concerned with *jus in bello*.

It was at this time that human rights moved from a "vision in the minds of some men, of an ideal aspiration towards universal values of law," to the reality of a world that began to acknowledge the existence and validity of international human rights. Next to the U.N. Charter, the primary document that frames the basic principles, as well as the future aspirations, for an international legal corpus for human rights is the U.N. Universal Declaration of Human Rights. The Universal Declaration was passed unanimously (eight abstentions) by the General Assembly in 1948, just three years after the creation of the United Nations.

Unlike the U.N. Charter, the U.N. Universal Declaration of Human Rights is not yet regarded as legally binding among the nations of the world. The Universal Declaration is a declaration of the international body relating to moral and political issues of governments. Although it is not legally binding, the Universal Declaration has gained considerable authority as a legal guide to all member states and serves as a foundation for future expansion of international human rights law.

Another problem with the Universal Declaration is that it possesses no machinery for enforcing any of the human rights that it lists. The Universal Declaration has, however, inspired two major covenants which contain more detailed assertions of fixed categories of human rights. Approved by the General Assembly in 1966, these are the International Covenant on Civil and Political Rights and the International Covenant on Economic, Social, and Cultural Rights. Both of these covenants continue to receive growing acceptance from many nations of the world community.

Other treaties that relate to human rights speak to a whole series of specific concerns such as the International Convention on the Elimination of All Forms of Racial Discrimination, the Convention on the Elimination of All Forms of Discrimination Against Women, the Convention on the Prevention and Punishment of the Crime of Genocide, and the Torture Convention.

Obviously, the evolution of the international corpus for human rights law is still ongoing. As with all aspects of international law, international human rights law develops as States become bound by treaty or by custom. Even absent consent via treaty, nations can still be obligated. Again, when a norm or standard has reached widespread acceptance in the international community, it is said to have passed into the realm of customary international law. For example, in respect to the U.N. Charter, even those few nations who are not members of the United Nations are bound by the provisions of the Charter under the concept of customary international law.

9.5 The Corpus of Human Rights Law

What then is the current corpus of human rights and how much of it falls into the category of recognized international human rights law? Many scholars view human rights as chronologically evolving in "generations." For the purposes of this study, it is particularly helpful to divide human rights into three generations.

The first generation of human rights deals basically with the individual's right to be secure in the most sacred asset of all—his person. All nations are bound by treaty and custom to observe these basic protections which are clearly included as the most fundamental of international human rights. Specifically, a State violates international human rights law if, as a matter of State policy, it practices, encourages, or condones seven types of actions that have gained universal recognition. Codified in the Restatement (Third) of the Foreign Relations Law of the United States (1987), Section 702, Customary International Law of Human Rights, those actions consist of:

1. genocide;
2. slavery or slave trade;
3. the murder or causing the disappearance of individuals;
4. torture or other cruel, inhuman, or degrading treatment or punishment;
5. prolonged arbitrary detention;

6. systematic racial discrimination; and
7. a consistent pattern of gross violations of internationally recognized human rights.

Any nation who violates these first generation human rights is deemed to have committed a "gross violation of international human rights."

The second generation of human rights is related to political and civil claims. In short, the individual has the right to be free from the State in his all of his civil and political endeavors. Second category rights are set forth in the International Covenant on Civil and Political Rights and include the broader civil and political freedoms of religion, movement, peaceful assembly, association, expression, privacy, family rights, fair and public trial, and participation in government—all sacred principles related directly to democratic principles of freedom. Unfortunately, while many countries have adopted these rights, nations who do not enter into international agreements to follow these rights are not obligated to do so. In other words, second generation rights are not yet customary international law.

Second generation human rights are fundamental to the complete development of the individual, for without the basic guarantees of freedom which these rights speak to, the full potential of the individual will never be realized. However, for those who mistakenly equate human rights with social equality, second generation rights are a paradox, as each individual is free to enjoy the consequences of his own decisions without government interference, good or bad. Furthermore, second generation human rights directly parallel the fundamental freedoms that are never offered under totalitarianism. A government committed to second generation human rights is tantamount to a democracy.

In contrast to the second generation of human rights, there is no great or growing international movement toward agreeing on the status of the third generation of human rights. Third generation rights are different from first and second generation rights because they move from restricting governmental behavior toward the individual, to mandating that the government perform numerous social and welfare actions for the individual. Third generation rights include such issues as working conditions, social security, education, health care, resource development, food, the environment, humanitarian assistance and peace.

Finally, while good government can certainly be measured by how closely it protects and provides for first and second generation human rights, it is not at all clear that the promotion of the third category of human rights is beneficial to society as a whole, especially over the long term. Apart from very basic obligations for any government to provide for the general welfare, many would argue that the obligation of the State is not to provide third generation human rights such as food, shelter, or employment to its citizens, but to protect the individual's freedom in the lawful pursuit of these things. Under this reasoning, the primary function of the State is to protect, not to give.

9.6 United Nations Efforts to Promote Human Rights

Thomas Paine once wrote: "Had we a place to stand upon, we might raise the world." If a program's success is ultimately measured by how effectively its goals are achieved, it is clear that the world community, embodied especially in the United Nations, has so far failed to develop any viable program to assist in institutionalizing the observance of first and second generation human rights in many of its member States. In short, the United Nations has not materialized as Paine's place upon which to stand.

To be sure, the United Nations has been extremely effective in codifying a body of binding international law so that basic human rights are clearly defined. Nevertheless, restricted by the sovereignty of its members, this tremendous contribution to the advancement of human rights has not been followed by a viable mechanism to ensure compliance with human rights standards within the community of nations. The United Nations thus far has proven to be more suited to building consensus among States about the nature of human rights than to enforcing observance of these rights by individual countries. If the new paradigm for war and terrorism avoidance is to flourish, gaining individual State commitment to at least first generation human rights must be the foundational basis of a workable and realistic plan of action.

One of the major challenges of the War on Terror will be what steps the United Nations can take to encourage member countries, particularly the Islamic and Arab nations, to follow human rights standards. The question, of course, is whether the United Nations has both the will and ability to offer the type of long-term assistance that is needed. The answer seems to be no.

Although a key purpose of the United Nations is to promote and encourage respect for human rights, the human rights provisions that actually guide the United Nations are set out in extremely general terms. Nowhere in the Charter is the term human rights defined; this work is left to later conventions and declarations. Article 1, paragraph 3, of the U.N. Charter lists as the purposes of the organization: "To achieve international cooperation in solving international problems of an economic, social, cultural, or humanitarian character, and in promoting and encouraging respect for human rights and fundamental freedoms for all without distinction as to race, sex, language, or religion." Article 55 of the U.N. Charter provides:

> With a view to the creation of conditions of stability and well-being which are necessary for peaceful and friendly relations among nations based on respect for the principle of equal rights and self-determination of peoples, the United Nations shall promote ... universal respect for, and observance of, human rights and fundamental freedoms for all without distinction as to race, sex, language, or religion.

In turn, Article 56 states that "[a]ll members pledge themselves to take joint and separate action in cooperation with the Organization for the achievement of purposes set forth in Article 55." The burden for enforcement and compliance is clearly placed on the individual states.

Under the U.N. Charter, the U.N. General Assembly does have a defined role with respect to the promotion of human rights. Article 13 of the U.N. Charter provides that the General Assembly "shall initiate studies and make recommendations for the purpose of ... assisting in the realization of human rights and fundamental freedoms for all without distinction as to race, sex, language, or religion." Within the framework of this mandate, the General Assembly's role has been to adopt numerous declarations or conventions concentrating on human rights matters.

Since the adoption of the Charter, the General Assembly has expended considerable effort to codify principles of human rights that nations should follow to guarantee the prosperity and well being of their citizens. These principles now form an important part of international law. Although codification has been a major contribution, so no nation can seriously contend that first generation human rights are not binding universal international law, mechanisms to curb the actual violations of these codified principles have been difficult to establish. In fact, the United Nations currently relies chiefly on what some have termed the "mobilization of shame"—the embarrassment of being under investigation, or even condemned, by the United Nations—as the primary means of motivating governments to comply with internationally recognized standards of human rights in the treatment of their citizens. Obviously, public condemnation means very little to totalitarian regimes, as was so clearly demonstrated by a decade of indifference by Saddam Hussein to almost twenty Security Council resolutions. Paradoxically, it is democracies such as the United States, who have far superior records in respecting human rights, that are often singled out for criticism. Driven by political agendas, the world body of the United Nations often looks at the speck of sand and ignores the boulder in the eye of dictatorships.

During the Cold War, the United Nations seemed to restrict its active concerns to resolving disputes between sovereign States, thereby not dealing with human rights abuses committed within the borders of sovereign States. Even in the process of resolving international disputes, U.N. forces had to be invited to play such a role by both parties to a conflict. While the term is not used in the U.N. Charter, the phrase "peacekeeping" was coined to describe this process.

With the end of the Cold War, the United Nations has attempted to enlarge its active concern to "peace-building," a concept inexorably linked to human rights concerns. Peace-building involves "action to identify and support structures which will tend to strengthen and solidify peace in order to avoid a relapse into conflict." In this context, the United Nations has been involved in numerous peace-building operations designed to help alleviate the suffering of a particular State through promoting human rights, democratization, and economic development.

As with the United Nation's attempt to shift from peacekeeping to peace-building, the War on Terror demands strong new approaches to promote the observance of human rights in such emerging nations as the new Afghanistan and Iraq. Hopefully, strong approaches will come under the United Nations' umbrella.

Always reluctant to employ or authorize the more forceful categories of sanctions such as the use of military force or embargoes, the United Nations traditionally draws on a series of weak sanctions based on embarrassing the government that has engaged in human rights violations. To better track human rights violators, the United Nations relies on several commissions and committees that derive their authority from key international human rights instruments or from the U.N. Charter itself.

Because many of the instruments that established these organizations are not binding or, if binding, drafted in terms that are ambiguous with respect to the responsibilities of individual member States, it is sometimes difficult to evaluate the specific obligations of individual U.N. member States. Also, each United Nations committee or commission generally has the task of reporting, commenting and studying only a specific category of human rights. As a result, these organizations have proven adept in developing human rights principles in specific areas of concern, but have been of little use in working toward the enforcement of these principles in practice.

The proponent for most actions taken by the General Assembly is the Economic and Social Council (ECOSOC). Under the terms of the U.N. Charter, the ECOSOC may:

1. make recommendations for the purpose of promoting respect for, and observance of, human rights and fundamental freedoms for all;
2. prepare draft conventions for submission to the General Assembly, with respect to matters falling within its competence; and
3. call ... international conferences on matters falling within its competence.

The ECOSOC may also ask member States to fully report on their own compliance with human rights obligations. The ECOSOC meets several times annually and matters related to human rights issues are typically handled by the ECOSOC's Second (Social) Committee. Under the U.N. Charter, the ECOSOC has the right to establish commissions for, *inter alia*, the promotion of human rights. Pursuant to this authority, the ECOSOC has formed two major commissions: the Commission on Human Rights (also known as the Human Rights Commission) and the Commission on the Status of Women. Of these two, the Commission on Human Rights has played the more significant role in the development and promotion of international human rights principles.

The ECOSOC established the Commission on Human Rights on February 16, 1946. The Human Rights Commission's role in the process of advancing human rights includes the following:

> Draft an international bill of rights; draft international declarations or conventions on civil liberties, the status of women, freedom of information and similar matters; protect minorities; prevent discrimination on grounds of race, sex, language, or religion; handle any other matter concerning human rights and ... assist the [ECOSOC] in coordination of activities concerning human rights in the United Nations System.

The crowning achievements of the Human Rights Commission include the drafting of the Universal Declaration of Human Rights, the International Covenant on Economic, Social and Cultural Rights, and the International Covenant on Civil and Political Rights. Taken together, these instruments comprise what has commonly become known as the International Bill of Human Rights.

In addition to functioning as a vehicle to codify and promote human rights, the Human Rights Commission also monitors and identifies human rights violations. However, since its enforcement powers are limited, the Human Rights Commission relies primarily on persuasion and dialogue to curb human rights violations.

The Human Rights Commission generally operates through the appointment of a special rapporteur or special envoy who acts as a fact-finder, investigating general human rights issues or a particular country's human rights record. The Human Rights Commission also recommends measures for State compliance and will act in an advisory capacity to governments that request such assistance. At other times, the special rapporteur will assist a particular government on specific human rights issues. The Human Rights Commission has also established several working groups which tackle such projects as drafting new international instruments.

Another organization under the United Nations umbrella is the Human Rights Committee. The Human Rights Committee serves as the chief administrator of the International Covenant on Civil and Political Rights. Established in 1977, the Human Rights Committee is responsible for studying, commenting and transmitting reports from United Nations member states to the Secretary General on the progress of implementing the obligations assumed by the member states under the International Covenant on Civil and Political Rights. Those obligations include:

1. ensuring to all individuals the rights enunciated in the covenant;
2. enacting legislation to give effect to those rights; and
3. guaranteeing to individuals remedies that can be exercised if those rights are violated.

The Human Rights Committee generally receives periodic reports from member nations in response to a series of questions and issues that the Committee wishes that nation to address. In compliance with Article 40 of the Covenant on Political and Civil Rights, the committee then passes a report on to the General Assembly. For example, in response to a Human Rights Committee request, a nation will usually send a delegation of public officials to Geneva with extensive written remarks on concerns raised by the Committee. The Committee will consider the written remarks and the oral input by the host nation delegation before issuing their report.

The Optional Protocol to the International Covenant on Civil and Political Rights contains provisions for the final implementation mechanism. In this regard, the Committee may consider individual complaints alleging human rights violations by State parties. Although the Committee may reach a decision on the merits and forward that decision to the State and individual concerned, it may not issue judgments. It is a paper tiger.

9.7 Non-Governmental Organizations Devoted to Human Rights

Non-governmental organizations (NGOs) serve an important function as watch dogs for human rights issues. The most widely recognized human rights NGO is Amnesty International. It is a worldwide movement that represents the main stream of NGOs and is premised on the "conviction that governments must not deny individuals their basic human rights." For its continuing efforts to promote worldwide observance of the Universal Declaration of Human Rights, Amnesty International was awarded the 1977 Nobel Peace Prize.

The three primary goals of Amnesty International are to work for:

1. the release of prisoners of conscience-men, women and children imprisoned for their beliefs, color, sex, ethnic origin, language or religion, provided they have neither used nor advocated violence;
2. fair and prompt trials for all political prisoners; and
3. an end to torture and executions in all cases.

With the exception of Amnesty International's opposition to the long recognized right of a State to exercise the death penalty, all of its goals are clearly consistent with the common body of first generation international human rights.

One powerful NGO that has attempted to actually implement human rights promotion programs in individual States is the International Committee of the Red Cross (ICRC). Beginning in 1976, the ICRC has sponsored scores of human rights symposia for numerous developing countries. From the establishment of the International Institute of Humanitarian Law in San Remo, Italy, to specific training programs for various militaries worldwide, the ICRC has taken the NGO lead in trying to promote institutional change. While other NGOs have sponsored human rights conferences, absolutely no organization has made as much progress as the ICRC in getting governments to at least address the issue of institutional change in the conduct of armed forces *vis-à-vis* human rights and the law of war. Unfortunately, because the ICRC constantly strives for neutrality, it can have difficulty establishing the necessary rapport with the host nation military to carry out significant training programs.

9.8 Regional Organizations to Promote Human Rights

In accordance with the provisions of the U.N. Charter regarding regional organizations, there are several major regional organizations that have been formed to better represent the desires of sovereign nations in the same geographic location. Like the United Nations approach in dealing with and enforcing compliance with human rights, all of the regional approaches rely simply on categorizing human rights abuses and little else.

For example, the Charter of the Organization of American States (OAS), which is the largest regional organization in the Americas (consisting of 32 members States), includes the same generalist human rights language that is found in the U.N. Charter. Article 3(j) holds that OAS member States will "proclaim the fundamental rights of the individual without distinction as to race, nationality, creed, or sex." Article 16 states that in exercising the right to freely develop its cultural, political, and economic life, the member States agree to "respect the rights of the individual and the principal of universal morality."

Similar to the United Nations approach to further define human rights by means of the Universal Declaration on Human Rights, the OAS passed the American Declaration of the Rights and Duties of Man (American Declaration) to provide a clear indication of what was meant by human rights. Indeed, when the OAS created the Inter-American Commission on Human Rights, it specified that the human rights listed in the American Declaration were the ones to be used by the Commission in evaluating evidence and issuing reports. The American Declaration includes in its list of human rights: the right to life, liberty, and security of person (Article 1); the protection from abusive attacks on honor, reputation, and family (Article 5); the inviolability of the home and correspondence (Articles 9 and 10); and due process of laws (Articles 18, 25, and 26).

As noted, the OAS has not created an enforcement mechanism. The OAS has passed the American Convention on Human Rights in 1978 which requires all members to respect "the rights and freedoms recognized herein and to ensure to all persons subject to their jurisdiction the free and full exercise of those rights and freedoms." To promote compliance, Articles 34 through 73 of the American Convention on Human Rights established the Inter-American Commission on Human Rights and the Inter-American Court on Human Rights. The Inter-American Commission on Human Rights is authorized to receive individual or state complaints alleging violations of human rights. After ensuring that all domestic remedies have been exhausted, the Commission can conduct investigations, make reports, and release information.

The Inter-American Court on Human Rights, located in San Jose, Costa Rica, is authorized to hear human rights cases, but only from parties who voluntarily submit to the jurisdiction of the court. If the parties do submit to the courts' jurisdiction, they pledge obedience to the judicial findings which may include reparations.

9.9 Traditional Efforts of the United States in Promoting Human Rights

If the United Nations, NGOs, and regional organizations have been less than effective in developing a serious methodology to promote the institutionalization of first and second generation human rights in new democracies, the United States government has only been slightly more effective. Recognizing that promoting human rights is in its best interest, as well as a responsibility to the world community, the United States relies on two means to achieve this end—foreign assistance funding and political pressure.

Political pressure is difficult to gauge in its success and varies according to each situation. In terms of politics, for example, the United States has signaled that it will not subordinate perceived security interests in Asia to the desire to promote human rights; the consequences for regional stability could be jeopardized if China is the recipient of an intensified human rights crusade. Under both the Clinton and Bush Administrations, even linking China's trade benefits to its human rights record has been viewed as counterproductive—China might become resentful and retaliate in ways that would be destabilizing for the region, such as not cooperating in the Security Council or making irresponsible arms sales.

The traditional mechanism for encouraging countries to develop acceptable human rights records rests with the policy of denying foreign assistance aid or security assistance to countries who are human rights abusers. Security assistance is generally defined as the complete body of statutory programs and authorities under which the United States provides defense articles, military training, and other defense related services to foreign governments and international organizations for the purpose of enhancing American national policies and objectives. Without question, the security assistance program is a principal element of American foreign policy.

The main objective of security assistance is to enhance American strategic objectives, not only from a regional perspective, but also in key countries within the region. Thus, the basic elements of security assistance involve assisting allies and friendly nations in meeting security threats, securing route access over flight and base rights essential to rapid deployment of United States forces, promoting force commonalities, and improving or maintaining access to critical raw materials.

It is well known that there are also domestic benefits associated with the security assistance program. Not only does the production of defense items provide domestic employment, it generates capital investment and improves the nation's industrial defense mobilization base.

Although the Department of State is responsible for the operation of the security assistance program, it is the National Security Council (NSC) that establishes the overall strategic planning and goals of the program. From the military aspect of security assistance, the Defense Security Assistance Agency (DSAA) is the primary Department of Defense office.

Each United States military Unified Command (collectively they have responsibility for all major regions in the world where American forces are stationed) is required to develop a security assistance program for their region which will assist in achieving assigned strategic goals and missions. After developing a security assistance program, the Commander of each Unified (and Specified) Command (CINC) forwards his security assistance proposal to the Joint Chiefs of

Staff (JCS) in Washington where they are evaluated and passed to the NSC for final incorporation into the overall United States strategic plan.

The subordinate component commands of Unified Commands are responsible for the actual implementation of security assistance programs within individual countries in the region. Furthermore, in the countries that are major recipients of security assistance, a Security Assistance Organization (SAO) operates on the ground as part of the Country Team to the American Ambassador in the country. The SAO includes all DOD elements located in the foreign country with assigned responsibilities for carrying out the various security assistance programs for that country. Because of their position, SAOs are afforded a great deal of deference by both the host nation and other Americans working in the host country.

Chief among the legislative authorities for security assistance is the Foreign Assistance Act (FAA) of 1961 (as amended). This act authorizes five basic types of programs as follows:

1. The Foreign Military Financing Program (FMFP). Under this program, defense articles are transferred to friendly nations either through grants, loans, or sales. Defense articles include such things as weapons, munitions, aircraft, vessels, and military equipment.

2. International military education and training (IMET). This program allows the United States military to provide training to foreign military students, primarily in the United States. A primary goal of IMET is to expose the foreign military students to the benefits of a free and democratic society based on the rule of law. Key in this process is the demonstration to the foreign soldiers of how a military is properly subordinated to civilian control. Not only are channels of communication opened between United States and foreign nationals, but it is hoped that the personal contacts made as a result of the training will encourage the promotion of democratic values and human rights in the future.

3. Antiterrorism assistance. A relatively new program, the antiterrorism program attempts to assist those democratic nations that are plagued by terrorist organizations.

4. Economic support fund. This program provides direct grant monies to the recipient nation in an effort to assist in economic recovery or development.

5. Peacekeeping operations. This provision authorizes assistance in the form of personnel and equipment to friendly countries and international organizations for peacekeeping operations.

The second major piece of security assistance legislation is the Arms Export Control Act (AECA). The AECA directly ties in with the applicable provisions of the FAA and provides for the sale of defense articles and services to other countries. The definition of what constitutes a defense article remains the same as under the FAA. A defense service includes any service, test, inspection, repair, training, publication, or other assistance, or defense information used for the purpose of making military sales.

A key element in the AECA defense service definition is "training." As defined in the act:

> Training includes formal or informal instruction of foreign students in the United States or overseas by officers or employees of the United States, contract technicians, or contractors

(including instruction at civilian institutions), or by correspondence courses, technical, educational, or information publications and media of all kinds, training aid, orientation, training exercise, and military advice to foreign military units and forces.

Depending on the type of training mission, American training teams fall into one of three general types: (1) mobile training teams; (2) technical assistance teams; or (3) technical assistance field teams. A letter of offer and acceptance of the training is executed in all cases. Besides the standard issues related to providing the service, this letter also spells out the status DOD team members will have while performing training duties in the foreign country. The status is usually the same privileges and immunities accorded to the administrative and technical staff at the American embassy in that country.

As stated, the Department of State is the executive branch agency charged with the operation of security assistance. Congress, however, through its power over the authorization and appropriation of funds, has actually become the key policy player in the process. In fact, much to the chagrin of executive branch, Congress views security assistance as a prime opportunity to influence and even establish foreign policy.

Congress exercises its authority in two ways, through the budget process and through the legislative process. Under the budget process, Congress does not simply allocate a fixed sum of money to the Department of State to allow them to operate the security assistance program through DSAA. Exercising their "power of the purse," Congress engages in micro-management by earmarking specific dollar amounts to specific countries.

From the earmarking of about half of the security assistance budget in the 1980s, Congress now earmarks about 90 percent of all security assistance monies. In addition, not content with earmarking monies to individual recipient States, Congress increasingly directs through functional accounts exactly how the earmarked money for a particular country will be spent. This Congressional practice has taken almost all of the flexibility away from the State Department and hence, the security assistance administrators.

In an effort to further increase its management role, Congress now establishes "mission accounts." For example, under the IMET funding for fiscal year 1994, Congress set up specific mission accounts in which money could be spent for particular countries. These accounts were: Middle East Peace, Promotion of Democracy and Human Rights, Counter-narcotics, Regional Stability and Defense Cooperation, and Promote Professional Military Relationships. All IMET money had to be spent in one of these mission accounts or returned to the general treasury.

The second manner in which Congress has inserted itself in the process rests in myriad legislative prohibitions on providing security assistance. Apart from numerous country specific restrictions, a sampling of the general prohibitions reveals just how complex the administration of security assistance program has become:

1. The prohibition against American personnel performing defense services of a combatant nature. Set out at 21(c)(1) of the AECA, 22, "Personnel performing defense services sold under this act may not perform any duties of a combatant nature, including any duties related to training and advising that may engage United States personnel in combat activities outside the United States in connection with the performance of those defense services."

Thus, if American military personnel find themselves in any situation where hostilities occur, or are imminent, they must cease training and withdraw from the area. This has occurred on many occasions in the past, particularly in situations where Army Special Forces are training host nation soldiers in unstable countries.

2. The prohibition against American forces training police forces, found at Section 660 of the FAA, provides that foreign assistance funds cannot be used to "provide training, advice, or financial support to police, prisons, or other law enforcement forces of a foreign government or for any program of internal intelligence or surveillance on behalf of a foreign government." This section has been amended to allow such training to longtime democracies with no standing armed forces and which do not violate human rights. Costa Rica, for example, has no military.

3. The Kennedy Amendment, at 502B of the FAA, requires that all federal assistance be cut off to any country that "engages in a consistent pattern of gross violations of internationally recognized human rights."

4. The Hickenlooper Amendment, at 620(e)(1) of the FAA, deals with halting aid to any nation that engages in the expropriation of American property.

5. The Symington-Glenn Amendments, at 669 and 670 of the FAA, deals with issues associated with the transfer of and receipt of nuclear materials. The intent is to keep nuclear arms from spreading to other countries.

6. The Brooke Amendment, at 620(q) of the FAA, mandates the complete termination of foreign assistance (to include United States military assistance) to any country more than twelve months in arrears on payment of debts accrued.

As disruptive as these restrictions appear on the ability of the Executive Branch to conduct foreign affairs, the Congress has given the President special authorities in both the FAA and AECA that allow him to override almost all Congressional restrictions. Because the entire process of planning, budgeting, and delivering security assistance requires substantial lead-time, the President is given this special authority to deal with exigent circumstances. This authority is exercised only as an exception to the rule, generally requires written notification, and is limited by dollar ceilings.

Through a series of federal statutes and directives, the United States government is required to consider human rights in conducting foreign relations with other countries. Countries that engage in a consistent pattern of gross violations of human rights are generally restricted from American foreign aid—military and economic. Obviously, this advantage is significant only in those areas that receive foreign aid from the United States.

In regard to the major legislative authority through which foreign assistance is rendered, the Kennedy Amendment and Harkin Amendment leave no doubt that the promotion of human rights is a key objective of American foreign policy. Indeed, Section 502B(a)(3) of the Kennedy Amendment directs the President to administer security assistance in a manner which promotes human rights and avoids "identification of the United States … with governments which deny to their people internationally recognized human rights and fundamental freedoms …."

Section 502B(a)(1) establishes as "a principal goal of the foreign policy of the United States ... to promote the increased observance of internationally recognized human rights by all countries." Section 502B(a)(2) prohibits security assistance to countries which "engage in a consistent pattern of gross violations of internationally recognized human rights."

As with most pieces of legislation, there is a limited exception clause in the Kennedy Amendment. Section 502B(e) allows the president to waive the restrictions imposed if he finds that "extraordinary circumstances exist warranting provision of such assistance," or if the president finds "that the human rights record in that country has significantly improved."

Similarly, Section 116(e) authorizes and encourages the President to identify and conduct "programs and activities which will encourage or promote increased adherence to civil rights, as set forth in the Universal Declaration of Human Rights ...." The Harkin Amendment also has an exception clause which prohibits economic assistance to "the government of any country which engages in a consistent pattern of gross violations of internationally recognized human rights ... unless such assistance will directly benefit the needy people of such country."

Gross violations of internationally recognized human rights are defined under both Sections 502B(d)(1) and 116(a) as the types of violations falling under the first generation of international human rights. The language describes gross violations as:

> [A] consistent pattern of gross violations of internationally recognized human rights, including torture or cruel, inhuman, or degrading treatment or punishment, prolonged detention without charges, causing the disappearance of persons by the abduction and clandestine detention of those persons, or other flagrant denial of the right to life, liberty, and the security of person.

Finally, both Sections 502B and 116 require the State Department to submit to Congress an annual status report on human rights for all countries receiving economic or security assistance. The process of collecting information for the report is conducted by the Assistant Secretary of State for Human Rights and Humanitarian Affairs. Information is gathered chiefly from the applicable American embassy and various respected human rights NGOs.

There exist numerous other legislative provisions that deal with the issue of providing assistance to nations that exhibit an unwillingness to abide by first generation human rights. For example, Section 701 of the International Financial Institutions Act requires the United States to do everything in its power to influence international financial institutions to prevent the grant of economic aid to countries whose governments engage in "a consistent pattern of gross violations of internationally recognized human rights." Because the United States exercises tremendous influence in organizations like the World Bank and International Finance Corporation over loans and grants to specific countries, it is able to act as an overseer for human rights issues.

Congress also enacts country-specific legislation which attempts to link American assistance to a particular country and that country's compliance with specific human rights standards. This conditional funding may be triggered by an unacceptable country report issued by the State Department. These violations mirror those found in Common Article 3 of the Geneva Conventions:

1. violence to life and person, in particular, murder of all kinds, mutilation, cruel treatment, and torture;

2. taking hostages;
3. outrages upon personal dignity, in particular, humiliating and degrading treatment;
4. the passing of sentences and carrying out of executions without previous judgment pronounced by a regularly constituted court affording all the judicial guarantees which are recognized as indispensable by civilized peoples.

History has shown that one of the most vital components of any democratic society is its military establishment. True democracy cannot exist without a military establishment dedicated to the principles associated with civilian control of the military and respect for fundamental human rights. While such principles are taken for granted in societies resting on stable democratic traditions, this is not the case in the militaries of totalitarian States. The antithesis of a democratic military, the military under the totalitarian system wields tremendous power over the internal affairs of the State; in many cases they are the government.

For better or worse, the United States has entered a period of profound change in the use of military capabilities to meet the new circumstances of the War on Terror. Not only has the use of overt military force as a tool of national security reemerged, but the War on Terror has led to a rethinking of military roles and missions with a search for "force multipliers." The term force multipliers applies in many ways, but in the War on Terror there are two significant force multipliers. First, the American strategy of using local indigenous fighters to help displace totalitarian regimes is a tremendous force multiplier in the short term. Coupled with a small cadre of United States Special Operations Forces, President George W. Bush has correctly used these local forces in conjunction with America's strongest military suit—its fantastic air and sea power.

The military campaign in Afghanistan was easily won and the new government easily established because the war was seen more as American help for the oppressed people to retake their own country than as an American invasion. Now that the War on Terror has reached Iraq, the elements are similar despite the continuing sectarian and al-Qa'eda sponsored violence. Considering that the city of Baghdad has over five million people, it is clear that the vast majority of Iraqis are not in conflict with the coalition forces or the new Iraqi government; they want a better life that offers freedom.

The other force multiplier speaks to the long-term goal of developing and institutionalizing a democratic ethos in the new militaries of the liberated lands. One of the greatest force multipliers imaginable would be to develop a methodology to encourage the growth of democracies throughout the community of nations. Since, for all practical purposes, democracies do not engage in aggressive warfare or terrorism, it is only logical for the United States to find ways to encourage the solidification of the new democracies that have emerged in the post-Cold War era and might emerge in the wake of the War on Terror.

The use of the United States military to promote democracy and human rights values to newly liberated countries will take on a much added significance in the War on Terror. In particular, the new governments of Afghanistan and Iraq look to American soldiers to assist them in establishing both order in the land and a law based military whose policies, rules, and practices are rooted in human rights. For now, many of these efforts are being conducted by American Special Operations Forces.

Although the terms human rights and democratic values do not immediately bring to mind images of Special Forces soldiers in action, the decade of the '90s actually witnessed, for example, the use of "Green Berets" in missions that clearly reflect America's desire to inculcate human rights values within the militaries of our friends and allies. Special Forces soldiers have proved themselves to be a premier vehicle in this regard and are now heavily engaged in Afghanistan and Iraq in this same effort. Given the new paradigm of democracy building, promoting human rights is clearly a priority mission for which Special Forces are uniquely qualified.

9.10 New Non-Traditional Roles—Human Rights as a Force Multiplier

Rubricated by the disintegration of the USSR in 1991, the world has changed drastically and with breathtaking speed. Just thirteen years ago, the free world was focused on containing a heavily armed and expansionist Soviet Empire. Suddenly, primarily through internal aspirations for greater human rights (first and second generation), the Soviet Union and its ideology of repression were gone, and the attendant winds of freedom have blown to peoples and nations throughout the world. While these winds did not much impact the Middle East, other formerly repressed peoples of the world have expressed aspirations leading to hurried attempts to establish democratic governments and free market economies, the principal coins of the realm of human rights.

The Cold War period was the classic example of the traditional use of military force to deter aggression-combat soldiers trained and prepared to go to war at any moment. The American armed forces were war-fighters, pure and simple.

As the Soviet Union began to implode, the free world realized that it was not only the military might of the United States that defeated communism—it was the ideals represented by the United States. It was what Americans have always represented to the world—respect for human rights and freedom. It can be argued that the United States military fixed the Soviets in place, but freedom ultimately caused Soviet communism to disintegrate.

Unfortunately, the United States entered the post-Cold War era with only a vague and ill defined understanding that fostering democracies was vital to American national security interests. Nevertheless, in the War on Terror, the export of human rights values is a powerful weapon against those renegade nations and peoples who still seek to wage war and terrorism. Without question, democratic values and promoting human rights are needed force multipliers in the War on Terror, primarily because the new-styled terrorists cannot be deterred by the threat of force.

The promise of a new era, where the world strives to be free from the constant evils of war, terrorism and human rights abuse, demands that the United States military expand its traditional role of war-fighter and actively enter into new, nontraditional roles. Indeed, beginning in the 1980s, the United States military has in limited areas responded by assisting in such things as drug reduction, disaster relief, humanitarian assistance, peace operations, and nation building.

In the War on Terror, the United States military has a much-needed role to play in two key force multipliers—humanitarian assistance and nation building. In fact, the concern for human rights in general mirrors the overall United States national security policy of peacetime engagement by maintaining contacts with allies and friendly governments for the purpose of imparting values and ideals associated with democratic principles. These forces must also be brought to bear on terrorist regimes.

One of the force multipliers in the War on Terror is the use of the United States military for humanitarian peacemaking missions or peace operations. The term peace operation is now defined in United States military doctrine. The United States military definition is drafted in broad terms to capture the full range of possible activities associated with maintaining or restoring peace. According to the United States Army's Center for Strategy and Force Evaluation, the term "peace operation" is defined as:

> The umbrella term encompassing observers and monitors, traditional peacekeeping, preventive deployment, internal conflict resolution, security assistance to a civil authority, protection and delivery of humanitarian relief, guaranteeing and denial of movement, imposing sanctions, peace enforcement, high intensity operations, and any other military, paramilitary or non-military action taken in support of a diplomatic peacemaking process.

In assessing the efficacy of a peace operation, from both a legal and a practical perspective, it is preferable to engage the backing and support of the United Nations as well as the financial assistance of fellow states. Not only do deepening fiscal concerns at home militate against the United States becoming the policeman for the world, common sense dictates that if the world is to move forward, all peace loving nations must join together in the effort. For these reasons, it is critical that other nations also share the burden and responsibility of future peace operations.

The other nontraditional role of the United States military is in the realm of nation building. This is what is happening in Afghanistan and in Iraq, although the continuing violence has slowed the efforts. The United States military defines nation building as "assisting a host nation in its efforts to restructure, reinforce, or rebuild its formal and informal institutions." Starting in the 1960s, the United States military has been involved in providing nation assistance, through the Foreign Assistance Act of 1961 and other Congressional authority, to friends and allies throughout the world.

In the War on Terror, many of these activities will be centered on helping new nations develop the military capability to defend themselves from internal and external aggression. The United States military is currently utilizing special Congressional authority to undertake activities designed to improve the standard of living for the inhabitants of Afghanistan and Iraq. As a result of this specific authority, United States military forces are engaged in numerous humanitarian and civic action (HCA) projects such as road building, medical care, well drilling, and other minor construction projects.

The hope for conducting these humanitarian efforts is that by raising the standard of living for the local population, the causes of internal unrest associated with conflict can be curtailed before they start. This concept has reaped tremendous benefits in fledgling democracies as far apart as Honduras and Thailand.

Of course, the most immediate concern in fostering the new Afghan and Iraqi governments is the formation of a military establishment that respects human rights and adheres to democratic principles. The new militaries of Afghanistan and Iraq have little frame of reference for a nation, or, for that matter, a military establishment that is ruled by law and guided by human rights concerns. These new militaries will undoubtedly be absolutely essential in protecting the fledgling nations as they find their paths on the road to democracy. Ironically, although totalitarian based militaries were the chief violators of international human rights in the old non-democratic Hussein and Taliban systems, the new military forces of Afghanistan and Iraq must establish themselves as the most influential institutions during their transition periods to democracy.

Because the chief violators of human rights in the old Taliban and Hussein systems were the military, it is absolutely essential that the new military arm of the Afghan and Iraqi governments be fully exposed to the basic norms and standards of behavior commonly held by militaries in a democratic society. At a minimum, they must be apolitical, respectful of human rights, personally accountable, and responsive to the civilian leadership in a democratic process.

The hallmark of a successful democracy is the military's acceptance of human rights concerns. In a democracy, the military cannot be an abuser of human rights; it must respect human rights and be held accountable to civilian authority under a rule of law for the way it carries out its missions. The military must understand that soldiers are not just people who have technical and fighting skills, but citizens who understand their role as a member of an organization with rights and responsibilities in a constitutional democracy.

Obviously, this goal can only be achieved through a systemic program designed to institutionalize these concepts. In past efforts with other emerging democracies since the fall of the Soviet Union, the United States relied on a variety of military security assistance programs to try to instill human rights values compatible with democratic principles in the host nation military. Since the United States effort was geared only at exposing the individual foreign soldier to human rights ideals, institutional reform within the host nation military never occurred. Essentially, the promotion of human rights and democracy was an indirect benefit at best, rather than explicit goals.

By their very nature, the promotion of human rights and democratization of the new Afghan and Iraqi governments involves matters that cannot be assigned to the jurisdiction of any single department of the United States government. However, the promotion of human rights and democratic principles in the military of any new democracy is best left to the United States military.

The primary concern for the Afghan and Iraqi governments rests with how, over the long term, the host nation military can be encouraged to accept a reduced and more professional role appropriate to a democracy. Ideally, this concern exceeds the minimally accepted standards for human rights and extends to the fullest possible range of meaningful human rights. These rights include freedom of religion, freedom of association, freedom of speech, and all of those principles indicative of a truly democratic society.

One of the major obstacles in imparting concepts relating to human rights and democratic principles is the fact that both Afghanistan and Iraq are faced with the social and economic turmoil traditionally associated with lesser developed countries—from economic chaos to actual armed insurgency by bands of terrorists and bandits. Thus, the effectiveness of any program of assistance must be measured against the realities associated with the specific problems facing Afghanistan and Iraq.

A successful strategy for achieving these democratization goals must be based on three clearly focused themes directed to the host nation military (and appropriate civilian government officials):

1. instilling a greater respect for internationally recognized standards for human rights;
2. fostering greater respect for and an understanding of the principle of civilian control of the military; and
3. improving military justice systems and procedures to comport with internationally recognized standards of human rights.

More than any other single endeavor one might imagine, the institutionalization of human rights values has the potential to directly reduce the threat of aggressive warfare. To be sure, true democracy cannot exist without a military establishment dedicated to the principles associated with a healthy respect for human rights. In his book on warfare in the twenty-first century, *Race to the Swift*, Richard Simpkin encapsulates this concept by noting that the militaries of democratic governments "rest on the rule of law, [of which human rights is the core] and must so rest." While such values may be taken for granted in societies resting on stable democratic traditions, this is clearly not the case in Afghanistan, Iraq or other nondemocratic states wishing to abandon totalitarian rule.

It is a simple fact that those militaries who truly abide by human rights will support and not threaten democratic development. In turn, healthy democracies are less likely to resort to aggressive warfare to settle international disputes.

9.11 The Role of Special Forces

The goal of creating a law based Afghan and Iraqi military has, to be sure, many challenges. Apart from the issue of funding such a force, they must be properly trained. Nevertheless, the training aspect is not as difficult as it may sound due to the fact that in large part, militaries of many emerging democracies have always looked to the American military in general, and the Army Special Forces in particular, as a model to assist them in defining how human rights concerns should properly function in their respective military establishments and how the military itself should fit into a more democratic form of government.

The genesis of modern Special Forces is most closely identified with President Kennedy who first officially authorized the wearing of the distinctive green beret for Army Special Forces. Although the entire force structure virtually disappeared with the end of the Vietnam era, revitalization of Special Forces occurred in the 1980s, culminating with the 1987 Congressional creation of a separate unified command—the United States Special Operations Command. This command has direct responsibility for every type of special operational force in the Navy, Army, Air Force and Marines. Congress further helped structure the types of forces and named specific mission activities: direct action, strategic reconnaissance, unconventional warfare, foreign internal defense, counterterrorism, civil affairs, psychological operations, humanitarian assistance, theater search and rescue, and other activities. Army Special Forces are one component of Special Operations Forces. They are elite professionals, trained to operate in any type of environment. Because they know the language, culture, and environment, the soldiers foster an atmosphere of unity with the indigenous people.

The public mystique of the Green Beret as the ultimate jungle fighter capable of single-handedly defeating entire enemy battalions clearly belies the real importance of these specialized and highly skilled soldiers. While they certainly have significant wartime missions, Special Forces are most effective when executing their dual peacetime roles of prevention and deterrence. Paradoxically, when executing their peacetime role, it is in part because of, not in spite of, the aura of invincibility that they enjoy public support and successes far in excess of what their limited numbers would imply. Currently, the Army has five active-duty, brigade-size Special Forces groups, each group operationally directed toward a particular segment of the world. In the War on Terror, prevention and deterrence roles are proving just as important as the fighting mission.

The Special Forces' role covers a full range of activities in the Third World, the principle purpose being to prevent escalation of conflict. This is done by training indigenous people to defend themselves and, to a lesser degree, engaging in limited humanitarian missions in the more remote parts of the country. This civic action includes providing medical and veterinary aid, conducting various public services, and other activities aimed at improving living conditions. The primary mission in the prevention role is training. It was during the Vietnam era that Special Forces earned the coveted reputation of being premier trainers of indigenous forces in military skills. Thousands of tribesmen and local Vietnamese were successfully organized into effective self-defense forces. Then, as now, the secret to their achievements was hard training, common sense, and empathy. These professionals were required not only to be experts in their technical skills, but they also had to be proficient in the host language, totally familiar with the culture, and able to literally live in the same, often-times primitive, environments. To accomplish these tasks, these men underwent extensive, intensive, and expensive training.

Carrying on this tradition, Special Forces continue to teach host nation forces fundamental military skills, as well as more advanced tactics in desert, jungle and urban warfare. The training activities are directly aimed at assisting the host nation through long-term, in-depth courses and instruction. Accordingly, the mission to train and help organize indigenous local forces remains the cornerstone of modern Special Forces. The efforts crystallize as the host nation is better prepared to deal with overt manifestations of conflict through strengthened military capabilities.

When used in their preventive capacity, Special Forces are inherently successful in establishing an excellent rapport with the local population. This, quite naturally, helps defeat terrorism at its roots. One Special Forces medic conducting missions in Honduras described the typical attitude of the locals, "[I]t is also a morale boost for them [Hondurans]; if we're out in the field with them, sweat with them, eat their food and drink their beer, then, by God, they appreciate what we're doing and what we're going through."

The other critical role of Special Forces is that of deterrence, a role that is particularly important in a crisis situation. In this role, the Special Forces are used to "wave the flag," to be nothing less than concrete evidence that America is strongly committed to the host nation. A good illustration of this function occurred in 1987. Soldiers from the 1st Special Forces Group were sent to Thailand at the request of that government in order to demonstrate American support. At the time, the Thais were fighting North Vietnamese forces seeking to exert control over Cambodian resistance fighters. In keeping with the deterrent function, the Special Forces were directed to perform numerous well-publicized mass parachute jumps and exercises with their Thai counterparts along the Cambodian border. More recently this role of deterrence assigned to Special Forces has been illustrated by numerous events in Afghanistan. Special Forces operatives assigned to a bodyguard detail for Afghan President Karzi thwarted an assassination attempt on Karzi. These Special Forces soldiers killed the would-be assailant, while sustaining only one casualty to an American soldier.

Show of force functions are relatively well-suited to the Special Forces, due again in part to their universal reputation as America's elite fighters. In 1987 the *Soviet Military Review* described them as being "professional killers ... with ... a brutal hatred of the Communist countries." Such puffing aside, these soldiers never fail to make an impression; no matter the story line, headlines always start with the same two words: "Green Berets."

Now, in the War on Terror, Special Forces are the preferred weapon of choice when it comes to ground operations with local counterparts and just as critical, in the task of promoting democratic values. Host nation forces that join the fight against terrorism instinctively turn to United States Army Special Forces for the following reasons.

First, Army Special Forces are uniquely positioned to influence the attitudes and, in some cases, even the structure and function of the host nation military. Why? Because they go where no other element of the United States military can. As noted by Major General Kenneth R. Bowra, the former commanding general of the Army's Special Forces (1996–1998), "Other than Special Forces, there is no element of the United States military forces that is capable of instilling human rights into the militaries of emerging democracies."

Special Forces soldiers perform hundreds of missions each year in support of the war fighting combatant commands and other government agencies. These operations span the entire spectrum of conflict, to include direct action, foreign internal defense, special reconnaissance, unconventional warfare, security assistance training, humanitarian assistance, counter-narcotics, de-mining, and combating terrorism. Simply put, when it comes to operating with host nation forces, Green Berets are everywhere, doing everything. The deployment figures tell the tale. In fiscal year (FY) 2001, for instance, United States Army Special Forces soldiers were deployed on over 2,500 missions to over 200 countries throughout the world.

Second, since Special Forces soldiers are extensively trained in the language, culture, religion, and politics of the countries in which they operate, they are best able to foster genuine military-to-military relationships. This fact applies to individual host nations, as well as to the geographic region as a whole. Thus, based on cultural nuances only they can appreciate, Special Forces can tailor each particular mission in order to make the maximum impression on their military counterparts regarding the importance of human rights concerns.

Third, more than any other arm of the United States military, Special Forces exemplify to foreign militaries the success story of how a professional military force can maintain a superb operational record while functioning in accordance with human rights concerns. Almost without exception, foreign soldiers are deeply impressed with how human rights and military efficiency can go hand-in-hand. Foreign forces know that, for the Green Berets, concern for human rights has always been the *sine que non* for United States military operations.

Indeed, the promotion of international human rights and democratic behavior has long been a critical theme of the United States Army's Special Forces, regardless of the mission that they happen to be performing. President Kennedy routinely praised this unique quality, and no one who has followed the success story of Army Special Forces soldiers in Operations Provide Comfort

(Iraq/Turkey), Restore Hope (Somalia), Just Cause (Panama), Desert Storm (Middle East), Uphold Democracy (Haiti), IFOR (Bosnia), Enduring Freedom (Afghanistan) and Iraqi Freedom (Iraq) can doubt their value in this regard.

In short, Army Special Forces soldiers are universally recognized and respected as efficient, professional, and humanitarian. The former United States Army Special Operations Commander, Lieutenant General (ret.) James T. Scott, stressed this truism during a speech given in the summer of 1996, "I can tell you that Special Forces soldiers will ... continue to serve as the conscience and the example for lesser developed nations regarding human rights."

The motto of Special Forces, *De Oppresso Liber* (To Free the Oppressed), reflects a profound concern for the inherent dignity of those who are denied international human rights. Crossing all cultural and societal boundaries, this mentality makes Special Forces soldiers an ideal model as they train host nation forces and assist in alleviating many of the conditions that breed human rights abuses. By word and deed, Special Forces promote the message that the hallmark of a professional military serving the interests of a democratic nation is its commitment to human rights. This message is not lost on the host nation.

The four basic themes taught and stressed to the developing Afghan and Iraqi militaries are:

1. human rights abuses are never tolerated by a democratic populace;
2. such violations do not shorten a conflict, be it internal or external in nature, but usually have the opposite effect;
3. the soldiers guilty of human rights violations must be punished, or similar abuses will certainly follow; and
4. in order to maintain discipline and esprit de corps, the chain of command must constantly train soldiers to respect internationally recognized human rights and the law of war.

Shortly after assuming command of the Army Special Forces Command at Fort Bragg, North Carolina, Major General Bowra took affirmative action to ensure that all Special Forces soldiers thoroughly understood their rights and responsibilities regarding human rights *vis-à-vis* any host nation military. A first ever Special Forces Human Rights Policy Memorandum was issued by General Bowra, directing that all Special Forces soldiers who deploy overseas must:

1. be trained in the full range of human rights issues, both generally and as they may apply to the host nation to which they are deploying; and
2. report through the chain of command all gross violations of human rights they may encounter while overseas.

The four-page policy memorandum also requires commanders, whenever practicable, to integrate human rights training as a part of the training provided to the host nation military. In addition, senior commanders must review all exercise and deployment "after action reports" to evaluate the impact that human rights training initiatives have had on host nation military forces and then make recommendations for improvements to higher headquarters.

Special Forces soldiers and their commanders have many resources available to them to promote human rights. The most important resource, other than a soldier's solid moral compass, is the group judge advocate (GJA) assigned to each of the Special Forces groups. Each GJA is thoroughly trained in human rights law and has compiled an extensive collection of information dealing with human rights issues related to the group's area of responsibility. Apart from providing the mandatory pre-deployment legal briefings to all soldiers deploying to foreign soil, these specialized military attorneys stay abreast of current doctrine in the form of international agreements, human rights doctrine, and political and social changes in the region concerned. They are currently on the ground in Afghanistan and Iraq, taking a proactive view and performing crucial implementation missions with the local Afghan and Iraqi leaders as new Afghan and Iraqi militaries stand up.

9.12 New Challenges and New Thinking

In terms of promoting peace and advancing human rights, the Middle East remains the most difficult area of the world for the United States to influence. A continuing pattern of violence and bloodshed accurately defines the character of the region, a pattern which was brought home to Americans with the heinous attacks by al-Qa'eda operatives on the United States, on September 11, 2001, and continues with terror attacks by Islamic radicals against United States forces in Afghanistan and Iraq.

Until the War on Terror, the policy of the United States toward the Middle East was rooted primarily on maintaining stability in this oil-rich region, with human rights concerns taking a back seat to financial concerns. To accomplish this, the United States still spends billions dollars each year (in equal amounts) in military and economic assistance for the two major powers in the region—Israel and Egypt.

Unfortunately, Islamic radicalism that engages in hostilities against the United States and its allies is seeking to fill the ideological power vacuum in the region left by the decline of communism and could easily engulf other Arab countries in the same manner as it did with Iran, Afghanistan and the Sudan. Islamic radicalism, which is diametrically opposed to most of the normative values of human rights, is offered as the only alternative to the moderate, yet non-democratic Muslim and Arab leaders who are unwilling or unable to address the economic and social disparities of their people.

In the context of advancing human rights issues in the region, only Israel can be considered as a stable democratic environment. Egypt by constitution is a socialist democratic republic in which the Islamic Sharia is the principal source of legislation. Unfortunately, Egypt has shown little willingness to improve its record. Tragically, the majority of countries considered by the State Department of the United States as sponsors of terrorism are located in the Middle East (e.g., Iran, Syria and Sudan).

The pivot for democratic advancement is certainly at stake in Iraq and Afghanistan. Only time will tell if the policy of bringing a more democratic form of government is a "bridge too far."

9.13 Questions for Discussion

1. *Causes of aggression.* Dr. Stanton E. Samenow, Jr., INSIDE THE CRIMINAL MIND (1984):

> Criminals cause crime—not bad neighborhoods, inadequate parents, television, schools, drugs, or unemployment. Crime resides in the minds of human beings and is not caused by social conditions. Once we as a society recognize this simple fact, we shall take measures radically different from current ones. To be sure, we shall continue to remedy intolerable social conditions for this is worthwhile in and of itself. But we shall not expect criminals to change because of such efforts.

Is Dr. Samenow's observation correct?

2. *Correct analysis but flawed execution?* Reflecting the fact that democracies do not engage in aggression and do a better job at promoting human rights concerns, democratization has been a central core of the Bush Administration's policy for the Middle East. How can democratization be achieved when it appears that centrifugal forces of violence have now been unleashed in many parts of the Middle East? By the end of 2006, despite the successful establishment of an Iraqi government and the greater deployment of the new Iraq military, Iraqis were dying at the rate of 100 a day.

3. *Has Mideast democracy concepts provided a boost to religious Islamic militants*? 2006 elections in Lebanon provided Hizbollah, an Iranian Shiite backed terrorist organization, seats in the parliament and a post in the government's Cabinet. Similarly, Hamas' rise to power in the "free" elections in the Palestinian territories replaced the secular Fatah party. Discuss.

Selected Bibliography

Burns, John F. *Traces of Terror: Kandahar and Kabul; Afghan President Escapes Bullets; 25 Killed by Bomb*, NY TIMES, Sept. 6, 2002, at A1.

Defense Institute of Security Assistance Management. THE MANAGEMENT OF SECURITY ASSISTANCE. 12th ed. 1992.

Foreign Assistance Act of 1961, as amended, 22 U.S.C. 2347, which provides the authority for security assistance under the International Military Education and Training (IMET) program.

Halberstadt, H. GREEN BERETS: UNCONVENTIONAL WARRIORS. 1988.

Howard, A.E. Dick. CONSTITUTION MAKING IN EASTERN EUROPE. 1993.

Humphrey, John T. NO DISTANT MILLENNIUM: THE INTERNATIONAL LAW OF HUMAN RIGHTS. 1989.

Hutchins, Robert Maynard, ed. GREAT BOOKS OF THE WESTERN WORLD. 1952.

Klare, Michael T., and Peter Kornbluh, eds. LOW-INTENSITY WARFARE. 1988.

Lesser, Ian O., et al. COUNTERING THE NEW TERRORISM. RAND, 1999.

Lillich, Richard B., and Frank C. Newman. INTERNATIONAL HUMAN RIGHTS. 1991.

O'Brien, William V. THE CONDUCT OF JUST AND LIMITED WAR. 1981.

Oppenheim, Lassa. INTERNATIONAL LAW: A TREATISE. 1955.

Privileged Killers, SOVIET MILITARY REVIEW, Jan. 1987, at 4.

Russett, B. GRASPING THE DEMOCRATIC PEACE: PRINCIPLES FOR A POST-COLD WAR WORLD. 1993.

Simpkin, Richard. RACE TO THE SWIFT: THOUGHTS ON TWENTY-FIRST CENTURY WARFARE. 1985.

Thieme, Robert B., Jr. THE INTEGRITY OF GOD. Houston, TX: R.B. Thieme. 1979. (an excellent discussion of the grace mechanics of salvation vs. the concept of human effort to achieve salvation.)

U.S. Army's Center for Strategy and Force Evaluation. PEACEKEEPING OPERATIONS. Sept. 1993.

USASFC (A) Policy Memorandum, dated August 13, 1996. SPECIAL FORCES HUMAN RIGHTS POLICY. Issued by MG Kenneth Bowra, CG, USASFC (A).

USASFC (A) HUMAN RIGHTS HANDBOOK (on file with the OSJA, USASFC(A), Fort Bragg, NC).

Chapter 10
Leading the Way—Pax Americana or the Rule of Law?

Let he who desires peace, prepare for war.

—Flavius Vegetius Renatus (first century A.D.)

The fact that the United States saved Western Europe and the free world in two World Wars by the use of its magnificent military establishment, coupled with its even greater industrial complex, does not imply that the ongoing military campaigns in the War on Terror will set the stage for a pax Americana. Much like President Roosevelt's attempt to color the participation of the United States in World War II with a far greater purpose than national self-interest, President Bush's concern for protecting the United States is also cognizant of promoting world stability. To his great credit, President Bush has chosen the rule of law as his rallying point and has not fallen into the trap of embracing issues and matters that appeal to utopian ideals beyond the scope of the War on Terror. This error was made by his father, President George H. Bush, in his desire to advance an idea known as the *New World Order* in the context of the Gulf War.

10.1 The United States Global Strategic View
Although the War on Terror has seen a dramatic shift to homeland security as the primary mission of the United States military, the overall strategy since the end of the Cold War has been one of active engagement or deterrence through power projection. At least in theory, active engagement also has a positive aim of promoting democracy, regional stability and economic prosperity. However, in the context of conducting "operations other than war," the orientation has shifted from containing the menace posed by an expansionist Soviet Union to responding to regional conflicts throughout the world.

Since regional conflicts may vary and are far less monolithic than the old Soviet threat, ad hoc coalitions have replaced formal alliances. This was seen in the Gulf War as well as in the ongoing War on Terror. To support the active engagement theory, force generation has also changed from forward deployment to forward presence—no longer are large numbers of United States forces permanently stationed in foreign countries to ensure the peace. Despite the presence of a large force in Iraq, the new strategy in the War on Terror envisions a force projection of small contingents of American forces deployed on the foreign soil of our allies, such as Yemen and the Philippines, to assist in blunting the impact of al-Qa'eda forces and other like-minded terrorist groups.

Another purpose of these small scale deployments of American fighters is to deter aggression simply by being present in the region. Ultimately, deterrence remains a key component of strategic policy in the War on Terror, with the United States able and ready to use full scale force to punish aggression should the challenge arise.

Undoubtedly, the projection of its forces in this engagement strategy requires a strong leadership role by the United States. In the post-Cold War era, the cement of anti-communism that held democratic alliances together is no longer valid and many allies and friends no longer have the same degree of need for American protection. Consequently, America is required to walk a thinner line between leadership and arrogant dominance, as selected coalitions are temporarily built to deal with the threat of terrorism. Furthermore, to be successful under the collective engagement strategy, American leadership must be exercised in conjunction with the interests of the people of the host nation. Indeed, the strongest coalition partners in defeating a totalitarian terrorist regime are the people enslaved in their own country.

Still, in the face of drastic military reductions in United States military forces since the 1990s, the elite ground forces available for these unique missions are being stretched to the breaking point. Demanding that the military do more with less causes many to express skepticism about maintaining the required effectiveness to fight and win a conflict with the ever elusive al-Qa'eda and the renegade States like Iran who seek access to weapons of mass murder.

One fact stands certain. The United States cannot continue the War on Terror or take a strong leadership role in promoting democracy in liberated lands with an emasculated military. There is no historical basis to validate the proposition that a nation can successfully increase its influence in the world while simultaneously reducing its armed forces. In the context of deterring future aggression and winning the War on Terror this proposition is extremely disturbing. If history has proven anything, it is that the machinations of aggressor nations bent on expansion are not stopped by negotiation or peace overtures. In dealing with aggressor nations, the avenues of unilateral military reduction, negotiation, or appeasement do not lead to the path of peace—all are false concepts. The shared revulsion against war and terrorism that all free people possess will have no good effect unless it is coupled with an enforcement mechanism.

10.2 Collective Security

Collective security has always required a dominant leader with a sufficient military establishment. Devoid of any military arm of its own, the United Nations could not deal with, for example, Saddam Hussein and his continued violations of international law. In the twentieth century, that has always meant the United States. This is true in every case in which international collective security has functioned. The lesson of the War on Terror is the same as that of the 1991 Gulf War and the Korean War: the United Nations does not have the capacity to guarantee the security of its members absent the direct participation of the United States.

In the real world, the question will be the same as it has always been. Will the people of the United States continue to possess the resolve to assist in the struggle to halt major acts of aggression in the future? As demonstrated in the War on Terror, it is probable that a majority of Americans will continue to possess such resolve. Apart from matters of self-interest, the United States of America does have a continuing responsibility to the world to enforce the rule of law. Judged by any positive standard, be it in the field of human rights, self-determination, economic opportunity, or privacy related to property and person, the United States stands out as the pearl of all that is possible for any given nation to achieve. Furthermore, America, like great nations before it, has related all of these positive values to a strong heritage of law. The framers of the nation established certain democratic values, and subsequent generations have generally exhibited the discipline and courage to maintain and expand those values.

America's most fundamental asset does not reside in her military might or industrial complex. Those pillars merely provide support for the United States' most precious commodity—freedom as related to the rule of law. Although the United States military most certainly deterred the aggressiveness of the Soviet Empire from 1945 to 1991, it was the beacon of American freedom that ultimately dispelled the darkness of communism. To the world, then, the United States offers a pattern of prosperity and freedom under the rule of law. This is the message that the United States must continue to send to the world.

The world is still a very dangerous place and, as never before, it is time for forward thinking in the long term as the nation prosecutes the War on Terror. Coming out of the Cold War just over a decade ago, millions of people in Central Asia and Eastern Europe still have little frame of reference for a nation or, for that matter, a world that is ruled by law. Indeed, the governments of the Middle East lag far behind in fulfilling the requirements of first and second generation human rights.

Under the leadership of President George W. Bush, the United States has so far successfully validated the logic and necessity for following the rule of law. Undeniably, the legitimate interest of the United States in halting international terrorism in the era of weapons of mass destruction has benefited the entire civilized world. For freedom loving peoples everywhere, the victory in Afghanistan and Iraq ensured that the cost of maintaining freedom was paid by another generation of patriotic Americans. To a large degree, this sacrifice not only enforces the rule of law, but undoubtedly serves as a deterrent to other tyrants and terrorists.

10.3 Peace, Freedom and Appeasement—Lessons from the Gulf War of 1991

It is a fundamental principle that all free States have a common interest in maintaining peace. However, peace, like security, is a precious commodity rarely attained without great sacrifice. In addition, peace is far more than the absence of war; it is an elusive intangible which only takes on meaning when related to freedom. Although the goal of abolishing war, like eradicating crime, is certainly commendable, given the basic nature of man, neither goal is totally feasible. As long as there are demagogues like Sennacherib, Hitler, Stalin or Saddam Hussein, nation-states must have strong military establishments to protect themselves. Under this truism, the symbol of freedom for Americans is not a cracked Liberty Bell in Philadelphia, but the military uniform of its soldiers.

Accepting the premise that human beings are morally flawed creatures, it stands to reason that the best that mankind can ever hope to achieve is to control aggression. Like criminals, aggressive nations and terrorists can only be deterred through the proper functioning of two principles:

(1) the threat of lawful force; or (2) the application of lawful force. To the extent that the function of these two principles fail, wars will certainly continue to exist. Paradoxically, those groups who resist this truism, demonstrated by irrational demands for peace through the continued restriction of all categories of force, blissfully lay the groundwork for the next war.

The oft-heard saying "violence never solves anything" is a favorite catch phrase for so-called "peace activists." Of course, as is the case for many such glib expressions, it is a falsehood that does not stand up to reason or historical scrutiny. As illustrated by the Allied defeat of the Axis powers in World War II, only the application of lawful violence ultimately solved the problem of Axis aggression and murder. In short, the use of lawful violence in self-defense is a hard reality of life that must always remain a legitimate option to secure the peace. While nonviolence expressed in the form of public demonstrations, boycotts, "sit-ins," etc., may be efficacious when confronting social injustice in certain organizations and governments that are based to some degree on democratic foundations, such activities seldom make any progress when used to confront committed totalitarian forces. Even Martin Luther King, the great American champion of nonviolence, conceded that this tactic would be useless against tyrants.

> I felt that while war could never be a positive or absolute good, it could serve as a negative good in the sense of preventing the spread and growth of an evil force. War, as horrible as it is, might be preferable to surrender to a totalitarian system—Nazi, Fascist, or Communist.

Sadly, in the course of the human experience, it is sometimes the case that nothing except the employment of lawful violence will thwart the use of aggressive violence and the correct moral course is to employ lawful violence. Understanding this truth is fundamental to penetrating the state of mind of those who simply reject violence under any circumstance. Tragically, those most devoted to peace above all values seem ill prepared to recognize that the cost of not using lawful violence may only ensure a continuation of aggressive violence that could spiral out of control.

Peace activists who use religion (primarily their reading of Christianity) to justify a rejection of force come in many varieties. Some try to mask their refusal to engage in violence with Bible verses taken out of context, while others simply make broad religious generalizations about the matter. For instance, William H. De Lancey, bishop of the Episcopal Diocese of New York, wrote a letter to President Abraham Lincoln in 1863 invoking religion to avoid participating in the American Civil War. He demanded that he and all other bishops and priests be exempted from the federal draft laws. De Lancey wrote, "[I]t is contrary to their consciences as officers of Christ's kingdom to bear arms as soldiers and shed blood." Continuing with the letter, Bishop De Lancey reminded Lincoln that in the garden of Gethsemane on the occasion of his arrest, Christ told Peter in Matt. 26:52 that "[t]hey that take the sword shall perish with the sword." Of course, in making his case, the bishop rejected the more sensible view that this passage refers to the societal consequences of criminal behavior, i.e., criminals will be lawfully executed by the State for their crimes, and not the lawful use of force in combat activities.

If peace at any price, with compromise as the only means to achieve it, is the major concern of a national entity, then the destruction of that nation will be the inevitable consequence. Freedom, not peace, must always be the issue for free nations; when nations are no longer willing to pay the price of freedom, then they, too, will lose their freedom. As Woodrow Wilson so wisely reflected in May of 1917: "It is not an army that we must train for war; it is a nation."

Tragically, every democratic nation has within it the very seeds which will eventually destroy it, for the choice between freedom or peace must be made by each successive generation. With freedom, war is periodically inevitable. By choosing peace without maintaining the power to enforce the peace, however, war will come more often and with a greater probability of resulting in the annihilation of the nation. Just as crime increases when society gets sentimental about the criminal and forgets about the victim, so to will the probability of war increase as the nation emphasizes peace instead of freedom.

When Spain was attacked by a series of coordinated bombings in March 2004, killing almost 200 commuters, the response to the al-Qa'eda linked terrorists was to withdraw all Spanish military personnel from Iraq. This step signaled to the terrorists that terror attacks can produce a desired outcome. In quick step, the terrorists used terror threats and acts of terror to intimidate the Philippines who withdrew their forces early from Iraq in response to a kidnapping and threat of beheading. On the other hand, threats to Italy and Australia to withdraw from Iraq have not been successful. In July of 2004, the Australians were warned that "we will shake the earth under your feet as we did in Indonesia [referring to the 2002 Bali bombing which killed over 200 people, mostly Australians on vacation], and lines of car bombs will not cease." Similarly, the Abu Jafs al-Masri Brigades threat to "shake the earth" everywhere in Italy, unless the Italians withdrew from Iraq has not caused the Italians to budge. The Italian and Australian leadership remember the lesson of Munich—appeasement only encourages aggression.

Ultimately, the cost of achieving freedom can only be understood by those who have paid the price. Indeed, there is no permanent guarantee that the United States will continue to function as a national entity beyond a strong military-industrial complex coupled with the people who have the will to fight if necessary.

For this reason, it is dangerous rhetoric to blur the fundamental distinction between the need for the legitimate use of force and unlawful aggression. Despite disclaimers that the concept of "world peace" should not be related to restricting the use of force or promoting unilateral disarmament, the connotation is otherwise. No anti-war movement has ever been premised on maintaining a strong and viable military, and no proponent of the use of lawful violence can ever hope to be immune from the wishful thinking of those who demand the dismantling of the very forces that sustain and protect the freedom of the nation—the military establishment.

On the other hand, the concept of the rule of law does not necessarily carry with it the connotation that man is ever capable of achieving the panacea of world peace. For the rule of law, it is enough if aggressive war can be controlled. As one expert in international law noted during the Gulf War of 1991, "At the root of United States policy in the Gulf War was the principle of upholding the Rule of Law. Article 2(4) of the U.N. Charter outlaws armed international aggression, and the massive Iraqi invasion of Kuwait was a direct challenge to that principle."

In short, how does one react to those nations or groups who either contemplate the use of unlawful force or who actually engage in such unlawful force? To date, the U.N. Charter is undeniably the foremost tool in dealing with and deterring aggression; it is an integral component of the rule of law. The classic McDougal and Feliciano, *Law and Minimum Public Order*, states:

> The most difficult problem which today confronts world public order is that of characteriz-ing and preventing unlawful violence. The history is familiar how over the centuries— through *bellum justum*, the Covenant of the League of Nations, the Pact of Paris, the judg-ments at Nuremberg and Tokyo, and the U.N. Charter—the public order of the world com-munity has at long last come to a prohibition of certain coercion as a method of interna-tional change and to a distinction between permissible and nonpermissible coercion.

Although history has proven time and again that the curtailment of aggression can only come through the threat of force, or the application of force, the authority for those responses must be firmly rooted in law. Despite this truism, the necessity for and legality of Article 51 is, nonethe-less, constantly under attack by those groups who intentionally blur the difference between lawful and unlawful uses of force. In their search for the panacea of brotherhood, various peace groups refuse to acknowledge any distinction regarding the use of force. Left unchallenged, this attitude will only encourage aggression, not forestall it.

President Bush has done an admirable job in the continuing task of articulating to the world the distinction between the unlawful use of force by an aggressor and the lawful use of force un-der the rule of law by civilized nations. In fact, those who advocate ending war by destroying the forests of bayonets (i.e., unilateral disarmament) hinder the validity of the rule of law to that ex-tent.

Historically, the desire of numerous organizations to curtail or eliminate the use of force as a national option, regardless of the justification for the employment of that force, is always present in any debate on how to best answer aggression. While these voices are helpful if kept in proper perspective, appeasement is nothing new. The Biblical prophet Jeremiah heard the same voices almost 2,500 years ago as peace activists in the Southern Kingdom of Judah proposed how to deal with the aggression of Chaldean militarism. Jeremiah analyzed the peace at any cost advocates as follows: "They allege to solve the problems of my people, [they cry] 'Peace, peace' when there is no peace."

Similarly, the voices in the War on Terror who call for peace at any price say nothing new— the same voices occurred in the Gulf War of 1991, although far more loudly. Calling for peace in the Gulf War at any price, some paid little regard for even the most clearly worded rules and norms associated with the rule of law as it applies to the lawful use of force. This phenomenon extended all the way from the highest levels of the United Nations to, as to be expected, an assort-ment of politically active anti-war groups.

At the top echelon, this phenomenon was brought out rather dramatically on November 8, 1990, when none other than the Secretary General of the United Nations, Perez de Cuellar, opined that because no nation had taken military action against Iraq since the occupation of Kuwait in August 1990, "the passage of three months time had terminated the right of individual states to use force against Iraq under the 'collective self-defense' provisions of Article 51." Not only did de Cuellar's statement exhibit a gross misunderstanding of the U.N. Charter, it did nothing but encourage the continued aggression of the Iraqi military.

Certainly, de Cuellar knew that Article 51 did not create the right of self-defense, but that such a right was an inherent right which Article 51 simply acknowledged and reinforced. Furthermore, Iraq's aggression did not end on August 2, 1990, but was a continuing offense, since none of the Security Council resolutions demanding that Iraq leave Kuwait had succeeded in "maintaining international peace and security."

The policy implications of the Secretary General's position reveal its total absurdity; a rule that requires nations to respond immediately to an armed attack or else forfeit their rights to take defensive action effectively nullifies the principles embodied in Article 2(3) and 2(4) of the U.N. Charter. By making a mockery of this critical rule of law, de Cuellar sent two disastrous signals, one to Saddam Hussein and one to the community of nations. First, the Secretary General's total misreading of Article 51 only encouraged Iraq's continuing occupation of Kuwait and was completely counterproductive to the international movement to force Iraq out of Kuwait short of armed force. Second, the requirement that nations act immediately in self-defense is the antithesis of what the United Nation encourages, i.e., the peaceful settlement of disputes through diplomacy and every other peaceful channel for resolution of conflict. Finally, the longer the hesitation in the use of legitimate force (give peace a chance), the more probable that the same peace activists will view the coalition forces as the aggressor!

The more common variety of anti-war groups also hoped that the end of the Cold War would be the catalyst for their simplistic notions concerning the abolition of war. Advocating peace, but having no concept of what the concept must necessarily entail—the willingness to fight for peace—numerous anti-war activists demanded appeasement. Paradoxically, the loud demands for peace during the six month Iraqi occupation of Kuwait probably ensured that the threat of force as a deterrence would most surely fail, leaving no alternative but the use of lawful violence.

As Saddam Hussein held firm in Kuwait with no signs of withdrawal, various religious groups also voiced dismay over those who contemplated the exercise of lawful armed force against Iraq under Article 51. For example, both the Vatican daily newspaper, *Losservatore Romano*, and the official publication of the Jesuit order, *La Civilta Cattolica*, spoke out against using force to expel Iraq from Kuwait. On November 17, 1990, *La Civilta Cattolica* wrote, "The [coming] war in the Gulf will be a moral shame and a political disaster."

In his traditional Christmas message, Pope John Paul II gave the following heartfelt warning to those who contemplated the use of force to expel Saddam Hussein: "May leaders be convinced that war is an adventure with no return. By reasoning, patience and dialogue with respect for the inalienable rights of people and nations, it is possible to identify and travel the paths of understanding and peace." In the final analysis, the Pope's sincere desire for "[n]o more war, war never again" is a beautiful ideal but, unfortunately, can sometimes prove counterproductive in the maintenance of world peace. Often, such signals encourage aggression if no room is left for the use of lawful force to halt aggression *ab initio* or to challenge aggression once it has become entrenched. In fact, one commentator observed that of the thirty-eight times the Pope spoke out against the Gulf War, "[t]here was not an echo of a hint of a suggestion that the United States and its allies (including Italy) were in a battle against a tyrant who had just invaded and [sic] occupied and brutally destroyed a small neighbor ...."

Some religious leaders, emotionally obsessed by the fact that large numbers of soldiers were going to be killed in war, irrationally concluded that all war in the modern era was immoral, regardless of the motivation. Fueled by reports that some Iraqi soldiers had been buried alive in their defensive positions by American tanks, a religious publicist, Guy Munger, concluded that "any discussion of whether Desert Storm was a just war seem[s] to border on the insane. Indeed, practical application of the theory may have ended with the crossbow." According to Munger, "modern war is always immoral." Of course, the argument is totally fallacious for two reasons. First, long before the crossbow, battle casualties could easily mount into the hundreds of thousands. For example, during the Second Punic War (219–202 B.C.), the Carthaginian forces under Hannibal killed in combat over 60,000 Roman soldiers in a single day. And second, Munger fails to understand the real world consequences associated with a refusal to defend oneself.

Claiming to be a spokesperson for morality and justice, the wife of Martin Luther King, Jr., Coretta King, attempted to derail the United States-led military coalition to eject Saddam Hussein from Kuwait. She referred to the American actions as a "low [point] since the death of Dr. King." Speaking on January 11, 1991, Mrs. King called on a new anti-war movement to be launched on January 15, 1991, the date of the United Nations' deadline for Iraq to withdraw from Kuwait or face the use of force: "And so I am urging everyone who believes in Martin Luther King, Jr.'s dream of peace to use this holiday to launch a new anti-war movement that will not rest until a peaceful resolution of the conflict in the Persian Gulf is secured."

Failing to elaborate on how this peace movement could force a brutal dictator to relinquish his death grip on Kuwait, Mrs. King called the American participation in the Gulf War "wrong and immoral." Like the other peace activists who refuse to consider the application of force under any circumstances, Mrs. King's call for "peace-loving people everywhere to accelerate their efforts to stop it" did nothing except encourage the ruthlessness of the Iraqi occupation.

Similarly, the president of the Southern Christian Leadership Conference, Reverend Joseph Lowery, objected to the United States military action on moral grounds saying, "Let us call upon the nations to spend our resources on medical supplies, not military supplies; to make tractors, not tanks; to beat missiles into morsels of bread to feed the hungry; to build housing, not foxholes." Again, if history has demonstrated anything, it has demonstrated that utopian rhetoric about turning "swords into plowshares" is not helpful in deterring people and nations who exhibit aggressive tendencies.

Obviously, man is always confronted with aggression; a world without conflict is not something that is in the here and now. Those who wish to enter a new world order in which "swords are turned in plowshares" need to recall the comments of Haynes Johnson of the *Washington Post*: "[this] is not the millennium; the new world order has not arrived." Unfortunately, the sincere but unrealistic belief that war can be curtailed by third-party dispute settlement processes or by massive disarming processes was not buried in the lessons of the Gulf War of 1991.

10.4 Peace, Freedom and Appeasement—Lessons from War on Terror

Closer in time, a sampling of remarks during the Global War on Terrorism is all that is necessary to address the theme of those who call for peace at any price, with little or no regard for the long standing norms and rules associated with the lawful use of force. In her 2006 book, *The Mighty and the Almighty*, even the liberal minded Madeleine Albright opposed the voices of appeasement that protested the pending military campaign against the Taliban regime in Afghanistan following the attacks of 9/11. Not only did she disagree with the official 2001 call by the World Council of Churches to not strike back against the terrorists, but she also questioned the soundness of prize winning author Alice Walker's naïve admonishment that "the only punishment that works is love."

In November of 2002, as the United States and its coalition of the willing were gearing up to expand the Global War on Terrorism to Iraq, over 70 religious leaders in the United States and the United Kingdom issued a joint statement that condemned the contemplated use of what they termed "preemptive war" against the regime of Saddam Hussein. Recognizing that the Iraqi government had a duty to "stop its internal repression, to end its threats to peace, to abandon its efforts to develop weapons of mass destruction, and to respect the legitimate role of the United Nations in ensuring that it does so," the religious leaders nevertheless insisted that as "Christians" they were certain that the United States, Britain and the international community could only employ the tools of "moral principles, political wisdom, and international law" to confront Saddam.

> As Christians, we seek to be guided by the vision of a world in which nations do not attempt to resolve international problems by making war on other nations. It is a long held Christian principle that all governments and citizens are obliged to work for the avoidance of war.

In closing the statement, the group quoted the familiar Biblical passage "nation shall not lift up sword against nation," which, although very popular in anti-war circles, is grossly distorted from its proper scriptural context. The passage clearly deals with eschatological teachings about the future and not the current world we reside in. They wrote, "We reaffirm our religious hope for a world in which 'nation shall not lift up sword against nation.' We pray that our governments will be guided by moral principles, political wisdom, and legal standards, and will step back from their calls for war."

Similarly, in late 2002, the President of the United Methodist Council of Bishops wrote a pastoral letter to the United Methodist congregation, of which President Bush and Vice President Cheney are both members, stating that "war by the United States against a nation like Iraq goes against the very grain of *our understanding of the gospel*, our church's teachings, and our conscience [emphasis added]."

With the defeat of Saddam Hussein and the end of the international armed conflict with Iraq in May 2003, the Bush Administration was faced with an unexpected deadly level of sectarian violence fueled in part by a variety of criminal groups, al-Qa'eda terrorists and Saddam loyalists. Nevertheless, the theme of religious based anti-war activists remains the same. When Reverend Al Sharpton met anti-war activist Cindy Sheehan at an interfaith service on Sunday, August 28, 2005, outside of Crawford, Texas, he did so based on his "moral obligation" to oppose the war. In March of 2003, two well known bishops and one church official were among 65 people arrested during an anti-war protest near the White House. United Methodist Bishop Joseph Sprague; Jim Winkler, the general secretary of the United Methodist Board of Church and Society; and Roman Catholic Bishop Thomas Gumbleton of Detroit were included among those arrested. Winkler said that his religious board had "stated that the war is wrong."

After receiving the 2002 Nobel Peace Prize in Oslo, Norway, former President Jimmy Carter concluded his December 10, 2002 remarks by asserting that God gives mankind the capacity for choice and that war is always an evil, even when necessary, and "never a good."

> War may sometimes be a necessary evil. But no matter how necessary, it is always an evil, never a good. We will not learn to live together in peace by killing each other's children. The bond of our common humanity is stronger than the divisiveness of our fears and prejudices. God gives us the capacity for choice. We can choose to alleviate suffering. We can choose to work together for peace. We can make these changes—and we must.

While many leading religious leaders have issued statements condemning the use of force in both Iraq and in Afghanistan, the majority of Christians prior to the war in Iraq supported the use of force. For example, the 16 million-strong Southern Baptist Convention, the largest denomination in America (made up of Southern conservatives), sent a letter to President Bush "assuring him that the Iraqi threat satisfied the conditions of a 'just war.'" (Current opposition by the American public is not based on moral or religious grounds, but on a sense that the mission of bringing democratic reforms cannot be accomplished.) In addition, George Weigel, a biographer of Pope John Paul II as well as a leading Catholic commentator and Senior Fellow of the Ethics and Public Policy Center, also believed that the 2003 war against Iraq was justified.

> In the case of Iraq, the crucial issue in the moral analysis is what we mean by an "aggression under way." When a vicious regime that has not hesitated to use chemical weapons against its own people and against a neighboring country, a regime that has no concept of the rule of law and that flagrantly violates its international obligations, works feverishly to obtain and deploy further weapons of mass destruction, I think a compelling moral case can be made that this is a matter of an "aggression under way." The nature of the regime, which is the crucial factor in the analysis, makes that plain. It surely makes no moral sense to say that the U.S. or the international community can only respond with armed force when an Iraqi missile carrying a weapon of mass destruction has been launched, or is being readied for launch. To be sure, there are serious questions of prudence to be addressed in thinking through the question of military action against the Iraqi regime. At the level of moral principle, however, it seems to me that there are, in fact, instances where it is not only right to "go first," but "going first" may even be morally obligatory. And I think this may well be one of those instances.

Weigel also criticized other "clerical opponents of war ... [as giving] themselves over to a functional pacifism, a conviction that there are virtually no circumstances in which the proportionate and discriminate use of armed force can serve the goals of peace, order, justice and freedom." Indeed, some of the more extreme pacifists go so far as to blame the "Christian God" and President Bush as instigating an "American Inquisition" in the War on Terror.

For the committed pacifist, there simply should be no relationship between religion and warfare. Their interpretation of religion prohibits all forms of violence whatsoever. Further, they steadfastly oppose people who invoke God to justify violence in self defense. While one can certainly agree with the utopian idea that war, crime, poverty, and a whole hosts of evils should not exist in the world, it is a fact that they do. When asked by his disciples what would be the signs that would signal His second coming to the world, Jesus Christ himself declared that wars would continue to be a part of the landscape until His return: "And you will be hearing of wars and rumors of wars; see that you are not frightened, for those things must take place, but that is not yet the end."

To some, pacifism is a fundamental aspect of being a Christian. Nevertheless, to use the Bible to justify an uncompromising belief in pacifism requires one to distort, ignore, or otherwise explain away vast areas of scripture that speaks approvingly of specific instances where violence is justified and necessary to protect various values and objects. Jesus Christ himself engaged in violence and would be considered by religious pacifists as quite "anti-Christian" in his dealings with the religious leaders and legalists of the day—calling them, among other things, "of your father the Devil" (Jn. 8:44a).

A fair understanding of the Bible does not support the human viewpoint expressed by the religious anti-war activist. In A.D. 425, Augustine, the Bishop of Hippo, strongly affirmed the idea that the Bible does not prohibit or condemn a Christian from engaging in combat on the battlefield. In a letter to a Roman Christian by the name of Boniface, Augustine told him to fight the invading tribes called the Vandals because "[w]ar is waged in order that peace may be obtained." As stated in Ecclesiastes and echoed throughout the Bible, in the affairs of mankind there is clearly "[a] time for war, and a time for peace." The hope is that when a soldier goes to war, he will be militarily prepared, per Psalms 144:1—"[God] teach my hands to war and my fingers to fight"—and that the national leadership will heed Proverbs 20:18, by choosing to—"make war by wise guidance."

10.5 Stay with the Rule of Law

To a large degree, history is defined by the workings of spheres of power which are commonly categorized into eras. Within these eras, the trends of history are replete with great wars whose goal was to end all wars. While the natural tendency of mankind is to promote and to nourish the resulting periods of peace between wars, history gives no encouragement to the notion that war will be no more or that peace will be more than a mere handful of years. The collective memory of the world has traditionally proved to be very short.

With the liberation of Kuwait in 1991, President George H. Bush became the primary proponent of an ambiguous phrase which he called the "New World Order." President George H. Bush attempted to advance this phrase as an international rallying cry for the future of the world. The New World Order was to herald a new era in international affairs, an era of collective security sponsored and reinforced by the United Nations. Expectations for the fulfillment of this goal were understandably high and recalled the old Roman proverb, "For he who desires to become rich also wishes that desire to be soon accomplished." In reality, however, the natural desire to create some form of a New World Order quickly met with failure. Even more disturbing, the promotion of the term New World Order by President Bush served only to minimize or cast doubt on the viability of the rule of law. President George W. Bush has been careful not to repeat this mistake as the War on Terror progresses. Catchy utopian phrases are counterproductive to the critical mission of promoting the rule of law and democratic behavior.

To the serious student of history, the concept New World Order is neither new in its origin, nor, as the concept might imply, universal in its interpretation; it has existed in many forms. From the *pax Romana* of ancient Rome to the *novus ordo seclorum* printed on the reverse side of the one-dollar bill, the concept of the New World Order has been used by public figures to represent a variety of agendas associated, of course, with a vision for how the world should be ruled.

In the past century, both the Germans under Adolph Hitler and the British under Winston Churchill used the concept to describe their respective notions about the world's future. Although both were seeking to rally public opinion to support a particular objective, they were diametrically opposed in their meaning and application of the concept. Hitler envisioned *Die neue Ordnung* (the New Order) as a world ruled by the master German race, while Churchill wielded it as a sword of international force against Nazi expansionism.

Addressing the League of Nations in 1936, Churchill warned of Hitler's continued pattern of aggression and announced that the "fateful moment [had] arrived for choice between the New Age and the Old." For Churchill, the new age for the world was squarely based on establishing a defensive alliance to defeat the Nazi's quest of conquering Europe and the world.

Adolph Hitler employed the concept in its most aggressive connotation and irrationally believed that he had a sacred mission to establish a New Order through terror, violence and warfare. The Axis powers set out the parameters of their New Order for the world by signing a joint agreement in Berlin, January 1942. Linking their New Order to economic prosperity, the Germans envisioned the world divided into four *Grossraumwirtschaften* (great economics), each led by an authoritarian leader under the ultimate control of Germany. Once the Axis forces had won World War II, "a conclave was to be held in Vienna to legalize Nazi Germany's hegemony within the New Order." Hitler's New Order would initially be made up of German dominated Europe, Africa and the Near East, but ultimately it would encompass the entire world.

In the end, Hitler's "New Order for the World" collapsed in a bloody inferno while "Churchill's New Age for the World" silently slipped into the bookshelves of history after it helped to inspire the formation of the United Nations. Although the concepts were similar, the meanings were not.

The New World Order witnessed its latest reincarnation during the Iraqi invasion of Kuwait in August of 1990. In an unprecedented use of the United Nations, President George H. Bush used the concept of the New World Order as the focal point for gathering world opinion against the Iraqi occupation of Kuwait. In an effort to consolidate support for the possible use of military force against Iraq, President Bush not only followed Churchill's example against Hitler, but simultaneously offered this old term to describe American foreign policy in the post-Cold War era.

Just a month after the invasion, President George H. Bush proclaimed that the New World Order "would be a world where the rule of law supplants the rule of the jungle. A world in which nations recognize the shared responsibility for freedom and justice. A world where the strong respect the rights of the weak." As the months passed and Iraq became more entrenched in Kuwait, the Bush Administration increased the usage of the concept. In a statement delivered on December 5, 1990, before the Senate Foreign Relations Committee, Secretary of State James Baker said, "Historically, we must stand with the people of Kuwait so that the annexation of Kuwait does not become the first reality that mars our vision of the new world order."

Without a doubt, America's vision of the New World Order was to be firmly rooted in the new founded efficacy of the United Nations to function as the primary legal instrument for maintaining peace in the world, the assumption being that Gorbachev's Russia would no longer use its veto power to hinder the effectiveness of the Security Council. By the close of the Gulf War, the tenets of the New World Order were set: "Peaceful settlements of disputes, solidarity against aggression, reduced and controlled arsenals and just treatment of all peoples."

Unfortunately, from the viewpoint of epistemology, the concept of New World Order was not very successful for the administration of President George H. Bush. First, although the New World Order was undeniably catchy, the concept was not really a simple phrase to understand. In reality, the New World Order stood for a whole regime of policies, ranging all the way from universal human rights issues to the peaceful settlement of international disputes. Apart from a handful of scholars devoted to the study of those topics, the hope that a wider audience would understand the concept, without fully grasping the categories behind it, was the primary failure of its proponents.

Second, because President George H. Bush chose as his rallying cry a phrase that, throughout the past hundred years, had been used to stand for various propositions, he should have necessarily exerted an even greater amount of time and effort to achieve a minimum amount of association to his meaning. In other words, if a concept is to gain acceptance, the rate of forgetting must not exceed the rate of learning. This, too, was never accomplished, reflected in part by a remarkable lack of attention given to the phrase by the public media.

In his September 1991 address to the United Nations, President Bush specifically stressed the concept New World Order several times, even deliberately choosing the theme of the New World Order to close out his final remarks to the world body. Seeking to establish a straightforward definition, the President dramatically spelled out the elements of the New World Order.

> [The] new world order [is] an order in which no nation must surrender one iota of its own sovereignty; an order characterized by the rule of law rather than the resort to force; the cooperative settlement of disputes, rather than anarchy and bloodshed; and an unstinting belief in human rights.

Unfortunately, this definition was not really the same given at the close of the Gulf War. Then it was "peaceful settlements of disputes, solidarity against aggression, reduced and controlled arsenals and just treatment of all people." In addition, despite a conscious effort by President Bush to fully sponsor the phrase, the domestic media concentrated on the President's condemnation of Iraqi interference with United Nations inspection teams and the ill-conceived "Zionism is racism" General Assembly resolution. Predictably, the news reports that followed Bush's speech failed to mention the New World Order even once. While one might criticize the news media for exhibiting a total failure to publicize the concept, judged by the standards of keeping it simple and promoting repetition, the blame also rested with the Bush administration.

As to simplicity, President George H. Bush erred by expanding his initial meaning of the New World Order, most associated with the enforcement of the international rule of law against the raw aggression of Iraq, to a definition which equated the New World Order to various categories of international principles, each requiring a sophisticated level of comprehension. By lumping other concepts ranging from nuclear disarmament to human rights with the concept of the New World Order, the vast majority of the public had no idea what the New World Order "really" entailed. At the time, Harvard's Joseph S. Nye, Jr., remarked, "No one really knows what it means."

Most of the world can quickly grasp the idea of halting an aggressor who has broken the law (e.g., Iraq broke the most critical provision of the rule of law, the prohibition of aggression, in its use of force against Kuwait). But, when one adds, for example, the concept of creating norms for international human rights to the concept of the New World Order, the audience is lost. A brief survey of the concept of humanitarian law reveals that it is, at best, an evolving idea that is not very well understood.

As to repetition, when the public was told that President George H. Bush was going to issue a major address to the nation on sweeping nuclear arms initiatives, many "New World Order watchers" anticipated that the concept would be woven throughout the speech. Set for September 27, 1991, the address would follow soon after the United Nations address, which provided President Bush with the perfect opportunity to promote the concept, but this time at the domestic level. Indeed, in President Bush's September 1990 address to the United Nations, he had already set the precedent and employed the concept of the New World Order to urge a worldwide ban on chemical weapons and to continue the efforts to stop the proliferation of nuclear and biological weapons. At that time, President Bush said, "It is in our hands to leave these dark machines [nuclear, chemical and biological weapons] behind, in the dark ages where they belong ... to cap a historic movement toward a new world order, and a long era of peace."

When the 1991 address to the nation was made, President George H. Bush did not invoke the concept New World Order even once. President Bush concentrated on an entirely new concept called "the new age." Pointing out that not only had the Cold War ended, but the Soviet Union was undergoing drastic change, President Bush preferred to justify his proposals for disarmament as in keeping with the new age. Once against the press exhibited no interest in reporting unfamiliar terminology; the new age was unmentioned.

In summation, after a full year-and-a-half of being in the market place of ideas, the New World Order was still unfamiliar to the American public. Consequently, the general domestic understanding of what the New World Order really meant remained inexorably clouded. Of course, if the American public could not understand the New World Order, it was certain the rest of the world was at an even greater disadvantage. This was especially true for emerging democracies. For example, having a vague frame of reference for the notion of a state ruled by law, the vast territories of the old Soviet Empire had only just begun to awaken from a seventy-year nightmare of the most vicious brutality. Although the republics had renounced the twisted and flawed premise upon which the Communist party had rested for seven decades, there was tremendous confusion. Indeed, even with the dawn of the twenty-first century it will be sometime before the former communist states will be able to implement many of the components associated with democratic values. It is difficult enough for them to grasp the concept of being ruled by law and not by force.

The first application of the New World Order was against Iraq in 1991, but it was only partially successful. The Gulf War drove Saddam Hussein out of Kuwait, but also drove him to ruthlessly turn his military on his own people. In addition, the failure of the international community to press for international war crimes trials for Saddam Hussein and his henchmen dealt a major blow to the most central ideal of the New World Order.

The second application of the New World Order envisioned the formation of a joint defense force, composed of Arabs and Americans, to deter future aggression in the Middle East. This application of the New World Order never materialized. The Damascus Declaration, hammered out just days after the war ended, called for Syrian and Egyptian participation in the Arab security force. As quickly as the Declaration was adopted, however, the age old problems of distrust and animosity emerged. The Declaration died less than a month after its birth. Similarly, the New World Order visions of a new Kuwait based on more democratic principles and self-reliance have not been fulfilled. Outside of some limited Israeli-Arab peace talks, the region has essentially returned to its pre-war status. Except for a new found respect for the military power of the United States, "[c]enturies-old attitudes have not changed, new alliances have not jelled, and the historic suspicion of Western influence has receded only slightly."

As the failures of the New World Order mounted, the phrase lost any power it may have had and quickly faded into history as a small footnote. On the other hand, breaches of the rule of law do not necessarily weaken the utility of the term rule of law; failures only reinforce the continued need for deterrence and enforcement of the rule of law. Simply put, the New World Order proved to be the jargon of politicians. The rule of law is the tool of nations.

The hope that the victory in the Gulf War set the pattern of some sort of a New World Order in which the United Nations would guarantee the security of its members through collective security was sophomoric. The response to the al-Qa'eda and their supporters in the War on Terror was the exact same response taken against the aggression of Saddam Hussein a decade ago—the application of the rule of law in the context of the lessons learned in Munich.

Despite the missed opportunity to promote the concept, the rule of law, not the New World Order, emerged from the dust of the Gulf War. As in former times, the New World Order quickly faded into history where it will silently await its next master to call it forward; the shallowness of the concept sealed its own fate.

Catchy phrases such as the New World Order have nothing positive to offer those who seek to foster, strengthen and advance the rule of law. If the United States is serious about promoting the rule of law as the basis for its war on terror, then it must stand as the chief champion of the rule of law as the basis for the War on Terror. The challenge must be to abandon all such new age and new world phrases and to concentrate fully on the never ending business of promoting the rule of law in word as well as deed. In the never ending struggle to move the credibility of the concept forward, the United States must exhibit a faithful sponsorship of the rule of law in every international forum available.

Many of the most fundamental values, particularly those dealing with the illegality of aggressive war, have been translated into well-rooted rules of law at the cost of untold blood and fortune. Hope remains that many more democratic values will be added to that book, and that the attendant sacrifices will not have been in vain. Although there is no need to speak of the United States as the world's policeman, there is a need for the United States to fully sponsor the rule of law, which remains the best hope to those nations that wish to exist in a sphere of freedom. As the

United States fights the War on Terror, it must continuously place emphasis on the rule of law and avoid the use of any descriptive phrase that casts doubt on the supreme function of the rule of law.

10.6 America Must Stay the Course

Since the events of September 11, 2001, the world has entered into a period fraught with uncertainty and yet, strangely, there shines a renewed hope to enlarge the peace and advance human rights. Although it is true that the chief characteristic of the War on Terror is the fact that the United States stands alone as the worlds only remaining superpower, this is not the central focus of the post-9/11 era. The central hope rests in the great promise of a world more fully based on governments who adhere to human rights and democratic values.

Unlike other historical eras, the War on Terror offers a chance to advance human rights and democracy in areas of the world heretofore untouched. There is an intense global interest in securing the blessings of peace, prosperity and human rights that the West has so long enjoyed. The positive aspect of the War on Terror is that it will create one of those rare moments in history where a window of opportunity opens for the world to make serious and lasting strides toward the ever elusive goals of controlling aggressive warfare and terrorism, and at the same time improving respect for human rights.

If the international community led by the United States does not find ways to realistically promote and foster at least the most fundamental categories of human rights, the horrific terrorism exemplified by the attacks on America is sure to be only a taste of things to come. Global terrorism will only meet its end because of the efforts of America. However, battlefield victories alone will not bring a peace that can extend beyond a handful of years. Long-term periods of peace and stability require an attendant advance in institutionalizing the blessings of human rights.

America must learn to take the long view of history and ignore the snap-shots which invariably portray the American led effort as a failure or a Viet Nam-like quagmire. Unfortunately, the news item of the day seldom takes the long view of things. For example, an article in *Life Magazine* by one of their star correspondents, John Dos Passos, dated January 7, 1946, featured a major story entitled: "Americans are Losing the Victory in Europe." The article then went on to catalogue all of the mistakes that were being made in occupied Germany and how the war had been a waste. Of course, as it turned out, the American effort to promote democracy in Germany was a resounding success story. Certainly, winning the War on Terror will require patience, leadership and optimism, but it can be accomplished. As in all wars, strategic and tactical errors have been made in the War on Terror, particularly in Iraq. But the al-Qa'eda-styled terrorists will not allow America to retreat to "a live and let live policy."

Assisting in the incorporation of human rights values into the institutional framework of, for example, the new Afghan and Iraqi governments is not merely an end worthy unto itself, but in the quest for war avoidance and promoting the full range of human rights benefits it creates a society which can peacefully coexist with the whole of the world community. It appears fundamentally obvious that activities pursued by democracies are substantially better than the activities pursued by totalitarian regimes like Cuba, North Korea, Sudan, Iran and Syria. While it has long been suspected that stable democracies firmly committed to human rights do not make war on each other, nor do they abuse their own people, the empirical evidence now demonstrates this correlation. Debate on this point is over.

Thus, the central question now becomes how best to quickly impress solid human rights values on other national entities. Most certainly, human rights values become solid and irreversible only through the development of institutions designed to promote them. Institutionalization must be the criterion. While the desires for freedom will ultimately destroy a totalitarian system, freedom and human rights are not self perpetuating; they can only be sustained through the creation of concrete law-based institutions.

In order to foster democratic ideals and human rights in countries like Afghanistan and Iraq, the United States must learn from its recent failure to liberate the people of Iraq from the evil of Saddam Hussein at the close of the 1991 Gulf War. The United States must accept that it has an obligation to assist any country endeavoring to create governments grounded in basic human rights. Liberated nations in the War on Terror will eagerly embrace the principles of liberal democracy and self-determination, but will need immediate assistance to implement an institutional framework to accommodate their desires for the full range of human rights. Without meaningful assistance to translate the battle cry of human rights into an institutional framework, it is naive to assume that democratic values and human rights will germinate.

Apart from the normal pressures associated with building democratic institutions, the escalating and often uncontrollable level of disorder and violence in many of the new democracies forcefully supports the idea that the United States must assist in the creation and maintenance of fledgling democratic governments. Aside from country specific issues, whether one concentrates on sectarian fragmentation or religious bias, the euphoric hope for instant world peace and greater human rights in the wake of the War on Terror is presumptuous—the globe is a dangerous place. Indeed, the danger of global terrorism is far more pronounced than ever before. Today, due to the growth of terrorist activities throughout the world, it is not only uncertain where the next attack will occur, but virtually impossible to take a defensive posture against every potential attack. The modern al-Qa'eda-styled terrorist cannot be deterred by the threat of force—these murderers welcome death.

In the minds of much of the world, the vision of freedom is synonymous with the words—the United States of America. People yearn for governments that can guarantee the social, political, and economic freedoms of human rights. Does this mean, however, that the United States should take the lead in assisting these nations to translate desire into reality? Should the United Nations, another nation, or another group of nations fulfill the mission?

In a pragmatic light, true collective security has always required a dominant leader. In the twentieth century, that has often meant the United States, particularly since World War II. In truth, the lesson of the 1991 Gulf War was the same as the Korean War, the United Nations or any other coalition does not have the capacity to guarantee the security of its members absent the direct participation of the United States. In the first major challenge of world terrorism, it was the active influence of the United States that built the necessary coalition force to respond.

The contention that America stands as the role model for the world is only part of the truth. To a substantial degree, the tyranny of communism met its end precisely because America generally has always been the world's beacon for broad principles of human rights. These principles of human rights are now necessary to ensure the destruction of terrorism as well. From this perspective, the United States has a continuing responsibility to the community of nations to promote human rights. The United States cannot afford to be indifferent to the moral values that are the true source of its global influence. Judged by any positive standard, be it in the field of human rights, self-determination, economic opportunity, or privacy related to property and person, the United States stands out as a positive model. But America's most fundamental value does not reside in her military might or industrial complex. Those mighty pillars merely provide support for the United States' most enduring commodity—human rights flourishing under a systemic respect for the rule of law.

America, like great nations before her, has related all of these positive human rights values to a strong heritage of law institutionalized into its government. The founders of the nation established certain fundamental democratic institutions, and subsequent generations have generally exhibited the moral values and discipline required to maintain those institutions. American democracy continues to boast that men can rise to eminence in nearly any profession unaided by the advantages related to hereditary preferment. For over 200 years, this boast of freedom and human rights has echoed throughout the world, penetrating even the strongest iron curtain of communism. As a consequence, together with American force of arms, several totalitarian regimes have been swept into the dust of history. More than any other nation, America has demonstrated that human rights and the by-products of human rights—economic success and social well being—are worth promoting and protecting.

Therefore, if democracies shun aggression, terrorism and hate, it is in the best interest of the United States to expend the necessary time, effort, and money to adequately assist those nations who have exhibited the will to embark on democracy's path. In this context, the United States has rapidly assessed the ramifications of this important responsibility and offered assistance to the fledgling Afghan government before the window of opportunity closed and the chance for democracy is lost. The most significant danger in the War on Terror is that the global movement toward democratic reform, which started with the collapse of the Soviet Union, will fail, signaling a return to totalitarianism, a more dangerous world, or even a Third World War.

Arguments that the Western European nations should take the lead in fostering the development of greater human rights and democracy have proven to be contentious. One need look no further than the conflict in the backyard of the European community itself, the former Yugoslavia, to conclude that either individually or collectively, Western Europe is not able to quickly solve even its own problems. Although Germany may be best suited to take on a leadership role in Europe, the historical suspicion of German militarism makes such an event highly unlikely.

For similar reasons, the Far East will not allow Japan, a powerhouse of the region, to assert a more dominant leadership role. It remains for the United States to continue to extend its influence in the region, particularly in the face of the destabilizing effect of an aggressive and nuclear armed North Korea.

It is far too early to tell if the United Nations might one day fill some part of the vacuum. Hopes that the United Nations might evolve into a truly effective world collective security organization have not materialized and given its track record, it seems unlikely that the United Nations can fulfill such a position. Clearly, an organization that allows totalitarian regimes an equal voice is inherently flawed.

In the final analysis, there is as yet no viable substitute for United States dominance in the international arena. For the time being, it is apparent that history has chosen the United States as the nation most suited to assist in promoting human rights in the War on Terror. This is true for three reasons. First, the United States emerged from the Cold War as the foremost power in the world, a power that possesses the necessary capability to influence change. Second, many governments in Western Europe, East Asia, and the Middle East, whether allies of the United States or not, want the United States to continue to lead. Third, despite its own internal faults and shortcomings in the realm of human rights, it is well recognized that the United States has always been the foremost champion of values related to human rights and democratic ideals.

Interestingly, many of these impressions have not been made by the civilian arm of the United States, but by its military forces stationed throughout the world. The United States military has been—and continues to be—an excellent ambassador for positive change.

Finally, those who argue that the United States should not become involved in assisting the growth of human rights and democratic movements because there is no domestic benefit are incorrect. The United States chose not to become involved after World War I, and the resulting costs in terms of life lost and property destroyed were extremely high. Conversely, as pointed out in an article by Brigadier General James R. Harding and John A. Pitts (*Military Review* July 1999), the United States did choose to become actively engaged after World War II and the resulting benefits were substantial, producing "the longest period of uninterrupted peace in Europe in 400 years, the highest level of economic prosperity and sustained economic growth in the history of the Western World, and the defeat of totalitarianism in Eastern Europe." The United States wisely rolled up its sleeves and rooted out Nazi ideology, Italian fascism and Japanese militarism. These evils were replaced with liberal democratic values which led to strongly rooted constitutional democracies at peace with their people and with the world community.

The spread of human rights and democracy around the world helps United States security, improves global stability, and increases economic prosperity. Thus, promoting governments who desire human rights and democracy benefits American national security directly—a more democratic world is a safer world. President George W. Bush has demonstrated an understanding of the paradigm of terrorism and war avoidance; his administration must stay the course and develop viable programs to fully promote the paradigm.

Gauged in terms of maintaining peace and stability—critical goals in the world community— it is time for the United States to exercise new thinking in terms of pursuing a foreign policy that promotes real programs to assist new democracies institutionalize human rights principles. Armed with the fact that human rights is the cornerstone of democracy and democracy is the foundation of building a better world, the United States must shift its role as the chief advocator of human rights to the chief promoter.

The United States has an opportunity and an obligation to assist in the historic potential for advancing human rights throughout the world community. Without question, the opening for constructive change is far wider than after the First or Second World Wars or the end of the Cold War. The events of September 11, 2001, initially unleashed a tremendous moral clarity in America and the civilized world for the creation of governments that are truly based on protecting human rights and living with their neighbors in peace and prosperity. Unfortunately, as the War on Terror grinds on into its sixth year, many have "hit the snooze button" and fallen into a false sense of security. The fight against the rather substantial forces of al-Qa'eda-styled terrorism will not end with the signing of a peace treaty with the enemy visibly vanquished. This war will follow our children into adulthood.

In order to push the global movement towards expanding human rights, America must develop a strong and practical strategy that can truly assist the struggling and emerging governments to get out of the totalitarian shadows in which they stand by institutionalizing human rights values. If the doctrines of human rights can be inculcated, for example, in Afghanistan and Iraq, the benefits will lead to two stabilized countries capable of contributing as full partners to a more peaceful, humane, and free world. This goal may or may not be achieved in the short term, but there is no other alternative.

On the homefront, the balance between civil liberties and security demands has changed. To be sure, the debate on where the balance should rest must be deliberate and inclusive of all voices, but the hard premise that accentuates the call for robust debate must rubricate the discussion— these al-Qa'eda-styled fanatics are in our midst and mean to slaughter us wholesale if they can. Many well know this fact. Yet they are naïve in considering the real world ramifications of advocating that no revisions need be made to existing authorities, laws and processes. For certain, the world of pre-9/11 will never return and evil forces of terror remain fixed on the horizon. Unfortunately, in the technological age of weapons of mass destruction, we need only be unlucky once for catastrophe to cripple the nation and the civilized world. As General Tommy Franks warned, such an event would "cause our population to question our own Constitution and to begin to militarize our country in order to avoid [another weapon of mass destruction event]."

The quote by former Chief Justice William H. Rehnquist cited at the Introduction to the book speaks to the challenge of achieving or maintaining a proper balance between freedom and order in time of national crisis. Rehnquist's words bear repeating: "In wartime, reason and history both suggest that this balance shifts to some degree in favor of order—in favor of the government's ability to deal with conditions that threaten the national well-being." While his observation is undoubtedly correct in terms of past wars in our history the uniqueness of the War on Terror poses a far more difficult dilemma for those concerned with civil liberties. In brief, the War on Terror may never "be over" so that the on-going conflict presents a fundamentally new and potentially devastating threat to civil liberties. If the War on Terror has no end in sight, Rehnquist's premise that order must trump freedom in wartime could mean that freedoms quickly relinquished in this war may never return. Accordingly, calls for greater "order" must be carefully weighed, debated and incrementally enacted. Another Chief Justice of the United States, Warren E. Burger (1969–1986), noted in his capacity as the Chairman for the Commission on the Bicentennial of the United States Constitution, "Ever since people began living in tribes and villages, they have had to balance order with liberty, individual freedom had to be weighed against the need for security of all."

More importantly, America's strongest weapon in the War on Terror does not rest with our military might or police functions. In the long run, America's strongest weapon is our uncompromising commitment to the freedoms and civil liberties embodied in our Constitution and reflected in the U.N. Charter. If we engage in tactics that violate the democratic principles that make up our rule of law, are we different from the terrorists at our gates? The United States of America can only ride the crests of the waves of history so long as it follows a rule of law rooted in human rights and democratic principles. America will drown in the sea of hypocrisy if it trades civil liberties for a mess of pottage. Terrorism consultant Brian Jenkins agrees that the best defense against the terrorists calls for a "continuing commitment to the basic values that ... the nation stands for." The real genius of the United States is that it is a nation of immigrants that has managed to unite its disparate parts through common values. These values are embodied in the Constitution and in the Declaration of Independence's expression of a people yearning to be free and to develop the talents given them by their Creator.

10.7 Questions for Discussion

1. *What is the proper role of nationalism in war?* See Edward Gibbons, THE HISTORY OF THE DECLINE AND FALL OF THE ROMAN EMPIRE, Vol. I, 85-86 (1914). Literally, the "peace of Rome. *Pax Romana* refers to the peace and prosperity in the known world, i.e., the Mediterranean, brought about by Roman rule from 27 B.C. to 180 A.D. Gibbon, widely recognized as the foremost modern scholar on the Roman empire, places the high point of *pax Romana* at 96 to 180 A.D., the period of the Antonine Caesars:

    If a man were called to fix the period in the history of the world during which the condition of the human race was most happy and prosperous, he would without hesitation, name that which elapsed from the death of Domitian [A.D. 96] to the accession of Commodus [A.D. 180]. The vast extent of the Roman Empire was governed by absolute power, under the guidance of virtue and wisdom. The armies were restrained by the firm but gentle hand of four successive emperors, whose characters and authority commanded in voluntary respect. The forms of the civil administration were carefully preserved by Nerva, Trajan, Hadrian, and the Antonines [Pius], who delighted in the image of liberty, and were pleased with considering themselves as the accountable ministers of the law.

2. *Is President Bush conducting the War on Terror under the banner of a religion? See* James Reston, Jr., *The American Inquisition*, USA TODAY, April 18, 2006, at 13A.

    It is not surprising that a leader who believes that his Christian God chose him to be president at the moment in history and that his Almighty speaks directly to him, should preside over this American Inquisition. Bush's messianic bent came to light vividly in June 2003, when he announced that his God had inspired him to go fight those terrorists and to end the tyranny in Iraq.

3. *Should foreign policy be only concerned with human rights? See* Madeleine Albright, THE MIGHTY AND THE ALMIGHTY (2006). In her chapter entitled, Good Intentions Gone Astray: Vietnam and the Shah, Albright talks about how the Carter policy of not sufficiently supporting the Shah of Iran in the late 1970s led to far greater human rights abuses under the mullahs.

    Many rejoiced when the monarch was brought down, but from any objective standpoint, the practices of Iran's successor governments with regard to human rights have been far worse than the shah's. In the first few years alone, thousands of people were executed for political dissent and "moral crimes." The shah's secret police were replaced by religious "guardians of the faith," who were even more ruthless.

Selected Bibliography

Ajami, Fouad. *Where the Warrior Comes to Rest*, U.S. NEWS AND WORLD REPORT. Oct. 7, 1991, at 10.

Albright, Madeleine. THE MIGHTY AND THE ALMIGHTY 18-32. 2006.

Bonds, Russell S. *Pawn Takes Bishop*, CIVIL WAR TIMES. May 2006, at 53.

Campanile, Carl. *Rev. Al Will Join GI Ma in Anti-War Texas Vigil*, N.Y. POST. Aug. 26, 2005, at 10.

Carty, Anthony, and Gennady Danilenko. *Perestroika and International Law*, CURRENT ANGLO-SOVIET AP-PROACHES TO INTERNATIONAL LAW, 1. 1990.

Coates, Sam. *Sharpton Adds Voice to Antiwar*, WASH. POST. Aug. 29, 2005, at A4.

Colombo, Furio. *Vatican: The Pope's War Record*, NEW REPUBLIC. Apr. 8, 1991, at 12. (The article compiled some of the Pope's statements about the use of force by the United States and its allies. On January 10, 1991: "This war is an adventure with no return." On January 16: "International law cannot be seen as a protection for hegemonic interests." On January 21: "The intoxication of war has prevailed over the courage of peace." On January 26: "This war is a threat to humanity." On February 4: "This war is a virus of death.")

Duke, Lynne. *Coretta Scott King Deplores Decision*, WASH. POST. Jan. 17, 1991, at A30 (quoting Rev. Joseph Lowery).

Elsner, Alan. *Christian Leaders Prominent in Anti-War Movement*, REUTERS. Feb. 8, 2003.

Gellman, Barton. *Reaction to Tactic They Invented Baffles 1st Division Members*, WASH. POST. Sept. 13, 1991, at A21.

Haberman, Clyde. *Pope, In Christmas Message, Warns on a Gulf War*, NEW YORK TIMES, 26. Dec. 1990, at A19 (quoting Pope John Paul II).

Interview by Zenit Daily Dispatch with George Weigel, a biographer of Pope John Paul II as well as a leading Catholic commentator, and Senior Fellow of the Ethics and Public Policy Center, Washington, D.C. Sept. 22, 2002. (discussing the Catholic moral teaching regarding what many claimed to be a preemptive strike in Iraq and the Catholic views of just war theory).

Jackson, Fred, and Jody Brown. *Arrest of Anti-War Methodist Leaders Called 'Embarrassment' for Denomination: Bishop, others from 'Radical Fringe' Protest Near White House*, AGAPE PRESS, *available at* http://headlines.agapepress.org/archive/3/282003a.asp. Mar. 28, 2003.

Johnson, Haynes. *Renewed Perils to Peace*, WASH. POST. Sept. 27, 1991, at A2.

King, Martin Luther, Jr. STRIDE TOWARD FREEDOM: THE MONTGOMERY STORY. 1958. Martin Luther King, Jr., a religious leader and civil rights crusader, advocated the use of non-violence to confront de-facto and de-jure segregation throughout the United States in the 1950's and 60's. At the age of thirty-five, Martin Luther King, Jr., became the youngest man in history to win the Nobel Peace Prize.

Kramer, Michael. *Kuwait: Back to the Past*, TIME. Aug. 5, 1991, at 32.

Munger, Guy. *Lessons From the Desert Death Plow*, NC CATHOLIC. Sept. 22, 1991, at 4.

President Orders Sweeping Reductions in Strategic and Tactical Nuclear Arms, WASH. POST. Sept. 28, 1991, at A1.

Przetacznik, Frank. *The Catholic Concept of Peace as a Basic Collective Human Right*, 39 REVUE DE DROIT MILITAIRE ET DE DROIT DE LA GUERRE, 523, 559. 1990.

Rich, Norman. HITLER'S WAR AIMS. 1973.

Safire, William. *The New New World Order*, NEW YORK TIMES. Feb. 17, 1991, at 14 (quoting President George H. Bush).

Schaff, Philip, ed. St. Augustine, Nicene and Post-Nicene Fathers of the Christian Church 553-554. 1983.

Smothers, Ronald. *Thousands Recall Quest for Equality*, New York Times. Jan. 22, 1991, at A18.

Steinfels, Peter. *War in the Gulf: Religious Leaders; Cardinal Says Iraqi's Acts Prove Bush Right*, New York Times. Jan. 26, 1991, at A9 (quoting Pope John Paul II).

Turner, Robert F. *The Gulf War—and Its Fallout*, Freedom Rev. May–June 1991, at 17, 19.

U.S. and U.K. Statement. *Disarm Iraq Without War: A Statement from Religious Leaders in the United States and United Kingdom,* Sojourners. Nov. 26, 2002.

Walker, Richard. *Martin Luther King's Widow Urges New Anti-War Movement*, Reuter Library Rep. Jan. 11, 1991.

We Stand ... Before a New World of Hope and Possibility for Our Children, Wash. Post. Dec. 26, 1991, at A35.

Wilgoren, Debbie. *Peaceful Protest Ends in Peaceful Arrest: Nobel Winners Among 68 Detained Activists*, Wash. Post. Mar. 27, 2003, at B.01.

Chapter 11
Civil Litigation

In the face of this universal criminal liability it is hardly a stretch to ask how the civil justice system might more effectively also contribute to deterrence against such heinous acts [international terrorism].

—John Norton Moore

Synopsis
11.1 Tort Liability Against Affected Targets
11.2 Suits Against State Sponsors of Terrorism
11.3 Questions for Discussion
Selected Bibliography

The area of civil litigation encompasses two major themes in the realm of terrorism. The first relates to cases brought by victims of terrorism against an "affected target" of terrorism under the sphere of tort law. The second relates to lawsuits directed against those individuals, groups, or States (or State agents) who commit or sponsor a terrorist attack. To be sure, the new and developing area of civil liability in either context is an open invitation for the courts to play a significant role in the realm of terrorism law.

11.1 Tort Liability Against Affected Targets
As in all cases of tort law, suits brought by individual victims against an affected target of terrorism, such as a building or an airline, must satisfy the common law elements of basic tort law: the affected target owed a duty to the plaintiff; the duty was breached; there existed a causal relationship between the breach and the resulting injury; and the plaintiff suffered an actual loss.

The most notable case currently in the court system related to these types of "terrorism" negligence claims is *In re SEPTEMBER 11*. *In re September 11th* is a major tort liability case in which the victims who were injured, survivors of victims who where killed and some who sustained property damage in the al-Qa'eda terror attacks on September 11, 2001, brought civil action against airlines, airport security companies, owners and operators of buildings destroyed in the crash and aircraft manufacturers. While the case has yet to be resolved, the federal district court has rendered some significant insight in early rulings: (1) under New York law, the duty of airlines and airport security companies to secure aircraft against potential terrorists and weapons smuggled aboard extended to ground victims of crashes; (2) the crash of the planes hijacked by terrorists was within the class of foreseeable hazards resulting from negligently performed security screening by airlines; (3) federal statutes and regulations providing for protection of passengers and property on aircraft in the event of air piracy did not preempt plaintiff's negligence claim under New York law; (4) owners and operators of office buildings owed a duty under New York law to the building's occupants to create and implement adequate fire safety measures; (5) plaintiffs pleaded sufficient facts to alleged legal proximate cause against owners and operators; (6) plaintiff's allegations were sufficient to establish manufacturer's duty under Virginia and Pennsylvania law; and (7) the failure of manufacturers to design an impenetrable cockpit door was a proximate cause of the crashes.

In re SEPTEMBER 11

United States District Court, S.D. New York

280 F.Supp.2d 279 (Sep. 9th 2003)

OPINION BY: HELLERSTEIN, J.

The injured, and the representatives of the thousands who died from the terrorist-related aircraft crashes of September 11, 2001, are entitled to seek compensation. By act of Congress, they may seek compensation by filing claims with a Special Master established pursuant to the Air Transportation Safety and System Stabilization Act of 2001, Pub.L. No. 107-42, 115 Stat. 230 (2001) (codified at 49 U.S.C. § 40101) "the Act." Or they may seek compensation in the traditional manner, by alleging and proving their claims in lawsuits, with the aggregate of their damages capped at the limits of defendants' liability insurance. If they choose the former alternative, their claims will be paid through a Victim Compensation Fund from money appropriated by Congress, within a relatively short period after filing. Claimants will not have to prove fault or show a duty to pay on the part of any defendant. The amount of their compensation, however, may be less than their possible recovery from lawsuits, for non-economic damages are limited to $250,000, economic damages are subject to formulas that are likely to be less generous than those often allowable in lawsuits, and punitive damages are unavailable. I have discussed, and upheld, certain portions of the Act and regulations related to the Fund in *Colaio v. Feinberg*, *262 F.Supp.2d 273 (S.D.N.Y.2003)*, appeal filed, June 6, 2003. Approximately seventy of the injured and representatives of those who died, and ten entities which sustained property damage, have chosen to bring lawsuits against defendants whom they claim are legally responsible to compensate them: the airlines, the airport security companies, the airport operators, the airplane manufacturer, and the operators and owners of the World Trade Center. The motions before me challenge the legal sufficiency of these lawsuits, and ask me to dismiss the complaints because no duty to the plaintiffs existed and because the defendants could not reasonably have anticipated that terrorists would hijack several jumbo jet airplanes and crash them, killing passengers, crew, thousands on the ground, and themselves. I discuss in this opinion the legal duties owed by the air carriers, United and American Airlines, and other airlines and airport security companies affiliated with the air carriers to the plaintiffs who were killed and damaged on the ground in and around the Twin Towers and the Pentagon; by the Port Authority of New York and New Jersey "Port Authority" and World Trade Center Properties LLC "WTC Properties" to those killed and injured in and around the Twin Towers; and by the Boeing Company, the manufacturer of the "757" jets that were flown into the Pentagon and the field near Shanksville, Pennsylvania, to those killed and injured in the two crashes. I hold in this opinion that each of these defendants owed duties to the plaintiffs who sued them, and I reject as well defendants' alternative arguments for dismissal.

I. Background

A. Exclusive Jurisdiction and the Governing Law

The Air Transportation Safety and System Stabilization Act of 2001, Pub.L. No. 107-42, 115 Stat. 230 (2001) (codified at 49 U.S.C. § 40101) "the Act", passed in the weeks following the September 11 attacks, provides that those who bring suit "for damages arising out of the hijacking and subsequent crashes" must bring their suits in the United States District Court for the Southern District of New York. The Southern District has "original and exclusive jurisdiction" "over all actions brought for any claim (including any claim for loss of property, personal injury, or death) resulting from or relating to the terrorist-related aircraft crashes of September 11, 2001," with the exception of claims to recover collateral source obligations and claims against terrorists and their aiders, abettors and conspirators, Act § 408(c). The Act provides that the governing law shall be "derived from the law, including choice of law principles, of the State in which the crash occurred unless such law is inconsistent with or preempted by Federal law." Act § 408(b)(2). Thus, all cases, whether arising out of the crashes in New York, Virginia, or Pennsylvania, must be brought in the Southern District of New York, to be decided in accordance with the law of the state where the crash occurred.

B. The Complaints

Plaintiffs' individual pleadings have been consolidated into five master complaints, one for the victims of each crash and one for the property damage plaintiffs. Plaintiffs allege that the airlines, airport security companies, and airport operators negligently failed to fulfill their security responsibilities, and in consequence, the terrorists were able to hijack the airplanes and crash them into the World Trade Center, the Pentagon, and the field in Shanksville, Pennsylvania, killing passengers, crew, and thousands in the World Trade Center and the Pentagon and causing extensive property damage. The complaints allege that the owners and operators of the World Trade Center, World Trade Center Properties LLC and the Port Authority of New York and New Jersey, negligently designed, constructed, maintained, and operated the buildings, failing to provide adequate and effective evacuation routes and plans. Plaintiffs who died in the crashes of American flight 77 and United flight 93 also sue Boeing, the manufacturer of the two "757" airplanes, for strict tort liability, negligent product design, and breach of warranty.

C. Motions to Dismiss

I heard oral argument on May 1 and 2, 2003 on six motions by the several categories of defendants. I previously have decided three of the motions, by most of the airport operators, by three airlines that did not carry any of the victims or alleged hijackers, and by Fiduciary Trust Company International and Franklin Templeton Investments, an employer of one of the victims. The three motions which remain, and which I now decide are: by the airlines and airport security companies (the "Aviation Defendants"); by the Port Authority and World Trade Center Properties LLC (together, the "WTC Defendants"); and by Boeing.

The airport operators that joined in this motion are: the Massachusetts Port Authority, the Metropolitan Washington Airport Authority, the City of Portland, Maine, and the Port Authority of New York and New Jersey. I denied their joint motion without prejudice. (Order of May 5, 2003, *In re September 11 Litigation, 21 MC 97.*) The City of Portland, Maine and the Port Authority of New York and New Jersey brought separate supplementary motions to dismiss. I granted Portland's motion, dismissing it as a defendant from those cases where plaintiffs had failed to file a timely notice of claim. *In re September 11 Litigation, 265 F.Supp.2d 208 (S.D.N.Y.2003).* The Port Authority's supplementary motion will be decided herein, see infra Part II.B.iv.

The three non-carrier airlines are Continental Airlines, Air Canada, and America West Airlines. I denied their motion for summary judgment without prejudice. (Order of May 5, 2003, *In re September 11* (Order of May 13, 2003, *Greene-Wotton v. Fiduciary Trust Co. Int'l, 02 Civ. 7245.*) The plaintiff's husband had worked for Fiduciary Trust/Franklin Templeton in Tower Two and was allegedly asked to remain at the office after Tower One had been struck. I held that the New York workers' compensation statute precluded plaintiff's negligence claims and that she had failed to state a claim for intentional infliction of emotional distress.

The Aviation Defendants who joined in the motion to dismiss include: AirTran Airlines, American Airlines, America West Airlines, AMR Corp., Argenbright Security, Atlantic Coast Airlines, Burn International Services Corp., Burns International Security Services Corp., Colgan Air, Continental Airlines, Delta Air Lines, Globe Aviation Services Corp., Globe Airport Security Services, Inc., Huntleigh USA Corp., Northwest Airlines, Pinkerton's Inc., and United Air Lines.

The Aviation Defendants concede that they owed a duty to the crew and passengers on the planes, but contend that they did not owe any duty to "ground victims." The Port Authority and WTC Properties argue that they did not owe a duty to protect occupants in the towers against injury from hijacked airplanes and, even if they did, the terrorists' actions broke the chain of proximate causation, excusing any negligence by the WTC Defendants. Boeing argues that it did not owe a duty to ground victims or passengers, and that any negligence on its part was not the proximate cause for the harms suffered by the plaintiffs.

II. Discussion

Defendants' motions were made pursuant to Fed.R.Civ.P. 12(b)(6). A Rule 12(b)(6) motion requires the court to determine if plaintiff has stated a legally sufficient claim. A motion to dismiss under Rule 12(b)(6) may be granted only if "it appears beyond doubt that the plaintiff can prove no set of facts in support of his claim which would entitle him to relief." *Conley v. Gibson, 355 U.S. 41, 45-46, 78 S.Ct. 99, 2 L.Ed.2d 80 (1957); Branum v. Clark, 927 F.2d 698, 705 (2d Cir.1991).* …

A. Aviation Defendants' Motion to Dismiss

The Aviation Defendants argue that they did not owe a duty to the ground victims; that the injuries suffered by the plaintiffs were beyond the scope of any foreseeable duty that may have been owed; and that the federal laws that regulate aviation preempt any state law to the contrary.

i. Choice of Law

Section 408(b)(2) of the Act provides that the substantive law "shall be derived from the law, including choice of law principles, of the State in which the crash occurred unless such law is inconsistent with or preempted by Federal law." Ground victims of the planes that crashed into the World Trade Center and the Pentagon have filed suit against the Aviation Defendants, and thus the choice of law principles of New York and Virginia apply.

New York typically analyzes choice-of-law issues in tort cases according to two categories of rules: conduct-regulating and loss-allocating. The issue of duty—whether duty exists and its scope—is conduct-regulating. New York choice of law dictates that the state in which the tort took place has the strongest interest in applying its conduct-regulating rules. *Schultz v. Boy Scouts of*

Am., Inc., *65 N.Y.2d 189, 491 N.Y.S.2d 90, 480 N.E.2d 679, 684- 85 (1985)*. Thus, the substantive law of New York governs the issue of duty in relation to the crashes at the World Trade Center.

Virginia's choice of law rules apply to the ground damage claims arising from the crash of American flight 77 into the Pentagon. Under Virginia law, the substantive law of the place of the tort controls. *McMillan v. McMillan, 219 Va. 1127, 253 S.E.2d 662, 664 (1979)*. The parties agree that the law of Virginia does not differ materially from New York law with respect to the issue of duty and rely on New York law for their arguments.

ii. Existence of Duty to Ground Victims

"The threshold question in any negligence action is: does the defendant owe a legally recognized duty of care to plaintiff?" *Hamilton v. Beretta U.S.A. Corp., 96 N.Y.2d 222, 727 N.Y.S.2d 7, 750 N.E.2d 1055, 1060 (2001)*. In New York, the existence of a duty is a "legal, policy-laden declaration reserved for judges." *Palka v. Servicemaster Mgmt. Servs. Corp., 83 N.Y.2d 579, 611 N.Y.S.2d 817, 634 N.E.2d 189, 192 (1994)*. The injured party must show that a defendant owed not merely a general duty to society but a specific duty to the particular claimant, for "without a duty running directly to the injured person there can be no liability in damages, however careless the conduct or foreseeable the harm." *Lauer v. City of New York, 95 N.Y.2d 95, 711 N.Y.S.2d 112, 733 N.E.2d 184, 187 (2000)*. Courts traditionally "fix the duty point by balancing factors, including the reasonable expectations of parties and society generally, the proliferation of claims, the likelihood of unlimited or insurer-like liability, disproportionate risk and reparation allocation, and public policies affecting the expansion or limitation of new channels of liability." *Palka, 611 N.Y.S.2d 817, 634 N.E.2d at 193*.

New York courts have been cautious in extending liability to defendants for their failure to control the conduct of others, "even where as a practical matter [the] defendant can exercise such control." *D'Amico v. Christie, 71 N.Y.2d 76, 524 N.Y.S.2d 1, 518 N.E.2d 896, 901 (1987)*. "This judicial resistance to the expansion of duty grows out of practical concerns both about potentially limitless liability and about the unfairness of imposing liability for the acts of another." *Hamilton, 727 N.Y.S.2d 7, 750 N.E.2d at 1061*. However, courts have imposed a duty when the defendant has control over the third party tortfeasor's actions, or the relationship between the defendant and plaintiff requires the defendant to protect the plaintiff from the conduct of others. As the New York Court of Appeals ruled, "The key in each [situation] is that the defendant's relationship with either the tortfeasor or the plaintiff places the defendant in the best position to protect against the risk of harm." *Id.* One additional consideration, the Court of Appeals added, is that "the specter of limitless liability is not present because the class of potential plaintiffs to whom the duty is owed is circumscribed by the relationship." *Id.*

Plaintiffs allege that the Aviation Defendants negligently failed to carry out their duty to secure passenger aircraft against potential terrorists and weapons smuggled aboard, enabling the terrorists to hijack and crash four airplanes. Plaintiffs argue that the Aviation Defendants employed their security measures specifically to guard against hijackings, and knew or should have known that the hijacking of a jumbo jet would create substantial risks of damage to persons and property, not only to passengers and crew, but also to people and property on the ground. Plaintiffs assert also that terrorism was a substantial international concern, and that suicidal acts by terrorists seeking to cause death, injury and havoc to as many innocent people as possible had become a frequently used strategy.

I must test this dispute over duty even before a record has been established. In New York, duty is a legal question, for the judge to decide. I must assume, for the purpose of the motion, that all well-pleaded facts about the defendants' negligence are true and will in time be proved, and that defendants' negligence proximately caused the injuries and deaths upon which plaintiffs filed their lawsuits.

Airplane crashes in residential areas are not unknown. In January 1952, an American Airlines Convair crashed into a residential area of Elizabeth, New Jersey on its approach to Newark airport, killing passengers and crew, as well as seven residents of houses it struck. Elizabeth Recalls First of 3 Crashes, N.Y. Times, Dec. 17, 1952, at 27. A month later, another plane out of Newark, a National Airlines DC-6, struck an apartment house in New Jersey, killing 29 passengers and four tenants of the apartment house. Id. Military airplanes have had to make emergency landings on highways, and have collided with automobiles. See *Rehm v. United States, 196 F.Supp. 428 (E.D.N.Y.1961)*. On July 9, 1982, a Pan American World Airways jet crashed shortly after takeoff, killing all on board and eight individuals on the ground. The airline and the government acknowledged liability for the crash, which was caused by windy conditions. Pan Am and U.S. Accept Responsibility for Crash, N.Y. Times, May 13, 1983, at 6. In January 1990, a Columbian passenger airplane exhausted its fuel supply while circling La Guardia Airport waiting for clearance to land, and crashed into a residential backyard in Long Island's populated North shore. See *In re Air Crash Disaster at Cove Neck, 885 F.Supp. 434 (E.D.N.Y.1995)*. On November 12, 2001, two months after the aircraft crashes of September 11, 2001, a jumbo-jet passenger airplane lost its stability in take-off from JFK airport and crashed into a populated area of the Rockaways, causing the deaths of over two hundred passengers and crew members and five people on the ground. Dan Barry and Elissa Gootman, 5 Neighbors Gone, N.Y. Times, Nov. 14, 2001, at D11. Such incidents are inevitable in the context of the sheer number of miles flown daily in the United States. None matches the quantity or quality of tragedy arising from the terrorist-related aircraft crashes of September 11.

Airlines typically recognize responsibility to victims on the ground. See, e.g., *Rehm, 196 F.Supp. at 428; Cove Neck, 885 F.Supp. at 439-40*. Assuming negligence and assuming there is damage to houses on the ground that is the type of traditional ground damage negligent maintenance cases in which the courts have imposed duty.... [W]e would concede in those circumstances assuming the facts of liability are proven there is a legal duty. (Tr. of May 1, 2003 at 8.) However, counsel did not concede duty in relation to those killed and injured on the ground in the September 11, 2001 aircraft crashes. The "potential for a limitless liability to an indeterminate class of plaintiffs," he argued, made the instant cases distinguishable. Id. The distinction, in his opinion, is "no[t][a] difference in kind," but "the law of extraordinary consequences [which] can sometimes draw a distinction based on degree." *Id.* at 9-10. He explained:

> We are in an area of policy and there are lines to be drawn that may occasionally seem arbitrary. But what really distinguishes our case from [the hypothetical example of an airplane crash into Shea Stadium while taking off from, or landing at, La Guardia airport] is the intentional intervening acts of the third party terrorists.

While defense counsel raised the issue of proximate causation during the oral argument, the issue was not briefed. Counsel suggested, without legal citation, that the extraordinary nature of the attacks, involving intervening acts by the terrorists, should negate the duty air carriers owed to ground victims. Id. As defense counsel commented, "we are in an area of policy," where "the existence and scope of a tortfeasor's duty is ... a legal question for the courts," *532 Madison Ave. Gourmet Foods, Inc. v. Finlandia Center, Inc., 96 N.Y.2d 280, 727 N.Y.S.2d 49, 750 N.E.2d 1097, 1101 (2001)* (Kaye, Ch. J.). It is the court's job to "fix the duty point by balancing factors," including the following: the reasonable expectations of parties and society generally, the proliferation of claims, the likelihood of unlimited or insurer-like liability, disproportionate risk and reparation allocation, and public policies affecting the expansion or limitation of new channels of liability. *Id.* (citation omitted). *532 Madison Avenue* involved collapses of a high-rise office building and a 48-story construction elevator tower, both in midtown Manhattan and both causing busy areas of the city to be closed for a two-week period. The lawsuits sought recovery of financial losses resulting from the closures; plaintiffs had not suffered personal injury or property damage. Applying the considerations set out above, the Court of Appeals limited the scope of defendants' duty "to those who have, as a result of these events, suffered personal injury or property damage," but held that those who suffered merely financial losses could not recover. *Id.* at 1103. The Court of Appeals acknowledged that "[p]olicy-driven line-drawing is to an extent arbitrary because, wherever the line is drawn, invariably it cuts off liability to persons who foreseeably might be plaintiffs." Id. If those who suffered financial losses were to be allowed to sue, the Court of Appeals held, "an indeterminate group in the affected areas" would be able to recover. Id. If, however, the field of plaintiffs was to be limited to those who "suffered personal injury or property damage" as a result of defendants' negligence, the limitation would "afford[ ] a principled basis for reasonably apportioning liability," and be "historically" consistent with New York precedents. *Id.*

The cases before me involve claims to recover for personal injuries, death, or property damage. They fall within the line drawn by the New York Court of Appeals in *532 Madison Avenue*. There may be more plaintiffs within the ambit of duty at issue here than those contemplated under the rule set forth in *532 Madison Avenue*, but that is not a principled basis of distinction. I therefore hold that the Aviation Defendants owed a duty of care, not only to their passengers to whom they concede they owed this duty, but also to victims on the ground.

In terms of the *532 Madison Avenue* analysis, plaintiffs are favored by the first of the factors set out above, for plaintiffs and society generally could have reasonably expected that the screening performed at airports by the Aviation Defendants would be for the protection of people on the ground as well as for those in airplanes. Ours is a complicated and specialized society. We depend on others charged with special duties to protect the quality of the water we drink and the air we breathe, to bring power to our neighborhoods, and to enable us to travel with a sense of security over bridges, through tunnels and via subways. We live in the vicinity of busy airports, and we work in tall office towers, depending on others to protect us from the willful desire of terrorists to do us harm. Some of those on whom we depend for protection are the police, fire and intelligence departments of local, state and national governments. Others are private companies, like the Aviation Defendants. They perform their screening duties, not only for those boarding airplanes, but also for society generally. It is both their expectation, and ours, that the duty of screening was performed for the benefit of passengers and those on the ground, including those present in the Twin Towers on the morning of September 11, 2001.

Nothing that I hold or say should be considered as any form of ruling on the reasonableness of the Aviation Defendants' conduct. Nor should it be construed as a finding on whether their conduct was the proximate cause of plaintiffs' damages, or whether that of the terrorists' constituted an intervening act breaking the chain of causation. I simply hold that the Aviation Defendants, and plaintiffs and society generally, could reasonably have expected that the screening methods at

Logan, Newark, and Dulles airports were for the protection of people on the ground as well as for those on board the airplanes that the terrorists hijacked.

...

The fourth factor of *532 Madison Avenue* is "disproportionate risk and reparation allocation." This inquiry probes who was best able to protect against the risks at issue and weighs the costs and efficacy of imposing such a duty. The airlines, and the airport security companies, could best screen those boarding, and bringing objects onto, airplanes. The same activities reasonably necessary to safeguard passengers and crew are those that would protect the public as well. Hijacking presents a substantial elevation of risks, not only to those aboard the hijacked airplane, but also to those on the ground. This case is thus distinguishable from other cases where courts did not find a duty to protect against third-party conduct. *In Waters v. New York City Housing Authority*, the court held that the owner of a housing project did not owe a duty to a passerby when she was dragged off the street into the building and assaulted. *69 N.Y.2d 225, 513 N.Y.S.2d 356, 505 N.E.2d 922 (1987)*. Imposing such a duty on landowners would do little to minimize crime, and the social benefits to be gained did not warrant the extension of the landowner's duty. See *id.* at 924. Similarly, in *Hamilton*, 727 N.Y.S.2d 7, 750 N.E.2d at 1062, the court held that gun manufacturers did not owe a duty to victims of gun violence for negligent marketing and distribution of firearms. The connection between the manufacturers, criminal wrongdoers, and victims was too remote, running through many links in a long chain, from manufacturer, distributor or wholesaler, retailer, legal purchasers, unlawful possessors, and finally to the victims of gun violence.

...

Unlike *Hamilton* and *Waters*, the *Aviation* Defendants could best control the boarding of airplanes, and were in the best position to provide reasonable protection against hijackings and the dangers they presented, not only to the crew and passengers, but also to ground victims. Imposing a duty on the Aviation Defendants best allocates the risks to ground victims posed by inadequate screening, given the Aviations Defendants' existing and admitted duty to screen passengers and items carried aboard.

Lastly, recognition of a duty on the part of the Aviation Defendants would not substantially expand or create "new channels of liability," the fifth and last factor of *532 Madison Avenue*. New York courts have found on other occasions that aircraft owners and operators owe a duty to those on the ground who may be harmed or sustain property damage resulting from improper or negligent operation of an aircraft.

...

The Second Circuit has recognized that airlines have a duty not only to passengers on the flights they operate, but also to passengers on connecting flights, and thus may be liable when they allow terrorists to board planes. In *Stanford v. Kuwait Airways Corp.*, 89 F.3d 117 (2d Cir.1996), the airline failed adequately to screen passengers against terrorists. The hijacking occurred, not on the airplane initially boarded, but on the connecting flight. The Second Circuit, relying on general tort principles including New York law, upheld the air carrier's duty of care as to the passengers on the connecting flight. *Id.* at 125. Clearly, the duty of care extends to cover those embraced by the risk of the terrorists' conduct.

Accordingly, I hold on the pleadings that the Aviation Defendants owed a duty of care to the ground victim plaintiffs.

iii. Scope of Duty to Ground Victims: the Issue of Foreseeability

Defendants argue that the ground victims lost their lives and suffered injuries from an event that was not reasonably foreseeable, for terrorists had not previously used a hijacked airplane as a suicidal weapon to destroy buildings and murder thousands. Defendants contend that because the events of September 11 were not within the reasonably foreseeable risks, any duty of care that they would owe to ground victims generally should not extend to the victims of September 11.

The scope of duty to a particular class of plaintiffs depends on the relationship to such plaintiffs, whether plaintiffs were within a zone of foreseeable harm, and whether the harm was within the class of reasonably foreseeable hazards that the duty exists to prevent. *Di Ponzio v. Riordan, 89 N.Y.2d 578, 657 N.Y.S.2d 377, 679 N.E.2d 616, 618 (1997)* (citations omitted). See also *Palsgraf v. Long Island R.R. Co., 248 N.Y. 339, 162 N.E. 99, 100-01 (1928)....*

In order to be considered foreseeable, the precise manner in which the harm was inflicted need not be perfectly predicted. As *Di Ponzio v. Riordan* explained: "Where an individual breaches a legal duty and thereby causes an occurrence that is within the class of foreseeable hazards that the duty exists to prevent, the individual may be held liable, even though the harm may have been brought about in an unexpected way. On the other hand, no liability will result when the occurrence is not one that is normally associated with such hazards...."

...

Construing the factual allegations in the light most favorable to the plaintiffs, I conclude that the crash of the airplanes was within the class of foreseeable hazards resulting from negligently performed security screening. While it may be true that terrorists had not before deliberately flown airplanes into buildings, the airlines reasonably could foresee that crashes causing death and destruction on the ground was a hazard that would arise should hijackers take control of a plane. The intrusion by terrorists into the cockpit, coupled with the volatility of a hijacking situation, creates a foreseeable risk that hijacked airplanes might crash, jeopardizing innocent lives on the ground as well as in the airplane. While the crashes into the particular locations of the World Trade Center, Pentagon, and Shanksville field may not have been foreseen, the duty to screen passengers and items brought on board existed to prevent harms not only to passengers and crew, but also to the ground victims resulting from the crashes of hijacked planes, including the four planes hijacked on September 11.

Defendants point to two decisions in cases brought against manufacturers and distributors of ammonium nitrate utilized in the Oklahoma City bombing and the 1993 attack on the World Trade Center. Relying on either New York or New Jersey law and on Oklahoma law, the courts found that the fertilizer products were not themselves dangerous and served socially useful purposes. *In Gaines-Tabb v. ICI Explosives USA, Inc.*, the district court ruled that the manufacturer did not owe a duty to the plaintiffs because the manufacturer did not expose the plaintiffs to a "recognizable high degree of risk of harm through the misconduct of third persons which a reasonable person would take into account." *995 F.Supp. 1304, 1317 (W.D.Okla.1996)* (citation omitted). On appeal, the Tenth Circuit affirmed, but on the ground that the terrorists' actions served as the supervening cause for the plaintiffs' injuries. 160 F.3d 613, 620 (10th Cir.1998). *In Port Authority of New York and New Jersey v. Arcadian Corp.*, the Third Circuit held that the manufacturers and distributors of ammonium nitrate did not owe a duty to the plaintiffs, because the product had been substantially altered after leaving the defendants' control, and because only the altered product created the danger to the plaintiff. 189 F.3d 305, 317 (3d Cir.1999). "[D]efendants' products were not in and of themselves dangerous but were merely the raw materials or components that terrorists used in combination with other ingredients to build a bomb." *Id.* at 313.

The cases are distinguishable. Ammonium nitrate is a socially and economically useful product. To require manufacturers to prevent the appropriation of their products for an unintended purpose when manufacturers have no control over who purchases and alters the fertilizer would be an undue burden. Unlike the manufacturers, however, the Aviation Defendants controlled who came onto the planes and what was carried aboard. They had the obligation to take reasonable care in screening precisely because of the risk of terrorist hijackings, and the dangerous consequences that would inevitably follow. The consequences that in fact followed were within the scope of the duty that the Aviation Defendants undertook to carry out.

I hold at this stage of the litigation, on the pleadings and before any discovery has taken place, that the injuries suffered by the ground victims arose from risks that were within the scope of the duty undertaken by the Aviation Defendants.

…

B. World Trade Center Defendants' Motions to Dismiss

i. Background

The Port Authority of New York and New Jersey and WTC Properties LLC move to dismiss all claims brought against them as owners and operators of the World Trade Center for loss of life, personal injury, and damage to nearby property and businesses resulting from the collapse of the Twin Towers. The claims are alleged in two Master Complaints regarding Flights 11 and 175 in the consolidated litigation, and in numerous individual complaints. Plaintiffs allege that the WTC Defendants: 1) failed to design and construct the World Trade Center buildings according to safe engineering practices and to provide for safe escape routes and adequate sprinkler systems and fireproofing; 2) failed to inspect, discover, and repair unsafe and dangerous conditions, and to maintain fireproofing materials; 3) failed to develop adequate and safe evacuation and emergency management plans; 4) failed to apply, interpret and/or enforce applicable building and fire safety codes, regulations and practices; and 5) instructed Tower Two occupants to return to their offices and remain in the building even while the upper floors of Tower One were being consumed by uncontrolled fires following the airplane crash into Tower One. See Plaintiffs' Flight 11 Master Liability Complaint ¶ 85; Plaintiffs' Flight 175 Master Liability Complaint ¶ 82.

A number of other defendants whose interests are aligned with the Port Authority and World Trade Center Properties LLC—those who were named as defendants because they designed, constructed, operated, or maintained the World Trade Center buildings - were voluntarily dismissed earlier in the litigation.

The WTC Defendants argue that the complaints against them should be dismissed because they had no duty to anticipate and guard against deliberate and suicidal aircraft crashes into the Towers, and because any alleged negligence on their part was not a proximate cause of the plaintiffs' injuries. The Port Authority argues also that it is entitled to immunity because the complained-of conduct essentially consisted of governmental functions.

…

ii. Existence and Scope of Duty

The WTC Defendants contend that they owed no duty to "anticipate and guard against crimes unprecedented in human history." Plaintiffs argue that defendants owed a duty, not to foresee the crimes, but to have designed, constructed, repaired and maintained the World Trade Center structures to withstand the effects and spread of fire, to avoid building collapses caused by fire and, in designing and effectuating fire safety and evacuation procedures, to provide for the escape of more people.

The existence of a duty owed by the WTC Defendants to its lessees and business occupants has been clearly set out in New York law. "A landowner has a duty to exercise reasonable care under the circumstances in maintaining its property in a safe condition,"

....

The duty of landowners and lessors to adopt fire-safety precautions applies to fires caused by criminals. "[L]andowners have a duty to protect tenants, patrons or invitees from foreseeable harm caused by the criminal conduct of others while they are on the premises." ....

The criteria for establishing the existence of duty, discussed previously in the context of the Aviation Defendants' duty to ground victims, applies as well to the duty of landowners to lessees and business occupants. See *532 Madison Ave., Gourmet Foods, Inc. v. Finlandia Ctr., 96 N.Y.2d 280, 727 N.Y.S.2d 49, 750 N.E.2d 1097, 1101 (2001); Palka v. Servicemaster Mgmt. Servs. Corp., 83 N.Y.2d 579, 611 N.Y.S.2d 817, 634 N.E.2d 189, 193 (1994).* First, the parties and society would reasonably expect that the WTC Defendants would have a duty to the occupants of the Twin Towers in designing, constructing, repairing and maintaining the structures, in conforming to appropriate building and fire safety codes, and in creating appropriate evacuation routes and procedures should an emergency occur. Second, although a large number of claims have been filed against the WTC Defendants, there is no danger that the number will proliferate beyond those who died in the collapse of the structures or were injured while trying to escape. Similarly, the WTC Defendants are not subject to unlimited or insurer-like liability, for they can be held liable only after a showing of fault and only to those who suffered death, personal injury, or property damage resulting from their alleged negligence. Furthermore, by specific provision of the Air Transportation Safety and System Stabilization Act, their liability is limited to their insurance coverage. Act § 408(a)(1). Fourth, the defendants' relationship with the plaintiffs, as their landlord or the landlord of their employer, placed the WTC Defendants in the best position to protect against the risk of harm. And fifth, as discussed above, imposing a duty on the WTC Defendants in the situation at hand will not create new channels of liability, for the New York courts have held traditionally that landlords owe duties of safety and care to the occupants of leased premises and their invitees.

A finding of duty also requires a consideration of the nature of plaintiffs' injuries, and the likelihood of their occurrence from a particular condition. "Defining the nature and scope of the duty and to whom the duty is owed requires consideration of the likelihood of injury to another from a dangerous condition or instrumentality on the property; the severity of potential injuries; the burden on the landowner to avoid the risk; and the foreseeability of a potential plaintiff's presence on the property." *Kush, 462 N.Y.S.2d 831, 449 N.E.2d at 727.* The criteria are clearly satisfied, for the severity and likelihood of potential injuries of people unable to escape from a heavily occupied building before fires envelope evacuation routes is high. The more difficult question is whether the injuries arose from a reasonably foreseeable risk.

Plaintiffs argue that the WTC Defendants had a duty to exercise reasonable care in order to mitigate the effects of fires in the Twin Towers. They allege that defendants knew about the fire safety defects in the Twin Towers, as evident by the Allied litigation concerning inadequate fireproofing in the construction of the buildings; that defendants could have reasonably foreseen crashes of airplanes into the Towers, given the near miss in 1981 of an Aerolineas Argentinas Boeing 707 and the studies conducted during the Towers' construction reporting that the Towers would be able to withstand an aircraft crash; that defendants were aware of numerous fires and evacuations that had occurred at the World Trade Center since its creation, including arson fires in 1975 and the 1993 terrorist-caused explosion in the garage under Tower One; and that the World Trade Center continued to be a prime target of terrorists. A finding of duty does not require a defendant to have been aware of a specific hazard. See *Sanchez v. State of New York, 99 N.Y.2d 247, 754 N.Y.S.2d 621, 784 N.E.2d 675, 679-81 (2002).* It is enough to have foreseen the risk of serious fires within the buildings and the goal of terrorists to attack the building.

This is a very early point in the litigation. There has been no discovery, and defendants' motions to dismiss accept, as they must, all allegations of the complaints. I hold that the WTC Defendants owed a duty to the plaintiffs, and that plaintiffs should not be foreclosed from being able to prove that defendants failed to exercise reasonable care to provide a safe environment for its occupants and invitees with respect to reasonably foreseeable risks.

iii. Proximate and Supervening Causation

The WTC Defendants argue that even if they are held to have owed a duty to the plaintiffs and even if a jury ultimately finds that they acted negligently, their negligence was not the proximate cause of plaintiffs' damages. This is because, they claim, the terrorist-related aircraft crashes into the Twin Towers were so extraordinary and unforeseeable as to constitute intervening and superceding causes, severing any link of causation to the WTC Defendants.

When an intervening act "is of such an extraordinary nature or so attenuates defendants' negligence from the ultimate injury that responsibility for the injury may not be reasonably attributed to the defendant," proximate cause is lacking. *Kush v. City of Buffalo, 59 N.Y.2d 26, 462 N.Y.S.2d 831, 449 N.E.2d 725, 729 (1983).* Thus, "when such an intervening cause 'interrupts the natural sequence of events, turns aside their course, prevents the natural and probable result of the original act or omission, and produces a different result that could not have been reasonably anticipated,' it will prevent a recovery on account of the act or omission of the original wrongdoer." *Sheehan v. City of New York, 40 N.Y.2d 496, 387 N.Y.S.2d 92, 354 N.E.2d 832, 835-36 (1976)* (citations omitted). The "negligence complained of must have caused the occurrence of the accident from which the injuries flow." *Rivera v. City of New York, 11 N.Y.2d 856, 227 N.Y.S.2d 676, 182 N.E.2d 284, 285 (1962).*

Generally, an intervening intentional or criminal act severs the liability of the original tortfeasor. *Kush, 462 N.Y.S.2d 831, 449 N.E.2d at 729.* But that "doctrine has no application when the intentional or criminal intervention of a third party or parties is reasonably foreseeable." *Id.* In *Bonsignore v. City of New York,* a New York City police officer shot and seriously wounded his wife. *683 F.2d 635 (2d Cir.1982).* The wife sued the City, alleging that it was negligent in failing to identify officers who were unfit to carry guns and who would likely use them without proper restraint and in inappropriate circumstances, and in not recognizing that her husband was such an officer. The City defended on the ground of independent and supervening cause, arguing that the officer's intentional and criminal act severed any link of causation to its own alleged negligence. The Court of Appeals held in favor of the wife, ruling that since the officer's act was precisely that which the City should reasonably have foreseen, the police officer's intentional and criminal act was not an independent and supervening break between the City's negligence and the plaintiff's injury. See *id.* at 637-38.

At this early stage of the case and in the absence of a factual record, I find that plaintiffs have pleaded sufficient facts to allege legal proximate cause....

iv. Governmental Immunity

The Port Authority claims that it is immune from liability to the extent that the plaintiffs complain that the Port Authority was negligent in its performance of governmental functions such as planning for public safety and responding to a public emergency. The Port Authority agrees, however, that it does not enjoy a blanket immunity to suit. See N.Y. Unconsol. Laws § 7106 (2003) ("Although the port authority is engaged in the performance of governmental functions, the said two states [NY and NJ] consent to liability on the part of the port authority in such suits, actions or proceedings for tortious acts committed by it and its agents to the same extent as though it were a private corporation"). The allegations and proofs have to be parsed in order to determine whether, and to what extent, the defense of government immunity applies.

The defense of governmental immunity requires a court to scrutinize specific claims. "It is the specific act or omission out of which the injury is claimed to have arisen and the capacity in which that act or failure to act occurred which governs [governmental] liability, not whether the agency involved is engaged generally in proprietary activity or is in control of the location in which the injury occurred." *Weiner v. Metro. Transp. Auth.*, 55 N.Y.2d 175, 448 N.Y.S.2d 141, 433 N.E.2d 124, 127 (1982). The inquiry is to determine a point "along a continuum of responsibility," one side of which may be considered as proprietary, and the other, governmental. See *Miller v. State,* 62 N.Y.2d 506, 478 N.Y.S.2d 829, 467 N.E.2d 493, 496 (1984). "[The continuum] begins with the simplest matters directly concerning a piece of property for which the entity acting as landlord has a certain duty of care, for example, the repair of steps or the maintenance of doors in an apartment building. The spectrum extends gradually out to more complex measures of safety and security for a greater area and populace, whereupon the actions increasingly, and at a certain point only, involve governmental functions, for example, the maintenance of general police and fire protection." *Id.* When a public entity acts in a proprietary capacity as a landlord, it is held to the same duty as private landlords. See id.

Miller illustrates the issue. The plaintiff, a student at a SUNY college, was assaulted in the college dormitory by an intruder and sued the State for the university's failure to keep doors locked and maintain adequate security. *478 N.Y.S.2d 829, 467 N.E.2d at 495.* The Court of Appeals held that while the state could not be liable for failure to provide police protection, the state in its capacity as landowner had the duty to maintain minimal security measures to protect occupants against foreseeable criminal intrusions. See *id.* at 496.

As a landowner, the State must act as a reasonable [person] in maintaining his property in a reasonably safe condition in view of all the circumstances, including the likelihood of injury to others, the seriousness of the injury, and the burden of avoiding the risk. Under this standard, a landlord has a duty to maintain minimal security measures, related to a specific building itself, in the face of foreseeable criminal intrusion upon tenants. *Id.* at 497 (citations omitted).

Plaintiffs allege negligence by the Port Authority in a number of respects: 1) failure to design and construct the World Trade Center buildings according to safe engineering practices and to provide for safe escape routes and adequate sprinkler systems and fireproofing; 2) failure to inspect, discover, and repair unsafe and dangerous conditions, and to maintain fireproofing materials; 3) failure to develop an adequate and safe evacuation plan and emergency management plan; 4) failure to apply, interpret and/or enforce applicable building and fire safety codes, regulations and practices; and 5) instructing Tower Two occupants to remain in the building rather than evacuate. See Plaintiffs' Flight 11 Master Liability Complaint ¶ 85; Plaintiffs' Flight 175 Master Liability Complaint ¶ 82. Based only on the pleadings and before any discovery has occurred, I have been given no basis to determine where, on the continuum between functions that are essentially proprietary and those that are essentially governmental, these various allegations should fall. It would seem, from the pleadings alone, that it would be difficult for the Port Authority to establish its defense with respect to claims of negligent design, construction, inspection, repair, maintenance, and application and enforcement of building codes, for these functions are not likely to differ from those required of private landowners. The same is true regarding allegations relating to inadequate evacuation and emergency management plans and procedures, but these allegations may touch also upon the functions of the Port Authority police force within the Twin Towers, and come closer to the governmental end of the continuum. This may be even more so for the allegation that occupants of Tower Two were told, before the crash into that Tower, to return to, and remain in, their offices, rather than evacuate. The record does not yet show who gave this instruction, whether a member of the Port Authority's security force or some other employee, and for what reasons the instruction was given.

...

At this point, the Port Authority has not shown that it will prove its defense of governmental immunity as to the negligence allegations made by WTC occupants.

The Port Authority argues also that it should have immunity in its capacity as operator of Newark Airport, for alleged negligence in permitting terrorists and weapons aboard United Air Lines flight 93, and for the hijacking and deaths that resulted. The Port Authority claims that it was performing a governmental function. Again, however, the Port Authority has not shown that it was performing a governmental function with respect to the "specific act or omission out of which the injury is claimed to have arisen and the capacity in which that act or failure to act occurred." *Weiner*, 448 N.Y.S.2d 141, 433 N.E.2d at 127. Further development of the record is required.

For the reasons stated, I deny the WTC Defendants' motion to dismiss the complaints.

C. Boeing's Motions to Dismiss

Some of those who were injured and the successors of those who died in the Pentagon, in American Airlines flight 77 which crashed into the Pentagon, and in United Air Lines flight 93 which crashed into the Shanksville, Pennsylvania field, claim the right to recover against Boeing, the manufacturer of the two "757" jets flown by United and American. Plaintiffs allege that Boeing manufactured inadequate and defective cockpit doors, and thus made it possible for the hijackers to invade the cockpits and take over the aircraft. Boeing moves to dismiss the lawsuits.

I hold that plaintiffs have alleged legally sufficient claims for relief under the laws applicable to the claims, Virginia and Pennsylvania, respectively. I therefore deny the motion except for certain claims, as discussed below.

...

ii. Motion to Dismiss Claims Arising out of the Crash of American Airlines Flight 77

a. Background

Thus far, three individual complaints have been filed with respect to the flight 77 crash. They charge Boeing with strict tort liability and negligent design based on an unreasonably dangerous design of the cockpit doors. See *Edwards v. American Airlines, Inc.*, No. 02 Civ. 9234 (brought on behalf of a decedent who was a passenger on flight 77); *Powell v. Argenbright Security, Inc.*, No.

02 Civ. 10160 (brought on behalf of a decedent who died while working at the Pentagon); *Gallop v. Argenbright Security, Inc., No. 03 Civ. 1016* (plaintiffs injured at the Pentagon site).

The Plaintiffs' First Amended Flight 77 Master Liability Complaint contains three counts applicable to Boeing. Count Six alleges strict tort liability for an unreasonably dangerous design of the cockpit doors. Count Seven alleges that Boeing breached its duty of care by failing to design the cockpit doors and accompanying locks in a manner that would prevent hijackers and/or passengers from accessing the cockpit. Count Eight alleges that Boeing violated its express or implied warranty that the aircraft structure and frame, with respect to the cockpit doors, were fit for the purposes for which they were designed, intended and used.

b. Strict liability claims

Virginia does not permit recovery on a strict liability theory in product liability cases. See *Sensenbrenner v. Rust, Orling & Neale, Architects, Inc., 236 Va. 419, 374 S.E.2d 55, 57 n. 4 (1988).* Thus, Count Six in the Flight 77 Master Complaint, and the underlying related claims in the individual complaints—Count Three in *Edwards*, Count Five in *Powell*, and Count Five in *Gallop*—are all dismissed.

c. Negligent design and breach of warranty claims

Boeing moves to dismiss both the claims of negligent design and breach of warranty, arguing that it did not owe a duty to prevent the use of the plane as a weapon, and that the independent and supervening acts of the terrorists, not Boeing's acts, caused the injuries of the plaintiffs. A plaintiff, to state a claim of negligence, must allege the existence of a legal duty, violation of that duty, and proximate causation which results in injury. *Marshall v. Winston, 239 Va. 315, 389 S.E.2d 902, 904 (1990).* In order to state a claim of breach of warranty, plaintiff may invoke the Virginia law of an implied warranty of merchantability, which guarantees that a product "was reasonably safe for its intended use when it was placed in the stream of commerce." *Turner v. Manning, Maxwell & Moore, Inc., 216 Va. 245, 217 S.E.2d 863, 868-69 (1975).*

In order to recover under either a negligence or breach of warranty theory against a product manufacturer, "a plaintiff must show (1) that the goods were unreasonably dangerous either for the use to which they would ordinarily be put or for some other reasonably foreseeable purpose, and (2) that the unreasonably dangerous condition existed when the goods left the manufacturer's hands." *Morgen Indus., Inc. v. Vaughan, 252 Va. 60, 471 S.E.2d 489, 492 (1996).* Thus, a manufacturer owes a duty to supply a product "fit for the ordinary purposes for which it is to be used" and safe notwithstanding a reasonably foreseeable misuse that could cause injury, *Jeld-Wen, Inc. v. Gamble, 256 Va. 144, 501 S.E.2d 393, 396 (1998).* However, "a manufacturer is not required to supply an accident-proof product." *Besser Co. v. Hansen, 243 Va. 267, 415 S.E.2d 138, 144 (1992)* (citation omitted).

The existence of duty in the products liability context is a question of law. "[T]he purpose of making the finding of a legal duty as a prerequisite to a finding of negligence, or breach of implied warranty, in products liability is to avoid the extension of liability for every conceivably foreseeable accident, without regard to common sense or good policy." *Jeld-Wen, 501 S.E.2d at 396* (citations omitted). Legal duty may extend to a user of the product, as well as to its purchaser. See *Morgen Indus., 471 S.E.2d at 492.*

...

Boeing argues that its design of the cockpit was not unreasonably dangerous in relation to reasonably foreseeable risks, and that the risk of death to passengers and ground victims caused by a terrorist hijacking was not reasonably foreseeable. The record at this point does not support Boeing's argument. There have been many efforts by terrorists to hijack airplanes, and too many have been successful. The practice of terrorists to blow themselves up in order to kill as many people as possible has also been prevalent. Although there have been no incidents before the ones of September 11, 2001 where terrorists combined both an airplane hijacking and a suicidal explosion, I am not able to say that the risk of crashes was not reasonably foreseeable to an airplane manufacturer. Plaintiffs have alleged that it was reasonably foreseeable that a failure to design a secure cockpit could contribute to a breaking and entering into, and a take-over of, a cockpit by hijackers or other unauthorized individuals, substantially increasing the risk of injury and death to people and damage to property. I hold that the allegation is sufficient to establish Boeing's duty.

Boeing also argues that the regulations of the Federal Aviation Administration ("FAA") relating to design of passenger airplanes did not require an impenetrable cockpit door, and thus its designs, which satisfied FAA requirements, could not be defective. However, the only support provided by Boeing for its argument is an after-the-fact FAA policy statement, issued to explain why the FAA, in 2002, was requiring airplane manufacturers to provide such doors even though the FAA previously had not done so.

Flight crew compartment doors on transport category airplanes have been designed principally to ensure privacy, so pilots could focus their entire attention to their normal and emergency flight duties. The doors have not been designed to provide an impenetrable barrier between the cabin and the flight crew compartment. Doors have not been required to meet any significant security threat, such as small arms fire or shrapnel, or the exercise of brute force to enter the flight crew compartment. *67 Fed.Reg. 12,820-12,824 (Mar. 19, 2002)*.

Boeing has not proffered the parameters that existed when it manufactured its "757" jumbo-jet airplanes that United and American flew on September 11, 2001. Boeing also has not shown the extent to which FAA regulations determined how passenger airplanes were to be constructed. Although a FAA promulgation of standards for the design and manufacture of passenger aircraft may be entitled to weight in deciding whether Boeing was negligent, see, e.g., *Curtin v. Port Auth. of N.Y. and N.J.*, 183 F.Supp.2d 664, 671 (S.D.N.Y.2002) (concluding that the standard of care with respect to aircraft evacuation procedures is a matter of federal, not state, law), statements by the FAA characterizing what its former regulations required does not dictate the totality of the duty owed by aircraft manufacturers. Boeing's argument is not sufficient to support its motion to dismiss the complaints against it.

d. Proximate Causation

Boeing next argues that its design of the cockpit doors on its "757" passenger aircraft, even if held to constitute an "unreasonably dangerous condition," was not the proximate cause of plaintiffs' injuries. Boeing argues that the criminal acts of the terrorists in hijacking the airplanes and using the airplanes as weapons of mass destruction constituted an "efficient intervening cause" which broke the "natural and continuous sequence" of events flowing from Boeing's allegedly inadequate design. See *Sugarland Run Homeowners Ass'n v. Halfmann, 260 Va. 366, 535 S.E.2d 469, 472 (2000)* (a "proximate cause of an event is that 'act or omission which, in natural and continuous sequence, unbroken by an efficient intervening cause, produces the event, and without which that event would not have occurred,' " quoting *Beale v. Jones, 210 Va. 519, 171 S.E.2d 851, 853*

(1970)). Plaintiffs have the burden to prove proximate cause and, generally, the issue is a question of fact to be resolved by a jury. *Sugarland, 535 S.E.2d at 472.* However, when reasonable people cannot differ, the issue becomes a question of law for the court. *Id.*

The record at this point does not support Boeing's argument that the invasion and take-over of the cockpit by the terrorists must, as a matter of law, be held to constitute an "efficient intervening act" that breaks the "natural and continuous sequence" flowing from Boeing's allegedly inadequate design. Plaintiffs allege that Boeing should have designed its cockpit door to prevent hijackers from invading the cockpit, that acts of terrorism, including hijackings of airplanes, were reasonably foreseeable, and that the lives of passengers, crew and ground victims would be imminently in danger from such hijackings. Virginia law does not require Boeing to have foreseen precisely how the injuries suffered on September 11, 2001 would be caused, as long as Boeing could reasonably have foreseen that "some injury" from its negligence "might probably result." See *Blondel v. Hays, 241 Va. 467, 403 S.E.2d 340, 344 (1991)* ("[A] reasonably prudent [person] ought under the circumstances to have foreseen that some injury might probably result from that negligence"). Given the critical nature of the cockpit area, and the inherent danger of crash when a plane is in flight, one cannot say that Boeing could not reasonably have foreseen the risk flowing from an inadequately constructed cockpit door.

…

In re Korean Air Lines Disaster of September 1, 1983, No. 83-3442, 1985 WL 9447, 1985 U.S. Dist. LEXIS 17211 (D.D.C.1985), involved lawsuits by the legal successors of passengers who died when Korean Airlines passenger flight 007 was shot down by Russian fighter planes. The passenger plane had flown off course and over a sensitive military zone in Russia. Russian fighter pilots intercepted the plane and, instead of following international protocol for causing the plane to return to international routes over the high seas or to land at a selected landing field, shot it down. Plaintiffs sued Boeing, the manufacturer of the airplane, alleging that a product defect in its navigation systems caused it to fly off course and over Soviet territory, and that Boeing's improper and unsafe design was therefore the proximate cause of plaintiffs' damages. The court dismissed the complaint, holding that Boeing could not foresee that the Soviet Union would destroy an intruding aircraft in violation of international conventions, and had no ability to guard against such conduct. See *id., 1985 WL 9447, **5-6, 1985 U.S. Dist. LEXIS 17211, at *17-20.* The court held, consequently, that Boeing did not owe a duty to passengers with respect to such risks, and that the actions of the Russian pilots were independent and supervening causes that broke the chain of causation.

…

Accordingly, I deny Boeing's motion to dismiss the complaints against it arising from the crash of flight 77 into the Pentagon.

iii. Motion to Dismiss Claims Arising out of the Crash of United Air Lines Flight 93

a. Background

The successors of the passengers who died in the crash of United Air Lines flight 93 in Shanksville have filed four lawsuits: *Burnett v. Argenbright, 02 Civ. 6168; Lyles v. Argenbright, 02 Civ. 7243; Cashman v. Argenbright, 02 Civ. 7608; and Driscoll v. Argenbright, 02 Civ. 7912.* Their allegations are encapsulated in Plaintiffs' Flight 93 Master Liability Complaint, which mirrors the Plaintiffs' First Amended Flight 77 Master Liability Complaint. The Flight 93 Master Complaint alleges claims against Boeing based on strict tort liability, for an unreasonably dangerous design of the cockpit doors (Count Five); negligence, for failure to design cockpit doors and accompanying locks in a manner that would prevent hijackers and/or passengers from accessing the cockpit (Count Six); and express or implied warranty, for creating a product that was unfit for the purposes for which it was designed, intended and used (Count Seven).

b. Strict tort liability and breach of warranty claims

Under Pennsylvania law, following section 402A of the Restatement (Second) of Torts, a plaintiff pressing a product liability or strict tort liability claim must allege and prove that the product was defective, that the defect existed when it left the defendant, and that the defect proximately caused the harm. See *Weiner v. American Honda Motor Co. Inc., 718 A.2d 305, 307 (Pa.Super.1998).* The elements of breach of warranty and strict product liability are the same. *Cucchi v. Rollins Protective Servs. Co., 377 Pa.Super. 9, 546 A.2d 1131, 1136 (1998),* rev'd on other grounds, *524 Pa. 514, 574 A.2d 565 (1990).*

...

Because the decision of whether the product was unreasonably dangerous and unsafe for its intended use is a question of law, Boeing argues that the judge should not be influenced by conclusory allegations of the complaint. The reason, Boeing argues, is that "the trial court is not bound by any party's legal conclusions as to the intended purpose of a product, even if those conclusions are couched as averments of fact or presented as expert evidence. To hold otherwise would force trial courts (and reviewing courts) to accept unrealistic, generalized or distorted views of the product's purpose simply because they are presented as factual evidence." *Schindler, 774 A.2d at 773.*

But this is not the situation in the case before me. The cockpit door, like any door, is intended as a separation, a "movable barrier of wood or other material, consisting either of one piece, or of several pieces framed together, usually turning on hinges or sliding in a groove, and serving to close or open a passage into a building, room, etc." Oxford English Dictionary (2d ed.1999). A door may be fitted with, and without, locks, depending on who may be allowed to enter and in what circumstances. The intended users of a door, and in particular a locked door, are those within, in order to assure their privacy, and possibly those without who may have an interest in allowing those within to perform their jobs without unwanted intrusion.

Boeing asks me to hold that since the terrorists who hijacked the airplanes were not the intended users of the cockpit doors, one cannot say that the doors were unreasonably dangerous or unsafe in relation to the use that terrorists would be expected to make of the doors. Clearly, however, the intended users of the cockpit doors were not the terrorists who broke through them, but the pilots who had the right to protection from unwanted intrusion, and the passengers who had the right to believe that the pilots could continue to guide the plane, free from intrusion, to ensure their safe arrival at their intended destination. If, as Boeing argues, a person who breaks through a door is considered to be an unintended user, no manufacturer of a door and lock system could ever be liable. The intended user of a door is the person who wishes it to be closed and stay closed, not the person who can easily force it open. The pilots and passengers are not mere "casual bystanders," but people with a vital stake in the door's performing its intended purpose. See Restatement (Second) Torts § 402A, Comments (l) and (o) (intended users include "those who are passively enjoying the benefit of the product, as in the case of passengers in automobiles or airplanes .... casual bystanders, and others who may come in contact with the product, as in the case of employees of the retailer, or a passer-by injured by an exploding bottle, or a pedestrian hit by an automobile have been denied recovery").

Boeing may be able to show that the cockpit doors were not unreasonably dangerous, and that it was not unreasonable to design them to provide privacy without making them impenetrable. At this point, it would be inappropriate for a judge to make this determination. The record will have to be developed to show if the cockpit doors, incapable of keeping out unwanted intruders, were unreasonably dangerous, taking into consideration: 1) the gravity of the danger posed by the design; 2) the likelihood that the danger would occur; 3) the feasibility of a safer design; 4) the adverse consequences to the product and to the consumer that would result from a safer design; 5) the usefulness and desirability of the product; 6) the likelihood that the product will cause injury and the probable seriousness of the injury; 7) the availability of a substitute product which meets the same needs and is not unsafe; 8) the manufacturer's ability to eliminate the unsafe character of the product without impairing usefulness or making the product too expensive; 9) the user's ability to avoid danger by the exercise of care in the use of the product; 10) the user's anticipated awareness of the dangers inherent in the product and their avoidability; and 11) the ability of the manufacturer to spread loss through price-setting or insurance coverage. See *Schindler, 774 A.2d at 772; Riley, 688 A.2d at 225.*

In order to prevail on their strict liability and breach of warranty claims, the plaintiffs must also show that the defect was the proximate cause for the injuries; this will be discussed in the negligent design analysis below. *Weiner, 718 A.2d at 307.*

c. Negligent design claims

Boeing argues that the plaintiffs' negligent design claims must be dismissed because it did not owe a duty of care to the plaintiffs, and because its alleged negligence was not the proximate cause of plaintiffs' damages. The elements of a claim of negligence are: the existence of a duty to plaintiffs; the breach of that duty; a causal relationship between the breach and the resulting injury; and actual loss by the plaintiff. See *Brisbine v. Outside In School, 2002 PA Super 138, 799 A.2d 89, 93 (2002)* (citation omitted). Because Pennsylvania and Virginia law do not appear to differ significantly, the analysis is similar to that for Flight 77.

Duty is "imposed on all persons not to place others at risk of harm through their actions. The scope of this duty is limited, however, to those risks which are reasonably foreseeable by the actor in the circumstances of the case." *J.E.J. v. Tri-County Big Brothers/Big Sisters, Inc., 692 A.2d 582, 584 (1997)* (citation omitted). "In the context of duty, the concept of foreseeability means the likelihood of the occurrence of a general type of risk rather than the likelihood of the occurrence of the precise chain of events leading to the injury." *Huddleston v. Infertility Ctr. of Am., Inc., 700 A.2d 453, 460 (Pa.Super.1997)* (citation omitted). Plaintiffs have alleged that Boeing reasonably should have foreseen that a negligently designed cockpit door, permitting unauthorized individuals to enter the cockpit, would lead to risk of injury or death. For the same reasons as I have discussed previously, Boeing's motion to dismiss based on the absence of a duty of care to plaintiffs is denied.

To determine whether proximate cause exists, "the court must determine whether the injury would have been foreseen by an ordinary person as the natural and probable outcome of the act complained of." *Reilly v. Tiergarten Inc., 430 Pa.Super. 10, 633 A.2d 208, 210 (1993).* The existence of a concurring cause responsible for producing injury does not relieve a defendant of liability, if "a jury could reasonably believe that a defendant's actions were a substantial factor in bringing about the harm." *Powell v. Drumheller, 539 Pa. 484, 653 A.2d 619, 622 (1995)*. "Among the factors to consider in determining whether a subsequent force is an intervening or superseding cause are whether the force is operating independently of any situation created by the first actor's negligence and whether it is a normal result of that situation." *Rabutino v. Freedom State Realty Co. Inc., 809 A.2d 933, 942 (Pa.Super.2002)*. Plaintiffs allege that without defendant's negligence, the hijackers would not have been able to intrude into the cockpit and take over the airplane. Again, for the reasons previously discussed, the terrorists' unauthorized entry into the cockpit was not unforeseeable, and did not constitute an "intervening" or "superseding" cause that could, as a matter of law, break the chain of causation.

Accordingly, I deny Boeing's motion to dismiss the complaints against it arising from the crash of flight 93 into Shanksville.

III. Conclusion

For the reasons stated, the motions to dismiss the complaints by the Aviation Defendants and the WTC Defendants are denied. The motion of Boeing to dismiss Counts Four and Six in the Flight 77 Master Complaint, Count Four in the Flight 93 Master Complaint, Count Three in *Edwards v. American Airlines, Inc.*, No. 02 Civ. 9234, Count Five in *Powell v. Argenbright Security, Inc.*, No. 02 Civ. 10160, and Count Five in *Gallop v. Argenbright Security, Inc.*, No. 03 Civ. 1016, is granted; the remainder of the motion is denied.

By this decision, substantially all preliminary matters have been resolved, with the exception of the Port Authority's motion to dismiss Mayore Estates LLC, 02 Civ. 7198(AKH). We are now ready to proceed with the discovery stages of the lawsuits. To this end, I will meet with all counsel for case management purposes on September 26, 2003, at 9:30 A.M., in Courtroom 14D, 500 Pearl Street, New York, N.Y. 10007. Liaison Counsel shall submit a proposed agenda by September 24, 2003.

SO ORDERED.

11.2 Suits Against State-Sponsors of Terrorism

The second type of civil action associated with terrorism law suits are those claims brought against one of three categories: (1) purely non-State actors; (2) State's that sponsor terrorism, or their agents (Flatow Amendment); or (3) so-called non-FSIA defendants (State actors committing acts of terrorism outside their official capacity). For the purposes of al-Qa'eda-styled terrorism, the first two categories are most at play. *Boim v. Quranic Literacy Institute* is a civil action related to the first category and *Acree v. Republic of Iraq* relates to the second category, although with a significant shift. Although "terrorism" law suits are growing in number, plaintiffs face strenuous challenges in establishing liability and collecting on judgments (in some instances, the successful plaintiff may now execute judgments via any foreign State property used of a commercial activity in the United States).

As seen in *Boim*, bringing civil litigation against a non-State actor can involve individuals as well as groups. While many plaintiffs win by default, the defendants in *Boim* offered a spirited defense touching a number of important statutory and Constitutional issues.

Joyce BOIM and Stanley Boim, Individually and as Administrator of the Estate of David Boim, Plaintiffs-Appellees,

v.

QURANIC LITERACY INSTITUTE AND HOLY LAND FOUNDATION FOR RELIEF AND DEVELOPMENT

United States Court of Appeals

Seventh Circuit

Defendants-Appellants.

Argued Sept. 25, 2001.

Decided June 5, 2002.

OPINION BY ROVNER, J

In this case of first impression, the parents of a young United States citizen murdered in Israel by Hamas terrorists have sued several individuals and organizations for the loss of their son. Two of the organizational defendants moved to dismiss the complaint, and the district court denied the motion. In this interlocutory appeal, we are asked to consider the viability of a claim brought under the never-tested *18 U.S.C. §2333*, which allows U.S. nationals who have been injured "by reason of an act of international terrorism" to sue therefor and recover treble damages. We affirm the district court's denial of the defendants' motion to dismiss....

I Background

David Boim was the son of Joyce and Stanley Boim, who are United States citizens. David held dual citizenship in the United States and Israel. In 1996, the Boims were living in Israel, where seventeen-year-old David was studying at a yeshiva. On May 13, 1996, David was murdered as he waited with other students at a bus stop near Beit El in the West Bank. He was struck by bullets fired from a passing car, and was pronounced dead within an hour of the shooting. His two attackers were later identified as Amjad Hinawi and Khalil Tawfiq Al-Sharif. The Palestinian Authority apprehended Hinawi and Al-Sharif, and temporarily imprisoned them in early 1997. They were released shortly thereafter, apparently pending trial. Al-Sharif subsequently killed himself and five civilians and injured 192 other people in a suicide bombing in Jerusalem on September 4, 1997. Two other suicide bombers joined him in this action. Hinawi, who confessed to participating in the shooting of David Boim, was eventually tried for David's murder by a Palestinian Authority court and was sentenced to ten years' imprisonment on February 17, 1998.

Both Hinawi and Al-Sharif were known members of the military wing of Hamas. The Boims describe Hamas as an extremist, Palestinian militant organization that seeks to establish a fundamentalist Palestinian state. The group is divided into two branches, one political and one military. The military branch receives orders and material support from the political branch. Hamas seeks to advance its political objectives through acts of terrorism and works to undermine the Middle East peace process through violent attacks on civilians. Hamas has a global presence, and terrorist operatives in Gaza and the West Bank receive their instructions, funds, weapons and practical support for their missions from Hamas organizers throughout the world. The Boims believe that

Hamas has command and control centers in the United States, Britain and several Western European countries. The leaders of these control centers coordinate fund-raising efforts from sympathetic parties in these various countries and then launder and channel the money to Hamas operatives in Gaza and the West Bank. They also arrange for the purchase of weapons and for the recruitment and training of military personnel. They work with local commanders in the West Bank and Gaza to plan terrorist attacks. Hamas was designated a terrorist organization by President William Jefferson Clinton in 1995 by Executive Order. In 1997, Hamas was designated a foreign terrorist organization pursuant to *8 U.S.C. §1189.*

The Boims allege that Hamas' military wing depends on foreign contributions, with approximately one-third of its multi-million dollar annual budget coming from fund-raising in North America and Western Europe. The Boims believe that the Quranic Literacy Institute ("QLI") and the Holy Land Foundation for Relief and Development ("HLF"), along with other defendants not involved in this appeal, are the main fronts for Hamas in the United States. They allege that these organizations' allegedly humanitarian functions mask their core mission of raising and funneling money and other resources to Hamas operatives in support of terrorist activities.

QLI is an Illinois not-for-profit corporation that purports to translate and publish sacred Islamic texts, but the Boims believe it is also engaged in raising and laundering money for Hamas. QLI also employed another defendant, Mohammed Abdul Hamid Khalil Salah, nominally as a computer analyst. The FBI has seized $1.4 million in cash and property from Salah, who is the admitted United States based leader of the military branch of Hamas. He has been prosecuted for channeling money to Hamas and for recruiting, organizing and training terrorist operatives in Israel. Salah is named on a list of Specially Designated Terrorists compiled by the United States Treasury Department's Office of Foreign Assets Control.

HLF is also a not-for-profit corporation, whose ostensible mission is to fund humanitarian relief and development efforts. HLF's director has acknowledged providing money to Hamas, and the Boims allege that, although HLF purports to have a charitable purpose, its true function is to raise and channel money to Hamas for terrorist activities. The U.S. base of HLF's operations is in Texas. HLF also has offices in Jerusalem and in Illinois. HLF, QLI and the other organizational defendants are linked by interlocking directorates and by ties to Salah and Mousa Mohammed Abu Marzook, another individual defendant (not involved in this appeal) who has a leadership role in the military branch of Hamas.

According to the Boims, money flows from American contributors to Hamas in a three-step process: first, the front organizations solicit contributions; second, the leaders arrange for the money to be laundered and wired overseas; and third, Hamas operatives in Gaza and the West Bank use the money to finance terrorist activities. Because it is illegal to provide financial support to recognized terrorist groups, the money flows through a series of complicated transactions, changing hands a number of times, and being commingled with funds from the front organizations' legitimate charitable and business dealings. The funds are laundered in a variety of ways, including through real estate deals and through Swiss bank accounts. The Boims allege that money raised by HLF and QLI was transferred to Hamas terrorists using these various methods in order to finance terrorist activities. Hamas used the money raised in this way to purchase weapons to carry out terrorist attacks, including the attack on David Boim. Hamas regularly drew money from a pool of laundered funds in order to finance training, weapons purchases, lodging, false identification, communications equipment, lethal substances, explosives, personnel, transportation and other material support for terrorist operations. The Boims believe that expenditures from this pool of funds paid for the vehicle, machine guns and ammunition used to kill David Boim, and also paid for the training of Hinawi, Al-Sharif and other Hamas operatives involved in the attack on David Boim. The funds were also used to provide a stipend for Al-Sharif's family, as it is a common practice to pay the families of suicide bombers in order to encourage others to volunteer for these activities.

The Boims bring their suit against HLF, QLI and other organizational and individual defendants pursuant to *18 U.S.C. §2333*. They charge that all of the defendants are civilly liable for David's murder. They name Hinawi and Al-Sharif as the persons who actually killed David, but allege that the other defendants aided, abetted and financed Hinawi and Al-Sharif. They assert that the organizational defendants provided material support or resources to Hamas as those terms are defined in *18 U.S.C. §§2339A and 2339B*. The Boims seek compensation for the extreme physical pain David suffered before his death, and for the cost of his funeral and the loss of accretion to his estate due to his death at age seventeen. They also seek damages for their own extreme mental anguish and loss of the society of their son. They ask for $100,000,000 compensatory damages, $100,000,000 punitive damages, plus costs and attorney's fees, and request the trebling of damages pursuant to the statute.

...

The district court granted HLF and QLI's motion for a certificate of appealability, and we subsequently granted them leave to file an interlocutory appeal. See *28 U.S.C. §1292(b)*....

In this case, the district court correctly certified three issues for appeal:

(1) Does funding, simpliciter, of an international terrorist organization constitute an act of terrorism under *18 U.S.C. §2331*?
(2) Does *18 U.S.C. §2333* incorporate the definitions of international terrorism found in *18 U.S.C. §§2339A* and *2339B*?
(3) Does a civil cause of action lie under *18 U.S.C. §§2331* and *2333* for aiding and abetting international terrorism?

...

II Discussion

The Boims seek to recover against HLF and QLI pursuant to 18 U.S.C. §2333, which provides, in relevant part:

> Any national of the United States injured in his or her person, property, or business by reason of an act of international terrorism, or his or her estate, survivors, or heirs, may sue therefor in any appropriate district court of the United States and shall recover threefold the damages he or she sustains and the cost of the suit, including attorney's fees.

18 U.S.C. §2333(a). "International terrorism," in turn, is a defined term:
[T]he term "international terrorism" means activities that—

(A) involve violent acts or acts dangerous to human life that are a violation of the criminal laws of the United States or of any State, or that would be a criminal violation if committed within the jurisdiction of the United States or of any State;

(B) appear to be intended-

    (i) to intimidate or coerce a civilian population;

    (ii) to influence the policy of a government by intimidation or coercion; or

    (iii) to affect the conduct of a government by assassination or kidnapping; and

(C) occur primarily outside the territorial jurisdiction of the United States, or transcend national boundaries in terms of the means by which they are accomplished, the persons they appear intended to intimidate or coerce, or the locale in which their perpetrators operate or seek asylum. *18 U.S.C. §2331(1)*. These provisions became law in 1992.

    We turn now to the Boims' three theories of liability under *section 2333: (1)* that funding Hamas, without more, is an act of international terrorism because it is conduct that involves violent acts or acts dangerous to human life; (2) that funding Hamas constitutes the provision of material support or resources to a terrorist organization in violation of the criminal provisions set forth in *sections 2339A* and *2339B*, and that violations of these criminal provisions give rise to civil liability under *section 2333*; and (3) that aiding and abetting an act of terrorism gives rise to civil liability under *section 2333*.

A.

The plaintiffs' first theory is that the simple provision of funds to Hamas by QLI and HLF constitutes an act of international terrorism because it "involve[s] violent acts or acts dangerous to human life." The Boims liken payments to Hamas to murder for hire: the person who pays for the murder does not himself commit a violent act, but the payment "involves" violent acts in the sense that it brings about the violent act and provides an incentive for someone else to commit it. The Boims urge us to adopt a very broad definition of "involves" that would include any activity that touches on and supports a violent act. They argue that David's murder was indisputably a violent act, and we have no quarrel with that premise. But they further argue that the provision of money or in-kind services to persons outside the country who set up the infrastructure used to recruit and train David's murderers, buy their weapons, and compensate their families also "involves" violent acts. The defendants, in turn, urge us to read the statute to hold liable only those who actually commit a violent act.

    No court has yet considered the meaning or scope of *sections 2331* and *2333*, and so we write upon a tabula rasa. The starting point in all statutory analysis is the plain language of the statute itself. *United States v. Wagner, 29 F.3d 264, 266 (7th Cir.1994)*. We look to the language in order to determine what Congress intended, and we also look to the statute's structure, subject matter, context and history for this same purpose. *Almendarez-Torres v. United States, 523 U.S. 224, 228, 118 S.Ct. 1219, 140 L.Ed.2d 350 (1998)* ("We therefore look to the statute before us and ask what Congress intended.... In answering this question, we look to the statute's language, structure, subject matter, context, and history—factors that typically help courts determine a statute's objectives and thereby illuminate its text."). The controversy here centers on the definition of international terrorism, and in particular on the definition of the word "involve," which is susceptible to many meanings. The statutory definition of international terrorism in *section 2331(1)* is drawn verbatim from the Foreign Intelligence Surveillance Act, *50 U.S.C. §1801(c)* ("FISA"). No court has yet expounded on the meaning or scope of "international terrorism" as it is used in FISA either, so we are not aided by that origin. A dictionary definition of "involve" demonstrates the many levels of participation that could constitute involvement. To involve is: to enfold or envelop so as to encumber; to engage as a participant; to oblige to take part; to occupy (as oneself) absorbingly; to commit emotionally; to relate closely; to have within or as part of itself; to require as a necessary accompaniment; to have an effect on. Webster's Ninth New Collegiate Dictionary (1983). Because of these many possibilities, we agree with the district court that we must look to the structure, context and legislative history of the statute to determine what Congress intended.

The government, in its very helpful amicus curiae brief, delineates some of the legislative history of *sections 2331* and *2333*. That history, in combination with the language of the statute itself, evidences an intent by Congress to codify general common law tort principles and to extend civil liability for acts of international terrorism to the full reaches of traditional tort law. *See 137 Cong. Rec. S4511-04 (April 16, 1991)* ("The [antiterrorism act] accords victims of terrorism the remedies of American tort law, including treble damages and attorney's fees."); *Antiterrorism Act of 1990, Hearing Before the Subcommittee on Courts and Administrative Practice of Committee on the Judiciary, United States Senate, 101st Congress, Second Session, July 25, 1990* (hereafter "Senate Hearing"), *Testimony of Joseph Morris, at 136* ("[T]he bill as drafted is powerfully broad, and its intention ... is to ... bring [in] all of the substantive law of the American tort law system.") In particular, the statute itself contains all of the elements of a traditional tort: breach of a duty (i.e., committing an act of international terrorism); injury to the person, property or business of another; and causation (injured "by reason of"). Although the statute defines the class of plaintiffs who may sue, it does not limit the class of defendants, and we must therefore look to tort law and the legislative history to determine who may be held liable for injuries covered by the statute.

The legislative record is replete with references to the then-recent decision in *Klinghoffer v. Palestine Liberation Organization, 739 F.Supp. 854 (S.D.N.Y.1990)*, vacated, *937 F.2d 44 (2d Cir.1991)*. *See Senate Hearing at 1, 12, 17, 79, 83, 122, 133; H.R. Rep. 102-1040, at 5 (1992); 137 Cong. Rec. S4511-04 (April 16, 1991); 136 Cong. Rec. S4568-01 (1990)*. Leon Klinghoffer was a U.S. citizen who was murdered in a terrorist attack on a cruise ship in the Mediterranean Sea. The district court found that his survivors' claims were cognizable in federal court under federal admiralty jurisdiction and the Death on the High Seas Act because the tort occurred in navigable waters. *739 F.Supp. at 858-59*. The repeated favorable references to *Klinghoffer* indicate a desire on the part of Congress to extend this liability to land-based terrorism that occurred in a foreign country. *See Senate Hearing at 12, Testimony of Alan Kreczko, Deputy Legal Advisor, Department of State* ("This bill ... expands the *Klinghoffer* opinion."); *H.R. Rep. 102-1040, at 5 (1992)* ("Only by virtue of the fact that the [*Klinghoffer*] attack violated certain Admiralty laws and the organization involved—the Palestinian Liberation Organization—had assets and carried on activities in New York, was the court able to establish jurisdiction over the case. A similar attack occurring on an airplane or in some other locale might not have been subject to civil action in the U.S. In order to facilitate civil actions against such terrorists the Committee [on the Judiciary] recommends [this bill]."); *137 Cong. Rec. S4511-04* (April 16, 1991), *Statement of Senator Grassley (section 2333* would "codify [the *Klinghoffer*] ruling and makes the right of American victims definitive"); *136 Cong. Rec. S4568-01 (1990)*.

The statute clearly is meant to reach beyond those persons who themselves commit the violent act that directly causes the injury. The Senate report on the bill notes that "[t]he substance of [an action under *section 2333*] is not de fined by the statute, because the fact patterns giving rise to such suits will be as varied and numerous as those found in the law of torts. This bill opens the courthouse door to victims of international terrorism." *S. Rep.102-342, at 45 (1992)*. This same report also remarks that the legislation, with "its provisions for compensatory damages, treble damages, and the imposition of liability at any point along the causal chain of terrorism," would "interrupt, or at least imperil, the flow of money." *Id.* at 22 (emphasis added). *See also Statement of Senator Grassley, 136 Cong. Rec. S4568-01 at S4593* ("With the enactment of this legislation, we set an example to the world of how the United States legal system deals with terrorists. If terrorists have assets within our jurisdictional reach, American citizens will have the power to seize them."); *Senate Hearing at 17, Statement of Alan Kreczko* ("[F]ew terrorist organizations are likely to have cash assets or property located in the United States that could be attached and used to fulfill a civil judgment. The existence of such a cause of action, however, may deter terrorist groups from maintaining assets in the United States, from benefitting from investments in the U.S. and from soliciting funds within the U.S."); *Senate Hearing at 79, Statement of Joseph Morris* ("[A]nything that could be done to deter money-raising in the United States, money laundering in the United States, the repose of assets in the United States, and so on, would not only help benefit victims, but would also help deter terrorism.") All of this history indicates an intent by Congress to allow a plaintiff to recover from anyone along the causal chain of terrorism.

But to the extent that the Boims urge a reading of the statute that would lead to liability for merely giving money to Hamas, a group which then sponsored a terrorist act in the manner the Boims have alleged, we agree with the district court, the defendants and the government that those allegations would be inadequate. To say that funding simpliciter constitutes an act of terrorism is to give the statute an almost unlimited reach. Any act which turns out to facilitate terrorism, however remote that act may be from actual violence and regardless of the actor's intent, could be construed to "involve" terrorism. Without also requiring the plaintiffs to show knowledge of and intent to further the payee's violent criminal acts, such a broad definition might also lead to constitutional infirmities by punishing mere association with groups that engage in terrorism, as we shall discuss later in addressing the First Amendment concerns raised here.

Additionally, the statute itself requires that in order to recover, a plaintiff must be injured "by reason of" an act of international terrorism. The Supreme Court has interpreted identical language to require a showing of proximate cause. See *Holmes v. Securities Investor Protection Corp., 503 U.S. 258, 265-68, 112 S.Ct. 1311, 117 L.Ed.2d 532 (1992)* (interpreting "by reason of" language in civil RICO provision to require a showing that the defendant's conduct proximately caused the plaintiff's injury). Foreseeability is the cornerstone of proximate cause, and in tort law, a defendant will be held liable only for those injuries that might have reasonably been anticipated as a natural consequence of the defendant's actions. *Suzik v. Sea-Land Corp., 89 F.3d 345, 348 (7th Cir.1996)*; Restatement (2d) of Torts, §§ 440-447. In the circumstances of this case, the Boims cannot show that David Boim was injured "by reason of" the defendants' payments to Hamas in the traditional tort sense of causation unless they can also show that murder was the reasonably foreseeable result of making the donation. To hold the defendants liable for donating money without knowledge of the donee's intended criminal use of the funds would impose strict liability. Nothing in the language of the statute or its structure or history supports that formulation. The government, in its amicus brief, maintains that funding may be enough to establish liability if the plaintiff can show that the provider of funds was generally aware of the donee's terrorist activity, and if the provision of funds substantially assisted the terrorist act in question. See *Halberstam v. Welch, 705 F.2d 472, 477 (D.C.Cir.1983)* (describing the standards for joint liability for tortious acts). We will consider the government's proposed standard separately in our discussion of aiding and abetting liability. For now we note only that the complaint cannot be sustained on the theory that the defendants themselves committed an act of international terrorism when they donated unspecified amounts of money to Hamas, neither knowing nor suspecting that Hamas would in turn financially support the persons who murdered David Boim. In the very least, the plaintiffs must be able to show that murder was a reasonably foreseeable result of making a donation. Thus, the Boims' first theory of liability under *section 2333*, funding simpliciter of a terrorist organization, is insufficient because it sets too vague a standard, and because it does not require a showing of proximate cause.

B.

The Boims' second theory of liability is that the defendants' violation of *sections 2339A* and *2339B*, the criminal counterparts to *section 2333*, gives rise to civil liability under *section 2333*. The Boims further contend that *sections 2339A* and *2339B* demonstrate Congress' intent to include the provision of material support to terrorist organizations in the definition of international terrorism for the purposes of *section 2333*. The district court concluded that Congress viewed violations of *sections 2339A* and *2339B* as "activities involving violent acts or acts dangerous to human life," and therefore found that violations of *sections 2339A* and *2339B* gave rise to civil liability under *section 2333*. Because much of the conduct the Boims alleged occurred before the passage of *sections 2339A* and *2339B*, however, the district court ruled that the Boims would have to rely primarily on their aiding and abetting theory.

In 1994, Congress passed *18 U.S.C. §2339A*, which criminalizes the provision of material support to terrorists:

> Whoever, within the United States, provides material support or resources or conceals or disguises the nature, location, source, or ownership of material support or resources, knowing or intending that they are to be used in preparation for, or in carrying out, a violation of *section 32, 37, 81, 175, 351, 831, 842(m) or (n), 844(f) or (i), 930(c), 956, 1114, 1116, 1203, 1361, 1362, 1363, 1366, 1751, 1992, 2155, 2156, 2280, 2281, 2332, 2332a, 2332b, 2332c,* or *2340A* of this title or *section 46502 of title 49*, or in preparation for, or in carrying out, the concealment or an escape from the commission of any such violation, shall be fined under this title, imprisoned not more than 10 years, or both.

18 U.S.C. §2339A(a). "Material support or resources" is a defined term:

> In this section, the term "material support or resources" means currency or other financial securities, financial services, lodging, training, safehouses, false documentation or identification, communications equipment, facilities, weapons, lethal substances, explosives, personnel, transportation, and other physical assets, except medicine or religious materials. *18 U.S.C. §2339A(b)*.

Two years later, Congress extended criminal liability to those providing material support to foreign terrorist organizations:

> Whoever, within the United States or subject to the jurisdiction of the United States, knowingly provides material support or resources to a foreign terrorist organization, or attempts or conspires to do so, shall be fined under this title or imprisoned not more than 10 years, or both.

18 U.S.C. §2339B(a)(1). Section 2339B adopts the definition of "material support or resources" provided in *section 2339A*, and looks to *8 U.S.C. §1189* for the definition of "terrorist organization."

HLF and QLI, of course, protest the district court's conclusion that funding may form the basis for a *section 2333* civil action if the funding meets the standards for criminal liability under *sections 2339A* or *2339B*. The defendants also fault the district court for relying on Congress' repeal of the jurisdictional immunity of a foreign state that has been designated a state sponsor of terrorism as evidence of Congressional intent to allow a *section 2333* civil action against persons who violate *sections 2339A* and *2339B*. See *28 U.S.C. § 1605(a)(7)*. HLF and QLI present a number of puzzling arguments against the Boims' theory of civil liability through violations of these criminal statutes. According to HLF and QLI, Congress neither expressly nor impliedly amended the definition of "international terrorism" when it enacted *section 2339A* and *2339B* because (1) these sections set forth criminal offenses separate from the statute making violent acts of international terrorism illegal under U.S. law; (2) these sections provide for relatively minor criminal penalties compared to the penalties for violent terrorist acts; (3) nothing in the text of either *sections 2339A* or *2339B* suggests that violations of these provisions are acts of international terrorism remediable under *section 2333*; (4) the inclusion of *sections 2339A* and *2339B* in the terrorism section of Title 18 alone does not mean that Congress intended for violations of these provisions to constitute acts of international terrorism for the purposes of *section 2333*; and (6) *section 2339B* contains a separate remedial scheme that does not include a private right of action but instead provides for civil enforcement by the United States. The defendants also argue that even if violations of *sections 2339A* and *2339B* create civil liability under *section 2333*, the Boims have insufficiently alleged violations of those criminal statutes.

Most of these arguments are tautologous. For example, *sections 2339A* and *2339B* certainly do proscribe different conduct than sections 2332, *2332a*, *2332b* and *2332d*. These latter provisions address the primary perpetrators of violent acts of terrorism, while *sections 2339A* and *2339B* apply to those persons who provide material support to the primary perpetrators of violent acts of terrorism. When it passed *sections 2339A* and *2339B*, Congress undoubtedly intended that the persons providing financial support to terrorists should also be held criminally liable for those violent acts. Indeed, as we have already noted, the Congressional record for *section 2333* indicates an intention to cut off the flow of money in support of terrorism generally. *S. Rep.102-342 at 22 (1992). Sections 2339A* and *2339B* further this goal by imposing criminal liability for financial support of terrorist activities and organizations. The fact that Congress imposed lesser criminal penalties for the financial supporters indicates perhaps that they found the financiers less dangerous or less culpable than the terrorists they finance, but it does not in any way indicate that Congress meant to limit civil liability to those who personally committed acts of terrorism. On the contrary, it would be counterintuitive to conclude that Congress imposed criminal liability in *sections 2339A* and *2339B* on those who financed terrorism, but did not intend to impose civil liability on those same persons through *section 2333*.

Section 2339A prohibits the provision of material support for an extensive list of violent crimes associated with terrorism—assassination, kidnapping, arson, destruction of aircraft—that make clear what types of conduct Congress had in mind when it defined "international terrorism" in *section 2331(1)* as not just the violent acts themselves, but also "activities that involve violent acts or acts dangerous to human life." There is no textual, structural or logical justification for construing the civil liability imposed by section 2333 more narrowly than the corresponding criminal provisions. Because Congress intended to impose criminal liability for funding violent terrorism, we find that it also intended through *sections 2333* and *2331(1)* to impose civil liability for funding at least as broad a class of violent terrorist acts. If the plaintiffs could show that HLF and QLI violated either *section 2339A* or *section 2339B*, that conduct would certainly be sufficient to meet the definition of "international terrorism" under *sections 2333* and *2331*. Such acts would give rise to civil liability under *section 2333* so long as knowledge and intent are also shown, as we shall discuss shortly in the context of aiding and abetting.

We hasten to add that, although proof of a criminal violation under *sections 2339A* or *2339B* might satisfy the definition of international terrorism under *section 2333*, such proof is not necessary to sustain a *section 2333* claim. As we discuss in the context of aiding and abetting, we believe Congress intended for civil liability for financing terrorism to sweep more broadly than the conduct described in *sections 2339A* and *2339B*. We also note that the district court seems to have inadvertently redefined the term "material" in the context of *sections 2339A* and *2339B* as meaning substantial or considerable. The statute itself defines "material support or resources" as "currency or other financial securities, financial services, lodging, training, safehouses, false documentation or identification, communications equipment, facilities, weapons, lethal substances, explosives, personnel, transportation, and other physical assets, except medicine or religious materials." *18 U.S.C. §2339A(b)*. Thus, the term relates to the type of aid provided rather than whether it is substantial or considerable. For civil liability, *section 2333* requires that the plaintiff be injured "by reason of" the act of international terrorism. Because we believe Congress intended to import standard tort law into *section 2333*, causation may be demonstrated as it would be in traditional tort law. Congress has made clear, though, through the criminal liability imposed in *sections 2339A* and *2339B*, that even small donations made knowingly and intentionally in support of terrorism may meet the standard for civil liability in *section 2333*. Congress' goal of cutting off funding for terrorism would be seriously compromised if terrorist organizations could avoid liability by simply pooling together small donations to fund a terrorist act.

We turn finally to *28 U.S.C. §1605(a)(7)*. In relevant part, the statute provides:

> A foreign state shall not be immune from the jurisdiction of courts of the United States or of the States in any case ... in which money damages are sought against a foreign state for personal injury or death that was caused by an act of torture, extrajudicial killing, aircraft sabotage, hostage taking, or the provision of material support or resources (as defined in *section 2339A of title 18*) for such an act if such act or provision of material support is engaged in by an official, employee, or agent of such foreign state while acting within the scope of his or her office, employment, agency[.]

Contrary to the defendants' characterization, the district court did not rely solely on the passage of *section 1605(a)(7)* in finding that Congress viewed the provision of material support and resources as an act of international terrorism. After finding support in both the text and the structure of *sections 2333* and *2331* for this proposition, the court found further reasons in *section 1605(a)(7)*. As the district court noted, "Considering that Congress has permitted foreign states that have been designated state sponsors of terrorism to be sued in United States courts for violating § 2339A, it is hard to argue that Congress did not intend to include such violations in its definition of 'terrorism' under the statutory scheme." *Boim, 127 F.Supp.2d at 1016*. We take the district court to mean that section 1605(a)(7) implies a foreign state may be sued in the United States for acts that would give rise to criminal liability under *section 2339A*, not that *section 2339A* itself has a civil provision. The mechanism for suing a foreign state for these acts that would give rise to criminal liability under *section 2339A* is *section 2333*. The defendants complain that Congress did not specifically mention *section 2333* as the device by which plaintiffs might sue foreign governments for violations of *section 2339A*, but they fail to point to any other source of civil liability. We agree that Congress made clear in *section 1605(a)(7)* its intent to characterize violations of *section 2339A* as acts of international terrorism under *section 2333*.

The district court believed there was a timing problem for the Boims in making their case under these criminal provisions because much of the funding conduct allegedly committed by HLF and QLI occurred prior to the passage of *sections 2339A* and *2339B*. Indeed, Hamas was not designated a terrorist organization under section 1189 until 1997, after David's murder. Certainly

HLF and QLI could not be held criminally liable for conduct that occurred before the statutes were enacted, but that argument misses the point. We are using *sections 2339A* and *2339B* not as independent sources of liability under section 2333 , but to amplify what Congress meant by "international terrorism." *Sections 2339A* and *2339B* merely lend further support to our finding that Congress considered the provision of material support to terrorists an act of international terrorism. This reading simply amplifies the conclusion we have already reached by examining the language and legislative history of *section 2333*. *Sections 2339A* and *2339B* provide criminal liability for the provision of material support, and *section 2333* provides civil liability. The Boims may thus show that QLI and HLF committed an act of international terrorism subject to civil liability under section 2333 by proving that QLI and HLF provided material support to terrorist organizations. No timing problem arises because *sections 2339A* and *2339B* merely elucidate conduct that was already prohibited by *section 2333*.

C.

We turn next to the Boims' theory that HLF and QLI may be held civilly liable under *section 2333* for aiding and abetting an act of international terrorism.

…

Finally, if we failed to impose liability on aiders and abettors who knowingly and intentionally funded acts of terrorism, we would be thwarting Congress' clearly expressed intent to cut off the flow of money to terrorists at every point along the causal chain of violence. *S. Rep. 102-342, at 22* (by imposing "liability at any point along the causal chain of terrorism, it would interrupt, or at least imperil, the flow of money."). Unlike section 10(b) where Congress' intent could be met without imposing liability on aiders and abettors, Congress' purpose here could not be met unless liability attached beyond the persons directly involved in acts of violence. The statute would have little effect if liability were limited to the persons who pull the trigger or plant the bomb because such persons are unlikely to have assets, much less assets in the United States, and would not be deterred by the statute. See *Central Bank, 511 U.S. at 188, 114 S.Ct. 1439* (policy considerations may be used to interpret the text and structure of a statute when a literal reading would lead to a result so bizarre that Congress could not have intended it). Also, and perhaps more importantly, there would not be a trigger to pull or a bomb to blow up without the resources to acquire such tools of terrorism and to bankroll the persons who actually commit the violence. Moreover, the organizations, businesses and nations that support and encourage terrorist acts are likely to have reachable assets that they wish to protect. The only way to imperil the flow of money and discourage the financing of terrorist acts is to impose liability on those who knowingly and intentionally supply the funds to the persons who commit the violent acts. For all of these distinguishing reasons, we do not think *Central Bank* controls the result here, but that aiding and abetting liability is both appropriate and called for by the language, structure and legislative history of *section 2333*.

D.

The defendants raise two First Amendment objections to this *section 2333* action against them. First, they argue that the Boims seek to hold them liable for their mere association with Hamas. Harking back to a line of cases involving the Communist party, HLF and QLI contend that, when an organization has both legal and illegal aims, a person may not be punished for mere membership in or association with that organization, but may be held civilly liable only if he or she possesses the specific intent to further the organizations' illegal purposes. Second, they contend that, to the extent the Boims' claim is founded on a violation of *section 2339B*, it cannot withstand First Amendment scrutiny because *section 2339B* fails to account for the intent and the associational rights of the contributors who donate money for humanitarian purposes. The National Coalition to Protect Political Freedom and the Center for Constitutional Rights have jointly filed an amicus brief in support of the defendants' First Amendment arguments, and we will consider their contentions as well.

1.

HLF and QLI begin their argument with the well-established proposition that the Constitution protects against the imposition of liability based solely upon association with a group. See *NAACP v. Claiborne Hardware Co., 458 U.S. 886, 920, 102 S.Ct. 3409, 73 L.Ed.2d 1215 (1982)* ("[c]ivil liability may not be imposed merely because an individual belonged to a group, some members of which committed acts of violence."); *Healy v. James, 408 U.S. 169, 185-86, 92 S.Ct. 2338, 33 L.Ed.2d 266 (1972)* ("the Court has consistently disapproved governmental action imposing criminal sanctions or denying rights and privileges solely because of a citizen's association with an unpopular organization."); *United States v. Robel, 389 U.S. 258, 265, 88 S.Ct. 419, 19 L.Ed.2d 508 (1967)* (where a statute establishes guilt by association alone, the inhibiting effect on First Amendment rights is clear); *Scales v. United States, 367 U.S. 203, 229, 81 S.Ct. 1469, 6 L.Ed.2d 782 (1961)* (a blanket prohibition of association with a group having both legal and illegal aims presents a real danger that legitimate political expression or association would be impaired). We have no quarrel with that general proposition or with its corollary, that in order to impose liability on an individual for association with a group, it is necessary to establish that the group possessed unlawful goals and that the individual held a specific intent to further those illegal aims.

...

HLF and QLI protest that the Boims have not alleged their specific intent to further the illegal activities of Hamas, and that the claim does not, therefore, survive First Amendment scrutiny. Rather, HLF complains, the Boims have simply alleged that HLF has admitted providing funds to Hamas, that HLF functions as a front organization for Hamas, that HLF raises and channels funds to Hamas to finance terrorist activities in Israel, and that HLF solicits donations over the internet. HLF protests that even if these allegations suffice to show a present intent to further terrorist acts, they do not show that HLF had that intent prior to David Boim's murder. Rather, HLF believes the Boims are lumping their organization in with other groups that may have had an intent to commit illegal acts, and that the Boims are seeking to hold them liable for their mere association with these other organizations. QLI similarly argues that the Boims have not alleged a specific intent on the part of QLI to further the illegal goals of Hamas, and that they may not be held liable for merely associating with organizations that might have intended to aid the illegal operations of Hamas.

Amici also emphasize that individuals may not be penalized for their association with a political organization that engages in both lawful and unlawful ends, absent a showing of specific intent to further the organization's illegal goals. *Claiborne Hardware, 458 U.S. at 919-20, 102 S.Ct. 3409*. The arguments of the defendants and amici beg the question, though, because *section 2333* does not seek to impose liability for association alone but rather for involvement in acts of international terrorism. The defendants nonetheless object that the definition of acts of international terrorism is so broad that they might be held liable for involvement in terrorist activity when all they intended was to supply money to fund the legitimate, humanitarian mission of Hamas or other organizations. To resolve the tension that arises when a group engages in both protected advocacy and unprotected criminal acts…. Civil liability may not be imposed merely because an individual belonged to a group, some members of which committed acts of violence. For liability to be imposed by reason of association alone, it is necessary to establish that the group itself possessed unlawful goals and that the individual held a specific intent to further those illegal aims.

We have already held that the Boims may prevail on their claim by showing, among other things, that the defendants aided and abetted David's murder. This requires them to prove that the defendants knew of Hamas' illegal activities, that they desired to help those activities succeed, and they engaged in some act of helping the illegal activities. See *Zafiro, 945 F.2d at 887*. If the Boims are able to prove the defendants aided and abetted terrorist acts, liability would not offend the principles announced in Claiborne Hardware. The Boims have alleged that HLF and QLI supplied money to Hamas to fund terrorist operations, that they are "front" organizations with ostensibly legitimate purposes which are actually engaged in fund-raising and money laundering in support of terrorist activities. They have alleged that HLF and QLI provided the money to purchase the weapons and train the men who killed David Boim. HLF and QLI, of course, deny these allegations and argue that as a factual matter, Hamas is primarily a humanitarian organization, and that any money supplied to Hamas by QLI and HLF was intended to fund humanitarian efforts, not terrorism. This is a classic factual dispute, not suitable for resolution on a motion to dismiss for failure to state a claim. If the Boims are able to prove their allegations, that HLF and QLI provided legitimate-looking fronts for raising money to support the terrorist operation that resulted in David Boim's murder, their claim will not run afoul of the First Amendment. The Boims are not seeking to hold HLF and QLI liable for their mere association with Hamas, nor are they seeking to hold the defendants liable for contributing money for humanitarian efforts. Rather, they are seeking to hold them liable for aiding and abetting murder by supplying the money to buy the weapons, train the shooters, and compensate the families of the murderers. That Hamas may also engage in legitimate advocacy or humanitarian efforts is irrelevant for First Amendment purposes if HLF and QLI knew about Hamas' illegal operations, and intended to help Hamas accomplish those illegal goals when they contributed money to the organization.

…

2.

We turn next to the defendants' contention that any *section 2333* claim founded on a violation of *section 2339B* must fail because *section 2339B* violates the First Amendment. As we noted above, *section 2339B* subjects to criminal liability anyone who, within the United States or subject to the jurisdiction of the United States, knowingly provides material support or resources to a foreign terrorist organization, or attempts or conspires to do so. *18 U.S.C. § 2339B(a)(1)*. The defendants complain that, because *section 2339B* imposes liability without regard to the intent of the donor, it violates the First Amendment. They maintain that *section 2339B* unnecessarily interferes with the associational rights of contributors who donate money solely for humanitarian purposes by failing to limit liability to those who intend to support the illegal goals of an organization. They contend that *section 2339B* will chill legitimate fund-raising for humanitarian purposes if a charitable organization could be prosecuted for providing food for the needy in the Middle East that happens to make its way into the mouths of the families of terrorists. They urge us to reject the reasoning of the Ninth Circuit in *Humanitarian Law Project v. Reno, 205 F.3d 1130 (9th Cir.2000)*, cert. denied, *532 U.S. 904, 121 S.Ct. 1226, 149 L.Ed.2d 136 (2001)*, in upholding the constitutionality of section 2339B against a First Amendment challenge. They argue that *Humanitarian Law Project* is inconsistent with *Claiborne Hardware*, and that even if it is not, it is factually distinguishable from the instant case.

These arguments miss the mark because the constitutionality of *section 2339B* is not before us. The defendants have not been charged with a criminal violation of *section 2339B*. As we discussed above, *section 2339B* is relevant to the Boims' claim only to the extent that it helps define what conduct Congress intended to include in its definition of "international terrorism." *Section 2339B* provides further support to the Boims' theory that Congress meant to include funding terrorism as an act "involving" violence. It is the constitutionality of section 2333 that concerns us today, and as we have just found, funding that meets the standard for aiding and abetting terrorist acts does not offend the First Amendment. We take the defendants' argument to be that a *section 2333* claim founded solely on conduct that would render a person criminally liable under *section 2339B* would violate the First Amendment. With this refinement to the question, we turn to the Ninth Circuit's analysis of *section 2339B*.

The plaintiffs in *Humanitarian Law Project* were organizations and individuals who wished to provide money to two groups that had been designated as foreign terrorist organizations under *8 U.S.C. §1189*. They sought a preliminary injunction barring enforcement of *section 2339B* against them, and maintained that they intended only to support the nonviolent humanitarian and political activities of the designated groups. They argued, as HLF and QLI do here, that *2339B* violates the First Amendment because it imposes liability on persons who provide material support to terrorist organizations regardless of whether the donor intends to further the unlawful goals of the organization. The plaintiffs relied on *Claiborne Hardware* for the proposition that "[f]or liability to be imposed by reason of association alone, it is necessary to establish that the group itself possessed unlawful goals and that the individual held a specific intent to further those illegal aims." *Humanitarian Law Project, 205 F.3d at 1133* (*Claiborne Hardware* and the similar cases we have discussed supra apply to situations where the government seeks to impose liability on the basis of association alone, i.e., on the basis of membership alone or because a person espouses the views of an organization that engages in illegal activities. Conduct giving rise to liability under *section 2339B*, of course, does not implicate associational or speech rights. *Humanitarian Law Project, 205 F.3d at 1133*. Under *section 2339B*, and indeed under *section 2333*, HLF and QLI may, with impunity, become members of Hamas, praise Hamas for its use of terrorism, and vigorously advocate the goals and philosophies of Hamas. *Section 2339B* prohibits only the provision of material support (as that term is defined) to a terrorist organization. There is no constitutional right to provide weapons and explosives to terrorists, nor is there any right to provide the resources with which the terrorists can purchase weapons and explosives. *205 F.3d at 1133*.

Advocacy is always subject to the highest levels of scrutiny under the First Amendment, but donations are not always equivalent to advocacy and are subject to greater government regulation. In *Buckley v. Valeo, 424 U.S. 1, 96 S.Ct. 612, 46 L.Ed.2d 659 (1976)*, the Supreme Court upheld the $1000 limit on political contributions to candidates for federal offices by individual donors. The Court acknowledged the expressive element of a contribution to a political campaign, noting that a contribution serves as a general expression of support for a candidate and the candidate's views, but does not communicate the underlying basis for the support. *424 U.S. at 21, 96 S.Ct. 612*. Because the expression involved in donating money "rests solely on the undifferentiated, symbolic act of contributing," the size of the donation provides only a very rough estimate of the intensity of the contributor's support for the candidate. *424 U.S. at 21, 96 S.Ct. 612*. The Court concluded that a limitation on the amount of money a person may contribute thus involved little direct restraint on the donor's political communication. Any size contribution will permit a symbolic expression of support, but a limitation on the size does not infringe the contributor's freedom to discuss issues. The Court acknowledged that the funds might be used by the candidate to present views to voters, but "the transformation of contributions into political debate involves speech by someone other than the contributor." *424 U.S. at 21, 96 S.Ct. 612*. The Court found that associational interests were also implicated because making a contribution affiliates a person with a candidate, and enables like-minded people to pool their resources to further political goals. *424 U.S. at 22, 96 S.Ct. 612*. Setting the standard for reviewing governmental regulation in this context, the Court held that "[e]ven a significant interference with protected rights of political association may be sustained if the State demonstrates a sufficiently important interest and employs means closely drawn to avoid unnecessary abridgement of associational freedoms." *424 U.S. at 25, 96 S.Ct. 612* (internal quote marks omitted).

Applying the *Buckley* standard to *section 2333* claims founded on conduct that would give rise to criminal liability under *section 2339B*, we conclude that the government's interest in preventing terrorism is not only important but paramount. *Humanitarian Law Project, 205 F.3d at 1135*. Although that interest has been made all the more imperative by the events of September 11, 2001, the terrorist threat to national security was substantial in 1992 when Congress passed *section 2333* and in 1996 when Congress passed section 2339B. That interest is unrelated to suppressing free expression. A *section 2333* suit founded on conduct violating *section 2339B* does not punish membership in a designated terrorist organization, or penalize the expression of views held by these organizations. Rather, such a suit is aimed at prohibiting the funding of violent acts that these organizations wish to carry out. *205 F.3d at 1135*.

The only remaining question is whether a *section 2333* action based on conduct that violates *section 2339B* employs means closely drawn to avoid unnecessary abridgement of associational freedoms. *Section 2339B* forbids the provision of any amount of "material support or resources" to a foreign terrorist organization. "Material support or resources" includes, among other things, money, training, weapons, lethal substances, explosives and personnel. Congress determined that "foreign organizations that engage in terrorist activity are so tainted by their criminal conduct that any contribution to such an organization facilitates that conduct." *Pub.L. 104-132, Section 301*. Terrorist organizations use funds for illegal activities regardless of the intent of the donor, and Congress thus was compelled to attach liability to all donations to foreign terrorist organizations. In order to be designated a terrorist organization, a group must engage in terrorist activity that threatens the security of United States nationals or the national security of the United States. *8 U.S.C. §1189(a)*. "Terrorist activity" is defined, in relevant part, as unlawful activity which involves any of the following: the hijacking or sabotage of any aircraft, vessel or vehicle; the seizing, detaining or threatening to kill, injure or continue detaining an individual in order to compel a third person to do or abstain from doing any act as a condition for the release of the individual detained; a violent act upon an internationally protected person; an assassination; the use of any biological agent, chemical agent, nuclear weapon or device, or explosive or firearm, with intent to endanger the safety of one or more individuals or cause substantial damage to property. *8 U.S.C. § 1182(a)(3)(B)(ii)*. Given the stringent requirements that must be met before a group is designated a foreign terrorist organization, Congress carefully limited its prohibition on funding as narrowly as possible in order to achieve the government's interest in preventing terrorism. We note that Congress did not attach liability for simply joining a terrorist organization or zealously espousing its views. By prohibiting funding alone, Congress employed means closely drawn to avoid unnecessary abridgement of associational freedoms. A *section 2333* action founded on conduct violating *section 2339B* is sufficiently tailored to achieve an important government interest and does not run afoul of the First Amendment. *Humanitarian Law Project, 205 F.3d at 1136.*

III Conclusion

In short, we answer the three questions certified by the district court as follows: funding, *simpliciter*, of a foreign terrorist organization is not sufficient to constitute an act of terrorism under *18 U.S.C. § 2331*. However, funding that meets the definition of aiding and abetting an act of terrorism does create liability under *sections 2331* and *2333*. Conduct that would give rise to criminal liability under *section 2339B* is conduct that "involves" violent acts or acts dangerous to human life, and therefore may meet the definition of international terrorism as that term is used in *section 2333*. Finally, as we have set forth the elements of an action under *section 2333*, civil liability for funding a foreign terrorist organization does not offend the First Amendment so long as the plaintiffs are able to prove that the defendants knew about the organization's illegal activity, desired to help that activity succeed and engaged in some act of helping. The plaintiffs have not yet had an opportunity to develop the facts of their case. Today we hold that dismissal would be premature at this stage of the litigation because we can envision a set of facts in support of the claim they have alleged that would entitle them to relief.

Affirmed.

Bringing a civil action against a State that sponsors terrorism is addressed squarely by Congressional statute. The 1996 Antiterrorism and Effective Death Penalty Act (AEDPA) amends the Foreign Sovereign Immunities Act (FSIA) so that victims of international terrorism may sue a foreign State or (as later amended) any "official, employee, or agent of a foreign State" who acts in the scope of his official duties, for money damages. Under the law, the federal district court may hear such claims so long as the State is designated as a State-sponsor of terrorism at the time the terrorist act occurred (or later designated). In addition, State responsibility for terrorism does not end with a change in government. The *Acree* case is instructive because it deals with a variety of issues to include the role of the Executive Branch. In *Acree* American prisoners of war (POWs) during the 1991 Gulf War and their immediate family members sued the Republic of Iraq, its president and its intelligence service, seeking compensatory and punitive damages for injuries allegedly suffered as result of torture inflicted on the POWs while in Iraqi captivity. The United States District Court for the District of Columbia granted default judgment for the plaintiff POWs and denied a federal government post-judgment motion to intervene.

United States Court of Appeals,

District of Columbia Circuit.

Clifford ACREE, Colonel, et al., Appellees,

v.

REPUBLIC OF IRAQ, et al.,

United States of America, Appellant

No. 03-5232.

Argued April 7, 2004.

Decided June 4, 2004.

Rehearing En Banc Denied August 19, 2004.

Holdings: The Court of Appeals held that:

(1) denial of government' s motion to intervene was abuse of discretion;

(2) President' s exercise of Congressional mandate to suspend economic sanctions against Iraq did not make terrorism exception to Foreign Sovereign Immunities Act (FSIA) inapplicable with respect to Iraq; and

(3) neither terrorism exception to FSIA nor Flatow Amendment, nor both of them considered in tandem, creates private right of action against foreign government.

Intervention judgment reversed; default judgment vacated; case dismissed.

OPINION BY EDWARDS, J

Appellees in this case are 17 American soldiers, joined by their close family members, who were captured and held as prisoners of war by the Iraqi Government while serving in the Gulf War in early 1991. Appellees brought suit in the District Court under the terrorism exception to the Foreign Sovereign Immunities Act ("FSIA"), 28 U.S.C. § 1605(a)(7) (2000), against the Republic of Iraq, the Iraqi Intelligence Service, and Saddam Hussein, in his official capacity as President of Iraq (collectively "Iraq"), seeking compensatory and punitive damages for the horrific acts of torture they suffered during their captivity. After Iraq failed to appear, the District Court examined appellees' evidentiary submissions and entered judgment in their favor. The District Court awarded damages against Iraq totaling over $959 million.

Two weeks after the District Court entered its judgment for appellees, the United States filed a motion to intervene for the purpose of contesting the District Court' s subject matter jurisdiction. The United States argued that recently enacted provisions of the Emergency Wartime Supplemental Appropriations Act, Pub. L. No. 108-11, § 1503, 117 Stat. 559, 579 (2003), made the terrorism exception to the FSIA inapplicable to Iraq and thereby stripped the District Court of its jurisdiction over appellees' lawsuit. The District Court denied the United States' motion to intervene as un-timely, and the United States now appeals.

We hold that the District Court abused its discretion in finding the United States' motion to intervene to be untimely and erred in denying that motion. The United States possesses weighty foreign policy interests that are clearly threatened by the entry of judgment for appellees in this case. Although the United States filed its motion after the District Court had entered its judgment, appellees have asserted no prejudice arising from the intervention. On the merits of the United States' jurisdictional challenge, we hold that the District Court properly exercised jurisdiction in appellees' lawsuit. Although it presents a close question of statutory interpretation, we conclude that the disputed language in the emergency supplemental appropriations act does not encompass the terrorism exception to the FSIA.

We nevertheless conclude that the District Court's judgment in favor of appellees must be vacated and their lawsuit dismissed for failure to state a cause of action. The District Court's judg-ment against Iraq rests solely on causes of action purportedly arising under the terrorism exception and the Flatow Amendment to the FSIA. Neither appellees' complaint, nor their submissions to this court, nor the District Court's decision in their favor offers any other coherent alternative causes of action in support of appellees' claims against Iraq. Our recent decision in *Cicippio-Puleo v. Islamic Republic of Iran, 353 F.3d 1024 (D.C.Cir.2004)* ("*Cicippio*"), makes it plain that the ter-rorism exception to the FSIA is merely a jurisdictional provision and does not provide a cause of action against foreign states. *Cicippio* also holds that the Flatow Amendment to the FSIA, which provides a cause of action against an "official, employee, or agent of a foreign state," 28 U.S.C. § 1605 note (2000), does not afford a cause of action against a foreign state itself. We are therefore constrained to vacate the judgment of the District Court and dismiss appellees' suit for failure to state a cause of action.

I. Background

A. The POW Lawsuit

The facts in this case are undisputed. While serving in the Gulf War following the Iraqi invasion of Kuwait, Colonel Clifford Acree and 16 other American soldiers who are appellees in this case were captured and held as prisoners of war in Kuwait and the Republic of Iraq between January and March 1991. On April 4, 2002, these POWs and their close family members filed a complaint in the District Court against the Republic of Iraq, the Iraqi Intelligence Service, and Saddam Hussein, in his official capacity as President of Iraq, for personal injuries caused to them and their family members as a result of their treatment by Iraq. In their complaint, the POW plaintiffs de-scribed brutal and inhumane acts of physical and psychological torture suffered during their cap-tivity, including severe beatings, starvation, mock executions, dark and unsanitary living condi-tions, and other violent and shocking acts. By these alleged atrocities, the plaintiffs' captors cre-ated a "climate [of] humiliation and degradation," in which the POWs "liv[ed] in constant fear of death and torture." Compl. ¶ 5, reprinted in Joint Appendix ("J.A.") 35.

Jurisdiction in the plaintiffs' lawsuit was based on the terrorism exception to the Foreign Sov-ereign Immunities Act, 28 U.S.C. § 1605(a)(7). Under the FSIA, foreign states enjoy immunity from suit in American courts, unless that immunity has been waived or abrogated pursuant to an exception enumerated in the FSIA. See 28 U.S.C. § 1604; see also 28 U.S.C. § 1330(a) (limiting the district courts' jurisdiction over suits against foreign states to cases in which the foreign state is not entitled to immunity under the FSIA). Section 1605(a)(7), added to the FSIA in 1996, creates an exception to foreign sovereign immunity in civil suits "in which money damages are sought against a foreign state for personal injury or death that was caused by an act of torture" or other terrorist acts. 28 U.S.C. § 1605(a)(7). This exception applies only if the defendant foreign state was designated as a state sponsor of terrorism at the time the alleged acts of torture occurred. See 28 U.S.C. § 1605(a)(7)(A). Pursuant to § 6(j) of the Export Administration Act, 50 U.S.C.App. § 2405(j) (1988 & Supp. I 1989), the Republic of Iraq was designated as a state sponsor of terrorism on September 13, 1990, shortly after the Iraqi invasion of Kuwait and before the events took place that formed the basis of the plaintiffs' claims. See 55 Fed. Reg. 37,793 (Sep. 13, 1990). Iraq was therefore amenable to suit in federal court under the FSIA at the time the plaintiffs commenced their lawsuit.

Citing several decisions of the District Court, the plaintiffs - appellees herein - premised their cause of action on § 1605(a)(7), as amended by the so-called "Flatow Amendment," which was adopted shortly after § 1605(a)(7) was added to the FSIA in 1996. See Compl. ¶ 596, J.A. 143. The Flatow Amendment provides that:

> [A]n official, employee, or agent of a foreign state designated as a state sponsor of terrorism ... while acting within the scope of his or her office, employment, or agency shall be liable to a United States national or the national's legal representative for personal injury or death caused by acts of that official, employee, or agent for which the courts of the United States may maintain jurisdiction under [§ 1605(a)(7)] for money damages which may include economic damages, solatium, pain, and suffering, and punitive damages if the acts were among those described in [§ 1605(a)(7)].

28 U.S.C. § 1605 note. Appellees alleged that the acts of torture set forth in their complaint constituted "traditional torts of assault, battery and intentional infliction of emotional distress," Compl. ¶ 597, J.A. 143, and requested compensatory and punitive damages for each of the POW plaintiffs and their family members.

Appellees effected proper service of process through diplomatic channels, pursuant to 28 U.S.C. § 1608. The Iraqi defendants failed to appear, and the Clerk of the District Court accordingly entered default against the defendants on September 25, 2002. On March 31, 2003, appellees submitted evidence to support their assertion of liability and claim for damages. These submissions provided further details regarding the factual basis of appellees' claims and again asserted the existence of a cause of action based on § 1605(a)(7), as amended by the Flatow Amendment, for assault, battery, and intentional infliction of emotional distress. See Pls.' Proposed Findings of Fact and Conclusions of Law at 80-90.

On July 7, 2003, the District Court entered final judgment in favor of appellees. See *Acree I, 271 F.Supp.2d 179*. The District Court held that "[s]uits brought under § 1605(a)(7) may be based on conventional common law torts." *Id.* at 215. Based on extensive findings of fact regarding the specific injuries suffered by each plaintiff, the District Court awarded compensatory and punitive damages to all of the POW plaintiffs and their family members totaling over $959 million. *Id.* at 224-25.

B. Legal and Military Developments in Iraq

As the proceedings in the District Court were running their course, the legal and military situation in Iraq was changing rapidly. In connection with Iraq's designation as a state sponsor of terrorism in September 1990, Congress had passed various statutes imposing sanctions on Iraq and prohibiting the United States Government and private parties from sending assistance to Iraq or conducting business or trade with Iraq. Most notably, Congress enacted the Iraq Sanctions Act of 1990, which condemned the Iraqi invasion of Kuwait and provided for the maintenance of a trade embargo and economic sanctions against Iraq. See Pub. L. No. 101-513, §§ 586-586J, 104 Stat. 1979, 2047-55 (1990) (codified at 50 U.S.C. § 1701 note (2000)) ("ISA"). These provisions required that all assistance, exports, loans, credits, insurance, or other guarantees be denied to Iraq, with exceptions for limited humanitarian relief. Section 586F(c) of the ISA also required full enforcement against Iraq of § 620A of the Foreign Assistance Act of 1961, which prohibits the grant of any assistance to any country determined by the Secretary of State to have "repeatedly provided support for acts of international terrorism," Pub. L. No. 87-195, § 620A, as added Pub. L. No. 94-329, § 303, 90 Stat. 729, 753 (1976) (codified as amended at 22 U.S.C. § 2371) ("FAA"). Along with the FAA, the ISA required that several other enumerated provisions of law be fully enforced against Iraq, as well as "all other provisions of law that impose sanctions against a country which has repeatedly provided support for acts of international terrorism." ISA § 586F(c), 104 Stat. 1979, 2051.

Both the Iraq Sanctions Act and the Foreign Assistance Act provide for rescission of the prohibitions they impose on aid to Iraq and other designated states, but only after the President certifies to Congress that there has been a fundamental change in the government or policies of the designated state and that the leadership is no longer supporting acts of terrorism. See ISA § 586H, 104 Stat. 1979, 2052-53; FAA, 22 U.S.C. § 2371(c) (2000). A similar certification is required to rescind the Secretary of State's determination under the Export Administration Act that Iraq is a country that has repeatedly provided support for acts of international terrorism.

Shortly after the commencement of the most recent military action against Iraq in 2003, which resulted in the ouster of Saddam Hussein's regime, the United States' policy toward Iraq changed to reconstructing Iraq's government and rebuilding the country's infrastructure. In furtherance of these new objectives, Congress took several steps to eliminate restrictions on the ability of the United States Government and private parties to provide assistance to or conduct business with Iraq. In April 2003, Congress enacted the Emergency Wartime Supplemental Appropriations Act ("EWSAA" or "Act"), which appropriated additional funding for military operations in Iraq, homeland security efforts in the United States, and bilateral economic assistance to America's allies in the war in Iraq. The bulk of the $78.5 billion appropriated in this Act was allocated to national defense activities. In addition, the Act appropriated nearly $2.5 billion for a new Iraq Relief and Reconstruction Fund, to be used for the development of physical and government infrastructure and humanitarian activities in Iraq. The Act provided that assistance to Iraq under the Iraq Relief and Reconstruction Fund and other aid programs could be provided "notwithstanding any other provision of law."

Of particular relevance to this appeal, § 1503 of the EWSAA authorized the President to "suspend the application of any provision of the Iraq Sanctions Act of 1990." EWSAA § 1503, 117 Stat. 559, 579. Section 1503 "[p]rovided further, [t]hat the President may make inapplicable with respect to Iraq section 620A of the Foreign Assistance Act of 1961 or any other provision of law that applies to countries that have supported terrorism." *Id.* The suspension of these provisions would permit American assistance to Iraq to proceed without awaiting completion of the lengthy certification process required to rescind the Secretary of State' s previous determination as to Iraq' s status as a sponsor of terrorism.

On May 7, 2003, President Bush carried out the authority granted in § 1503 of the EWSAA by issuing Presidential Determination No. 2003-23, which "ma[d]e inapplicable with respect to Iraq section 620A of the Foreign Assistance Act of 1961 ... and any other provision of law that applies to countries that have supported terrorism." Presidential Determination No. 2003-23 of May 7, 2003, 68 Fed. Reg. 26,459 (May 16, 2003). In a message to Congress delivered on May 22, 2003, President Bush explained the need to protect Iraqi assets from attachment, judgment, or other judicial process, and stated his view that the May 7 Determination applied to, inter alia, the terrorism exception to the FSIA, 28 U.S.C. § 1605(a)(7). See Message to the Congress Reporting the Declaration of a National Emergency With Respect to the Development Fund for Iraq, 39 Weekly Comp. Pres. Doc. 647, 647-48 (May 22, 2003).

C. The United States' Motion to Intervene

On July 21, 2003, two weeks after the District Court entered judgment for appellees, the United States moved to intervene for the sole purpose of contesting the subject matter jurisdiction of the District Court. This challenge rested on legal developments that had occurred in the wake of the United States' invasion of Iraq in March 2003. The United States argued that § 1605(a)(7) is a "provision of law that applies to countries that have supported terrorism" within the meaning of § 1503 of the EWSAA, as implemented by the May 7 Presidential Determination, and was therefore made inapplicable to Iraq by operation of those provisions. The District Court, the Government argued, was therefore divested of jurisdiction over appellees' lawsuit as of May 7, 2003, two months prior to the entry of judgment against the Iraqi defendants.

On August 6, 2003, the District Court denied the Government's motion to intervene as untimely.. The District Court noted that the United States had waited 75 days after the Presidential Determination to file its motion, and the court was particularly reluctant to permit the Government to intervene after appellees' case had proceeded to final judgment. See *Id.* The District Court further held that, even if the United States' motion was not untimely, appellees' lawsuit did not threaten to impair any cognizable interest of the United States and that allowing the Government to intervene at that late stage would cause undue delay and prejudice to the parties. See *Id.* at 99-102. Finally, the District Court considered its own subject matter jurisdiction and concluded that it retained jurisdiction under the FSIA, despite the EWSAA and the Presidential Determination. See *Id.* at 100-01. On August 22, 2003, the United States filed this appeal of the District Court' s decision.

D. Related Developments

Just before the United States moved to intervene, appellees filed a second suit in the District Court against the Secretary of the Treasury, seeking to satisfy their newly won judgment against Iraq by attaching funds from seized Iraqi bank accounts, pursuant to the Terrorism Risk Insurance Act of 2002 ("TRIA"). Section 201(a) of the TRIA provides that a person who has obtained a judgment against a foreign state designated as a state sponsor of terrorism may seek to attach the blocked assets of that state in satisfaction of an award of compensatory damages based on an act of terrorism. Although appellees initially prevailed in obtaining a temporary restraining order, precluding the Secretary of the Treasury from spending down the United States' seized Iraqi assets, the District Court ultimately awarded summary judgment to the United States. The District Court held that § 1503 of the EWSAA, as implemented by the May 7 Determination, made the TRIA inapplicable to Iraq and therefore unavailable to appellees as a mechanism for satisfying their judgment.

This court affirmed the decision of the District Court by judgment. The court did not address the applicability or effect of the EWSAA and the Presidential Determination. Rather, the court adopted the reasoning of the Second Circuit's decision in *Smith v. Federal Reserve Bank of New York, 346 F.3d 264 (2d Cir.2003)*. In that case, the Second Circuit held that plaintiffs proceeding under the TRIA to attach seized Iraqi assets in satisfaction of a judgment were precluded from doing so because the President had previously confiscated the blocked assets and vested title in them in the United States Department of the Treasury, thereby rendering those funds insusceptible to execution or attachment. The Second Circuit - and by extension this court - therefore did not reach the issue of whether § 1503 or the Presidential Determination made the TRIA inapplicable to Iraq and expressed no views on the scope or validity of those provisions. See *Id.*

In another important development, this court issued its decision in *Cicippio, 353 F.3d 1024*, three months before oral argument in this case. That case presented the question whether 28 U.S.C. § 1605(a)(7) or the Flatow Amendment, 28 U.S.C. § 1605 note, created a cause of action against a foreign state. Several decisions in the District Court had held or assumed that these provisions did create a cause of action against foreign states. See *Cicippio, 353 F.3d at 1032* (citing cases). The court of appeals had not previously affirmed any of these judgments, however, or otherwise squarely confronted the issue.

In *Cicippio,* this court definitively ruled that "neither 28 U.S.C. § 1605(a)(7) nor the Flatow Amendment, nor the two considered in tandem, creates a private right of action against a foreign government." *353 F.3d at 1033.* We held that § 1605(a)(7) merely waived the immunity of foreign states, without creating a cause of action against them, and that the Flatow Amendment provides a cause of action only against officials, employees, and agents of a foreign state, not against the foreign state itself. See *Id.* We further held that "insofar as the Flatow Amendment creates a private right of action against officials, employees, and agents of foreign states, the cause of action is limited to claims against those officials in their *individual,* as opposed to their official, capacities." *Id.* at 1034. Because of its clear relevance to the instant case, in which the only named defendants are the Republic of Iraq, the Iraqi Intelligence Service, and Saddam Hussein in his official capacity as President of Iraq, we ordered the parties here to consider the implications of our ruling in *Cicippio* for appellees' suit and to be prepared to discuss the issue at oral argument. See *Acree v. Republic of Iraq, No. 03-5232 (D.C.Cir. Apr. 5, 2004).*

II. Discussion

This case requires us to consider whether § 1503 of the EWSAA, as implemented by the May 7 Presidential Determination, makes the terrorism exception to the FSIA inapplicable with respect to Iraq. While it is a close question, we agree with appellees that 28 U.S.C. § 1605(a)(7) is not a provision of law that falls within the scope of § 1503. The District Court therefore properly exercised jurisdiction over appellees' lawsuit under the FSIA. Having reached this conclusion, we need not address the additional issues debated by the parties concerning the retroactive scope and constitutional validity of § 1503 and the Presidential Determination.

Although we find that the District Court had jurisdiction in this matter, the judgment for appellees must nonetheless be vacated. This court's recent decision in *Cicippio* makes it clear that plaintiffs cannot state a cause of action against a foreign state under § 1605(a)(7) or the Flatow Amendment, the sole bases for appellees" action in this case. Although *Cicippio* was decided after the District Court's judgment in this case, it is nonetheless the controlling precedent to which we must look in determining whether appellees have stated a cause of action. Because appellees' action fails under *Cicippio,* we conclude that the District Court's judgment in favor of appellees must be vacated and their suit dismissed for failure to state a cause of action....

A. The Motion to Intervene

The District Court's denial of a motion to intervene is an appealable final order. Our standard of review in such an appeal is mixed. We review pure questions of law *de novo,* findings of fact for clear error, and discretionary issues such as timeliness for abuse of discretion. See *Id.* In this case, we find that the District Court abused its discretion in finding the United States' motion to be untimely and erred in denying the motion.

Under Rule 24 of the Federal Rules of Civil Procedure, a prospective intervenor must be permitted to intervene as of right if the applicant claims an interest relating to the subject matter of the case, if the disposition of the case stands to impair that interest, and if the applicant's interest is not adequately represented by the existing parties. Alternatively, an applicant may be permitted to intervene if his claim shares a question of law or fact in common with the underlying action and if the intervention will not unduly delay or prejudice the rights of the original parties. Under either test, the prospective intervenor's motion must be "timely." Evaluation of the timeliness of a motion to intervene lies within the sound discretion of the District Court.

Courts are generally reluctant to permit intervention after a suit has proceeded to final judgment, particularly where the applicant had the opportunity to intervene prior to judgment. The timeliness of a motion to intervene must be considered in light of all the circumstances of the case, however, including the purpose for which intervention is sought, the need for intervention as a means of preserving the applicant's rights, and the possibility of prejudice to the existing parties, Post-judgment intervention is often permitted, therefore, where the prospective intervenor's interest did not arise until the appellate stage or where intervention would not unduly prejudice the existing parties. In particular, courts often grant post-judgment motions to intervene where no existing party chooses to appeal the judgment of the trial court. See *Id.*

In *Smoke,* we reversed the District Court's denial of a post-judgment motion to intervene where the existing party indicated it might not bring an appeal. In doing so, we noted that the would-be intervenor's interests, which had been consonant with those of the existing party, were no longer adequately represented by that party's litigation of the case. In those circumstances, we found the post-judgment motion to intervene for the purpose of prosecuting an appeal to be timely, because " the potential inadequacy of representation came into existence only at the appellate stage." In this case, the District Court denied the United States' motion to intervene largely because it came after the court had already entered judgment in the case. The District Court noted that approximately two months had intervened between the May 7 Presidential Determination and the entry of final judgment for appellees, during which time the United States could have filed its motion. See *Id.* However, in reaching this judgment, the District Court failed to consider adequately the unique circumstances of this case. In particular the District Court failed to weigh the importance of this case to the United States' foreign policy interests and the purposes for which the Government sought to intervene. This is not a case in which the United States was simply seeking to weigh in on the merits. Rather, the Government's sole purpose in intervening was to raise a highly tenable challenge to the District Court's subject matter jurisdiction in a case with undeniable impact on the Government's conduct of foreign policy and to preserve that issue for appellate review.

In the face of these weighty interests, appellees assert no prejudice arising from the United States' intervention. Nor could they, given the District Court's independent obligation to assure itself of its own jurisdiction. The only result achieved by denial of the motion to intervene in this case is the effective insulation of the District Court's exercise of jurisdiction from all appellate review. In these circumstances, we find that the District Court abused its discretion in denying the United States' motion as untimely. We therefore reverse the decision of the District Court denying the United States' motion to intervene and turn to the merits of the Government's jurisdictional challenge.

B. Subject Matter Jurisdiction Under the FSIA

It is uncontested that at the time appellees commenced their lawsuit in April 2002, the District Court had jurisdiction over the case under § 1605(a)(7), because appellees sought damages for injuries arising from alleged acts of torture that occurred while Iraq was designated as a state sponsor of terrorism. The United States now argues that § 1503 of the EWSAA, as implemented by the May 7 Presidential Determination, made § 1605(a)(7) inapplicable to Iraq and thereby divested the District Court of its jurisdiction in appellees' case. Appellees respond that § 1605(a)(7) is not a provision of law that falls within the scope of § 1503 of the EWSAA. Appellees alternatively contend that § 1503 and the Presidential Determination cannot be applied against them in this case without resulting in impermissible retroactive effects or violating constitutional principles of separation of powers. We review the District Court's exercise of jurisdiction *de novo*. In our view, while it is an exceedingly close question, the language of § 1503 of the EWSAA does not embrace the terrorism exception to the FSIA. We conclude that § 1503, read in the context of the EWSAA as a whole and its legislative history, is aimed at legal provisions that present obstacles to assistance and funding for the new Iraqi Government and was not intended to alter the jurisdiction of the federal courts under the FSIA.

This issue presents us with a basic question of statutory interpretation. We therefore begin with the language of the EWSAA. Section 1503 provides, in its entirety:

> The President may suspend the application of any provision of the Iraq Sanctions Act of 1990: Provided, That nothing in this section shall affect the applicability of the Iran-Iraq Arms Non-Proliferation Act of 1992, except that such Act shall not apply to humanitarian assistance and supplies: Provided further, That the President may make inapplicable with respect to Iraq section 620A of the Foreign Assistance Act of 1961 or any other provision of law that applies to countries that have supported terrorism: Provided further, That military equipment, as defined by title XVI, section 1608(1)(A) of Public Law 102-484, shall not be exported under the authority of this section: Provided further, That section 307 of the Foreign Assistance Act of 1961 shall not apply with respect to programs of international organizations for Iraq: Provided further, That provisions of law that direct the United States Government to vote against or oppose loans or other uses of funds, including for financial or technical assistance, in international financial institutions for Iraq shall not be

construed as applying to Iraq: Provided further, That the President shall submit a notification 5 days prior to exercising any of the authorities described in this section to the Committee on Appropriations of each House of the Congress, the Committee on Foreign Relations of the Senate, and the Committee on International Relations of the House of Representatives: Provided further, That not more than 60 days after enactment of this Act and every 90 days thereafter the President shall submit a report to the Committee on Appropriations of each House of the Congress, the Committee on Foreign Relations of the Senate, and the Committee on International Relations of the House of Representatives containing a summary of all licenses approved for export to Iraq of any item on the Commerce Control List contained in the Export Administration Regulations, including identification of end users of such items: Provided further, That the authorities contained in this section shall expire on September 30, 2004, or on the date of enactment of a subsequent Act authorizing assistance for Iraq and that specifically amends, repeals or otherwise makes inapplicable the authorities of this section, whichever occurs first.

EWSAA § 1503, 117 Stat. 559, 579 (citations omitted) (emphasis added). The controversy in this case concerns the second proviso of § 1503, authorizing the President to "make inapplicable with respect to Iraq section 620A of the Foreign Assistance Act of 1961 or any other provision of law that applies to countries that have supported terrorism." *Id.* (emphasis added). The United States argues that this language embraces the authority to make § 1605(a)(7) inapplicable to Iraq, and that the President carried out that authority in the May 7 Presidential Determination.

The logic of this interpretation is straightforward: Section 1605(a)(7) creates an exception to the sovereign immunity normally enjoyed by foreign states in American courts for suits based on acts of torture or other terrorist acts. This exception applies only if the defendant foreign state was designated as a sponsor of terrorism at the time the acts took place. Section 1605(a)(7) is thus a "provision of law that applies to countries that have supported terrorism." The EWSAA authorizes the President to make such provisions inapplicable to Iraq, which authority the President exercised in the May 7 Determination. Section 1605(a)(7) therefore no longer applies to Iraq and cannot provide a basis for jurisdiction in appellees' case. *Quod erat demonstrandum.*

The difficulty with this view is that it focuses exclusively on the meaning of one clause of § 1503, divorced from all that surrounds it. This approach violates "the cardinal rule that a statute is to be read as a whole, since the meaning of statutory language, plain or not, depends on context." *King v. St. Vincent's Hosp., 502 U.S. 215, 221, 112 S.Ct. 570, 574, 116 L.Ed.2d 578 (1991)* (citations omitted). In interpreting any statute, we must " ' consider not only the bare meaning' of the critical word or phrase ' but also its placement and purpose in the statutory scheme.' *Holloway, 526 U.S. at 6, 119 S.Ct. at 969.*

Traditional interpretive canons likewise counsel against a reading of the second proviso of § 1503 that ignores the context of § 1503 and the EWSAA as a whole. In particular, the canons of *noscitur a sociis* and *ejusdem generis* remind us that "[w]here general words follow specific words in a statutory enumeration, the general words are construed to embrace only objects similar in nature to those objects enumerated by the preceding specific words." *Wash. State Dep't of Soc. & Health Servs. v. Guardianship Estate of Keffeler, 537 U.S. 371, 384, 123 S.Ct. 1017, 1025, 154 L.Ed.2d 972 (2003)* (internal quotation marks and citations omitted). In addition, where statutory language is phrased as a proviso, the presumption is that its scope is confined to that of the principal clause to which it is attached..

Applying the foregoing principles, we conclude that the scope of § 1503 is narrower than the Government suggests. The primary function of the EWSAA was to provide emergency appropriations in support of the United States' military operations in Iraq. The Act also provided additional funding for homeland security activities in the United States. Chapter 5 of the Act, entitled "Bilateral Economic Assistance," appropriated funds for a variety of assistance programs to Iraq and other American allies. See EWSAA, ch. 5, 117 Stat. 559, 572-81. In addition to the Iraq Relief and Reconstruction Fund, these programs included the Child Survival and Health Programs Fund, International Disaster Assistance, the Economic Support Fund (providing assistance to the governments of Jordan, Egypt, Turkey, the Philippines, and Afghanistan), Loan Guarantees to Israel, the Emergency Refugee and Migration Assistance Fund, peacekeeping operations, and similar activities. Thus, each program funded in Chapter 5 of the EWSAA addresses matters of bilateral economic assistance to Iraq and other countries. The United States points to nothing in this portion of the Act - or elsewhere in the EWSAA, for that matter - that addresses the jurisdiction of the federal courts.

Section 1503 is one of several "general provisions" within Chapter 5 of the EWSAA. See EWSAA §§ 1501-1506, 117 Stat. 559, 578-81. These "general provisions" all supply specific instructions or impose conditions upon the outlays of money appropriated throughout the Chapter. For example, § 1501 provides that the President has authority to transfer money between the several programs funded in the Chapter, upon proper notification to Congress. Section 1502 provides that "[a]ssistance or other financing under this chapter may be provided for Iraq notwithstanding any other provision of law," subject to certain provisos. Section 1504 authorizes the President to export certain nonlethal military equipment to Iraq, notwithstanding any other provision of law, subject to certain conditions and reporting requirements. Section 1503 thus finds itself situated among several other provisions that govern the distribution of assistance to Iraq within the context of ongoing military operations and against a backdrop of legal obstacles that would otherwise prohibit such assistance.

Section 1503 itself authorizes the President to suspend the application of any provision of the Iraq Sanctions Act of 1990, subject to eight provisos. See EWSAA § 1503, 117 Stat. 559, 579. Three of the provisos impose notification or reporting requirements and provide for expiration of the suspension authority granted in § 1503. The remaining provisos are each responsive to a specific aspect of the ISA or other statutes that are implicated by the suspension authority granted in § 1503, thereby resolving potential ambiguities that may arise in the statutory landscape as a result of the suspension of the ISA. Thus, the first proviso, stating that nothing in § 1503 shall affect the applicability of the Iran-Iraq Arms Non-Proliferation Act of 1992, reflects the fact that portions of the Non-Proliferation Act incorporate the ISA by reference and are to remain in effect despite suspension of the ISA. See Iran-Iraq Arms Non-Proliferation Act of 1992, Pub. L. No. 102-484, §§ 1601-1608, 106 Stat. 2315, 2571-75 (codified at 50 U.S.C. § 1701 note (2000)). Similarly, the fifth proviso states that "provisions of law that direct the United States Government to vote against or oppose loans or other uses of funds, including for financial or technical assistance, in international financial institutions for Iraq shall not be construed as applying to Iraq." This language responds in part to § 586G(a)(5) of the ISA, which requires the United States to oppose any loan or financial or technical assistance to Iraq by international financial institutions, pursuant to other provisions of law incorporated into the ISA. See ISA § 586G(a)(5), 104 Stat.1979, 2052. This fifth proviso thus makes clear that the President may suspend not only the ISA, but also those provisions of law that are incorporated by reference into the ISA' s prohibition on American support for assistance to Iraq from international financial institutions. The remaining provisos are similarly tied to specific features of the ISA and the other statutes with which the ISA interacts.

The second proviso of § 1503 - which lies at the heart of the controversy in the instant case - provides that "the President may make inapplicable with respect to Iraq section 620A of the Foreign Assistance Act of 1961 or any other provision of law that applies to countries that have supported terrorism." Just like the other provisos in § 1503, this language is responsive to a particular section of the ISA. As we have seen, the ISA required that certain enumerated provisions of law, including § 620A of the Foreign Assistance Act of 1961, and "all other provisions of law that impose sanctions against a country which has repeatedly provided support for acts of international terrorism" be fully enforced against Iraq. See ISA § 586F(c), 104 Stat.1979, 2051. The second proviso in § 1503 thus makes clear that the authority in § 1503 to suspend the ISA includes the authority to make inapplicable to Iraq § 620A of the FAA and those additional provisions of law incorporated into § 586F(c) of the ISA.

As previously noted, § 620A of the FAA prohibits the grant of assistance to any country determined by the Secretary of State to have "repeatedly provided support for acts of international terrorism." 22 U.S.C. § 2371(a). A survey of the other provisions enumerated in § 586F(c) of the ISA indicates that all of those provisions deal with restrictions on assistance to state sponsors of terrorism. These provisions include § 40 of the Arms Export Control Act, 22 U.S.C. § 2780 (2000); §§ 555 and 556 of the Foreign Operations, Export Financing, and Related Programs Appropriations Act of 1991, Pub. L. No. 101-513, §§ 555-556, 104 Stat. 1979, 2021-22 (1990); and § 555 of the International Security and Development Cooperation Act of 1985, Pub. L. No. 99-83, § 555, 99 Stat. 190, 227. Each of these provisions calls for the imposition of economic sanctions on countries that are determined to have supported international terrorism, including restrictions on exports, aviation boycotts, and prohibitions on loans, credits, or other financial assistance. Read within this context, the reference in the ISA to "all other provisions of law that impose sanctions against a country which has repeatedly provided support for acts of international terrorism" is best read to denote provisions of law that call for economic sanctions and prohibit grants of assistance to state sponsors of terrorism.

To recapitulate, the meaning of the disputed language in § 1503, like each of the other substantive provisos in that section, is thus illuminated by consideration of the corresponding provisions of the ISA. See *Morrow, 266 U.S. at 534-35, 45 S.Ct. at 174-75* ("The general office of a proviso is to except something from the enacting clause, or to qualify and restrain its generality and prevent misinterpretation. Its grammatical and logical scope is confined to the subject-matter of the principal clause.") (citations omitted). The reference in § 586F(c) of the ISA to § 620A of the FAA and "all other provisions of law" that impose sanctions on state sponsors of terrorism appears clearly to encompass laws which, like the FAA and the other enumerated provisions, impose obstacles to assistance to designated countries. None of these provisions remotely suggests any relation to the jurisdiction of the federal courts. Thus, when read in juxtaposition with this portion of the ISA, the second proviso of § 1503 is more persuasively interpreted as sharing a similar scope. That is, it authorizes the President to make inapplicable with respect to Iraq those provisions of law that impose economic sanctions on Iraq or that present legal obstacles to the provision of assistance to the Iraqi Government. This interpretation reflects a central function of Chapter 5 of the EWSAA, which is to provide for relief and reconstruction in post-war Iraq.

Although sparse, the legislative history of § 1503 of the EWSAA likewise supports our interpretation of the disputed language in § 1503. The EWSAA began as a request from the President to Congress for emergency supplemental appropriations to support Department of Defense operations in Iraq and for other purposes. See Letter from President George W. Bush to Rep. Dennis

Hastert, Speaker of the House of Representatives (Mar. 25, 2003), reprinted in H.R. DOC. No. 108-55, at 1 (2003). The portion of the President's request dealing with bilateral economic assistance included language repealing the Iraq Sanctions Act of 1990, subject to the proviso "[t]hat the President may make inapplicable with respect to Iraq section 620A of the Foreign Assistance Act of 1961, as amended, or other provision of law that applies to countries that have supported terrorism." H.R. DOC. No. 108-55, at 24. The request explained that this language would "authorize the President to make inapplicable with respect to Iraq section 620A, and section 620G, and section 307 of the Foreign Assistance Act." Id.

One week after the President issued this request for supplemental appropriations, the Committees on Appropriations of the Senate and House reported bills that each contained language similar to that proposed by the President. The Senate version, reported on April 1, 2003, repeated exactly the language of the President's request, repealing the ISA and authorizing the President to "make inapplicable with respect to Iraq section 620A of the Foreign Assistance Act of 1961, as amended, or other provision of law that applies to countries that have supported terrorism." S. 762, 108th Cong. § 503 (2003). The accompanying committee report explained that this section of the Senate bill "provide[d] the request for the repeal of the Iraqi Sanctions Act of 1990 [sic], and other limitations on assistance for Iraq." S. Rep. No. 108-33, at 21 (2003) (emphasis added). The House version, reported on April 2, 2003, included the same language that became § 1503 of the EWSAA. *See* H.R. 1559, 108th Cong. § 1402 (2003). The committee report accompanying the House bill explained that this language was "similar to the authority requested by the President that would repeal the Iraq Sanctions Act of 1990 and authorize the President to make inapplicable with respect to Iraq section 620A and section 307 of the Foreign Assistance Act." H.R. Rep. No. 108-55, at 30 (2003).

The Conference Committee agreed to the language proposed in the House version of the supplemental appropriation. See H.R. Conf. Rep. No. 108-76, at 21 (2003). The conferees reported that § 1503 of the conference agreement "would make inapplicable the Iraq Sanctions Act of 1990 and authorize the President to make inapplicable with respect to Iraq section 620A and section 307 of the Foreign Assistance Act." *Id.* at 76. The language of the conference agreement was passed by both houses on April 12, 2003, without further amendment to § 1503, and signed by the President on April 16, 2003.

While not conclusive, this legislative history bolsters our conclusion as to the scope of § 1503. There is no reference in the legislative history to the FSIA in particular or to federal court jurisdiction in general. Rather, the legislative history of the EWSAA reflects an underlying legislative concern with eliminating statutory restrictions on aid and exports needed for the reconstruction of Iraq. This concern is easily understood. Any effort by the United States Government or private businesses in the United States to provide assistance or conduct business with the new Iraqi regime, in the absence of § 1503, would be barred by numerous provisions of law until such time as the President and the Secretary of State could make the necessary certifications to Congress to remove Iraq's designation as a state sponsor of terrorism. See, e.g., 22 U.S.C. § 2371(c) (rescission provisions of the Foreign Assistance Act of 1961); 50 U.S.C.App. § 2405(j)(4) (rescission provisions of the Export Administration Act). Section 1503 permits assistance and reconstruction efforts to proceed without waiting for this lengthy and complex certification process to run its course by setting aside the ISA and "other limitations on assistance for Iraq," S. Rep. No. 108-33, at 21 (2003). This legislative history, along with the other provisions in § 1503, the EWSAA as a whole, and the complex web of economic sanctions and prohibitions on assistance that previously applied to Iraq thus supports our interpretation that the general reference in § 1503 to "other provision[s] of law that appl[y] to countries that have supported terrorism" embraces only those provisions of law that constitute legal restrictions on assistance to and trade with Iraq.

Because we find, as a matter of statutory interpretation, that § 1503 does not make the terrorism exception to the FSIA inapplicable to Iraq, we need not consider whether § 1503 operates retroactively to appellees' pending lawsuit. Nevertheless, comparison of the temporal scope of 28 U.S.C. § 1605(a)(7) with that of § 1503 lends further support to our resolution of the statutory interpretation issue. The language of § 1503 is broad, general, and unclear. Yet, the United States seeks to employ it to supersede the much more precise language of § 1605(a)(7), which already provides in quite specific terms for the prospective restoration of sovereign immunity once a country is decertified as a sponsor of terrorism. Specifically, § 1605(a)(7) provides that the terrorism exception to foreign sovereign immunity arises only when a defendant country is designated as a sponsor of terrorism "at the time the act occurred, unless later so designated as a result of such act." 28 U.S.C. § 1605(a)(7)(A). Thus, the FSIA specifically provides that when a country, once designated as a state sponsor of terrorism, is subsequently restored to good standing, that country is still amenable to suit for acts that took place prior to the restoration of its sovereign immunity. As the United States would have it, however, waiver of § 1605(a)(7) in the case of Iraq pursuant to § 1503 would restore Iraq's immunity even for acts that occurred while Iraq was still considered a sponsor of terrorism.

This perplexing result appears even more bizarre when the sunset provisions of § 1503 are taken into account. The final proviso in § 1503 states that "the authorities contained in this section shall expire on September 30, 2004, or on the date of enactment of a subsequent Act authorizing assistance for Iraq and that specifically amends, repeals or otherwise makes inapplicable the authorities of this section, whichever occurs first." EWSAA § 1503, 117 Stat. 559, 579. If the United States were correct in its interpretation of § 1503, then this sunset provision would mean that, absent intervening events, § 1605(a)(7) would once again be available as a basis of jurisdiction after September 30, 2004. At such time, the District Court would properly have jurisdiction over a suit against Iraq based on events that occurred while Iraq was designated as a state sponsor of terrorism. It makes little sense to say that between the date of the May 7 Presidential Determination and the date of expiration of the authorities conferred in § 1503, there is no federal court jurisdiction for suits against Iraq, but that after that period elapses, such suits will again be available. Yet, this is precisely the result that follows if one imposes the unwieldy language of § 1503 upon the otherwise careful and precise scheme established under the FSIA. Thus, considerations of temporal scope weigh in favor of an interpretation of § 1503 that avoids this conflict.

The United States contends that, even if the disputed clause in § 1503 must be construed to reach only those provisions of law that are similar in nature to the legal restrictions on assistance to Iraq that are enumerated elsewhere in § 1503, the terrorism exception to the FSIA still falls within the scope of provisions the President is authorized to make inapplicable to Iraq. Specifically, the United States points out that § 1605(a)(7) shares a "criterion of similarity" with the other provisions mentioned in § 1503, Reply Br. at 17, namely, that it is a provision of law that imposes penalties on foreign nations as a result of their designation as sponsors of terrorism. This contention has some attraction, because § 1605(a)(7) arguably poses a threat of a sort to American reconstruction efforts in Iraq by providing jurisdiction in American courts for cases seeking huge liability judgments against the Iraqi Government. Under this view, it is plausible to suggest that § 1503 encompasses the terrorism exception to the FSIA.

It is true that section 1605(a)(7) is not totally dissimilar to laws imposing economic sanctions or prohibitions on assistance and trade, in that it penalizes countries designated as supporters of terrorism. However, even if the FAA and the other economic penalties discussed above could be said to share this single common attribute with § 1605(a)(7), the FSIA's rules of federal court jurisdiction would still be several steps removed from those other provisions, which are all much more closely analogous to one another. Because § 1503, the EWSAA as a whole, and the relevant legislative history all reflect an overriding concern for economic assistance, trade, and reconstruction in Iraq, we find that this context counsels against a reading of § 1503 that stretches so far as to reach a law, like the FSIA, that is largely dissimilar to all of the "look-alike" provisions affected by § 1503.

We conclude that when § 1503 is read in the context of the other provisions of the EWSAA and its legislative history, as it must be, that provision is best understood as applying only to legal restrictions on assistance and funding for the new Iraqi Government. There is nothing in the language of § 1503, the EWSAA as a whole, or its legislative history to suggest that Congress intended by this statute to alter the jurisdiction of the federal courts under the FSIA. We acknowledge that this is a close question. We nevertheless conclude that § 1503 was not intended to apply to § 1605(a)(7). The scope of the May 7 Presidential Determination is immaterial, because it cannot exceed the authority granted in § 1503. We therefore affirm the District Court's exercise of jurisdiction over appellees' claims under 28 U.S.C. § 1605(a)(7).

C. Cause of Action

Having concluded that jurisdiction in this case properly lies in the District Court, we arrive at the clear conflict between the District Court's judgment in favor of appellees and this court's recent holding in *Cicippio-Puleo v. Islamic Republic of Iran, 353 F.3d 1024*. In *Cicippio*, we held that neither § 1605(a)(7) nor the Flatow Amendment, nor the two considered together, supplies a cause of action against foreign states. See *353 F.3d at 1033*. In the instant case, the District Court predicated its finding of liability on precisely those provisions, and appellees point to no alternative cause of action. We therefore conclude that appellees have failed to state a cause of action.

Because of the default of the Iraqi defendants, no party questioned the existence of appellees' cause of action during the proceedings in the District Court. Nor did the United States raise this issue in its motion to intervene. Nevertheless, no party contests this court's discretion to reach this issue on our own motion in light of the intervening change in law.

Appellees rightly contend that non-jurisdictional defenses such as the failure to state a cause of action are waivable and that courts generally do not permit parties to raise such issues for the first time on appeal. The right of a party to advance this objection is not coextensive with the discretion of the court to consider the issue, however. As we have held, "[c]ourts of appeals are not rigidly limited to issues raised in the tribunal of first instance; they have a fair measure of discretion to determine what questions to consider and resolve for the first time on appeal." *Roosevelt v. E.I. Du Pont de Nemours & Co., 958 F.2d 416, 419 n. 5 (D.C.Cir.1992)* (addressing the existence of a cause of action for the first time on appeal in light of a relevant intervening Supreme Court decision). Thus, while we will ordinarily refrain from reaching non-jurisdictional questions that have not been raised by the parties or passed on by the District Court, we may do so on our own motion in "exceptional circumstances." *Id.*

Our intervening decision in *Cicippio,* which definitively resolved a previously open question of law that we find to be dispositive in appellees' case, surely qualifies as the type of exceptional circumstance that justifies our exercise of discretion. See *Id.* at 419. The issue before us is "purely one of law important in the administration of federal justice, and resolution of the issue does not depend on any additional facts not considered by the district court." *Id.* at 419 n.5. The circumstances of this case are even more extraordinary when one considers the stakes: Appellees have obtained a nearly-billion dollar default judgment against a foreign government whose present and future stability has become a central preoccupation of the United States' foreign policy. In these circumstances, it would be utterly unseemly for this court to ignore the clear implications of our holding in *Cicippio.* We therefore find it appropriate to exercise our discretion to determine whether appellees' case must be dismissed for failure to state a cause of action.

In their complaint, appellees premised their claim of liability on § 1605(a)(7), as amended, asserting that this provision "creates a federal cause of action for torture ... of American nationals, or for the benefit of American national claimants, when such acts are committed by a foreign state designated as a state sponsor of terrorism." Compl. ¶ 596, J.A. 143. The complaint pointed to several decisions of the District Court that proceeded on the assumption that § 1605(a)(7), as amended by the Flatow Amendment, "not only waives sovereign immunity and provides jurisdiction but also creates a cause of action within its scope of applicability." *Id.* While appellees also alluded to the "traditional torts of assault, battery and intentional infliction of emotional distress" in their generic form, Compl. ¶ 597, J.A. 143, they did not point to any other specific source in state, federal, or foreign law for their cause of action.

The District Court similarly relied on § 1605(a)(7) and the Flatow Amendment, finding that those provisions "create[ ] a federal cause of action against officials, employees and agents of a foreign state, as well as the state and its agencies and instrumentalities themselves." *Acree I, 271 F.Supp.2d at 215.* In company with appellees, the District Court reasoned that "[s]uits brought under § 1605(a)(7) may be based on conventional common law torts such as assault, battery, and intentional infliction of emotional distress," *Id.,* and found that the facts appellees alleged satisfied the elements of several such torts, see *Id.* at 215-17. The District Court cited no alternative cause of action.

In *Cicippio,* we held that neither § 1605(a)(7) nor the Flatow Amendment, nor the two together, creates a cause of action against foreign states themselves. See *Cicippio, 353 F.3d at 1033.* This holding applies also to suits against "agenc[ies] or instrumentalit[ies]" of a foreign state, which are included in the FSIA's definition of "foreign state," see 28 U.S.C. § 1603(a), (b); see also *Roeder, 333 F.3d at 234* (explaining that an official state entity whose core functions are governmental is treated as the foreign state itself for purposes of the FSIA); Compl. ¶ 3, J.A. 33 (stating that the Iraqi Intelligence Service is an agency or instrumentality of Iraq and therefore also a "foreign state" within the meaning of the FSIA). *Cicippio* also made clear that any suit against an official of a foreign state must be a suit in that official's *personal* capacity. See *353 F.3d at 1034; cf.* Com pl. ¶¶ 2-3, J.A. 31-33 (naming as a defendant Saddam Hussein "in his official capacity as President of the Republic of Iraq."). The causes of action advanced by appellees before the District Court therefore do not suffice to state claims for which relief may be granted.

In response to our order to consider this issue in preparation for oral argument, appellees did not advance any alternative causes of action. At oral argument, counsel for appellees gestured again toward generic common law torts, see Oral Argument Tr. at 23-29, but generic common law cannot be the source of a federal cause of action. The shared common law of the states may afford useful guidance as to the rules of decision in a FSIA case where a cause of action arises from some specific and concrete source of law. But there is no support for the proposition that generic common law itself may furnish the cause of action. Rather, as in any case, a plaintiff proceeding under the FSIA must identify a particular cause of action arising out of a specific source of law. Appellees failed to do so in this case.

Here, appellees pointed to no source of liability other than § 1605(a)(7) and the Flatow Amendment. When pressed repeatedly at oral argument, appellees offered no coherent alternative. We therefore find no cause to remand this case to the District Court in order to allow appellees to amend their complaint to state a cause of action under some other source of law. See *Cicippio, 353 F.3d at 1036*. In *Cicippio*, we permitted such a remand because the state of the law at the time of that appeal "may have ... misled" the plaintiffs in that case into assuming that the Flatow Amendment afforded a cause of action against the foreign state defendant. See *Id.* In addition, we noted that amici in that case had advanced the possibility that an alternative source of law might supply a viable cause of action. *See Id.* In this case, by contrast, our decision in *Cicippio* and our order to the parties prior to oral argument put appellees on notice of this issue. Despite this notice, appellees offered no alternative cause of action when asked to do so at oral argument. Accordingly, appellees' suit must be dismissed for failure to state a cause of action.

III. Conclusion

We are mindful of the gravity of appellees' allegations in this case. That appellees endured this suffering while acting in service to their country is all the more sobering. Nevertheless, we cannot ignore the magnitude of their default judgment or its impact on the United States' conduct of foreign policy where the law is indisputably clear that appellees were not legally entitled to this judgment. We reverse the order of the District Court denying the United States' motion to intervene, *Acree II, 276 F.Supp.2d. 95*. We vacate the District Court's judgment for appellees, *Acree I, 271 F.Supp.2d 179*, and dismiss appellees' suit against the Republic of Iraq, the Iraqi Intelligence Service, and Saddam Hussein in his official capacity as President of Iraq on the grounds that appellees have failed to state a cause of action.

So ordered.

Supreme Court of the United States
Clifford ACREE, et al., petitioners,
v.
REPUBLIC OF IRAQ, et al.
No. 04-820.
April 25, 2005.

Motion of Washington Legal Foundation, et al., for leave to file a brief as *amici curiae* granted. Motion of St. Mary's University School of Law, et al., for leave to file a brief as *amici curiae* granted. Motion of Center for Justice & Accountability and International Law Scholars for leave to file a brief as *amici curiae* granted. Petition for writ of certiorari to the United States Court of Appeals for the District of Columbia Circuit denied.

11.3 Questions for Discussion

1. *Litigation as a deterrence to State-sponsored terrorism.* Some have argued that allowing civil actions against States who sponsor international terrorism is an important deterrence tool. See Wendy Bay Lewis, *Civil Litigants as Citizen Diplomats*, Voir Dire, Spring 2003:

> Litigation is an important weapon for several reasons. First, it opens a judicial front in the war against terrorism which supplements military, political, and economic sanctions. Second, as the result of globalization, there is an intricate network of individuals, groups, corporations, and nation-states which facilitate terrorism and make military and political measures less than adequate. Third, given the supremacy of the rule of law in a democracy, judicial outcomes eventually put pressure on the other two branches of government to be more accountable to the voters. For example, when the Pan Am plaintiffs' lawsuit initially faltered because Libya had immunity as a sovereign nation, Congress amended antiterrorism statutes to preclude immunity pleas by state sponsors of terrorism.

On the other hand, has Congress opened the door for other nations to sue the United States for "terrorism?"

2. *What impact has the concept of civil liability against affected targets had on the development of new anti-terrorism technology?* Consider the impact of the SAFTEY Act.

3. *Costs and Benefits.* Because enforcing a monetary judgment is often impossible, what would be the other benefits to the plaintiff of going through the process of a civil action?

Selected Bibliography

Lewis, Wendy Bay, *Civil Litigants as Citizen Diplomats*, Voir Dire, Spring 2003.

Moore, John Norton (ed), *Civil Litigation Against Terrorism*, 2004.

Murphy, John F., *Punishing International Terrorists: The Legal Framework for Policy Initiatives*, 1985.

Chapter 12
Responses to Bioterrorism and the Legal Ramifications

TSWKY

[T]he whole people covenants with each citizen, and each citizen with the whole people, that all shall be governed by certain laws for the 'common good.'

—John Marshall Harlan II

Synopsis

Terrorists are continuously expanding their capabilities and methods turning to new and old tools to threaten death and chaos. The use of biological agents to cause death is so feared in the War on Terror that a new term has entered the lexicon - bioterrorism. While the use of infectious substances as a tool of terror is not new–the British were alleged to have spread smallpox to American soldiers during the War for Independence–the United States has yet to suffer a major biological attack from terrorists. Nevertheless, the potential for harm is so great that federal, state, local and tribal government officials have expended considerable efforts to establish effective response plans and to improve preemptive tools already in place. In the event of a significant biological attack a variety of containment procedures would most certainly be employed to prevent or slow the spread of death and disease. Such measures would include quarantine, isolation, vaccination, decontamination, destruction of infected property, eviction, specimen testing, mandatory health information disclosure, mandatory health care responses, etc. All of these measures give rise to significant policy and legal issues. The purpose of this chapter is to explore the realities of a biological attack and to examine the local, state and federal responsibilities in preventing and reacting to the event – prevention and containment.

12.1 Defining Bioterrorism
Bioterrorism is a deadly specter that looms on the horizon. It can affect any living creature and cause mass destruction across great physical expanses. While there are a variety of definitions of the term, the best is found in the Model State Emergency Health Powers Act (MSEHPA), drafted in 2001 by the Center for Law and the Public's Health at Johns Hopkins and Georgetown Universities:

Def {

[T]he intentional use of any organism, virus, infectious substance, or biological product…to cause death, disease, or other biological malfunction in a human, an animal, a plant, or another living organism in order to influence conduct of government or to intimidate or coerce a civilian population.

Biological agents occur both naturally and may be manufactured by man. Not all biological agents are capable of causing death or harm; therefore, not all biological agents may be suited to function as "weapons" in a bioterrorist attack. Still, harmful biological agents can be produced and disseminated with tremendous ease and can target animals, plants, crops and material supplies. Recognizing the vast potential for widespread harm associated with harmful biological agents, Chapter 18 of the United States Code makes the possession of biological agents or devices which may be utilized to spread biological agents a federal crime. Section 178 defines a biological agent as:

[A]ny microorganism (including, but not limited to, bacteria, viruses, fungi, rickettsiae or protozoa), or infectious substance, or any naturally occurring, bioengineered or synthesized component of any such microorganism or infectious substance, capable of causing—
    (A) death, disease, or other biological malfunction in a human, an animal, a plant, or another living organism;
    (B) deterioration of food, water, equipment, supplies, or material of any kind; or
    (C) deleterious alteration of the environment.

Bioterrorism is the poor man's "atomic bomb." The use of harmful biological agents is attractive to terrorists for a variety of reasons: (1) many biological agents can do great harm with only a small amount of material; (2) some agents may be harvested directly from the natural environment; (3) there are numerous methods of "weaponizing" the material for release into the environment; (4) it is difficult or impossible to trace the agent to its source; (5) some harmful agents can be developed or synthesized in laboratories, stolen from company supplies or stockpiles, or genetically manipulated. In addition, biological agents are capable of changing naturally. For example, influenza is a virus that is continuously mutating and taking on new forms, most recently a form know as Avian flu originated in Asia. In short, the availability, accessibility and alterability of certain harmful biological agents makes them a particularly dangerous weapon in the hands of terrorists.

Biological agents can be delivered to the environment utilizing a wide variety of methods. One method a terrorist may use is releasing a harmful biological agent through aerosol form in a ventilation system in a building, school, airplane, or mass transit system. Since many ventilation systems are enclosed they contribute to the spread of the harmful material. Food and water systems are also attractive targets for biological terrorism. The consequences associated with the natural occurrence of Mad Cow disease is some indication of the panic that could quickly spread should a significant attack target the food sources of the nation. Another method of disseminating a harmful biological agent is through physical contact with the agent itself or something that is contaminated with the agent. For instance, the anthrax in the mail attacks in 2001, saw the death of at least five people (several were postal workers) when individuals came into contact with letters and envelopes containing the harmful agent. Although anthrax is not contagious, the small-pox virus is highly contagious.

Diseases that are easily spread through contact between humans, animals, or insects are known as infections or communicable diseases. Communicable diseases are transmitted from person to person through physical contact with the infectious bacteria or virus by means of bodily fluids, coughing, sneezing and feces. Because the virus or bacteria is easily and rapidly spread, requiring only a small quantity to infect a small portion of the population, terrorists could introduce the harmful agent and watch as it spread like wildfire. Furthermore, as an added bonus, there is always the probability that the disease may mutate naturally and adapt to stifle vaccines. The possibility that a terrorist could start what would become a global pandemic is not far fetched.

12.2 Government Responsibilities and Authority

The consensus among those who study the threat of a wide spread biological epidemic – whether it occurs naturally or via a terrorist - is that the United States is not prepared. Among other matters, the lack of national procedures, policies, response plans, medical facilities and medicine contribute to this assessment. On the other hand, the world community is even less prepared.

The last major pandemic to strick the globe was the Spanish flu of 1918. Incredibly, the flu killed about 500,000 in the United States and anywhere from 20 million to 50 million people world wide! This tragic event, coupled with the use of poison gas in World War I, prompted the civilized world to realize the dangers of biological warfare and the need to prevent or limit the availability and use of these weapons of mass destruction. In 1925, the Protocol for the Prohibition of the Use in War of Asphyxiating, Poisonous or other Gases, and of Bacteriological Methods of Warfare was introduced and subsequently adopted by most of the world. The treaty prohibits of the use of chemical and biological weapons in warfare, but is silent with regards to the development, manufacture, storage and transfer of these weapons. In an effort to remedy the deficiencies of this treaty and to eliminate the existence of chemical and biological weapons entirely, the United Nations developed the 1972 Convention on the Prohibition of the Development, Production and Stockpiling of Bacteriological (Biological) and Toxin Weapons and on Their Destruction. Not only does this treaty ban all development, manufacture, storage and transfer of biological weapons, it also mandates that all stockpiles of biological weapons and biological agents be peaceably and safely destroyed or legitimately diverted to peaceful purposes within nine months of entry into force of the treaty. The United States ratified this treaty in 1975.

At the domestic level the federal government has concentrated efforts associated with the most harmful communicable biological agents. The federal government is authorized to take official action in response to a communicable disease only if the disease is specifically designated by Presidential executive order. Executive Order 13295, as amended by Executive Order 13375, in April 2005, lists all of the communicable diseases that mandate official action:

> Cholera, diphtheria, infectious tuberculosis, plague, smallpox, yellow fever, viral hemorrhagic fevers (Marburg, Ebola, and Congo-Crimean), Severe Acute Respiratory Syndrome (SARS), and influenza caused by novel or reemergent influenza viruses that are causing or have the potential to cause a pandemic.

The first responders to a bioterrorist attack will be local emergency room personnel, physicians and health departments. These first responders must be trained to recognize the symptoms in sick individuals as early as possible to ensure that these listed highly communicable diseases are detected as quickly as possible.

The Constitution of the United States grants each state the power to regulate the health, safety and welfare of its citizens. This authority is generally known as the police powers and is specifically reserved to the states by the 10th Amendment. These powers empower the state with the ability to develop rules, regulations, policies, procedures and plans to prepare the state's response within its own borders to an outbreak of a highly communicable disease. Each state operates differently to meet the needs of its citizens; as a result each state has a slightly different response plan. However, since harmful agents do not recognize state borders, it is imperative that states adopt a standardized set of rules that will allow better cooperation and the ability of federal agencies to lend aid more efficiently. In addition, streamlined procedures, information sharing and compatible response plans can help states and federal agencies identify biological agents that are the result of a bioterrorism as opposed to disease outbreaks that are naturally occurring.

As noted, the MSEHPA was drafted to provide states with a uniformed framework for passing Emergency Health Powers Acts of their own. As of 2006, the MSEHPA has been introduced either in whole or in part in legislation in 44 states and has been enacted in whole or in part in 38 states including the District of Columbia. While the MSEHPA is not enacted verbatim in every state, the wide acceptance of many of the main principles and policies set forth in the model help to prevent conflict between state laws. Although it is beyond the scope of this chapter to detail the plans of individual states, an overview of the MSEHPA is helpful. The MSEHPA grants emergency powers to the state governor and public health officials which are subject to legislative veto. The appropriate state officials have the authority to prevent, detect, manage and contain any biological or health threats that arise within the state borders. At the same time, the MSEHPA recognizes that state officials have the duty to protect individuals from undue interference with their civil rights and liberties. While the ultimate goal is to protect the health, safety and welfare of individuals, state officials should simultaneously develop an environment that fosters respect for all social groups and individuals from every background. State police powers under MSEHPA are restricted to communicable disease outbreaks that are wholly contained within the state's borders and naturally occurring (it may take some time before a disease can be traced to a terrorist).

If a naturally occurring disease spreads past a single state's borders or is introduced via foreign arrival from another country, the Centers for Disease Control (CDC), a part of the Department of Health and Human Services (HHS), has the authority to assert federal authority under Title 42 (Public Health and Welfare) U.S.C. § 264. The use of this authority is at the discretion of the Surgeon General, who must have approval of the Secretary of HHS and also may not authorize actions to address any communicable diseases other than those listed in the aforementioned Executive Orders. In the event that the CDC takes command and control the Code of Federal Regulations (C.F.R.) provides a variety of tools that the CDC can utilize. These are found in Parts 70 (Interstate Quarantine) and 71 (Foreign Quarantine) of Title 42 (Public Health).

While the CDC is designated as the lead agency to prevent and control the spread of the listed communicable diseases when they occur naturally, the aforementioned laws and regulations do not control in the event of a terrorist attack. The CDC would monitor public health threats, but the FBI would take the lead for crisis management. The Federal Emergency Management Agency, now part of the DHS, would coordinate the overall national response to a terror biological attack.

On February 28, 2003, President George W. Bush signed Homeland Security Presidential Directive 5 (HSPD-5) which mandated the development and implementation of a National Response Plan (NRP) that would supersede the FRP. The NRP was developed and released in 2004 and has been updated on a regular basis. The purpose of the NRP is to provide a national system for prevention, preparedness, response and recovery in the event of any national disasters, including terrorist and bioterrorist attacks. If a biological outbreak occurs in the United States, the NRP Biological Incident Annex provides the guiding procedures and policies to be followed by federal agencies in aiding state, local and tribal governments. Biological outbreaks are unique in nature as compared to most other possible national disasters. For that reason:

> Actions described in [the Biological Incident] Annex take place with or without a Presidential…declaration or a public health emergency declaration by the Secretary of Heath and Human Services.

Governmental response to any biological outbreak must be timely, strong and effective. Accordingly, at the state level the Governor has the authority to order isolation, quarantine, or social-distancing requirements to prevent the spread of certain communicable diseases. At the federal level, §264 of Title 42 of the U.S.C. empowers the Surgeon General of the United States to order "inspection, fumigation, disinfection, sanitation, pest extermination, destruction of animals or articles found to be so infected or contaminated as to be sources of dangerous infection to human beings, and other measures, as…may be necessary" to prevent the spread of any of the listed communicable diseases across state lines. In addition, § 70.6 of Title 42 of the C.F.R. authorizes the "detention, isolation, quarantine, or conditional release of individuals" when the purpose is to prevent the spread of any of the listed communicable diseases within the United States. Part 71 of Title 42 of the C.F.R. provides for the detention, isolation and quarantine of individuals, goods, animals and other items at ports and airports to prevent the introduction or spread of any of the listed communicable deceases.

12.3 The Goal of Quarantine

Quarantine is a critical tool that governmental agencies may utilize in the event of a biological outbreak to prevent the continuing spread of the subject communicable disease to new individuals. The MSEHPA defines quarantine as:

> The physical separation and confinement of an individual or groups of individuals, who are or may have been exposed to a contagious or possibly contagious disease and who do not show signs or symptoms of a contagious disease, from non-quarantined individuals, to prevent or limit the transmission of the disease to non-quarantined individuals.

By definition, quarantine may be used to restrict the movement and actions of individuals who are not yet ill, and may not ever become ill, but have been exposed to the disease. Quarantine is different from isolation, which is the isolation of individuals who have become infected, or ill, from the communicable disease. Obviously, the main goal of quarantine is to separate people who are potential carriers of a communicable disease from coming into contact with those individuals who have never come into contact with the disease. Utilizing quarantine prevents the spread of communicable diseases during incubation periods when individuals do not exhibit any symptoms of the illness.

The concept of quarantine is not new. For instance, the Old Testament commands the separation of lepers from the camps of the people and specifies specific instructions on how and when they may be returned to society. The term quarantine is derived from the Italian words *quaranta giorni*, meaning 40 days. It is believed that the Italian phrase was used to describe the practice of requiring ships that arrived in Venice from infected ports during the fourteenth century plague outbreaks to weigh anchor outside the port for forty days before the ship could dock. During the 2003 SARS (severe acute respiratory syndrome) virus outbreak, many countries implemented quarantine procedures to include Canada, China, Hong Kong and Singapore.

Although the United States did not utilize the quarantine tool during the SARS outbreak, the President did add, by Executive Order, SARS to the list of quarantinable communicable diseases. In addition, the Executive Order also listed an extremely broad based category to cover all possible future influenza viruses: "influenza caused by novel or reemergent influenza viruses that are causing or have the potential to cause a pandemic."

12.4 The Legality of Quarantine

As noted, federal authority to establish quarantine in the event of a bioterrorist attack or biological outbreak rests in the Surgeon General and the Secretary of HHS pursuant to § 264 of Title 42 of the U.S.C., which has been conferred to the CDC. The law explicitly limits quarantine authority to those cases in which the purpose of the quarantine is to prevent the introduction, transmission, or spread of the communicable diseases set out in Executive Orders. States, through their police powers, have reserved the right to establish quarantines for communicable disease outbreaks wholly contained within the state borders and which are not the result of a terrorist attack.

Quarantine is not always a mandatory order. Several times in history, including the more recent SARS epidemic, the government has instead suggested voluntary quarantine by individuals who believe they have come in contact with the subject communicable disease. While many individuals may choose to voluntarily quarantine themselves, legal concerns do not arise from these actions. Legal concerns involving quarantine arise only when the government issues a mandatory quarantine.

The 14th Amendment of the Constitution of the United States guarantees that no person shall be deprived of life, liberty or property without due process of law. This guarantee has long protected individuals' freedom from physical restraint. The United States Supreme Court has interpreted the preservation of due process to include a balancing test that weighs private interests against government interests. In *Jacobson v. Commonwealth of Massachusetts*, 197 U.S. 11 (1905), a case involving mandatory small pox vaccinations, the Supreme Court said:

> But the liberty secured by the Constitution of the United States to every person within its jurisdiction does not import an absolute right in each person to be, at all times and in all

circumstances, wholly freed from restraint. There are manifold restraints to which every person is necessarily subject for the common good. On any other basis organized society could not exist with safety to its members.

While the individual right to due process and freedom against physical restraint are not absolute, the government may not impose mandatory quarantine orders without restraint. In every instance of quarantine the government and the courts that review governmental actions will have to weigh individual interests in privacy, freedom and due process against the government's interests in protecting the safety and health of all citizens. In *Parham v. J.R.*, 442 U.S. 584 (1979), the Supreme Court noted: "What process is constitutionally due cannot be divorced from the nature of the ultimate decision that is being made."

The main goals of quarantine authority in United States law are constructed in ways that aim to protect individual due process to the greatest extent possible. The Supreme Court in *Goldberg v. Kelly*, 397 U.S. 254, discusses four requirements of due process: (1) reasonable and adequate notice; (2) opportunity to be heard within a reasonable manner and time; (3) available legal counsel; and (4) review of governmental actions by an impartial decision maker. Because quarantine necessarily interferes with an individuals' right to be free from restraint, the government must utilize procedures that comport with these basic due process requirements.

Currently, 42 C.F.R Parts 70 and 71 lay out the federal regulations regarding quarantine and the process necessary to invoke quarantine. Specifically, § 70.6 states:

> Regulations prescribed in this part authorize detention, isolation, quarantine, or conditional release of individuals, for the purpose of preventing the introduction, transmission, and spread of communicable diseases listed in an Executive Order setting out a list of quarantinable communicable diseases, as provided under section 361(b) of the Public Health Service Act.

In addition to this authority, § 70.5 provides special travel restrictions on persons who have been exposed to cholera, plague, smallpox, typhus, or yellow fever.

Even a cursory view of the matter reveals that the current laws and regulations associated with quarantine are not settled, even at the federal level. In light of these major gaps, HHS issued a Proposed Rule on November 30, 2005, for public comment. The Proposed Rule would change and add to 42 C.F.R. Parts 70 and 71. Under the proposed version of Part 70, federal officials have several different types of tools–ranging in severity–to address a biological outbreak. For example, government officials may order measures that infringe on individual rights and liberties to a lesser degree than quarantine sanitary measures, like specific cleaning procedures or the destruction of infected materials. The proposed Part 70 provides measures to address vaccination clinics, screenings, travel restrictions and the establishment of hospitals and stations in the event of a biological outbreak. In addition to these measures, the proposed Part 70 establishes a specific process for ordering quarantine. A person may only be placed under what is termed "provisional quarantine" if the responsible government official has a reasonable belief that the individual has been exposed to a quarantinable communicable disease. Generally, individuals in such a situation will be asked to submit voluntarily to quarantine. However, if individuals refuse to submit voluntarily to quarantine, the official may order provisional quarantine via written order, verbal order, or actual physical movement restrictions. Individuals may be served with provisional quarantine orders either through personal service or the government officials may post or publish the order in a noticeable location. Under the proposed rule, provisional quarantine would last only three business days. If the government wished to extend the provisional quarantine, the official must serve the individual with a written quarantine order. The written quarantine order must explain the reasonable belief that the individual is in a communicable stage of a quarantinable disease based on medical evidence and that the quarantine is necessary to prevent the spread of the disease to non-infected individuals. The quarantine order must also specify the person(s) to be quarantined, the legal basis for the quarantine, the dates of quarantine and the location of the quarantine. Both the quarantine order and the provisional quarantine order must inform the person to be quarantined that they have the right to refuse any medical treatment offered, e.g., vaccination. In addition, the following rights are set out:

- The quarantine order must provide the person with notice that they have the right to request a hearing to review the quarantine order at any time during the quarantine.
- Following a request for a hearing, the government must hold a hearing within one business day of the request. The official will provide reasonable notice to inform the individual, and designate a hearing officer to review all the evidence available to the government and make findings to determine whether or not the quarantined individual is in a quarantinable stage of a communicable disease.
- The individual has the right to appoint a representative to provide other evidence to the hearing officer and the government must make reasonable accommodations to allow the individual to communicate with their representative.
- The hearing officer, upon reviewing all the evidence, will make a written recommendation to the government regarding release from quarantine. This final determination made by the government official is deemed to be final.
- Section 2241 of Title 28 of the U.S.C. provides that any individual that is detained may seek a writ of habeas corpus. The hearing officer is only authorized to review the factual, scientific, and medical basis for the quarantine; therefore, the writ of habeas corpus provides judicial review of the legal and constitutional concerns associated with the quarantine.

The MSEHPA provides a model quarantine process for state government officials. Under MSEHPA:

- The state officials may order a temporary quarantine or isolation by written directive.
- The temporary isolation or quarantine may not last more than ten days.
- Longer periods of quarantine require that state officials obtain a court order of quarantine or isolation. The court must hold a hearing to review the evidence presented by health officials as well as evidence provided by representatives of the quarantined or isolated persons within five days of the petition to the court.

- The court may issue a quarantine or isolation order only upon finding by a preponderance of the evidence that the quarantine or isolation is reasonably necessary to prevent the spread of the communicable disease.
- Should the court decide to issue the order, a quarantine or isolation order cannot be for a period longer than thirty days for any individual. If the State officials believe that quarantine is necessary for longer than the thirty day period, the state must file a petition for an extension, which may not last longer than thirty days.
- Individuals who are quarantined have the right to request the court show cause for the order of quarantine or isolation and why the individual should not be released. The court must either grant or deny the petition to show cause within forty-eight hours and, if the petition is granted, must issue an order to show cause within twenty-four hours.

During the quarantine or isolation period, the MSEHPA provides additional protections.

- State health officials must continuously monitor individuals for changes in their medical condition, and must release individuals immediately in the event that they are no longer in a medical state that poses a threat to others requiring quarantine or isolation.
- Isolated individuals and quarantined individuals shall be housed in separate locales.
- All quarantine and isolation measures should utilize the least restrictive means available to prevent the spread of the communicable disease.
- The state must provide food, clothing, shelter, means of communication, medical treatment and medication in a systematic and efficient manner to all individuals in quarantine or isolation.
- All quarantine or isolation locations must be kept clean and safe.
- The state should make every effort to ensure that cultural and religious beliefs of the quarantined or isolated persons are considered while addressing the needs and those individuals.

The Supreme Court has not squarely addressed the validity of quarantine laws and procedures enacted by states to prevent the spread of communicable diseases since 1902. In 1902, the Supreme Court heard a case from Louisiana regarding a quarantine law that prohibited a French vessel from entering a port that had been quarantined due to infestation. In *Compagnie Francaise de Navigation a Vapeur v. Louisiana State Board of Health*, 186 U.S. 380 (1902), the Court held:

> That from an early day the power of the States to enact and enforce quarantine laws for the safety and the protection of the health of their inhabitants has been recognized by Congress, is beyond question. That until Congress has exercised its power on the subject, such state quarantine laws and state laws for the purpose of preventing, eradicating or controlling the spread of contagious or infectious diseases, are not repugnant to the Constitution of the United States, although their operation affects interstate or foreign commerce, is not an open question.

In further examining whether such quarantine laws were unconstitutional, the Court stated:

It having been ascertained that the regulation was lawfully adopted and enforced the contention demonstrates its own unsoundness, since in the last analysis it reduces itself to the proposition that the effect of the Fourteenth Amendment was to strip the government, whether state or national, of all power to enact regulations protecting the health and safety of the people, or, what is equivalent thereto, necessarily amounts to saying that such laws when lawfully enacted cannot be enforced against person or property without violating the Constitution. In other words, that the lawful powers of government which the Constitution has conferred may not be exerted without bringing about a violation of the Constitution.

The case law regarding the quarantine of individuals is sparse because the United States has yet to face mass quarantine due to the spread of an epidemic, pandemic, or a bioterrorist attack. Clearly, the enactment of laws and regulations in the vein of the CDC's Proposed Parts 70 and 71 and the MSEHPA provide starting points from which the judicial branch can evaluate the issues.

UNITED STATES v. SHINNICK

U.S. District Court for the Eastern District of New York

219 F. Supp. 789 (E.D.N.Y. Aug. 2, 1963)

DOOLING, District Judge.

Petitioner, Helen Minkin, seeks on behalf of her mother, Ellen Siegel, an order, after inquiry, that respondents produce the body of relator before the court and that relator then be discharged from custody. Relator is presently being held at the United States Public Health Hospital at Stapleton, Staten Island, in this District; she is in isolation for the balance of the small pox incubation period of 14 days from July 25, 1963. She is being isolated because she was in Stockholm, a small pox infected local area, on July 25, 1963 and she did not present on arrival here from Stockholm on July 25, 1963, a valid certificate of vaccination against small pox; she stated in substance that the only vaccination to which she had reacted positively was her school entry vaccination, sixty-three years earlier; all later attempts at vaccination produced no positive reaction; the latest such 'unsuccessful' vaccination was on May 31, 1963 (Ex. 4).

The facts were found orally in tentative form at the conclusion of the hearing and that part of the hearing has been transcribed. There being no apparent dispute about the underlying facts, they are now found as transcribed with ink typographical corrections and with one material change.

The suspected small pox case in Stuttgart, a person who had been in Stockholm July 14 to 17, has now been ascertained to be a case of eczema, so that the last Stockholm case now known is that which was isolated June 22. Both counsel have supplied this datum by affidavit.

Stockholm is a small pox infected area and has been since before July 21-25, 1963 when Relator visited Stockholm (Ex. 3, 6 pp. 372, 376; 312, 328, 360). Under the International Sanitary Regulations (W H O Regulations No. 2) [FN1] Articles 3, 6 (Cf. 42 C.F.R. § 71.1(1)(0) [FN2] the declaration that a local area is infected and that it is free of local infection emanates from the health administration of the territory in which the infected local area is situated. It does not appear that others are legally competent to (as they would be hopelessly handicapped in seeking to) make a determination on such a question as whether or not Stockholm can now be regarded as not an infected local area on the basis that the last reported case went into isolation on June 22 and W H O Regulations No. 2 seems to provide for terminating a declaration of local infection twenty-eight days after the last reported case of small pox dies, recovers or is isolated; responsibility for applying that standard rests with the territorial health administration and depends on whether, also, all measures of prophylaxis have been taken and maintained to prevent recurrence of the disease. It is idle and dangerous to suggest that private judgment or judicial ipse dixit can, acting on the one datum of the date June 22 as the last identified and reported case, undertake to supercede the continuing declaration of the interested territorial health administration that Stockholm is still a small pox infected local area.

The Public Health Service Regulations do not conflict with W H O Regulations No. 2 although their arrangement is quite different. Relator did not arrive on an infected aircraft (42 C.F.R. § 71.87, W H O Reg. No. 2, Art. 84). Had she so arrived, isolation could have been directed on the basis of that fact, the authorities, however, taking into account previous vaccinations and the possibilities of her exposure to infection (42 C.F.R. § 71.87(b)(3); W H O Reg. No. 2, Art. 85 sd. 1(b). Where the aircraft is not infected, isolation may be imposed if the passenger is a 'suspect' (42 C.F.R. § 71.88; W H O Reg. No. 2, Art. 84, sd. 2). A 'suspect' is one who is considered by the health authority (medical officer in charge) as having been exposed to infection by a quarantinable disease and to be capable of spreading that disease (42 C.F.R. § 71.1(bb); W H O Reg. No. 2, Art. 1). While isolation is not to be substituted for surveillance unless the health authority considers the risk of transmission of the infection by the suspect to be exceptionally serious (42 C.F.R. § 71.70, W H O Reg. No. 2, Art. 39 sd. 2), the judgment required is that of a public health officer and not of a lawyer used to insist on positive evidence to support action; their task is to measure risk to the public and to seek for what can reassure and, not finding it, to proceed reasonably to make the public health secure. They deal in a terrible context and the consequences of mistaken indulgence can be irretrievably tragic. To supercede their judgment there must be a reliable showing of error. The words cautioning against light use of isolation are indeed strong but the three medical men who testified manifestly shared a concern that was evident and real and reasoned. [FN3] Their differentiation of the case of Mr. Siegel, Relator's husband, was forthright, reasoned and circumstantially reassuring. Their conclusion, reached in obvious good faith, cannot be challenged on the ground that they had no evidence of the exposure of Relator to the disease; they, simply, were not free and certainly not bound to ignore the facts that opportunity for exposure existed during four days in Stockholm, that no one on earth could know for fourteen days whether or not there had been exposure, and that Relator, with a history of unsuccessful vaccinations, was peculiarly in a position to have become infected and to infect others. Their action in no way discriminated against Relator or singled her out for treatment different from that accorded the few others similarly situated.

The petition for issuance of the writ is therefore denied. It is accordingly Ordered that Relator's petition be and it hereby is dismissed after hearing on the merits.

FN1. 7 United States Treaties and other International Agreements (1956) 2259-2296— cited 7 UST 2259-2296.

FN2. The Foreign Quarantine regulations (Part 71 of Title 42) appear to depend primarily from 42 U.S.C. § 264. Their adjustment to the W H O Regulations reflects, no doubt, the quasi-treaty status of regulations adopted under authority of the International Agreement creating the Organization,

62 Stat., Part 3, 2679, 2685; Congress authorized the President to accept membership and participate in the Organization 62 Stat. 441.

FN3. No negative inference, that voluntary submission to vaccination requires substitution of surveillance for isolation, can be drawn from 42 C.F.R. § 71.86(c); W H O Reg. No. 2, Art. 83, sd. 2.
The regulation states one condition warranting isolation: refusal of vaccination; and one procedure available when vaccination is accepted: continued surveillance notwithstanding vaccination.
The regulation does not exhaust the procedural alternatives nor straiten the authorities. Their procedure remains a function of the gravity of the situation as measured by their expert judgments
dispassionately formed.

12.5 Search and Seizure

The government also has the power to search and seize personal property in the event of the emergence of a named communicable disease. The 4th Amendment to the Constitution of the United
States provides that:

> The right of the people to be secure in their persons, houses, papers, and effects, against
> unreasonable searches and seizures, shall not be violated, and no Warrants shall issue, but
> upon probable cause, supported by Oath or affirmation, and particularly describing the
> place to be searched, and the persons or things to be seized.

As is often repeated, the right to be free from search and seizure conducted without probable
cause or warrant is not an absolute right. There are several situations in which the Supreme Court
has found that a government search and seizure without warrant or probable cause does not violate the Constitution. One instance when a warrant and probable cause are not necessary is when
a search and seizure is conducted with the consent of someone who is authorized to provide such
consent. Accordingly, an individual may consent to the search and seizure of personal property
which may be infected with biological agents.

Individuals in transit between states or at points of entry into the United States, occupy a
unique position when it comes to privacy expectations. Parts 70 and 71 of 42 C.F.R. afford government officials the authority to search individuals in transit between states or individuals attempting to enter the United States from foreign countries for the purpose of determining the
presence of communicable diseases. Indeed, inspections for communicable diseases are routine
at all international ports of entry and are required under the C.F.R. even without the presence of a
warrant or probable cause. Courts have made it clear that by the nature of being in transit or attempting to enter or leave the United States, individuals have a reduced expectation of privacy
and are subject to search and seizure of their person and effects without a warrant or probable
cause. The 7th Circuit, in *United States v. McDonald, 100 F. 3d 1320 (1996)*, found that individuals who are in transit on public transportation vehicles, like a bus, train, or airplane, have a greatly
reduced expectation of privacy as compared to individuals in a fixed place, like their homes. In
United States v. Berisha, 925 F. 2d 791 (1991), the 5th Circuit held found that individuals at the

border, both entering the United States and leaving the United States, are essentially on notice that their privacy may be invaded.

Closely regulated commercial industries have also been deemed by the Supreme Court to occupy a position of reduced expectation of privacy, primarily due to the fact that the nature of the business is highly regulated by the government. In *New York v. Burger, 482 U.S. 691 (1987)*, the Court set forth the standard.

> Because the owner or operator of a commercial premises in a "closely regulated" industry has a reduced expectation of privacy, the warrant and probable-cause requirements, which fulfill the traditional Fourth Amendment standard of reasonableness for a government search have lessened application in this context....This warrantless inspection...will be deemed to be reasonable only so long as three criteria are met. First, there must be a "substantial" government interest that informs the regulatory scheme pursuant to which the inspection is made. Second, the warrantless inspections must be "necessary to further [the] regulatory scheme".... Finally, "the statute's inspection program, in terms of certainty and regularity of its application, [must] provid[e] a constitutionally adequate substitute for a warrant." In other words, the regulatory statute must perform the two basic functions of a warrant: it must advise the owner of the commercial premises that the search is being made pursuant to the law and has a properly defined scope, and it must limit the discretion of the inspecting officers [citations omitted].

Finally, the requirements of the 4th Amendment that a warrant and probable cause are necessary to conduct a search and seizure may be unnecessary if the search and seizure was conducted in an effort to prevent an imminent threat to the health or safety of the general public. The Supreme Court upheld the seizure and destruction of food that was unfit for consumption to protect the public health in *North American Cold Storage Company v. City of Chicago, 211 U.S. 306 (1908)*. This decision suggests that in the event of a biological outbreak or bioterrorist attack, government officials may have a great amount of authority to inspect, seize and destroy personal property to prevent the spread of deadly communicable diseases. As noted, current provisions exist in 42 C.F.R. Parts 70 and 71 to provide for the search and seizure of property at ports of entry, but no federal laws or regulations have been passed to grant such carte blanche authority to government officials in the event of a bioterrorist attack or biological outbreak in the United States.

12.6 Other Legal Issues

A variety of other legal concerns may arise when government officials are faced with preventative and containment measures. Officials at any level of government–federal, state, local, or tribal–may infringe on individual civil liberties. Accordingly, the full range of possible actions available to the government should be complemented by a combination of limitations, safeguards and oversight provisions to ensure the protection of individual rights.

The MSEHPA recognizes that a major outbreak may quickly overwhelm the existing health care system of clinics and hospitals, requiring the government to procure property to provide for the care, treatment and housing of patients. In addition, the government may find it necessary to destroy entire facilities or private property and material that has become infected and poses a threat to the health of the general public. Private property may be taken by the government, even when the procurements are only utilized temporarily. However, when the government commits a taking of private property it must provide the rightful owner with just compensation. The MSEHPA suggests that the calculated compensation should include the value of the property at the eminent domain cost that would be afforded in a non-emergency setting.

Government officials will also be faced with patient concerns about protecting privacy rights. The conflicting goals of protecting privacy and preventing the spread of a communicable disease must be addressed. The MSEHPA as well as the Proposed Parts 70 and 71 of 42 C.F.R. provide for the maintenance of administrative records for each patient that will combine their legal quarantine orders, challenges, as well as their entire medical records. The protection of these records and maintenance of individual privacy should also be accounted for not only during the crisis but also in the aftermath. Use of the medical records should be limited to the provision of treatment, epidemiological research, or investigation of the cause of transmission of the communicable disease on a strict need to know basis.

Another issue of concern deals with the fact that health care providers may simply refuse to provide treatment to the infected, as occurred with some hospital personnel in Canada during the SARS outbreak in 2003. To be sure, in the event of an epidemic, pandemic, or bioterrorist attack, health care providers will be in high demand and short supply. The MSEHPA suggests that states pass laws that allow government officials to compel health care providers within the state to treat individuals who have fallen ill due to an epidemic, pandemic, or bioterrorist attack as a condition of the provider's licensing and ability to practice in that state. The MSEHPA also provides that the state officials should allow health care providers licensed in other states to assist during the crisis, in effect temporarily waiving jurisdictional and licensing concerns. Furthermore, the MSEHPA suggests that state actors, health care providers and others providing aid and assistance during an outbreak should be afforded immunity for negligent acts or omissions. Immunity would help foster action during a crisis situation that might otherwise be hindered by fear of legal repercussions. Nevertheless, immunity should not extend to gross negligence or willful misconduct or to any individual that in some way brought about the biological emergency.

Legal concerns do not cease when an infected individual dies. The Black Death of the fourteenth century killed 25 million Europeans in just five years, with corpses playing a large role in the spread of the virus. Since disease can spread from human remains, government officials must have a process to control and dispose of human remains that prevents the spread of the communicable disease while taking into account the religious, cultural, familial and individual beliefs of the deceased and their survivors.

Enforcement of any orders of quarantine will create a variety of problems and every mandatory quarantine order will see its violators. The MSEHPA suggests that violations pursuant to the state laws should constitute a misdemeanor. Federal law, in 42 U.S.C. § 271, states that violations of the enforcement provisions for 42 U.S.C. § 264, namely 42 C.F.R. Parts 70 and 71, will give rise to a fine not more than $1,000, imprisonment for not more than a year, or both. In addition, Subsection (b) of § 271 subjects vessels that violate orders pursuant to the aforementioned code and regulations to a fine that will not be more that $5,000. While these penalties can provide a framework for how to address non-compliance with mandatory quarantine orders, lawmakers should consider unintended consequences. For example, during the 2003 SARS outbreak in Singapore, the government ordered local law enforcement not to arrest individuals engaged in some illegal activities, like quarantine violation, so as to prevent those who may have been exposed from being pushed underground.

Funding issues are also a major concern. The majority of hospitals in the United States are privately owned and are simply not equipped, staffed, or willing to stretch the capabilities of the hospital to meet the enormous needs that would occur during a major epidemic. In addition, if the epidemic strikes Mexico, the United States could expect a flood of people streaming across the border for health care. Diseases that cause such mayhem do not discriminate in victim choice. Privately owned hospitals in the United States will need major financial support from the government.

Individuals ordered to quarantine also face the possibility that they will lose their employment. Will the government compensate those who suffer financial loss due to quarantine?

In summary, a plethora of legal issues stand hungrily at the door. They will not become fully apparent until the nation is in the middle of a biological outbreak. In the ensuing chaos, the government will have to utilize all the legal tools that are currently in place and quickly develop new tools. Certainly, the government entities at all levels should plan now for the worst case scenario. The United States has managed responses to a variety of disasters in recent years, both natural and terrorist, and each new disaster brings new legal issues that require executive, legislative and judicial attention and action. Like all issues associated with the war on terror, the goal in addressing these issues is always to ensure that the citizens of the United States are safe from the crisis as well as from an over active governmental response.

12.7 Questions for Discussion

1. *HHS Proposed Rules.* The proposed changes to 42 C.F.R. Parts 70 and 71, published by the HHS in November 2005, not only established more detailed procedures for quarantine by the CDC, the proposed changes also established authority in the CDC to mandate a variety of measures, including: the collection of passenger information by airlines; travel permits for individuals to travel to places the CDC deems a potential threat to the health of the public; the establishment of hospitals and clinics; implementation of sanitary measures; implementation of CDC control in the event the CDC perceives local control inadequate; and special powers given to the government in time of war. In the event of a confirmed bioterrorist attack, the FBI assumes control of all government actions in response to the attack, meaning the FBI will have all of the power that the proposed changes afford the CDC. Will the proposed rules give the government too much power? Will these regulations infringe upon rights guaranteed to individuals by the Constitution?

2. *Who oversees the government?* A bioterrorist attack on the United States would set in motion a governmental response machine that currently is not subject to oversight. Do the courts have

sufficient power to oversee the executive branch to ensure that individual civil liberties are secure during the government's response to a large scale bioterrorist attack? Will the courts exercise the power they may have even if they will appear to be acting contrary to the nationalist and patriotic trends of the times?

3. *Does Executive Order 13375 go too far?* President Bush's 2005 Executive Order 13375 lists a new and extremely broad based category to cover all possible future influenza viruses: "influenza caused by novel or reemergent influenza viruses that are causing or have the potential to cause a pandemic." What impact does such a broad based category present in terms of government power?

Selected Bibliography

Department of Health and Human Services, *Control of Communicable Diseases; Proposed Rule.* Fed. Reg. 70, 229 at 71891, Nov. 30, 2005.

Department of Homeland Security, *National Response Plan* 2004.

Gosten, Lawrence O., MODEL STATE EMERGENCY HEALTH POWERS ACT 2001.

O'Leary, N. Pieter M., *Cock-a-Doodle-Doo: Pandemic Avian Influenza and the Legal Preparation and Consequences of an H5N1 Influenza Outbreak*, HEALTH MATRIX: JOURNAL OF LAW-MEDICINE, Summer 2006.

O'Leary, N. Pieter M. , *Bioterrorism or Avian Influenza: California, the Model State Emergency Health Powers Act, and Protecting Civil Liberties During a Public Health Emergency*, CALIFORNIA WESTERN LAW REVIEW, Spring, 2006.

Pimentel, David and Marcia Pimentel, *Essay: Bioweapon Impacts on Public Health and the Environment*, WILLIAM AND MARY ENVIRONMENTAL LAW AND POLICY REVIEW, Spring, 2006.

Posner, Richard A., CATASTROPHE: RISK AND RESPONSE 2005.

Rosenstein, Mark et. al., *Quarantine and Isolation: Lessons Learned from SARS.* REPORT TO THE CENTERS FOR DISEASE CONTROL AND PREVENTION. 2003.

Sutton, Victoria, LAW AND BIOTERRORISM 2002.

Appendix A
Selected Provisions of the Charter of the United Nations

June 26, 1945, 59 Stat. 1031, T.S. 993, 3 Bevans 1153, entered into force Oct. 24, 1945.

PREAMBLE

WE THE PEOPLES OF THE UNITED NATIONS DETERMINED

- to save succeeding generations from the scourge of war, which twice in our life-time has brought untold sorrow to mankind, and
- to reaffirm faith in fundamental human rights, in the dignity and worth of the human person, in the equal rights of men and women and of nations large and small, and
- to establish conditions under which justice and respect for the obligations arising from treaties and other sources of international law can be maintained, and
- to promote social progress and better standards of life in larger freedom,

AND FOR THESE ENDS

- to practice tolerance and live together in peace with one another as good neighbors, and
- to unite our strength to maintain international peace and security, and
- to ensure by the acceptance of principles and the institution of methods, that armed force shall not be used, save in the common interest, and
- to employ international machinery for the promotion of the economic and social advancement of all peoples,

HAVE RESOLVED TO COMBINE OUR EFFORTS TO ACCOMPLISH THESE AIMS

Accordingly, our respective Governments, through representatives assembled in the city of San Francisco, who have exhibited their full powers found to be in good and due form, have agreed to the present Charter of the United Nations and do hereby establish an international organization to be known as the United Nations.

CHAPTER I
PURPOSES AND PRINCIPLES

Article 1

The Purposes of the United Nations are:

1. To maintain international peace and security, and to that end: to take effective collective measures for the prevention and removal of threats to the peace, and for the suppression of acts of aggression or other breaches of the peace, and to bring about by peaceful means, and in conformity with the principles of justice and international law, adjustment or settlement of international disputes or situations which might lead to a breach of the peace;

2. To develop friendly relations among nations based on respect for the principle of equal rights and self-determination of peoples, and to take other appropriate measures to strengthen universal peace;

3. To achieve international cooperation in solving international problems of an economic, social, cultural, or humanitarian character, and in promoting and encouraging respect for human rights and for fundamental freedoms for all without distinction as to race, sex, language, or religion; and

4. To be a center for harmonizing the actions of nations in the attainment of these common ends.

Article 2

The Organization and its Members, in pursuit of the Purposes stated in Article 1, shall act in accordance with the following Principles.

1. The Organization is based on the principle of the sovereign equality of all its Members.

2. All Members, in order to ensure to all of them the rights and benefits resulting from membership, shall fulfill in good faith the obligations assumed by them in accordance with the present Charter.

3. All Members shall settle their international disputes by peaceful means in such a manner that international peace and security, and justice, are not endangered.

4. All Members shall refrain in their international relations from the threat or use of force against the territorial integrity or political independence of any state, or in any other manner inconsistent with the Purposes of the United Nations.

5. All Members shall give the United Nations every assistance in any action it takes in accordance with the present Charter, and shall refrain from giving assistance to any state against which the United Nations is taking preventive or enforcement action.

6. The Organization shall ensure that states which are not Members of the United Nations act in accordance with these Principles so far as may be necessary for the maintenance of international peace and security.

7. Nothing contained in the present Charter shall authorize the United Nations to intervene in matters which are essentially within the domestic jurisdiction of any state or shall require the Members to submit such matters to settlement under the present Charter; but this principle shall not prejudice the application of enforcement measures under Chapter VII.

CHAPTER II
MEMBERSHIP

Article 3

The original Members of the United Nations shall be the states which, having participated in the United Nations Conference on International Organization at San Francisco, or having previously signed the Declaration by United Nations of January 1, 1942, sign the present Charter and ratify it in accordance with Article 110.

Article 4

1. Membership in the United Nations is open to all other peace-loving states which accept the obligations contained in the present Charter and, in the judgment of the Organization, are able and willing to carry out these obligations.

2. The admission of any such state to membership in the United Nations will be effected by a decision of the General Assembly upon the recommendation of the Security Council.

Article 5

A member of the United Nations against which preventive or enforcement action has been taken by the Security Council may be suspended from the exercise of the rights and privileges of membership by the General Assembly upon the recommendation of the Security Council. The exercise of these rights and privileges may be restored by the Security Council.

Article 6

A Member of the United Nations which has persistently violated the Principles contained in the present Charter may be expelled from the Organization by the General Assembly upon the recommendation of the Security Council.

CHAPTER III
ORGANS

Article 7

1. There are established as the principal organs of the United Nations: a General Assembly, a Security Council, an Economic and Social Council, a Trusteeship Council, an International Court of Justice, and a Secretariat.

2. Such subsidiary organs as may be found necessary may be established in accordance with the present Charter.

Article 8

The United Nations shall place no restrictions on the eligibility of men and women to participate in any capacity and under conditions of equality in its principal and subsidiary organs.

CHAPTER IV
THE GENERAL ASSEMBLY

Composition

Article 9

1. The General Assembly shall consist of all the Members of the United Nations.

2. Each member shall have not more than five representatives in the General Assembly.

Functions and Powers

Article 10

The General Assembly may discuss any questions or any matters within the scope of the present Charter or relating to the powers and functions of any organs provided for in the present Charter, and, except as provided in Article 12, may make recommendations to the Members of the United Nations or to the Security Council or to both on any such questions or matters.

Article 11

1. The General Assembly may consider the general principles of cooperation in the maintenance of international peace and security, including the principles governing disarmament and the regulation of armaments, and may make recommendations with regard to such principles to the Members or to the Security Council or to both.

2. The General Assembly may discuss any questions relating to the maintenance of international peace and security brought before it by any Member of the United Nations, or by the Security Council, or by a state which is not a Member of the United Nations in accordance with Article 35, paragraph 2, and, except as provided in Article 12, may make recommendations with regard to any such questions to the state or states concerned or to the Security Council or to both. Any such question on which action is necessary shall be referred to the Security Council by the General Assembly either before or after discussion.

3. The General Assembly may call the attention of the Security Council to situations which are likely to endanger international peace and security.

4. The powers of the General Assembly set forth in this Article shall not limit the general scope of Article 10.

Article 12

1. While the Security Council is exercising in respect of any dispute or situation the functions assigned to it in the present Charter, the General Assembly shall not make any recommendation with regard to that dispute or situation unless the Security Council so requests.

2. The Secretary-General, with the consent of the Security Council, shall notify the General Assembly at each session of any matters relative to the maintenance of international peace and security which are being dealt with by the Security Council and shall similarly notify the General Assembly, or the Members of the United Nations if the General Assembly is not in session, immediately the Security Council ceases to deal with such matters.

Article 13

1. The General Assembly shall initiate studies and make recommendations for the purpose of:
   a. promoting international cooperation in the political field and encouraging the progressive development of international law and its codification;
   b. promoting international cooperation in the economic, social, cultural, educational, and health fields, and assisting in the realization of human rights and fundamental freedoms for all without distinction as to race, sex, language, or religion.

2. The further responsibilities, functions and powers of the General Assembly with respect to matters mentioned in paragraph 1(b) above are set forth in Chapters IX and X.

Article 14

Subject to the provisions of Article 12, the General Assembly may recommend measures for the peaceful adjustment of any situation, regardless of origin, which it deems likely to impair the general welfare or friendly relations among nations, including situations resulting from a violation of the provisions of the present Charter setting forth the Purposes and Principles of the United Nations.

Article 15

1. The General Assembly shall receive and consider annual and special reports from the Security Council; these reports shall include an account of the measures that the Security Council has decided upon or taken to maintain international peace and security.
2. The General Assembly shall receive and consider reports from the other organs of the United Nations.

Article 16

The General Assembly shall perform such functions with respect to the international trusteeship system as are assigned to it under Chapters XII and XIII, including the approval of the trusteeship agreements for areas not designated as strategic.

Article 17

1. The General Assembly shall consider and approve the budget of the Organization.
2. The expenses of the Organization shall be borne by the Members as apportioned by the General Assembly.
3. The General Assembly shall consider and approve any financial and budgetary arrangements with specialized agencies referred to in Article 57 and shall examine the administrative budgets of such specialized agencies with a view to making recommendations to the agencies concerned.

Voting

Article 18

1. Each member of the General Assembly shall have one vote.
2. Decisions of the General Assembly on important questions shall be made by a two-thirds majority of the members present and voting. These questions shall in-

clude: recommendations with respect to the maintenance of international peace and security, the election of the non-permanent members of the Security Council, the election of the members of the Economic and Social Council, the election of members of the Trusteeship Council in accordance with paragraph 1(c) of Article 86, the admission of new Members to the United Nations, the suspension of the rights and privileges of membership, the expulsion of Members, questions relating to the operation of the trusteeship system, and budgetary questions.

3. Decisions on other questions, Composition including the determination of additional categories of questions to be decided by a two-thirds majority, shall be made by a majority of the members present and voting.

Article 19

A Member of the United Nations which is in arrears in the payment of its financial contributions to the Organization shall have no vote in the General Assembly if the amount of its arrears equals or exceeds the amount of the contributions due from it for the preceding two full years. The General Assembly may, nevertheless, permit such a Member to vote if it is satisfied that the failure to pay is due to conditions beyond the control of the Member.

Procedure

Article 20

The General Assembly shall meet in regular annual sessions and in such special sessions as occasion may require. Special sessions shall be convoked by the Secretary-General at the request of the Security Council or of a majority of the Members of the United Nations.

Article 21

The General Assembly shall adopt its own rules of procedure. It shall elect its President for each session.

Article 22

The General Assembly may establish such subsidiary organs as it deems necessary for the performance of its functions.

CHAPTER V
THE SECURITY COUNCIL

Article 23

1. The Security Council shall consist of fifteen Members of the United Nations. The Republic of China, France, the Union of Soviet Socialist Republics, the United Kingdom of Great Britain and Northern Ireland, and the United States of America shall be permanent members of the Security Council. The General Assembly shall elect ten other Members of the United Nations to be non-permanent members of the Security Council, due regard being specially paid, in the first instance to the contribution of Members of the United Nations to the maintenance of international peace and security and to the other purposes of the Organization, and also to equitable geographical distribution.

2. The non-permanent members of the Security Council shall be elected for a term of two years. In the first election of the non-permanent members after the increase of the membership of the Security Council from eleven to fifteen, two of the four additional members shall be chosen for a term of one year. A retiring member shall not be eligible for immediate re-election.

3. Each member of the Security Council shall have one representative.

Functions and Powers

Article 24

1. In order to ensure prompt and effective action by the United Nations, its Members confer on the Security Council primary responsibility for the maintenance of international peace and security, and agree that in carrying out its duties under this responsibility the Security Council acts on their behalf.

2. In discharging these duties the Security Council shall act in accordance with the Purposes and Principles of the United Nations. The specific powers granted to the Security Council for the discharge of these duties are laid down in Chapters VI, VII, VIII, and XII.

3. The Security Council shall submit annual and, when necessary, special reports to the General Assembly for its consideration.

Article 25

The Members of the United Nations agree to accept and carry out the decisions of the Security Council in accordance with the present Charter.

Article 26

In order to promote the establishment and maintenance of international peace and security with the least diversion for armaments of the world's human and economic resources, the Security Council shall be responsible for formulating, with the assistance of the Military Staff Committee referred to in Article 47, plans to be submitted to the Members of the United Nations for the establishment of a system for the regulation of armaments.

Voting

Article 27

1. Each member of the Security Council shall have one vote.
2. Decisions of the Security Council on procedural matters shall be made by an affirmative vote of nine members.
3. Decisions of the Security Council on all other matters shall be made by an affirmative vote of nine members including the concurring votes of the permanent members; provided that, in decisions under Chapter VI, and under paragraph 3 of Article 52, a party to a dispute shall abstain from voting.

Procedure

Article 28

1. The Security Council shall be so organized as to be able to function continuously. Each member of the Security Council shall for this purpose be represented at all times at the seat of the Organization.
2. The Security Council shall hold periodic meetings at which each of its members may, if it so desires, be represented by a member of the government or by some other specially designated representative.
3. The Security Council may hold meetings at such places other than the seat of the Organization as in its judgment will best facilitate its work.

Article 29

The Security Council may establish such subsidiary organs as it deems necessary for the performance of its functions.

Article 30

The Security Council shall adopt its own rules of procedure, including the method of selecting its President.

Article 31

Any Member of the United Nations which is not a member of the Security Council may participate, without vote, in the discussion of any question brought before the Security Council whenever the latter considers that the interests of that Member are specially affected.

Article 32

Any Member of the United Nations which is not a member of the Security Council or any state which is not a Member of the United Nations, if it is a party to a dispute under consideration by the Security Council, shall be invited to participate, without vote, in the discussion relating to the dispute. The Security Council shall lay down such conditions as it deems just for the participation of a state which is not a Member of the United Nations.

CHAPTER VI
PACIFIC SETTLEMENT OF DISPUTES

Article 33

1. The parties to any dispute, the continuance of which is likely to endanger the maintenance of international peace and security, shall, first of all, seek a solution by negotiation, enquiry, mediation, conciliation, arbitration, judicial settlement, resort to regional agencies or arrangements, or other peaceful means of their own choice.
2. The Security Council shall, when it deems necessary, call upon the parties to settle their dispute by such means.

Article 34

The Security Council may investigate any dispute, or any situation which might lead to international friction or give rise to a dispute, in order to determine whether the continuance of the dispute or situation is likely to endanger the maintenance of international peace and security.

Article 35

1. Any Member of the United Nations may bring any dispute, or any situation of the nature referred to in Article 34, to the attention of the Security Council or of the General Assembly.
2. A state which is not a Member of the United Nations may bring to the attention of the Security Council or of the General Assembly any dispute to which it is a party

if it accepts in advance, for the purposes of the dispute, the obligations of pacific settlement provided in the present Charter.

3. The proceedings of the General Assembly in respect of matters brought to its attention under this Article will be subject to the provisions of Articles 11 and 12.

Article 36

1. The Security Council may, at any stage of a dispute of the nature referred to in Article 33 or of a situation of like nature, recommend appropriate procedures or methods of adjustment.
2. The Security Council should take into consideration any procedures for the settlement of the dispute which have already been adopted by the parties.
3. In making recommendations under this Article the Security Council should also take into consideration that legal disputes should as a general rule be referred by the parties to the International Court of Justice in accordance with the provisions of the Statute of the Court.

Article 37

1. Should the parties to a dispute of the nature referred to in Article 33 fail to settle it by the means indicated in that Article, they shall refer it to the Security Council.
2. If the Security Council deems that the continuance of the dispute is in fact likely to endanger the maintenance of international peace and security, it shall decide whether to take action under Article 36 or to recommend such terms of settlement as it may consider appropriate.

Article 38

Without prejudice to the provisions of Articles 33 to 37, the Security Council may, if all the parties to any dispute so request, make recommendations to the parties with a view to a pacific settlement of the dispute.

CHAPTER VII
ACTION WITH RESPECT TO THREATS TO THE PEACE, BREACHES OF THE PEACE, AND ACTS OF AGGRESSION

Article 39

The Security Council shall determine the existence of any threat to the peace, breach of the peace, or act of aggression and shall make recommendations, or decide what measures shall be taken in accordance with Articles 41 and 42, to maintain or restore international peace and security.

Article 40

In order to prevent an aggravation of the situation, the Security Council may, before making the recommendations or deciding upon the measures provided for in Article 39, call upon the parties concerned to comply with such provisional measures as it deems necessary or desirable. Such provisional measures shall be without prejudice to the rights, claims, or position of the parties concerned. The Security Council shall duly take account of failure to comply with such provisional measures.

Article 41

The Security Council may decide what measures not involving the use of armed force are to be employed to give effect to its decisions, and it may call upon the Members of the United Nations to apply such measures. These may include complete or partial interruption of economic relations and of rail, sea, air, postal, telegraphic, radio, and other means of communication, and the severance of diplomatic relations.

Article 42

Should the Security Council consider that measures provided for in Article 41 would be inadequate or have proved to be inadequate, it may take such action by air, sea, or land forces as may be necessary to maintain or restore international peace and security. Such action may include demonstrations, blockade, and other operations by air, sea, or land forces of Members of the United Nations.

Article 43

1. All Members of the United Nations, in order to contribute to the maintenance of international peace and security, undertake to make available to the Security Council, on its call and in accordance with a special agreement or agreements, armed forces, assistance, and facilities, including rights of passage, necessary for the purpose of maintaining international peace and security.

2. Such agreement or agreements shall govern the numbers and types of forces, their degree of readiness and general location, and the nature of the facilities and assistance to be provided.

3. The agreement or agreements shall be negotiated as soon as possible on the initiative of the Security Council. They shall be concluded between the Security Council and Members or between the Security Council and groups of Members and shall be subject to ratification by the signatory states in accordance with their respective constitutional processes.

Article 44

When the Security Council has decided to use force it shall, before calling upon a Member not represented on it to provide armed forces in fulfillment of the obligations assumed under Article 43, invite that Member, if the Member so desires, to participate in the decisions of the Security Council concerning the employment of contingents of that Member's armed forces.

Article 45

In order to enable the United Nations to take urgent military measures Members shall hold immediately available national air-force contingents for combined international enforcement action. The strength and degree of readiness of these contingents and plans for their combined action shall be determined, within the limits laid down in the special agreement or agreements referred to in Article 43, by the Security Council with the assistance of the Military Staff Committee.

Article 46

Plans for the application of armed force shall be made by the Security Council with the assistance of the Military Staff Committee.

Article 47

1. There shall be established a Military Staff Committee to advise and assist the Security Council on all questions relating to the Security Council's military requirements for the maintenance of international peace and security, the employment and command of forces placed at its disposal, the regulation of armaments, and possible disarmament.
2. The Military Staff Committee shall consist of the Chiefs of Staff of the permanent members of the Security Council or their representatives. Any Member of the United Nations not permanently represented on the Committee shall be invited by the Committee to be associated with it when the efficient discharge of the Committee's responsibilities requires the participation of that Member in its work.
3. The Military Staff Committee shall be responsible under the Security Council for the strategic direction of any armed forces placed at the disposal of the Security Council. Questions relating to the command of such forces shall be worked out subsequently.
4. The Military Staff Committee, with the authorization of the Security Council and after consultation with appropriate regional agencies, may establish regional subcommittees.

Article 48

1. The action required to carry out the decisions of the Security Council for the maintenance of international peace and security shall be taken by all the Members of the United Nations or by some of them, as the Security Council may determine.

2. Such decisions shall be carried out by the Members of the United Nations directly and through their action in the appropriate international agencies of which they are members.

Article 49

The Members of the United Nations shall join in affording mutual assistance in carrying out the measures decided upon by the Security Council.

Article 50

If preventive or enforcement measures against any state are taken by the Security Council, any other state, whether a Member of the United Nations or not, which finds itself confronted with special economic problems arising from the carrying out of those measures shall have the right to consult the Security Council with regard to a solution of those problems.

Article 51

cf p 73

Nothing in the present Charter shall impair the <u>inherent</u> right of individual or collective self-defense if an armed attack occurs against a Member of the United Nations, until the Security Council has taken measures necessary to maintain international peace and security. Measures taken by Members in the exercise of this right of self-defense shall be immediately reported to the Security Council and shall not in any way affect the authority and responsibility of the Security Council under the present Charter to take at any time such action as it deems necessary in order to maintain or restore international peace and security.

CHAPTER VIII
REGIONAL ARRANGEMENTS

Article 52

1. Nothing in the present Charter precludes the existence of regional arrangements or agencies for dealing with such matters relating to the maintenance of international peace and security as are appropriate for regional action, provided that

such arrangements or agencies and their activities are consistent with the Purposes and Principles of the United Nations.

2. The Members of the United Nations entering into such arrangements or constituting such agencies shall make every effort to achieve pacific settlement of local disputes through such regional arrangements or by such regional agencies before referring them to the Security Council.

3. The Security Council shall encourage the development of pacific settlement of local disputes through such regional arrangements or by such regional agencies either on the initiative of the states concerned or by reference from the Security Council.

4. This Article in no way impairs the application of Articles 34 and 35.

Article 53

1. The Security Council shall, where appropriate, utilize such regional arrangements or agencies for enforcement action under its authority. But no enforcement action shall be taken under regional arrangements or by regional agencies without the authorization of the Security Council, with the exception of measures against any enemy state, as defined in paragraph 2 of this Article, provided for pursuant to Article 107 or in regional arrangements directed against renewal of aggressive policy on the part of any such state, until such time as the Organization may, on request of the Governments concerned, be charged with the responsibility for preventing further aggression by such a state.

2. The term enemy state as used in paragraph 1 of this Article applies to any state which during the Second World War has been an enemy of any signatory of the present Charter.

Article 54

The Security Council shall at all times be kept fully informed of activities undertaken or in contemplation under regional arrangements or by regional agencies for the maintenance of international peace and security.

...

IN FAITH WHEREOF the representatives of the Governments of the United Nations have signed the present Charter.
DONE at the city of San Francisco the twenty-sixth day of June, one thousand nine hundred and forty-five.

Appendix B

Selected Provisions of the 2002 National Security Strategy of the United States of America

The great struggles of the twentieth century between liberty and totalitarianism ended with a decisive victory for the forces of freedom—and a single sustainable model for national success: freedom, democracy, and free enterprise. In the twenty-first century, only nations that share a commitment to protecting basic human rights and guaranteeing political and economic freedom will be able to unleash the potential of their people and assure their future prosperity. People everywhere want to be able to speak freely; choose who will govern them; worship as they please; educate their children—male and female; own property; and enjoy the benefits of their labor. These values of freedom are right and true for every person, in every society—and the duty of protecting these values against their enemies is the common calling of freedom-loving people across the globe and across the ages.

Today, the United States enjoys a position of unparalleled military strength and great economic and political influence. In keeping with our heritage and principles, we do not use our strength to press for unilateral advantage. We seek instead to create a balance of power that favors human freedom: conditions in which all nations and all societies can choose for themselves the rewards and challenges of political and economic liberty. In a world that is safe, people will be able to make their own lives better. We will defend the peace by fighting terrorists and tyrants. We will preserve the peace by building good relations among the great powers. We will extend the peace by encouraging free and open societies on every continent.

Defending our Nation against its enemies is the first and fundamental commitment of the Federal Government. Today, that task has changed dramatically. Enemies in the past needed great armies and great industrial capabilities to endanger America. Now, shadowy networks of individuals can bring great chaos and suffering to our shores for less than it costs to purchase a single tank. Terrorists are organized to penetrate open societies and to turn the power of modern technologies against us.

To defeat this threat we must make use of every tool in our arsena—military power, better homeland defenses, law enforcement, intelligence, and vigorous efforts to cut off terrorist financing. The war against terrorists of global reach is a global enterprise of uncertain duration. America will help nations that need our assistance in combating terror. And America will hold to account nations that are compromised by terror,

443

including those who harbor terrorists—because the allies of terror are the enemies of civilization. The United States and countries cooperating with us must not allow the terrorists to develop new home bases. Together, we will seek to deny them sanctuary at every turn.

The gravest danger our Nation faces lies at the crossroads of radicalism and technology. Our enemies have openly declared that they are seeking weapons of mass destruction, and evidence indicates that they are doing so with determination. The United States will not allow these efforts to succeed. We will build defenses against ballistic missiles and other means of delivery. We will cooperate with other nations to deny, contain, and curtail our enemies' efforts to acquire dangerous technologies. And, as a matter of common sense and self-defense, America will act against such emerging threats before they are fully formed. We cannot defend America and our friends by hoping for the best. So we must be prepared to defeat our enemies' plans, using the best intelligence and proceeding with deliberation. History will judge harshly those who saw this coming danger but failed to act. In the new world we have entered, the only path to peace and security is the path of action.

As we defend the peace, we will also take advantage of an historic opportunity to preserve the peace. Today, the international community has the best chance since the rise of the nation-state in the seventeenth century to build a world where great powers compete in peace instead of continually prepare for war. Today, the world's great powers find ourselves on the same side—united by common dangers of terrorist violence and chaos. The United States will build on these common interests to promote global security. We are also increasingly united by common values. Russia is in the midst of a hopeful transition, reaching for its democratic future and a partner in the war on terror. Chinese leaders are discovering that economic freedom is the only source of national wealth. In time, they will find that social and political freedom is the only source of national greatness. America will encourage the advancement of democracy and economic openness in both nations, because these are the best foundations for domestic stability and international order. We will strongly resist aggression from other great powers—even as we welcome their peaceful pursuit of prosperity, trade, and cultural advancement.

Finally, the United States will use this moment of opportunity to extend the benefits of freedom across the globe. We will actively work to bring the hope of democracy, development, free markets, and free trade to every corner of the world. The events of September 11, 2001, taught us that weak states, like Afghanistan, can pose as great a danger to our national interests as strong states. Poverty does not make poor people into terrorists and murderers. Yet poverty, weak institutions, and corruption can make weak states vulnerable to terrorist networks and drug cartels within their borders.

The United States will stand beside any nation determined to build a better future by seeking the rewards of liberty for its people. Free trade and free markets have proven their ability to lift whole societies out of poverty—so the United States will work with individual nations, entire regions, and the entire global trading community to build a world that trades in freedom and therefore grows in prosperity. The United States will deliver greater development assistance through the New Millennium Challenge Account to nations that govern justly, invest in their people, and encourage economic freedom. We will also continue to lead the world in efforts to reduce the terrible toll of HIV/AIDS and other infectious diseases.

In building a balance of power that favors freedom, the United States is guided by the conviction that all nations have important responsibilities. Nations that enjoy freedom must actively fight terror. Nations that depend on international stability must help prevent the spread of weapons of mass destruction. Nations that seek international aid must govern themselves wisely, so that aid is well spent. For freedom to thrive, accountability must be expected and required.

We are also guided by the conviction that no nation can build a safer, better world alone. Alliances and multilateral institutions can multiply the strength of freedom-loving nations. The United States is committed to lasting institutions like the United Nations, the World Trade Organization, the Organization of American States, and NATO as well as other long-standing alliances. Coalitions of the willing can augment these permanent institutions. In all cases, international obligations are to be taken seriously. They are not to be undertaken symbolically to rally support for an ideal without furthering its attainment.

Freedom is the non-negotiable demand of human dignity; the birthright of every person—in every civilization. Throughout history, freedom has been threatened by war and terror; it has been challenged by the clashing wills of powerful states and the evil designs of tyrants; and it has been tested by widespread poverty and disease. Today, humanity holds in its hands the opportunity to further freedom's triumph over all these foes. The United States welcomes our responsibility to lead in this great mission.

George W. Bush
THE WHITE HOUSE
September 17, 2002

I. Overview of America's International Strategy

> *Our Nation's cause has always been larger than our Nation's defense. We fight, as we always fight, for a just peace—a peace that favors liberty. We will defend the peace against the threats from terrorists and tyrants. We will preserve the peace by building good relations among the great powers. And we will extend the peace by encouraging free and open societies on every continent.*

President Bush
West Point, New York
June 1, 2002

The United States possesses unprecedented—and unequaled—strength and influence in the world. Sustained by faith in the principles of liberty, and the value of a free society, this position comes with unparalleled responsibilities, obligations, and opportunity. The great strength of this nation must be used to promote a balance of power that favors freedom.

For most of the twentieth century, the world was divided by a great struggle over ideas: destructive totalitarian visions versus freedom and equality.

That great struggle is over. The militant visions of class, nation, and race which promised utopia and delivered misery have been defeated and discredited. America is now threatened less by conquering states than we are by failing ones. We are menaced less by fleets and armies than by catastrophic technologies in the hands of the embittered few. We must defeat these threats to our Nation, allies, and friends.

This is also a time of opportunity for America. We will work to translate this moment of influence into decades of peace, prosperity, and liberty. The U.S. national security strategy will be based on a distinctly American internationalism that reflects the union of our values and our national interests. The aim of this strategy is to help make the world not just safer but better. Our goals on the path to progress are clear: political and economic freedom, peaceful relations with other states, and respect for human dignity.

And this path is not America's alone. It is open to all. To achieve these goals, the United States will:

- champion aspirations for human dignity;
- strengthen alliances to defeat global terrorism and work to prevent attacks against us and our friends;
- work with others to defuse regional conflicts;

- prevent our enemies from threatening us, our allies, and our friends, with weapons of mass destruction;
- ignite a new era of global economic growth through free markets and free trade;
- expand the circle of development by opening societies and building the infrastructure of democracy;
- develop agendas for cooperative action with other main centers of global power; and
- transform America's national security institutions to meet the challenges and opportunities of the twenty-first century.

...

V. Prevent Our Enemies from Threatening Us, Our Allies, and Our Friends with Weapons of Mass Destruction

The gravest danger to freedom lies at the crossroads of radicalism and technology. When the spread of chemical and biological and nuclear weapons, along with ballistic missile technology—when that occurs, even weak states and small groups could attain a catastrophic power to strike great nations. Our enemies have declared this very intention, and have been caught seeking these terrible weapons. They want the capability to blackmail us, or to harm us, or to harm our friends—and we will oppose them with all our power.

President Bush
West Point, New York
June 1, 2002

The nature of the Cold War threat required the United States—with our allies and friends—to emphasize deterrence of the enemy's use of force, producing a grim strategy of mutual assured destruction. With the collapse of the Soviet Union and the end of the Cold War, our security environment has undergone profound transformation.

Having moved from confrontation to cooperation as the hallmark of our relationship with Russia, the dividends are evident: an end to the balance of terror that divided us; an historic reduction in the nuclear arsenals on both sides; and cooperation in areas such as counterterrorism and missile defense that until recently were inconceivable.

But new deadly challenges have emerged from rogue states and terrorists. None of these contemporary threats rival the sheer destructive power that was arrayed against us by the Soviet Union. However, the nature and motivations of these new adversaries, their determination to obtain destructive powers hitherto available only to the world's strongest states, and the greater likelihood that they will use weapons of mass destruction against us, make today's security environment more complex and dangerous.

In the 1990s we witnessed the emergence of a small number of rogue states that, while different in important ways, share a number of attributes. These states:

- brutalize their own people and squander their national resources for the personal gain of the rulers;
- display no regard for international law, threaten their neighbors, and callously violate international treaties to which they are party;
- are determined to acquire weapons of mass destruction, along with other advanced military technology, to be used as threats or offensively to achieve the aggressive designs of these regimes;
- sponsor terrorism around the globe; and
- reject basic human values and hate the United States and everything for which it stands.

At the time of the Gulf War, we acquired irrefutable proof that Iraq's designs were not limited to the chemical weapons it had used against Iran and its own people, but also extended to the acquisition of nuclear weapons and biological agents. In the past decade North Korea has become the world's principal purveyor of ballistic missiles, and has tested increasingly capable missiles while developing its own WMD arsenal. Other rogue regimes seek nuclear, biological, and chemical weapons as well. These states' pursuit of, and global trade in, such weapons has become a looming threat to all nations.

We must be prepared to stop rogue states and their terrorist clients before they are able to threaten or use weapons of mass destruction against the United States and our allies and friends. Our response must take full advantage of strengthened alliances, the establishment of new partnerships with former adversaries, innovation in the use of military forces, modern technologies, including the development of an effective missile defense system, and increased emphasis on intelligence collection and analysis.

Our comprehensive strategy to combat WMD includes:

- *Proactive counterproliferation efforts.* We must deter and defend against the threat before it is unleashed. We must ensure that key capabilities—detection, active and passive defenses, and counterforce capabilities—are integrated into our defense transformation and our homeland security systems. Counterproliferation must also be integrated into the doctrine, training, and equipping of our forces and those of our allies to ensure that we can prevail in any conflict with WMD-armed adversaries.

- *Strengthened nonproliferation efforts to prevent rogue states and terrorists from acquiring the materials, technologies, and expertise necessary for weapons of mass destruction.* We will enhance diplomacy, arms control, multilateral export controls, and threat reduction assistance that impede states and terrorists seeking WMD, and when necessary, interdict enabling technologies and materials. We will continue to build coalitions to support these efforts, encouraging their increased political and financial support for nonproliferation and threat reduction programs. The recent G-8 agreement to commit up to $20 billion to a global partnership against proliferation marks a major step forward.

- *Effective consequence management to respond to the effects of WMD use, whether by terrorists or hostile states.* Minimizing the effects of WMD use against our people will help deter those who possess such weapons and dissuade those who seek to acquire them by persuading enemies that they cannot attain their desired ends. The United States must also be prepared to respond to the effects of WMD use against our forces abroad, and to help friends and allies if they are attacked.

It has taken almost a decade for us to comprehend the true nature of this new threat. Given the goals of rogue states and terrorists, the United States can no longer solely rely on a reactive posture as we have in the past. The inability to deter a potential attacker, the immediacy of today's threats, and the magnitude of potential harm that could be caused by our adversaries' choice of weapons, do not permit that option. We cannot let our enemies strike first.

In the Cold War, especially following the Cuban missile crisis, we faced a generally status quo, risk-averse adversary. Deterrence was an effective defense. But deterrence based only upon the threat of retaliation is less likely to work against leaders of rogue states more willing to take risks, gambling with the lives of their people, and the wealth of their nations.

- In the Cold War, weapons of mass destruction were considered weapons of last resort whose use risked the destruction of those who used them. Today, our enemies see weapons of mass destruction as weapons of choice. For rogue states these weapons are tools of intimidation and military aggression against their neighbors. These weapons may also allow these states to attempt to blackmail the United States and our allies to prevent us from deterring or repelling the aggressive behavior of rogue states. Such states also see these weapons as their best means of overcoming the conventional superiority of the United States.

- Traditional concepts of deterrence will not work against a terrorist enemy whose avowed tactics are wanton destruction and the targeting of innocents; whose so-called soldiers seek martyrdom in death and whose most potent protection is statelessness. The overlap between states that sponsor terror and those that pursue WMD compels us to action.

For centuries, international law recognized that nations need not suffer an attack before they can lawfully take action to defend themselves against forces that present an imminent danger of attack. Legal scholars and international jurists often conditioned the legitimacy of preemption on the existence of an imminent threat—most often a visible mobilization of armies, navies, and air forces preparing to attack.

We must adapt the concept of imminent threat to the capabilities and objectives of today's adversaries. Rogue states and terrorists do not seek to attack us using conventional means. They know such attacks would fail. Instead, they rely on acts of terror and, potentially, the use of weapons of mass destruction—weapons that can be easily concealed, delivered covertly, and used without warning.

The targets of these attacks are our military forces and our civilian population, in direct violation of one of the principal norms of the law of warfare. As was demonstrated by the losses on September 11, 2001, mass civilian casualties is the specific objective of terrorists and these losses would be exponentially more severe if terrorists acquired and used weapons of mass destruction.

The United States has long maintained the option of preemptive actions to counter a sufficient threat to our national security. The greater the threat, the greater is the risk of inaction—and the more compelling the case for taking anticipatory action to defend ourselves, even if uncertainty remains as to the time and place of the enemy's attack. To forestall or prevent such hostile acts by our adversaries, the United States will, if necessary, act preemptively.

The United States will not use force in all cases to preempt emerging threats, nor should nations use preemption as a pretext for aggression. Yet in an age where the enemies of civilization openly and actively seek the world's most destructive technologies, the United States cannot remain idle while dangers gather. We will always proceed deliberately, weighing the consequences of our actions. To support preemptive options, we will:

- build better, more integrated intelligence capabilities to provide timely, accurate information on threats, wherever they may emerge;

- coordinate closely with allies to form a common assessment of the most dangerous threats; and

- continue to transform our military forces to ensure our ability to conduct rapid and precise operations to achieve decisive results.

The purpose of our actions will always be to eliminate a specific threat to the United States or our allies and friends. The reasons for our actions will be clear, the force measured, and the cause just.

Appendix C
War Powers Resolution

Public Law 93-148, 93rd Congress, H. J. Res. 542, November 7, 1973

Joint Resolution

Concerning the war powers of Congress and the President.

Resolved by the Senate and the House of Representatives of the United States of America in Congress assembled,

SHORT TITLE

SECTION 1.

PURPOSE AND POLICY

SEC. 2.

(a) It is the purpose of this joint resolution to fulfill the intent of the framers of the Constitution of the United States and insure [sic] that the collective judgement of both the Congress and the President will apply to the introduction of United States Armed Forces into hostilities, or into situations where imminent involvement in hostilities is clearly indicated by the circumstances, and to the continued use of such forces in hostilities or in such situations.

(b) Under article I, section 8, of the Constitution, it is specifically provided that the Congress shall have the power to make all laws necessary and proper for carrying into execution, not only its own powers but also all other powers vested by the Constitution in the Government of the United States, or in any department or officer thereof.

(c) The constitutional powers of the President as Commander-in-Chief to introduce United States Armed Forces into hostilities, or into situations where imminent involvement in hostilities is clearly indicated by the circumstances, are exercised only pursuant to (1) a declaration of war, (2) specific statutory authorization, or (3) a national emergency created by attack upon the United States, its territories or possessions, or its armed forces.

CONSULTATION

SEC. 3.

The President in every possible instance shall consult with Congress before introducing United States Armed Forces into hostilities or into situation where imminent involvement in hostilities is clearly indicated by the circumstances, and after every such introduction shall consult regularly with the Congress until United States Armed Forces are no longer engaged in hostilities or have been removed from such situations.

REPORTING

SEC. 4.

(a) In the absence of a declaration of war, in any case in which United States Armed Forces are introduced—

   (1) into hostilities or into situations where imminent involvement in hostilities is clearly indicated by the circumstances;

   (2) into the territory, airspace or waters of a foreign nation, while equipped for combat, except for deployments which relate solely to supply, replacement, repair, or training of such forces; or

   (3) in numbers which substantially enlarge United States Armed Forces equipped for combat already located in a foreign nation; the president shall submit within 48 hours to the Speaker of the House of Representatives and to the President pro tempore of the Senate a report, in writing, setting forth—

      (A) the circumstances necessitating the introduction of United States Armed Forces;

      (B) the constitutional and legislative authority under which such introduction took place; and

      (C) the estimated scope and duration of the hostilities or involvement.

(b) The President shall provide such other information as the Congress may request in the fulfillment of its constitutional responsibilities with respect to committing the Nation to war and to the use of United States Armed Forces abroad

(c) Whenever United States Armed Forces are introduced into hostilities or into any situation described in sub section (a) of this section, the President shall, so long as such armed forces continue to be engaged in such hostilities or situation, report to the Congress periodically on the status of such hostilities or situation as well as on the scope and duration of such hostilities or situation, but in no event shall he report to the Congress less often than once every six months.

CONGRESSIONAL ACTION

SEC. 5.

(a) Each report submitted pursuant to section 4(a)(1) shall be transmitted to the Speaker of the House of Representatives and to the President pro tempore of the Senate on the same calendar day. Each report so transmitted shall be referred to the Committee on Foreign Affairs of the House of Representatives and to the Committee on Foreign Relations of the Senate for appropriate action. If, when the report is transmitted, the Congress has adjourned sine die or has adjourned for any period in excess of three calendar days, the Speaker of the House of Representatives and the President pro tempore of the Senate, if they deem it advisable (or if petitioned by at least 30 percent of the membership of their respective Houses) shall jointly request the President to convene Congress in order that it may consider the report and take appropriate action pursuant to this section.

(b) Within sixty calendar days after a report is submitted or is required to be submitted pursuant to section 4(a)(1), whichever is earlier, the President shall terminate any use of Untied States Armed Forces with respect to which such report was submitted (or required to be submitted), unless the Congress

(1) has declared war or has enacted a specific authorization for such use of United States Armed Forces,

(2) has extended by law such sixty-day period, or

(3) is physically unable to meet as a result of an armed attack upon the United States. Such sixty-day period shall be extended for not more than an additional thirty days if the President determines and certifies to the Congress in writing that unavoidable military necessity respecting the safety of United States Armed Forces requires the continued use of such armed forces in the course of bringing about a prompt removal of such forces.

(c) Notwithstanding subsection (b), at any time that United States Armed Forces are engaged in hostilities outside the territory of the United States, its possessions and territories without a declaration of war or specific statutory authorization, such forces shall be removed by the President if the Congress so directs by concurrent resolution.

CONGRESSIONAL PRIORITY PROCEDURES FOR JOINT RESOLUTION OR BILL

SEC. 6.

(a) Any joint resolution or bill introduced pursuant to section 5(b) at least thirty calendar days before the expiration of the sixty-day period specified in such section shall be referred to the Committee on Foreign Affairs of the House of Representatives or the Committee on Foreign Relations of the Senate, as the case may be, and such committee shall report one such joint resolution or bill, together with its recommendations, not later than twenty-four calendar days before the expiration of the sixty-day period specified in such section, unless such House shall otherwise determine by the yeas and nays.

(b) Any joint resolution or bill so reported shall become the pending business of the House in question (in the case of the Senate the time for debate shall be equally divided between the proponents and the opponents), and shall be voted on within three calendar days thereafter, unless such House shall otherwise determine by yeas and nays.

(c) Such a joint resolution or bill passed by one House shall be referred to the committee of the other House named in subsection (a) and shall be reported out not later than fourteen calendar days before the expiration of the sixty-day period specified in section 5(b). The joint resolution or bill so reported shall become the pending business of the House in question and shall be voted on within three calendar days after it has been reported, unless such House shall otherwise determine by yeas and nays.

(d) In the case of any disagreement between the two Houses of Congress with respect to a joint resolution or bill passed by both Houses, conferees shall be promptly appointed and the committee of conference shall make and file a report with respect to such resolution or bill not later than four calendar days before the expiration of the sixty-day period specified in section 5(b). In the event the conferees are unable to agree within 48 hours, they shall report back to their respective Houses in disagreement. Notwithstanding any rule in either House concerning the printing of conference reports in the Record or concerning any delay in the consideration of such reports, such report shall be acted on by both Houses not later than the expiration of such sixty-day period.

CONGRESSIONAL PRIORITY PROCEDURES FOR CONCURRENT RESOLUTION
SEC. 7.

(a) Any concurrent resolution introduced pursuant to section 5(b) at least thirty calendar days before the expiration of the sixty-day period specified in such section shall be referred to the Committee on Foreign Affairs of the House of Representatives or the Committee on Foreign Relations of the Senate, as the case may be, and one such concurrent resolution shall be reported out by such committee together with its recommendations within fifteen calendar days, unless such House shall otherwise determine by the yeas and nays.

(b) Any concurrent resolution so reported shall become the pending business of the House in question (in the case of the Senate the time for debate shall be equally divided between the proponents and the opponents), and shall be voted on within three calendar days thereafter, unless such House shall otherwise determine by yeas and nays.

(c) Such a concurrent resolution passed by one House shall be referred to the committee of the other House named in subsection (a) and shall be reported out by such committee together with its recommendations within fifteen calendar days and shall thereupon become the pending business of such House and shall be voted on within three calendar days after it has been reported, unless such House shall otherwise determine by yeas and nays.

(d) In the case of any disagreement between the two Houses of Congress with respect to a concurrent resolution passed by both Houses, conferees shall be promptly appointed and the committee of conference shall make and file a report with respect to such concurrent resolution within six calendar days after the legislation is referred to the committee of conference. Notwithstanding any rule in either House concerning the printing of conference reports in the Record or concerning any delay in the consideration of such reports, such report shall be acted on by both Houses not later than six calendar days after the conference report is filed. In the event the conferees are unable to agree within 48 hours, they shall report back to their respective Houses in disagreement.

INTERPRETATION OF JOINT RESOLUTION

SEC. 8.

(a) Authority to introduce United States Armed Forces into hostilities or into situations wherein involvement in hostilities is clearly indicated by the circumstances shall not be inferred—

   (1) from any provision of law (whether or not in effect before the date of the enactment of this joint resolution), including any provision contained in any appropriation Act, unless such provision specifically authorizes the introduction of United States Armed Forces into hostilities or into such situations and stating that it is intended to constitute specific statutory authorization within the meaning of this joint resolution; or

   (2) from any treaty heretofore or hereafter ratified unless such treaty is implemented by legislation specifically authorizing the introduction of United States Armed Forces into hostilities or into such situations and stating that it is intended to constitute specific statutory authorization within the meaning of this joint resolution.

(b) Nothing in this joint resolution shall be construed to require any further specific statutory authorization to permit members of United States Armed Forces to participate jointly with members of the armed forces of one or more foreign countries in the headquarters operations of high-level military commands which were established prior to the date of enactment of this joint resolution and pursuant to the United Nations Charter or any treaty ratified by the United States prior to such date.

(c) For purposes of this joint resolution, the term "introduction of United States Armed Forces" includes the assignment of member of such armed forces to command, coordinate, participate in the movement of, or accompany the regular or irregular military forces of any foreign country or government when such military forces are engaged, or there exists an imminent threat that such forces will become engaged, in hostilities.

(d) Nothing in this joint resolution—

    (1) is intended to alter the constitutional authority of the Congress or of the President, or the provision of existing treaties; or

    (2) shall be construed as granting any authority to the President with respect to the introduction of United States Armed Forces into hostilities or into situations wherein involvement in hostilities is clearly indicated by the circumstances which authority he would not have had in the absence of this joint resolution.

SEPARABILITY CLAUSE

SEC. 9.

If any provision of this joint resolution or the application thereof to any person or circumstance is held invalid, the remainder of the joint resolution and the application of such provision to any other person or circumstance shall not be affected thereby.

EFFECTIVE DATE

SEC. 10.

This joint resolution shall take effect on the date of its enactment.

Appendix D
United Nations Security Council Resolution 1441 (2002)

The Security Council,

Recalling all its previous relevant resolutions, in particular its resolutions 661 (1990) of 6 August 1990, 678 (1990) of 29 November 1990, 686 (1991) of 2 March 1991, 687 (1991) of 3 April 1991, 688 (1991) of 5 April 1991, 707 (1991) of 15 August 1991, 715 (1991) of 11 October 1991, 986 (1995) of 14 April 1995, and 1284 (1999) of 17 December 1999, and all the relevant statements of its President,

Recalling also its resolution 1382 (2001) of 29 November 2001 and its intention to implement it fully,

Recognizing the threat Iraq's noncompliance with Council resolutions and proliferation of weapons of mass destruction and long-range missiles poses to international peace and security,

Recalling that its resolution 678 (1990) authorized Member States to use all necessary means to uphold and implement its resolution 660 (1990) of 2 August 1990 and all relevant resolutions subsequent to Resolution 660 (1990) and to restore international peace and security in the area,

Further recalling that its resolution 687 (1991) imposed obligations on Iraq as a necessary step for achievement of its stated objective of restoring international peace and security in the area,

Deploring the fact that Iraq has not provided an accurate, full, final, and complete disclosure, as required by resolution 687 (1991), of all aspects of its programmes to develop weapons of mass destruction and ballistic missiles with a range greater than one hundred and fifty kilometres, and of all holdings of such weapons, their components and production facilities and locations, as well as all other nuclear programmes, including any which it claims are for purposes not related to nuclear-weapons-usable material,

Deploring further that Iraq repeatedly obstructed immediate, unconditional, and unrestricted access to sites designated by the United Nations Special Commission (UNSCOM) and the International Atomic Energy Agency (IAEA), failed to cooperate fully and unconditionally with UNSCOM and IAEA weapons inspectors, as required by resolution 687 (1991), and ultimately ceased all cooperation with UNSCOM and the IAEA in 1998,

Deploring the absence, since December 1998, in Iraq of international monitoring, inspection, and verification, as required by relevant resolutions, of weapons of mass destruction and ballistic missiles, in spite of the Council's repeated demands that Iraq provide immediate, unconditional, and unrestricted access to the United Nations Monitoring, Verification and Inspection Commission (UNMOVIC), established in resolution 1284 (1999) as the successor organization to UNSCOM, and the IAEA, and regretting the consequent prolonging of the crisis in the region and the suffering of the Iraqi people,

Deploring also that the Government of Iraq has failed to comply with its commitments pursuant to resolution 687 (1991) with regard to terrorism, pursuant to resolution 688 (1991) to end repression of its civilian population and to provide access by international humanitarian organizations to all those in need of assistance in Iraq, and pursuant to resolutions 686 (1991), 687 (1991), and 1284 (1999) to return or cooperate in accounting for Kuwaiti and third country nationals wrongfully detained by Iraq, or to return Kuwaiti property wrongfully seized by Iraq,

Recalling that in its resolution 687 (1991) the Council declared that a ceasefire would be based on acceptance by Iraq of the provisions of that resolution, including the obligations on Iraq contained therein,

Determined to ensure full and immediate compliance by Iraq without conditions or restrictions with its obligations under resolution 687 (1991) and other relevant resolutions and recalling that the resolutions of the Council constitute the governing standard of Iraqi compliance,

Recalling that the effective operation of UNMOVIC, as the successor organization to the Special Commission, and the IAEA is essential for the implementation of resolution 687 (1991) and other relevant resolutions,

Noting the letter dated 16 September 2002 from the Minister for Foreign Affairs of Iraq addressed to the Secretary General is a necessary first step toward rectifying Iraq's continued failure to comply with relevant Council resolutions,

Noting further the letter dated 8 October 2002 from the Executive Chairman of UNMOVIC and the Director General of the IAEA to General Al-Saadi of the Government of Iraq laying out the practical arrangements, as a follow-up to their meeting in

Vienna, that are prerequisites for the resumption of inspections in Iraq by UNMOVIC and the IAEA, and expressing the gravest concern at the continued failure by the Government of Iraq to provide confirmation of the arrangements as laid out in that letter,

Reaffirming the commitment of all Member States to the sovereignty and territorial integrity of Iraq, Kuwait, and the neighbouring States,

Commending the Secretary General and members of the League of Arab States and its Secretary General for their efforts in this regard,

Determined to secure full compliance with its decisions,

Acting under Chapter VII of the Charter of the United Nations,

1. *Decides* that Iraq has been and remains in material breach of its obligations under relevant resolutions, including resolution 687 (1991), in particular through Iraq's failure to cooperate with United Nations inspectors and the IAEA, and to complete the actions required under paragraphs 8 to 13 of resolution 687 (1991);

2. *Decides*, while acknowledging paragraph 1 above, to afford Iraq, by this resolution, a final opportunity to comply with its disarmament obligations under relevant resolutions of the Council; and accordingly decides to set up an enhanced inspection regime with the aim of bringing to full and verified completion the disarmament process established by resolution 687 (1991) and subsequent resolutions of the Council;

3. *Decides* that, in order to begin to comply with its disarmament obligations, in addition to submitting the required biannual declarations, the Government of Iraq shall provide to UNMOVIC, the IAEA, and the Council, not later than 30 days from the date of this resolution, a currently accurate, full, and complete declaration of all aspects of its programmes to develop chemical, biological, and nuclear weapons, ballistic missiles, and other delivery systems such as unmanned aerial vehicles and dispersal systems designed for use on aircraft, including any holdings and precise locations of such weapons, components, sub-components, stocks of agents, and related material and equipment, the locations and work of its research, development and production facilities, as well as all other chemical, biological, and nuclear programmes, including any which it claims are for purposes not related to weapon production or material;

4. *Decides* that false statements or omissions in the declarations submitted by Iraq pursuant to this resolution and failure by Iraq at any time to comply with, and cooperate fully in the implementation of, this resolution shall constitute a further material breach of Iraq's obligations and will be reported to the Council for assessment in accordance with paragraphs 11 and 12 below;

5. *Decides* that Iraq shall provide UNMOVIC and the IAEA immediate, unimpeded, unconditional, and unrestricted access to any and all, including underground, areas, facilities, buildings, equipment, records, and means of transport which they wish to inspect, as well as immediate, unimpeded, unrestricted, and private access to all officials and other persons whom UNMOVIC or the IAEA wish to interview in the mode or location of UNMOVIC's or the IAEA's choice pursuant to any aspect of their mandates; further decides that UNMOVIC and the IAEA may at their discretion conduct interviews inside or outside of Iraq, may facilitate the travel of those interviewed and family members outside of Iraq, and that, at the sole discretion of UNMOVIC and the IAEA, such interviews may occur without the presence of observers from the Iraqi government; and instructs UNMOVIC and requests the IAEA to resume inspections no later than 45 days following adoption of this resolution and to update the Council 60 days thereafter;

6. *Endorses* the 8 October 2002 letter from the Executive Chairman of UNMOVIC and the Director General of the IAEA to General Al-Saadi of the Government of Iraq, which is annexed hereto, and decides that the contents of the letter shall be binding upon Iraq;

7. *Decides* further that, in view of the prolonged interruption by Iraq of the presence of UNMOVIC and the IAEA and in order for them to accomplish the tasks set forth in this resolution and all previous relevant resolutions and notwithstanding prior understandings, the Council hereby establishes the following revised or additional authorities, which shall be binding upon Iraq, to facilitate their work in Iraq:

   • UNMOVIC and the IAEA shall determine the composition of their inspection teams and ensure that these teams are composed of the most qualified and experienced experts available;

   • All UNMOVIC and IAEA personnel shall enjoy the privileges and immunities, corresponding to those of experts on mission, provided in the Convention on Privileges and Immunities of the United Nations and the Agreement on the Privileges and Immunities of the IAEA;

   • UNMOVIC and the IAEA shall have unrestricted rights of entry into and out of Iraq, the right to free, unrestricted, and immediate movement to and from inspection sites, and the right to inspect any sites and buildings, including immediate, unimpeded, unconditional, and unrestricted access to Presidential Sites equal to that at other sites, notwithstanding the provisions of resolution 1154 (1998);

   • UNMOVIC and the IAEA shall have the right to be provided by Iraq the names of all personnel currently and formerly associated with Iraq's chemical, biological, nuclear, and ballistic missile programmes and the associated research, development, and production facilities;

- Security of UNMOVIC and IAEA facilities shall be ensured by sufficient UN security guards;

- UNMOVIC and the IAEA shall have the right to declare, for the purposes of freezing a site to be inspected, exclusion zones, including surrounding areas and transit corridors, in which Iraq will suspend ground and aerial movement so that nothing is changed in or taken out of a site being inspected;

- UNMOVIC and the IAEA shall have the free and unrestricted use and landing of fixed- and rotary-winged aircraft, including manned and unmanned reconnaissance vehicles;

- UNMOVIC and the IAEA shall have the right at their sole discretion verifiably to remove, destroy, or render harmless all prohibited weapons, subsystems, components, records, materials, and other related items, and the right to impound or close any facilities or equipment for the production thereof; and

- UNMOVIC and the IAEA shall have the right to free import and use of equipment or materials for inspections and to seize and export any equipment, materials, or documents taken during inspections, without search of UNMOVIC or IAEA personnel or official or personal baggage;

8. *Decides* further that Iraq shall not take or threaten hostile acts directed against any representative or personnel of the United Nations or the IAEA or of any Member State taking action to uphold any Council resolution;

9. *Requests* the Secretary General immediately to notify Iraq of this resolution, which is binding on Iraq; demands that Iraq confirm within seven days of that notification its intention to comply fully with this resolution; and demands further that Iraq cooperate immediately, unconditionally, and actively with UNMOVIC and the IAEA;

10. *Requests* all Member States to give full support to UNMOVIC and the IAEA in the discharge of their mandates, including by providing any information related to prohibited programmes or other aspects of their mandates, including on Iraqi attempts since 1998 to acquire prohibited items, and by *recommending* sites to be inspected, persons to be interviewed, conditions of such interviews, and data to be collected, the results of which shall be reported to the Council by UNMOVIC and the IAEA;

11. *Directs* the Executive Chairman of UNMOVIC and the Director General of the IAEA to report immediately to the Council any interference by Iraq with inspection activities, as well as any failure by Iraq to comply with its disarmament obligations, including its obligations regarding inspections under this resolution;

12. *Decides* to convene immediately upon receipt of a report in accordance with paragraphs 4 or 11 above, in order to consider the situation and the need for full compliance with all of the relevant Council resolutions in order to secure international peace and security;

13. *Recalls*, in that context, that the Council has repeatedly warned Iraq that it will face serious consequences as a result of its continued violations of its obligations;

14. *Decides* to remain seized of the matter.

Appendix E
United Nations Security Council Resolution 1483 (2003)

The Security Council,

Recalling all its previous relevant resolutions,

Reaffirming the sovereignty and territorial integrity of Iraq,

Reaffirming also the importance of the disarmament of Iraqi weapons of mass destruction and of eventual confirmation of the disarmament of Iraq,

Stressing the right of the Iraqi people freely to determine their own political future and control their own natural resources, *welcoming* the commitment of all parties concerned to support the creation of an environment in which they may do so as soon as possible, and *expressing* resolve that the day when Iraqis govern themselves must come quickly,

Encouraging efforts by the people of Iraq to form a representative government based on the rule of law that affords equal rights and justice to all Iraqi citizens without regard to ethnicity, religion, or gender, and, in this connection,
recalls resolution 1325 (2000) of 31 October 2000,

Welcoming the first steps of the Iraqi people in this regard, and noting in this connection the 15 April 2003 Nasiriyah statement and the 28 April 2003 Baghdad statement,

Resolved that the United Nations should play a vital role in humanitarian relief, the reconstruction of Iraq, and the restoration and establishment of national and local institutions for representative governance,

Noting the statement of 12 April 2003 by the Ministers of Finance and Central Bank Governors of the Group of Seven Industrialized Nations in which the members recognized the need for a multilateral effort to help rebuild and develop Iraq and for the need for assistance from the International Monetary Fund and the World Bank in these efforts,

Welcoming also the resumption of humanitarian assistance and the continuing efforts of the Secretary-General and the specialized agencies to provide food and medicine to the people of Iraq,

Welcoming the appointment by the Secretary-General of his Special Advisor on Iraq,

Affirming the need for accountability for crimes and atrocities committed by the previous Iraqi regime,

Stressing the need for respect for the archaeological, historical, cultural, and religious sites, museums, libraries, and monuments,

Noting the letter of 8 May 2003 from the Permanent Representatives of the United States of America and the United Kingdom of Great Britain and Northern Ireland to the President of the Security Council (S/2003/538) and recognizing the specific authorities, responsibilities, and obligations under applicable international law of these states as occupying powers under unified command (the "Authority"),

Noting further that other States that are not occupying powers are working now or in the future may work under the Authority,

Welcoming further the willingness of Member States to contribute to stability and security in Iraq by contributing personnel, equipment, and other resources under the Authority,

Concerned that many Kuwaitis and Third-State Nationals still are not accounted for since 2 August 1990,

Determining that the situation in Iraq, although improved, continues to constitute a threat to international peace and security,

Acting under Chapter VII of the Charter of the United Nations,

1. *Appeals* to Member States and concerned organizations to assist the people of Iraq in their efforts to reform their institutions and rebuild their country, and to contribute to conditions of stability and security in Iraq in accordance with this resolution;

2. *Calls upon* all Member States in a position to do so to respond immediately to the humanitarian appeals of the United Nations and other international organizations for Iraq and to help meet the humanitarian and other needs of the Iraqi people by providing food, medical supplies, and resources necessary for reconstruction and rehabilitation of Iraq's economic infrastructure;

3. *Appeals* to Member States to deny safe haven to those members of the previous Iraqi regime who are alleged to be responsible for crimes and atrocities and to support actions to bring them to justice;

4. *Calls upon* the Authority, consistent with the Charter of the United Nations and other relevant international law, to promote the welfare of the Iraqi people through the effective administration of the territory, including in particular working towards the restoration of conditions of security and stability and the creation of conditions in which the Iraqi people can freely determine their own political future;

5. *Calls upon* all concerned to comply fully with their obligations under international law including in particular the Geneva Conventions of 1949 and the Hague Regulations of 1907;

...

8. *Requests* the Security-General to appoint a Special Representative for Iraq whose independent responsibilities shall involve reporting regularly to the Council on his activities under this resolution, coordinating activities of the United Nations in post-conflict processes in Iraq, coordinating among the United Nations in post-conflict processes in Iraq, coordinating United Nations and international agencies engaged in humanitarian assistance and reconstruction activities in Iraq, and, in coordination with the Authority, assisting the people of Iraq through:

   (a) coordinating humanitarian and reconstruction and reconstruction assistance by United Nations agencies and between United Nations agencies and non-governmental organizations;

   (b) promoting the safe, orderly, and voluntary return of refugees and displaced persons;

   (c) working intensively with the Authority, the people of Iraq, and others concerned to advance efforts to restore and establish national and local institutions for representative governance, including by working together to facilitate a process leading to an internationally recognized, representative government in Iraq;

   (d) facilitating the reconstruction of key infrastructure, in cooperation with other international organizations;

   (e) promoting economic reconstruction and the conditions for sustainable development, including through coordination with national and regional organizations, as appropriate, civil society, donors, and the international financial institutions;

   (f) encouraging international efforts to contribute to basic civilian administration functions;

   (g) promoting the protection of human rights;

(h) encouraging international efforts to rebuild the capacity of the Iraqi civilian police force; and

(i) encouraging international efforts to promote legal and judicial reform;

9. *Supports* the formation, by the people of Iraq with the help of the Authority and working with the Special Representative, of an Iraqi interim administration as a transitional administration run by Iraqis, until an internationally recognized, representative government is established by the people of Iraq and assumes the responsibilities of the Authority;

...

16. *Requests* also that the Secretary-General, in coordination with the Authority, continue the exercise of his responsibilities under Security Council resolution 1472 (2003) of 28 March 2003 and 1476 (2003) of 24 April 2003, for a period of six months following the adoption of this resolution, and terminate within this time period, in the most cost effective manner, the ongoing operations of the "Oil-for-Food" Programme (the "Programme"), both at headquarters level and in the field, transferring responsibility for the administration of any remaining activity under the Programme to the Authority, including by taking the following necessary measures:

(a) to facilitate as soon as possible the shipment and authenticated delivery of priority civilian goods as identified by the Secretary-General and representatives designated by him, in coordination with the Authority and the Iraqi interim administration, under approved and funded contracts previously concluded by the previous Government of Iraq, for the humanitarian relief of the people of Iraq, including, as necessary, negotiating adjustments in the terms or conditions of these contracts and respective letters of credit as set forth in paragraph 4 (d) of resolution 1472 (2003);

(b) to review, in light of changed circumstances, in coordination with the Authority and the Iraqi interim administration, the relative utility of each approved and funded contract with a view to determining whether such contracts contain items required to meet the needs of the people of Iraq both now and during reconstruction, and to postpone action on those contracts determined to be of questionable utility and the respective letters of credit until an internationally recognized, representative government of Iraq is in a position to make its own determination as to whether such contracts shall be fulfilled;

(c) to provide the Security Council within 21 days following the adoption of this resolution, for the Security Council's review and consideration, an estimated operating budget based on funds already set aside in the account established pursuant to paragraph 8 (d) of resolution 986 (1995) of 14 April 1995, identifying:

(i) all known and projected costs to the United Nations required to ensure the continued functioning of the activities associated with implementation of the present resolution, including operating and administrative expenses associated with the relevant United Nations agencies and programmes responsible for the implementation of the Programme both at Headquarters and in the field;

(ii) all known and projected costs associated with termination of the Programme;

(iii) all known and projected costs associated with restoring Government of Iraq funds that were provided by Member States to the Secretary-General as requested in paragraph 1 of resolution 778 (1992); and

(iv) all known and projected costs associated with the Special Representative and the qualified representative of the Secretary-General identified to serve on the International Advisory and Monitoring Board, for the six month time period defined above, following which these costs shall be borne by the United Nations;

(d) to consolidate into a single fund the accounts established pursuant to paragraphs 8 (a) and 8 (b) of resolution 986 (1995);

(e) to fulfil all remaining obligations related to the termination of the Programme, including negotiating, in the most cost effective manner, any necessary settlement payments which shall be made from the escrow accounts established pursuant to paragraphs 8 (a) and 8 (b) of resolution 986 (1995), with those parties that previously have entered into contractual obligations with the Secretary-General under the Programme, and to determine, in coordination with the Authority and the Iraqi interim administration, the future status of contracts undertaken by the United Nations and related United Nations agencies under the accounts established pursuant to paragraphs 8 (b) and 8 (d) of resolution 986 (1995);

(f) to provide the Security Council, 30 days prior to the termination of the Programme, with a comprehensive strategy developed in close coordination with the Authority and the Iraqi interim administration that would lead to the delivery of all relevant documentation and the transfer of all operational responsibility of the Programme to the Authority;

...

27. *Decides* to remain seized of this matter.

Appendix F
United Nations Security Council Resolution 1546 (2004)

The Security Council,

Welcoming the beginning of a new phase in Iraq's transition to a democratically elected government, and *looking forward* to the end of the occupation and the assumption of full responsibility and authority by a fully sovereign and independent Interim Government of Iraq by 30 June 2004,

Recalling all of its previous relevant resolutions on Iraq,

Reaffirming the independence, sovereignty, unity, and territorial integrity of Iraq,

Reaffirming also the right of the Iraqi people freely to determine their own political future and control their own natural resources,

Recognizing the importance of international support, particularly that of countries in the region, Iraq's neighbours, and regional organizations, for the people of Iraq in their efforts to achieve security and prosperity, and noting that the successful implementation of this resolution will contribute to regional stability,

Welcoming the efforts of the Special Adviser to the Secretary-General to assist the people of Iraq in achieving the formation of the Interim Government of Iraq, as set out in the letter of the Secretary-General of 7 June 2004 (S/2004/461),

Taking note of the dissolution of the Governing Council of Iraq, ands welcoming the progress made in implementing the arrangements for Iraq's political transition referred to in resolution 1511 (2003) of 16 October 2003,

Welcoming the commitment of the Interim Government of Iraq to work towards a federal, democratic, pluralist, and unified Iraq, in which there is full respect for political and human rights,

Stressing the need for all parties to respect and protect Iraq's archaeological, historical, cultural, and religious heritage,

Affirming the importance of the rule of law, national reconciliation, respect for human rights including the rights of women, fundamental freedoms, and democracy including free and fair elections,

Recalling the establishment of the United Nations Assistance Mission for Iraq (UNAMI) on 14 August 2003, and affirming that the United Nations should play a leading role in assisting the Iraqi people and government in the formation of institutions for representative government,

Recognizing that international support for restoration of stability and security is essential to the well-being of the people of Iraq as well as to the ability of all concerned to carry out their work on behalf of the people of Iraq, and *welcoming* Member State contributions in this regard under resolution 1483 (2003) of 22 May 2003 and resolution 1511 (2003),

Recalling the report provided by the United States to the Security Council on 16 April 2004 on the efforts and progress made by the multinational force,

Recognizing the request conveyed in the letter of 5 June 2004 from the Prime Minister of the Interim Government of Iraq to the President of the Council, which is annexed to this resolution, to retain the presence of the multinational force,

Recognizing also the importance of the consent of the sovereign Government of Iraq for the presence of the multinational force and of close coordination between the multinational force and that government,

Welcoming the willingness of the multinational force to continue efforts to contribute to the maintenance of security and stability in Iraq in support of the political transition, especially for up coming elections, and to provide security for the United Nations presence in Iraq, as described in the letter of 5 June 2004 from the United States Secretary of State to the President of the Council, which is annexed to this resolution,

Noting the commitment of all forces promoting the maintenance of security and stability in Iraq to act in accordance with international law, including obligations under international humanitarian law, and to cooperate with relevant international organizations,

Affirming the importance of international assistance in reconstruction and development of the Iraqi economy,

Recognizing the benefits to Iraq of the immunities and privileges enjoyed by Iraqi oil revenues and by the Development Fund for Iraq, and noting the importance of providing for continued disbursements of this fund by the Interim Government of Iraq and its successors upon dissolution of the Coalition Provisional Authority,

Determining that the situation in Iraq continues to constitute a threat to international peace and security,

Acting under Chapter VII of the Charter of the United Nations,

1. *Endorses* the formation of a sovereign Interim Government of Iraq, as presented on 1 June 2004, which will assume fill responsibility and authority by 30 June 2004 for governing Iraq while refraining from taking any action actions affecting Iraq's destiny beyond the limited interim period until an elected Transitional Government of Iraq assumes office as envisaged in paragraph four below;

2. *Welcomes* that, also by 30 June 2004, the occupation will end and the Coalition Provisional Authority will cease to exist, and that Iraq will reassert its full sovereignty;

3. Reaffirms the right of the Iraqi people freely to determine their own political future and to exercise full authority and control over their financial and natural resources;

4. *Endorses* the proposed timetable for Iraq's political transition to democratic government including:

    (a) formation of the sovereign Interim Government of Iraq that will assume governing responsibility and authority by 30 June 2004;

    (b) convening of a national conference reflecting the diversity of Iraqi society; and

    (c) holding of direct democratic elections by 31 December 2004 if possible, and in no case later than 31 January 2005, to a Transitional National Assembly, which will, inter alia, have responsibility for forming a Transitional Government of Iraq and drafting a permanent constitution for Iraq leading to a constitutionally elected government by 31 December 2005;

5. *Invites* the Government of Iraq to consider how the convening of an international meeting could support the above process, and *notes* that it would welcome such a meeting to support the Iraqi political transition and Iraqi recovery, to the benefit of the Iraqi people and in the interest of stability in the region;

6. *Calls on* all Iraqis to implement these arrangements peaceably and in full, and on all States and relevant organizations to support such implementation;

7. *Decides* that in implementing, as circumstances permit, their mandate to assist the Iraqi people and government, the Special Representative of the Secretary-

General and the United Nations Assistance Mission for Iraq (UNAMI), as requested by the Government of Iraq, shall:

(a) play a leading role to:

(i) assist in convening, during the month of July 2004, of a national conference to select a Consultative Council;

(ii) advise and support the Independent Electoral Commission of Iraq, as well as the Interim Government of Iraq and the Transitional National Assembly, on the process for holding elections;

(iii) promote national dialogue and consensus-building on the drafting of a national constitution by the people of Iraq;

(b) and also:

(i) advise the Government of Iraq in the development of effective civil and social services;

(ii) contribute to the coordination and delivery of reconstruction, development, and humanitarian assistance;

(iii) promote the protection of human rights, national reconciliation, and judicial and legal reform in order to strengthen the rule of law in Iraq; and

(iv) advise and assist the Government of Iraq on initial planning for the eventual conduct of a comprehensive census;

8. *Welcomes* ongoing efforts by the incoming Interim Government of Iraq to develop Iraqi security forces including the Iraqi armed forces (hereinafter referred to as "Iraqi security forces"), operating under the authority of the Interim Government of Iraq and its successors, which will progressively play a greater role and ultimately assume full responsibility for the maintenance of security and stability in Iraq;

9. *Notes* that the presence of the multinational force in Iraq is at the request of the incoming Interim Government of Iraq and therefore reaffirms the authorization for the multinational force under unified command established under resolution 1511 (2003), having regard to the letters annexed to this resolution;

10. *Decides* that the multinational force shall have the authority to take all necessary measures to contribute to the maintenance of security and stability in accordance with the letters annexed to this resolution expressing, inter alia, the Iraqi request for the continued presence of the multinational force and setting out its tasks, including by preventing and deterring terrorism, so that, inter alia, the United Nations can fulfil its role in assisting the Iraqi people as outlined in paragraph seven above and the Iraqi people can implement freely and without intimidation the timetable and programme for the political process and benefit from reconstruction and rehabilitation activities;

11. *Welcomes*, in this regard, the letters annexed to this resolution stating, inter alia, that arrangements are being put in place to establish a security partnership be-

tween the sovereign Government of Iraq and the multinational force and to ensure the coordination between the two, and notes also in this regard that Iraqi security forces are responsible to appropriate Iraqi ministers, that the Government of Iraq has authority to commit Iraqi security forces to the multinational force to engage in operations with it, and that the security structures described in the letters will serve as the fora for the Government of Iraq and the multinational force to reach agreement on the full range of fundamental security and policy issues, including policy on sensitive offensive operations, and will ensure full partnership between Iraqi security forces and the multinational force, through close coordination and consultation;

12. *Decides* further that the mandate for the multinational force shall be reviewed at the request of the Government of Iraq or twelve months from the date of this resolution, and that this mandate shall expire upon the completion of the political process set out in paragraph four above, and declares that it will terminate this mandate earlier if requested by the Government of Iraq;

13. *Notes* the intention, set out in the annexed letter from the United States Secretary of State, to create a distinct entity under unified command of the multinational force with a dedicated mission to provide security for the United Nations presence in Iraq, *recognizes* that the implementation of measures to provide security for staff members of the United Nations system working in Iraq would require significant resources, and *calls upon* Member States and relevant organizations to provide such resources, including contributions to that entity;

14. *Recognizes* that the multinational force will also assist in building the capability of the Iraqi security forces and instructions, through a programme of recruitment, training, equipping, mentoring, and monitoring;

15. *Requests* Member States and international and regional organizations to contribute assistance to the multinational force, including military forces, as agreed with the Government of Iraq, to help meet the needs of the Iraqi people for security and stability, humanitarian and reconstruction assistance, and to support the efforts of UNAMI;

16. *Emphasizes* the importance of developing effective Iraqi police, border enforcement, and the Facilities Protection Service, under the control of the Interior Ministry of Iraq, and, in the case of the Facilities Protection Service, other Iraqi ministries, for the maintenance of law, order, and security, including combating terrorism, and *requests* Member States and international organizations to assist the Government of Iraq in building the capability of these Iraqi institutions;

...

32. *Decides* to remain actively seized of the matter.

Appendix G
The United States Constitution
(Selected Provisions)

We the People of the United States, in Order to form a more perfect Union, establish Justice, insure domestic Tranquility, provide for the common defence, promote the general Welfare, and secure the Blessings of Liberty to ourselves and our Posterity, do ordain and establish this Constitution for the United States of America.

Article I

Section 1

All legislative Powers herein granted shall be vested in a Congress of the United States, which shall consist of a Senate and House of Representatives.

...

Section 8

Clause 1: The Congress shall have Power To lay and collect Taxes, Duties, Imposts and Excises, to pay the Debts and provide for the common Defence and general Welfare of the United States; but all Duties, Imposts and Excises shall be uniform throughout the United States;

Clause 2: To borrow Money on the credit of the United States;

Clause 3: To regulate Commerce with foreign Nations, and among the several States, and with the Indian Tribes;

Clause 4: To establish an uniform Rule of Naturalization, and uniform Laws on the subject of Bankruptcies throughout the United States;

Clause 5: To coin Money, regulate the Value thereof, and of foreign Coin, and fix the Standard of Weights and Measures;

Clause 6: To provide for the Punishment of counterfeiting the Securities and current Coin of the United States;

Clause 7: To establish Post Offices and post Roads;

Clause 8: To promote the Progress of Science and useful Arts, by securing for limited Times to Authors and Inventors the exclusive Right to their respective Writings and Discoveries;

Clause 9: To constitute Tribunals inferior to the supreme Court;

Clause 10: To define and punish Piracies and Felonies committed on the high Seas, and Offences against the Law of Nations;

Clause 11: To declare War, grant Letters of Marque and Reprisal, and make Rules concerning Captures on Land and Water;

Clause 12: To raise and support Armies, but no Appropriation of Money to that Use shall be for a longer Term than two Years;

Clause 13: To provide and maintain a Navy;

Clause 14: To make Rules for the Government and Regulation of the land and naval Forces;

Clause 15: To provide for calling forth the Militia to execute the Laws of the Union, suppress Insurrections and repel Invasions;

Clause 16: To provide for organizing, arming, and disciplining, the Militia, and for governing such Part of them as may be employed in the Service of the United States, reserving to the States respectively, the Appointment of the Officers, and the Authority of training the Militia according to the discipline prescribed by Congress;

Clause 17: To exercise exclusive Legislation in all Cases whatsoever, over such District (not exceeding ten Miles square) as may, by Cession of particular States, and the Acceptance of Congress, become the Seat of the Government of the United States, and to exercise like Authority over all Places purchased by the Consent of the Legislature of the State in which the Same shall be, for the Erection of Forts, Magazines, Arsenals, Dock-Yards, and other needful Buildings;—And

Clause 18: To make all Laws which shall be necessary and proper for carrying into Execution the foregoing Powers, and all other Powers vested by this Constitution in the Government of the United States, or in any Department or Officer thereof.

...

Article II

Section 1

Clause 1: The executive Power shall be vested in a President of the United States of America. He shall hold his Office during the Term of four Years, and, together with the Vice President, chosen for the same Term, be elected, as follows

...

Section 2

Clause 1: The President shall be Commander in Chief of the Army and Navy of the United States, and of the Militia of the several States, when called into the actual Service of the United States; he may require the Opinion, in writing, of the principal

Officer in each of the executive Departments, upon any Subject relating to the Duties of their respective Offices, and he shall have Power to grant Reprieves and Pardons for Offences against the United States, except in Cases of Impeachment.

Clause 2: He shall have Power, by and with the Advice and Consent of the Senate, to make Treaties, provided two thirds of the Senators present concur; and he shall nominate, and by and with the Advice and Consent of the Senate, shall appoint Ambassadors, other public Ministers and Consuls, Judges of the supreme Court, and all other Officers of the United States, whose Appointments are not herein otherwise provided for, and which shall be established by Law: but the Congress may by Law vest the Appointment of such inferior Officers, as they think proper, in the President alone, in the Courts of Law, or in the Heads of Departments.

...

GO. WASHINGTON—President and deputy from Virginia

[Signed also by the deputies of twelve States.]

Appendix H
Universal Declaration of Human Rights

PREAMBLE

Whereas recognition of the inherent dignity and of the equal and inalienable rights of all members of the human family is the foundation of freedom, justice and peace in the world,

Whereas disregard and contempt for human rights have resulted in barbarous acts which have outraged the conscience of mankind, and the advent of a world in which human beings shall enjoy freedom of speech and belief and freedom from fear and want has been proclaimed as the highest aspiration of the common people,

Whereas it is essential, if man is not to be compelled to have recourse, as a last resort, to rebellion against tyranny and oppression, that human rights should be protected by the rule of law,

Whereas it is essential to promote the development of friendly relations between nations,

Whereas the peoples of the United Nations have in the Charter reaffirmed their faith in fundamental human rights, in the dignity and worth of the human person and in the equal rights of men and women and have determined to promote social progress and better standards of life in larger freedom,

Whereas Member States have pledged themselves to achieve, in cooperation with the United Nations, the promotion of universal respect for and observance of human rights and fundamental freedoms,

Whereas a common understanding of these rights and freedoms is of the greatest importance for the full realization of this pledge,

Now, therefore,

The General Assembly,

Proclaims this Universal Declaration of Human Rights as a common standard of achievement for all peoples and all nations, to the end that every individual and every organ of society, keeping this Declaration constantly in mind, shall strive by teaching and education to promote respect for these rights and freedoms and by progressive measures, national and international, to secure their universal and effective recognition and observance, both among the peoples of Member States themselves and among the peoples of territories under their jurisdiction.

Article 1

All human beings are born free and equal in dignity and rights. They are endowed with reason and conscience and should act towards one another in a spirit of brotherhood.

Article 2

Everyone is entitled to all the rights and freedoms set forth in this Declaration, without distinction of any kind, such as race, colour, sex, language, religion, political or other opinion, national or social origin, property, birth or other status.
Furthermore, no distinction shall be made on the basis of the political, jurisdictional or international status of the country or territory to which a person belongs, whether it be independent, trust, non-self-governing or under any other limitation of sovereignty.

Article 3

Everyone has the right to life, liberty and security of person.

Article 4

No one shall be held in slavery or servitude; slavery and the slave trade shall be prohibited in all their forms.

Article 5

No one shall be subjected to torture or to cruel, inhuman or degrading treatment or punishment.

Article 6

Everyone has the right to recognition everywhere as a person before the law.

Article 7

All are equal before the law and are entitled without any discrimination to equal protection of the law. All are entitled to equal protection against any discrimination in violation of this Declaration and against any incitement to such discrimination.

Article 8

Everyone has the right to an effective remedy by the competent national tribunals for acts violating the fundamental rights granted him by the constitution or by law.

Article 9

No one shall be subjected to arbitrary arrest, detention or exile.

Article 10

Everyone is entitled in full equality to a fair and public hearing by an independent and impartial tribunal, in the determination of his rights and obligations and of any criminal charge against him.

Article 11

1. Everyone charged with a penal offence has the right to be presumed innocent until proved guilty according to law in a public trial at which he has had all the guarantees necessary for his defence.
2. No one shall be held guilty of any penal offence on account of any act or omission which did not constitute a penal offence, under national or international law, at the time when it was committed. Nor shall a heavier penalty be imposed than the one that was applicable at the time the penal offence was committed.

Article 12

No one shall be subjected to arbitrary interference with his privacy, family, home or correspondence, nor to attacks upon his honour and reputation. Everyone has the right to the protection of the law against such interference or attacks.

Article 13

1. Everyone has the right to freedom of movement and residence within the borders of each State.
2. Everyone has the right to leave any country, including his own, and to return to his country.

Article 14

1. Everyone has the right to seek and to enjoy in other countries asylum from persecution.
2. This right may not be invoked in the case of prosecutions genuinely arising from non-political crimes or from acts contrary to the purposes and principles of the United Nations.

Article 15

1. Everyone has the right to a nationality.
2. No one shall be arbitrarily deprived of his nationality nor denied the right to change his nationality.

Article 16

1. Men and women of full age, without any limitation due to race, nationality or religion, have the right to marry and to found a family. They are entitled to equal rights as to marriage, during marriage and at its dissolution.
2. Marriage shall be entered into only with the free and full consent of the intending spouses.
3. The family is the natural and fundamental group unit of society and is entitled to protection by society and the State.

Article 17

1. Everyone has the right to own property alone as well as in association with others.
2. No one shall be arbitrarily deprived of his property.

Article 18

Everyone has the right to freedom of thought, conscience and religion; this right includes freedom to change his religion or belief, and freedom, either alone or in community with others and in public or private, to manifest his religion or belief in teaching, practice, worship and observance.

Article 19

Everyone has the right to freedom of opinion and expression; this right includes freedom to hold opinions without interference and to seek, receive and impart information and ideas through any media and regardless of frontiers.

Article 20

1. Everyone has the right to freedom of peaceful assembly and association.
2. No one may be compelled to belong to an association.

Article 21

1. Everyone has the right to take part in the government of his country, directly or through freely chosen representatives.
2. Everyone has the right to equal access to public service in his country.

3. The will of the people shall be the basis of the authority of government; this will shall be expressed in periodic and genuine elections which shall be by universal and equal suffrage and shall be held by secret vote or by equivalent free voting procedures.

Article 22

Everyone, as a member of society, has the right to social security and is entitled to realization, through national effort and international co-operation and in accordance with the organization and resources of each State, of the economic, social and cultural rights indispensable for his dignity and the free development of his personality.

Article 23

1. Everyone has the right to work, to free choice of employment, to just and favourable conditions of work and to protection against unemployment.
2. Everyone, without any discrimination, has the right to equal pay for equal work.
3. Everyone who works has the right to just and favourable remuneration ensuring for himself and his family an existence worthy of human dignity, and supplemented, if necessary, by other means of social protection.
4. Everyone has the right to form and to join trade unions for the protection of his interests.

Article 24

Everyone has the right to rest and leisure, including reasonable limitation of working hours and periodic holidays with pay.

Article 25

1. Everyone has the right to a standard of living adequate for the health and well-being of himself and of his family, including food, clothing, housing and medical care and necessary social services, and the right to security in the event of unemployment, sickness, disability, widowhood, old age or other lack of livelihood in circumstances beyond his control.
2. Motherhood and childhood are entitled to special care and assistance. All children, whether born in or out of wedlock, shall enjoy the same social protection.

Article 26

1. Everyone has the right to education. Education shall be free, at least in the elementary and fundamental stages. Elementary education shall be compulsory.

Technical and professional education shall be made generally available and higher education shall be equally accessible to all on the basis of merit.

2. Education shall be directed to the full development of the human personality and to the strengthening of respect for human rights and fundamental freedoms. It shall promote understanding, tolerance and friendship among all nations, racial or religious groups, and shall further the activities of the United Nations for the maintenance of peace.

3. Parents have a prior right to choose the kind of education that shall be given to their children.

Article 27

1. Everyone has the right freely to participate in the cultural life of the community, to enjoy the arts and to share in scientific advancement and its benefits.

2. Everyone has the right to the protection of the moral and material interests resulting from any scientific, literary or artistic production of which he is the author.

Article 28

Everyone is entitled to a social and international order in which the rights and freedoms set forth in this Declaration can be fully realized.

Article 29

1. Everyone has duties to the community in which alone the free and full development of his personality is possible.

2. In the exercise of his rights and freedoms, everyone shall be subject only to such limitations as are determined by law solely for the purpose of securing due recognition and respect for the rights and freedoms of others and of meeting the just requirements of morality, public order and the general welfare in a democratic society.

3. These rights and freedoms may in no case be exercised contrary to the purposes and principles of the United Nations.

Article 30

Nothing in this Declaration may be interpreted as implying for any State, group or person any right to engage in any activity or to perform any act aimed at the destruction of any of the rights and freedoms set forth herein.

Appendix I
International Covenant on Civil and Political Rights

Adopted and opened for signature, ratification and accession by General Assembly resolution 2200A (XXI) of 16 December 1966.

Entry into force 23 March 1976, in accordance with Article 49

PREAMBLE

The States Parties to the present Covenant,

Considering that, in accordance with the principles proclaimed in the Charter of the United Nations, recognition of the inherent dignity and of the equal and inalienable rights of all members of the human family is the foundation of freedom, justice and peace in the world,

Recognizing that these rights derive from the inherent dignity of the human person,

Recognizing that, in accordance with the Universal Declaration of Human Rights, the ideal of free human beings enjoying civil and political freedom and freedom from fear and want can only be achieved if conditions are created whereby everyone may enjoy his civil and political rights, as well as his economic, social and cultural rights,

Considering the obligation of States under the Charter of the United Nations to promote universal respect for, and observance of, human rights and freedoms,

Realizing that the individual, having duties to other individuals and to the community to which he belongs, is under a responsibility to strive for the promotion and observance of the rights recognized in the present Covenant,

Agree upon the following articles:

Part I

Article 1

1. All peoples have the right of self-determination. By virtue of that right they freely determine their political status and freely pursue their economic, social and cultural development.

2. All peoples may, for their own ends, freely dispose of their natural wealth and resources without prejudice to any obligations arising out of international economic co-operation, based upon the principle of mutual benefit, and international law. In no case may a people be deprived of its own means of subsistence.

3. The States Parties to the present Covenant, including those having responsibility for the administration of Non-Self-Governing and Trust Territories, shall promote the realization of the right of self-determination, and shall respect that right, in conformity with the provisions of the Charter of the United Nations.

Part II

Article 2

1. Each State Party to the present Covenant undertakes to respect and to ensure to all individuals within its territory and subject to its jurisdiction the rights recognized in the present Covenant, without distinction of any kind, such as race, colour, sex, language, religion, political or other opinion, national or social origin, property, birth or other status.

2. Where not already provided for by existing legislative or other measures, each State Party to the present Covenant undertakes to take the necessary steps, in accordance with its constitutional processes and with the provisions of the present Covenant, to adopt such laws or other measures as may be necessary to give effect to the rights recognized in the present Covenant.

3. Each State Party to the present Covenant undertakes:

   (a) To ensure that any person whose rights or freedoms as herein recognized are violated shall have an effective remedy, notwithstanding that the violation has been committed by persons acting in an official capacity;

   (b) To ensure that any person claiming such a remedy shall have his right thereto determined by competent judicial, administrative or legislative authorities, or by any other competent authority provided for by the legal system of the State, and to develop the possibilities of judicial remedy;

   (c) To ensure that the competent authorities shall enforce such remedies when granted.

Article 3

The States Parties to the present Covenant undertake to ensure the equal right of men and women to the enjoyment of all civil and political rights set forth in the present Covenant.

Article 4

1. In time of public emergency which threatens the life of the nation and the existence of which is officially proclaimed, the States Parties to the present Covenant may take measures derogating from their obligations under the present Covenant to the extent strictly required by the exigencies of the situation, provided that such measures are not inconsistent with their other obligations under international law and do not involve discrimination solely on the ground of race, colour, sex, language, religion or social origin.

2. No derogation from articles 6, 7, 8 (paragraphs I and 2), 11, 15, 16 and 18 may be made under this provision.

3. Any State Party to the present Covenant availing itself of the right of derogation shall immediately inform the other States Parties to the present Covenant, through the intermediary of the Secretary-General of the United Nations, of the provisions from which it has derogated and of the reasons by which it was actuated. A further communication shall be made, through the same intermediary, on the date on which it terminates such derogation.

Article 5

1. Nothing in the present Covenant may be interpreted as implying for any State, group or person any right to engage in any activity or perform any act aimed at the destruction of any of the rights and freedoms recognized herein or at their limitation to a greater extent than is provided for in the present Covenant.

2. There shall be no restriction upon or derogation from any of the fundamental human rights recognized or existing in any State Party to the present Covenant pursuant to law, conventions, regulations or custom on the pretext that the present Covenant does not recognize such rights or that it recognizes them to a lesser extent.

Part III

Article 6

1. Every human being has the inherent right to life. This right shall be protected by law. No one shall be arbitrarily deprived of his life.

2. In countries which have not abolished the death penalty, sentence of death may be imposed only for the most serious crimes in accordance with the law in force at the time of the commission of the crime and not contrary to the provisions of the present Covenant and to the Convention on the Prevention and Punishment of the Crime of Genocide. This penalty can only be carried out pursuant to a final judgement rendered by a competent court.

3. When deprivation of life constitutes the crime of genocide, it is understood that nothing in this article shall authorize any State Party to the present Covenant to derogate in any way from any obligation assumed under the provisions of the Convention on the Prevention and Punishment of the Crime of Genocide.

4. Anyone sentenced to death shall have the right to seek pardon or commutation of the sentence. Amnesty, pardon or commutation of the sentence of death may be granted in all cases.

5. Sentence of death shall not be imposed for crimes committed by persons below eighteen years of age and shall not be carried out on pregnant women.

6. Nothing in this article shall be invoked to delay or to prevent the abolition of capital punishment by any State Party to the present Covenant.

Article 7

No one shall be subjected to torture or to cruel, inhuman or degrading treatment or punishment. In particular, no one shall be subjected without his free consent to medical or scientific experimentation.

Article 8

1. No one shall be held in slavery; slavery and the slave-trade in all their forms shall be prohibited.

2. No one shall be held in servitude.

3. (a) No one shall be required to perform forced or compulsory labour;

(b) Paragraph 3(a) shall not be held to preclude, in countries where imprisonment with hard labour may be imposed as a punishment for a crime, the performance of hard labour in pursuance of a sentence to such punishment by a competent court;

(c) For the purpose of this paragraph the term "forced or compulsory labour" shall not include:

(i) Any work or service, not referred to in subparagraph (b), normally required of a person who is under detention in consequence of a lawful order of a court, or of a person during conditional release from such detention;

(ii) Any service of a military character and, in countries where conscientious objection is recognized, any national service required by law of conscientious objectors;

(iii) Any service exacted in cases of emergency or calamity threatening the life or well-being of the community;

(iv) Any work or service which forms part of normal civil obligations.

Article 9

1. Everyone has the right to liberty and security of person. No one shall be subjected to arbitrary arrest or detention. No one shall be deprived of his liberty except on such grounds and in accordance with such procedure as are established by law.

2. Anyone who is arrested shall be informed, at the time of arrest, of the reasons for his arrest and shall be promptly informed of any charges against him.

3. Anyone arrested or detained on a criminal charge shall be brought promptly before a judge or other officer authorized by law to exercise judicial power and shall be entitled to trial within a reasonable time or to release. It shall not be the general rule that persons awaiting trial shall be detained in custody, but release may be subject to guarantees to appear for trial, at any other stage of the judicial proceedings, and, should occasion arise, for execution of the judgement.

4. Anyone who is deprived of his liberty by arrest or detention shall be entitled to take proceedings before a court, in order that court may decide without delay on the lawfulness of his detention and order his release if the detention is not lawful.

5. Anyone who has been the victim of unlawful arrest or detention shall have an enforceable right to compensation.

Article 10

1. All persons deprived of their liberty shall be treated with humanity and with respect for the inherent dignity of the human person.

2. (a) Accused persons shall, save in exceptional circumstances, be segregated from convicted persons and shall be subject to separate treatment appropriate to their status as unconvicted persons;

(b) Accused juvenile persons shall be separated from adults and brought as speedily as possible for adjudication.

3. The penitentiary system shall comprise treatment of prisoners the essential aim of which shall be their reformation and social rehabilitation. Juvenile offenders shall be segregated from adults and be accorded treatment appropriate to their age and legal status.

Article 11

No one shall be imprisoned merely on the ground of inability to fulfil a contractual obligation.

Article 12

1. Everyone lawfully within the territory of a State shall, within that territory, have the right to liberty of movement and freedom to choose his residence.
2. Everyone shall be free to leave any country, including his own.
3. The above-mentioned rights shall not be subject to any restrictions except those which are provided by law, are necessary to protect national security, public order (ordre public), public health or morals or the rights and freedoms of others, and are consistent with the other rights recognized in the present Covenant.
4. No one shall be arbitrarily deprived of the right to enter his own country.

Article 13

An alien lawfully in the territory of a State Party to the present Covenant may be expelled therefrom only in pursuance of a decision reached in accordance with law and shall, except where compelling reasons of national security otherwise require, be allowed to submit the reasons against his expulsion and to have his case reviewed by, and be represented for the purpose before, the competent authority or a person or persons especially designated by the competent authority.

Article 14

1. All persons shall be equal before the courts and tribunals. In the determination of any criminal charge against him, or of his rights and obligations in a suit at law, everyone shall be entitled to a fair and public hearing by a competent, independent and impartial tribunal established by law. The press and the public may be excluded from all or part of a trial for reasons of morals, public order (ordre public) or national security in a democratic society, or when the interest of the private lives of the parties so requires, or to the extent strictly necessary in the opinion of the court in special circumstances where publicity would prejudice the interests of justice; but any judgement rendered in a criminal case or in a suit at law shall be made public except where the interest of juvenile persons otherwise requires or the proceedings concern matrimonial disputes or the guardianship of children.
2. Everyone charged with a criminal offence shall have the right to be presumed innocent until proved guilty according to law.
3. In the determination of any criminal charge against him, everyone shall be entitled to the following minimum guarantees, in full equality:

(a) To be informed promptly and in detail in a language which he understands of the nature and cause of the charge against him;

(b) To have adequate time and facilities for the preparation of his defence and to communicate with counsel of his own choosing;

(c) To be tried without undue delay;

(d) To be tried in his presence, and to defend himself in person or through legal assistance of his own choosing; to be informed, if he does not have legal assistance, of this right; and to have legal assistance assigned to him, in any case where the interests of justice so require, and without payment by him in any such case if he does not have sufficient means to pay for it;

(e) To examine, or have examined, the witnesses against him and to obtain the attendance and examination of witnesses on his behalf under the same conditions as witnesses against him;

(f) To have the free assistance of an interpreter if he cannot understand or speak the language used in court;

(g) Not to be compelled to testify against himself or to confess guilt.

4. In the case of juvenile persons, the procedure shall be such as will take account of their age and the desirability of promoting their rehabilitation.

5. Everyone convicted of a crime shall have the right to his conviction and sentence being reviewed by a higher tribunal according to law.

6. When a person has by a final decision been convicted of a criminal offence and when subsequently his conviction has been reversed or he has been pardoned on the ground that a new or newly discovered fact shows conclusively that there has been a miscarriage of justice, the person who has suffered punishment as a result of such conviction shall be compensated according to law, unless it is proved that the non-disclosure of the unknown fact in time is wholly or partly attributable to him.

7. No one shall be liable to be tried or punished again for an offence for which he has already been finally convicted or acquitted in accordance with the law and penal procedure of each country.

Article 15

1. No one shall be held guilty of any criminal offence on account of any act or omission which did not constitute a criminal offence, under national or international law, at the time when it was committed. Nor shall a heavier penalty be imposed than the one that was applicable at the time when the criminal offence was committed. If, subsequent to the commission of the offence, provision is made by law for the imposition of the lighter penalty, the offender shall benefit thereby.

2. Nothing in this article shall prejudice the trial and punishment of any person for any act or omission which, at the time when it was committed, was criminal according to the general principles of law recognized by the community of nations.

Article 16

Everyone shall have the right to recognition everywhere as a person before the law.

Article 17

1. No one shall be subjected to arbitrary or unlawful interference with his privacy, family, home or correspondence, nor to unlawful attacks on his honour and reputation.
2. Everyone has the right to the protection of the law against such interference or attacks.

Article 18

1. Everyone shall have the right to freedom of thought, conscience and religion. This right shall include freedom to have or to adopt a religion or belief of his choice, and freedom, either individually or in community with others and in public or private, to manifest his religion or belief in worship, observance, practice and teaching.
2. No one shall be subject to coercion which would impair his freedom to have or to adopt a religion or belief of his choice.
3. Freedom to manifest one's religion or beliefs may be subject only to such limitations as are prescribed by law and are necessary to protect public safety, order, health, or morals or the fundamental rights and freedoms of others. 4. The States Parties to the present Covenant undertake to have respect for the liberty of parents and, when applicable, legal guardians to ensure the religious and moral education of their children in conformity with their own convictions.

Article 19

1. Everyone shall have the right to hold opinions without interference.
2. Everyone shall have the right to freedom of expression; this right shall include freedom to seek, receive and impart information and ideas of all kinds, regardless of frontiers, either orally, in writing or in print, in the form of art, or through any other media of his choice.

3. The exercise of the rights provided for in paragraph 2 of this article carries with it special duties and responsibilities. It may therefore be subject to certain restrictions, but these shall only be such as are provided by law and are necessary:

   (a) For respect of the rights or reputations of others;

   (b) For the protection of national security or of public order (ordre public), or of public health or morals.

Article 20

1. Any propaganda for war shall be prohibited by law.

2. Any advocacy of national, racial or religious hatred that constitutes incitement to discrimination, hostility or violence shall be prohibited by law.

Article 21

The right of peaceful assembly shall be recognized. No restrictions may be placed on the exercise of this right other than those imposed in conformity with the law and which are necessary in a democratic society in the interests of national security or public safety, public order (ordre public), the protection of public health or morals or the protection of the rights and freedoms of others.

Article 22

1. Everyone shall have the right to freedom of association with others, including the right to form and join trade unions for the protection of his interests.

2. No restrictions may be placed on the exercise of this right other than those which are prescribed by law and which are necessary in a democratic society in the interests of national security or public safety, public order (ordre public), the protection of public health or morals or the protection of the rights and freedoms of others. This article shall not prevent the imposition of lawful restrictions on members of the armed forces and of the police in their exercise of this right.

3. Nothing in this article shall authorize States Parties to the International Labour Organization Convention of 1948 concerning Freedom of Association and Protection of the Right to Organize to take legislative measures which would prejudice, or to apply the law in such a manner as to prejudice, the guarantees provided for in that Convention.

Article 23

1. The family is the natural and fundamental group unit of society and is entitled to protection by society and the State.

2. The right of men and women of marriageable age to marry and to found a family shall be recognized.

3. No marriage shall be entered into without the free and full consent of the intending spouses.

4. States Parties to the present Covenant shall take appropriate steps to ensure equality of rights and responsibilities of spouses as to marriage, during marriage and at its dissolution. In the case of dissolution, provision shall be made for the necessary protection of any children.

Article 24

1. Every child shall have, without any discrimination as to race, colour, sex, language, religion, national or social origin, property or birth, the right to such measures of protection as are required by his status as a minor, on the part of his family, society and the State.

2. Every child shall be registered immediately after birth and shall have a name.

3. Every child has the right to acquire a nationality.

Article 25

Every citizen shall have the right and the opportunity, without any of the distinctions mentioned in article 2 and without unreasonable restrictions:

(a) To take part in the conduct of public affairs, directly or through freely chosen representatives;

(b) To vote and to be elected at genuine periodic elections which shall be by universal and equal suffrage and shall be held by secret ballot, guaranteeing the free expression of the will of the electors;

(c) To have access, on general terms of equality, to public service in his country.

Article 26

All persons are equal before the law and are entitled without any discrimination to the equal protection of the law. In this respect, the law shall prohibit any discrimination and guarantee to all persons equal and effective protection against discrimination on any ground such as race, colour, sex, language, religion, political or other opinion, national or social origin, property, birth or other status.

Article 27

In those States in which ethnic, religious or linguistic minorities exist, persons belonging to such minorities shall not be denied the right, in community with the other members of their group, to enjoy their own culture, to profess and practice their own religion, or to use their own language.

Part IV

Article 28

1. There shall be established a Human Rights Committee (hereafter referred to in the present Covenant as the Committee). It shall consist of eighteen members and shall carry out the functions hereinafter provided.
2. The Committee shall be composed of nationals of the States Parties to the present Covenant who shall be persons of high moral character and recognized competence in the field of human rights, consideration being given to the usefulness of the participation of some persons having legal experience.
3. The members of the Committee shall be elected and shall serve in their personal capacity.

...

Part V

Article 46

Nothing in the present Covenant shall be interpreted as impairing the provisions of the Charter of the United Nations and of the constitutions of the specialized agencies which define the respective responsibilities of the various organs of the United Nations and of the specialized agencies in regard to the matters dealt with in the present Covenant.

Article 47

Nothing in the present Covenant shall be interpreted as impairing the inherent right of all peoples to enjoy and utilize fully and freely their natural wealth and resources.

Part VI

Article 48

1. The present Covenant is open for signature by any State Member of the United Nations or member of any of its specialized agencies, by any State Party to the Statute of the International Court of Justice, and by any other State which has been invited by the General Assembly of the United Nations to become a Party to the present Covenant.
2. The present Covenant is subject to ratification. Instruments of ratification shall be deposited with the Secretary-General of the United Nations.

3. The present Covenant shall be open to accession by any State referred to in paragraph 1 of this article.

4. Accession shall be effected by the deposit of an instrument of accession with the Secretary-General of the United Nations.

5. The Secretary-General of the United Nations shall inform all States which have signed this Covenant or acceded to it of the deposit of each instrument of ratification or accession.

Article 49

1. The present Covenant shall enter into force three months after the date of the deposit with the Secretary-General of the United Nations of the thirty-fifth instrument of ratification or instrument of accession.

2. For each State ratifying the present Covenant or acceding to it after the deposit of the thirty-fifth instrument of ratification or instrument of accession, the present Covenant shall enter into force three months after the date of the deposit of its own instrument of ratification or instrument of accession.

Article 50

The provisions of the present Covenant shall extend to all parts of federal States without any limitations or exceptions.

Article 51

1. Any State Party to the present Covenant may propose an amendment and file it with the Secretary-General of the United Nations. The Secretary-General of the United Nations shall thereupon communicate any proposed amendments to the States Parties to the present Covenant with a request that they notify him whether they favour a conference of States Parties for the purpose of considering and voting upon the proposals. In the event that at least one third of the States Parties favours such a conference, the Secretary-General shall convene the conference under the auspices of the United Nations. Any amendment adopted by a majority of the States Parties present and voting at the conference shall be submitted to the General Assembly of the United Nations for approval.

2. Amendments shall come into force when they have been approved by the General Assembly of the United Nations and accepted by a two-thirds majority of the States Parties to the present Covenant in accordance with their respective constitutional processes.

3. When amendments come into force, they shall be binding on those States Parties which have accepted them, other States Parties still being bound by the provisions of the present Covenant and any earlier amendment which they have accepted.

Article 52

Irrespective of the notifications made under article 48, paragraph 5, the Secretary-General of the United Nations shall inform all States referred to in paragraph I of the same article of the following particulars:

(a) Signatures, ratifications and accessions under article 48;

(b) The date of the entry into force of the present Covenant under article 49 and the date of the entry into force of any amendments under article 51.

Article 53

1. The present Covenant, of which the Chinese, English, French, Russian and Spanish texts are equally authentic, shall be deposited in the archives of the United Nations.

2. The Secretary-General of the United Nations shall transmit certified copies of the present Covenant to all States referred to in article 48.

Appendix J
President's Letter to Congress on American Response to Terrorism

Office of the Press Secretary
October 9, 2001

President's Letter to Congress on American Response to Terrorism

Text of a Letter from the President to the Speaker of the House of Representatives and the President Pro Tempore of the Senate
October 9, 2001

Dear Mr. Speaker: (Dear Mr. President:)

At approximately 12:30 p.m. (EDT) on October 7, 2001, on my orders, U.S. Armed Forces began combat action in Afghanistan against Al Qaida terrorists and their Taliban supporters. This military action is a part of our campaign against terrorism and is designed to disrupt the use of Afghanistan as a terrorist base of operations.

We are responding to the brutal September 11 attacks on our territory, our citizens, and our way of life, and to the continuing threat of terrorist acts against the United States and our friends and allies. This follows the deployment of various combat-equipped and combat support forces to a number of locations in the Central and Pacific Command areas of operations, as I reported to the Congress on September 24, to prepare for the campaign to prevent and deter terrorism.

I have taken these actions pursuant to my constitutional authority to conduct U.S. foreign relations as Commander in Chief and Chief Executive. It is not possible to know at this time either the duration of combat operations or the scope and duration of the deployment of U.S. Armed Forces necessary to counter the terrorist threat to the United States. As I have stated previously, it is likely that the American campaign against terrorism will be lengthy. I will direct such additional measures as necessary in exercise of our right to self-defense and to protect U.S. citizens and interests.

I am providing this report as part of my efforts to keep the Congress informed, consistent with the War Powers Resolution and Public Law 107-40. Officials of my Administration and I have been communicating regularly with the leadership and other members of Congress, and we will continue to do so. I appreciate the continuing support of the Congress, including its enactment of Public Law 107-40, in these actions to protect the security of the United States of America and its citizens, civilian and military, here and abroad.

Sincerely,
GEORGE W. BUSH

Appendix K
Treaty Providing for the Renunciation of War as an Instrument of National Policy (Kellogg-Briand Pact)

Signed in Paris, August 27, 1928

Entered into force 24 July 1929

The President of the German Reich, the President of the United States of America, His Majesty the King of the Belgians, the President of the French Republic, His Majesty the King of Great Britain Ireland and the British Dominions beyond the seas, Emperor of India, His Majesty the King of Italy, His Majesty the Emperor of Japan, the President of the Republic of Poland, the President of the Czechoslovak Republic.

Deeply sensible of their solemn duty to promote the welfare of mankind; Persuaded that the time has come when a frank renunciation of war as an instrument of national policy should be made to the end that the peaceful and friendly relations now existing between their peoples may be perpetuated;

Convinced that all changes in their relations with one another should be sought only by pacific means and be the result of a peaceful and orderly process, and that any signatory Power which shall hereafter seek to promote its national interests by resort to war should be denied the benefits furnished by this treaty;

Hopeful that, encouraged by their example, all the other nations of the world will join in this humane endeavor and by adhering to the present treaty as soon as it comes into force bring their peoples within the scope of its beneficent provisions, thus uniting the civilized nations of the world in a common renunciation of war as an instrument of their national policy;

Have decided to conclude a treaty and for that purpose have appointed as their respective plenipotentiaries:

The President of the German Reich: Dr. Gustav Stresemann, Minister for Foreign Affairs;

The President of the United States of America: The Honorable Frank B. Kellogg, Secretary of State;

503

His Majesty the King of the Belgians: Mr. Paul Hymans, Minister for Foreign Affairs, Minister of State;

The President of the French Republic: Mr. Aristide Briand, Minister for Foreign Affairs;

His Majesty the King of Great Britain, Ireland and the British Dominions beyond the seas, Emperor of India: For Great Britain and Northern Ireland and all parts of the British Empire which are not separate members of the League of Nations: The Right Honourable Lord Cushendun, Chancellor of the Duchy of Lancaster, Acting Secretary of State for Foreign Affairs;

For the Dominion of Canada: The Right Honourable William Lyon Mackenzie King, Prime Minister and Minister for External Affairs;

For the Commonwealth of Australia: The Honourable Alexander John McLachlan, Member of the Executive Federal Council;

For the Dominion of New Zealand: The Honourable Sir Christopher James Parr, High Commissioner for New Zealand in Great Britain;

For the Union of South Africa: The Honourable Jacobus Stephanus Smit, High Commissioner for the Union of South Africa in Great Britain; .

For the Irish Free State: Mr. William Thomas Cosgrave, President of the Executive Council;

For India: The Right Honourable Lord Cushendun, Chancellor of the Duchy of Lancaster, Acting Secretary of State for Foreign Affairs.

His Majesty the King of Italy: Count Gaetano Manzoi, His Ambassador Extraordinary and Plenipotentiary at Paris;

His Majesty the Emperor of Japan: Count Uchida, Privy Councillor;

The President of the Republic of Poland: Mr. A. Zaleski, Minister for Foreign Affairs;

The President of the Czechoslovak Republic: Dr. Eduard Benes, Minister for Foreign Affairs;

who, having communicated to one another their full powers found in good and due form have agreed upon the following articles:

Article 1

The high contracting parties solemnly declare in the names of their respective peoples that they condemn recourse to war for the solution of international controversies, and renounce it as an instrument of national policy in their relations with one another.

Article 2

The high contracting parties agree that the settlement or solution of all disputes or conflicts of whatever nature or of whatever origin they may be, which may arise among them, shall never be sought except by pacific means.

Article 3

The present treaty shall be ratified by the high contracting parties Named in the preamble in accordance with their respective constitutional requirements, and shall take effect as between them as soon as all their several instruments of ratification shall have been deposited at Washington.

This treaty shall, when it has come into effect as prescribed in the preceding paragraph, remain open as long as may be necessary for adherence by all the other Powers of the world. Every instrument evidencing the adherence of a Power shall be deposited at Washington and the treaty shall immediately upon such deposit become effective as between the Power thus adhering and the other Powers parties hereto.

It shall be the duty of the Government of the United States to furnish each government named in the preamble and every government subsequently adhering to this treaty with a certified copy of the treaty and of every instrument of ratification or adherence. It shall also be the duty of the Government of the United States telegraphically to notify such governments immediately upon the deposit with it of each instrument of ratification or adherence. In faith whereof the respective Plenipotentiaries have signed this Treaty in the French and English languages both texts having equal force, and hereunto affix their seals.

Appendix L
Military Commissions Act of 2006

An Act

To authorize trial by military commission for violations of the law of war, and for other purposes.

Be it enacted by the Senate and House of Representatives of the United States of America in Congress assembled,

SECTION 1. SHORT TITLE; TABLE OF CONTENTS.

(a) Short Title- This Act may be cited as the "Military Commissions Act of 2006."

(b) Table of Contents- The table of contents for this Act is as follows:

SEC. 2. CONSTRUCTION OF PRESIDENTIAL AUTHORITY TO ESTABLISH MILITARY COMMISSIONS.

The authority to establish military commissions under chapter 47A of title 10, United States Code, as added by section 3(a), may not be construed to alter or limit the authority of the President under the Constitution of the United States and laws of the United States to establish military commissions for areas declared to be under martial law or in occupied territories should circumstances so require.

SEC. 3. MILITARY COMMISSIONS.

...

Sec. 948a. Definitions

In this chapter:

(1) UNLAWFUL ENEMY COMBATANT-

(A) The term "unlawful enemy combatant" means—

> (i) a person who has engaged in hostilities or who has purposefully and materially supported hostilities against the United States or its co-belligerents who is not a lawful enemy combatant (including a person who is part of the Taliban, al Qaeda, or associated forces); or

> (ii) a person who, before, on, or after the date of the enactment of the Military Commissions Act of 2006, has been determined to be an unlawful enemy combatant by a Combatant Status Review Tribunal or another competent tribunal established under the authority of the President or the Secretary of Defense.

(B) CO-BELLIGERENT- In this paragraph, the term "co-belligerent," with respect to the United States, means any State or armed force joining and directly engaged with the United States in hostilities or directly supporting hostilities against a common enemy.

(2) LAWFUL ENEMY COMBATANT- The term "lawful enemy combatant" means a person who is—

(A) a member of the regular forces of a State party engaged in hostilities against the United States;

(B) a member of a militia, volunteer corps, or organized resistance movement belonging to a State party engaged in such hostilities, which are under responsible command, wear a fixed distinctive sign recognizable at a distance, carry their arms openly, and abide by the law of war; or

(C) a member of a regular armed force who professes allegiance to a government engaged in such hostilities, but not recognized by the United States.

(3) ALIEN- The term "alien" means a person who is not a citizen of the United States.

(4) CLASSIFIED INFORMATION- The term "classified information" means the following:

(A) Any information or material that has been determined by the United States Government pursuant to statute, Executive order, or regulation to require protection against unauthorized disclosure for reasons of national security.

(B) Any restricted data, as that term is defined in section 11 y. of the Atomic Energy Act of 1954 (42 U.S.C. 2014(y)).

(5) GENEVA CONVENTIONS- The term "Geneva Conventions" means the international conventions signed at Geneva on August 12, 1949.

Sec. 948b. Military commissions generally

(a) Purpose- This chapter establishes procedures governing the use of military commissions to try alien unlawful enemy combatants engaged in hostilities against the United States for violations of the law of war and other offenses triable by military commission.

(b) Authority for Military Commissions Under This Chapter- The President is authorized to establish military commissions under this chapter for offenses triable by military commission as provided in this chapter.

(c) Construction of Provisions- The procedures for military commissions set forth in this chapter are based upon the procedures for trial by general courts-martial under chapter 47 of this title (the Uniform Code of Military Justice). Chapter 47 of this title does not, by its terms, apply to trial by military commission except as specifically provided in this chapter. The judicial construction and application of that chapter are not binding on military commissions established under this chapter.

(d) Inapplicability of Certain Provisions-

(1) The following provisions of this title shall not apply to trial by military commission under this chapter:

(A) Section 810 (article 10 of the Uniform Code of Military Justice), relating to speedy trial, including any rule of courts-martial relating to speedy trial.

(B) Sections 831(a), (b), and (d) (articles 31(a), (b), and (d) of the Uniform Code of Military Justice), relating to compulsory self-incrimination.

(C) Section 832 (article 32 of the Uniform Code of Military Justice), relating to pretrial investigation.

(2) Other provisions of chapter 47 of this title shall apply to trial by military commission under this chapter only to the extent provided by this chapter.

(e) Treatment of Rulings and Precedents- The findings, holdings, interpretations, and other precedents of military commissions under this chapter may not be introduced or considered in any hearing, trial, or other proceeding of a court-martial convened under chapter 47 of this title. The findings, holdings, interpretations, and other precedents of military commissions under this chapter may not form the basis of any holding, decision, or other determination of a court-martial convened under that chapter.

(f) Status of Commissions Under Common Article 3- A military commission established under this chapter is a regularly constituted court, affording all the necessary 'judicial guarantees which are recognized as indispensable by civilized peoples' for purposes of common Article 3 of the Geneva Conventions.

(g) Geneva Conventions Not Establishing Source of Rights- No alien unlawful enemy combatant subject to trial by military commission under this chapter may invoke the Geneva Conventions as a source of rights.

Sec. 948c. Persons subject to military commissions

Any alien unlawful enemy combatant is subject to trial by military commission under this chapter.

Sec. 948d. Jurisdiction of military commissions

(a) Jurisdiction- A military commission under this chapter shall have jurisdiction to try any offense made punishable by this chapter or the law of war when committed by an alien unlawful enemy combatant before, on, or after September 11, 2001.

(b) Lawful Enemy Combatants- Military commissions under this chapter shall not have jurisdiction over lawful enemy combatants. Lawful enemy combatants who violate the law of war are subject to chapter 47 of this title. Courts-martial established under that chapter shall have jurisdiction to try a lawful enemy combatant for any offense made punishable under this chapter.

(c) Determination of Unlawful Enemy Combatant Status Dispositive- A finding, whether before, on, or after the date of the enactment of the Military Commissions Act of 2006, by a Combatant Status Review Tribunal or another competent tribunal established under the authority of the President or the Secretary of Defense that a person is an unlawful enemy combatant is dispositive for purposes of jurisdiction for trial by military commission under this chapter.

(d) Punishments- A military commission under this chapter may, under such limitations as the Secretary of Defense may prescribe, adjudge any punishment not forbidden by this chapter, including the penalty of death when authorized under this chapter or the law of war.

...

SUBCHAPTER II—COMPOSITION OF MILITARY COMMISSIONS

...

Sec. 948h. Who may convene military commissions

Military commissions under this chapter may be convened by the Secretary of Defense or by any officer or official of the United States designated by the Secretary for that purpose.

...

Sec. 948k. Detail of trial counsel and defense counsel

(a) Detail of Counsel Generally-

    (1) Trial counsel and military defense counsel shall be detailed for each military commission under this chapter.

    (2) Assistant trial counsel and assistant and associate defense counsel may be detailed for a military commission under this chapter.

    (3) Military defense counsel for a military commission under this chapter shall be detailed as soon as practicable after the swearing of charges against the accused.

    (4) The Secretary of Defense shall prescribe regulations providing for the manner in which trial counsel and military defense counsel are detailed for military commissions under this chapter and for the persons who are authorized to detail such counsel for such commissions.

(b) Trial Counsel- Subject to subsection (e), trial counsel detailed for a military commission under this chapter must be—

    (1) a judge advocate (as that term is defined in section 801 of this title (article 1 of the Uniform Code of Military Justice) who—

        (A) is a graduate of an accredited law school or is a member of the bar of a Federal court or of the highest court of a State; and

        (B) is certified as competent to perform duties as trial counsel before general courts-martial by the Judge Advocate General of the armed force of which he is a member; or

    (2) a civilian who—

        (A) is a member of the bar of a Federal court or of the highest court of a State; and

        (B) is otherwise qualified to practice before the military commission pursuant to regulations prescribed by the Secretary of Defense.

(c) Military Defense Counsel- Subject to subsection (e), military defense counsel detailed for a military commission under this chapter must be a judge advocate (as so defined) who is—

    (1) a graduate of an accredited law school or is a member of the bar of a Federal court or of the highest court of a State; and

    (2) certified as competent to perform duties as defense counsel before general courts-martial by the Judge Advocate General of the armed force of which he is a member.

(d) Chief Prosecutor; Chief Defense Counsel-

    (1) The Chief Prosecutor in a military commission under this chapter shall meet the requirements set forth in subsection (b)(1).

    (2) The Chief Defense Counsel in a military commission under this chapter shall meet the requirements set forth in subsection (c)(1).

(e) Ineligibility of Certain Individuals- No person who has acted as an investigator, military judge, or member of a military commission under this chapter in any case may act later as trial counsel or military defense counsel in the same case. No person who has acted for the prosecution before a military commission under this chapter may act later in the same case for the defense, nor may any person who has acted for the defense before a military commission under this chapter act later in the same case for the prosecution.

. . .

Sec. 948m. Number of members; excuse of members; absent and additional members

(a) Number of Members- (1) A military commission under this chapter shall, except as provided in paragraph (2), have at least five members.

. . .

SUBCHAPTER III—PRE-TRIAL PROCEDURE

. . .

Sec. 948q. Charges and specifications

(a) Charges and Specifications- Charges and specifications against an accused in a military commission under this chapter shall be signed by a person subject to chapter 47 of this title under oath before a commissioned officer of the armed forces authorized to administer oaths and shall state—

    (1) that the signer has personal knowledge of, or reason to believe, the matters set forth therein; and

    (2) that they are true in fact to the best of the signer's knowledge and belief.

(b) Notice to Accused- Upon the swearing of the charges and specifications in accordance with subsection (a), the accused shall be informed of the charges against him as soon as practicable.

Sec. 948r. Compulsory self-incrimination prohibited; treatment of statements obtained by torture and other statements

(a) In General- No person shall be required to testify against himself at a proceeding of a military commission under this chapter.

(b) Exclusion of Statements Obtained by Torture- A statement obtained by use of torture shall not be admissible in a military commission under this chapter, except against a person accused of torture as evidence that the statement was made.

(c) Statements Obtained Before Enactment of Detainee Treatment Act of 2005- A statement obtained before December 30, 2005 (the date of the enactment of the Defense Treatment Act of 2005) in which the degree of coercion is disputed may be admitted only if the military judge finds that—

   (1) the totality of the circumstances renders the statement reliable and possessing sufficient probative value; and

   (2) the interests of justice would best be served by admission of the statement into evidence.

(d) Statements Obtained After Enactment of Detainee Treatment Act of 2005- A statement obtained on or after December 30, 2005 (the date of the enactment of the Defense Treatment Act of 2005) in which the degree of coercion is disputed may be admitted only if the military judge finds that—

   (1) the totality of the circumstances renders the statement reliable and possessing sufficient probative value;

   (2) the interests of justice would best be served by admission of the statement into evidence; and

   (3) the interrogation methods used to obtain the statement do not amount to cruel, inhuman, or degrading treatment prohibited by section 1003 of the Detainee Treatment Act of 2005.

...

SUBCHAPTER IV—TRIAL PROCEDURE

...

Sec. 949a. Rules

(a) Procedures and Rules of Evidence- Pretrial, trial, and post-trial procedures, including elements and modes of proof, for cases triable by military commission under this chapter may be prescribed by the Secretary of Defense, in consultation with the Attorney General. Such procedures shall, so far as the Secretary considers practicable or consistent with military or intelligence activities, apply the principles of law and the rules of evidence in trial by general courts-martial. Such procedures and rules of evidence may not be contrary to or inconsistent with this chapter.

(b) Rules for Military Commission- (1) Notwithstanding any departures from the law and the rules of evidence in trial by general courts-martial authorized by subsection (a), the procedures and rules of evidence in trials by military commission under this chapter shall include the following:

   (A) The accused shall be permitted to present evidence in his defense, to cross-examine the witnesses who testify against him, and to examine and respond to evidence admitted against him on the issue of guilt or innocence and for sentencing, as provided for by this chapter.

   (B) The accused shall be present at all sessions of the military commission (other than those for deliberations or voting), except when excluded under section 949d of this title.

   (C) The accused shall receive the assistance of counsel as provided for by section 948k.

   (D) The accused shall be permitted to represent himself, as provided for by paragraph (3).

(2) In establishing procedures and rules of evidence for military commission proceedings, the Secretary of Defense may prescribe the following provisions:

   (A) Evidence shall be admissible if the military judge determines that the evidence would have probative value to a reasonable person.

   (B) Evidence shall not be excluded from trial by military commission on the grounds that the evidence was not seized pursuant to a search warrant or other authorization.

   (C) A statement of the accused that is otherwise admissible shall not be excluded from trial by military commission on grounds of alleged coercion or compulsory self-incrimination so long as the evidence complies with the provisions of section 948r of this title.

   (D) Evidence shall be admitted as authentic so long as—

      (i) the military judge of the military commission determines that there is sufficient basis to find that the evidence is what it is claimed to be; and

      (ii) the military judge instructs the members that they may consider any issue as to authentication or identification of evidence in determining the weight, if any, to be given to the evidence.

   (E)(i) Except as provided in clause (ii), hearsay evidence not otherwise admissible under the rules of evidence applicable in trial by general courts-martial may be admitted in a trial by military commission if the proponent of the evidence makes known to the adverse party, sufficiently in advance to provide the adverse party with a fair opportunity to meet the evidence, the intention of the proponent to offer the evidence, and the particulars of the evidence (including information on the general circumstances under which the evidence was obtained). The disclosure of evidence under the preceding sentence is subject to the requirements and limitations applicable to the disclosure of classified information in section 949j(c) of this title.

(ii) Hearsay evidence not otherwise admissible under the rules of evidence applicable in trial by general courts-martial shall not be admitted in a trial by military commission if the party opposing the admission of the evidence demonstrates that the evidence is unreliable or lacking in probative value.

(F) The military judge shall exclude any evidence the probative value of which is substantially outweighed—

(i) by the danger of unfair prejudice, confusion of the issues, or misleading the commission; or

(ii) by considerations of undue delay, waste of time, or needless presentation of cumulative evidence.

(3)(A) The accused in a military commission under this chapter who exercises the right to self-representation under paragraph (1)(D) shall conform his deportment and the conduct of the defense to the rules of evidence, procedure, and decorum applicable to trials by military commission.

(B) Failure of the accused to conform to the rules described in subparagraph (A) may result in a partial or total revocation by the military judge of the right of self-representation under paragraph (1)(D). In such case, the detailed defense counsel of the accused or an appropriately authorized civilian counsel shall perform the functions necessary for the defense.

...

Sec. 949c. Duties of trial counsel and defense counsel

(a) Trial Counsel- The trial counsel of a military commission under this chapter shall prosecute in the name of the United States.

(b) Defense Counsel- (1) The accused shall be represented in his defense before a military commission under this chapter as provided in this subsection.

(2) The accused shall be represented by military counsel detailed under section 948k of this title.

(3) The accused may be represented by civilian counsel if retained by the accused, but only if such civilian counsel—

(A) is a United States citizen;

(B) is admitted to the practice of law in a State, district, or possession of the United States or before a Federal court;

(C) has not been the subject of any sanction of disciplinary action by any court, bar, or other competent governmental authority for relevant misconduct;

(D) has been determined to be eligible for access to classified information that is classified at the level Secret or higher; and

(E) has signed a written agreement to comply with all applicable regulations or instructions for counsel, including any rules of court for conduct during the proceedings.

(4) Civilian defense counsel shall protect any classified information received during the course of representation of the accused in accordance with all applicable law governing the protection of classified information and may not divulge such information to any person not authorized to receive it.

(5) If the accused is represented by civilian counsel, detailed military counsel shall act as associate counsel.

(6) The accused is not entitled to be represented by more than one military counsel. However, the person authorized under regulations prescribed under section 948k of this title to detail counsel, in that person's sole discretion, may detail additional military counsel to represent the accused.

(7) Defense counsel may cross-examine each witness for the prosecution who testifies before a military commission under this chapter.

Sec. 949d. Sessions

(a) Sessions Without Presence of Members- (1) At any time after the service of charges which have been referred for trial by military commission under this chapter, the military judge may call the military commission into session without the presence of the members for the purpose of—

(A) hearing and determining motions raising defenses or objections which are capable of determination without trial of the issues raised by a plea of not guilty;

(B) hearing and ruling upon any matter which may be ruled upon by the military judge under this chapter, whether or not the matter is appropriate for later consideration or decision by the members;

(C) if permitted by regulations prescribed by the Secretary of Defense, receiving the pleas of the accused; and

(D) performing any other procedural function which may be performed by the military judge under this chapter or under rules prescribed pursuant to section 949a of this title and which does not require the presence of the members.

(2) Except as provided in subsections (c) and (e), any proceedings under paragraph (1) shall—

   (A) be conducted in the presence of the accused, defense counsel, and trial counsel; and

   (B) be made part of the record.

(b) Proceedings in Presence of Accused- Except as provided in subsections (c) and (e), all proceedings of a military commission under this chapter, including any consultation of the members with the military judge or counsel, shall—

(1) be in the presence of the accused, defense counsel, and trial counsel; and

(2) be made a part of the record.

(c) Deliberation or Vote of Members- When the members of a military commission under this chapter deliberate or vote, only the members may be present.

(d) Closure of Proceedings- (1) The military judge may close to the public all or part of the proceedings of a military commission under this chapter, but only in accordance with this subsection.

(2) The military judge may close to the public all or a portion of the proceedings under paragraph (1) only upon making a specific finding that such closure is necessary to—

   (A) protect information the disclosure of which could reasonably be expected to cause damage to the national security, including intelligence or law enforcement sources, methods, or activities; or

   (B) ensure the physical safety of individuals.

(3) A finding under paragraph (2) may be based upon a presentation, including a presentation ex parte or in camera, by either trial counsel or defense counsel.

(e) Exclusion of Accused From Certain Proceedings- The military judge may exclude the accused from any portion of a proceeding upon a determination that, after being warned by the military judge, the accused persists in conduct that justifies exclusion from the courtroom—

(1) to ensure the physical safety of individuals; or

(2) to prevent disruption of the proceedings by the accused.

(f) Protection of Classified Information-

(1) NATIONAL SECURITY PRIVILEGE- (A) Classified information shall be protected and is privileged from disclosure if disclosure would be detrimental to the national security. The rule in the preceding sentence applies to all stages of the proceedings of military commissions under this chapter.

   (B) The privilege referred to in subparagraph (A) may be claimed by the head of the executive or military department or government agency concerned based on a finding by the head of that department or agency that—

      (i) the information is properly classified; and

(ii) disclosure of the information would be detrimental to the national security.

(C) A person who may claim the privilege referred to in subparagraph (A) may authorize a representative, witness, or trial counsel to claim the privilege and make the finding described in subparagraph (B) on behalf of such person. The authority of the representative, witness, or trial counsel to do so is presumed in the absence of evidence to the contrary.

(2) INTRODUCTION OF CLASSIFIED INFORMATION-

(A) ALTERNATIVES TO DISCLOSURE- To protect classified information from disclosure, the military judge, upon motion of trial counsel, shall authorize, to the extent practicable—

(i) the deletion of specified items of classified information from documents to be introduced as evidence before the military commission;

(ii) the substitution of a portion or summary of the information for such classified documents; or

(iii) the substitution of a statement of relevant facts that the classified information would tend to prove.

(B) PROTECTION OF SOURCES, METHODS, OR ACTIVITIES- The military judge, upon motion of trial counsel, shall permit trial counsel to introduce otherwise admissible evidence before the military commission, while protecting from disclosure the sources, methods, or activities by which the United States acquired the evidence if the military judge finds that (i) the sources, methods, or activities by which the United States acquired the evidence are classified, and (ii) the evidence is reliable. The military judge may require trial counsel to present to the military commission and the defense, to the extent practicable and consistent with national security, an unclassified summary of the sources, methods, or activities by which the United States acquired the evidence.

(C) ASSERTION OF NATIONAL SECURITY PRIVILEGE AT TRIAL- During the examination of any witness, trial counsel may object to any question, line of inquiry, or motion to admit evidence that would require the disclosure of classified information. Following such an objection, the military judge shall take suitable action to safeguard such classified information. Such action may include the review of trial counsel's claim of privilege by the military judge in camera and on an ex parte basis, and the delay of proceedings to permit trial counsel to consult with the department or agency concerned as to whether the national security privilege should be asserted.

(3) CONSIDERATION OF PRIVILEGE AND RELATED MATERIALS- A claim of privilege under this subsection, and any materials submitted in support thereof, shall, upon request of the Government, be considered by the military judge in camera and shall not be disclosed to the accused.

(4) ADDITIONAL REGULATIONS- The Secretary of Defense may prescribe additional regulations, consistent with this subsection, for the use and protection of classified information during proceedings of military commissions under this chapter. A report on any regulations so prescribed, or modified, shall be submitted to the Committees on Armed Services of the Senate and the House of Representatives not later than 60 days before the date on which such regulations or modifications, as the case may be, go into effect.

Sec. 949e. Continuances

The military judge in a military commission under this chapter may, for reasonable cause, grant a continuance to any party for such time, and as often, as may appear to be just.

Sec. 949f. Challenges

(a) Challenges Authorized- The military judge and members of a military commission under this chapter may be challenged by the accused or trial counsel for cause stated to the commission. The military judge shall determine the relevance and validity of challenges for cause. The military judge may not receive a challenge to more than one person at a time. Challenges by trial counsel shall ordinarily be presented and decided before those by the accused are offered.

(b) Peremptory Challenges- Each accused and the trial counsel are entitled to one peremptory challenge. The military judge may not be challenged except for cause.

(c) Challenges Against Additional Members- Whenever additional members are detailed to a military commission under this chapter, and after any challenges for cause against such additional members are presented and decided, each accused and the trial counsel are entitled to one peremptory challenge against members not previously subject to peremptory challenge.

Sec. 949g. Oaths

(a) In General- (1) Before performing their respective duties in a military commission under this chapter, military judges, members, trial counsel, defense counsel, reporters, and interpreters shall take an oath to perform their duties faithfully.

(2) The form of the oath required by paragraph (1), the time and place of the taking thereof, the manner of recording the same, and whether the oath shall be taken for all cases in which duties are to be performed or for a particular case, shall be as prescribed in regulations of the Secretary of Defense. Those regulations may provide that—

(A) an oath to perform faithfully duties as a military judge, trial counsel, or defense counsel may be taken at any time by any judge advocate or other person certified to be qualified or competent for the duty; and

(B) if such an oath is taken, such oath need not again be taken at the time the judge advocate or other person is detailed to that duty.

(b) Witnesses- Each witness before a military commission under this chapter shall be examined on oath.

Sec. 949h. Former jeopardy

(a) In General- No person may, without his consent, be tried by a military commission under this chapter a second time for the same offense.

(b) Scope of Trial- No proceeding in which the accused has been found guilty by military commission under this chapter upon any charge or specification is a trial in the sense of this section until the finding of guilty has become final after review of the case has been fully completed.

Sec. 949i. Pleas of the accused

(a) Entry of Plea of Not Guilty- If an accused in a military commission under this chapter after a plea of guilty sets up matter inconsistent with the plea, or if it appears that the accused has entered the plea of guilty through lack of understanding of its meaning and effect, or if the accused fails or refuses to plead, a plea of not guilty shall be entered in the record, and the military commission shall proceed as though the accused had pleaded not guilty.

(b) Finding of Guilt After Guilty Plea- With respect to any charge or specification to which a plea of guilty has been made by the accused in a military commission under this chapter and accepted by the military judge, a finding of guilty of the charge or specification may be entered immediately without a vote. The finding shall constitute the finding of the commission unless the plea of guilty is withdrawn prior to announcement of the sentence, in which event the proceedings shall continue as though the accused had pleaded not guilty.

Sec. 949j. Opportunity to obtain witnesses and other evidence

(a) Right of Defense Counsel- Defense counsel in a military commission under this chapter shall have a reasonable opportunity to obtain witnesses and other evidence as provided in regulations prescribed by the Secretary of Defense.

(b) Process for Compulsion- Process issued in a military commission under this chapter to compel witnesses to appear and testify and to compel the production of other evidence—

(1) shall be similar to that which courts of the United States having criminal jurisdiction may lawfully issue; and

(2) shall run to any place where the United States shall have jurisdiction thereof.

(c) Protection of Classified Information- (1) With respect to the discovery obligations of trial counsel under this section, the military judge, upon motion of trial counsel, shall authorize, to the extent practicable—

  (A) the deletion of specified items of classified information from documents to be made available to the accused;

  (B) the substitution of a portion or summary of the information for such classified documents; or

  (C) the substitution of a statement admitting relevant facts that the classified information would tend to prove.

(2) The military judge, upon motion of trial counsel, shall authorize trial counsel, in the course of complying with discovery obligations under this section, to protect from disclosure the sources, methods, or activities by which the United States acquired evidence if the military judge finds that the sources, methods, or activities by which the United States acquired such evidence are classified. The military judge may require trial counsel to provide, to the extent practicable, an unclassified summary of the sources, methods, or activities by which the United States acquired such evidence.

(d) Exculpatory Evidence- (1) As soon as practicable, trial counsel shall disclose to the defense the existence of any evidence known to trial counsel that reasonably tends to exculpate the accused. Where exculpatory evidence is classified, the accused shall be provided with an adequate substitute in accordance with the procedures under subsection (c).

(2) In this subsection, the term 'evidence known to trial counsel', in the case of exculpatory evidence, means exculpatory evidence that the prosecution would be required to disclose in a trial by general court-martial under chapter 47 of this title.

Sec. 949k. Defense of lack of mental responsibility

(a) Affirmative Defense- It is an affirmative defense in a trial by military commission under this chapter that, at the time of the commission of the acts constituting the offense, the accused, as a result of a severe mental disease or defect, was unable to appreciate the nature and quality or the wrongfulness of the acts. Mental disease or defect does not otherwise constitute a defense.

(b) Burden of Proof- The accused in a military commission under this chapter has the burden of proving the defense of lack of mental responsibility by clear and convincing evidence.

(c) Findings Following Assertion of Defense- Whenever lack of mental responsibility of the accused with respect to an offense is properly at issue in a military commission under this chapter, the military judge shall instruct the members of the commission as to the defense of lack of mental responsibility under this section and shall charge them to find the accused—

(1) guilty;

(2) not guilty; or

(3) subject to subsection (d), not guilty by reason of lack of mental responsibility.

(d) Majority Vote Required for Finding- The accused shall be found not guilty by reason of lack of mental responsibility under subsection (c)(3) only if a majority of the members present at the time the vote is taken determines that the defense of lack of mental responsibility has been established.

Sec. 949l. Voting and rulings

(a) Vote by Secret Written Ballot- Voting by members of a military commission under this chapter on the findings and on the sentence shall be by secret written ballot.

(b) Rulings- (1) The military judge in a military commission under this chapter shall rule upon all questions of law, including the admissibility of evidence and all interlocutory questions arising during the proceedings.

(2) Any ruling made by the military judge upon a question of law or an interlocutory question (other than the factual issue of mental responsibility of the accused) is conclusive and constitutes the ruling of the military commission. However, a military judge may change his ruling at any time during the trial.

(c) Instructions Prior to Vote- Before a vote is taken of the findings of a military commission under this chapter, the military judge shall, in the presence of the accused and counsel, instruct the members as to the elements of the offense and charge the members—

(1) that the accused must be presumed to be innocent until his guilt is established by legal and competent evidence beyond a reasonable doubt;

(2) that in the case being considered, if there is a reasonable doubt as to the guilt of the accused, the doubt must be resolved in favor of the accused and he must be acquitted;

(3) that, if there is reasonable doubt as to the degree of guilt, the finding must be in a lower degree as to which there is no reasonable doubt; and

(4) that the burden of proof to establish the guilt of the accused beyond a reasonable doubt is upon the United States.

Sec. 949m. Number of votes required

(a) Conviction- No person may be convicted by a military commission under this chapter of any offense, except as provided in section 949i(b) of this title or by concurrence of two-thirds of the members present at the time the vote is taken.

(b) Sentences- (1) No person may be sentenced by a military commission to suffer death, except insofar as—

(A) the penalty of death is expressly authorized under this chapter or the law of war for an offense of which the accused has been found guilty;

(B) trial counsel expressly sought the penalty of death by filing an appropriate notice in advance of trial;

(C) the accused is convicted of the offense by the concurrence of all the members present at the time the vote is taken; and

(D) all the members present at the time the vote is taken concur in the sentence of death.

(2) No person may be sentenced to life imprisonment, or to confinement for more than 10 years, by a military commission under this chapter except by the concurrence of three-fourths of the members present at the time the vote is taken.

(3) All other sentences shall be determined by a military commission by the concurrence of two-thirds of the members present at the time the vote is taken.

(c) Number of Members Required for Penalty of Death-

(1) Except as provided in paragraph (2), in a case in which the penalty of death is sought, the number of members of the military commission under this chapter shall be not less than 12.

(2) In any case described in paragraph (1) in which 12 members are not reasonably available because of physical conditions or military exigencies, the convening authority shall specify a lesser number of members for the military commission (but not fewer than 9 members), and the military commission may be assembled, and the trial held, with not fewer than the number of members so specified. In such a case, the convening authority shall make a detailed written statement, to be appended to the record, stating why a greater number of members were not reasonably available.

Sec. 949n. Military commission to announce action

A military commission under this chapter shall announce its findings and sentence to the parties as soon as determined.

Sec. 949o. Record of trial

(a) Record; Authentication- Each military commission under this chapter shall keep a separate, verbatim, record of the proceedings in each case brought before it, and the record shall be authenticated by the signature of the military judge. If the record cannot be authenticated by the military judge by reason of his death, disability, or absence, it shall be authenticated by the signature of the trial counsel or by a member of the commission if the trial counsel is unable to authenticate it by reason of his death, disability, or absence. Where appropriate, and as provided in regulations prescribed by the Secretary of Defense, the record of a military commission under this chapter may contain a classified annex.

(b) Complete Record Required- A complete record of the proceedings and testimony shall be prepared in every military commission under this chapter.

(c) Provision of Copy to Accused- A copy of the record of the proceedings of the military commission under this chapter shall be given the accused as soon as it is authenticated. If the record contains classified information, or a classified annex, the accused shall be given a redacted version of the record consistent with the requirements of section 949d of this title. Defense counsel shall have access to the unredacted record, as provided in regulations prescribed by the Secretary of Defense.

SUBCHAPTER V—SENTENCES

...

Sec. 949s. Cruel or unusual punishments prohibited

Punishment by flogging, or by branding, marking, or tattooing on the body, or any other cruel or unusual punishment, may not be adjudged by a military commission under this chapter or inflicted under this chapter upon any person subject to this chapter. The use of irons, single or double, except for the purpose of safe custody, is prohibited under this chapter.

Sec. 949t. Maximum limits

The punishment which a military commission under this chapter may direct for an offense may not exceed such limits as the President or Secretary of Defense may prescribe for that offense.

Sec. 949u. Execution of confinement

(a) In General- Under such regulations as the Secretary of Defense may prescribe, a sentence of confinement adjudged by a military commission under this chapter may be carried into execution by confinement—

(1) in any place of confinement under the control of any of the armed forces; or

(2) in any penal or correctional institution under the control of the United States or its allies, or which the United States may be allowed to use.

(b) Treatment During Confinement by Other Than the Armed Forces- Persons confined under subsection (a)(2) in a penal or correctional institution not under the control of an armed force are subject to the same discipline and treatment as persons confined or committed by the courts of the United States or of the State, District of Columbia, or place in which the institution is situated.

SUBCHAPTER VI—POST-TRIAL PROCEDURE AND REVIEW OF MILITARY COMMISSIONS

...

Sec. 950c. Appellate referral; waiver or withdrawal of appeal

(a) Automatic Referral for Appellate Review- Except as provided under subsection

(b), in each case in which the final decision of a military commission (as approved by the convening authority) includes a finding of guilty, the convening authority shall refer the case to the Court of Military Commission Review. Any such referral shall be made in accordance with procedures prescribed under regulations of the Secretary.

...

Sec. 950d. Appeal by the United States

(a) Interlocutory Appeal- (1) Except as provided in paragraph (2), in a trial by military commission under this chapter, the United States may take an interlocutory appeal to the Court of Military Commission Review of any order or ruling of the military judge that—

  (A) terminates proceedings of the military commission with respect to a charge or specification;

  (B) excludes evidence that is substantial proof of a fact material in the proceeding; or

  (C) relates to a matter under subsection (d), (e), or (f) of section 949d of this title or section 949j(c) of this title.

(2) The United States may not appeal under paragraph (1) an order or ruling that is, or amounts to, a finding of not guilty by the military commission with respect to a charge or specification.

(b) Notice of Appeal- The United States shall take an appeal of an order or ruling under subsection (a) by filing a notice of appeal with the military judge within five days after the date of such order or ruling.

(c) Appeal- An appeal under this section shall be forwarded, by means specified in regulations prescribed the Secretary of Defense, directly to the Court of Military Commission Review. In ruling on an appeal under this section, the Court may act only with respect to matters of law.

...

Sec. 950f. Review by Court of Military Commission Review

(a) Establishment- The Secretary of Defense shall establish a Court of Military Commission Review which shall be composed of one or more panels, and each such panel shall be composed of not less than three appellate military judges. For the purpose of reviewing military commission decisions under this chapter, the court may sit in panels or as a whole in accordance with rules prescribed by the Secretary.

(b) Appellate Military Judges- The Secretary shall assign appellate military judges to a Court of Military Commission Review. Each appellate military judge shall meet the qualifications for military judges prescribed by section 948j(b) of this title or shall be a civilian with comparable qualifications. No person may be serve as an appellate military judge in any case in which that person acted as a military judge, counsel, or reviewing official.

(c) Cases To Be Reviewed- The Court of Military Commission Review, in accordance with procedures prescribed under regulations of the Secretary, shall review the record in each case that is referred to the Court by the convening authority under section 950c of this title with respect to any matter of law raised by the accused.

(d) Scope of Review- In a case reviewed by the Court of Military Commission Review under this section, the Court may act only with respect to matters of law.

Sec. 950g. Review by the United States Court of Appeals for the District of Columbia Circuit and the Supreme Court

(a) Exclusive Appellate Jurisdiction- (1)(A) Except as provided in subparagraph (B), the United States Court of Appeals for the District of Columbia Circuit shall have exclusive jurisdiction to determine the validity of a final judgment rendered by a military commission (as approved by the convening authority) under this chapter.

   (B) The Court of Appeals may not review the final judgment until all other appeals under this chapter have been waived or exhausted.

(2) A petition for review must be filed by the accused in the Court of Appeals not later than 20 days after the date on which—

   (A) written notice of the final decision of the Court of Military Commission Review is served on the accused or on defense counsel; or

   (B) the accused submits, in the form prescribed by section 950c of this title, a written notice waiving the right of the accused to review by the Court of Military Commission Review under section 950f of this title.

(b) Standard for Review- In a case reviewed by it under this section, the Court of Appeals may act only with respect to matters of law.

(c) Scope of Review- The jurisdiction of the Court of Appeals on an appeal under subsection (a) shall be limited to the consideration of—

(1) whether the final decision was consistent with the standards and procedures specified in this chapter; and

(2) to the extent applicable, the Constitution and the laws of the United States.

(d) Supreme Court- The Supreme Court may review by writ of certiorari the final judgment of the Court of Appeals pursuant to section 1257 of title 28.

...

Sec. 950i. Execution of sentence; procedures for execution of sentence of death

(a) In General- The Secretary of Defense is authorized to carry out a sentence imposed by a military commission under this chapter in accordance with such procedures as the Secretary may prescribe.

(b) Execution of Sentence of Death Only Upon Approval by the President- If the sentence of a military commission under this chapter extends to death, that part of the sentence providing for death may not be executed until approved by the President. In such a case, the President may commute, remit, or suspend the sentence, or any part thereof, as he sees fit.

(c) Execution of Sentence of Death Only Upon Final Judgment of Legality of Proceedings- (1) If the sentence of a military commission under this chapter extends to death, the sentence may not be executed until there is a final judgment as to the legality of the proceedings (and with respect to death, approval under subsection (b)).

(2) A judgment as to legality of proceedings is final for purposes of paragraph (1) when—

(A) the time for the accused to file a petition for review by the Court of Appeals for the District of Columbia Circuit has expired and the accused has not filed a timely petition for such review and the case is not otherwise under review by that Court; or

(B) review is completed in accordance with the judgment of the United States Court of Appeals for the District of Columbia Circuit and—

(i) a petition for a writ of certiorari is not timely filed;

(ii) such a petition is denied by the Supreme Court; or

(iii) review is otherwise completed in accordance with the judgment of the Supreme Court.

(d) Suspension of Sentence- The Secretary of the Defense, or the convening authority acting on the case (if other than the Secretary), may suspend the execution of any sentence or part thereof in the case, except a sentence of death.

Sec. 950j. Finality or proceedings, findings, and sentences

(a) Finality- The appellate review of records of trial provided by this chapter, and the proceedings, findings, and sentences of military commissions as approved, reviewed, or affirmed as required by this chapter, are final and conclusive. Orders publishing the proceedings of military commissions under this chapter are binding upon all departments, courts, agencies, and officers of the United States, except as otherwise provided by the President.

(b) Provisions of Chapter Sole Basis for Review of Military Commission Procedures and Actions- Except as otherwise provided in this chapter and notwithstanding any other provision of law (including section 2241 of title 28 or any other habeas corpus provision), no court, justice, or judge shall have jurisdiction to hear or consider any claim or cause of action whatsoever, including any action pending on or filed after the date of the enactment of the Military Commissions Act of 2006, relating to the prosecution, trial, or judgment of a military commission under this chapter, including challenges to the lawfulness of procedures of military commissions under this chapter.

SUBCHAPTER VII—PUNITIVE MATTERS

...

Sec. 950p. Statement of substantive offenses

(a) Purpose- The provisions of this subchapter codify offenses that have traditionally been triable by military commissions. This chapter does not establish new crimes that did not exist before its enactment, but rather codifies those crimes for trial by military commission.

(b) Effect- Because the provisions of this subchapter (including provisions that incorporate definitions in other provisions of law) are declarative of existing law, they do not preclude trial for crimes that occurred before the date of the enactment of this chapter.

...

(b) Offenses- The following offenses shall be triable by military commission under this chapter at any time without limitation:

(1) MURDER OF PROTECTED PERSONS- Any person subject to this chapter who intentionally kills one or more protected persons shall be punished by death or such other punishment as a military commission under this chapter may direct.

(2) ATTACKING CIVILIANS- Any person subject to this chapter who intentionally engages in an attack upon a civilian population as such, or individual civilians not taking active part in hostilities, shall be punished, if death results to one or more of the victims, by death or such other punishment as a military commission

under this chapter may direct, and, if death does not result to any of the victims, by such punishment, other than death, as a military commission under this chapter may direct.

(3) ATTACKING CIVILIAN OBJECTS- Any person subject to this chapter who intentionally engages in an attack upon a civilian object that is not a military objective shall be punished as a military commission under this chapter may direct.

(4) ATTACKING PROTECTED PROPERTY- Any person subject to this chapter who intentionally engages in an attack upon protected property shall be punished as a military commission under this chapter may direct.

(5) PILLAGING- Any person subject to this chapter who intentionally and in the absence of military necessity appropriates or seizes property for private or personal use, without the consent of a person with authority to permit such appropriation or seizure, shall be punished as a military commission under this chapter may direct.

(6) DENYING QUARTER- Any person subject to this chapter who, with effective command or control over subordinate groups, declares, orders, or otherwise indicates to those groups that there shall be no survivors or surrender accepted, with the intent to threaten an adversary or to conduct hostilities such that there would be no survivors or surrender accepted, shall be punished as a military commission under this chapter may direct.

(7) TAKING HOSTAGES- Any person subject to this chapter who, having knowingly seized or detained one or more persons, threatens to kill, injure, or continue to detain such person or persons with the intent of compelling any nation, person other than the hostage, or group of persons to act or refrain from acting as an explicit or implicit condition for the safety or release of such person or persons, shall be punished, if death results to one or more of the victims, by death or such other punishment as a military commission under this chapter may direct, and, if death does not result to any of the victims, by such punishment, other than death, as a military commission under this chapter may direct.

(8) EMPLOYING POISON OR SIMILAR WEAPONS- Any person subject to this chapter who intentionally, as a method of warfare, employs a substance or weapon that releases a substance that causes death or serious and lasting damage to health in the ordinary course of events, through its asphyxiating, bacteriological, or toxic properties, shall be punished, if death results to one or more of the victims, by death or such other punishment as a military commission under this chapter may direct, and, if death does not result to any of the victims, by such punishment, other than death, as a military commission under this chapter may direct.

(9) USING PROTECTED PERSONS AS A SHIELD- Any person subject to this chapter who positions, or otherwise takes advantage of, a protected person with the intent

to shield a military objective from attack, or to shield, favor, or impede military operations, shall be punished, if death results to one or more of the victims, by death or such other punishment as a military commission under this chapter may direct, and, if death does not result to any of the victims, by such punishment, other than death, as a military commission under this chapter may direct.

(10) USING PROTECTED PROPERTY AS A SHIELD- Any person subject to this chapter who positions, or otherwise takes advantage of the location of, protected property with the intent to shield a military objective from attack, or to shield, favor, or impede military operations, shall be punished as a military commission under this chapter may direct.

(11) TORTURE-

(A) OFFENSE- Any person subject to this chapter who commits an act specifically intended to inflict severe physical or mental pain or suffering (other than pain or suffering incidental to lawful sanctions) upon another person within his custody or physical control for the purpose of obtaining information or a confession, punishment, intimidation, coercion, or any reason based on discrimination of any kind, shall be punished, if death results to one or more of the victims, by death or such other punishment as a military commission under this chapter may direct, and, if death does not result to any of the victims, by such punishment, other than death, as a military commission under this chapter may direct.

(B) SEVERE MENTAL PAIN OR SUFFERING DEFINED- In this section, the term 'severe mental pain or suffering' has the meaning given that term in section 2340(2) of title 18.

(12) CRUEL OR INHUMAN TREATMENT-

(A) OFFENSE- Any person subject to this chapter who commits an act intended to inflict severe or serious physical or mental pain or suffering (other than pain or suffering incidental to lawful sanctions), including serious physical abuse, upon another within his custody or control shall be punished, if death results to the victim, by death or such other punishment as a military commission under this chapter may direct, and, if death does not result to the victim, by such punishment, other than death, as a military commission under this chapter may direct.

...

(13) INTENTIONALLY CAUSING SERIOUS BODILY INJURY-

(A) OFFENSE- Any person subject to this chapter who intentionally causes serious bodily injury to one or more persons, including lawful combatants, in violation of the law of war shall be punished, if death results to one or more of the victims, by death or such other punishment as a military commission under this chapter may direct, and, if death does not result to any of the victims, by such punishment, other than death, as a military commission under this chapter may direct.

    (B) SERIOUS BODILY INJURY DEFINED- In this paragraph, the term serious bodily injury' means bodily injury which involves—

        (i) a substantial risk of death;

        (ii) extreme physical pain;

        (iii) protracted and obvious disfigurement; or

        (iv) protracted loss or impairment of the function of a bodily member, organ, or mental faculty.

(14) MUTILATING OR MAIMING- Any person subject to this chapter who intentionally injures one or more protected persons by disfiguring the person or persons by any mutilation of the person or persons, or by permanently disabling any member, limb, or organ of the body of the person or persons, without any legitimate medical or dental purpose, shall be punished, if death results to one or more of the victims, by death or such other punishment as a military commission under this chapter may direct, and, if death does not result to any of the victims, by such punishment, other than death, as a military commission under this chapter may direct.

(15) MURDER IN VIOLATION OF THE LAW OF WAR- Any person subject to this chapter who intentionally kills one or more persons, including lawful combatants, in violation of the law of war shall be punished by death or such other punishment as a military commission under this chapter may direct.

(16) DESTRUCTION OF PROPERTY IN VIOLATION OF THE LAW OF WAR- Any person subject to this chapter who intentionally destroys property belonging to another person in violation of the law of war shall punished as a military commission under this chapter may direct.

(17) USING TREACHERY OR PERFIDY- Any person subject to this chapter who, after inviting the confidence or belief of one or more persons that they were entitled to, or obliged to accord, protection under the law of war, intentionally makes use of that confidence or belief in killing, injuring, or capturing such person or persons shall be punished, if death results to one or more of the victims, by death or such other punishment as a military commission under this chapter may direct, and, if death does not result to any of the victims, by such punishment, other than death, as a military commission under this chapter may direct.

(18) IMPROPERLY USING A FLAG OF TRUCE- Any person subject to this chapter who uses a flag of truce to feign an intention to negotiate, surrender, or otherwise suspend hostilities when there is no such intention shall be punished as a military commission under this chapter may direct.

(19) IMPROPERLY USING A DISTINCTIVE EMBLEM- Any person subject to this chapter who intentionally uses a distinctive emblem recognized by the law of war

for combatant purposes in a manner prohibited by the law of war shall be punished as a military commission under this chapter may direct.

(20) INTENTIONALLY MISTREATING A DEAD BODY- Any person subject to this chapter who intentionally mistreats the body of a dead person, without justification by legitimate military necessity, shall be punished as a military commission under this chapter may direct.

(21) RAPE- Any person subject to this chapter who forcibly or with coercion or threat of force wrongfully invades the body of a person by penetrating, however slightly, the anal or genital opening of the victim with any part of the body of the accused, or with any foreign object, shall be punished as a military commission under this chapter may direct.

(22) SEXUAL ASSAULT OR ABUSE- Any person subject to this chapter who forcibly or with coercion or threat of force engages in sexual contact with one or more persons, or causes one or more persons to engage in sexual contact, shall be punished as a military commission under this chapter may direct.

(23) HIJACKING OR HAZARDING A VESSEL OR AIRCRAFT- Any person subject to this chapter who intentionally seizes, exercises unauthorized control over, or endangers the safe navigation of a vessel or aircraft that is not a legitimate military objective shall be punished, if death results to one or more of the victims, by death or such other punishment as a military commission under this chapter may direct, and, if death does not result to any of the victims, by such punishment, other than death, as a military commission under this chapter may direct.

(24) TERRORISM- Any person subject to this chapter who intentionally kills or inflicts great bodily harm on one or more protected persons, or intentionally engages in an act that evinces a wanton disregard for human life, in a manner calculated to influence or affect the conduct of government or civilian population by intimidation or coercion, or to retaliate against government conduct, shall be punished, if death results to one or more of the victims, by death or such other punishment as a military commission under this chapter may direct, and, if death does not result to any of the victims, by such punishment, other than death, as a military commission under this chapter may direct.

(25) PROVIDING MATERIAL SUPPORT FOR TERRORISM-

(A) OFFENSE- Any person subject to this chapter who provides material support or resources, knowing or intending that they are to be used in preparation for, or in carrying out, an act of terrorism (as set forth in paragraph (24)), or who intentionally provides material support or resources to an international terrorist organization engaged in hostilities against the United States, knowing that such organization has engaged or engages in terrorism (as so set forth), shall be punished as a military commission under this chapter may direct.

(B) MATERIAL SUPPORT OR RESOURCES DEFINED- In this paragraph, the term 'material support or resources' has the meaning given that term in section 2339A(b) of title 18.

(26) WRONGFULLY AIDING THE ENEMY- Any person subject to this chapter who, in breach of an allegiance or duty to the United States, knowingly and intentionally aids an enemy of the United States, or one of the co-belligerents of the enemy, shall be punished as a military commission under this chapter may direct.

(27) SPYING- Any person subject to this chapter who with intent or reason to believe that it is to be used to the injury of the United States or to the advantage of a foreign power, collects or attempts to collect information by clandestine means or while acting under false pretenses, for the purpose of conveying such information to an enemy of the United States, or one of the co-belligerents of the enemy, shall be punished by death or such other punishment as a military commission under this chapter may direct.

(28) CONSPIRACY- Any person subject to this chapter who conspires to commit one or more substantive offenses triable by military commission under this chapter, and who knowingly does any overt act to effect the object of the conspiracy, shall be punished, if death results to one or more of the victims, by death or such other punishment as a military commission under this chapter may direct, and, if death does not result to any of the victims, by such punishment, other than death, as a military commission under this chapter may direct.

Sec. 950w. Perjury and obstruction of justice; contempt

(a) Perjury and Obstruction of Justice- A military commission under this chapter may try offenses and impose such punishment as the military commission may direct for perjury, false testimony, or obstruction of justice related to military commissions under this chapter.

(b) Contempt- A military commission under this chapter may punish for contempt any person who uses any menacing word, sign, or gesture in its presence, or who disturbs its proceedings by any riot or disorder.

...

SEC. 7. HABEAS CORPUS MATTERS.

(a) In General- Section 2241 of title 28, United States Code, is amended by striking both the subsection (e) added by section 1005(e)(1) of Public Law 109-148 (119 Stat. 2742) and the subsection (e) added by added by section 1405(e)(1) of Public Law 109-163 (119 Stat. 3477) and inserting the following new subsection (e):

(e)(1) No court, justice, or judge shall have jurisdiction to hear or consider an application for a writ of habeas corpus filed by or on behalf of an alien detained by the

United States who has been determined by the United States to have been properly detained as an enemy combatant or is awaiting such determination.

(2) Except as provided in paragraphs (2) and (3) of section 1005(e) of the Detainee Treatment Act of 2005 (10 U.S.C. 801 note), no court, justice, or judge shall have jurisdiction to hear or consider any other action against the United States or its agents relating to any aspect of the detention, transfer, treatment, trial, or conditions of confinement of an alien who is or was detained by the United States and has been determined by the United States to have been properly detained as an enemy combatant or is awaiting such determination.

(b) Effective Date- The amendment made by subsection (a) shall take effect on the date of the enactment of this Act, and shall apply to all cases, without exception, pending on or after the date of the enactment of this Act which relate to any aspect of the detention, transfer, treatment, trial, or conditions of detention of an alien detained by the United States since September 11, 2001.

...

Appendix M

DOD Department of Defense DIRECTIVE NUMBER 2310.01E September 5, 2006

SUBJECT: The Department of Defense Detainee Program

References:
(a) DoD Directive 2310.01, "DoD Program for Enemy Prisoners of War (EPOW) and Other Detainees," August 18, 1994 (hereby canceled)
(b) DoD Directive 5101.1,""DoD Executive Agent," September 3, 2002
(c) Secretary of Defense Memorandum,""Office of Detainee Affairs," July 16, 2004 (hereby superseded)
(d) DoD Directive 2311.01E, "DoD Law of War Program," May 9, 2006
(e) through (k), see Enclosure 1

1. REISSUANCE AND PURPOSE

This Directive:

1.1. Reissues Reference (a) to revise policy and responsibilities within the Department of Defense (DoD) for a Detainee Program to ensure compliance with the laws of the United States, the law of war, including the Geneva Conventions of 1949, and all applicable policies, directives, or other issuances, consistent with References (d) through (k).

1.2. Re-designates, according to Reference (b), the Secretary of the Army as the DoD Executive Agent for the Administration of Department of Defense Detainee Operations Policy.

1.3. Supersedes Reference (c) and establishes the responsibilities of the Under Secretary of Defense for Policy (USD(P)) as the lead proponent in developing, coordinating, and implementing policies and guidance pertaining to detainee operations.

2. APPLICABILITY

2.1. This Directive applies to:

2.1.1. The Office of the Secretary of Defense (OSD), the Military Departments, the Chairman of the Joint Chiefs of Staff, the Combatant Commands, the Office of the Inspector General of the Department of Defense, the Defense Agencies, the DoD Field Activities, and all other organizational entities in the Department of Defense (hereafter collectively referred to as the "DoD Components").

2.1.2. DoD contractors assigned to or supporting the DoD Components engaged in, conducting, participating in, or supporting detainee operations.

2.1.3. Non-DoD personnel as a condition of permitting access to internment facilities or to detainees under DoD control.

2.1.4. All detainee operations conducted by DoD personnel (military and civilian), contractor employees under DoD cognizance, and DoD contractors supporting detainee operations.

2.2. This Directive applies during all armed conflicts, however such conflicts are characterized, and in all other military operations.

3. <u>DEFINITIONS</u>

Terms used in this Directive are defined, and are to be interpreted, in accordance with U.S. law and the law of war. Specific terms found in this directive are provided in Enclosure 2.

4. <u>POLICY</u>

It is DoD policy that:

4.1. All detainees shall be treated humanely and in accordance with U.S. law, the law of war, and applicable U.S. policy.

4.2. All persons subject to this Directive shall observe the requirements of the law of war, and shall apply, without regard to a detainee's legal status, at a minimum the standards articulated in Common Article 3 to the Geneva Conventions of 1949 (References (g) through (j),full text of which is found in Enclosure 3), as construed and applied by U.S. law, and those found in Enclosure 4, in the treatment of all detainees, until their final release, transfer out of DoD control, or repatriation. Note that certain categories of detainees, such as enemy prisoners of war, enjoy protections under the law of war in addition to the minimum standards prescribed in Common Article 3 to References (g) through (j).

4.3. Captured or detained persons will be removed as soon as practicable from the point of capture and transported to detainee collection points, holding areas, or other detention locations operated by the DoD Components.

4.4. Detainees and their property shall be accounted for and records maintained according to applicable law, regulation, policy, or other issuances.

4.4.1. Detainees shall be assigned an Internment Serial Number (ISN) as soon as possible after coming under DoD control, normally within 14 days of capture. DoD Components shall maintain full accountability for all detainees under DoD control.

4.4.2. Detainee records and reports shall be maintained, safeguarded, and provided to USD(P) and other DoD Components as appropriate.

4.5. No person subject to this Directive shall accept the transfer of a detainee from another U.S. Government Department or Agency, coalition forces, allied personnel, or other personnel not affiliated with the Department of Defense or the U.S. Government, except in accordance with applicable law, regulation, policy, and other issuances.

4.6. No detainee shall be released or transferred from the care, custody, or control of a DoD Component except in accordance with applicable law, regulation, policy, and other issuances.

4.7. Where doubt exists as to the status of a detainee, the detainee's status shall be determined by a competent authority.

4.8. Detainees under DoD control who do not enjoy prisoner of war protections under the law of war shall have the basis for their detention reviewed periodically by a competent authority.

4.9. All persons subject to this Directive shall:

4.9.1. Receive instruction and complete training, commensurate with their duties, in the laws, regulations, policies, and other issuances applicable to detainee operations, prevention of violations of same, and the requirement to report alleged or suspected violations thereof that arise in the context of detainee operations.

4.9.2. Receive instruction and complete training in advance of conducting, participating in, or supporting detainee operations, and annually thereafter. Training requirements and certifications of completion shall be documented according to applicable law and policy.

4.10. All persons subject to this Directive shall report possible, suspected, or alleged violations of the law of war, and/or detention operations laws, regulations, or policy, for which there is credible information, or conduct, during military operations other than war, that would constitute a violation of law or policy if it occurred during an armed conflict, in accordance with References (d) and (k).

4.11. The International Committee of the Red Cross (ICRC) shall be allowed to offer its services during an armed conflict, however characterized, to which the United States is a party.

5. RESPONSIBILITIES

5.1. The USD(P) shall:

5.1.1. Review, ensure coordination of, and approve all implementing policies or guidance to the DoD Detainee Program, including all detainee matters involving interaction between the Department of Defense and other U.S. Government Departments or Agencies.

5.1.2. Review, ensure coordination of, and approve all implementing policy or guidance developed pursuant to this Directive by DoD Components. DoD Components will forward copies of such documents to USD(P) for review prior to issuance.

5.1.3. Serve as the principal DoD interlocutor with the ICRC and develop policy and procedures to ensure the proper and timely reporting of ICRC communications to appropriate DoD and U.S. Government officials.

5.2. The Under Secretary of Defense for Personnel and Readiness (USD(P&R)) shall:

5.2.1. Develop and oversee policy to ensure education and training programs satisfy DoD Component requirements in the areas of language, culture, customs, and related matters and to assure that persons subject to this directive have been provided requisite training, knowledge, and skills, necessary to perform detainee operations duties.

5.2.2. Ensure the Assistant Secretary of Defense for Health Affairs develops policies, procedures, and standards for medical program activities and issues DoD instructions consistent with this Directive for medical program activities required by the DoD Detainee Program.

5.2.3. Ensure the Assistant Secretary of Defense for Reserve Affairs develops policies, procedures, and standards for Reserve Components and issues DoD Instructions consistent with this Directive for National Guard and Reserve activities required for the DoD Detainee Program.

5.3. The Under Secretary of Defense for Acquisition, Technology, and Logistics (USD(AT&L)) shall:

5.3.1. Establish policies and procedures, in coordination with USD(P), the General Counsel, and the appropriate DoD Components, to ensure all DoD contracts pursuant to which contractor employees interact with detainees include a requirement that such contractor employees receive training regarding the international obligations and laws of the United States applicable to detention operations.

5.3.2. Ensure contractor employees accompanying DoD Components in conducting, participating in, or supporting detainee operations complete training and receive information on the law, regulations, and policies applicable to detention operations, and the requirements to report possible, suspected, or alleged violations that arise in the context of detention operations, in accordance with References (d) and (k).

5.4. The Under Secretary of Defense for Intelligence (USD(I)) shall:

5.4.1. Exercise primary responsibility for developing policy pertaining to DoD intelligence interrogations, detainee debriefings, and tactical questioning according to Reference (k).

5.4.2. Act as primary liaison between the Department of Defense and other agencies of the Intelligence Community on intelligence matters pertaining to detainees.

5.5. The General Counsel of the Department of Defense shall coordinate with the Department of Justice and other agencies regarding detainee-related litigation matters and on matters pertaining to detainees who may be U.S. citizens, dual-nationals with U.S. citizenship, or U.S. resident aliens, as appropriate.

5.6. The Heads of the DoD Components shall ensure that all personnel are properly trained
and certified in detainee operations commensurate with their duties, maintaining records of such training and certification.

5.7. The Secretary of the Army is hereby designated as the Executive Agent for the Administration of Department of Defense Detainee Operations Policy and in that role shall:

5.7.1. Ensure all Executive Agent responsibilities and functions for the administration of DoD detainee operations policy are assigned and executed according to Reference (b) and this Directive.

5.7.2. Develop and promulgate guidance, regulations, and instructions necessary for the DoD-wide implementation of detainee operations policy in coordination with USD(P).

5.7.3. Communicate directly with the Heads of the DoD Components as necessary to carry out assigned functions. The Chairman of the Joint Chiefs of Staff shall be informed of communications to the Commanders of the Combatant Commands.

5.7.4. Designate a single point of contact within the Department of the Army for detainee operations policy, who shall also provide advice and assistance to USD(P).

5.7.5. Plan for and operate a national-level detainee reporting center and its elements (e.g., theater and lower levels) to account for detainees. Coordinate with USD(P) to provide reports on detainee operations to the Secretary of Defense and others as appropriate.

5.7.6. Recommend DoD-wide detainee operations-related planning and programming guidance to the USD(P), USD(AT&L), USD(I), USD(P&R), the Under Secretary of Defense (Comptroller), the Assistant Secretary of Defense for Networks and Information Integration, the Director of Program Analysis and Evaluation, and the Chairman of the Joint Chiefs of Staff. Provide information copies of such guidance to the Secretaries of the Military Departments.

5.7.7. Establish detainee operations training and certification standards, in coordination with the Secretaries of the Military Departments and the Joint Staff.

5.7.8. Develop programs to ensure all DoD detainee operations policy; doctrine; tactics, techniques, and procedures; and regulations or other issuances are subject to periodic review, evaluation, and inspection for effectiveness and compliance with this Directive.

5.8. The Chairman of the Joint Chiefs of Staff shall:

5.8.1. Provide appropriate oversight to the Commanders of the Combatant Commands to ensure their detainee operations policies and procedures are consistent with this Directive.

5.8.2. Designate a single point of contact within the Joint Staff for matters pertaining to the implementation of this Directive.

5.8.3. Ensure that operational exercises routinely test the capabilities of the DoD Components to conduct, participate in, and support detainee operations, consistent with this Directive.

5.9. The Commanders of the Combatant Commands shall:

5.9.1. Plan, execute, and oversee Combatant Command detainee operations in accordance with this Directive and implementing issuances.

5.9.2. Develop programs and issue appropriate guidance and orders implementing this Directive. All such programs and guidance shall be subjected to periodic review and evaluation for compliance and efficacy.

5.9.3. When detainee internment facilities, holding areas, collection points, or interrogation facilities are in their area of responsibility:

5.9.3.1. Ensure procedures are established for the treatment of detainees consistent with this Directive.

5.9.3.2. Ensure detainees are provided with information, in their own language, concerning the rights, duties, and obligations of their detention, which may include applicable provisions of the Geneva Conventions.

5.9.3.3. Ensure periodic unannounced and announced inspections of internment facilities, including temporary holding areas and collection points, are conducted to provide continued oversight of detainee operations.

6. <u>EFFECTIVE DATE</u>

This Directive is effective immediately.

Gordon England
Deputy Secretary of Defense

DEFINITIONS

E2.1. <u>Detainee</u>. Any person captured, detained, held, or otherwise under the control of DoD personnel (military, civilian, or contractor employee). It does not include persons being held primarily for law enforcement purposes, except where the United States is the occupying power. A detainee may also include the following categories:

E2.1.1. <u>Enemy Combatant</u>. In general, a person engaged in hostilities against the United States or its coalition partners during an armed conflict. The term "enemy combatant" includes "both" "lawful enemy combatants" and "unlawful enemy combatants."

E2.1.1.1. <u>Lawful Enemy Combatant</u>. Lawful enemy combatants, who are entitled to protections under the Geneva Conventions, include members of the regular armed forces of a State party to the conflict; militia, volunteer corps, and organized resistance movements belonging to a State party to the conflict, which are under responsible command, wear a fixed distinctive sign recognizable at a distance, carry their arms openly, and abide by the laws of war; and members of regular armed forces who profess allegiance to a government or an authority not recognized by the detaining power.

E2.1.1.2. <u>Unlawful Enemy Combatant</u>. Unlawful enemy combatants are persons not entitled to combatant immunity, who engage in acts against the United States or its coalition partners in violation of the laws and customs of war during an armed conflict. For purposes of the war on terrorism, the term Unlawful Enemy Combatant is defined to include, but is not limited to, an individual who is or was part of or supporting Taliban or al Qaeda forces or associated forces that are engaged in hostilities against the United States or its coalition partners.

E2.1.2. <u>Enemy Prisoner of War</u>. Individuals under the custody and/or control of the Department of Defense according to Reference (g), Articles 4 and 5.

E2.1.3. <u>Retained Person</u>. Individuals under the custody and/or control of the Department of Defense according to Reference (g), Article 33.

E2.1.4. <u>Civilian Internee</u>. Individuals under the custody and/or control of the Department of Defense according to Reference (h), Article 4.

E2.2. <u>Law of War</u>. That part of international law that regulates the conduct of armed hostilities and occupation. It is often called the "law of armed conflict" and encompasses all international law applicable to the conduct of hostilities that is binding on the United States or its individual citizens, including treaties and international agreements to which the United States is a party (e.g., the Geneva Conventions of 1949), and applicable customary international law.

E3. <u>ENCLOSURE</u> 3

ARTICLE 3 COMMON TO THE GENEVA CONVENTIONS OF 1949
E3.1. The text of Common Article 3 to the Geneva Conventions of 1949 is as follows:

In the case of armed conflict not of an international character occurring in the territory of one of the High Contracting Parties, each Party to the conflict shall be bound to apply, as a minimum, the following provisions:

(1) Persons taking no active part in the hostilities, including members of armed forces who have laid down their arms and those placed *hors de combat* by sickness, wounds, detention, or any other cause, shall in all circumstances be treated humanely, without any adverse distinction founded on race, colour, religion or faith, sex, birth or wealth, or any other similar criteria.

To this end, the following acts are and shall remain prohibited at any time and in any place whatsoever with respect to the above-mentioned persons:

(a) violence to life and person, in particular murder of all kinds, mutilation, cruel treatment and torture;

(b) taking of hostages;

(c) outrages upon personal dignity, in particular humiliating and degrading treatment;

(d) the passing of sentences and the carrying out of executions without previous judgment pronounced by a regularly constituted court, affording all the judicial guarantees which are recognized as indispensable by civilized peoples.

(2) The wounded and sick shall be collected and cared for.

An impartial humanitarian body, such as the International Committee of the Red Cross, may offer its services to the Parties to the conflict.

The Parties to the conflict should further endeavour to bring into force, by means of special agreements, all or part of the other provisions of the present Convention. The application of the preceding provisions shall not affect the legal status of the

Parties to the conflict.

E4. <u>ENCLOSURE</u> 4

DETAINEE TREATMENT POLICY

E4.1. In addition to the requirements in paragraph 4.2 and Enclosure 3, DoD policy relative to the minimum standards of treatment for all detainees in the control of DoD personnel (military, civilian, or contractor employee) is as follows:

E4.1.1. All persons captured, detained, interned, or otherwise in the control of DoD personnel during the course of military operations will be given humane care and treatment from the moment they fall into the hands of DoD personnel until release, transfer out of DoD control, or repatriation, including:

E4.1.1.1. Adequate food, drinking water, shelter, clothing, and medical treatment;

E4.1.1.2. Free exercise of religion, consistent with the requirements of detention;

E4.1.1.3. All detainees will be respected as human beings. They will be protected against threats or acts of violence including rape, forced prostitution, assault and theft, public curiosity, bodily injury, and reprisals. They will not be subjected to medical or scientific experiments. They will not be subjected to sensory deprivation. This list is not exclusive.

E4.1.2. All persons taken into the control of DoD personnel will be provided with the protections of Reference (g) until some other legal status is determined by competent authority.

E4.1.3. The punishment of detainees known to have, or suspected of having, committed serious offenses will be administered in accordance with due process of law and under legally constituted authority.

E4.1.4. The inhumane treatment of detainees is prohibited and is not justified by the stress of combat or deep provocation.

About the Author

Jeffrey F. Addicott is currently the Associate Dean for Administration (2006-2007) at St. Mary's University School of Law and the Director of the Center for Terrorism Law at St. Mary's University School of Law (www.stmarytx.edu/ctl), San Antonio, Texas, where he teaches a variety of courses to include Terrorism Law. An active duty Army officer in the Judge Advocate General's Corps for twenty years (he retired in 2000 at the rank of Lieutenant Colonel), Professor Addicott spent a quarter of his career as a senior legal advisor to the United States Army's Special Forces. An internationally recognized authority in terrorism law, Professor Addicott not only lectures and participates in professional and academic organizations both in the United States and abroad, he is a frequent contributor to national and international news shows to include FOX News Channel and MSNBC. Professor Addicott is a prolific author, publishing over 20 books, articles and monographs on a variety of legal topics. Among his many contributions to the field, Professor Addicott pioneered the teaching of law of war and human rights courses to the militaries of numerous nascent democracies in Eastern Europe and Latin America. For these efforts he was awarded the Legion of Merit, named the 1993 Army Judge Advocate of the year and honored as a co-recipient of the American Bar Association's Hodson award. He has served in senior legal positions in Germany, Korea, Panama and throughout the United States. Professor Addicott holds a Doctor of Juridical Science (SJD) and Master of Laws (LLM) from the University of Virginia School of Law. He also received a Master of Laws (LLM) from the Judge Advocate General's School, a Juris Doctor (JD) from the University of Alabama School of Law and a bachelor of arts with honors in government (BA) from the University of Maryland.

Index